D0141591

British Academy Monographs in Archaeology no.3

In Memoriam

Crystal-M. Bennett, OBE, FSA
(1918–1987)

STUDIES ON ROMAN AND ISLAMIC 'AMMĀN

The Excavations of Mrs C-M Bennett
and Other Investigations

VOLUME I

History, Site and Architecture

Alastair Northedge
with contributions by
Julian Bowsher, Ulrich Hübner,
Henry Innes MacAdam,
and Jason Wood

Published for
the British Institute in Amman for Archaeology and History
by Oxford University Press

Oxford University Press Walton Street, Oxford OX2 6DP
Oxford New York Toronto
Delhi Bombay Calcutta Madras Karachi
Kuala Lumpur Singapore Hong Kong Tokyo
Nairobi Dar es Salaam Cape Town
Melbourne Auckland Madrid
and associated companies in
Berlin Ibadan

Oxford is a trade mark of Oxford University Press

Published in the United States
by Oxford University Press Inc., New York

Copyright © Alastair Northedge 1992

All rights reserved. No part of this publication may be reproduced, stored in a retrieval system, or transmitted, in any form or by any means, electronic, mechanical, photocopying, recording, or otherwise, without the prior permission of the author

British Library Cataloguing in Publication Data
Northedge, Alastair
(data available)
ISBN 0-19-727002 6

Printed by PJ Reproductions, London

Studies in Roman and Islamic ʻAmmān

Errata

Page 64 In the last line رحمة should read رحمه

Page 148 The last line of text should appear as the first line of the section 'Area D' on page 149

Fig.41 The image has been reversed left to right. The correct orientation is shown below.

Fig.137 No.4 is at a scale of 1:3

Fig.146 Caption should read:
Cross-section of the street in Area B, showing development of surfaces from Stratum VIII (Byzantine) to Stratum III (AA–AA on figs 145 and 156)

Fig.154 Caption should read:
Section of Room D, Building D (CC–CC on figs 145 and 156) (1:30)

Plate 77A The photograph is incorrect (a repetition of Plate 75A).
The correct photograph is shown below.

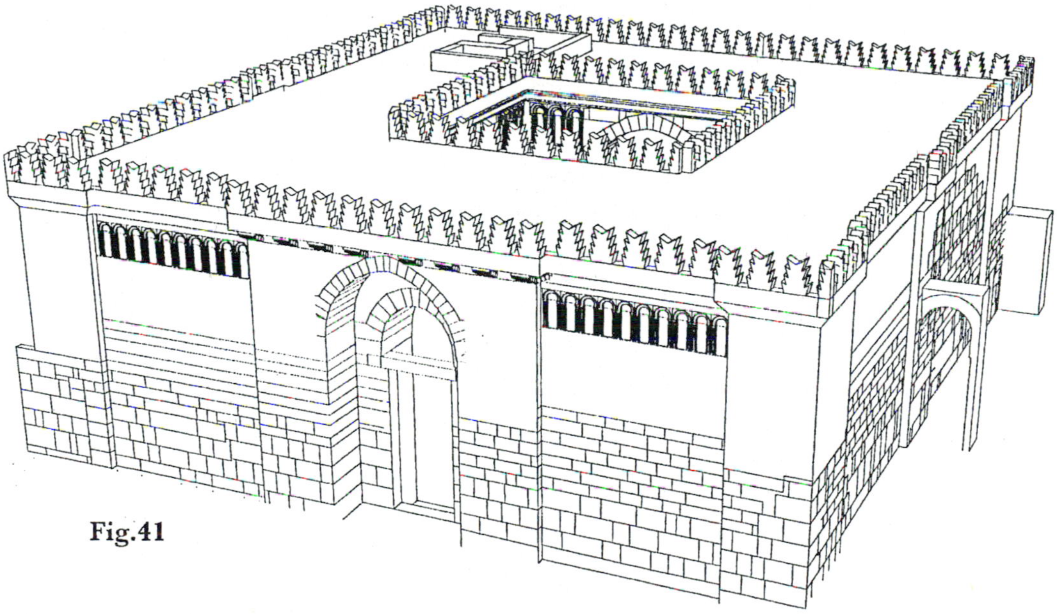

Fig.41

Plate 77A

CONTENTS

List of Tables

List of Figures

List of Plates

looking south.
B. Fatimid bread oven in the northwest corner of the courtyard in unit 1 in Umayyad Building C.
C. Plastered drain and cistern in Umayyad Building D (trench B19).
75. A. Fatimid Stratum III reconstruction of Umayyad Building D, looking south. Note bread oven in upper-right corner.
B. Byzantine (Stratum VIII) steps underlying Umayyad Building D, looking west.
76. A. Umayyad remains east of the B area street in trench B52, looking east.
B. Ayyubid surface levels in Room D, Umayyad Building D, looking east.
77. A. Tower E in Area D, looking north.
B. Abbasid-Fatimid (Stratum IVb–III) house overlying Tower E in Area D.
78. A. Detail of drains adjacent to Tower E.
B. Abbasid basin, drain and cistern in Area D.
79. A. Qal'a, Church, looking southeast.
B. Apse of the Citadel church, looking northeast.
80. A. Open Cistern belonging to the Umayyad construction.
B. Open Cistern, detail of steps.

Strata of the Excavations

Strata	*Name*	*Dating*
I	Modern	20th century.
IIa	pre-modern	Ill-defined post-occupation collapse deposits.
IIb	Ayyūbid	Defined by presence of Pseudo-prehistoric ware, and coin group of al-Malik al-ʿĀdil (d.1218).
IIIa	Late Fātimid	Late occupation of Stratum III buildings terminating in earthquake destruction *c.* 1100 +/–30 years.
IIIb	Early Fātimid	Coins of al-Ḥākim and al-Ẓahir (first quarter of the 5th/11th century).
IVa		Undated deposits between V and III.
IVb	ʿAbbāsid	Pottery with parallels in the 3rd/9th and 4th/10th centuries.
Va	Late Umayyad	Post-construction occupation, and rebuilding. Destruction by earthquake of 129–30/747–8.
Vb	Umayyad	Superstructure of Umayyad Citadel, dated by architecture of Umayyad palace to 115/735 +/–10 years.
VI	Umayyad	Levelling fills for the buildings of Vb, dated by architecture of Umayyad palace to 115/735 +/–10 years.
VII	Early Umayyad	Provable post-Conquest deposits, predating construction of the Umayyad Citadel (635–735).
VIIIa	Byzantine	Byzantine urban settlement; *c.* 6th-century deposits.
VIIIb	Byzantine	Byzantine urban settlement; *c.* 4th-century deposits.
IXa	Roman	Occupation of 2nd-century Roman reconstruction of the Citadel.
IXb	Roman	2nd-century Roman reconstruction of the Citadel, construction and levelling fills.
X	Early Roman	1st-century (Decapolis period) occupation.
XI	Iron Age	Iron Age II deposits, defined by late Ammonite pottery.
XII	MB/LB	Late Middle Bronze Age deposits, defined by red-painted ware, *c.* 1550 BC.

Period Terminology

Early Roman	1st century AD
Late Roman	2nd–3rd centuries AD
Early Byzantine	4th–5th centuries AD
Late Byzantine	6th century–14/635
Early Islamic	14/635–middle 5th/11th centuries
Umayyad	14/635–132/750 including the Orthodox Caliphs (*al-Khulafāʾ al-Rāshidūn*)
Early ʿAbbāsid	132/750–221/836
Sāmarran	221/836–end of 3rd/9th century
Post-Samarran	4th/10th century
Middle Islamic	Middle 5th/11th century–8th/14th century
5th/11th century	5th/11th century
6th/12th century	6th/12th century
Early Crusader	6th/12th century
Ayyūbid	Late 6th/12th–658/1260
Late Crusader	7th/13th century
Early Mamluk	658/1260–8th/14th century
Early Modern	9th/15th century–1342/1918
Late Mamlūk	9th/15th century–923/1517
Ottoman	923/1517–1342/1918

Acknowledgements

We would like to acknowledge the help of the Department of Antiquities of the Hashemite Kingdom of Jordan, in particular the successive past Directors-General, Ya'qub 'Uways, who died in 1977, Dr 'Adnan al-Hadidi, Dr Ghazi Bishe, and the present Director-General, Dr Safwan Tell.

We would also like to thank the British Institute at 'Ammān for Archaeology and History, for encouraging and sponsoring this publication, in particular: Dr P. R. S. Moorey, Dr J. A. J. Raby, Mr P. Parr, and the former Director of the Institute in 'Ammān, Dr Andrew Garrard.

A great many individuals took part in the excavations, and we hope that we have succeeded in identifying all of them in the following list, which is intended as an appropriate recognition of their work.

1975 Chris Davey (architect), Rosalind Wade.
1976 Naomi Assinder (draughtswoman), Rosalind Wade (senior Field supervisor), Michael Upton (architect), Prof. Kalayan (architect), Harry Russell (acting deputy director), Robert Killick, Simon Khano, Fr Florentino Diez, Juliet Dearbergh, Liza Johnston. Department Representative: Ghassan Ramahi.
1977 Naomi Assinder (draughtswoman), Susan Balderstone (architect), Simon Lamb (photographer), Rosalind Wade, A. Budeiri, P. Assinder, Virginia Segreti, Liza Johnston. Department Representative: Ghassan Ramahi.
Palace Survey: Mark Watts. Department Representative: Ghassan Ramahi. Funding: British Institute at Ammān; Wright Fund, Cambridge University.
1978 Naomi Assinder (draughtswoman), Susan Balderstone (architect), Alan Walmsley (photographer), Alastair Killick, Andrina Bamber, Vanessa Clewes, Jim Irvine, Michel Kuypers, Struan Reid. Department Representative: Ghassan Ramahi.
Palace Survey: Susan Balderstone. Department Representative: Ghassan Ramahi. Funding: Dept. of Antiquities.
1979 (Area B) Robert Killick (assistant director), Naomi Assinder (draughtswoman), Jane Killick, Alastair Killick, Julian Bowsher. Department Representative: Ghassan Ramahi.
(Area E) Virginia Segreti, Andrina Bamber, Susan Balderstone (architect), Neil Mackenzie. Department Representative: Ghassan Ramahi.
1981 Elizabeth Errington (pottery), Abigail Jones, Timothy Crump, Jason Wood (fortification survey), Richard Brotherton (Temple of Hercules survey), and Judith MacKenzie (architectural fragments). Department Representative: Ghassan Ramahi.

Pottery drawings in this volume are by Naomi Assinder, with a few by Elizabeth Errington. Site drawings were contributed by many team members, notably Susan Balderstone and Jason Wood, but also by Richard Brotherton and Judith MacKenzie. Unsigned drawings are by the author.

Many thanks are owed to my wife, Andrina Bamber, for much tolerance and decoration drawings.

Alastair Northedge

Note on Conventions

The Arabic transcription used is that of the *Encyclopaedia of Islam*, with the usual changes, thus 'q' instead of 'k', 'j' instead of 'dj', and 'sh', 'kh' instead of 'sh', 'kh', etc. The definite article of names has often been omitted, but not always (e.g. 'Walid' rather than 'al-Walid'). Arabic terms have been italicized. However, in the case of archaeological sites, if there is a form of the Arabic name used by their excavators, that form has been used to avoid confusion.

Dates associated with Islamic history are quoted with the *hijrī* date first, separated by a stroke from the date according to the Christian era, e.g. 117/735. Otherwise dates are only given in the Christian era.

The following is a glossary of the terminology of the archaeological periods used. It is a terminology of period concepts that often overlap and which only represent approximate periods of time: it does not represent a systematic periodization of the Islamic era. Rather it was felt that although a periodization is essential to archaeological description, excessive precision would tend to distort the subtleties of change that are evident in the relatively recent archaeological materials.

INTRODUCTION

'Ammān has always been one of the most significant city sites in Jordan. This importance dates back not merely to its establishment as the capital of Jordan in the 1920s, but back across the centuries through the medieval Islamic period, through the Byzantine, Roman and Hellenistic periods, through the Iron Age, to the period when 'Ammān first became important in the middle of the 2nd millennium BC.

It is often the case that where cities continue to preserve today the importance they first gained many millennia ago, that only a relatively small part of the ancient city is open to modern investigation, and that the archaeology and history are extremely complex. This is true of 'Ammān, where in recent years the Citadel, or, to use its Arabic form, the Qal'a, has been the main centre of archaeological work – although considerable work has also taken place around the forum, with its theatre and odeon. The archaeology of 'Ammān has certainly proved to be extremely complex, and presents multiple periods of occupation that are often accessible to the excavator in only limited areas.

In spite of the obvious importance of 'Ammān as an archaeological site, it has been poorly served by publication. The last general, detailed, account of the archaeology of the city was by H. C. Butler at the beginning of the century, and that account is often vitiated by his lack of interest in periods other than those of Graeco-Roman culture. The work of Butler was followed up by a large-scale Italian mission in the 1930s, principally directed by Bartoccini, but this work was never published in any extensive way. More recent work by a Spanish mission has at least been published, although the publication is limited to a specific aspect of the Qal'a: the Umayyad palace.

The present study does not pretend to be the successor of Butler, but it attempts a degree of synthesis for at least the later periods, principally because the longer the work on the ground continued, the more unknown aspects of the archaeology of 'Ammān appeared. It was impossible to ignore these elements, although even today not all of them have been properly explored.

The origin of this volume lies in a number of small archaeological projects. In 1975 the then Director-General of Antiquities, Ya'qub 'Uways, invited the late Mrs C-M. Bennett OBE FSA, who was at the time Director of the British School of Archaeology in Jerusalem, to conduct rescue excavations on behalf of the Department of Antiquities of the Hashemite Kingdom of Jordan.

Mrs Bennett's excavations led to further work, intended to elucidate the character of the remains, and the results of these investigations are also incorporated in this volume. The present writer conducted a short survey of the Umayyad palace in 1977 and 1978. In 1979 and 1981 the writer directed a survey and excavation of the Roman and Islamic fortifications of the site.

The present writer also completed a PhD thesis about the Qal'a in the Islamic period,[1] and that dissertation forms the heart of this volume, together with the reports on the fieldwork.

As a result, this volume is partly primary archaeological report, and partly secondary synthesis and analysis. The aim is to elucidate the complex archaeology and history of 'Ammān. It was thought wise to invite outside specialists to make contributions to the volume, because no one archaeologist or historian can hope to offer a considered judgement on such a long history. As a result, the structure of the work is looser than might have been the case had there been a single author.

As in many city-sites of long occupation in the Middle East, there are three main cultural periods: firstly the ancient Near Eastern culture of prehistory, and the Bronze and Iron Ages, secondly the Hellenistic and Roman era, and thirdly Islam. For 'Ammān, a proper study demands contributions from specialists in all three periods. As it happens, the results of the fieldwork have led to a concentration in this publication on the third, Islamic, phase. Nevertheless there is substantial attention paid to the Romano-Byzantine period. It seems to be the case that the Roman architecture and plan of the Citadel is by no means as straightforward and standard as once used to be thought.

It remains very difficult to say much about the archaeology of Bronze and Iron Age 'Ammān, outside of the pottery sequence and other isolated finds. A brief study by Hübner of pre-Hellenistic 'Ammān has been included, but it is appropriate to refer the reader to Hübner's own publication for a more complete explanation of the earlier periods.[2]

This study, though it ranges much more broadly, is therefore essentially one of the history, origins and implications of a single event at the Qal'a of 'Ammān: the construction of a grand citadel towards the end of the Umayyad Caliphate, within a few years of 117/735. Without doubt, this project of construction deeply altered the physical appearance of the citadel, and the fact that it remained unrecognized for so long hindered the classical studies of Butler and Bartoccini, and possibly also those of subsequent excavators. The surface remains of the Upper Citadel today are in fact largely composed of the reoccupied ruins of the Umayyad citadel. There are areas where these traces have eroded to expose earlier remains; other areas where excavators have dug through the Umayyad levels; and yet others where nothing was ever built, such as on the Lower Citadel, or over the robbed remains of the Temple of Hercules. But it is the plan of the Umayyad citadel that gives pattern and structure to the site today.

The Field Projects

In 1975 rescue excavations were planned by the Department of Antiquities of the Hashemite Kingdom of Jordan in two areas of the Upper Citadel, to prepare for the construction of a new national archaeological museum[3] – a project that has not yet come to fruition.[4] As part of the same project Dr Fawzi Zayadine of the Department of Antiquities excavated in a further area, Area A, and the results have already been published in the Annual of the Department of Antiquities of Jordan.[5] Mrs Bennett's excavations lasted from 1975 to 1979, with two short seasons in 1975, a six month season in 1976, and further seasons in 1977, 1978, and 1979. The present writer was assistant director of the excavations between 1976 and 1978. The excavations took place in the areas labelled B, C, and D (fig. 28).[6]

The writer conducted a short survey of the area of the Roman *temenos* at the north end of the Citadel, now known to contain the Umayyad palace, in 1977 and 1978.[7] The original aim was simply to record a number of apparently Umayyad buildings, but it soon became evident that the arrangement of these structures was organized, and represented a palace. The area, and the writer's conclusions, were subsequently taken over by the Spanish mission mentioned above.

In 1979 and 1981 the writer directed a survey and excavation of the Roman and Islamic fortifications of the site.[8] In fact the excavation was limited to a relatively small area, called Area E, which lay south and east of the Temple of Hercules. However, a survey conducted by Jason Wood in 1981 was made of the entire line of the Roman and Islamic fortifications, including the recording of all architectural blocks reused in the walls.

The original excavations by Mrs Bennett were conducted on behalf of the Department of Antiquities; the author's fieldwork was jointly sponsored by the Department and the British Institute at 'Ammān for Archaeology and History. This publication has been sponsored by the British Institute, with the agreement of the Department of Antiquities.

PREVIOUS WORK ON 'AMMAN

1. Travellers and Surveys

By the time that Western visitors first began to describe the site the city of 'Ammān was nearly deserted, though there had been a *khān* on a branch of the *ḥajj* road *(darb al-ḥajj al-Shāmī)* from perhaps the Mamlūk period up until the 19th century.

Ulrich von Seetzen visited the site of 'Ammān in 1806, but his description is not extensive. An early version of his travels was published in English in 1810, and a fuller version in German in 1854.[9]

John Lewis Burckhardt visited 'Ammān in 1812, and wrote a lengthy and interesting account published in 1822, with a schematic plan. His account of the lower city provides interesting details, but he only had the opportunity to see the south side of the Qal'a, and did not visit the more northerly remains.[10]

James Silk Buckingham's visit in 1821 has left the earliest account of the Umayyad Reception Hall.[11]

In 1826 Leon de Laborde, who published in 1837, made two fine etchings of the Qabr al-Sulṭān and the theatre.[12]

In November 1863 the Frenchman F. de Saulcy spent three days at 'Ammān, with a small group including a photographer and a military surveyor, Capt. d'État Major Gélis.[13] Although de Saulcy himself was restrained by illness, Gélis drew up a plan at a scale of 1: 6000 that contains a remarkable quantity of archaeological detail (fig.2).

A further plan of 'Ammān was published to illustrate the report of a visit by the Rev. A. E. Northey in the Palestine Exploration Fund Quarterly Statement of 1872.[14] The plan was the product of a visit by Lt. Charles Warren in July-August 1867 (fig.3).

The efforts of de Saulcy were carried forward by the

Palestine Exploration Fund (PEF) as part of the survey of Eastern Palestine during a week in October 1881, under the leadership of C. R. Conder.[15] A plan was made of the site, entitled ‘Special Survey of Ammān’, together with plans of all the monuments (fig. 4). As the latest work before the appearance of the modern settlement a year or two later, and as the product of a relatively long period spent on site, the survey is of particular value. The site plan of the expedition formed the basis of the subsequent plan made by Butler, and was republished as recently as 1978 as a site plan of ancient ‘Ammān.[16]

The Princeton Archaeological Expedition to Syria visited ‘Ammān in 1904, and made a detailed survey, ‘when it became apparent that the ruins had suffered great depredations since the last publications of them were made, and were likely to perish entirely under the hands of the recent Circassian settlers’.[17] Howard Crosby Butler’s compendious description has formed the basic text for the classical monuments of ‘Ammān since its publication, but it omits the Islamica, and so Conder’s survey remains the latest of the early accounts of the Islamic structures.

2. Early Photography of ‘Ammān
by Henry Innes MacAdam

Because of the modern development of the city of ‘Ammān, early photographs have proved to be an important source of information on the ancient remains. This is partly because the monumental architecture was either still in existence, or in a much better state of preservation, at the time that the photographs were taken; and partly because the photographs provide evidence for the lie and disposition of the ruins, and the extent of the ancient city.

Although de Saulcy notes that his photographer had already photographed ‘Ammān in November 1863, these photographs have not been located.[18] The earliest known surviving photographs seem to be those taken by Phillips for Lt. Charles Warren for the Palestine Exploration Fund in July-August 1867 (pls 7a–b, 8a, 17b,20a, 42a, 65b).[19] A further early series was taken on 18 October 1875 by Tancrède Dumas for the American Palestine Exploration Society.[20] Most of those were photographs of the lower city taken from the citadel, and clearly depict the extant remains (pls 3, 4, 64a). In October 1881 further Palestine Exploration Fund photographs were taken by the Survey of Eastern Palestine (pls 26, 14a, 61a).[21] About ten years later Félix Bonfils took several wider-angle photographs of the forum, odeon and theatre.[22] Later photographic studies of ‘Ammān and its region were made by the Brünnow and von Domaszewski expedition (1897/98; pl.16), and the Princeton University Expedition of 1904/05.[23] Political and historical photographs of early 20th-century ‘Ammān are preserved in the Middle East Centre, St Anthony’s College, Oxford.

Aerial photography of the city and surrounding area dating from the first half of this century has not yet been thoroughly explored. Most of that early photography is connected with British military activity in Jordan during the two World Wars. While many photograph files were subsequently destroyed by the very agencies that produced them, dozens of such photographs still exist. David Kennedy drew attention to their potential at the First International Conference on the History and Archaeology of Jordan a decade ago.[24] In addition, at least one German air photograph from the First World War is known (pl.2a).[25]

Following the Second World War, Hunting Aerosurveys, in the course of contractual work for the Hashemite Kingdom of Jordan, took vertical stereo and oblique photographs of ‘Ammān in the early 1950s (pl.1).[26] Thanks to the efforts of the Spanish Archaeological Mission, an aerial photographic survey of central ‘Ammān was conducted in 1978.[27]

3. Excavations

After the foundation of the Amirate of Transjordan, the Missione Scientifiche Italiana in Levante embarked upon a major excavation at the Qal‘a over five seasons between 1927 and 1938. The first director was Giacomo Guidi, but beginning with the second season in 1929 the work was headed by Renato Bartoccini. The scope of this work was considerable: every major monument known from the Qal‘a was partially or wholly excavated by the Mission.

At the north end of the Qal‘a, approximately half of the structures on the site of the *temenos* of the Northern Temple and the palace were excavated over the five seasons. In 1933 the Reception Hall was cleared and consolidated. In the same year work on the Temple of Hercules was begun, and an area on the lower terrace was excavated to reveal what was called ‘David’s City’. Probably in 1938, a Byzantine church was also excavated, a building since further excavated by Dr Fawzi Zayadine.[28] Although these excavations were of major importance for the site, little of the work was published. The total publication amounts to three short notes and a longer preliminary article, without plans, on the first four seasons, together with a conference paper delivered in 1935.[29] Finally, in 1983, Almagro published the architectural drawings made by Ceschi in 1930 of the Roman monuments.[30]

After the Second World War, in 1949, rescue excavations were carried out by Gerald Lankester Harding, then Director of Antiquities, on the site of the present Jordan Archaeological Museum at the Qal'a.[31] In addition, Harding excavated a number of rock tombs of Middle Bronze Age, Iron Age II, Nabataean and Roman date.[32]

From 1964 to 1967 Dr Adnan Hadidi, then at the University of Jordan and subsequently the Director-General of Antiquities, directed excavations in the Roman forum, concurrently with a restoration of the theatre.[33]

In 1969 R. Dornemann, then Director of the American Center of Oriental Research, carried out small-scale excavations at the Qal'a. These included new work on the Temple of Hercules, a small trench on an Iron Age fortification wall at the north end, and part of a Roman house on the lower terrace.[34]

Between 1968 and 1973 Dr Fawzi Zayadine excavated two areas on the south side of the lower terrace; one of these has been published.[35]

This already complex excavation history was added to in 1974 when a Spanish Archaeological Mission, headed by Dr Martin Almagro and his son Antonio, carried out a photogrammetric survey of the Reception Hall. Spanish work was resumed in 1978 with further excavation and consolidation of that building. In addition a group of rooms on the east side of the Hall was excavated, together with a small adjacent mosque that dated from a later period. The main rooms of the North Building were excavated in 1979, and a trench was excavated to the south of the Reception Hall in 1981. The results have been published as *El Palacio Omeya de Ammān*, a three-volume series of which the first two volumes have so far appeared.[36] In 1989–90 excavation was resumed by Antonio Almagro, with excavation in Building 7 of the palace.

In 1987 the Department of Antiquities carried out further rescue excavations on the lower terrace of the Qal'a, on the site proposed for a school.[37] Since then a further project of excavations under the direction of Humbert of the École Biblique in Jerusalem has been begun, adjacent to Dr Zayadine's Area A on the Lower Citadel, and this work has been directed towards elaborating the early sequence of the Citadel.[38]

In 1990 and 1991 a new project was embarked on, funded by USAID, for the study and restoration of the Temple of Hercules. This project was led initially by Dr Khair Yassine and R. Dornemann, but the most recent active excavators have been Dr Muhammad Najjar and (the late) Dr Kenneth W. Russell.

Alastair Northedge
Maître de Conférences
Université de Paris-Sorbonne (Paris IV)

I

THE PHYSICAL TOPOGRAPHY OF 'AMMĀN

by Alastair Northedge

THE REGION

Jordan is part of the Fertile Crescent, that arc of cultivable land that stretches from Gaza on the Levantine coast of the Mediterranean, to Basra in Iraq at the head of the Gulf.[1] The country lies at the southern end of the Levant, divided from the coastal strip of Palestine by the depression containing the River Jordan, the Dead Sea and Wādī 'Araba. It constitutes the Levant's last extremity in the direction of the Arabian Peninsula. It may also be regarded as the furthest limit of Arabia in the direction of the Fertile Crescent.

Such an area of transition might be thought to have little regional identity (fig. 1). The present form of Jordan is certainly the creation of modern politics, in that it is a result of the settlement at the end of the First World War that produced the Palestine Mandate. The Hashemite Kingdom of Jordan has inherited the Mandate's boundaries. Nevertheless, there are reasons for supposing that what is now Jordan represents a genuine and distinct regional entity within the Levant: the thin strip of cultivable land that stretches down the eastern rim of the Jordan-'Araba depression.

The nature of this entity is worth emphasizing, because the present-day state, formulated in the modern idiom with linear boundaries, also includes the eastern side of the Jordan-Araba depression and a part of the Syrian desert, the latter constituting over 83 per cent of Jordan's land area. Both these areas today are being developed extensively. In the past, however, they tended to act as boundaries themselves, by virtue of their physical characteristics, although one must not forget that these boundary areas were also exploited as territories. It is only in the north that the generally similar terrain of the Ḥawrān, shading into the hinterland of Damascus, makes for an ill-defined boundary.

The hinterland of 'Ammān stretches from the deep cut of Wādī Zarqā' in the north to the equally deep incision of Wādī Mūjib in the south, and from the rim of the Jordan Valley in the west almost to Azraq in the east. Since the rise of Arabic as the dominant language, this area has been called al-Balqā' ('the piebald', probably from the mixture of black basalts and white limestones that characterize the area), although this name today is restricted to the district of al-Salṭ.[2]

Within the area defined above four different types of terrain are found (fig. 7):[3]

The Limestone Desert

To the east of 'Ammān lies a section of the Syrian Desert *(Bādiyat al-Shām)*, a plateau of low relief with a gentle decline of elevation to the east. The main topographical feature is an inland drainage basin centering on Azraq, where springs have formed a series of surface pools. Although to the northeast of Azraq the terrain consists of basalt boulder fields, the area between Azraq and 'Ammān has a low-relief terrain of chert desert pavement (*ḥammāda*),[4] developed from chalks and soft limestones, banded with chert.[5] The desert pavement is intersected with sandy wadis leading down to Azraq, and these carry the only vegetation.

The Steppe Region

The inland desert-edge steppe extends from the desert border to the rim of the plateau in the region of Mādabā.[6] To the north it runs past 'Ammān, and includes all of the plateau east of the 900m contour, linking with the plain of the Ḥawrān. The terrain here is a rolling plateau, to the southwest intersected by deeply incised wadis leading down to the Dead Sea and the lower Jordan Valley. The main difference between this area and the desert is the amount of rainfall in the steppe region, ranging from the 200mm isohyet to the east to 355mm at Mādabā (fig. 9).

The Northwest Uplands

The Northwest Uplands of northern Jordan are a dissected highland area between 'Ammān and Irbid, with two distinct highland masses separated by Wādī Zarqā', and centred on 'Ajlūn and al-Salṭ. The southern area has a maximum elevation of 1113m near to al-Salṭ. The vegetation here makes a transition from the Irano-Turanian steppe to a Mediterranean type, with a climax of oaks and scrub. Rainfall is higher, ranging from 378mm on the west side of 'Ammān to 655mm at Salṭ (fig.8).

The Jordan Valley

The Jordan depression to the west is a part of the Rift Valley that extends from northern Syria down to the Red Sea. From the freshwater lake of Tiberias at *c.*-212m, the River Jordan winds its way south to the salty sterile Dead Sea (-392m; fig. 6). The section close to 'Ammān is a tropical environment, with mean temperatures 5°C higher than 'Ammān, and Saharo-Sindian vegetation.[7]

Although 'Ammān in the past had links with all these environments, its principal focus seems to have been south and east of the city, south to Mādabā, and east to Muwaqqar and Zarqā' in the steppelands. The city is therefore not like Jarash, which belongs to a Mediterranean environment; rather, it is open to the people of the steppe and the desert, and this is expressed by al-Muqaddasī's description of 'Ammān as lying *'alā sīf al-bādiya* ('on the border of the desert').[8] However, it is true that the terrain as far north as the Wādī Zarqā', including the small Baq'a plain and the area of al-Salṭ, have played an important part in the city's history.

PHYSICAL TOPOGRAPHY OF THE CITY SITE

The site of the city (31° 55' N; 35° 55' E) is on the Wādī 'Ammān, part of the upper basin of the Wādī Zarqā', a stream with a permanent flow, incised into a rolling plateau of hard limestones (fig. 13).[9]

In the centre of the city the main wadi flows southwest–northeast. On the north side is a tributary wadi which splits into two. This is named on the Palestine Exploration Fund survey as 'Misdar al-Madheneh' (fig. 4); the eastern branch is today occupied by Shāri' al-Salṭ, and the western by Shāri' Wādī al-Sīr. To the east is a second tributary wadi on the north side, Wādī al-Ḥaddāda, which curves around to the west (fig. 14).

The main spring for 'Ammān is located one kilometre southwest of the ancient town at Rās al-'Ayn (fig. 14). The spring was estimated in 1938 to produce an average of 3.8 million cubic metres per annum.[10] In recent years the spring was a main water-source for modern 'Ammān, but its capacity has been overtaken by the growth of the city. The spring feeds into the wadi bed and, supplemented by further ill-defined sources to the east, provides a year-round flow.

According to Conder, the spring was covered by an alcove or apse *c.*7m in diameter.[11] Although no longer extant, one might suppose that this construction was Roman. In pre-modern times water was brought into the city by two 'aqueducts' or channels recorded by Conder. The northern channel led into the mosque, and the southern channel had a branch leading into a mill that was probably of Middle Islamic or Ottoman date (pls 3–4). The available evidence suggests, therefore, that these channels were Islamic, and so for the moment we do not have any evidence of the Roman water supply.

No natural spring is known on the top of the Qal'a or Citadel: the steep topography suggests that any aquifers would emerge as a spring at the base of the hill, not on the top. Nor is there any known well dug down through the rock to an aquifer. However there are cisterns, of which seventeen have been identified; but this is almost certainly a small proportion of the total. The Qal'a would have depended on them when there was no access to outside water; this possibility is suggested by the story in Polybius, that while Antiochus was besieging the city in 218 BC, the defenders maintained access to an external water supply by means of an underground passage.[12] It has been suggested that the site of this passage and water source be identified with a large multi-chamber cistern outside the north wall of the Qal'a, which contains evidence of use in the Iron Age.[13]

'Ammān has always been a city built of stone. There are good quality outcrops of Tertiary limestones in the immediate vicinity. Although the locations of the ancient quarries are not precisely known, some indication can be derived from the identification of quarrying by early Western visitors. The Palestine Exploration Fund map of 1881 (fig. 4), followed by the Baedeker map of 1912, identifies quarries on the south side of Jabal al-Tāj, to the southeast of the Qal'a. But it is also possible that the modern quarries to the south of Jabal Naẓīf, and west of Waḥdāt, conceal earlier ancient workings.

PHYSICAL TOPOGRAPHY OF THE JABAL AL-QAL'A (CITADEL HILL)

The site of the Citadel Hill (Jabal al-Qal'a) (fig.28; pls 2a, 11, 12) is located between the two wadis of Wādī Shāri' al-Salṭ and Wādī Ḥaddāda. It is thus an isolated hill, only linked with the surrounding high ground at the northwest, where there is a saddle to Jabal Ḥusayn. Although the hill is overlooked on the south side by the greater elevations of Jabal Ashrafiyya and Jabal Jawfa, and on the north by Jabal Ḥusayn, the site is an excellent defensive position, for it is almost entirely surrounded by slopes that vary from 35% on the southwest to 70% to the northeast. Only at the saddle is there a gentle slope of approximately 8.5%. The hill is composed of three plateaus, an upper terrace oriented northwest, approximately 370 × 150m, and two lower terraces, oriented east northeast, approximately 330 × 100m and 350 × 80m. The total area within the fortification walls is about 89,980 sq.m.

Like the surrounding hills, the natural structure of the Citadel Hill is composed of hard grey Tertiary limestones. The strata were folded subsequent to deposition, but the visible angles of folding – which are only exposed in excavation areas – do not exceed 20°.

The Upper Terrace

The upper terrace can be said to consist of two parts: the double enclosure of the palace, about 126m × 126m at its maximum dimensions, and the hexagon of the main area, approximately 250m north to south, by 150m east to west. The area of the double enclosure is about 15,200 sq.m., and that of the hexagon about 40,860 sq.m.

The double enclosure of the palace, as it stands today, is an artificial platform built out from the north end of the hill, extending from the level of the bedrock at its southern end, to a maximum height of 11m above the natural hill at its northern end. The construction of the platform is discussed further in Chapter 7.

The hexagon to the south is a plateau-like area surrounded by the Roman and Umayyad fortification walls. Although the area appears level in air photographs (pls 2a, 11), there is in fact considerable variation in height; the bedrock of the hill rises in the centre to a height of *c.* 848m above Mean Sea Level (MSL), and at the edge of the hill, by the fortification wall in Area C, the bedrock is at *c.* 834m, a difference of 14m.[14]

The plateau-like appearance is a product of terracing, though of a more limited kind than the platform of the double enclosure. The terracing was carried out partly in the Roman period, when it seems that the centre of the ancient tell was flattened, as was noted by Harding,[15] and can be seen clearly in the stratigraphic sequence. In the centre of the hill (Area B), the Byzantine remains are founded directly on the bedrock, with only faint traces of earlier occupation. The rectangular *temenos* of the Temple of Hercules seems to have been levelled by means of cuts and fills. In addition, limited terracing was carried out in the Umayyad period (Area C: Stratum VI). Nevertheless, such a steep site could not be entirely levelled, and a peak of bedrock remains to the east of the present archaeological museum.

The Lower Terrace

The first terrace of the eastern limb of the hill, approximately 330m long and 100m wide, is a rectangular plateau at levels between 824 and 827.5m above MSL. The area of the terrace is about 33,860 sq.m. Today, the area also has the appearance of a plateau, although there is no direct evidence for terracing, as exists for the upper terrace. It is possible that the fortification walls which surround this lower terrace have to some extent resisted the erosion of the archaeological deposits that have accumulated over the centuries.

The Easternmost Terrace

To the east of the Lower Terrace there is a further lower terrace, 350 × 80m, which in late periods, at least, was outside the wall-line, and which is today covered by houses. According to early plans of 'Ammān, there was a fosse dividing it from the fortified area to the west. It is at present uncertain whether this terrace was ever included within the walls; however, it may be said that this terrace does have traces of archaeological occupation, mainly from the Iron Age and the Hellenistic – Early Roman periods.

2

'AMMĀN BEFORE THE HELLENISTIC PERIOD

by Ulrich Hübner

Up until the present, little has been discovered about the beginnings of the settlement of 'Ammān – that is, of the Citadel and its immediate vicinity – and the same is true for the settlement throughout the Bronze Age (*c.*3200–1200 BC), Iron Age (*c.*1200–539 BC) and the Persian period (*c.*539–333 BC).[1] This is to be attributed on the one hand to the Hellenistic, Roman, Byzantine and Arabo-Islamic inhabitants of 'Ammān, who cleared away the older settlement remains and reused them as building material. On the other hand, it is also due to the fact that so far only a few excavation deposits have produced remains of pre-Hellenistic occupation *in situ*. Thus, archaeologically speaking, the pre-Hellenistic periods of 'Ammān's history have been investigated mainly through sherds and other small finds (most of which are nothing more than surface finds), or by material from Bronze and Iron Age graves, much less often from the remains of buildings or material which was found *in situ*.

Moreover, nearly every excavation that has produced any evidence of the early history of 'Ammān has either not been published, or has only been published in the form of short preliminary excavation reports that do not provide the detail necessary for study purposes.[2] To be added to these large gaps in the archaeological evidence is the almost complete silence of the literary sources during the entire Bronze Age and the Achaemenid Period, and the similarly scarce literary and epigraphic sources from the Iron Age.

The earliest provable remains of settlement in 'Ammān date back to the late Chalcolithic Period,[3] as do some of the dolmens found in the immediate vicinity of the city.[4] Whether or not this evidence should be considered a part of the earliest settlement of 'Ammān can only be verified or discounted by further excavation.[5] In any case it has been shown that 'Ammān was almost continuously inhabited throughout the Bronze and Iron Ages. However, the little material recovered so far hardly permits any historical statements other than the mere determination of the period under consideration. There are many other questions, such as when 'Ammān became an urban settlement; what area the urban settlement of 'Ammān covered during the various early periods; what type and what degree of civilization it had at any given time, or when and how often the settlements were destroyed by external force or earthquakes, and then rebuilt. All of these questions can only be answered more or less hypothetically for the time being.

By analogy to other sites in Palestine,[6] the village-like settlement structures of Rabbath Ammon might have become a city towards the end of Early Bronze I (*c.*3200–3000 BC).[7] At any rate, the existence of settlement during Early Bronze II and III (*c.*3000–2300 BC) on the Upper and Lower Terraces of the Citadel has been confirmed.[8] The following so-called non-urban intermediate Early Bronze IV – Middle Bronze I Period (*c.*2200–2000 BC)[9] has been documented primarily through graves on the Citadel,[10] and its immediate[11] and more distant surroundings.[12]

The earliest fortifications on the Citadel of 'Ammān so far identified date to Middle Bronze I (*c.*2000–1500 BC). This is a massive wall, with a glacis on its outside face, which has been excavated on both the Lower and the Upper Terraces.[13] Furthermore, settlement of the same period has been substantiated by a series of graves found on, and in the vicinity of, the Citadel. The finds of this period are richer and more varied than those of the previous periods, a point which probably documents the growing prosperity and the increasing importance of the town.[14]

A part of the late Middle Bronze II finds from 'Ammān can also be dated to the Late Bronze Age I (*c.*1550–1400 BC).[15] This clearly shows the continuity of the transition from the late Middle Bronze Age to the early Late Bronze Age settlement. Nevertheless, according to our present state of knowledge, it appears that the Citadel of 'Ammān did not enjoy the same importance during Late Bronze I and particularly Late Bronze II (*c.*1400–1200 BC),[16] as it did in Middle Bronze II. Among the few Egyptian itineraries from the time of the New Kingdom that mention geographical names of the Transjordanian plateau, the long 'Palestine List' of

Thutmoses III (No.96) does not mention Rabbath Ammon;[17] however a certain *krmn* (Abel Keramim, cf. Jud. 11:33) is mentioned (*ANET*^{3} *242*),[18] which is probably to be identified with Saḥāb.[19] From this, it seems that the Canaanite city-state of Rabbath Ammon could only have been of small territorial extent (at least to the southeast), and of correspondingly small political significance. It apparently stood in the shadow of, or at least was obliged to compete with, the city-state of Saḥāb.[20]

Hardly anything is known about the settlement of ʻAmmān during Iron Age I (*c*.1200–1000 BC).[21] Some of the finds seem to point to a continuum between the Late Bronze Age and the Early Iron Age.[22] There are also hardly any literary sources which shed any light upon this period: neither the traditions dealing with Jephthah (Jud. 11:1–40) nor the ones discussing Saul (I Sam. 11:1–11) reveal anything about the history of the city of Rabbath Ammon.

At the beginning of the 10th century BC, the Israelite king David conquered Ammon as part of his expansionist policy, and crowned himself king of both Israel and Ammon (II Sam. 8:12; 10:1–19; 11:1–27; 12:26–31). During the siege of Rabbath Ammon he ordered his general, Joab, to occupy the so-called 'City of the Waters' (II Sam. 2:27) before he gave the command to storm the city itself, a tactic which Antiochus III was to use successfully against *Rabbatamana* centuries later.[23] The term 'City of the Waters' (*ʻyr h-mym*) suggests a settlement outside the Citadel walls, which might have been situated on the site which the later Roman Forum was to occupy, where many sherds from the 8th to the 6th centuries have been found.[24] When the only water-system on the Citadel so far known was constructed still remains a mystery – though it was probably in use during Iron IIB–C.[25]

David married his son Solomon to an Ammonite princess named Naʻamah (I Kings 14:21, 31; II Chr. 12:13), who was probably the daughter of the Ammonite king Hanun (LXX: II Kings 12:24a), and left him with a political union which Solomon's heir, Rehaboam, the product of this Israelite–Ammonite mixed marriage, could not hold together for long. With the division of the united kingdom of Israel into the southern kingdom of Judah and the northern kingdom of Israel, round about the middle of the 10th century BC, Ammon was able to regain its independence. Rabbath Ammon became the capital of an Ammonite state. However hardly any archaeological material can be dated with any certainty to the period of Israelite predominance, or the following two centuries (Iron Age IIA–B: *c*.1000–*c*.850 BC).[26] Arabo-Islamic traditions commemorate Uriah (cf. II Sam. 11:17), or rather his alleged grave, as well as Solomon, who supposedly built the Roman theatre (Muqaddasī 175; Yāqūt III: 760). Another tradition names Lot as the founder of Rabbath Ammon (Yāqūt III: 719, Abū al-Fidāʼ: 247; Gen. 19:30–38). Equally unhistorical are the various traditions of the Old Testament that deal with the pre-Ammonite period of Rabbath Ammon. This is reflected for example in the Israelite legends concerning Rabbath Ammon found in the later antiquarian comments on the *rpʼym* (Deut. 2:20; 3:11), who appear here as the pre-Ammonite inhabitants of middle and upper East Jordan. By way of analogy with the Ugaritic texts, however, they are to be understood as deified heroes or ancestors. Nor is Og's bed, described as '9 cubits long and 4 cubits wide', anything more than a polemical late Israelite back-projection of a neo-Babylonian temple-inventory into the pre-Ammonite period.[27]

With the beginning of Iron Age IIC (*c*.850–582 BC), the history of the city of Rabbath Ammon can be reconstructed not only through archaeology, but also from literary and epigraphic sources. As its history is more or less the same as that of the land – or rather the kingdom – of Ammon,[28] the history will be considered as background material, while the Iron Age archaeological finds from ʻAmmān will be emphasized here.

Rabbath Ammon was certainly fortified on the Upper and Lower Terraces of the Citadel[29] – this probably encompassed the area of the present Jabal al-Qalʻa. Little is known, though, about the internal urban development.[30] Most of our present knowledge comes from the many graves[31] found along the slopes of the Citadel and its vicinity, from chance finds, and from finds not discovered *in situ*.[32]

During the 9th/8th to 7th centuries BC Rabbath Ammon was the production-centre of stone male and female statues of high artistic quality.[33] One such statue boasts an inscription on its base, according to which the figure depicted was an Ammonite King: *] m̊ẘ Yrḥʻzr/ [r̊ z̊k̊r br švnp̊*;[34] it is probable that the grandfather of *Yrḥʻzr* is the same king as the one who is mentioned as *ᴵSa-ni-pu/bu* in the Neo-Assyrian records of Tilgathpileser III in 733 BC (*ANET*^{3} *282*). The *pax assyriaca* during the 8th and 7th centuries BC provided the necessary political framework,[35] within which the capital of the Ammonite state embarked on an era of cultural and economic prosperity: nearly all of the known Ammonite inscriptions from ʻAmmān originate from this period,[36] particularly the various epigraphic seals,[37] the inscribed jars,[38] and the 'Theatre Inscription'.[39] Cultural influences – or rather Ammonite adaptations of Mesopotamian practices – can be seen in such things as burial in slipper coffins,[40] or the Neo-Babylonian seals[41] found in ʻAmmān.[42] Up till now, five anthropomorphic ceramic sarcophagi dating to the 8th–7th centuries BC have been found at Jabal al-Quṣūr,[43] for which there is a series of Iron Age parallels in Transjordan (Saḥāb, Dibon, Khirbat al-Mukhayyit, Pella) and Palestine. Various anthropomorphic and theriomorphic terracotta figurines,[44] clay model shrines,[45] cosmetic palettes of the normal style,[46] as well as palettes decorated with figural designs,[47] often found in and around ʿAmmān, demonstrate the strong connection between the culture and religion of ʿAmmān, and that of its Moabite, Edomite, Israelite and other neighbours.[48]

During the era of Assyrian supremacy, the Ammonite kings remained loyal vassals of Mesopotamian power, and paid their tribute punctually. We know this, for example, in the case of *ᴵP/Bu-du-ilu (*Pādāʾil)*, who is mentioned in texts from Esarhaddon's time (*ANET³ 291*), and is probably also mentioned on an Ammonite official's seal of unknown provenance.[49] The Ammonite kings also provided Assurbanipal with auxiliary troops in his campaign against Pharaoh Taharqa (*ANET³ 294*), and most likely also for his wars against *Yuhaiṯiʿ* of Arabia (*ANET³ 298*), which took place partly in Ammonite territory.

The end of Assyrian predominance, or rather the advent of Babylonian supremacy, heralded no new autonomy for the Ammonites; rather it brought about their political demise, thanks to what the Babylonians saw as Ammonite opportunistic policies (2 Kings 24:1 f.; Jer. 27:1ff.). The last known king of Ammon, Baʿalis (Jer. 40:14), also known from the impression of an Ammonite official's seal, found at Tell al-ʿUmeiri, as *bʿlyšʿ (*Baʿalyiṯaʿ)*,[50] is recorded in the Old Testament as having taken part in the assassination of the Babylonian puppet Gadalya in 586 BC. In any case, Nebuchadnezzar II (605–562 BC) conquered Rabbath Ammon during his twenty-third regnal year, i.e. five years after his conquest of Jerusalem, in 582/581 BC[51] – an event which brought about the end of the Ammonite state and throne, and their incorporation into the Babylonian provincial system. Thus Rabbath Ammon ceased to be the capital of a state, or the seat of a king.

When Neo-Babylonian control over Palestine came to an end (539 BC), the Babylonian province of Ammon was transferred straight into the hands of the Achaemenids (*c.*539–333 BC). During this period, Ammon was a sub-province of the Persian province of Samaria, as emerges from the few remarks about Tobiya, the Governor of Samaria's vassal, *h-ʿbd h-ʿm(w)ny* (especially Neh. 2:10, 19).[52] After this period, there is no further record of the toponym Rabbath Ammon, and from the Citadel in ʿAmmān there are so far no traces of occupation from the Persian period. As the pottery of the Late Iron Age hardly differs from that of the (early) Persian period,[53] and as a substantial series of settled sites are known from Ammonitis during this period, it would be rather peculiar if ʿAmmān, of all places, was not settled at all. Further excavations and a better knowledge of Ammonite pottery are here particularly necessary.

It remains to express the hope that the pre-Hellenistic periods of ʿAmmān's history will receive their due attention in future excavations – and their published final reports! Since its foundation, ʿAmmān has been the focal point of central Trans-Jordan, and the ancient Canaanite toponym *Ammon* has survived to give us the name of the modern capital, *ʿAmmān*. Yet very little information has been gleaned from the Citadel itself, despite the fortuitous absence of modern construction. When one compares the Citadel of ʿAmmān to other local capitals, such as Bosra (Buseira), Jerusalem or Samaria, then it becomes apparent both how little is actually known about pre-Hellenistic ʿAmmān, and how great the rewards of further research could be.

3

THE HISTORY OF PHILADELPHIA IN THE CLASSICAL PERIOD

by Henry Innes MacAdam

ALEXANDER AND AFTER: THE HELLENISTIC AGE

Alexander's expedition to and from Egypt in 332–331 BC held to the coastal road and ignored the inland portions of Syria-Palestine. Rabbath Ammon and its imposing acropolis were of no strategic importance for the conquest of Persia, and accordingly played no role in that campaign. Syria (in its broadest geographical sense) was administered from Damascus as a satrapy until Alexander's premature death in 323 BC.[1] Immediately thereafter Rabbath Ammon and all of Transjordania fell within the bounds of the Greek kingdom (centred on Egypt) that had been carved from Alexander's empire by his resourceful marshal Ptolemy (Sōtēr). The Near Eastern segments of Ptolemy's domain were immediately contested by several other of Alexander's 'Successors', foremost among them Seleucus (Nicatōr). It would be another generation, concluding with the Battle of Ipsus in 301, before the frontiers between the Seleucid and Ptolemaic kingdoms solidified.

1. Ptolemaic Ammanitis

Ptolemaic Syria included all of Phoenicia and Palestine, and the territory east of the River Jordan from Damascus to the Red Sea. Ptolemy I Sotēr (d.283) consolidated his hold on that territory, but there is no evidence of close administrative control during his reign. Rabbath Ammon was one of the larger settlements within Ptolemaic territory east of the Jordan. Like Bostra to the northeast and Pella to the northwest it could boast of a history stretching back to the Bronze Age and perhaps beyond (see Chapter 2). An ethnographical work of late antiquity informs us that the city was 'first [called] Ammana, then Astartē, then Philadelphia'.[2] The same source goes on to say that the official dynastic name Philadelphia ('Brother/Sister-Loving') derives from Ptolemy II Philadelphus (283–246 BC), who thus honoured either himself or his sister/wife Arsinoë II. St Jerome's commentary on Ezekiel also notes that the city's name was associated with Ptolemy II: 'Rabbath, which today is named Philadelphia, from the king of Egypt, Ptolemy [called] Philadelphus'.[3]

Had Rabbath Ammon been refounded as a Ptolemaic colony it would have received a sizeable Greek population, a Greek constitution, and perhaps the privilege of coining. There is no evidence for any of this during the Hellenistic age, though the city did attain the status of *polis* in the Roman era (see below). The change of name seems to have been purely propagandistic symbolism, and was perhaps made simply to advertise Ptolemaic possession of a strategic site. Third and second century sources ignore 'Philadelphia' and use instead the pre-Ptolemaic name 'Rabbatammana'.[4] Much the same was undoubtedly true for other towns such as the port of Aela/'Aqaba (which received the name Berenice) and the Phoenician religious centre at Ba'albek (renamed Heliopolis). Only cities which had already enjoyed autonomy would have maintained any special civic status, i.e. Akko (renamed Ptolemais), Pella (Berenice) and Bethshan (Scythopolis).[5] The date at which Rabbatammana became Philadelphia remains uncertain. Akko received its dynastic name no later than 261 BC,[6] and it may be that all such honorary benefactions (except perhaps the two Berenices), date to the 260s.[7] But there is indirect evidence that Philadelphia was not known as such until as late as the end of the Second Syrian War (255 BC).

Professor A.H.M. Jones observed that traces of the administrative system in the Ptolemaic Near East are evident in some of the district names attested in Hellenistic and later sources.[8] Such names end in *-ites* or *-itis*, common topographical suffixes used by Greeks in Egypt. Most of those names are regional, e.g. *Samareitis* in Palestine, or *Trachonitis*, *Auranitis* and *Gaulanitis* in the south of modern Syria, or *Gabalitis* and *Moabitis* in south-central Jordan. But a few are named after cities. That distinction may indicate their importance to the Ptolemies. *Esbonitis* refers to Ḥisbān and its vicinity, and *Ammanitis* designates the region of Rabbatammana. Ammanitis is in fact the oldest attested of these terms, occurring in several papyrus documents of the mid-third century BC (see below).[9] Certainly all the major towns would have been under Ptolemaic authority, either directly through royal garrisons or less directly through local chieftains commanding resident Greek or Macedonian veterans. Philadelphia would have been no exception.[10]

The Ptolemies were content to administer their portion of Syria in much the same fashion as they governed Egypt, that is, through a centralized bureaucracy responsible to the crown. The official name for the entire region was 'Syria and Phoenicia', but unofficially the name remained simply 'Syria'. Ptolemaic Syria's financial affairs are known to have been overseen by a *dioiketēs* ('treasurer'), not, as in the other Ptolemaic possessions, by an *oikonomos* ('manager'). But the pattern of administration in other regions under Ptolemaic control (e.g. Lycia, Cyprus, Cyrenaica) suggests that Syria would also require a *stratēgos* (military commandant) as overall 'governor'.[11] There is some support for this from the fact that once Ptolemaic Syria passed to the Seleucids an inscription attests a named '*stratēgos* and *archiereus* (high priest) of Coele Syria and Phoenicia'.[12] Therefore it is likely, though as yet unattested, that Ammanitis and the other 'districts' of Ptolemaic Syria were governed collectively by a *stratēgos* with full civil, and perhaps some religious, authority. This would be fully consonant with the region's 'frontier' position vis à vis the Seleucids.

The smallest administrative unit in Ptolemaic Syria, as in Egypt, was the village (*kōmē*). At village level the official in charge was the *kōmarchos* (headman or *shaykh*).[13] The unit of intermediate size was called a *hyparchia*, not (as Jones supposed) a *nomos* or *toparchia*.[14] We may assume, in the absence of formal proof, that Ammanitis was one such *hyparchia*. The official in charge of this administrative unit is nowhere named in contemporary sources, but we know that each *hyparchia* had at the head of its financial affairs an *oikonomos*. Each of those, in turn, was responsible to the provincial *dioiketēs*, who then reported to the king's finance minister.

2. Ammanitis in the Zenōn Archive

The unique structure of the administrative system in Ptolemaic Syria indicates that the region was particularly important to the crown. Not only was Syria the largest of the provinces, it was among the wealthiest. Agriculturally rich areas such as the Massyas (Biqā') Valley in eastern Phoenicia, and the Esdraelon Valley in northern Palestine, must have commanded the utmost attention from Egypt. The export of wine, grain and oil was a standard feature of commerce between those two regions and Alexandria. The commercial wealth of the Phoenician city-states was also a major factor in the close attention paid to the internal affairs of Ptolemaic Syria. But it is less easy to discern the economic importance of Ammanitis and the other territories east of the Jordan, where pastoralism was prevalent outside the few urban settlements. A recent archaeological survey of western Ammanitis reported that the number of inhabited sites dropped from 145 in the Iron Age to only 35 in the Persian-Hellenistic period.[15]

Some aspects of social and economic life may be found in the remarkable corpus of papyrus business documents known as the Zenōn Correspondence or the Zenōn Archive. This was among the earliest of the papyrological collections discovered in the Fayyūm district of Egypt, and it has been published in a scattered and piecemeal fashion over the last 75 years. The archive consists of letters, sale contracts, expense accounts, customs payments and the like. One of these recorded the sale of a young slave-girl to Zenōn, the business agent of Egypt's Finance Minister under Ptolemy II. The bright light this document casts on the internal affairs of Ammanitis at this time (259 BC) makes it worth quoting at length:

> In the twenty-seventh year of Ptolemy [II] son of Ptolemy [I]... in the month Xandicus [April-May], at Birta of Ammanitis. Nicanor son of Xenocles, Cnidian, in the service of Tobias, has sold to Zenōn son of Agreophon, Caunian, in the service of Apollonius the *dioiketēs*, a [Sid]onian (?) girl named Sphragis, about seven years of age, for fifty drachmae. Guarantor: ...son of Ananias, Persian, *kleruchos*, of the horsemen of Tobias. Witnesses:...(a judge) the son of Agathon, Persian, and Polemon son of Straton, Macedonian, *klerouchoi* [both], among the horsemen of Tobias; Timopolis son of Botes, Milesian; Heraclitus son of Philippus, Athenian, Zenōn son of Timarchus, Colophonian, Demostratus son of Dionysius, Aspendian, all four in the service of Apollonius the *dioiketēs*. [Verso] Sale of a female slave.[16]

'Birta' transcribes Aramaic *bīrtā*, itself a loan-word from Akkadian *bīrtu*, the primary meaning of which is 'fortress' or 'citadel'.[17] Since Père Vincent identified it with 'Araq al-Amīr, 17 km southwest of modern 'Ammān, Birta has become what Claude Orrieux calls a *mot magique* for archaeologists, historians and philologists.[18] The ruins of large and splendidly built structures at 'Araq al-Amīr caught the imagination of all early visitors. The physical remains and the archaeological dating accord well with Josephus' description (*AJ* 12.4.11) and chronology of the construction that he attributes to the Tobiad prince Hyrcanus (187–175 BC). Josephus calls the site Tyros (not Birta), which presumably transliterates an older Canaanite place-name 'Sōr' (Phoenician Sōr: Gk. Tyros). 'Sōr' is preserved in the modern name of Wādī Sīr, the watercourse which flows past the site.[19] Josephus mentions in particular the *baris* ('palace', not 'fortress') constructed of white marble.[20]

Excavations in the 1960s established that the major structures did indeed date from the first quarter of the second century BC. Since 1976 joint French-Jordanian excavations have confirmed this mid-Hellenistic date.[21] The only earlier evidence for permanent occupation at 'Araq al-Amīr dates from the 11th century BC. That conclusion would seem to undermine the identification of Birta, a place-name (cf. Birtha on the Euphrates)[22] evoking a military stronghold, with a site yielding no evidence of fortifications or permanent habitation at the time Zenōn purchased the slave-girl.

Siegfried Mittmann saw this difficulty and suggested instead that 'Araq al-Amīr would better be identified with another place-name,[23] perhaps 'Sōrabitta' (also 'Sourabitta'), known from related documents in the Zenōn archive.[24] Such an identification had been proposed earlier, but that resulted in three distinct place-names being equated with 'Araq al-Amīr.[25] Mittmann eliminated one by proposing that the phrase 'Birta of Ammanitis' should be understood as the 'Zitadelle von 'Ammān', and that the transaction described in the document quoted above actually took place within the military stronghold of the district capital.

That conjecture has more recently been accepted by a noted papyrologist and several of the French team excavating at 'Araq al-Amīr.[26] 'Birta of Ammanitis' would thus specify the Ptolemaic sector of Rabbatammana, in particular the fortress on the acropolis. That same distinction seems to have obtained in an earlier period, when the 'royal city' (the acropolis) and 'the city of waters' (the settlement around the Wādī 'Ammān?) are noted separately in the Israelite capture of Rabbath Ammon (2 Sam. 12:26–8). 'Rabbatammana' would include both the acropolis and the residential area below. Some comments on the social background of this document will demonstrate that Mittmann's supposition is sound.

By the time of this slave-sale the name 'Tōbīah' had already been associated with Ammanitis for several centuries. Descendants of the same family (the son and grandson of our Tobias) were prominent in the political affairs of Palestine in the late third and early second century.[27] Tobias in 259 BC was an important element in the Ptolemaic administrative system in Ammanitis. His ancestral home at 'Araq al-Amīr/Tyros was unquestionably a show-piece; indeed the name *TWBYH* (*Tōbīah*) appears twice carved above cave-entrances at the site.[28] Thus it may well have served Tobias and his entourage as a Persian-style *paradeisos*, a place where royal officials such as Zenōn could be entertained and impressed.[29]

The three cavalrymen in the service of Tobias were military settlers, each with his *kleros* or allotted homestead. The two designated as 'Persians' may have been Persian-*born*, but are clearly not ethnic Persians. The patronymic (Hananiah) of the 'guarantor' is Hebrew. The other (the judge) is almost certainly Greek or Macedonian. He may well have had jurisdiction within the Greek community of Ammanitis. The man from whom the slave is purchased would seem to be a civilian in Tobias' employ. These are not local villagers related by birth or marriage to a *kōmarchos*. They are resident foreigners 'in the service of' a local man of considerable authority. Tobias himself is given no title in this or any other document in the Zenōn archive, so his exact status and the geographical extent of his authority (i.e. 'the [land] of Tobias'[30]) are conjectural.

How much prestige he enjoyed is evident from another document in the Zenōn collection. In a letter written to Apollonius in 257 BC, Tobias appended a note to Ptolemy II regarding a gift of animals. Though the note was relayed to the king by the finance minister, it is nevertheless significant that Tobias wrote in the certain expectation that the king himself would read it. Considerable imagination has been expended in assigning an appropriate title to Tobias: 'Ammonite (or Transjordanian) *shaykh* (or *chef*)', *judische Scheikh*, *seigneur féodal* or *Feudalherr*,[31] 'local prince' or 'Jewish aristocrat'[32] and even military ranks such as *stratēgos*, *Reiteroberst* or *Reitergeneral*.[33]

With military control went administrative duties. The military and administrative centre of Tobias' dominions cannot have been at 'Araq al-Amīr at the time of this document. The district 'capital' of Ammanitis was Rabbatammana/Philadelphia. It is there that we can expect Tobias to have transacted business involving a deputy of Egypt's minister of finance, and there that the requisite witnesses and guarantors would be found. In spite of its seeming awkwardness, the phrase 'Birta of Ammanitis' must represent what in the Old Testament was 'Rabbat of the Ammōnites'[34] and is today the 'Qal'a of 'Ammān'. Support for this comes very recently from a thorough study of the term *bīrtā* by Lemaire and Lozachmeur (1987). They argue convincingly that from the Persian period on the term has not only a military sense, but also an important administrative aspect as well. At the time of this contract Birta would refer not only to the Ptolemaic fortress on the acropolis at Philadelphia, but by extension to the administrative authority which emanated from it.[35]

Though the slave-girl is presumably a Near Easterner, her name is Greek. The low sale price indicates that she is untrained. Zenōn expected a substantially increased resale value in Egypt once she acquired skills. Ammanitis and neighbouring regions were themselves the source of slaves. A Minaean inscription of early Hellenistic date from Ma'īn in South Arabia attests a number of foreign women, probably brought there for service as temple-slaves. From among the dozens of names and places of origin are 'Adanat from 'Ammon' (*'DNT bn 'MN*) and 'Ya'ya from Moāb' (*Y'Y bn M'B*).[36] The Zenōn Archive also abounds with references to slaves. One of these (*PSI* 406.13, *c.*258 BC) records a nameless slave-girl whom 'they [i.e. agents of Zenōn] took away from [the land of] Ammōn; they sold her in Ptolemais (Acco).'[37] This, then, is probably the single most important aspect of Egyptian interest in Transjordania.[38] Of secondary but still considerable concern was livestock. There are indications elsewhere in the Zenōn papyri that horses and related species were a regular regional export, with Philadelphia perhaps the central market.[39] More exotic animals, also probably transhipped through Philadelphia, were sold or given as diplomatic gifts to the royal zoo at Alexandria.[40]

For the next half-century we know nothing of Philadelphia's history. During the same year in which this slave-sale was recorded, Seleucid and Ptolemaic forces clashed in what became the Second Syrian War (259–255 BC). The outcome of that struggle was far from decisive. An uneasy peace between the rival kingdoms was formalized by inter-dynastic marriage. Philadelphia seems to have played no part in that struggle, but we may assume that its military garrison was maintained and that fortifications on the acropolis were built or rebuilt. The civilian settlement which must have flourished in the area of the later Roman forum is known only through its pottery.[41]

3. Seleucid Ammanitis

Our next glimpse of the city is during the Seleucid campaign into Trans-Jordan in the penultimate year of the Third Syrian War (221–217 BC). Antiochus III swept through Palestine in 218, capturing major Ptolemaic cities such as Philoteria and Scythopolis. The fortified towns beyond the Jordan had to be taken before an invasion of Egypt could be launched. Antiochus' forces were aided by Arab tribes in the vicinity. Polybius (*Hist.* 5.71–2) tells us that Gadara (Umm Qays) on its high bluff overlooking the confluence of the Yarmūk and Jordan Rivers 'was reckoned the strongest [town] in that region'. That estimation proved to be false; the city fell after a short siege. Learning that a major contingent of Ptolemaic forces was operating from 'Rabbatammana in Arabia' the king made its capture a priority.

The Seleucid army encamped below the citadel and reconnoitered the city's defences. Battering rams were brought forward and set to work at two sections of wall deemed vulnerable.[42] But even though the outer defences were breached, the number and determination of the defenders held the acropolis during successive attacks 'by night and by day'. The city fell only through treachery. A captured prisoner revealed the location of an underground passageway by which the defenders of Philadelphia reached a hidden water source. Sappers broke into the tunnel and blocked it with 'wood, stones and other such material'. The thirsty defenders, confronted with a typically rainless summer, surrendered. A Seleucid garrison was installed and the king withdrew to Ptolemais on the coast, awaiting the spring and the planned invasion of Egypt.

The mention of Arabs as allies of the Seleucids, reference to Philadelphia as 'Rabbatammana', and the identification of that city as 'in Arabia', are interesting features of whatever source or sources Polybius utilized. The Nabataean Arabs of Petra had by this time established themselves as a growing power in the Jordanian plateau. They had foiled several attacks (motivation unknown) by Macedonian forces in 312 BC.[43] A half-century later slave-dealers in the employ of Zenōn had encountered Nabataeans in the Syrian Ḥawrān.[44] Nabataean inscriptions of Hellenistic date from that same area are still awaiting publication.[45] The 'Arab' allies of the Seleucids may or may not have been Nabataeans. In either event, ultimately the Seleucids would be obliged to confront the Nabataeans. The Third Syrian War ended with a Seleucid defeat at Raphia in 217 BC. Control of Ammanitis undoubtedly passed again to the Ptolemies, who would not have left such an important district in Seleucid control.

4. Nabataean Ammanitis

All of this changed when Ptolemaic Syria fell to the Seleucids at the end of the Fourth Syrian War in 200 BC. It is possible that Philadelphia was then given over to Nabataean control as a reward for military assistance against the Ptolemies. Soon thereafter western Ammanitis was neither Seleucid nor Nabataean. A descendant of the Tobiad family, Hyrcanus, re-established hegemony in 'Araq al-Amīr and its vicinity *c.*187 BC, and did not relinquish control until his suicide *c.*175 BC. Josephus offers many details of the massive building programme initiated by Hyrcanus, remains of which can still be seen.[46]

A late Hellenistic document clearly reveals that Philadelphia was not under direct Seleucid control during the reign of Antiochus IV (175–164 BC). About 172 BC the Hellenizing Jewish High Priest, Jason, was deposed and 'forced to flee into the region of Ammanitis' (2 Macc. 4:26–27). Some years later Jason led a failed uprising against Seleucid forces in Jerusalem. He was again forced to take refuge in Ammanitis (2 Macc. 5:7–8). But then, we are told, his luck ran out. Accusations brought him before 'Aretas, tyrant of the Arabs'. Jason fled yet again, this time to Egypt (2 Macc. 5:8–9). Aretas the *tyrannos* can only mean Aretas I, the earliest attested Nabataean king.[47] The implications are clear. Jason had fled to Nabataean-controlled territory. Seleucid displeasure at a rebel finding refuge in the territory of a client-kingdom led to the tribunal before Aretas and the subsequent exile of the Hasmonaean prince.[48]

This was not the last time that the Nabataeans would become involved in the political affairs of Palestine. Within a few years of Jason's ignominious departure, Ammanitis was attacked by forces under Judas Maccabaeus (*c.*165–160 BC). The motive appears to have been territorial aggrandizement. When Judas had subdued areas of Palestine:

> ...he moved against the Ammanites, finding there strong forces and a sizeable population, under the command of Timotheus. [Judas] fought against them many times... [eventually] he captured Jazer and its villages, and turned back to Judaea (1 Macc. 5:6–8).

A parallel account of this campaign (2 Macc. 12:17–19) has Judas besiege and destroy the stronghold of Charax and 'the garrison that Timotheus had left within [it]', in the region of 'the Tobiad Jews' (i.e. near 'Araq al-Amīr). The identity of Timotheus remains a mystery. He may have been a Greek or Macedonian mercenary, perhaps the *stratēgos* of Ammanitis in the pay of the Nabataean king.[49] Timotheus ultimately launched a reprisal against Judas, and was slain (1 Macc. 5:34–44). Jazer (Yazer, Gazara) is also known from the Old Testament (e.g. Num. 32:1). It has been identified with Khirbat Sār, 15 km west of 'Ammān.[50] Charax may be the newly discovered Hellenistic/Herodian fortress at Sūr (see below).

Such is the literary evidence for Nabataean rule in Ammanitis early in the Seleucid period. We may assume Ammanitis was administered as part of the Nabataean realm centred on Petra. During the next century of Seleucid decline Nabataean influence expanded northward to Damascus and westward into the Negev Desert, while the Hasmonaean dynasty consolidated its control of central Palestine. Philadelphia stood at the crossroads of the lucrative trade with inner Arabia, some of which may have come westward through the Wādī Sirhān and the Azraq Oasis. The bulk of it came northward through Petra from the Ḥijāz and the Ḥismā. Philadelphian merchants transhipped those goods northwest through Gerasa to Pella and Scythopolis and then on to the Palestinian coast.[51]

It would have been essential to the Nabataeans to control such an important emporium, either directly through a *stratēgos* appointed by the king, or indirectly through a local *shaykh*. In the late second century (*c.*135 BC) we hear of a Zenōn Cotylas and his son Theodorus who were 'tyrants' of Philadelphia.[52] Zenōn may or may not be a Semitic name.[53] His Greek nickname of Cotylas ('drinking-cup') would be appropriate in the context of Nabataean banqueting.[54] Theodorus might be a rough translation of some Semitic name, e.g. 'Abdallah. The ethnic identity of Zenōn and Theodorus remains ambiguous, but Nabataean military commanders with Hellenized names are well-attested.[55] Elsewhere Josephus informs us that Gerasa, Gadara and Amathus were also controlled by Theodorus.[56] Gerasa later fell to the Hasmonaeans. The Nabataean hold on Philadelphia was strong enough to withstand sustained attacks on the city by Alexander Jannaeus (103–76 BC).[57] Perhaps the Hellenistic fortification walls on the lower terrace, dated to the second century BC by Zayadine (see Chapters 5 and 8 below), were instrumental in the city's successful defence.

Proof that Philadelphia was still Nabataean on the eve of the Roman conquest of Syria lies in a careful reading of Josephus' account of the Nabataean involvement in Hasmonaean affairs in 65 BC. Pompey's lieutenant, M. Aemilius Scaurus, was sent to Jerusalem in that year to relieve the Nabataean siege of the city. The Nabataean king, Aretas III, had intervened in the dynastic struggle between Jannaeus' sons Aristobulus and Hyrcanus. Scaurus threatened a Roman invasion of Nabataea unless the Nabataean forces withdrew. 'Aretas', says Josephus, 'terrified, fled from Judaea to Philadelphia.'[58] Clearly the city was an integral part of Aretas' dominions east of the Jordan. There is every reason to believe that Philadelphia was Nabataean from the very beginning of the second century and remained so until the end of Seleucid rule in Syria.[59]

The territory of early Hellenistic Philadelphia must have been enormous. It included all the villages and land within the city's effective control, but its exact dimensions remain unknown. Gerasa/Gerasenē to the north and Esbus/Esbonitis to the south were the nearest cities possessing territories of their own. Presumably the territories of all three cities were larger before the period of Hasmonaean expansion into the area east of the Jordan (the Peraea) in the late second century BC. Jones has pointed out that both Ammanitis and Esbonitis lost some western territory when Alexander Jannaeus annexed the Peraea.[60] The Hasmonaeans retained possession of the Peraea (including a portion of western Gerasenē and parts of Moabitis as well) throughout the period of Nabataean hegemony in Ammanitis. The Peraea included the towns of Amathus west of Gerasa, Gadara (Tell Jadūr, near Salṭ) west of Philadelphia, Julias/Livias west of Ḥisbān, and Abila west of Mādabā.[61] Those four towns were the centres of the region's four toparchies.

Evidence for Nabataean influence in Philadelphia and Gerasa (and elsewhere in the region) has recently been reviewed by David Graf and Pierre-Louis Gatier.[62] Gatier concentrates exclusively on the literary sources, whereas Graf includes a brief account of the steadily increasing archaeological data. In the case of Philadelphia, it should be noted that no Nabataean material – ceramic or numismatic – from an archaeological context can be safely dated any earlier than the first century AD.[63] Nabataean epigraphy is so far completely absent. One may also add that the *amount* of material so far discovered is limited. But given the witness of Maccabees and Josephus, discussed above, there is no reason to doubt that physical evidence for the late Hellenistic period will yet be found.[64] For the rest of Ammanitis there is little reason to hope for important discoveries. The French survey of the region centred on 'Araq al-Amīr reported that neither pottery nor coins are plentiful enough to demonstrate occupancy between *c.*150–50 BC.[65] The chaotic political and economic conditions of that century may have been responsible for a decline in population. Those circumstances were rectified only by direct Roman intervention.

POMPEY AND AFTER: THE EARLY ROMAN PERIOD

Pompey's restructuring of Eastern affairs in 64/63 BC profoundly affected the subsequent history of Philadelphia. We have only the barest outlines of the internal affairs of Roman Syria at this time. As the political heirs of the Seleucids the Romans found themselves in direct control of northern Syria and in nominal control of the southern portion. In south Syria they encountered three native kingdoms, the Ituraeans in Phoenicia and the lava-lands south of Damascus, the Hasmonaeans in Palestine, and the Nabataeans. Phoenician Ituraea was reduced in size to just the territory of 'Arqa and its mountainous hinterland near Tripolis. The Ituraeans in Trachonitis were likewise left under the rule of a native prince. Both areas eventually became part of the Herodian kingdom.

The history of hostility between the Hasmonaeans and the Nabataeans during the century preceding Roman intervention presented Pompey with a dilemma. Outright annexation of either kingdom would have meant an additional burden on the provincial administrative system. Complete autonomy would encourage them to encroach on each other's territory. Pompey and his lieutenants Scaurus and Gabinius were content to accept the native dynasties in Jerusalem and Petra as clients once Roman hegemony was established. In one instance Pompey ordered Roman forces across the Jordan against 'the bandit strongholds and the treasuries of the *tyrannoi* … [one of which was located at] Lysias, and those near Philadelphia.'[66] Lysias is perhaps to be identified with the modern site of Sūr, 4 km southwest of 'Araq al-Amīr.[67] The fortifications there will be discussed below.

1. The Territory of Roman Philadelphia

Roman Philadelphia was a more circumscribed entity than its early Hellenistic predecessor. The southern and eastern boundaries are the most problematic. Esbus/Ḥisbān is only 20 km southwest of Philadelphia. The border between their territories may have lain along the Wādī Kifrayn or its tributary, the Wādī Ḥisbān. Neither watercourse presents a well-defined, natural line of demarcation. The eastern limits of Philadelphia's territory would have lain no further than the line of habitation before the edge of the Jordanian steppe-land. Zarqā' to the northeast, Quwaysma and Rajīb to the southeast, are modern villages that yield epigraphy of the Roman/Byzantine period.[68] There can be no doubt, because of their proximity, that they belonged to Philadelphia.[69]

There is less uncertainty about the northern and western limits of Philadelphia's territory. The Wādī Zarqā' is a major landmark that would have presented a natural boundary between the territories of Philadelphia and Gerasa. The Wādī 'Ammān, an important tributary of the Wādī Zarqā', flows northeast from 'Ammān and describes a huge loop out into the steppe near the village of Zarqā', before turning northwest and joining the larger Wādī Zarqā', which then runs directly west as a tributary of the Jordan. The great bulk of Philadelphia's territory, therefore, lay to the north of the city. The early Church historian, Eusebius, noted (*Onom.* 144.4–6) that the town of Ramōth (Khirbat Jal'ad), 23 km northwest of 'Ammān, belonged to Philadelphia.

To the west Philadelphia adjoined the region of the

Peraea. Gadara/Jadūr was the capital of the Peraea and central town of its own toparchy. How extensive its territory was may be gauged from Josephus' statement that the less important toparchy of Julias/Livias further south incorporated 14 villages. At some point between 'Ammān and Salṭ the territory of Roman Philadelphia and the region of the Peraea had a common border. This can be fixed at one point with some precision. Josephus (*AJ* 20.1.2–4) related that the Judaean procurator Cuspius Fadus (AD 44–45) had to settle a dispute between the Jewish residents of the Peraea and the city of Philadelphia 'concerning the boundaries of the village called Zia'. Zia is modern Zay, just a few kilometres northwest of Jadūr/Gadara.[70]

2. Philadelphia and the Decapolis

Certain cities belonging to the Hasmonaean and Nabataean kingdoms were designated as members of a Decapolis. Those cities and their territories were attached to the province of Syria.[71] One of the initial 'Ten Cities' was Philadelphia, whose calendrical system reckoned its foundation-year to be 64/63 BC precisely.[72] Just what membership of the Decapolis actually meant can only be surmised. Philadelphia was the southernmost of nine cities east of the Jordan. Gerasa and Gadara were its nearest neighbours to the north. Scythopolis, alone out of the Palestinian towns, was a charter member. Canatha, once under Ituraean rule, was also given membership. If the territories of all ten original members were contiguous, the Decapolis 'region' stretched from Damascus in the north to Philadelphia in the south, and from Scythopolis in the west to Canatha in the east. The standard view since the 19th century has been that the Decapolis was created as an 'anti-Semitic blockade' against Jewish and Arab cultural influence in Hellenized districts. In that sense it was taken to be a 'League' or 'Confederation'.[73]

Parker has argued against that well-entrenched belief, observing that Strabo, who wrote at length about the Lycian League, had nothing to say about the Decapolis. Parker thus concluded that 'Decapolis' was a geographic expression.[74] But Isaac reproduced epigraphic evidence demonstrating that the Decapolis was an administrative district of Syria in the late first century AD.[75] Graf contends that the Decapolis was created to keep its ten member cities out of Hasmonaean control.[76] Gatier, without knowledge of Graf's study, took the issue a step further. He argues that the Decapolis was created expressly to preclude either Hasmonaean or Nabataean political control of those cities by placing them within the administrative authority of the Syrian governor.[77] The Romans thereby gained control of the northern half of the 'King's Highway' – the main trade artery between Petra and Damascus.[78]

None of the new studies ascribes any ethnic or cultural motive to the creation of the Decapolis. That signals a significant challenge to prevailing opinion, and requires some comment. At the moment of Roman intervention the degree of Hellenization in most of the Ten Cities, especially ones which had fallen to the Hasmonaeans, must have been minimal. Gadara is the only city for which there is sufficient evidence (albeit exclusively literary) for advanced Hellenization prior to Roman intervention. Both Will and Rey-Coquais have recently drawn attention to this.[79] In the two centuries from *c*.250 BC – *c*.50 BC, Gadara produced thoroughly Hellenized poets, teachers, philosophers and orators (e.g. Meleager, Philodemus, Menippus and Theodorus, respectively), and its native sons brought fame to the city well into the third century AD. Extensive excavations of the site have revealed only monuments and epigraphy of the Roman/ Byzantine/Islamic city. There are as yet no traces of Meleager's 'Syrian Attica' of the pre-Roman period, which is perhaps some indication of the devastation that befell the city under Alexander Jannaeus.[80]

The earliest evidence for civic institutions in any of the Decapolis cities is of Neronian date. There are no coins or inscriptions of Hellenistic date from any of 'The Ten', including what Josephus called 'the greatest' city, Scythopolis.[81] The earliest dated inscription, found at Gerasa, is Tiberian.[82] Eventually all the cities of the Decapolis issued coins, but so far only those of Gadara date to the time of Pompey, i.e. to 'The Year One of Rome' (64/63 BC).[83] Those earliest Gadarene coins show immediate Greco-Roman influence in religious motifs.[84] But there are as yet no clear indications that the Hellenization process had made much headway elsewhere in the region, prior to Roman intervention.[85] Accordingly there is no need to suggest, as has often been done, that preservation of the Hellenized element in those cities was uppermost in Pompey's mind at the time the Decapolis was created.[86]

Just how the region was administered in that early period is unknown. The only evidence for any internal supervision dates from a century and a half later. This is a Greek inscription of *c*.AD 90 in which an equestrian official is attested as having jurisdiction in 'the Decapolis in Syria'.[87] How long that arrangement had obtained is conjectural. Isaac has theorized that the occasion of Herod's death (4 BC) and the reorganization of Judaean territory may have provided the right moment to place the region of the Decapolis under the direct supervision of an official responsible to the Syrian governor.[88] But Pliny the Elder, whose *Natural History*

(5.74) does devote some notes to the Decapolis, employs the geographical term *regio* rather than a precise administrative expression. Pliny, however, is notorious for using archaic sources. The *Gospel of Mark* (7:31), perhaps contemporary with the *Natural History*, uses the expression 'boundaries (*horia*) of the Decapolis', which is hardly more precise. Josephus refers to just 'the Decapolis' (e.g. *BJ* 3.9.7). The overall impression is vague indeed. If the Decapolis was an administrative district prior to AD 90, there is not the slightest hint of that from the available sources.

Pliny indicates that the number of cities remained constant at ten. But the implication is that the names of the ten might vary. This can only mean that certain cities had 'lost' membership and others 'gained' it in their place. Ptolemy of Alexandria (*c.*150 AD) registers *eighteen* cities under the combined heading 'Coele Syria and the Decapolis' in his *Geography* (5.14.22). Presumably that list includes cities which became part of the Decapolis when one or more original members lost that status. Our sources give only two instances when that occurred. In the settlement following the Battle of Actium (31 BC), Augustus ceded to Herod the Great certain towns and territories on both sides of the Jordan. Among those were Gadara and Hippos.[89] Both towns are thought to be foundation members of the Decapolis. At Herod's death Gadara and Hippos (along with Gaza) were separated from Judaea and made an appendage (*prosthēkē*) of Syria.[90] Early in the reign of Nero a town called Abila was added to the territory of King Agrippa II. That was probably Abila of the Decapolis.[91] In none of these accounts of territorial disposition is there mention of the Decapolis, nor is there any implication that the cities involved belonged to an association. It would therefore seem that no case can be made for the Decapolis, by that name, being a political unit before the time of Domitian.

3. Philadelphia from Augustus to Trajan

The historical outlines of this period are unfortunately very vague. Philadelphia remained on the periphery of larger political events unfolding across the Jordan. Pompey's punitive expedition into bandit territory on the western border of Ammanitis was an isolated event. Relations between the Hasmonaeans and Nabataeans were cordial until the last years of the struggle between opposing forces in the Roman civil war. Josephus relates that Cleopatra persuaded Mark Antony to pressure Herod the Great into war with Malichus I. The pretext was default of payments on the part of the Nabataean king; the underlying motive was the destruction of both monarchies. Herod's first campaign resulted in an ignominious defeat at Canatha in the Ḥawrān. The severe earthquake in the spring of 31 BC led to a Nabataean plundering of Herodian territory. That gave Herod the excuse he needed to launch a reprisal campaign, one which ended with a decisive victory on the borders of Ammanitis. 'Having encamped at Philadelphia ... [Herod] fought for possession of a fort captured by the Nabataeans' (*BJ* 1.19.5–6). It fell, and Herod's triumph was complete.

The fort in question may well be that recently surveyed by the French at Sūr, a site near 'Araq al-Amīr.[92] It is shaped somewhat like a spearhead, some 400m at its longest and about 250m at its widest, overlooking the Peraea and the Jordan Valley to the west and the route to the interior of Ammanitis to the east. A rectangular structure, approximately 25 × 30m (the 'citadel' of the fortress?), was constructed at the northern end. In the absence of excavation the fort cannot be dated precisely. The survey team believe it can be no earlier than the second century BC, and no later than the end of the first century AD. It may well have been in use, and modified, within those three centuries. It occupies a strategic point on the western border of Ammanitis. As such it was either intended to guard an entrance to the Peraea from the east (as Villeneuve thinks), or defended the western approaches to Ammanitis. Its identification with Strabo's Lysias is conjectural; it may instead be the camp called Charax, captured by Judas Maccabaeus in his campaign against Timotheus (2 Macc. 12.17). It may, indeed, be *both* unidentified strongholds.

The sources are silent concerning Philadelphia and Ammanitis between the time of Herod the Great and the outbreak of the first Jewish revolt. It was during that latter event that the ancient animosity between the Jews of Palestine and the Hellenized communities of western Transjordania (many of which now belonged to the Decapolis) surfaced with particular violence. Again our witness is Josephus. He relates that the massacre of Jews by the gentile population of Caesaraea Maritima prompted severe reprisals by their enraged countrymen. Mobs of Jewish insurgents moved across the Jordan, where they attacked 'Syrian villages *(kōmai)* and the nearby cities *(poleis)*' (*BJ* 2.18.1–2). Philadelphia heads the list of cities (most belonging to the Decapolis) thus assaulted.

This would appear to be exaggeration on the part of Josephus. It is unlikely that groups of untrained dissidents could either seriously or lastingly disrupt the activities of any large city. But we may certainly accept that villages within Ammanitis were harassed, if not damaged. Whatever the specific details, the Jewish incursions led in time to counter-reprisals against the Jewish inhabitants of the Decapolis. Entire families were slaughtered, property was confiscated or destroyed. Some residents escaped. Others stayed and survived, only to be expelled later. Philadelphia is not explicitly named among the communities exacting vengeance on its Jewish inhabitants, but neither is it noted as one of the few cities which (Josephus says) exercised restraint. We simply do not know the level or extent of Philadelphia's response in the midst of these appalling circumstances.

There is nothing to indicate that Philadelphia was directly or actively involved in the Jewish War (AD 66–73) which followed. Apparently only one minor campaign was conducted east of the Jordan. The sole reference to it is a laconic statement in Josephus (*BJ* 4.8.1–2) about the meeting in Jericho (in June of AD 68) between Vespasian and his general Traianus (father of the future Emperor). Traianus had with him 'the (military) force he brought from Peraea, (the region) beyond the Jordan already having been pacified.' Nevertheless, the protracted Judaean War seems to have affected the status of Philadelphia's population, and perhaps that of other cities of the Decapolis.

The evidence for this is the tombstones of two soldiers, both of whom were natives of Philadelphia. A Latin epitaph from the faraway province of Pannonia Superior in central Europe attests a certain 'Proculus the son of Rabilus, of (the tribe) *Collina*, (from) Philadel(phia)'. Proculus had served with the Roman army in Syria as an *optio* in the *cohors II Italica civium Romanorum*. He was transferred, as part of a special archery unit, to the military base at Carnuntum, near what is now Vienna, where he died at the age of twenty-six. He had served seven years in the military. The epitaph, which is undated, was set up by his brother Apuleius who presumably served with him in the same unit.[93]

The second epitaph (also Latin) is from Bostra, northeast of 'Ammān. The soldier, 'Titus Flavius Marcianus, the son of Marcus, of (the tribe) *Collina*, home(town) Philad(elphia)', had served as *optio* of the third-ranking centurion of the *Legio VI Ferrata*, and was remembered by his mother Luculla and his sister, Flavia Ialla. Again there is no date (*IGLS* 13.9179).

Proculus was from Syrian Philadelphia, either the city itself or a village in its territory. His name, and that of his brother, tell us nothing about their ethnic background, but the patronymic *Rabilus (Rab'el)* is a well-attested Nabataean name, both for royalty and for commoners.[94] Proculus and his family were Arabs. But in the case of Marcianus, whose father has a Latin name, the ethnic identity is unknown. It is also less certain that he is from Philadelphia of the Decapolis. The Latin tribal affiliation, Collina, is not specific enough, as it could be associated with Philadelphia/'Ammān, or with Lydian Philadelphia in western Asia Minor. The circumstantial evidence regarding Marcianus points to the former. He had served with a Syrian legion (eventually transferred to Palestine), and was buried in a neighbouring province. Thus in both cases we are dealing with 'locals' recruited into the Roman army.

Proculus' epitaph cannot be dated with certainty. But as earlier editors have noted, his service on the Danube could be connected with the movement of units from Syria (against Vitellius) by the consular governor, Licinius Mucianus, toward the end of AD 69.[95] That date is attractive since it would mean that Proculus joined the Roman army at about the time of the first phase of the Jewish War, i.e. in the years AD 66–69. His tribal identification would then be significant, providing a Flavian date for the bestowal of citizenship rights on Philadelphia. Vespasian very probably had conferred citizenship throughout the Decapolis in return for support in the war. Nevertheless, the transfer of Proculus' unit from Syria may have occurred as late as Trajan's Dacian Wars (AD 101–106).

The date of Marcianus' funerary inscription is equally uncertain. His presence at Bostra is probably connected with the annexation of the Nabataean kingdom in the early second century. His *praenomen* Titus, and the *nomen* Flavius/Flavia in his family, point to either Vespasian or Titus for the privilege of citizenship and enrolment in the same tribe as Proculus. This would have occurred during the Jewish War. The initial recipient of this benefaction would have been the father or even grandfather of Marcianus.

G. W. Bowersock has shown that the development of Syria's commercial and cultural potential was a Flavian priority in the immediate aftermath of the Judaean War.[96] Responsibility for that policy devolved upon the province's consular governors. The first of these was the elder Trajan, whose long tenure (AD 73/74–78/79) saw the securing of the Euphrates frontier and the active promotion of urban and commercial enterprises. Bowersock's study singled out the Syrian cities of Palmyra and Gerasa as *foci* of imperial and provincial attention, and Nabataean Bostra as a parallel case within the domains of that client-kingdom. Gerasa is of particular interest, since any developments there were bound to influence its sister-cities in the Decapolis. During the decade between AD 70 and 80, its urban layout was reoriented and an orthogonal street plan implemented. The city's fortification walls, once also thought to date to Flavian times, would appear to be some two centuries later.[97] But the northwest gate, dated epigraphically to AD 78/81, is articulated with the new street plan. Unless it was a free-standing monument there must have been earlier walls. With or without Flavian fortifications,

Gerasa became a 'show-case' of urban renewal.

For Philadelphia only the barest outlines of any important transformations are discernible. The grant of citizenship to the city may have occurred, as argued above, *c*.AD 66–69. The earliest coinage we know of appears with the date '143' of the Pompeian era (that is, AD 80/81) on the reverse. This is discussed below. The appointment of an equestrian official with jurisdiction within Philadelphia and other of the Ten Cities may have been roughly contemporary with the documented developments elsewhere in Syria. We know for certain of only one such official, the nameless individual noted above who served the governor of Syria in some capacity *c*.AD 90. No known structure of the upper or lower cities dates to the Flavian era. The city walls were undoubtedly rebuilt in Roman times. Some progress has been made in determining which portions of the present walls belong to the Roman period. A date in the second century seems probable (see Chapter 8 below). The earliest securely datable inscription is AD 150 (*IJ* 2.17).

4. Roman Philadelphia: Constitution, Calendar, and Coins

Along with an extensive territory, Philadelphia also enjoyed several other privileges of a constitutional *polis*. Among them were the prestige of civic institutions, a calendrical era and the privilege of minting. It is probable that all three were implemented at the time of Pompey, though the evidence for each is considerably later.

The City *(Polis)*, its Council *(Boulē)* and the People (*Dēmos*) of Philadelphia are attested in several Greek inscriptions. In one dedication (*IJ* 2.23), found when excavating the forum area, 'The City of Philadelphia ... built a triple portico (*tristoön*) in the year 252 (that is, AD 189/90)'. In another, of uncertain date, the city honoured an emperor (*IJ* 2.24). In each of these instances, the term *polis* collectively signifies the city's constituent government. We find the latter attested in the restoration of a damaged and undated Greek dedication (*IJ* 2. 29) in which 'The Council and the People, as a token of esteem', honour one Martas, son of Diogenēs. During the reign of Alexander Severus (AD 222–35) the Council and the People 'by decree' allowed a centurion to honour his dead daughter, perhaps with a statue (*IJ* 2.30). Less certain is the restoration of 'Council and People' in a badly-damaged and undated Greek inscription honouring Titus Flavius Longinus (*IJ* 2.28).

There is also an epigraphic attestation of individual members of the council and the specific magistracies they held. Martas, noted above, was 'Councillor and *Proedros*'. The latter term designates the 'President' or 'Chairman' of the city's Council. His father once held the office of *Gymnasiarchos*, normally a one-year appointment. The inscription is damaged where a second position, apparently held 'for life', was noted. Such distinctions are all the more remarkable since only at Gerasa and Canatha, among the cities of the Decapolis, are there parallels for these or other municipal offices.[98] Also worthy of mention is the mixture of Graeco-Roman and Semitic personal names in these civic inscriptions, a characteristic feature of urban onomastica throughout the Hellenized East. One may add that 'Philadelphus' as a personal name appears in several Greek inscriptions from nearby areas.[99]

Philadelphia and the villages within its territory utilized four different calendar-systems throughout the classical period. Most common were those based on the era of the Seleucids (dated from 312/11 BC) and on the Pompeian era (64/63 BC). Less frequent are examples of dating by regnal years of an emperor, and calculations according to the era of the province of Arabia (the latter only from AD 106). What little evidence there is indicates that Macedonian month-names were used.[100] The Pompeian era continued to be used in Ammanitis well into the Umayyad period. A Greek mosaic inscription (see below) from the floor of a church in the village of Quwaysma, six kilometres south of 'Ammān, is dated to 'the year 780' (that is, AD 717/718).[101]

Philadelphia issued coins from 80/81 in the reign of Titus until Elagabalus (218–222).[102] Two eras appear to be used for the dated varieties. Examples such as Spijkerman nos 1–3 and nos 7–10 are dated by the Pompeian era to 80/81. Spijkerman nos 4–5, dated by him to 441/442, cannot be based on that era, but would instead be of the Seleucid era (equating to 130/131).[103] The iconography of most 'quasi-autonomous' coins features pastoral motifs: woven baskets, laurel wreaths and corn-clusters appear on the reverse, and representations of Demeter on the obverse. The 'colonial' imagery draws heavily on Philadelphia's identification with Herakles and his mother Asteria. More 'neutral' are depictions of the city's Tychē,[104] the goddess Athena, and the divine twins *(Dioscuri)* Castor and Pollux. One 'quasi-autonomous' issue of 80/81 surrounds the date on the reverse with a laurel wreath; another (of smaller module) has as motif a palm tree and fruit. The obverse of the first displays a bust of Athena, and the second a bust of Nikē. Each bears the legend *Philadelpheōn.* On larger denominations of the same date the obverse features the head either of Titus or Domitian (as Caesar) with an inscription naming each, and the reverse displays a bust of Herakles or Tychē, respectively.[105]

On both types of coins, and in the city's epigraphy, the phrase 'Philadelphia of Coele Syria' is prominent. It appears in coin legends as early as Hadrian's reign, and in a dated inscription of the late second century.[106] Much has been written about the meaning of 'Coele Syria' in the historical geography of the classical Near East. At the simplest level the qualifying expression 'of Coele Syria' distinguishes *this* Philadelphia from several others, notably Philadelphia (Neocaesaraea) in western Asia Minor. Beyond that, the city's identification with 'Coele Syria' is specifically propagandistic. It evokes the political geography of the Hellenistic era, especially the Seleucid period when Philadelphia was nominally part of 'Coele Syria and Phoenicia'. If Rey-Coquais' analysis is correct, Philadelphia's explicit association with 'Coele Syria' also signals a conscious effort to reject the Nabataean element in the city's history and culture.[107] The identity with 'Coele Syria' also provided a way by which Philadelphia might proclaim its 'autonomy' when the Decapolis was dissolved and the city was assigned to the Roman province of Arabia in AD 106. Lastly 'Coele Syria' proclaimed membership in a new association *(koinon)* of Hellenized cities which participated in the imperial cult established by Augustus and revived by Hadrian.[108]

TRAJAN AND AFTER: THE LATER ROMAN PERIOD

By the end of the first century AD it was becoming evident that Rome's long tradition of client-kingship in the Near East was drawing to a close. The kingdom of Commagene had been re-annexed by Rome in AD 72. The last remnants of the Herodian kingdom reverted to Rome upon the death of Agrippa II *c.*94; the various portions were attached to Syria or Judaea. In AD 105/106, upon the death of King Rabbel II, the same fate befell the Nabataean kingdom. In that case the annexation involved military forces entering from Syria and Egypt. The disposition of Nabataean territory was also handled differently; the bulk of it became the Roman province of Arabia.[109]

A secondary aspect of this new dispensation was the dissolution of the Decapolis. The distribution of its various cities and their territories was dictated purely by their geographical location. The northernmost cities were attached to Syria, and the westernmost to Palestine. The southernmost two, Gerasa and Philadelphia, were assigned to the new province of Arabia.[110] The sources are absolutely silent regarding Philadelphia in the early decades of the second century. There is a break in coinage during the reigns of Nerva and Trajan, and a resumption beginning with Hadrian. That issue, as noted above, proclaims the city as 'Philadelphia of Coele Syria'. The same inscription appears on coins until minting ceased during the reign of Elagabalus.[111] By that time a Roman province with the official name of Coele Syria (the northern half of the old province of Syria) had already existed for several decades. What began as a conscious anachronism ended in a confusion of terminology. 'Philadelphia of Coele Syria' was the city's way of clinging to the aura of respectability it once had as a member of the Decapolis, a privilege enjoyed since the time of Pompey the Great.

1. Philadelphia and the Via Nova Traiana

One immediately visible sign of a Roman presence was the new highway between the ancient port of Aela/'Aqaba on the Red Sea and the provincial capital at Bostra. Construction of that *via nova Traiana* began immediately after the annexation of Nabataea. Newly discovered milestones at 'Aqaba indicate that the southern portion of the road (to Petra) was completed in AD 111/112.[112] This confirms the dating of other milestones on sections of the road north from 'Aqaba. Philadelphia was incorporated into the *via nova*. This is clear from milestones found just north of the city, and traces of an ancient road entering Philadelphia from the south. The section of road between Bostra and Philadelphia is better known because it was better preserved, and therefore was surveyed several times at the beginning of this century.

The traveller moving south along that road would enter the territory of Philadelphia at what is now the site of Qal'at Zarqā', just beyond the forty-first milestone. When the Princeton Expedition surveyed that section of road in the spring of 1909, it appeared that the *via nova* forked at the forty-eighth milestone. The main road ran due south toward Mādabā and Petra, but a branch road entered Philadelphia. It was also clear from dates on several milestones that the Bostra-Philadelphia segment was not completed until AD 114. Other milestones indicate road repairs north and south of Philadelphia undertaken during the reigns of Hadrian, Marcus Aurelius, Commodus, Pertinax, Septimius Severus, Caracalla, Elagabalus, Severus Alexander, Maximinus, Philip the Arab, Aurelian and Diocletian.[113] Milestone distances along the *via nova* were initially counted north from Petra to Bostra. Beginning with the reign of Commodus (the reason is not yet clear) distances were calculated from Bostra toward the south. This inevitably created some confusion regarding the mileage figures on certain stones.[114]

Philadelphia is also quite prominent on a famous road map of the early Roman empire, the Peutinger

Map. The present map is a medieval copy, incorporating features associated with the Christian Roman Empire of late antiquity. But other features are dateable to the first century AD, and the map's ultimate prototype may be as early as the reign of Augustus.[115] What is relevant here is that Philadelphia is depicted as an important stop for traffic moving north or south along the *via nova*. The distinction is made by the cartographer's vignette of the city: twin towered structures of some sort. The same stylized drawing is attached to other prominent cities in the region, e.g. Petra, Bostra and Damascus. The significance of the vignette has variously been interpreted as indicating a stop on the imperial post route, or perhaps the presence of a military detachment.[116]

Butler's observation that Philadelphia was connected to the main highway by a branch road which swung in a loop through the city is not refuted by the Peutinger Map. The latter was designed for the edification of the traveller, and as such indicates the regular stops along the major roads, with distances (in Roman miles) clearly specified between each. Alternative routes and 'by-passes' would not be shown. Also not indicated on the Peutinger Map is a second road north from Philadelphia, to Gerasa and then on to Adraa (modern Dar'cā), west of Bostra. Milestones from north and south of Gerasa have yielded Hadrianic dates for the initial construction of this road.[117] The absence of the Philadelphia-Gerasa road on the Peutinger Map strengthens the argument that its archetype is far earlier than the Byzantine date once taken for granted.

2. Philadelphia and the Roman Army in Arabia

There is no clear indication of Philadelphia's role in the provincial garrison. Arabia was a one-legion province, with the governor in command, for the first two centuries of its existence. The legionary headquarters, and the governor's official residence, were at Bostra. Legio III Cyrenaica, brought from Egypt at the time of annexation, was the province's garrison force. The bulk of that legion was headquartered at Bostra, but units were outstationed where needed. There is a possibility, noted below, that Philadelphia served as the permanent base for a unit of that legion, and perhaps as a temporary home for a detachment of a legion based in neighbouring Palestine.

Only a handful of the Greek and Latin inscriptions from Philadelphia are military in character. Three are dedications. The earliest, already touched upon above, dates to the reign of Alexander Severus (222–35). The Greek text notes that 'Herennius Moschus, centurion of the *Legio X Fretensis Severiana*, honours Herennia Eistha, his daughter prematurely dead, by decree of the Council and the People' (*IJ* 2.30). A veteran of that same legion, Aurelius Victor, is honoured in a damaged Greek inscription (*IJ* 2.26). The legion's imperial epithet is now *Gordiana*, dating the text to 238–44. The home base of the *Legio X Fretensis* was Jerusalem until *c.* 300, when it was moved to Aela/'Aqaba. It has been conjectured that a detachment of the legion was stationed at Philadelphia in the early third century as part of larger military movements on the eastern frontier.[118]

The third inscription is a well-preserved Latin dedication:

> To the most holy gods, Health and Asclepius, Terentius Heraclitus, *beneficiarius* of (the governor) Claudius Capitolinus, for the preservation of the imperial household and of his governor, and by the oracle of the god Jupiter, has completed his vow (*IJ* 2.13).

Capitolinus is attested elsewhere as legate of Arabia *c.*245. Heraclitus had been excused from normal military duties to assist the governor in some capacity.

An undated Latin tombstone (*IJ* 2.34) attests Tiberius Claudius Antoninus, a soldier of the *legio III Cyrenaica*, who had seventeen years of service. His burial at Philadelphia may suggest that a unit of the legion was on duty there. A badly damaged Greek funerary text (*IJ* 2.48) yields part of a man's name ([Theod]orus?) and his title, *cornicularius*. The latter may refer to either military or civilian duties, the former as adjutant to a senior officer, the latter as administrative assistant or secretary to some official.

However distasteful the relegation to provincial status might have been to her citizenry, Philadelphia prospered under Roman rule. A strong military presence in the lava-lands to the north, where banditry had been endemic, ensured the regular flow of commercial traffic between Philadelphia and Damascus. The city's greatest internal development coincided with the Antonine period. The evidence for this is primarily the remains of the major structures built during the period, and the epigraphic witness to known and unknown buildings of the era.

3. Philadelphia and Traditional Culture

Philadelphia celebrated and advertised its Hellenistic heritage with its dynastic name, its constitution and coins, and such structures as a theatre, an odeon, a gymnasium (as yet undiscovered), and a propylaeon. Its sense of Roman identity was linked to the forum, the baths, the temple complex on the citadel, the colonnaded streets, bridges, a splendidly engineered conduit, a military presence, dedications to emperors and governors, and the highways that ran through and near the city. The temples, nymphaeum and coin motifs were also evocative of Graeco-Roman culture. But in the midst of that it is well to keep in mind that the indigenous element, Arab and even pre-Arab, was a constant feature of life in late Roman Philadelphia. Two bits of evidence remind us of that.

One is an epigraphic discovery made at the site of Ziza (modern Jīza or Zizia), 27 km to the southeast of Philadelphia. From that site early this century came an undated bilingual (Nabataean-Greek) inscription of considerable interest.[119] Both texts are damaged, but one supplements the other nicely. Together they attest a certain Dēmas, son of Hellēl (?) and grandson of Dēmas, 'from 'Ammān' *('MWN)*, who built a temple dedicated to 'Zeus who is in Beelphegōr', and consecrated a shrine to another deity (*IJ* 2.154). The 'Zeus' for whom Dēmas built the temple is no doubt Ba'al Shamīn, localized near Mt Nebo as 'Ba'al of (Mt) Fogor'. The latter is familiar from the Old Testament.[120] A cube-shaped altar with sculpted reliefs, purportedly from 'Ammān, has recently been published. It is specifically attributed to worship of Zeus-Ba'alshamīn, and dated to the first or second century AD.[121] Dēmas, his father, and grandfather, are presumably Nabataean. The palaeography of both texts suggests a date in the second-century AD. It is striking that the older form of the city's name prevails in the Nabataean version.

Though the Nabataean element in Philadelphia and its territory was no doubt still strong, descendants of the pre-Arab people are also attested. This is apparent from our second piece of evidence. In the mid-second century the Christian apologist Justin Martyr, born in Neapolis (Nablus) in Palestine, remarked that 'there are now [i.e. at the time he wrote] a great number of Ammonites (Gk. *Amanitai* [sic])'.[122] The context of that statement is a discussion of Near Eastern ethnic groups or 'nationalities', among which are 'Arabians'. It is therefore clear that Justin distinguished between 'Ammonites' and the Arab/Nabataean element in the Transjordanian population of his own time. That a similar distinction was not made by Stephanus of Byzantium (who calls on the testimony of Josephus) some centuries later is of no concern.[123] What matters is that such evidence fits together nicely with the indigenous names of other Philadelphians such as Martas (noted above), Kaioumus (*IJ* 2.46) and Obaidus (*IJ* 2.49), and names such as Tzobeus and Abbibus (*IJ* 2.53) from a site close to 'Ammān. Eventually we can glimpse, however indistinctly, the continuity of local culture within the Hellenistic and Roman milieu.

DIOCLETIAN AND AFTER: THE BYZANTINE PERIOD

Our knowledge of the final phase of Philadelphia's pre-Islamic history is lamentably inadequate. The literary evidence is exceedingly sketchy, more so than for any earlier portion of the classical era. The reasons are clear enough. Byzantine Philadelphia was a prosperous and peaceful city. It was neither a political capital nor a 'centre' of church activity. There is no evidence that Philadelphia contributed to the philosophical or theological movements of late antiquity. Neither is there scandal or controversy associated with the name of the city. Like most of its sister cities in the once-famous and prestigious Decapolis, Philadelphia paid the price of obscurity for its modest success throughout the fourth, fifth, sixth and seventh centuries. To some extent we can fill in the shadows with the aid of epigraphy and archaeology, but even that evidence is limited and conspicuously centred on the church and church affairs.

1. Byzantine Arabia: Borders and Defences (fig. 10)

The reigns of Diocletian and Constantine saw major transformations in the Roman Empire. A second Rome was established, first at Nicomedia and later at Constantinople. Diocletian's reorganization of the provincial system *c.*300 had a dramatic effect on the province of Arabia, which had been created by Trajan and later enlarged by Septimius Severus. The entire southern two-thirds of Roman Arabia was administratively detached and transferred to the authority of the governors of Palestine. For two centuries the border lay along the line of the Wādī Ḥasā, and thereafter was redrawn along the Wādī Mūjib farther north. Arabia received a second legion, the IV Martia, which was installed in the newly constructed *castrum* called Betthoro, at modern Lejjūn (east of Karak). Philadelphia remained within the shrunken territory of what we may call Byzantine Arabia.[124] When Eusebius compiled his Onomasticon in the early fourth century he noted Philadelphia as a 'distinguished *(episēmos)* city of Arabia'.[125]

The introduction of a second legion reflected a massive increase of troop strength throughout the eastern provinces. A military road, officially styled the *Strata Diocletiana*, followed the edge of the desert, south from the Euphrates to the *castellum* and its subsidiary fortifications at the oasis of Azraq, 100 km directly east of Philadelphia.[126] The *Notitia Dignitatum* (compiled *c.*400), a 'directory' of civil and military posts throughout the empire, sets out the disposition of Byzantine forces province by province for the West

(Occidens) and East (Oriens). Under the list of troops commanded by the *Dux Arabiae* there is no entry for a unit stationed at Philadelphia, nor for any big city of the province except Bostra.

But the *Notitia* (*Oriens* 37.20) does register a unit at a place it calls Gadda. Luckily the same name appears on the Peutinger Map, where it is located thirteen Roman miles along the *via nova* north of Philadelphia. Gadda is probably to be identified with modern Ḥadīd or Qal'at Zarqā'. Both are the proper distance northeast of 'Ammān and are near the line of the ancient road. Gadda was the post of the *equites sagittarii indigenae*, a unit of mounted archers recruited locally. Gadda may have lain within or just beyond the *territorium* of Philadelphia; it obviously guarded the main approaches to that city from the north and east.[127]

2. Byzantine Ammanitis

The limited evidence that exists for economic growth and settlement patterns in Byzantine Arabia is primarily archaeological. Because of that, the published results are limited to certain sites or areas, and therefore fall short of creating a truly comprehensive cross-section of the province. The evidence from one region or site may contradict that from another. This is particularly true in the case of Ammanitis. Thus, it may be best to begin with some recent regional surveys of central Jordan, and then compare those results with similar studies undertaken in 'Ammān and elsewhere in Ammanitis.

Father Piccirillo has conveniently assessed the work done in various areas of Jordan during the past sixty years.[128] A comprehensive and detailed multi-volume study of excavations and other fieldwork in Jordan has been published.[129] From that rich harvest we may select some material relevant to the topic at hand. A survey of northern Ammanitis by Glueck, and of central Peraea by de Vaux and Benoit, were completed between the two World Wars. Most of the sites examined showed evidence of Byzantine occupation.

Within the past two decades three areas of the central plateau of Jordan have been extensively surveyed. Single-season surveys were conducted by a Belgian team in 1977, and by an American team from Emory University in the following year. The Belgians worked in the area between Ḥisbān and Karak, and the Americans investigated between the Wādī Mūjib and Karak.[130] Teams from Andrews University Seminary concentrated on sites in the region of Ḥisbān, and in the vicinity of Tell 'Umayri to the north, both of which lie in the Mādabā Plain. Their multi-season survey also included sites to the west of Ḥisbān, where the wadi systems drain toward the Jordan Valley.[131] As noted above, for more than a decade the French have been conducting a survey in the region of western Ammanitis, centred on the site of 'Araq al-Amīr.[132]

The results of the Belgian survey showed that of 30 sites investigated, only 16 yielded Byzantine material. But 21 of the 30 produced finds from the Roman period. This implied a twenty per cent decrease in settlement within that region during the Byzantine era. Emory University examined more than 30 sites, but the report does not include a complete list of places, nor a chronological breakdown of surface finds. The Andrews University team investigated 155 sites in five campaigns between 1968 and 1976. Most (125) of these lay within a ten kilometre radius of Tell Ḥisbān. But in 1976 they surveyed 30 different sites between Ḥisbān and 'Ammān, a number of which lay within the territory of Philadelphia. When the results of the entire survey were tabulated, the Byzantine period was found to be represented at 133 of the 155 sites. Only 99 sites showed signs of habitation in the Roman period.[133]

In 1984 Andrews University began a separate survey of Tell 'Umayrī and the surrounding area, on the very edge of the Mādabā plain where the territories of Ammanitis and Esbonitis meet.[134] Of interest here is the discovery that the settlement pattern at the tell and satellite sites 'reached its peak in the Byzantine era'.[135] The French survey found that about sixty per cent (83 of 145) of the sites they surveyed near 'Araq al-Amīr were inhabited in the Roman/Byzantine period.[136] Roman and Byzantine occupation patterns cannot be compared since the figure given is composite.

Though the results of the Belgian and French surveys would appear to conflict, the number of sites and the area surveyed by each are vastly different. Moreover, the majority of sites investigated by the Belgians lay well outside the orbit of urban centres. Overall, the pattern shows expanded settlement in the Byzantine age, an aspect of late antiquity reflected in the results of surveys in other areas of Jordan.[137]

Hugh Kennedy (1985) has argued for a general decline in the economic and social life of (geographical) Syria in the last century (540–640) before the Islamic conquest. He does not single out one factor as responsible, but suggests that the combined effects of imperial mismanagement, a devastating series of earthquakes and plagues, and other less perceptible causes were to blame. For Ammanitis itself we may adduce a relative decline in prosperity compared with the pronounced urban development in the Antonine era. What wealth there was had never been based on a vast agricultural hinterland (in contrast to Bostra, to the northeast). Trade and commerce must have been the mainstay of the economy.

We may observe that during the Byzantine period in Philadelphia no new fortifications were constructed on the acropolis, that many of the churches so far discovered were badly built, and that intensified agricultural expansion eventually eroded what soil-cover existed on the surrounding hillsides. All of this will be discussed in greater detail in Chapter 5 below. Suffice it to note that this progressive decline was one of several elements underlying the relative ease with which Islam supplanted Byzantine rule in Philadelphia and throughout the eastern provinces. It remains to be seen whether future fieldwork in Jordan and elsewhere will confirm or contradict Kennedy's thesis.

There are several epigraphic indications that pockets of prosperity did exist within the territory of Philadelphia. At Quwaysma, which is today on the southern edge of greater 'Ammān, a splendid Roman mausoleum shares pride of place at the site with the remains of two Byzantine churches. Three Greek inscriptions (all undated) appear within the sumptuous mosaics of Church B. One indicates clearly that a local benefactor is honoured:

> For the health, the peace and the long life of our master, Stephanus the tribune, and for his servant Matrona and her children. Bless them, Lord God, with a spiritual benediction in the heavenly prayers of holy Kērykos. Amen. Lord, give assistance to your servant Magnus and his wife (*IJ* 2.54b).

Stephanus was very much a *patronus* of this church, and probably of his community as well. The woman Matrona may have been his wife or sister. It is probable that 'the holy structure' referred to in a nearby inscription (54c) is the church itself, for the construction of which this grand seigneur was almost certainly responsible. In a similar church dedication (*IJ* 2.43) from central 'Ammān the phrase 'for the health and longevity of our masters' undoubtedly refers to wealthy Philadelphians who underwrote the construction costs. There are no dated Greek or Latin inscriptions from Philadelphia or its territory later than the Umayyad period. But new discoveries at Umm al-Raṣāṣ to the south (see below) reveal a Christian community constructing churches and creating mosaics with consummate skill in the late eighth century. That argues for continuity (at least for the community at Umm al-Raṣāṣ) through the onset of the Abbasid era. Whether Umm al-Raṣāṣ was an isolated phenomenon, or represents conditions obtaining elsewhere, is presently unknown.[138]

3. Christianity in Philadelphia

The story of Paul's conversion at Damascus (Acts 9: 1–26) would indicate that Christian belief had reached the area of the Decapolis at a very early date. Hans Bietenhard has even postulated that Paul's later sojourn 'in Arabia' (Gal.1:17)[139] was spent not in the 'Arabian desert' but in one or more of the Decapolis cities south of Damascus, and F. F. Bruce has argued that Paul's preaching in the synagogues of Damascus was paralleled by similar activity within Nabataean-controlled territory:

> Had he gone to Arabia to commune with God at Mt Horeb, like Moses and Elijah in earlier days, it is unlikely that he would have attracted the hostile attention of the Arabian authorities. Some activity of a more public nature is implied, and the tenor of his argument in Gal. 1:15-17 suggests that this public activity took the form of Gospel preaching.[140]

Christian communities such as that represented by Ananius at Damascus existed east of the Jordan a generation before the famous flight of the Jerusalem Christians to Pella at the onset of the First Jewish War (*HE* 3.5.3-4). But the evidence for early Christianity (i.e. during the first and second centuries) in Philadelphia is totally lacking. Nor do we hear of Philadelphia in the troubled third century, when churches in nearby cities such as Bostra were embroiled in doctrinal controversies (*HE* 6.33; 37) just prior to the outbreak of organized persecutions (*HE* 6.39).

Only at the onset of the fourth century is there any hint of a Christian community at Philadelphia. The evidence for that community is somewhat ambiguous and late, and falls within the genre of Byzantine literature known as 'hagiography' or, more accurately, 'martyrology'. (Of course, this raises the question of the historical value of such sources – a query not yet satisfactorily answered.)[141] Those martyrs noted here are numbered among the 'many holy martyrs' of Provincia Arabia who were later commemorated by the Church. Those of Philadelphia, in particular, were remembered by a *synodus martyrum*.[142]

One tale, a 'Passion' narrative,[143] involves six friends, all Christian, who met privately for worship in an as yet unidentified town in Roman Arabia.[144] Sometime after the outbreak of the Diocletianic persecution in 303 they were betrayed, taken prisoner by the Roman authorities, and eventually transported to Philadelphia. There they stood trial before Maximus, the governor (*hēgemōn*) of Arabia, and were executed on 5 August.

The names of the six fall neatly into two categories. Theodorus, Julian and Eubulus represent the 'Hellenized' Christian community, Malcamon, Mocimus and Salamones the 'Semitic'. Their sufferings were shared by two among the Philadelphian Christians,

Moses and Silvanus. The story has all the standard elements of a 'martyr's epic', which the editor of the document is quick to point out.[145] Yet there are details of geography and bureaucratic terminology that argue for a core of historical truth within the layers of pious embroidery. Other examples will demonstrate this.

A parallel narrative, the 'Passion of Saints Zenōn and Zenas', attests the deaths of two more martyrs at Philadelphia. Their martyrdom is dated to 'the year one of the Emperor Maximianus'.[146] Zenas was the slave/companion of Zenōn. Both were said to be, in the Latin rendition, *oriundi ex Philadelphia Arabiae*, i.e. native-born Philadelphians.[147] They too were brought to trial before Maximus, who must have held assizes regularly in the major cities of Arabia.[148] Their refusal to sacrifice resulted in their torture and a further review before Bogus (or Bonus), the military prefect *(dux)* of Arabia. This second interrogation took place in the *Hippicus*, perhaps a reference to a hippodrome, or the horse-market, of Philadelphia.[149] Zenōn and Zenas were sentenced to beheading in June 304. Of several others we know only the names and the fact that they were put to death most probably during that same great persecution. Such are 'the holy martyrs of Philadelphia in Arabia: Cyril, Aquila, Peter, Domitian, Rufus and Menander.'[150]

St Elianus has only recently become prominent among the known martyrs of Philadelphia, thanks to several Georgian manuscripts published (without translation) in 1946, and a translation and commentary based on additional manuscripts published seventeen years later.[151] Elianus is said to have had a shop *(taberna)* near the Gerasa gate of Roman Philadelphia 'not far from the church that was [later] built there'.[152] During a visit to the city by the provincial governor (Maximus), a group of Christians were arrested and jailed after an outbreak of violence. Elianus visited them in prison, and was himself taken captive. The inevitable public interrogation followed, said to have taken place 'in a large, circular paved area, where a bronze statue of Kronus stood upon a bronze pillar'.[153] Elianus' refusal to sacrifice to the pagan gods (particularly Kronus) led to his torture and eventual martyr's death (by fire) 'near the Mādabā gate' of Philadelphia.[154]

Christian Philadelphia is otherwise known through the churches, chapels or tombs so far discovered, the evidence of epigraphy associated with those buildings or in other ways identifiably Christian, and the various accounts of Philadelphia's church leaders at ecclesiastical councils. A detailed description of each structure identified as Christian is given in Chapter 5. Only the briefest of references will be offered here.

Some half-dozen buildings within the urban area of Byzantine Philadelphia have been identified as churches. One is located at or near the far end of the *cardo* (the northwest-southeast colonnaded street), on its northeastern side. It was long ago identified as such by Conder, and later by Butler. The second is the 'apsidal structure' just southwest of the nymphaeum, identified as a cathedral by Conder (fig.19; pl.76). Butler believed it was a church which had incorporated part or all of an earlier building. Subsequent opinion supports this, and the structure is generally accepted as the seat of Philadelphia's bishops. A nearby structure may have been a church. Neither of those poorly preserved churches, understandably, received a mention in Butler's posthumous *Early Churches in Syria* (1929). Remains of a sixth-century church were identified in the 1930s by Italian excavators on the citadel's upper terrace, just northeast of the Archaeological Museum.[155] Conder also identified a 'chapel', just south-west of the citadel.

Outside the ancient city limits a number of other churches are known. At Swafiyya, near the Sixth Circle on Jabal 'Ammān, portions of a sixth-century church have been uncovered.[156] The church floor was paved with an inscribed mosaic (9.5 × 5m) which was laid on an earlier mosaic floor. At Khuraybat al-Sūq, six kilometres south of the city centre, a late Roman temple of moderate size was converted into a church (with mosaic floor).[157] At Quwaysma, now a southeastern suburb of greater 'Ammān, two churches are known.[158] Church A, near the mausoleum at the site, has a mosaic floor inscribed in Greek and Aramaic. The Greek inscription (*IJ* 2.53) records repair work presumably associated with the great earthquake of January 717, which did considerable damage throughout Jordan and Palestine. Church B, which seems to date to the second half of the sixth century, also has an inscribed mosaic floor. At Jubayḥa, eight kilometres northwest of the city centre and near the University of Jordan campus, the remains of a Byzantine church with a mosaic floor were uncovered in 1976.[159] A similar church-floor mosaic from Yadūda, ten kilometres south of 'Ammān, records the installation of the mosaic 'in the year ?565' (AD ?502).[160]

Three other structures are worth noting: chapels, tombs and monasteries. At Jabal Akhḍar in the southern part of 'Ammān is what may have been a private chapel. There a small (1.42 × 0.5m) inscribed mosaic floor was found within a group of domestic structures that surrounds the 'Ammonite tower' at the site.[161] An undated Christian tomb was found at Jabal Jawfa in the southern part of 'Ammān in 1981.[162] Two painted scenes, now badly preserved, depict miraculous events from the New Testament. One is the raising of Lazarus, the other the healing of the blind. Two-word captions (*IJ* 2.47) identify each. The monastic life is represented by a complex of buildings from the village of Zia (Zay) near Salṭ.[163] Whether Zia lay within the territory or diocese of Gadara/Salṭ (as the excavators believe), or belonged to Philadelphia, is uncertain. No monastery has yet been identified at Quwaysma, though several scholars have postulated that one may have been associated with one or both of the churches at that site.[164]

Apart from the above buildings, there are certain inscriptions, explicitly or implicitly Christian, to consider. Many of these are entirely formulaic, but some are less so. At Jubayḥa a broken inscription (*IJ* 2.6) invokes 'The Lord to protect the entrance and the exit of this holy place' and to accept the offering made. Within the 'chapel' at Jabal Akhḍar was another inscribed invocation:

> 'Lord our God, King for Eternity, come to the aid of your servants Epiphanius, with his children and wife, and Kaioumus the deacon, by provision of [the latter]' (*IJ* 2.46).

The construction of a church was commemorated on a white marble plaque (*IJ* 2.43) found at Jabal Luwaybda ('Ammān) early this century:

> By the will of God, and the consent of A.mon... (?), priest of (the church of) St George, for the health and longevity of our masters, thanks to their generosity, this church has been built under (the aegis of) the holy bishop Polyeucte, through the zeal of Thalassamachias, a... (?)

The date of this inscription is much disputed, and the letters at the end of line one are quite problematic. Gatier has restored there the Greek words for 'most holy monk', i.e. *ha[g(iotatos) mon[achos]*. However, a personal name would be more usual, followed by the person's office (in this case 'priest of St George's'). The status of Thalassamachias is unclear; Gatier suggests 'archiprêtre'. The 'masters' *(despotai)*, like the *tribunus* Stephanus above, must be local gentry of some substance. The mention of a bishop is noteworthy: Polyeucte is not attested elsewhere. Two more names of otherwise unknown bishops appear in the epigraphy of Philadelphia and vicinity: 'the most holy' Thomas at Swafiyya (*IJ* 2.7), and 'the most pious and holy' Theodosius at Yadūda (*IJ* 2.56). The conciliar lists of the fourth and fifth centuries provide the names of two others. Cyrion attended both the Council of Nicaea in 325 and the Council of Antioch in 341; Eulogius represented Philadelphia at the Council of Chalcedon in 451.[165] Almost two centuries later Pope Martin I sent letters to a number of eastern dioceses, including one (AD 649) to 'Bishop John of Philadelphia'.[166]

4. Itineraries, Pilgrimages and Maps

Philadelphia would not have ranked among the most prominent sites in the topography of the 'Holy Land', but its Old Testament associations must have attracted some of the pious Christian travellers who, from the fourth century on, made their way to Jerusalem. Unfortunately we have no clear record of that. Michele Piccirillo has recently reviewed the literary and archaeological evidence for the pilgrim route between Palestine and Trans-Jordan.[167] From Jerusalem the standard itinerary led pilgrims to the River Jordan via Jericho, then on to some point where the Jordan was crossed. The two major attractions on the East Bank were Mt Nebo and the hot springs at Baaru (mod. Ḥammāmāt Ma'īn), which presumably offered spiritual and physical renewal, respectively. For many pilgrims Mt Nebo was the end of the journey. Such was the attitude of Egeria in the late fourth century, who turned back to Jerusalem. For the aged Peter the Iberian, a century later, Mt Nebo was an incidental pause on the way to Baruu via Mādabā.

The accounts of such pilgrims have been the focus of two recent studies.[168] But among the dozens of reports there is only one oblique reference to Philadelphia. Theodosius, an archdeacon and (probably) pilgrim of the early sixth century, produced a rather disorganized and much re-edited work, *De Situ Terrae Sanctae* (On the Topography of the Holy Land), which includes a list of places and routes, and occasional commentary on biblical passages. It has recently been argued by Yoram Tsafrir (1986) that much of Theodosius' topographical information was based on a map or maps used by contemporary tour-guides who conducted pilgrims from Palestine to sites in Transjordania, and that the Mādabā map (see below) used the same source or sources. Theodosius may have inserted information gained from his own travels, or by interviewing others who had made the trip. In chapter 24 of *De Situ*, thirteen cities of (Provincia) Arabia are noted, among them 'Filadelphia'. But there is not the slightest hint that Theodosius ever travelled to Philadelphia, or knew of any prior account of such a trip. The roll-call of martyrs, noted above, was not enough to put the city 'on the map' of tourist sites. Philadelphia was hardly alone in being ignored by the pious pilgrims who left a record of their journeys. Of the cities once belonging to the Decapolis, only Damascus and Scythopolis were regular stops on the pilgrimage itineraries.[169] Even Pella is absent from the travel reports, an omission difficult to understand. Pella had been a refuge for Palestinian Christians in the first century and still flourished in the Byzantine age. It would appear that Christian interest east of the Jordan centred on the Old Testament, and in particular on the burial place of Moses.

The famous mosaic map discovered at Mādabā at the end of the last century is the only visual representation we have of portions of the Near East from late antiquity.[170] The map was created sometime in the second half of the sixth century, and its *raison d'être* must be closely linked to Mādabā's fortuitous location near Mt Nebo. In its original state it displayed in colourful vignettes and cartouches all the names of towns and tribes, cities, rivers, mountains and deserts associated with the Old and New Testaments. In geographic extent it would have represented the Near East from Tyre and Damascus in the north to the Red Sea and the Nile Delta to the south, and from the Palestinian coast in the west to the Decapolis in the east. Unfortunately Philadelphia and virtually all the territory north of the River Arnon (Wādī Mūjib) and east of the Jordan is missing. The lacunae include, ironically, Mādabā itself.

How Philadelphia was depicted in very late antiquity may be inferred from a newly discovered eighth-century mosaic on the floor of the church of St Stephen at Umm al-Raṣāṣ, 30 km southeast of Mādabā.[171] This is not a mosaic map *per se*, but a geographical motif was used with great skill by the mosaicist. Two dedicatory Greek inscriptions give dates of AD 756 and 785. The church and its mosaics are technically from the early Abbasid era, but the tradition they represent is Byzantine Christian. Around the rectangular central panel (damaged sometime after AD 785) is an outer border consisting of eighteen city plans, all but one with the toponym spelled out beneath it. Eight are cities west of the Jordan, and ten (including Philadelphia) lie east of that river. An inner border of the central panel is a scenario from Egyptian geography: the Nile Delta region with ten of its cities and villages presented with captions.

Philadelphia, labelled as such, appears in the upper right-hand corner of the outer mosaic border. Above it is a depiction of a place labelled 'Castron Mefaa', which is now known to be the ancient name of Umm al-Raṣāṣ.[172] Below it is a representation of 'Midaba' (Mādabā). The panel in which Philadelphia appears measures about one metre in length and a half metre in width. The city is presented as one might view it from a nearby hillside, looking toward a city gate. The gate is flanked by towers, and a section of city wall is shown to the left and right of the towers. A number of buildings are shown within the city, in perspective, angled to the left and the right of the viewer, one behind the other. Behind the innermost building another section of wall is shown, with what appear to be the tops of two buttresses or towers above it. To either side of that building are two larger towers, with windows or arrow slits showing. It is difficult to know if those towers stand within the city, or are part of the outer defences.

The depiction of Philadelphia is strikingly different from that of the larger town plan of 'Castron Mefaa' above it. It is, however, similar to that of 'Midaba', both in size and layout, though there are enough details of difference to convince the viewer that the mosaicist was not simply reproducing a stereotype of a city plan. Indeed, the plans of the other fifteen cities are rendered with some attempt at individuality. Where the topography of a city is known from other representations or descriptions (e.g. Jerusalem and Neapolis), its depiction in the Umm al-Raṣāṣ mosaic is reasonably accurate. This is the only detailed representation we have of Philadelphia. The buildings shown, each with a tile roof, may be churches. The walls and gates are standard features of many, but not all, of the cities in the mosaic. This sketch may be more accurate than the stylized rendering of the walled citadel on the crown of the marble *Tychō* of Philadelphia, found in 1961.[173] Since we know that the physical appearance of Philadelphia (especially the citadel area) was transformed after the Islamic conquest, we may assume that the features shown at Umm al-Raṣāṣ are characteristic of the pre-Islamic period and are what travellers or pilgrims would have encountered before the Umayyad age.

5. Philadelphia's Byzantine Historian

Philadelphia produced one historian of 'international' stature in the early Byzantine period. This was Malchus (less certainly Malichus), who flourished in the late fifth and early sixth centuries.[174] It is worth noting that he was known by his native name only; Malchus transliterates either the Semitic word *malik (mlk)*, meaning 'king', or the well-known Arab name 'Mālik'.[175] His city of origin was said to be 'Philadelphia', which can only mean 'Ammān (not Philadelphia/Neocaesaraea in Lydia) in view of his name.[176] He apparently resided in Constantinople, where about the year 500 he compiled a Byzantine *History* ('Byzantiaká'; the exact title is uncertain). It survives only in fragments quoted by later sources, particularly the *Excerpta de Legationibus Romanorum* (10th century AD). Malchus' *History* was of unknown length, but it is likely that it covered events in the years 473–*c*.500. Its scope was nominally the entire Byzantine Empire, West and East, and the surviving fragments bear this out.[177]

Malchus was much praised by later commentators for his clarity, simplicity and orderly style of writing. That acclaim may be due in part to his 'classical' training as a sophist and 'rhetor'.[178] Among his models for composition were Herodotus and Thucydides,[179] and therefore lengthy speeches must have been woven into his narrative at regular intervals. There has been some scholarly debate regarding Malchus' religious background, with rival claims put forward for either his Christianity or his paganism.[180] The fragmentary nature of his *History* indicates only that he held a 'secular position in his narrative and in rendering his historical judgements'.[181] The historical sources used by Malchus can only be conjectured. His approach to historiography was annalistic.

The closest we get to an account of a contemporary event affecting the Byzantine Near East is Malchus' description (Frag. 1)[182] of the seizure of the island of Iotabe (mod. Ṭīrān), at the entrance to the Gulf of 'Aqaba, by an Arab chieftain, Amorkesos, in 472–3.[183] Amorkesos then petitioned Constantinople for recognition as 'phylarch of (Arabia) Petraea', a concession which he was granted upon his conversion to Christianity.[184] The Byzantine Emperor Leo is strongly criticized by Malchus, not for awarding federated status to Amorkesos and his tribe, but for inviting him to Constantinople and seating him among the Byzantine aristocracy. What the fragment reveals of Malchus' treatment of but one small incident in the history of his time makes the loss of his work especially regretful. Whether his native city of Philadelphia played any role in his *Byzantine History* is unknown. What is not doubtful is the high regard in which the *History* is held by several modern historians.[185]

Acknowledgements
I am indebted to Alastair Northedge for advice and encouragement during the preparation of this contribution. Grateful acknowledgement is also made to Dr Martin Price of the British Museum, and Dr Lawrence Keppie of the Hunterian Museum, for acute and helpful comments on numismatics and epigraphy, respectively. Professor Doron Mendecsls of the Hebrew University kindly brought to my attention several useful works concerning the Hellenistic period in Palestine/ Trans-Jordan.

4

THE HISTORY OF 'AMMĀN IN THE EARLY ISLAMIC PERIOD

by Alastair Northedge

The history of 'Ammān after the Islamic conquests has long been obscure. In 1979 Dr. Yusuf Ghawanma published a study of 'Ammān in the Islamic period, based upon textual sources, and this study demonstrated clearly that there is relatively little material in medieval Arabic texts on the history of the city.[1] In itself this point is not so important; it can be difficult to trace the history of events in many provincial cities of the Middle East, cities in which there was no local history written, and which were not centres of the *'ulamā'*, the religious scholars from whose circles much of medieval Arabic historical writing stemmed. To write the history of these cities one is forced to cull isolated items of information from a wide range of sources. However the history of 'Ammān is more difficult to recover than most, and is in strong contrast to the well-preserved archaeological remains of the Islamic period described later in this volume.

In the course of time, 'Ammān changed from being a substantial city in the Umayyad period, perhaps to be described as a city of second rank within Bilād al-Shām,[2] to being a mere village in the time of the Ayyūbids, and eventually disappeared altogether as a settlement at some time under the Mamlūks, probably in the late 8th/14th or 9th/15th centuries. It only re-emerged as a modern city as a result of settlement by Circassians about 1878–82, subsequently to achieve its present prominent position as a result of the establishment of the Amirate of Transjordan after the First World War.

Considering the importance of the Umayyads, and the importance of their leadership of the Islamic world in the first century and a half after the *Hijra*, there is very little detailed material in the historical sources which throws light on the functioning of the Umayyad metropolitan province of al-Shām, although it was the centre of an empire that stretched across the Middle East. Many of the early chronicle and geographical texts were written in the 'Abbāsid period, and in Iraq. By contrast, when 'Ammān had declined in importance, there is much material in the sources on the Ayyūbid and Mamlūk periods. In this sense the historical material on 'Ammān is deceptive, and there are as many references in the sources to 'Ammān in this later period as to when it was an important city.

There is a sharp divide between the history of the city in the Islamic period, and that of Roman times, simply in the form of the name. 'Ammān (عَمَّان) is the only form of the name in Arabic sources, and the Roman name of Philadelphia disappeared immediately. Deschamps identified two medieval French forms of the name, *Ahamant* and *Haman*, in documents of the Latin Kingdom of Jerusalem.[3] However in the circles of the Christian church, the bishopric continued to be named after Philadelphia. It is very probable that the name of Ammon had never been entirely abandoned among the Aramaic and Arabic-speaking population, and when the Hellenistic cultural overlay was removed, the earlier usage came back to life.

THE CONQUEST

The Balqā' was a traditional settlement area for Arab tribes: in the 4th century AD Salīḥ were *mulūk bi-bilād Mādabā* – 'kings in the territory of Mādabā'.[4] Iṣfahānī describes the territory of Salīḥ as *al-Madhāhib* (probably the desert-edge steppe south of Mādabā), the Balqā' and Muwaqqar. The Ghassānid Jabala b. al-Ḥārith is said to have built al-Qasṭal.[5]

Because of its geographical proximity, the area of modern Jordan was one of the first areas of Bilād al-Shām to be approached by the Muslim armies from the Arabian Peninsula. In addition to the early raid and battle at Mu'ta in 8/630, two of the major battles between the Byzantines and the Muslims had taken place within the territory of modern Jordan at Faḥl and Yarmūk.

According to al-Balādhurī, 'Ammān was conquered by Yazīd ibn Abī Sufyān, in the wake of the conquest of Damascus.[6] The date for the conquest of Damascus is given by different sources as 13/634 or 14/635.[7] Al-Balādhurī called it an easy conquest (*fatḥ yasīr*), reflecting the fact that 'Ammān was indefensible from the south and east, and may not even have had a citadel wall at this time.

'Ammān capitulated on terms similar to those of Buṣrā. At Buṣrā, 'its people came to terms stipulating that their lives, property and children be safe, and agreeing to pay the *jizya*. According to some reporters, the inhabitants of Busrā made terms agreeing to pay for each adult one *dīnār* and one *jarīb* of wheat.'[8]

As capitulation terms formed a basis for later taxation, the 3rd/9th century books of conquests, such as Balādhurī, should not be necessarily understood as containing the literal truth about the events of the conquest, as it was in the interests of people later to falsify the supposed terms of settlement. However this is the information which survives. On the basis of the archaeological evidence presented in this volume, which indicates the replacement of a Byzantine quarter of the city by a new citadel in the first half of the 2nd/8th century, one wonders whether in fact the terms of the capitulation were genuinely kept. It is questionable whether the governor apparently responsible for the construction carefully negotiated the purchase of all the complex property rights which must have existed. Even if the rights were purchased, rather than expropriated, at least some of the purchases must have been forced sales.

THE UMAYYAD PERIOD

Twenty-five years after the conquest, Mu'āwiya ibn Abī Sufyān, governor of Syria and senior member of the Meccan family of Banī Umayya, led the Syrians to victory in the First Civil War, and became Caliph in 41/661.

The period of the Umayyad Caliphate (41/661–132/750) was an important one for Jordan, one of the high points of its history before modern times, but it is very difficult to write a history of the region in this period in any detail. On the whole it was a peaceful region, and the dramatic conflicts of the period of the Umayyad Caliphate occurred elsewhere in the Middle East. Nevertheless very great changes had occurred by the time of the 'Abbāsid Revolution in 132/750, even if these can only dimly be perceived in a Jordanian context.

1. Government Organisation

Systematic descriptions of the administration and settlement of the region of modern Jordan appear in the town and district lists in the 3rd/9th century authors, Ibn Khurdādhbih, *Kitāb al-Mamālik wal-Masālik* (*c*.232/846), and al-Ya'qūbī, *Kitāb al-Buldān* (*c*.276/889). A shorter list may also be extracted from al-Balādhurī, *Kitāb Futūḥ al-Buldān* (before 279/892). These are set out in Table 1. These lists are obviously a century to a century and a half later than the end of the Umayyad period; Ibn Khurdādhbih has the most archaic situation, including the Arabic forms of the Decapolis cities of Gadara and Abila, which do not appear later.

Syria had been divided by the Umayyads into four, and later five, provinces (*jund*, pl.*ajnād*): Qinnasrīn, Ḥimṣ, Dimashq, Urdunn, and Filasṭīn.[9] According to these 3rd/9th century authors the East Bank of the Jordan was divided between two of the *ajnād*, Dimashq and Urdunn. The hill country north of Wādī Zarqā' belonged to Urdunn, and the remainder from 'Ammān to the Red Sea was part of Dimashq (Table 1 & fig.11).

It is worth noting that while the arrangement of the *ajnād* remained unreformed in theory until the Crusades, later authors have different accounts. In Iṣṭakhrī (*c*.340/951), al-Sharāt and al-Jibāl are part of Filasṭīn.[10] Muqaddasī (*c*.385/985) removes the East Bank completely from Dimashq: 'Ammān is part of Filasṭīn, and al-Sharāt is an independent entity (fig.12).[11] These differences might reflect contemporary political associations, or simple ignorance of the earlier arrangements: one suspects in any case that the *jund* system had lost any real significance in later times.

The Balqā', which Ya'qūbī tells us was the district belonging to 'Ammān, usually meant the steppe-land east and south of the city (Table 2). Al-Ṣalt, though later associated with the Balqā', was not included: this was probably the Jabal al-Ghawr of Ibn Khurdādhbih. The southern boundary most probably lay at Wādī Mūjib: both Ibn Khurdādhbih and Ya'qūbī agree that Ma'āb was a separate *kūra*. However there was a second wider interpretation of the Balqā'; this included nearly all the steppe-land to the south of 'Ammān, as far as Moab and Ma'ān.[12] This appears early, in a conquest account of Ma'āb,[13] and late, in Yāqūt. But it should predate the Crusades: later the Balqā' was a satellite of Karak, and the south belonged to the latter.

Under the Umayyads at least, the Balqā' and the south were under a united administration, based on 'Ammān. This administration formed a sub-governorate of Dimashq. The linkage is made clear by the account of the arrest of the 'Abbāsid Imām Ibrahīm ibn Muḥammad at Ḥumayma by Marwān II in 132/750: the governor of Damascus, al-Walīd ibn Mu'āwiya, is instructed to write to his *'āmil* in the Balqā' to send cavalry to Ḥumayma for the arrest.[14]

The list of known governors of the Balqā' (Table 3) is fragmentary: three under the Umayyads, three under the 'Abbāsids, and one each under the Ikhshīdids and Fāṭimids. Although only three Umayyad governors are known, the personalities are significant. Firstly Abān, a brother of the Caliph 'Abd al-Malik (dates not known), secondly, in the reign of 'Abd al-Malik (65/685–86/705), Muḥammad ibn 'Umar al-Thaqafī, brother of Yūsuf ibn 'Umar al-Thaqafī, later the famous governor of Iraq and the East under Hishām. Lastly Ḥārith ibn 'Amr al-Ṭā'ī, who was later governor of Armenia. All three were prominent men in the Umayyad Caliphate. The first two seem to be less important members of famous families, who could be given a safe but prestigious governorate. The third went on to do greater things on the northern frontier.

At the end of the Umayyad period, at least, there was a local garrison (*jund al-Balqā'*), which perhaps included the cavalry sent to Ḥumayma.[15]

Connected with this administration there was a treasury: in 126/744 Sulaymān, a son of the Caliph Hishām, who had been imprisoned by Walīd II in 'Ammān, presumably in the Qal'a, escaped to take part in the Civil War, 'and took the *amwāl* which were in 'Ammān'. *Amwāl* here means public monies.

'Ammān was an Umayyad mint, from which copper issues are known in some quantity.[16] Its history has been most recently treated by Bates, who concludes that an early type with two emperors on the obverse, and majuscule M on the reverse, did exist.[17] Pre-reform copper of the Standing Caliph type has been published: the issue has a standing Caliph on the obverse, and a cross modified on the reverse.[18] There are also two post-reform types, of which the first has the symbol of a trefoil on the reverse.[19] The significance of the trefoil for 'Ammān is unknown, although it incidentally appears among the decorative motives of the Reception Hall of the Umayyad Palace (see Chapter 7). Following the end of the Umayyad period, there may have been minting early in the 'Abbāsid period: one example has been published of a *fils* read as dated to 188/804 in the reign of the Caliph Hārūn al-Rashīd.[20] However 'Ammān was never a mint city later.[21] Lane-Poole published three Būyid *dirhams* attributed to 'Ammān;[22] but this is a misreading: they should be read 'Umān, conquered by Mu'izz al-Dawla in 356/967.

2. The Economy and Settlement of the Balqā' in the Umayyad period

To gain a view of the long-term trends of the period, three different topics should briefly be looked at: firstly, the cities of Roman Jordan and their survival in the Umayyad period, secondly, agricultural conditions in the area, and thirdly the new element of the Umayyad period – the desert castles or *quṣūr*.

Urban Occupation

Of the major Roman-Byzantine cities of Jordan, Petra appears to have been effectively abandoned before the Conquest. According to Parr, the decline of Petra took place during the 4th and 5th centuries AD, and was speeded by the earthquake of May 363.[23] No doubt the decline of Petra is to be connected with the increasing transfer of the trans-Arabian land route for the transport of South Arabian incense – a trade on which the Nabataeans had grown wealthy – to the cheaper maritime route up the Red Sea, by-passing Petra. The economy of Petra had always been fragile, and the existence of the city could not outlast the loss of this external trade by more than several centuries. This decline had important effects in the Jordanian area, for urban and agricultural settlement became increasingly concentrated in the north during the Byzantine and Early Islamic periods.

Further north, the cities had more diverse economic bases – market centres for the agricultural hinterland and industrial centres – and many of the major Roman-Byzantine cities have produced evidence of occupation in the Umayyad period. The list of major urban sites with evidence of Umayyad occupation in northern Jordan is: Pella/Faḥl,[24] Gadara/Umm Qays,[25] Gerasa/Jarash,[26] Esbus/Ḥisbān,[27] Abila/Ābil,[28] Capitolias/ Bayt Rās,[29] and Mādabā.[30]

All of these cities appear to have flourished in the period before the Conquest, with extensive evidence of building activity, most strongly marked in the construction of churches. For the Umayyad period there is evidence of occupation, pottery, coins and other artefacts. Precisely this kind of evidence appears in dramatic form in the recently excavated earthquake destruction deposits at Pella.[31] In addition there is some evidence of domestic construction. For example a newly constructed Umayyad residential quarter has been excavated at Jerash.[32] At Pella, also, there is a new phase of residential construction in the Umayyad period.

On the other hand, apart from 'Ammān, little evidence of monumental building has so far appeared in these cities: only a small mosque at Jarash, apparently built in the courtyard of an earlier building,[33] a point which contrasts strongly with the extensive evidence of church building in the century before the Conquest. While the construction of new churches was often prohibited under Islam, it is also true that by the 7th century there was an oversupply of churches in Jordan – more than could be staffed. It may be that there are more large Umayyad mosques still to find in Jordan, but it seems unlikely there will be many. It is more probable that the Muslim population of these cities was quite low, and that small mosques could satisfy the requirements.[34]

Nevertheless, if people have money, they will usually spend at least a part of it on building. In the Decapolis cities during the Umayyad period this did not occur. For this reason, one gains an impression of rather static economic conditions; the new expenditure was taking place elsewhere, notably on palatial residences for the Umayyad aristocracy.

The relative importance of different cities was also changing. Jerash, for example, which had evidently been wealthy before Islam, was less so after the conquest. 'Ammān, by contrast, came to the fore in the Umayyad period. At some time after the 'Abbāsid Revolution in 132/750 nearly all the cities went into a steep decline, with occupation almost terminated at some, a fact which suggests that economic conditions had not been good even before the Revolution.

Conditions on the Land

Our information about conditions on the land is much thinner, and our access to it is limited to the numbers of sites located by surface survey, a point which might be taken as in broad consonance with the extent of exploitation of the land. Surface survey work has been published by Mittmann from north Jordan, the hill country between Wādī Zarqā' and Wādī Yarmūk;[35] by Ibrahim, Sauer and Yassine from the east Jordan Valley;[36] plus reports on work in the Ḥisbān area,[37] from Moab,[38] and Wādī Ḥasā,[39] all referred to by MacAdam in the previous chapter.

The first important point is that density of settlement in the Byzantine period seems to have been extremely high: Mittmann reports 208 Byzantine sites, an increase of 100% over 103 Roman sites, in an area which a recent map shows to have 95 modern villages.[40] The east Jordan Valley survey found 55 sites with traces of Byzantine pottery of all kinds, though the authors suggest a decline in late Byzantine times.

For the Umayyad period however the numbers are lower. In the east Jordan Valley only 19 sites were found. In the Ḥisbān survey, against 133 sites showing traces of Byzantine occupation, there were 29 identifiably Umayyad.[41] In the Wādī Ḥasā survey there were virtually no Umayyad sites, although the Byzantine period had been the period of densest occupation.

Of course, the Byzantine period was longer than the Umayyad, and no account is taken of the possibility of one site succeeding another. There may also have been a change in the pattern of rural settlement, towards fewer, larger villages. Nevertheless it seems likely that, when the data from field surveys has been finally published, it will be confirmed that there was a contraction of the agricultural system between the Conquest and the end of the Umayyad period.[42]

The explanation of why this might have happened is not yet clear. There was flight from the land in Iraq during the Umayyad period. In 84/703 al-Ḥajjāj ibn Yūsuf ordered the return of new converts to Islam to their villages.[43] However conditions in Iraq were more disordered than in Jordan, and it is not until the end of the 2nd/8th century that we learn of peasants fleeing the land in Palestine.[44]

It is more likely that the high density of Byzantine rural settlement played a role. To support such a density of settlement even marginal land must have been cultivated; in northern Jordan such marginal land is often steeply sloped, and exposed to rapid erosion when the natural vegetation has been cleared. Within a limited period of time, such land would become uncultivable, forcing a reduction in the density of settlement.

Perhaps also the recurrent epidemics of plague, commencing with the plague of Justinian in 542, and continuing till the end of the Umayyad period, reduced the rural population, as proposed by Conrad.[45]

It is impossible to judge objectively whether the tax burden was heavier under the Umayyads than it had been before the Conquest, although there are many complaints in the Christian sources that this was the case.[46] The taxation system bore most heavily on the peasant cultivator. In the Umayyad period taxes were apparently assessed collectively on the community.[47] Urban residents could easily escape taxation, whereas the cultivator could not. One could avoid excessive taxation by converting to Islam, and moving to a city. In Iraq a growth of cities and decline of cultivated area between the Sāsānian and 'Abbāsid periods has been identified by Adams;[48] in Jordan a certain decline in the cultivated area is apparent, but there seems to be little evidence of an increase in the size of cities.

The Quṣūr or Desert Castles

There is one feature of the region of 'Ammān in the Umayyad period that does not seem to represent a continuation of settlement patterns from before the Conquest, and this is the construction of the Umayyad *quṣūr* (Ar. *qaṣr*, pl. *quṣūr*) or castles. In the past these buildings generated an extensive scholarly debate over their form and function, and that debate continues today.[49] One can say that a consensus among scholars on their interpretation has not yet been reached.

Ten sites are known for certain within the boundaries of present-day Jordan (Table 4; for distribution see fig.13). In addition there are eight more sites where it is reasonable to assume there was a castle, or there is Umayyad occupation in a Roman fort. As will appear, *quṣūr* were occupied by relatively minor figures in the Umayyad Caliphate, and some were no doubt too poor to reconstruct those forts extensively.

The architectural typology of these sites is well known. On the one hand there are square castles in the form of a fort, such as at Qaṣr Kharāna and al-Qasṭal. This pattern is developed in a more complex way at Mshattā, where there is a triple internal division, and at Qaṣr Ṭūba, where the castle pattern is doubled. At some sites there are small mosques. The second pattern is of small basilical audience halls, with a bath attached, as at Quṣayr 'Amra and Ḥammām al-Sarakh. As shown by Sauvaget, the buildings are often grouped into complexes with groups of houses, and service buildings, as at Jabal Says in Syria.[50] Elsewhere there are enclosures,[51] which may have been intended for gardens, that is, 'garden' in the sense of the Arabic *bustān*, a small scale area of irrigated horticulture also used for pleasure.

In recent years the interpretation proposed by Sauvaget in an unfinished posthumous article has been widely followed:[52] this links the *quṣūr* with historical accounts of Umayyad investment in agriculture, thus suggesting that they were productive agricultural units, with the castle as the main residence, a sort of Roman villa.[53] At least for the sites in Jordan, it is questionable whether agriculture was a major element. Agapius of Manbij, for example, tells us that the Caliph Hishām 'made extensive plantations in Jazīra and in Syria (*Shāmāt*), and the product of these properties exceeded the taxes of his empire.'[54] It is difficult to believe that the environment of the Jordanian steppe, in terms of soil and water, would have supported agricultural development on the large scale described. In fact many of the individual developments known are irrigation projects on the Syrian Euphrates.[55]

On the other hand, the historical texts furnish evidence that a number of members of the Caliphal clan of Banī Umayya, and their circles, lived in the Balqā'. Abū Sufyān Sakhr ibn Ḥarb owned the village of Biqinnīs before the Conquest.[56] Yazīd ibn 'Abd al-Malik (Caliph 101/720–105/724) lived at al-Muwaqqar.[57] Sulaymān ibn 'Abd al-Malik (Caliph 96/715–99/717) was in *Mashārif al-Balqā'* at the time of his accession.[58] Walīd ibn Yazīd (Caliph 125/743–126/744) is connected with al-Aghdaf, Zīzā', and Azraq.[59] Sulaymān ibn Hishām, very much a royal prisoner, was held at 'Ammān in 126/744.[60] Apart from the Umayyads themselves, a leading supporter, Yūsuf ibn 'Umar al-Thaqafī, governor of Iraq and the East from 120/738 to 126/744, had a house and agricultural land (*mazra'a*) in the Balqā'.[61] His brother, as we have seen, was governor of the Balqā' under 'Abd al-Malik. The 'Abbāsid family were settled at Ḥumayma before the revolution of 132/750. On a lower level, an Umayyad poet called Khālid ibn 'Abbād had a *ḥiṣn* (castle) in the village of Tanhaj in the Balqā'.[62] The life of poets was notoriously insecure, dependent on the irregular generosity of the Caliph. This point suggests that ownership of *quṣūr* may have been quite widespread in the circles around the Umayyad court. It is evident that the *quṣūr* are, on the one hand, largely the work of this elite, and, on the other hand, they are principally their residences.[63]

'Ammān, as can be seen from the distribution of *quṣūr* in Jordan (fig.13), concentrated in a quarter-circle south and east of the city, was a central place for these settlements. Although the castles seem to be isolated desert sites, they would have needed access to urban markets, and 'Ammān was also the administrative centre and major congregational mosque (See Chapter 6).

Such settlements should be regarded as a consuming rather than a producing sector of the economy. The building of the *quṣūr* apparently proved a heavy drain on resources. In his accession speech, the Caliph Yazīd ibn Walīd (126/744) had to promise not to lay 'stone on stone, brick on brick, or dig canals'. He also had to promise that he will not 'transfer revenues from one town to another', reflecting complaints by the provinces that revenues paid were not being spent locally, but transferred to Syria.[64] Provincials feared that their taxes were being used to pay for the *quṣūr* in the Balqā', and in this they were probably right.[65]

In addition a figure such as Yūsuf ibn 'Umar would have enriched himself personally from his tenure of the governorship of Iraq. The scale of Yūsuf ibn 'Umar's fortune can be judged from his offer to the Caliph Walīd ibn Yazīd of 50 million *dirhams* to settle the debts of his predecessor Khālid ibn 'Abdallah al-Qaṣrī.[66] Even ill-gotten gains are normally spent, and part would have been spent on his house and family in the Balqā'.

All of this probably represented a large external financial input into the economy of Umayyad Jordan, although one cannot make quantitative statements about it. The construction of palaces, and the maintenance of their occupants, created a demand for local goods and services.[67] No doubt the creation of a distinctive ceramic industry in Jordan during the Umayyad period, to be seen in the fine red-painted wares (fig.131), is to be connected with the existence of a market for the products in the region.

Herein lay the crux of the economic problems of Umayyad Jordan: if an interpretation of rather static conditions in the urban and rural sectors turns out to be correct, then the *quṣūr* and their occupants were supporting the local economy, rather than vice versa. The external stimulus created by the expenditure of tax revenues from other provinces was an important factor; it was withdrawn at the time of the 'Abbāsid Revolution in 132/750, and the kind of large-scale expenditure hitherto seen in the Syrian area began anew in Iraq with the construction of Baghdād, and, eventually, Sāmarrā'.

3. Overview of the Umayyad period

Before the Conquest, there was already a substantial population of Arab tribes in Jordan, and the Syrian area in general, and the events of the Conquest brought to power their ethnic relatives from Arabia. In the early years the linkages of power were based upon the tribal structures, and the Caliph Mu'āwiya ibn Abī Sufyān, for example, acted much as a tribal *shaykh*. But it is now well recognized that later in the Umayyad period, power depended on personal and family relationships, although the forms of tribal identity were retained, and power remained firmly in the hands of people of Arab tribal stock. The long-term effect was to impose an Arab tribal culture as the dominant culture, where previously late Hellenistic urban culture had been dominant. However the Caliphate itself also became more like a traditional Near Eastern monarchy, a process completed in the 'Abbāsid period. It is the realities of that transition that the limited textual evidence and the more extensive archaeological evidence about the Umayyad period depict.

In effect, the Umayyads in their eighty years of power created a new cultural, economic and administrative system in Jordan, centred on 'Ammān, a system which increasingly diverged from what had existed before Islam, and which subsisted until the Crusades. The driving force was, without doubt, the aristocracy which consisted of the Caliphal clan of Banī Umayya, and their associates and supporters. This group had access to large quantities of external funds through the taxation system of the Caliphate, and they spent the money partly on urban and rural palatial residences. In doing so, they created a new art and architecture; it is undeniable that, within the immediate area of Jordan, Qaṣr Mshattā and Khirbat al-Mafjar represent high points of artistic achievement. The expenditure must also have stimulated the local economy.

This system was intended for the benefit of the Muslim Arabs, though Christian Arabs were probably also privileged.[68] Nevertheless, although there was no doubt a much higher percentage of Muslim Arabs in Jordan during the Umayyad period than in some other parts of the Middle East, it seems unlikely that they constituted a majority of the population, with the possible exception of 'Ammān itself. It is the size and distribution of Umayyad mosques, in comparison with the continued use, redecoration with new mosaics, or new construction of churches, which will prove the most useful indicator on this question.[69] At the moment it seems that 'Ammān had the only large congregational mosque of the Umayyad period in Jordan, though perhaps one also existed at 'Aqaba.[70] The continued use of a number of churches at Jarash was balanced by the find of only a small mosque.

The Christian community does not seem to have taken part in the change and development of the Umayyad period, except in so far as it was somewhat reduced.[71] The evidence for the Christian community in the Umayyad period is charted in the previous chapter. On an artistic level, it is striking that the mosaic dated to AD 756 excavated in the church of St Stephen at Umm al-Raṣāṣ is quite uninfluenced by the contemporary stylistic developments in Islamic decoration.[72] As the Umayyad Islamic artistic tradition developed its own particular character, there were two separate artistic traditions in the same territory. In as far as artistic traditions represent a part of community identity, the real separation of the two communities was emphasized.

THE 'ABBĀSID REVOLUTION AND AFTER

The particular character of the development of Umayyad Jordan was checked by the 'Abbāsid revolution of 132/750. The last Umayyad Caliph, Marwān ibn Muḥammad (127/744 – 132/750), was finally defeated on the Zāb in northern Iraq in that year, and fled westwards, abandoning Syria to the armies of 'Abdallah ibn 'Alī.

Shortly before this event, the region of 'Ammān, the Jordan Valley, and Jerusalem was heavily affected by the severe earthquake dated variously between 746 and 749. The Qal'a of 'Ammān was damaged by the earthquake (fig.167), and the topic is treated in more detail below in Chapter 11. The effect of this catastrophe on one of the heartlands of Umayyad Syria was no doubt partly to reduce resistance to the 'Abbāsid armies, but more importantly it meant that the 'Abbāsids took over a land in ruins.

The response locally to the 'Abbāsid Revolution (132/750) was a revolt, that of Ḥabīb ibn Murra al-Marrī, a *qā'id* (commander) of Marwān ibn Muḥammad in Bathaniyya, Ḥawrān, and the Balqā' in 132/750.[73] A group from the Balqā' also participated in the defence of Damascus against 'Abdallah ibn 'Alī, the uncle of al-Manṣūr.[74] At the end of the year 'Abdallah ibn 'Alī sent an army to the Balqā', and killed Sulaymān ibn Yazīd ibn 'Abd al-Malik, one of the surviving Umayyads.[75]

Following the immediate establishment of 'Abbāsid rule in Syria, disturbances continued, and in these, two elements are distinguishable: firstly an Umayyad claim to the Caliphate, which acquired a certain messianic aspect. In the revolt of Abū al-Ward at Ḥimṣ in 132/750, the movement is called *tabyīḍ* (proclaiming the white), in obvious reaction to the 'Abbāsid *musawwada* (people of the black flags). The claim to the Caliphate was made in the name of Abū Muḥammad al-Sufyānī, and he is described as the 'Sufyānī who is mentioned'.[76] A similar description is known from the revolt of Abū al-'Amayṭir in Damascus in 195/810–11.[77]

The other element was *'aṣabiyya* (faction) between Qays and Yaman. Although fighting caused by *'aṣabiyya* had been a central problem of the Umayyad period, we have no record of it affecting the Balqā' then. However, under Hārūn al-Rashīd (170/786–193/809), there were outbreaks in the Balqā' in 176/792 and 180/796.[78] There was flight from the land in Filasṭīn under Rashīd.[79] Evidence of this insecurity might be seen in a hoard of 56 *dīnārs* found in 'Ammān, the latest minted in 171/787–8.[80]

In the reign of al-Ma'mūn (198/813–218/833) there was a revolt in the Balqā' that combined the two issues, that of an Umayyad, Sa'īd ibn Khālid al-'Uthmānī al-Fudaynī at Fudayn in the Ḥawrān (now al-Mafraq).[81] He attacked Qays and sided with Yaman, moved with a force to Zīzā', south of 'Ammān, and then to Māsūḥ, southeast of Mādabā. But he was driven out to Ḥisbān, where his supporters deserted him. He had claimed the Caliphate following Abū al-'Amayṭir.[82] This event, which is not well dated, may be connected with reports of anarchy west of the Jordan during the 'Abbāsid civil war (811–817), during which churches and monasteries were destroyed, and which led to an exodus of monks to Cyprus.[83] Possibly the Christian communities east of the Jordan suffered at the same time.

The reasons behind the continuing disturbances are not hard to see. The proud Arabs of Syria had lost the privileged position they had been accustomed to under the Umayyads. More specifically the influx of taxation money had ceased. The 'Abbāsids do not seem to have invested in reconstruction. One may compare al-Muqaddasī's story of the rebuilding of the Aqsa mosque: the Caliph claimed that there was insufficient in the treasury, and provincial amirs and generals were asked to build an arcade each.[84] At the same time, however, large sums of money were being spent on Baghdād.

Nevertheless, during the second half of the 2nd/8th century at least the Balqā' continued to preserve some of the status it had had under the Umayyads. We know the names of two governors in this period. The dismissal of Muḥammad ibn 'Ubaydallah ibn Muḥammad ibn Sulaymān ibn Muḥammad ibn 'Abd al-Muṭṭalib ibn Rabī'a ibn al-Ḥārith from the governorship of al-Balqā' is reported by Ṭabarī in 158/775 under al-Manṣūr, who sought to recover the unfortunate governor's personal gains.[85] The point of the story is that the man had only 2000 *dīnārs* and a few personal possessions, not the great wealth of the Balqā' that Manṣūr imagined he would have. This individual of noble origins was later governor of Yaman.

The second appointee known, Ṣāliḥ ibn Sulaymān, in 180/796 was a subordinate of Ja'far ibn Yaḥyā, one of the most famous of the Barmakid family of *wazīrs*. Ja'far ibn Yaḥyā had been appointed to settle the disturbances in Syria, and Ṣāliḥ ibn Sulaymān was one of his sub-appointments before he departed back again to Iraq. The ethnic origin of Ṣāliḥ ibn Sulaymān is unknown; he could have been Iraqi or of the same origin as the Barmakids themselves, who were east Iranians from Balkh.

At about this time the palace and citadel in 'Ammān were restored, obviously as the seat of the governor, and in Chapter 11 this event is proposed to be connected with one of these individuals, probably the latter. The example of an 'Abbāsid *fils* minted at 'Ammān in 188, mentioned above, might also be an indicator of the activity of Ṣāliḥ ibn Sulaymān.

From the early 3rd/9th century till the late 4th/10th century, however, very little is known from historical sources about events in the Balqā'. Banī Sulaym fled from Arabia to the Balqā' to hide from the 'Abbāsid general Bughā in 231/845.[86] In this time Syria had been taken over by the Ṭūlūnids in 264/878, and in 292/905 retaken by the 'Abbāsids. There was still an 'Abbāsid governor in 'Ammān: Muḥammad ibn Ṭughj, later founder of the Ikhshīdid dynasty in Egypt, was appointed to 'Ammān, al-Karmal and al-Sharāt' before 306/918–9, in which year he defeated a bedouin attack upon the *ḥajj*.[87]

Muḥammad ibn Ṭughj, after his appointment to Egypt in 323/935, gained control of the southern half of Syria, up to Damascus. The Fāṭimids also, succeeding the Ikhshīdids in 358/969, took control of southern Syria. Much of Fāṭimid history in the area consisted of struggles between varying combinations of three groups: the central government in Cairo, insubordinate Turkish governors in Damascus, and the Arab tribes. 'Ammān was described as an assembly point for the tribes in an incident of 378/988 in the reign of al-'Azīz. The Fāṭimid general Munīr al-Khādim was sent to 'Ammān to collect a force of tribesmen of Qays, 'Uqayl and Fazāra with the purpose of bringing down the governor of Damascus, Bakjūr. In a second incident of the same year the *wazir* Ya'qūb ibn Killīs sent instructions to an individual called Nāsiḥ al-Ṭabbākh at 'Ammān to attack Bakjūr at Ḥimṣ.[88] Under al-Mustanṣir in

460/1068 an attempt by the Armenian general Badr al-Jamālī to take revenge on an Alid Abū Ṭāhir Ḥaydara ibn Muḥtaṣṣ al-Dawla, led to the latter fleeing to 'Ammān to hide, but he was surrendered by the Lord of 'Ammān (*Ṣāḥib 'Ammān*), Badr ibn Ḥazim ibn 'Alī (cf. Table 3).

The main development of the 4th/10th century was the growing importance of the Arab tribes on the political scene. Ibn Ḥawqal (*c.*378/988) says of al-Jibāl and al-Sharāt in southern Jordan that the tribal Arabs dominate it.[89] In the Umayyad period, of course, the power of the Caliphs depended on their alliance with the tribes. In the 'Abbāsid period there had been a growing separation, and a reduction in the status of the Arab tribes; by the reign of al-Mu'taṣim (218/833–227/842), there were no tribal Arabs in the army, and thus on the state payroll.[90] The tribal resurgence, mainly of bedouin, was first marked by the Isma'īlī sect of the Qarāmiṭa, who began to terrorize the Fertile Crescent, commencing with a siege of Damascus in 290/903.[91] The manpower of the Qarāmiṭa was drawn from the tribes of the Syrian desert, and later from those of northern and eastern Arabia. But apart from the Qarāmiṭa, the tribe of 'Uqayl was important in the Damascus area, and under the Ikhshīdid Kāfūr (regent 334/946–357/968), Shabīb ibn Jarīr al-'Uqalī was governor of 'Ammān and the Balqā' until 348/959, when he rebelled and advanced on Damascus.[92]

More importantly, numbers of the tribe of Ṭayy moved from their original lands in central northern Arabia around modern Ḥā'il to Palestine, under the leadership of Banū al-Jarrāḥ.[93] There were implications east of the Jordan: the Balqā' also seems to have been under the control of Banū al-Jarrāḥ. The Lord of 'Ammān mentioned above in 460/1068, Badr ibn Ḥāzim ibn 'Alī, was from Banū al-Jarrāḥ.[94]

Settlement in the 'Abbāsid and Fāṭimid Periods

The assessment of settlement trends from archaeological evidence in the region of 'Ammān between the end of the Umayyad period and the First Crusade remains extremely difficult. It used to be thought that settled occupation virtually disappeared from Jordan, and that the country was taken over by bedouin.[95] Recently, however, a more optimistic picture has been painted, suggesting a contraction in the settled area, but a continuing pattern of settlement nonetheless.[96]

The problem lies in the fact that, for the 'Abbāsid and Fāṭimid periods, the recent archaeological surface surveys in Jordan have reported very few sites. The survey of the east Jordan valley found five sites.[97] In the Ḥisbān regional survey, only four 'Abbāsid sites, compared with 29 Umayyad, were found.[98] In the French archaeological survey of the region of 'Araq al-Amīr, virtually total abandonment occurred after the end of the Umayyad period.[99] However, 'Abbāsid deposits, when excavated, are often thin and small in quantity; they would not show up well in surface survey, although they have been found at a village site such as Khirbat Fāris.[100]

In addition it is evident that the Umayyad ceramic tradition – notably Umayyad red-painted ware (fig.131) – continued after the fall of the Umayyad Caliphate in 132/750, and it is not always easy to distinguish early 'Abbāsid occupation from Umayyad. Probably the main change in the ceramic tradition occurred at the time of the introduction of polychrome glazed ware, in the 3rd/9th century. 'Abbāsid remains have been found in an increasing number of excavations: at Pella/Faḥl,[101] the Umayyad palace of al-Muwaqqar,[102] and in large quantity at 'Aqaba.[103]

'Aqaba, however, is exceptional: it lay in a different environment from northern Jordan, being a port with a share in the developing trade of the Indian Ocean, and also a stop on the Egyptian pilgrimage route. For northern Jordan, one can conclude that, although it is very difficult to make firm statements, the settlement pattern continued to resemble that of the Umayyad period, but was reduced; the archaeological evidence is consonant with the textual evidence. In effect urban and rural settlement in Jordan did go through a severe recession in the 'Abbāsid and Fāṭimid periods. The contrast with the abundant 'Abbāsid remains of the 3rd/9th and early 4th/10th centuries found in the Gulf, Iraq and northern Syria is very striking. One is tempted to conclude that northern and central Jordan, having lost its role as a land of princes in the Umayyad period, did not find a new one until the time of the Crusades and the Ayyūbids.

THE CRUSADES AND AFTER

In the years after the creation of the Latin Kingdom of Jerusalem in 1099, the area of Jordan became a battleground between the Crusaders and the amirs of Damascus. In the view of Prawer they destroyed what they could not hold to the east of the Jordan.[104] In 500/1106–7 the amir al-Iṣfahīd al-Turkmānī, who had arrived in Damascus, was given an *iqṭā'* consisting of 'Wādī Mūsā, Ma'āb, al-Sharāt, al-Jibāl and al-Balqā'. 'The Franks had raided the area, and had killed, captured or plundered all they could lay their hands on. When he arrived he found the population in great fear and extremely poor condition from their sufferings at the hands of the Franks.'[105] The amir was subsequently defeated and killed by the Crusaders.

The early years of the Latin Kingdom saw periods of raiding, but also agreements to divide the revenues.[106] In the second agreement of 504/1110–11 it was agreed that Baudouin, King of Jerusalem, should have, in addition to what he already controlled, half of Jabal 'Awf (modern Jabal 'Ajlūn), the Sawād (i.e. North Jordan), and Jabāniyya, and the adjoining territories which were in the hands of the Arabs of Al Jarrāḥ. The last area probably includes the Balqā'.

For a period 'Ammān came under Crusader domination.[107] It is mentioned as Ahamant or Haman in two Latin charters of 1161 and 1166. In the first, dated 31st July 1161, Philip of Nablus exchanged his lands at Nablus and Tyre for Montreal (Shawbak), Crac (Karak) and Ahamant, from the Zarqā' (Lat. Zerca) to the Red Sea. In the second, dated 17th January 1166, Amalric I granted to the order of the Temple Haman, its territory, and half of what Philip of Nablus had held in the Balqā' (Lat. Belcha). Evidently 'Ammān was an outlying territory of the lordship of Oultrejourdain, based on Karak and Shawbak. The area of 'Ammān may have come into Crusader possession as early as a date between 1118 and 1128,[108] but was definitely lost by 1170.

At any rate, in the counter-offensive of Nūr al-Dīn Zengī and Saladin against Karak, 'Ammān and the Balqā' are only mentioned as springboards for attacks. In 565/1170 Nūr al-Dīn stopped in 'Ammān: the attractive point was the spring pasturage.[109] In 580/1184 the Balqā' was a good assembly point, particularly for the baggage.[110]

After the battle of Ḥaṭṭīn and the recapture of Jerusalem in 583/1187, new administrative arrangements appeared, which were descended from those of the Crusader lordship of Karak. In 584/1189 Saladin made over Karak as an *iqṭā'* to his brother al-Malik al-'Ādil, as far north as *minṭaqat al-Balqā' wal-Ṣalt.*[111] This *iqṭā'* then passed to al-Mu'aẓẓam 'Īsā. Both of these figures were responsible for much construction in the area, Qal'at al-Ṣalt,[112] Qaṣr al-Azraq, Qal'at 'Ajlūn,[113] to add to the extant Crusader castles of Karak and Shawbak.

The result was a country populated with fortified sites, and an unfortified town was of no significance. Nevertheless, according to the archaeological evidence, the Qal'a at 'Ammān had not been fortified since the 3rd/9th century. No castle or citadel was built at 'Ammān, rather, only a watchtower.

The position of 'Ammān was taken on the one hand by Karak, as the main centre east of the Jordan, and on the other by Ṣalt, as the local and subsequently main centre. Under the Mamlūks, according to Dimashqī (d. 727/1327) *mamlakat al-Karak* extended from al-Ṣalt, al-Balqā', and *madīnat 'Ammān* to the Red Sea, but he also includes 'Ammān and Ṣalt in the province of Damascus.[114] The area round 'Ammān is referred to as *al-Ṣalt wal-Balqā'*.[115] At about the beginning of the 8th/14th century the centre of administration in the Balqā' was moved to Ḥisbān.[116]

'Ammān appears to have enjoyed a certain revival in the middle of the 8th/14th century, when in 757/1357 the Mamlūk amir Sarghatmish restored the town, and made it a local centre again *(umm tilka al-bilād)*.[117] It is quite possible that some of the medieval architectural features of the lower city which survived into modern times – the minaret of the mosque, the ḥammām, and perhaps the khān – belonged to this work. Nevertheless there is nothing to indicate that 'Ammān was at this time much more than a small settlement.

By the next century the local governorate had settled permanently in Salt, where it stayed until 1921. In the Ottoman cadastral survey, *Daftar-i Jadīd* of 1596, studied by Hütteroth and Abdulfattah, 'Ammān is not mentioned at all.[118]

Nevertheless 'Ammān did not die entirely; a site with permanent flowing water is never unused. Although the history of the khān at 'Ammān is not well known at the moment, it seems certain that it lasted into the Ottoman period. The pilgrim road from Damascus to the Holy Cities in Arabia *(Darb al-Ḥajj al-Shāmī)* normally passed to the east of 'Ammān, along a route from Mafraq to Zarqā' and Zīzā'.[119] However it was only a short diversion to 'Ammān, which would have been often taken by travellers. More importantly, the khān lay on the road which led east across the Jordan from Jerusalem, if one were travelling to Buṣrā. Nevertheless all the accounts of Western travellers who visited the site of 'Ammān in the 19th century indicate that by that time the khān was in ruins (figs 2–4; pls 2b, 4). It was not until a date between 1878 and 1881 that a party of Circassian settlers arrived to refound 'Ammān.[120]

5

ARCHAEOLOGICAL TOPOGRAPHY

by Alastair Northedge

PHILADELPHIA IN THE CLASSICAL PERIOD

Substantial deposits of the Hellenistic and Decapolitan, that is, Early Roman, periods have been noted from 'Ammān. Excavations on the lower terrace revealed a two-phase occupation of the 2nd century BC, although nothing is yet known of the earlier Hellenistic period.[1]

The Hellenistic deposits from these excavations were overlaid by Early Roman deposits, assignable to the 1st centuries BC and AD. Remains of that period are quite common, and have also been found to underly the gate of the Temple of Hercules (Gate C, described in Chapter 8), as well as being present in Area C outside the fortification wall,[2] and in Area A.[3] The only monumental architecture that has been revealed is a masonry platform of uncertain purpose, which underlies the 2nd-century temple gate (Gate C: figs 97–8; pl.50a). At the southeast corner the trace of a Hellenistic fortification of two phases has been suggested;[4] and it is possible that the structures excavated in Area C outside the wall represent a tower of the fortifications. Elsewhere all that can be said is that the Hellenistic and Early Roman fortifications must have lain outside the line of the later works; in Area C and Area E Early Roman occupation is found outside the wall-line.

Under Antiochus III (223–187 BC) 'Ammān was subjected to a siege about 218 BC, in which the city was taken only by the discovery and blocking of an underground passage leading to a spring.[5] The topography of the account is interesting: the hill is described as 'having access at only two spots'. The location of one access point is clear, at the north, but where was the second? It is possible that the easternmost plateau, not included in the Umayyad defences, was also not walled in the Hellenistic period. The location of the passage has been suggested to be a large cistern at the north end outside the later walls.[6] This area, lying on one of the approaches, must have been a difficult location for secret access to water, but it remains the best candidate for locating this event; however it must be remembered that the extensive overlay of later remains at the Qal'a means that many similar cisterns could still lie concealed.

Topography of Roman Philadelphia

Many of the most enduring elements in the layout of the city appeared subsequent to AD 106, and most were constructed during the 2nd century. Although the city continued to include the Qal'a, this is the first period in which we can be certain that the city centre lay in the wadis, stretching from a gate below the eastern end of the Qal'a along the Wādī 'Ammān, and up the wadi to the west of the Qal'a. The Roman town-plan has been described principally by Butler, and revised by Hadidi.[7] It may be brought up to date by reference to the American Palestine Exploration Society panorama of the lower city taken in 1875 (pls 3–4).

The area of the ancient city is not defined by any surviving line of fortifications. Indeed, the evidence is very scant that the city as a whole was ever fortified, either in the Roman period or in Islamic times; no walls have appeared in the course of building operations.

Nevertheless, the Palestine Exploration Fund survey marks an East Gate, with a stretch of wall aligned north and south (fig.4).[8] The existence of a gate at this point is confirmed by de Saulcy in 1863 (fig.2), but we have no details of its appearance. A martyr of Philadelphia, St Elianus, had a shop by the Jarash gate.[9] Monumental gates could be built without accompanying fortifications, and it may be that 'gate' could also have a more metaphorical meaning, in the sense of 'exit from a city in a certain direction'.

Ammianus Marcellinus, in a geographical description of Provincia Arabia written *c.*AD 380, says that Philadelphia, Bostra and Gerasa are 'large and well-fortified with walls'.[10] This has usually been taken to refer to the Qal'a, in the absence of any substantial evidence for full fortifications. In our view the Qal'a shows evidence of a wall of the 2nd century, and this appears to confirm Ammianus' remark.[11] But it should also be noted that Ammianus was referring to more than one city, and his statement is less likely to be as precise as if it had referred to Philadelphia alone.

The organization of the town-plan was restricted by the hilly nature of the site, which precluded a regular grid of streets. There were two colonnaded streets; one, probably to be called the *decumanus,* ran from the East Gate, curving round the bend of the stream, southwest to a point roughly 100m southwest of the mosque. The eastern end of this street seems to have been much better preserved in Roman form than the western end, though it is apparent that the same line was used in Islamic times at the west end. The Propylaeon, which formed the approach to the Temple of Hercules, was placed on the north side of the street. Opposite it was a monumental column, and an approach to what may have been a bridge over the stream.

A second street, to be called the *cardo,* is proposed by Butler as having run at right angles to the *decumanus,* up the wadi west of the Citadel (fig.5). Unfortunately no pre-1882 photographs of this wadi have been found. The suggestion seems to rest solely on the survival of two standing columns to the north of the mosque (these are visible in plate 4); but the idea is still likely to be correct, as a modern track survived in the same place, and some kind of street must have led in the direction of Jarash.[12]

All that can be said about dating the construction of these streets is that the *terminus ante* for the *decumanus* is the building of the Temple of Hercules (reign of Marcus Aurelius, AD 161–166[13]), for the Propylaeon and the staircase of the approach are aligned with the street.

The stream was partly contained in a vaulted conduit, a short section of which stood until the 1960s (pl.6a). This conduit extended from the area of the Nymphaeum to opposite the Propylaeon, and appears to have been intended to maximise the land area in the wadi. Opposite to the Propylaeon, there seems to have been a bridge, although neither the photographic evidence nor the evidence of 19th-century plans is clear in demonstrating what the structure visible at this point was. Although one would expect the conduit to have extended further east to the area of the forum, the evidence is negative in this respect.

The various public buildings of the lower city in the Roman period were:

(i) Forum (or Agora: fig.15; pl.3)

The forum lies on the south side of the stream. It is trapezoid in shape, with dimensions of 100m on the south side, 48m on the west, and 50m on the east. There are three extant colonnades, belonging to two architectural phases, and they are dated by an inscription which refers to a *tristoön,* or triple portico. The inscription gives the date as the year 252 of, according to Zayadine and Rey-Coquais, the era of Pompey (i.e. counted from 63 BC, and therefore equal to AD 189).[14]

(ii) Theatre (fig.16; pl.3)

The theatre is set into the slope on the south of the forum, and thirty-three rows of seats could accommodate about 6000 spectators. Both the stage area and the *scaenae frons* had disappeared, though the lowest courses of the latter were visible in excavation. Hadidi's excavation produced a coin of Marcus Aurelius (type minted AD 169–177) from the foundations of the *scaena.* This coin gives a *terminus post* for the *scaena,* one of the last parts of the building to be erected, while the *terminus ante* is the erection of the triple portico of the forum in AD 189.

(iii) Odeum (fig.15; pl.5b)

A smaller free-standing theatre set on the east side of the forum, with an external diameter of 38m. The capacity of the Odeum has been estimated at *c.*500. According to Hadidi it should be dated to the early-middle 2nd century.

(iv) Nymphaeum (fig.18; pl.5a)

Lying to the west of the forum complex, this building survives, but is poorly preserved, being largely incorporated into modern buildings.[15] It is a half-octagon of large proportions, with a restored length of 68m. There were three semi-domed apses, each flanked with two tiers of shell niches. There were traces of a colonnade at the front and an arch underneath for the passage of wadi floods from the northwest. It was identified as a Nymphaeum by Butler and is compared by Hadidi to the Nymphaeum at Jarash (which is dated to AD 191 by inscription). An undated Greek dedication 'to the Nymphs and Muses' must honour the benevolent spirits associated with the Nymphaeum.[16]

Epigraphy also provides evidence for a public bath *(balneion)* and a quadruple portico *(tetrastoön),* which were apparently built and dedicated *c.*150.[17] The Department of Antiquities has conducted a rescue excavation of a bath to the east of the Odeum. The *tetrastoön* is so far undiscovered; even the provenance of the inscription which mentions it is unknown. We would suggest, because of its date, that it was a colonnade enclosing a second forum-like plaza in front of the Nymphaeum. The idea that there was a further open space here has already been proposed by Butler, and is a logical deduction from the fact that the Nymphaeum is set back from the line of the *decumanus.*[18] Further support for the suggestion can be gained from noting the position of the great church at this point (see below).

The monuments described, together with the two temples of the Citadel discussed later, appear to represent one well-defined phase in the city's history.

Those structures which can be closely dated all belong to the second half of the 2nd century; the remainder may well be of similar date. Thus, the Roman city of Philadelphia seems not to have developed over a period of centuries, like many of the other Roman cities of the Levant; instead, the monumental form of the city appeared as a result of a relatively brief burst of activity.

There are other, less well-dated, aspects of the Roman city that should be mentioned, in particular the cemeteries, as these were virtually ignored by Butler.

Philadelphia had a fine tradition of funerary architecture, and the tombs are discussed at length by the Palestine Exploration Fund survey.[19] There were three main concentrations of tombs: at the southern end of Jabal Ḥusayn; in the bottom of the Wādī 'Ammān, to the west of the ancient city; and on Jabal Ashrafiyya and Jabal Jawfa to the south. Burials were of four types: inhumations;[20] stone sarcophagi apparently placed in the open or on a built platform;[21] rock-cut tombs – the published tombs are all of this category;[22] and mausolea.

The most impressive of the mausolea, Qabr al-Sulṭān, was located at the east end of Wādī al-Ḥaddāda, and had a porch flanked by two alcoves, and a single interior chamber (pl.6b).[23] The remainder were square in plan and roofed with a dome or a barrel vault. Qaṣr al-Nuwayjis, located three kilometres northeast of the Qal'a on the 'Ayn al-Ghazal road, has a dome on pendentives, and four barrel-vaulted recesses. The result is a cruciform interior with *loculi* in the satellite spaces.[24] The Western Tomb was a simple cubical building, surmounted by a dome whose transition was managed by blocks laid across the corners (pl.7a).[25] Qaṣr al-Sab' at Quwaysma is similar, but with a barrel vault.[26] Conder records two more poorly preserved mausolea of similar style.[27]

In the absence of fortifications, which would have clearly delimited the site, the cemeteries may be used to calculate the size of the city – for Roman cemeteries were always located outside the city limits. The result, when combined with other topographical considerations, produces a rough approximation of the maximum possible area.

On the east side the East Gate and its north-south wall may be the most likely marker of the limit of settlement. On the south Jabal Jawfa and Jabal Ashrafiyya have numbers of tombs; this suggests that settlement did not extend up from the wadi bed, and the photographs of 1875 appear to confirm that there is no trace of debris from settlement at all on these two hills. To the west, settlement was delimited by sarcophagi on Jabal 'Ammān, and by the Western Tomb. Several of the 19th-century photographs suggest that there is debris to the west of the mosque in the base of the wadi as far as the Western Tomb (pls 2b, 4). To the northwest we have very little information; a tomb is published from Jabal Luwaybda,[28] but nothing is known of the extent of settlement in the bottom of the wadis. The Qal'a marked the limit of settlement to the north, for there were tombs on the saddle leading to Jabal Ḥusayn.[29] On the Qal'a itself, a 3rd-century burial found overlying earlier Roman occupation, and thus lying within the Qal'a fortifications, suggests only that the limits of the city had changed over time.[30]

The total area enclosed within the tomb line is 46.35 ha. Of this perhaps 5 ha are public buildings. Philadelphia then was smaller than Jarash (*c.*75 ha), and considerably smaller than the largest cities of Roman Palestine: Aelia Capitolina, 120 ha; Anthedon, 90 ha; Caesaraea Maritima, 95 ha; Gaza, 90 ha; Ptolemais, 100 ha; and Scythopolis, 110 ha. It was, rather, on a par with Tiberias (40 ha), Ascalon (52 ha), and Diocaesarea-Sepphoris 60 ha).[31]

Topography of Byzantine Philadelphia

The plan of the city as it appeared after the 2nd-century transformation was only lightly modified over the following 400 years, up until the Arab conquest. Our knowledge of change in the city is really limited to the churches, and to the appearance of residential quarters on the Qal'a. Six or seven churches are known.

(i) The 'Cathedral'[32]

Recorded and planned by the Palestine Exploration Fund survey in 1881, the only known photograph dates to the visit of Warren in 1867 (pl.7b). The plan reveals a basilica measuring 41.9 × 22.3m (fig.19). To the northwest a further wall may have belonged to an atrium with an off-axis entrance. In 1867 the apse, which was external, stood as high as three courses of the semi-dome, together with a section of the aisle end-wall on the east side.

The apse was flanked by pairs of shell niches in two tiers, making a total of eight. According to Conder, these niches are 'small apses or alcoves'.[33] The word 'niche' here reflects the evidence of a Palestine Exploration Fund photograph (no.560; see pl.7b), that these are set into the body of the wall, and should not properly appear in the ground-plan. The church did not therefore have five apses, as Conder describes it.

The building seems to have disappeared before 1900. In 1867 the apse wall was already leaning (see pl.6a).

(ii) Possible Church Adjacent to the 'Cathedral'

There is a further apsed building incorporated into the complex described as a *Khān,* which may have been a church, located between the 'Cathedral' and the Nymphaeum. The plan of 'Ammān drawn by Warren and published by the Rev. A. E. Northey, gives the clear impression of a church at this point (fig.3).

(iii) St Elianus' Church[34]

The Palestine Exploration Fund survey describes a columned basilica west of the Qal'a measuring 13.7 metres square. It had an external apse. Bagatti thought that it was dedicated to the martyr of Philadelphia, Elianus, who lived near the Jarash gate.

(iv) St George's Church[35]

A small basilical chapel built outside a rock-cut tomb on the southeastern tip of Jabal Luwaybda. The chapel is 19m long and outside the west end were four columns of a porch. Three columns of the aisles were seen by the Palestine Exploration Fund survey. The tomb contained one sarcophagus.

In 1908 Abel found an inscription, which may be a foundation inscription, referring to the priest of St George, and the Bishop Polieuktos. The inscription is published by F-M. Abel in the *Revue Biblique,* and commented on by Milik.[36] Milik believes that the priest of St George mentioned in the inscription belonged to another church, possibly the one in the Qal'a.

The site has been cleared, and is in the grounds of the Greek Catholic church; but no new plan has been made. It may be compared with the Memorial Church at Jarash;[37] it was presumably not a congregational church.

(v) Church Apse

The apse of a church was discovered in the forum excavations.[38]

(vi) Church on the Upper Citadel (see Chapter 11)

(vii) Church on the Lower Citadel (see Chapter 11)

THE TOPOGRAPHY OF 'AMMĀN IN ISLAMIC TIMES

The Islamic city of 'Ammān was a direct successor to classical Philadelphia. Thus there were two parts to the city, a settlement in the wadi of the *sayl 'Ammān,* and the Qal'a, which overlooked it.

There is one description of 'Ammān in Islamic times, written by al-Muqaddasī *c.*375/985, when the city was under tribal control but owed allegiance to Fatimid suzerainty:[39]

> 'Ammān lies on the edge of the desert, and possesses villages and farmlands. Its district is the Balqā', and it is a source of cereals and flocks. It has a number of streams and mills driven by water. There is a fine congregational mosque in the area of the market, the court of which is ornamented with mosaics. We have already stated that it resembles Mecca.[40] The Castle of Goliath (Qaṣr Jālūt) lies on a hill which overlooks the town. There also is the tomb of Uriah, over which is a mosque, and the Circus of Solomon. Prices are cheap and fruit is plentiful, but its people are ignorant, and difficult roads lead to it.

The picture presented is one of a small agricultural centre, with strong links to the desert, and smaller and less prosperous than in its greater days under the Umayyads.

The Circus of Solomon has been identified, probably correctly, with the Roman theatre.

Zayadine suggested that Qaṣr Jālūt was, in fact, the Temple of Hercules.[41] However, the temple was not standing at this time, and would not have been striking to the eye. Rather Qaṣr Jālūt must be the Qal'a itself, which dominated the city in this period. As with the Circus of Solomon, the appearance of a biblical association in the name of Qaṣr Jālūt suggests that Muqaddasī thought the Qal'a a relic of ancient times, rather than, as it was in fact in his day, a largely Umayyad structure. One might suppose from this that knowledge of the Umayyad period was heavily eroded by the late 4th/10th century.

Neither the tomb of Uriah, nor its mosque, have been satisfactorily located; and the text gives no indications as to where in the city the tomb was situated. The identification might have been with one of the Roman tombs, or with a feature of the Qal'a, where Uriah was killed, such as the Umayyad Reception Hall.

The evidence of al-Muqaddasī indicates that there should be a considerable overlay of Islamic archaeological remains on top of classical Philadelphia. With the exception of the Qal'a these have now been entirely covered by the modern city. There are two means of access to information about the extent of the city: firstly the spread of debris visible in the 19th-century photographs (pl.4), and secondly the descriptions of buildings provided by the Palestine Exploration Fund survey.

Buildings

(i) The Congregational Mosque (see Chapter 6)

(ii) Khān

This building disappeared before 1900, but was described by Conder,[42] and the site can be seen in plate 4:

> The Khan ... is a later building than the mosque. Its ruins are almost indistinguishable, but it consisted of a great court, with small surrounding

> chambers, occupying about 300 ft north and south by 170 ft east and west ... Some pointed arches remain, and in one case the keystone is nicked out below to form the point...

The building referred to by Conder as a *khān* was a courtyard building aligned with the ʻCathedral', and seemingly continuous with it. While the reference to pointed arches seems to indicate that there was late construction here, it may have been built in the already existing precincts of the ʻCathedral'. Conder's identification of the building as a *khān*, or caravanserai, reflects the requirements of the site in the Ayyubid period and after. ʻAmmān, although not directly lying on the main *Darb al-Ḥajj* from Damascus to the Holy Cities in Arabia, was only a brief diversion to a well-watered halt. Secondly ʻAmmān also lay on a road east from Jerusalem, at the head of the ascent from the Jordan Valley. There is no doubt that the site of ʻAmmān, even when it was not inhabited as a city, would have been an important site for a *khān*.

(iii) Ḥammām

This building also disappeared before 1900, but was described by Conder:[43]

> There are eight small low chambers, built of inferior masonry and apparently not very ancient. The block containing them measures 40 ft east and west, 50 ft north and south. The arches are pointed. The northern aqueduct seems to have supplied these baths with water.

The site of this building is visible in plate 4, but no close photographs of it have survived. Conder's assessment of it as an Islamic building may be accepted, and it may have belonged to the restoration of the city of ʻAmmān by the Mamlūk *amīr* Sarghatmish in 1357.

Discussion

The mosque and these two buildings were clustered together at the west end of the Roman lower city. Al-Muqaddasī tells us that the mosque was located in the area of the market, and that Qaṣr Jālūt overlooked the town; it seems likely that the centre of the Islamic town lay around the mosque at the junction of the two wadis, and not in the area of the Roman theatre where the forum lay. This point seems to perpetuate the situation of the Byzantine period, for the mosque is almost adjacent to the largest church, the supposed ʻCathedral'.

The extent of the lower city in the Islamic period may be detected from the lay of debris visible in plates 3 and 4, where there is a distinct change towards the west end of the lower city. There seems to have been settlement on the southern slopes of the Qalʻa, and vaults visible in plate 64a, on the west side of the Propylaeon, probably represent Islamic occupation. There must also have been occupation in the bottom of the wadi north from the mosque, and some of the wall-lines there recorded by the Special Survey plan of the Palestine Exploration Fund (fig.4) probably represent buildings of Islamic date. The approximate total area of the lower city in the Islamic period was 15.3 ha.

The area of the Qalʻa within the Umayyad walls was 9 ha, but only about 3.5 ha were occupied by buildings. The Qalʻa, as rebuilt in the Umayyad period, was more than half the size of the remainder of the city, and, as we shall see, it subsequently retained a settlement which must have been a suburb to the lower city. So the maximal extent of the city in the Umayyad period was about 24.3 ha. It should be emphasized that the proposed areas of the city given in this chapter are of a low order of accuracy, and are only intended to give a general idea.

Regrettably there is little comparative information on the sizes of early medieval Islamic provincial cities, especially in the Levant. In Iraq, where information is available, Abbasid provincial cities were much larger, for example Uskāf Banī Junayd covered 400 ha, ʻUkbarā' 130 ha, and Karkh Fayrūz, 190 ha.[44] However post-medieval Sāmarrā', a city of comparable status within its province, had an area of 35 ha.

6

THE UMAYYAD CONGREGATIONAL MOSQUE

by Alastair Northedge

The mosque was located at the junction of King Hussein and King Talal Streets, on the site of the present main mosque, the Jāmiʿ al-Ḥusaynī al-Kabīr, which was first built in 1923. Because the remains of the earlier mosque are no longer visible, the evidence about the building is limited, but it is enough to say something worthwhile about it. The evidence consists of two descriptions with drawings, an inscription, and photographs from the period between 1867 and 1922.

THE EVIDENCE

We have one textual reference to a mosque at ʿAmmān, by al-Muqaddasī in the *Aḥsan al-Taqāsīm fī Maʿrifat al-Aqālīm* (*c*.375/985):

> There is in the area of the market a fine mosque, whose courtyard is ornamented with mosaics.[1]

Apart from this contemporary reference, an understanding of the mosque is largely dependent on two early reports.

Conder's Description

In October 1881 the survey party of the Palestine Exploration Fund, under the direction of C. R. Conder, spent a week at ʿAmmān, planning the site of the ancient city. In the course of Conder's visit the party surveyed a large mosque. In the first and only volume of their publication, *The Survey of Eastern Palestine* (1889), there is a description with a plan and three further drawings (figs 20–21, 23).[2] In the Palestine Exploration Fund archive one photograph of the mosque is preserved (pl.8a), but this predates Conder's survey, having been taken by Phillips for Lt Warren in 1867, the year that Warren made his map of ʿAmmān; in addition, the mosque appears in two general photographs of the wadi in the archive (pl.8b).[3] One of these dates to Warren's visit in 1867, and the second to Conder's work in 1881.

Conder gives the following account of the structure of the mosque:

> The minaret is described by Lord Linsay as the 'lofty steeple' of a church, but this is an error. The plan of the mosque is quite distinct, with its mihrab and minaret; and the brackets which supported the gallery of the Muedhdhen remain intact. The mosque is of the typical form, with a large square court to the north, and a broad, short, covered building on the south. The court is 120 feet wide east and west, by 135 feet north and south inside; the covered part is 37 feet north and south, by 120 feet east and west. The court had three entrances, the middle one 10 feet wide, the side ones 7 feet. The roof of the mosque was supported on narrow arches which sprung from the wall, and were corbelled out in such a manner as to be apparently – but not structurally – of the Moorish form, or rather more than a half-circle or ellipse. The mihrab in the south wall is 11 feet 9 inches in diameter, and a smaller mihrab has been has been built up inside it. The arches of the entrance-gates are semi-circular in two cases, while the central one is segmental. The segmental arch has a lintel-stone 16 feet long beneath it, and a second lintel lower again forming the head of the door. The west entrance has a lintel 9 feet long, similar to this last. The arrangement of segmental relieving arch and lintel is similar to that so often found in Byzantine buildings, but is also not uncommon in Arab work. There are four windows in this north wall between the entrances, also with round arches. This wall is standing to its original height, but the others are ruined in parts; the masonry is of moderate size and finish, not drafted. The Ausâm, or tribe-marks, of all the principal tribes are found on the walls. ... The minaret of this mosque is on the north wall near the west end, and although the masonry in this structure is smaller than that in the wall, there seems no reason to suppose that the minaret is a later addition. The minaret is square on plan, a tower 10 feet side. A shaft of stone 14 inches in diameter in the centre supports the winding stair in a cylindrical well about 6 feet in total diameter, the

> stairs being only 2 feet wide. There are thirty-three steps, with a total height of 33 feet, leading to a platform with four windows, one in each wall. The total height is about 45 feet, and the top is crowned by a dome, which is concealed outside by an elegant octagonal shaft which springs from the corbels of the Muedhdhen's gallery above the windows. The windows are round-arched, and partly filled in with a balustrade of stone 3 feet high. The minaret stair is reached from a low door in the east wall having a lintel above it, on which is crudely incised an Arab inscription. … It is merely the formula: 'No God but Allah; Muhammed is the messenger of God.'…
>
> The use of round arches in this building seems to indicate (an) early date.…The mosque at 'Ammân would thus appear to be a building of the Ommiyeh Khalifs (661–750 AD), or more probably one of the 'Abbāside family (750–850 AD) at latest.

Butler's Description

After the foundation of the Circassian settlement at 'Ammān at about the time of the Palestine Exploration Fund survey in 1881, the prayer hall of the mosque was cleared out, and the roof rebuilt, for service as the mosque of 'Ammān. When H. C. Butler, leading the Princeton Archaeological Expedition to Syria, visited 'Ammān in 1904, the development of 'Ammān had meant that the north wall of the building had become separated from the restored prayer hall. As is apparent in the account below, Butler did not appreciate the unity of the building, and includes the north wall in the *Publications of the Princeton Archaeological Expedition* to Syria under the heading 'Ancient Wall near Mosque' (with two drawings; fig.24).[4]

> The best preserved of the fragments of buildings that are later than the great Roman period, is a fine section of wall, with three portals and four windows in it, that now forms the north side of the court-yard of the mosque. The wall is of great thickness (1.55m), laid dry, in courses of 45–50cm; the portals are high and spacious, two of them have flat lintels and stilted relieving arches, and the other, the middle one, has a lintel below a flat segmental arch. The windows are all roundheaded. The structure is devoid of ornament of any kind. To the north or outer face of the wall, near its west end, is attached a tower, or minaret, of later and poorer workmanship, built in courses 30 to 40 cm wide, laid in mortar. The entrance to this tower has been roughly cut through the ancient wall. The great central portal has been reduced in size by the insertion of new jambs and lintel. The wall, when mentioned by travellers, has always been considered as Mohammedan work, and part of the mosque. It has at present no further relation to the mosque, which is a small structure, and, as I imagine, not very ancient, further than that it bounds one side of the court before the mosque. The wall itself with its portals and windows was built to form one side, or the front, of a building; it is not a courtyard wall, and if it formed the front of an earlier mosque than the present one, as it may have done, the mosque was, in all likelihood, the one described in the 10th century by Mukaddasi. But even so the matter of the date of the wall is not settled. It is difficult for me to believe that the wall is Mohammedan work…but the character of the wall seems either very late Roman, or early Christian. The wall might easily have formed the north side of a large church…the typical side wall of Syrian basilicas.

In 1920 the mosque was visited and photographed by Creswell (pl.9),[5] but it has only proved possible to find a brief note by him of his observations:

> *Mosque at west end of Town.* Only the facades and minaret now exist. Although it is difficult to give an approximate date to this building, it is certainly ancient and worthy of conservation. The facade is well built of cut stone.[6]

In 1923 the site was also photographed by Garstang,[7] and St John Philby, while he was adviser to Amir 'Abdallah.[8]

Inscription (fig.22; pl.10a)

A building inscription was recorded by Littmann for the Princeton Expedition.[9] This was a stone, measuring probably 0.80 × 0.55m, found in a disturbed location in the mosque. A photograph by Garstang (pl.10a) shows that the text was placed in a *tabula ansata*-like frame, but the frame is oriented vertically in place of the normal Roman horizontal layout. The photograph is taken adjacent to the main central door of the mosque.

The script is Kufic, incised with pronounced serifs. The script has no diacritical marks:

1 بسم الله الرحمن الرحيم
2 مما سهل الله عزّ و
3 جلّ وله الحمد عما
4 رته علي يدي القائد
5 الحسن بن ابرهيم رحمة

6 الله ورحم من ترحم
7 عليه

Transcription:

1. *bism Allah al-Raḥmān al-Raḥīm*
2. *mimmā sahala Allah ʿazza wa*
3. *jalla wa-lahu al-ḥamd ʿimā-*
4. *ratuhu ʿalā yaday al-qāʾid*
5. *al-Ḥasan bn Ibrahīm raḥimahu*
6. *Allah wa-raḥima man taraḥḥama*
7. *ʿalayhi*

Translation:

> In the name of God the Merciful, the Compassionate/ this is among what God who is mighty and/ great, and to whom be praise facilitated to be/ built under the direction of the commander/ al-Ḥasan ibn Ibrahīm, may God have mercy/ upon him, and may He have mercy upon him who says God have mercy/ upon him.

The text is undated. The script may be compared to two gravestones published by Van Berchem which are attributed to either the 3rd/9th or 4th/10th centuries.[10] These scripts, however, lack serifs and are described as archaizing. A third gravestone in this style carries a date of AH 3?5, and it is suggested that this equates with 305/917–18.[11]

The executor of the construction work, al-Ḥasan ibn Ibrahīm, appears unknown to history. The name is Arab, but without a *nisba*. The title of *qāʾid* ('commander') denotes a military officer of the Caliphate or its successor states, but was not usual in the post-Crusading period.[12] This man ought to be an ʿAbbāsid, Ṭūlūnid, Ikhshīdid or possibly Fāṭimid general.

ASSESSMENT OF THE EVIDENCE

Although Butler's account, as quoted above, expresses itself as uncertain about the dating, and thus the identification of the building, he gave the impression in 1920 to the British Mandate authorities in Palestine that the building was definitely a church.[13] It was Butler's incorrect, but publicized, views that were the cause of confusion in the mind of Amir ʿAbdullah. ʿAbdullah had the building demolished and built a new mosque. The event caused a political controversy.

However, the photographs of 1867 and 1881 show clearly that the whole was a single building, and Conder's plan can be seen to give a generally accurate idea of its layout. The evidence of an early date of construction discussed later suggests that it is the same building as that mentioned by al-Muqaddasī.

Although we have a good idea of the courtyard and the north wall and minaret from the photographs, we have little evidence about the prayer hall, of which no close photographs have come to light.

As it stood in 1881, the mosque was a rectangular building measuring 57.1 × 39.7m. It was entered by three gates in the north wall. The two flanking entrances had stilted semi-circular arches, the western one having a stone lintel. The central entrance had a lintel and flat segmental arch. A secondary lower lintel and jambs had been fitted into this entrance. The wall was also pierced by four windows. Towards the northwest corner there was a square minaret. At the top there was an interior room lit by four windows, and approached by a spiral staircase. Above the square section there were the brackets for a gallery, and a further octagonal section, of which four courses survived.

The prayer hall in its final form measured 39.7 × 14 m, and was divided from the courtyard *(ṣaḥn)* by a solid wall with three entrances (fig.27). The central entrance was wider, but its arch was missing (pl.4).[14] The two side doors had round arches.[15] The *miḥrāb* was set in a salient, and a second smaller *miḥrāb* was built up inside it. Surprisingly, the arch fronting the semi-dome of the *miḥrāb* remained standing, clearly visible in photographs of the building. The springing of six arcades perpendicular to the *qibla* wall was observed by Conder, and these had the slight return of a horseshoe shape (fig.23). Warren's plan of ʿAmmān, dating to 1867, shows a single line of six columns down the centre of the prayer hall (fig.3).

Butler was probably wrong in suggesting that the masonry was laid dry; it is common for mortar to erode out of the joints, and for traces only to survive in the interior of the wall.

The photographs also show that Butler was certainly more correct than Conder in claiming the minaret to be a later addition (pl.8a).

RECONSTRUCTION OF THE PHASING

The mosque was in use over a long period of time, and clearly must have had a complex constructional history. We cannot hope to recover the phasing of construction in detail from the evidence available, but it is possible to gain a general outline.

The north wall was built of finely dressed plain limestone ashlars in courses 0.4–0.5m deep, and was 1.55m thick, according to Butler. The west and east exterior walls seem to have been of a similar quality, to judge from the photographs taken by Philby (pl.10b).

The rectangle of the exterior wall, as it stood in the 19th century, must have belonged to the original construction. The size of the mosque as delineated by this enclosure was 2255 square metres.

The enclosure wall stood 5.9m high in Butler's elevation drawing (figs 24, 26), but it is clear that the top of the foundation level on the inside was 1.0–1.2m lower, making a total surviving height of 7.0–7.1m.

There were three entrances in the north wall. The central entrance was not placed axially; rather its western jamb lay on the axis of the mosque. It was 3.55m wide, with a lintel and segmental relieving arch. The two flanking entrances were 2.3m wide. While only the western entrance preserved a lintel, it is clear that the eastern entrance originally had one also. Both had stilted semi-circular relieving arches. The wall was also pierced by four round-arched windows, 0.98m wide and 1.5m high.

Why the facade was not symmetrical is not at all clear. While it is possible that there was an earlier minaret that was later replaced, it should be remembered that the mosque was built in the centre of an already existing city, and it may be that limitations of the site demanded an asymmetric design.

A row of beam holes in the exterior facade over the doors and windows shows that the building once had a colonnaded porch (fig.26; pl.9b); although in an earlier version of this study it was not certain how long this porch was,[16] a photograph subsequently discovered shows the porch covered the area of the entrances only (pl.8a). The Jāmiʿ al-ʿUmarī at Buṣrā also has a similar porch in front of a triple entrance, probably to be dated later than the Umayyad period;[17] and the Umayyad mosque of Qaṣr al-Ḥallabāt has a porch around three sides of the building.[18]

At the top of the inside face there is a ledge (pl.9a); this should be interpreted as intended to carry the roofing timbers of an arcade for the *ṣaḥn*. The colonnaded porch and *riwāq* of the *ṣaḥn* disappeared before the construction of the minaret. The seating of the minaret on the wall overlaps the ledge that held the roof timbers of the *riwāq*.

The *qibla* end of the mosque is more of a problem. The *miḥrāb* was clear enough. It was set in a rectangular salient 4.9 × 0.75m, and there is no reason to suppose that the salient, which is visible in the Palestine Exploration Fund photographs, was not original (pl.8b). The *miḥrāb* itself was extremely large, measuring 3.58m in diameter. In its latest form there was a second *miḥrāb* built up inside it. As Conder's plan shows two full semicircles, it seems likely that the second *miḥrāb* was of later date (fig.20). The facade arch of the larger *miḥrāb* remained standing, to a height that cannot be precisely measured, but of the order of six to seven metres.

The Palestine Exploration Fund plan shows that the prayer hall measured 39.7 × 14m overall. The facade wall facing the *ṣaḥn* was a solid wall with only three entrances (fig.27). The side entrances were each about two metres wide; the central entrance was wider (about three metres), and was narrowed after 1881 (pl.9b).[19] The two side doors had round arches, and the facade was built of an ashlar masonry not dissimilar to that of the north wall.

If this facade wall of the prayer hall belonged to the first period of construction, then the plan would be unique among courtyard mosques: the usual architectural practice in areas with cold winters was an arched facade filled in with wooden doors. While it is possible that the building was unique, it would seem more likely that the facade was a rebuild. However, the use of round arches in this wall is surprising, if the wall is indeed later than the Umayyad period, and the photographs give no evidence of rebuilt masonry.

We have no way of knowing for certain whether this wall, if it was a rebuild, was on the same line as the original facade: examples of mosques are known where the width of the prayer hall has been increased, and decreased.[20] However, the size of the prayer hall in the mosque's final form, by comparison with other courtyard mosques, seems too small, and the *ṣaḥn* correspondingly too large. It seems likely, therefore, that when the mosque was rebuilt, the size of the prayer hall was reduced, and that a new facade wall was built out of the mosque's original masonry.

The way that this might have happened is suggested by the plan of the Umayyad mosque of Ruṣāfa, which is a close parallel to that of ʿAmmān.[21] The mosque of Ruṣāfa is of the same overall dimensions as that of ʿAmmān, 40 × 56m, and the *miḥrāb* is also set in a rectangular salient. At Ruṣāfa the prayer hall is 21m deep and the courtyard 35m deep. The prayer hall has two arcades placed parallel to the *qibla* wall, making a hall with three aisles, each seven metres wide. The second arcade is placed on the 14m line, as is the facade wall at ʿAmmān. It is possible, therefore, that when the mosque came to be rebuilt, a formerly three-aisled prayer hall was reduced to two aisles. The advantage of building the new facade wall on the line of the former arcade would have been, of course, that there was an already existing foundation for the new wall.

This hypothesis is consistent with the evidence that we have. The plan of ʿAmmān drawn by Lt Warren in 1867 indicates a line of six columns down the centre of the prayer hall (fig.3). The 1923 mosque, which appears to follow the plan of the mosque as repaired in the 1880s quite closely, was built with a single row of eight columns the length of the centre of the prayer hall. Both of these points could be relics of a prayer hall with two aisles parallel to the *qibla* wall.

Nevertheless the Palestine Exploration Fund plan shows the springing of six horseshoe arches perpendicular to the *qibla* wall, and not parallel to it. They are on centres 3.7m apart, with a wider axial nave 6.5m centre to centre. The 3.7m spacing fits perfectly with there having been two more arches in the original plan, making a total of eight. Although we are not told by Conder whether the springers were found attached the *qibla* wall or the facade wall of the prayer hall, it was the facade wall which survived to a greater height, sufficient for at least some of the springers to have survived (fig.25, pl.4).

Structural horseshoe arches are found before Islam in 6th-century churches, such as at Rusāfa, and in the Umayyad period at the Umayyad Mosque in Damascus,[22] and the mosque of Qaṣr al-Ḥayr al-Sharqī.[23] Decorative horseshoe arches are common, and are found in ʿAmmān in the niches of the Reception Hall of the palace in the Citadel. However, structural horseshoe arches are also particularly a feature of post-Umayyad architecture in Syria: the gates of the third period of walls at ʿAyn Zarba (now Anavarza in Turkey), attributed to Sayf al-Dawla in the middle of the 4th/10th century,[24] the Numayrid gateway in the Citadel of Ḥarrān (5th/11th century),[25] and the 6th/12th century facade of the mosque of Ḥarrān all have horseshoe arches.[26] If the facade wall of the sanctuary was rebuilt on a new line, then the horseshoe arches belong to a secondary phase, and the parallels of the 4th/10th–5th/11th centuries are relevant. It seems likely, then, that when the mosque was rebuilt, the direction of the arches was changed, and that the conclusions reached in the first version of this study should be modified.[27]

From the above it is apparent that there were at least two phases in the construction of the prayer hall before the 19th century: (1) the original construction, and (2) the reduction in size of the prayer hall and the construction of the horseshoe arches, with a single central line of columns.

The wider axial nave, which survived as part of the mosque's final form, must also have existed earlier. Both the standing *miḥrāb* arch, and the evidence of the masonry from the prayer hall facade's central doorway, require walling higher than the exterior enclosure wall, and it seems there must have been a clerestory.

The single detail from al-Muqaddasī, that the courtyard was ornamented with mosaic, surely also belongs to the original construction. These were presumably wall mosaics similar to those of the Dome of the Rock, or the Umayyad Mosque of Damascus.

The Palestine Exploration Fund survey calculated the *qibla* of the mosque to be 185°, that is, to the west of due south. The correct *qibla* from ʿAmmān is 165°, to the east of south. The *qibla* of the mosque was therefore apparently incorrect by 20°. However, there is some reason to believe that the survey's north point was incorrect. Comparison with the modern orientation of buildings also shown on the Special Survey plan suggests that the error was 11–12°. Magnetic variation since 1881 amounts to 2° 34'. The probable *qibla* was therefore about 173–174°, and inaccurate by 8–9°.[28] The mosque could be described as pointing roughly at Makka.

Tabulation of the Phasing

Period 1

The outer enclosure, with colonnaded porch, arcaded *ṣaḥn*, and first *miḥrāb*. The size of the prayer hall and its style of arcading are unknown, but there was probably a wider axial nave with clerestory.

Period 2

Much of the courtyard was abandoned, and the arcades collapsed. A secondary doorway was built in the central north entrance, and the two side doors were blocked up. The prayer hall was rebuilt smaller (39.7 × 14m), with horseshoe arches for arcades perpendicular to the *qibla* wall. A secondary *miḥrāb* was built inside the earlier one.

Period 3

The minaret was added.

DATING

The dating evidence for the original construction lies in the architecture, principally in the details of the north wall. The combination of round-arched windows, and doors with lintels and round relieving arches is typical of Umayyad religious architecture, for example the Dome of the Rock,[29] the Jāmiʿ al-ʿUmarī at Buṣrā,[30] the mosque of Qaṣr Ḥallabāt,[31] and the Umayyad Mosque in Damascus.[32] Outside the Umayyad period the parallels are earlier, particularly the cathedral at Buṣrā,[33] Qalb Lozeh,[34] and Qalʿat Simʿan.[35]

The masonry is also typically Umayyad, well-laid ashlar limestone masonry. This can also resemble Byzantine masonry, but in the context of a mosque, of course it can only be Umayyad.

These features would suggest that the original construction is Umayyad, and less strongly that it is an earlier rather than a later Umayyad building, before the more systematic introduction of the pointed arch towards the end of the period. For example, the architecture of this phase is quite different from the

Umayyad palace in the Citadel. The Reception Hall of that building has its parallels with late Umayyad construction, and probably belongs to the reign of the Caliph Hishām ibn ʿAbd al-Malik.[36] The most likely period for the construction of the mosque would be between the reigns of al-Walīd ibn ʿAbd al-Malik and Yazīd ibn ʿAbd al-Malik (86/705–105/724).

The work of early modification (Period 2) could have belonged to one programme of work, but equally it could have belonged to more than one period. Perhaps the mosque was damaged in an earthquake, similar to the damage known to have been caused in the Qalʿa, and only the prayer hall was restored. The mosque was reduced in size, and the *ṣaḥn* left unrebuilt.

The inscription of al-Hasan ibn Ibrahīm ought to apply to this work, and we would thus date it around the late 3rd/9th to early 4th/10th centuries. However al-Muqaddasī's description of the mosque as a fine building with a decorated *ṣaḥn* is difficult to reconcile with a collapse of the *riwāq*s, and a rebuild of the prayer hall. However, it is possible that this change post-dated the composition of the *Aḥsan al-Taqāsīm* (*c.*375/985). We need not place too great an emphasis on al-Muqaddasī's evaluation of the mosque as fine; the rebuilt mosque of Period 2 may have justified al-Muqaddasī's remark. As a reconstruction in the 5th/11th century is later than the likely date of the inscription, in that case the inscription would refer either to building operations of which we know nothing, or to the new *miḥrāb*.

The minaret resembled the usual Middle Islamic minarets of the Levant – a square tower surmounted by a short drum with a roofed gallery. In other minarets such a drum might be square, octagonal or round. The smaller drum and roofed gallery may have first appeared at the Saljuq minaret of the Great Mosque of Aleppo (483/1089).[37] Minarets of this form continued to be built into the 9th/15th century; particularly close parallels can be seen in the minarets of the Khanqah Salāḥiyya (820/1417),[38] and of the mosque of Afḍal ʿAlī in Jerusalem.[39] On the whole the small size of the masonry favours a later rather than an earlier date. Possibly the minaret is Mamlūk, late 7th/13th century or 8th/14th century, and the work might be identified as part of the restoration of ʿAmmān carried out by the *Amīr* Sarghatmish in AD 1357.

DISCUSSION

The congregational mosque of ʿAmmān was originally an Umayyad construction. One might divide Umayyad mosques into categories: the small private *masājid* (sing. *masjid*) in the palaces, and the *jawāmiʿ* (sing. *jāmiʿ*) of the cities. But the dividing line in the archaeological evidence is not clear; the larger planned settlements at ʿAnjar,[40] and Qaṣr al-Ḥayr al-Sharqī[41] have mosques intermediate in size between the two classes, and it is obvious that there was a gradation of size according to requirement.

ʿAmmān falls clearly under the heading of an urban *jāmiʿ*. We know the plans, or parts of the plans, of five similar buildings: Damascus, Jerusalem (al-Aqṣā), Buṣrā,[42] Rusāfa, and Ḥarrān. The *miḥrāb* was unusual among Umayyad mosques in being set in a rectangular salient. Only Ruṣāfa among other Umayyad mosques has this feature. At the other four quoted above, the *miḥrāb* is set into the wall, as also at ʿAnjar and Qaṣr al-Ḥayr al-Sharqī. The smaller mosques at Qaṣr Ḥallabāt, Umm al-Walīd,[43] and Jabal Says,[44] have curved salients.

A city's mosque can be an indicator of population changes. A *jāmiʿ*, if there is only one, ought to be able to hold a city's male Muslim population. Mosques were often rebuilt to accommodate larger congregations, for example the mosques of the Round City of Baghdad,[45] Sīrāf,[46] and Cordova. Of course, the proportional correspondence is likely to be far from exact, because of the long intervals between building and rebuilding. Also, in the early period the size of the Muslim population might be no guide to the size of the total population of the city.

The sequence of development of the ʿAmmān mosque was from a large Period 1 mosque (2255 sq.m.) to a much smaller Period 2 building (555 sq.m.), a size that was later maintained. The Period 1 building was considerably smaller than the mosques of the great cities of the early Islamic world – Damascus (15,750 sq.m.), Ḥarrān (*c.*10,000 sq.m.), or Wāsiṭ (10,795 sq.m.) in the Umayyad period; or Raqqa (10,042 sq.m.),[47] the first period at Cordova (7114 sq.m.), or the Mosque of ʿAmr (13,200 sq.m.),[48] in the ʿAbbāsid period. But it was comparable in size with those of other cities, the mosque of Ruṣāfa (2255 sq.m.) in the Umayyad period, and Period 1 at Sīrāf (2244 sq.m.), Susa (2726 sq.m.),[49] and Damghān (1739 sq.m.), all of which post-date the ʿAbbāsid revolution. It was larger than the Jāmiʿ al-ʿUmarī at the neighbouring city of Buṣrā (*c.*1190 sq.m.).

Taking into account its early date, this mosque was a building of some significance in the early Islamic world, but not one of the first rank. This evidence illustrates the importance of ʿAmmān in the Umayyad period. After the end of the Umayyad period, the mosque provides evidence of a population decline, for only a smaller building was required when the mosque came to be rebuilt.[50]

The mosque of ʿAmmān is the largest Umayyad mosque known from the area of the Hashemite Kingdom of Jordan. No monumental mosques are yet known from the other Roman cities of Jordan at which Umayyad occupation has been found – Jarash, Tabaqat Faḥl (Pella), Umm Qays (Gadara), Bayt Rās (Capitolias), and Ḥisbān. No doubt this was because 'Ammān was the seat of the governor of the Balqā', and the main centre of Jordan in the Umayyad period.

Taking into account the size of the city, and the fact that the proportion of Muslim population in the Umayyad period was not high, the mosque is quite large. As 'Amman was the main market centre for the desert palaces, Qusayr 'Amra, Qaṣr al-Ḥallabāt, al-Qasṭal, Muwaqqar, Mshattā, Qaṣr al-Kharāna, etc., it is possible to imagine that their inhabitants came to 'Ammān for the Friday prayers, if not every week, at least for the two festivals of 'Īd al-Fiṭr and 'Īd al-Aḍḥā. In a parallel example forty years later in Iraq, 'Īsā ibn Mūsā, an uncle of the Caliph al-Manṣūr:

> went out to an estate of his [which has been identified by Creswell with the great palace of al-Ukhayḍir], and only used to come into Kūfa in two months of the year, in Ramaḍān, to be present at the Friday prayers and the 'Īd, and then he would return to his estate, and in the beginning of Dhūal-Ḥijja; and when he had been present at the 'Īd, he returned to his estate.[51]

'Īsā ibn Mūsā was unusual in that he was famous for having become a recluse; his practice illustrates the minimum attendance that was acceptable.

7

THE UMAYYAD PALACE

by Alastair Northedge

The Umayyad palace at the north end of the Citadel has been the subject of two recent pieces of fieldwork. Firstly, the present author conducted a short survey in 1977–8, and secondly a project of photogrammetric survey, excavation and conservation was carried out by a Spanish archaeological mission in 1976 and 1978–80, under the direction of A. Almagro. The Spanish team resumed work quite recently, in 1989. The author's survey has only been published in preliminary form,[1] while two out of the three volumes the Spanish team expect to produce have so far appeared.[2] The latter are the product of fairly extensive work, and reflect that fact. The first volume, by Almagro, *El Palacio Omeya de Amman I, La Arquitectura,* can be described as an excellent record of the stonework, but as less strong on understanding the quite complex archaeological sequence of the area, and the interpretation of the remains.[3]

It seemed worthwhile to include another treatment of the Umayyad Palace in this publication for three reasons: the author's survey work was never published in its final form, and some aspects have not been taken into account by the Spanish publication; the palace area provides important evidence for understanding the development of the Citadel as a whole, and it would be impossible to explain this development adequately without reference to the palace; and some aspects of the palace can be described as having a distinctive cultural significance for the Umayyad period, and this significance needs to be brought out.

Architecture and Sequence

At the time of the First World War, much of the plan of the complex known today was already visible, despite being filled with rubble to a depth of two metres or more (pls 2a, 14a, 16). The Roman enclosure has been known since the 19th century, and was surveyed by Butler (fig.30).[4] Of the palace, the Reception Hall, standing with its vaults, has also been known since the beginning of the 19th century, but only Conder recognized that there might be further buildings connected with it,[5] and there was disagreement about its date.

The Italian Mission made this area one of the major objects of their excavation in the 1930s. In the course of these excavations the east half of the double enclosure was excavated, together with the Reception Hall of the palace. The expedition's plans of this area have not been published.[6] The Italian Mission implicitly accepted Butler's interpretation that there were only two major architectural units at the site: a Roman enclosure, with buildings; and the Reception Hall, which was described as an Arab building. However, they noted later construction in the enclosure.[7] It seems unlikely that Bartoccini, the director of the Italian excavations, ever worked out the implications of his own mission's discoveries.

However, a new interpretation emerged from the author's survey work of 1977–8, an interpretation subsequently taken up by Almagro,[8] and we can now see that there are two major constructions, superimposed on one another. The first phase consists of two courtyards of Roman date, and this superstructure is mounted on a substantial artificial platform that projects from the hill. Although the buildings do not always bond with one another, the later complex of buildings, the second major phase, can be said to represent a single architectural development – a palace of the Umayyad period.

1. PRE-PLATFORM TOPOGRAPHY

The natural outline of the north end of the Qal'a appears to have been a gentle declination of the ridge from a high point of 843.6m above Mean Sea Level (MSL) to the south of the complex, down to 822.4m at a saddle (an overall gradient of 8.5%), thereafter rising more steeply to Jabal Ḥusayn, which overlooks the

Qal'a. To east and west, steep slopes with a gradient of about 60% lead down to the wadis on either side of the hill. Before the construction of the platform the extent of the site in the direction of Jabal Ḥusayn had been rather greater. The lines of the city walls of Middle Bronze and Iron Age date have been identified at the north end, and they appear to curve around the hill to the north of the line of the present enclosure.[9]

2. THE ROMAN REMAINS

a. The Platform

The natural outline of the hill at this point has been changed by the erection of a massive artificial platform of a double trapezoid shape, projecting from the hill. The two trapezoids measure 78 × 126m and 48 × 104m.

On the south side the levelled area touches the bedrock of the hill, though there is no evidence of actual excavation of the rock. At its northern end the levelled surface (approximately 839m above MSL) stands between 6m and 18m above the immediately surrounding terrain. The marker of this platform is a monumental wall of rusticated ashlar masonry, at its one measurable point 1.85m thick. The wall survives to a maximum height of 13.8m. This wall is described in more detail in Chapter 8 as wall Sectors 1–7. In Sector 1, on the east side, the wall is faced with plain-dressed ashlar masonry, and in Sectors 4 and 5, on the north and west sides, up to five courses of plain-dressed ashlar masonry survive above the rusticated masonry. These appear to represent remnants of the superstructure wall. Some of this masonry is of a poorer quality, and may represent the reconstruction of the later period.

b. The Double Enclosure (fig.31)

The superstructure that was built on the platform is composed of two courtyards, divided by a wall. To judge from the continuity of the masonry, and the fit of the design, the platform was built specifically for the present enclosure.

The First Enclosure

The first enclosure is a trapezoid, measuring approximately 78 × 120–126m. The western limits are known partly from the platform wall (Sector 5), and partly from a wall of plain-dressed ashlar masonry (Sector 7) in the southwest corner of the enclosure. This links to a corner tower (Tower C) measuring 8.0 × 8.4m.

Two sections of the south wall are visible. To the west of the later Reception Hall a section 15m long is visible in the surface, and to the east the whole length of 29.8m stands to a maximum of 6.1m high. The wall is of plain-dressed ashlars 0.9m wide. There is one protruding bond, later utilized by the west wall of the Umayyad period Room 64. In addition, the Spanish excavations revealed the stylobate for a colonnade lining the south wall, 7m to the north of the wall, and 1.1m wide.[10] In the southeast corner, Tower A is a reconstruction of a Roman room or tower, and measures 8.0 × 8.15m (see Chapter 8).

The east wall is again a wall of plain-dressed ashlars 0.9m wide (Sector 1). Its northern end is strengthened with a buttress, whose dimensions are *c.* 8.85m × 0.45m.

Five rooms (E1–5) lining this wall have survived through their incorporation into the Umayyad development, and are the survivors of a line that probably extended the full length of the east side (pl.32c). The northernmost (E5) is a plain, almost square, room measuring 5.2 × 4.6m internally; from the evidence of the exterior buttress, it is possible that this was a tower, but no conclusive indications survive. There is evidence, from a photograph taken by Garstang (pl.38b), that there may have been a doorway in the facade of the Sector 2 wall to the west of the external buttress. What this led into, we do not know, but it is possible that there was a staircase down within Room E5. The next room (E4: 15 × 5.03m) is partly open-fronted, and partly closed, with a doorway; it was presumably originally divided in two. At its southern end the Italians discovered a mosaic, now gone.[11] The three remaining rooms (E1: 9.5 × 4.9m; E2: 8.5 × 4.9m; E3: 5.1 × 4.9m) are open-fronted. The ends of the side walls of these rooms each have a pair of square pilasters separated by a shell niche (fig.33). As suggested by Almagro, the open-fronted rooms may have had a colonnade.[12] The fact that the north wall foundation projects 4.4m beyond the facade of these rooms suggests that there was a further colonnade stretching the full length of the facade.

Rooms E1 and E2 were subsequently rebuilt with a front wall and doorway (Period 2). E1 was also provided with a second storey, supported by three arches that run parallel to the long axis of the room; one of these arches is still standing. Construction of this second period employs small limestone ashlars, including at least one recut Roman architectural fragment. A graffito cross is cut on the door-jamb of E2.

The north wall, dividing the two enclosures, was not lined with rooms. Rather, the facade was elaborately decorated, although the decoration has subsequently been partly cut away, and the remainder badly weathered (fig.32). The remains *in situ*, and fragments incorporated into the later palace, show that there was a series of rectangular podiums (3.42 × 1.5 × 0.9m). At the corner of each of these a rectangular pilaster is cut in relief on the wall; the front corners presumably carried small columns. Between each podium is a shell niche. There would have been no colonnade on this side. Two gateways are visible in the excavated section of the wall, 3.0 and 2.5m wide. Symmetry would suggest that there was a third gate on the west side, but no evidence of this can be seen at present.

On the line of the later columned street, paving of the original period has survived: limestone blocks in 0.55m rows are laid parallel to the wall dividing the two enclosures. A pair of ridges 0.7m wide and 5m apart appear in the paving, running at a slight angle to the present kerbing, and extending as far as the south wall: this seems to be the seating for an earlier colonnade, and indicates that the enclosure was divided by a columned way (fig.31). On the east side of this columned way, at least, there was no evidence of an adjoining wall or building to carry the roofing timbers of a colonnaded street. It is possible that this colonnade was merely ornamental, but otherwise we have to assume that it was the columned way itself that was covered.

The ridges lead in one direction to the western of the two gates in the dividing wall, and in the other to the site of the Reception Hall. The Spanish excavations on the east side of the Reception Hall found evidence of two periods of Roman-Byzantine construction underneath the building, which may have been a gate for the complex.[13]

In addition, at the south end of Sector 5 of the platform wall on the west side, there is a vertical break in the masonry before the Sector 6 wall, which appears to be a later insert. One might explain this feature by suggesting that the Sector 6 wall is a filling of an earlier entrance on this site also. The length of the Sector 6 wall visible is 14.5m, and would suggest a broad monumental entrance leading up by a staircase from the lower city.

The Second Enclosure

This enclosure is also of a trapezoidal shape, approximately 48 × 104m. With the exception of the wall dividing the two enclosures, none of the enclosure walls survive above surface level. Within the enclosure there is relatively little that can be attributed with confidence to the original period of construction. Two lines of foundations in the southeast corner are candidates: of these there is one line, 1.05m wide, parallel to the dividing wall, and this may be the stylobate for a colonnade. There is today a column base on it at the southeast corner, possibly placed there in modern times. However, it is open to doubt whether this line is part of the original Roman construction, as the line stands some 0.7m higher than the threshold level of the adjacent gate; in fact, the level of this possible stylobate equates more nearly with the foundation levels of the Umayyad buildings in the vicinity. It seems more likely that Roman blocks have been relaid as foundation for the Umayyad buildings. However two further lines not related to the Umayyad buildings might be the foundation of an altar (fig.31).

c. Discussion and Dating

Butler, in his survey of the complex, offers no comment on its purpose.[14] In his preliminary report on the excavation, Bartoccini thought it the forum of the Roman city,[15] but it has since been agreed that the forum was located in a more plausible position – in the lower city adjacent to the theatre.[16]

In fact, neither author appreciated the existence of an artificial platform, the full height of which was concealed under debris at that time. The existence of such a large platform, a considerable undertaking, shows that this complex was of substantial significance for the Roman city. The resulting structure would have resembled the Herodian platform for the Temple in Jerusalem, built perhaps more than a century earlier. Monumental platforms of this kind have a long history in the ancient Near East, and we need not suppose that the platform here was directly inspired by the example in Jerusalem.

The platform also provides the best evidence for the purpose of a complex whose main buildings have disappeared. Within the spectrum of forms of monumental architecture employed in the Decapolis, which was relatively standardized, it is difficult to imagine that such a significant complex could have been anything but a temple.[17] There are two possible locations for the temple itself: one in the second enclosure, facing east, and the second in the western half of the first enclosure, also facing east, with the columned way crossing the courtyard running in front.

The second enclosure, and its section of the platform, would not have been built as it was if it had not been intended for a main building. The columned way crossing the first enclosure, and leading to the second, also draws us to the northern area. The space available in the second enclosure, 48 × 104m, is in fact capable of accommodating a temple as large as the so-called Temple of Hercules (27m wide) on the south side of the Citadel. However, it is more likely that the building was somewhat smaller, and located in the western half of the enclosure.

It is more difficult to reconstruct the possible layout of the first enclosure, although the area is larger. The area is divided in two by the columned way: one must suppose that the eastern half was an open courtyard, perhaps with an altar. As regards the western half, we have seen that there is evidence that there may have been a monumental staircase in the west wall. Although we do not know the width of this possible entrance – it was at least 14.5m wide, but probably less than the potential maximum of 30m – the north side lay only three metres south of the wall dividing the two enclosures. The remaining space in the southwest quarter, approximately 40–50 × 75m, is adequate for a monumental building.

As there is a double courtyard, it seems quite possible that there were in fact two temples. A similar arrangement of two temples, with the main one in a second enclosure, is recorded at the temple of Dushare at Sīʿ in the Lajā.[18] If this were the case, then there would have been two entrances, one on the site of the later Reception Hall, for the approach from the Temple of Hercules and the forum, and a second on the west side, dividing the two buildings, and leading up from the western part of the lower city. However, it must be stressed that in our present state of knowledge we can only speak of possibilities.

An inscription that is probably connected with the temple has been published by Gatier.[19] This stone is a limestone block now set into the corner of Building 3, and is evidently reused from its original location. The stone, 0.66 × 0.9m, is now placed on its side. There are seven lines of inscription, covering the top 0.44m of the stone, while the remainder is plain. Both the beginnings and ends of the lines are damaged, making it difficult to be certain whether the inscription originally comprised more blocks. The letters are evenly and well cut on a flat block, and the alphabet varies between 30 and 35mm in height, cut to a depth of 2.5mm.

As edited by Gatier, the text reads:

> La cité de Philadelphie de Coele-Syrie honore l'empereur César...Auguste grand pontife, ayant la puissance tribunicienne pour la...fois, consul pour la...fois, père de la patrie.

There is no evidence from the inscription to date the complex, but the architectural decoration has been assessed to be Antonine, mid-2nd century AD (figs 33–4).[20] Nevertheless, the evidence of the sequence of the fortifications, discussed elsewhere in this volume, indicates that the construction predates that of the Roman period of the fortifications and the Temple of Hercules, now dated to AD 161–166. The date should therefore lie in the forty or so years before AD 161.

The grand construction does emphasize the point that this sanctuary must have been of about equal status to that of the Temple of Hercules, and must have been dedicated to one of the known cults of Philadelphia.

We do not know what effects the earthquakes of the Roman-Byzantine period, effects noted elsewhere in the Qalʿa in the course of our work, might have had upon this Roman complex. However, it is unlikely that any temple would have survived in good condition into the following period.

3. THE UMAYYAD PALACE (fig.35)

The Roman double enclosure underwent an extensive reconstruction in its third period. All the buildings inside the enclosure were removed, with the exception of the five rooms on the east side, and the corner towers. In addition, the mouldings of the dividing wall were cut flat, and the podiums that lined the wall were removed, except where blocks were required for wall-bonds and seats.

The general plan of the palace is one of an almost square hall (24.4 × 26.1m), built on the south side of the first enclosure wall (Reception Hall).[21] To the north of it there is a small court (Court 1) of the same dimensions, which leads into a short columned street. In the second enclosure there is a further hall (North Building) facing onto a second small court (Court 2: 10 × 24m). On the east side of the columned street and Court 1 are three residential units, the rooms of which are arranged around three sides of a small courtyard (Buildings 4, 5 and 6). Adjacent to the North Building are two more residential units on the east side (Buildings 2 and 3).

It will be recalled that the Italians excavated only the east side of the double enclosure. A general impression of the plan of the western half of the palace can at present best be recovered from an early air photograph from the First World War, showing in general where groups of rooms lay (pl.2a).[22] It can be deduced also from ground evidence that the pattern of three residential units on the east side was repeated on the west side of the street (Buildings 7, 8 and 9).[23]

There is in addition a passageway leading further to the west side. The tripartite division extended as far as the west wall, and there were three further enclosed spaces. There were rooms against the west wall, and parts of three of these are exposed through construction work. However, it is not certain that these spaces were filled with courtyard buildings similar to Buildings 2 to 9. They may have been open yards. It appears from the air photographs that there was at least one courtyard building, on the west side of the North Building, .

Though there is much of the palace yet to be excavated, two common elements of early Islamic palaces have not so far been found: a mosque or a bath.[24]

a. The Reception Hall (figs 37–56; pls 14–29)

The Reception Hall, attached to the south side of the double enclosure, is the finest of the buildings of the palace, and must have stood at the entrance, with a passageway through to the remainder of the complex. It is for this reason that the building has sometimes been described as a gatehouse or vestibule.[25]

It is well preserved, and is in fact the most complete building at the Qal'a (see pl.14a for its condition in the 19th century). All the vaults and semi-domes are standing, but the upper parts of the north and south walls have collapsed, together with several courses of the east and west walls. The interior remained substantially complete to the cornice until early this century, when the upper parts of the interior facades collapsed (shown complete in pls.16, 17b, 20a). Clemen's account of war damage in the First World War remarks that a bomb from a British air raid in 1918 hit the building.[26] However, it is probable that these facades had begun to be denuded before the First World War.

i. Earlier Descriptions and Assessments

The building has been known and discussed several times since the beginning of the 19th century.[27]

It was described by J. S. Buckingham in 1816 as:

> ...an open square court with arched recesses on each side...The recesses in the northern and southern walls were originally open passages, and had arched doorways facing each other, but the first of these we found wholly closed, and the last was partially filled up...There is no appearance of the central square court ever having been roofed...there are lines of small niches in the walls all around the inside of the building.[28]

Canon Tristram, in 1865, called it 'a perfect Greek church of the late Byzantine type', comparing it with the 12th-century cathedral in Athens.[29] This suggestion was repeated by the Rev. A. E. Northey in 1872.[30]

The building was surveyed by C. R. Conder in 1881 for the Palestine Exploration Fund. Conder notes the similarity of the niches to Persian building, and the use of the pointed arch. He dates the building to early 'Abbāsid times, the reign of al-Ma'mūn (198/813–218/833). Conder was the first to remark upon the existence of a second similar building at the site (the North Building).

Conder's work led to an article by Hayter Lewis, an architect, who remarked that 'the great arches over the recesses, and the wall spaces to each side, are designed in almost exactly the same way as those of the Tak Kesra at Ctesiphon'(cf. fig.72).[31]

This theme of Persian influence has been an important one in scholarship on the building. In the late 19th century, Dieulafoy thought that the structure was late Sasanian, as he considered it had none of the characteristics of the Islamic style.[32] A more specific version of this idea, that the building belonged to the Sasanian occupation of Syria under Khusraw Parvīz (AD 614–28) was proposed by Warren.[33] A further formulation of the idea of Persian influence was put forward by Godard, who called attention to the existence of a Shi'ite population in 'Ammān in the 4th/10th century, and thought the building might be the product of Persian Shi'ite traders of that period.[34] Shi'ism was to be found, of course, among both Persians and Arabs in the 4th/10th century, and many of the Arab tribes of the Syrian desert edge were Shī'a in that period.

The second theme of scholarly ideas about the building was that it was Ghassānid, the work of Banī Ghassān, who, as Byzantine vassals, managed the desert frontier in the 6th century. This idea was originally propounded by Brunnow and von Domaszewski, who compared the decoration with Qaṣr al-Abyaḍ (Khirbat al-Bayḍā') in the Ruḥba.[35] In effect the building would be dated to the Late Byzantine period.

The idea of a Ghassanid origin was, however, subsequently maintained only by Islamicists, not by classical scholars: Butler assumed it to be a 'Mohammedan building'.[36] Van Berchem thought that although the 'liwans are vaulted in the Persian style', the plan corresponded with the 'symmetrical ground-plan of some Byzantine and Syrian churches with two axes', and proposed that 'Ammān was the origin of the four-*īwān* layout of Cairene *madrasas*.[37] Creswell also thought it Ghassanid, comparing it directly with the basilica of al-Mundhir at Ruṣāfa.[38] In an unpublished report of 1976 Almagro also concluded that the building is Ghassanid,[39] although subsequently he changed his views.[40]

Some scholars did date the building to the Early Islamic period: Rivoira,[41] Diez,[42] and Gertrude Bell, who compared the niches with those of Ukhayḍir.[43] Herzfeld perceptively thought that 'Amman is an Umayyad building, Iranian in character, and it proves the existence of that (four-*īwān*) plan in Iran long before there was any madrasa'.[44]

The first modern detailed treatment of the Reception Hall, by Gaube, sees the building as an Umayyad *dār al-imāra* or governor's palace.[45] He compares it to the *dār al-imāra* of Abū Muslim at Merv, a building described in detail, including dimensions, by Iṣṭakhrī, but of which no archaeological remains are known.[46] The *dār al-imāra* of Merv is said to have had a central dome chamber, and four *īwāns* facing out onto courtyards; this is a different use of the four-*īwān* plan from 'Ammān, and one that is first known in archaeological evidence from the palace of Hiraqla outside Raqqa, which is dated by its excavator, Toueir, to 190/806 or soon after.[47]

The Reception Hall was excavated and consolidated by the Italians in 1933. Bartoccini thought the building to be of the 'IX–Xe secolo'.[48] One can only speculate about the basis of his dating. The pottery found above the floor in the course of the excavations would have been of the 9th–11th centuries; alternatively, he may have been influenced by Godard's theory.

ii. Constructional Methods

The basic building material is the local limestone, used universally for construction in the city. This varies in hardness. The grade used in Roman monumental architecture at the site is rather harder than that in this building. The stone dressing has been carried out with a plain tool without teeth.

Spolia have been used to a certain extent, mainly in the core and utilitarian locations; these are mostly distinguishable by the use of a toothed tool for dressing, but there are a few Roman architectural fragments. Nevertheless the main facades seem to be new stonework.

The same mortar is employed for both internal and visible work; it is a lime mortar mixed with ash that gives it a distinctive grey colour. A second type is a harder water-proof plaster mixed with chips of crushed red pottery. This appears as a facing in the spiral staircase, but is otherwise found only in water-channels at this site.

The foundations of the Hall consist of an overall bed of rubble, set in a mortar, which has a higher ash content and is therefore looser than usual. At one point this bed of rubble rests on the bedrock, approximately one metre beneath, but at another it rests merely on fill.[49] In fact, it is likely that the foundation bed does rest on bedrock over a good proportion of the building, giving it the stability that has enabled it to survive. The ground levels east, west and south of the Hall are approximately one metre higher than the inside, and this gives the impression of a single course of ashlar foundation.

The walling was then constructed of ashlars on a rubble core, and liberal amounts of mortar bound the whole together. Two thicknesses of walling are employed for the Hall: 1.65m for the exterior walls, and 2.2m for the interior. In fact, the latter are more like masses of masonry than walls. The bottom five courses on the outside, and two on the inside, are composed of much larger blocks: the lower courses vary between 0.5m and 1m, and above that there are 0.35m courses.

iii. The Plan (fig.37)

The building is nearly a square (24.4 × 26.1m), with main entrances north and south, the latter being recessed by 1.45m. The interior is defined by its cruciform centre, based on what is today an open court, 10.3m square. The arms of the cross are symmetrical, tunnel-vaulted north and south, semi-domed east and west. These arms all measure the same in plan, 6.2 × 5.4m, but the open mouth is narrowed by a rectangular buttress, 0.20–0.25 × 1.90m, that serves as a strengthener. The two main entrances are placed in the north and south tunnel-vaulted arms. The south entrance includes three steps down from a ground level that is approximately one metre higher.

The satellite spaces of the cross are then filled out by three tunnel-vaulted rooms, and a spiral staircase in the northwest corner. The two southern rooms measure 5 × 7m, and open onto the southern arm of the cross through arched doorways, 1.4m wide and 4.6m high. The northeast room is 5m square, and opens onto Court 1 to the north. Here, in the thickness of the wall, there is a short stair to an alley that runs along the east side. The spiral staircase is in the form of a 5m square, about a central pier of 2.2m. It runs anti-clockwise, through one complete turn, to the roof. It is lit by two slit windows that open to the west, and one to the north. There is a further slit through to the western arm of the cross.

The fact that both this stair and the northeast room do not open into the interior of the building, but rather onto Court 1 to the north, is an indicator that the Hall was not intended to be an independent structure, although it is not in fact bonded with the other palace buildings.

iv. The Exterior Facades

The south facade has a central main entrance recessed by 1.45m, with an arched door 6m high and 2.5m wide (pl.14b). From the inside it is apparent that there is a change of masonry from the remainder of the south arm, though from the outside this is not apparent. Some kind of change must have taken place in the course of construction. There are four buttresses 0.25m deep and 2.4m long. Adjacent to the entrance are two seats with the typical Early Islamic quarter-circle arm-rests; these are not bonded into the structure (pl.20c). A later rectangular building has been added to the west half of the facade.

The west facade has three buttresses, 0.25m deep and 2.4m, 2.35m and 2.5m long (pl.15a). The last of these, at the south end, is built into a double door-jamb with the springer of an arch. This must have belonged to a gateway that led to a further building on the west side, or to a street leading to Gate A. There are four visible courses of the large masonry, and six of the smaller. Above this point are five further courses of irregular ashlars, where the central buttress does not continue. This could represent a final completion of the building in inferior masonry, a not uncommon occurrence when money ran out; alternatively, it could represent a repair. Considering the evidence presented elsewhere for repair and modification of the palace shortly after it was constructed, the latter possibility of a repair is perhaps more likely.

The east facade also has three buttresses, measuring 0.25 × 2.9, 2.75, and 3.35m, respectively, from north to south (pl.14b). The northern buttress has a flat-lintelled doorway belonging to the stairway leading to Court 1. The central buttress has the springer of an arch linking the Hall with further buildings on the east side (fig.41).

The north facade is plain, with five courses of the larger ashlar masonry, and seven courses of the smaller masonry, surviving (pl.15b). In the centre is the main north entrance, an arched doorway 3m wide and 8m high. On the east side is a doorway, with a flat lintel, leading to the northeast room, and on the west a doorway, with a flat lintel and three blocks of a semi-circular relieving arch, leading to the spiral staircase.

v. The Interior

The centrepiece of the building is the central space, a square of 10.3m, from which the four arms of the cross extend (figs 37–40; pls 17–19). This is the most elaborately treated part of the building; there are four symmetrical facades, which stood at the beginning of this century to a height of 10.4m, each with a central arch flanked by tiers of decoration.

Of these facades the bottom 1.6m is a plain dado of large ashlars in two courses. There are few holes in the stone-work, so that it is unlikely that a marble or stucco revetment was attached. The second element is a projecting moulding, and above this is a register of blind niches that ran around the whole interior except for the south door.

This register (Register 1: fig.45) was originally composed of 106 niches 1.64m high, and 0.65m wide. These niches have a flat back (Block B), flanked on each side by a small engaged column, which has a rectangular block for base and capital (Block C). At the top of the niche is a horse-shoe arch, with two lines of dog-tooth moulding on the archivolt (Block A). The carving of these arches is rather uneven, and some are almost semi-circles. Register 1 is topped off with a second moulding, a horizontal line of the dog-tooth pattern.

Above this is a second register of niches (Register 2: fig.50), 4.05m high and 1.65m wide, approximately two and a half times the size of Register 1. There are eight of these niches, one on each side of each arm, and whereas Register 1 was prefabricated from separate blocks, Register 2 is a superficial carving on the masonry, and must have been carried out after the erection of the building, for the niches are cut into the voussoirs of the structural arches. In this register two pairs of engaged columns flank the niche back, which is only slightly recessed. But the same double line of dog-tooth moulding is found on the niche arch.

The type of niches found in Register 1 was then repeated at the top in Register 3, which totalled 24 niches (pls 16, 20a). The arch block (Block A) of the Register 3 niches is lower, and the arch fills the whole block (fig.46; pl.28). The spandrel panels (Aa) of the Register 1 niches are thus here reduced to small corner spaces. The facade is then finished off with a cornice that included dentils and a bead-and-reel moulding (pl.29). The whole of this third register, and the cornice, excepting one block of engaged columns in the northeast corner, are not now *in situ*.

The panels of the three registers and the cornice are carved with the decorations discussed in the second part of this chapter.

All four arms of the cross have the same groundplan: a rectangle 6.2 × 5.4m narrowed by a buttress at the open mouth measuring 0.20–0.25m × 1.9m. The north and south arms are roofed with tunnel vaults with an interior height of 9.15m.

The vaults are constructed of the same kind of masonry as used for the walls, and are slightly pointed; testing with a pair of compasses on a photograph indicates that the vaults are struck from two centres onetenth of the span apart (pls 18–9). Another estimate, by Warren, indicates that the degree of separation is one sixth: there may well be some variation.[50] The use of a two-centre pointed arch is clearly an intentional architectural style here.

Below the vaults there is a double string-line. These two tunnel-vaulted arms contain the main entrances; in the north arm the string-line is raised in a square pattern over the doorway (pl.19a). The masonry of the south doorway has no decoration (pls 16, 19b). The treatment of the arms is the same as for the central space up to the top of Register 1, that is, a plain dado, a projecting moulding, a register of niches, and a dog-tooth moulding.

The east and west arms, by contrast to those north and south, have ashlar semi-domes, with a similar degree of pointing. These are built up of horizontal courses; a semi-dome of horizontal coursing was standard for the apses of Byzantine churches in the area.

Elsewhere, radial coursing is also found in semi-domes; this is a more elegant but more complex way of building a semi-dome. Semi-circular apses with both kinds of coursing are found in the Bath Hall at Khirbat al-Mafjar.[51] At 'Ammān, however, the semi-dome is applied to a square plan, and the transition is managed by a pair of 'squinches' (pl.20b).

These 'squinches' are a distinctive feature of the building. The elliptical outline of a Sasanian squinch is cut in relief on the courses of masonry, but the 'squinch' is not structurally separate. According to Creswell, 'it is more accurate to describe it as a counterfeit squinch. It must have been executed by a Syrian mason to whom the form of a squinch had been described, but not the construction thereof'.[52] In other words, what is described as a 'squinch' might be better classified as part of the decoration. The actual structure of transition has been created by increasingly rounding five courses of masonry until the circular plan is achieved. There is apparently no particular arrangement of blocks common to all four 'squinches' that would indicate that the architect had a specific plan for coping with the problem of the loads of transition. As they stand the 'squinches' operate as a distortion of the domical curve, an arrangement which works only if the building is solid enough, as this one is.[53] Although the 'squinches' have suffered from some cracking down the centre, this rather awkward solution has survived in all four places.

The original flooring of the building remains a problem. The present surface is at about the level of the original floor, for a curve of plaster in the north arm meets it, and there is no further floor underneath. Naturally one would have expected flooring of mosaic or stone paving, but no trace of flooring has survived.[54] However there are traces in the north arm of a rubble foundation for a floor, and one must simply conclude that we do not know what the original flooring was.

vi. Later History

Occupation of the building continued after the Umayyad period. Nevertheless, the Hall as we see it is substantially the original structure, and there is no sign of radical alteration. One may note the following changes:

1. A careful blocking of the North Door with reused ashlar masonry.[55]
2. A secondary doorway cut from the central space through to the northeast room.[56]
3. The blocking of the entrance to the spiral staircase with a mortared wall.[57]
4. A series of beam holes cut into the spandrel panels of the second register of niches of the facades, just below the third register (fig.53; pls 20a, 27). There are four on the south facade, two on the west, four on the north, and two again on the east. The holes, cut horizontally, were presumably intended to receive four beams running from north to south across the space, and two from east to west. These beams may have supported a wooden roof, or an awning; or they might have been used for scaffolding, but there are no further holes lower in the facades, and this possibility is less likely. They must be secondary, for they are cut into the decoration of Register 2, which was carved after the erection of the building. In any case, if they had been original, the beams would have obscured the decoration.

With the exception of (4) all these changes can be shown to predate the *c.*1.5m fill of debris that the Italian excavators found, although they are not necessarily contemporary with one another. The blocking of the spiral stair is probably an early alteration because it used walling with the same lime mortar as the construction of the hall; and the same may be said of the cutting of the doorway to the northeast room, because it is associated with the original floor level. The sum of these alterations, however, marks a change from a hall that is part of a larger complex to a building that is an independent structure with a single entrance to the south – and thus is probably a private dwelling.

Subsequent to the appearance of collapse debris a wall and door of random rubble masonry were built closing off the north arm (pl.17b); in 1876 Merrill found a family from Salṭ living in the building.[58]

vii. Measurements and Setting Out

The measurement unit: A known local and contemporary measurement unit was the cubit of 44.75cm, measured from the water-gauge at al-Muwaqqar.[59] It has also been concluded that this unit was used at Khirbat al-Mafjar,[60] and al-Qasṭal.[61] A cubit of 44.75cm is apparently derived from the lesser cubit of the ancient Egyptian standard.[62] Egyptian influence in Palestine and Jordan was common in ancient times, and it is known that Egyptian craftsmen worked on Umayyad construction projects. Assuming the usual proportion of 2:3 between the foot and the cubit, a similar standard was found by Abel in a depiction of a foot measuring 30.89cm in a Byzantine inscription from Jerusalem.[63]

It is unlikely that the Muwaqqar cubit was used here. Some indication of the standards employed in 'Ammān during the Roman period can be derived from noting that the facade masonry of the Roman 2nd-century fortification wall is built of regular blocks, 0.34 × 0.34 × 0.7m. This suggests the standard foot employed in the Near East of 34.8cm; this foot is usually related, in a proportion of 2:3, to a cubit of about 51.5–52.5cm.[64] Although there is considerable variability in the coursing of the Reception Hall, much of the upper masonry is of 35cm courses. While on the exterior some of the masonry may be reused Roman blocks, 35cm coursing is also usual on the carved interior facades, which is almost certainly masonry newly cut for the building. For this reason, it seems likely that the standards of the foot of 34.8cm and the cubit of about 51.5–52.5cm were used, and this conclusion seems to be supported by the setting out. The unit of the foot is not known in Islamic textual sources, but there is no reason why it should not be found in the earliest Islamic buildings. The measurements are in fact easier to resolve in feet than in cubits.[65]

The setting out: The setting out appears to have been based on the overall rectangle of 24.4 × 26.1m, for this is drawn out again in Court 1. If the foot of 34.8cm were used, these measurements would be approximately equal to 70 × 75 feet, and are not easily resolvable in cubits (see figs 42–3 for a graphical presentation). The exterior walls are 1.85m wide, equal to 5 feet, but this is not a round figure in cubits. The inside face of the exterior wall is a rectangle of 20.7 × 22.45m, within 1% of 60 × 65 feet. This inside rectangle could be considered a square of 60 feet, with an extension to the south of 5 feet. A square of 10.3m or 30 feet (20 cubits), for the central space, was drawn in the centre of this presumed square, and its sides projected to the exterior. This in theory left corner spaces 5.2m or 15 feet (10 cubits) square, and side spaces of 10.3 × 5.2m or 30 × 15 feet (20 × 10 cubits). The northeast room and the spiral staircase fit these dimensions to within 5%, and the two southern side-rooms benefit from the extension from square to rectangle, to approximate to 15 × 20 feet to within 5%. In practice, the dimensions are 2–5% less than expected to facilitate a bond between the four central space facades. The vaults and semi-domes of the arms, and their supporting walls, are accommodated in the spaces of 30 × 15 feet to within 2%.

viii. Reconstruction of the Original Form

The Reception Hall is an exceptionally well-preserved building, and there is a substantial amount of evidence for reconstructing the original pattern of the building, although it is an unusual one. The most recent reconstruction, by Almagro, was based on the idea that the cruciform interior was related to Romano-Byzantine cruciform plans, and the Byzantine tradition in Umayyad architecture. Naturally, in as far as is possible, the reconstruction ought to be based on the evidence of the site, but there are points where parallels must be used, and the choice of appropriate parallels should be based on the parallels of existing features at the site.

From the exterior the building would have looked much like a square block (fig.41). The roof itself is flat and the exterior surfaces of the vaults are covered. The facades were relieved principally by rectangular buttresses on the west, south and east faces, but not on the north, which was plain. On the east side the facade masonry survives to what is very probably the last course before the cornice, and so it is certain that the buttresses continued to the full height of the facade.[66]

The south facade was without doubt the most elaborate, but the evidence is the least conclusive. Almagro proposed two solutions: that the buttresses were joined together by a blind arch, reflecting the vaults of the rooms inside; or that the buttresses were full height.[67] The solution of a blind arch was preferred by Almagro, but there is no evidence of a springer, nor does the alignment of the buttresses match the vaults of the interior.[68]

There are three fragments from niches composed of one block (fig.55), that cannot belong to the interior registers: these apparently belong to the exterior. These niches vary in width between 0.44 and 0.62m, averaging 0.52m. Although no full height survives, the proportion of height to width found in all three registers of the interior (1:2.15) would give a height of about 1.12m.

Almagro proposed that a pair of these niches flanked the south door, but there are more fragments than would be appropriate for this solution. In the Sasanian and post-Sasanian architectural tradition, to which the style of these niches belongs, a register of niches would have been located at the top of the wall. At Qaṣr al-Kharāna five niches are placed over the main entrance.[69] At al-Ukhayḍir there is a register of niches at the top of the main exterior wall. Only one section survives to the left of the north gate at Ukhayḍir, and it is not certain that the niches continued round the whole wall; they may have been limited to the north facade. Here at ʿAmmān a row of ten of these niches fits well into the space between the buttresses of the facade, and it would seem that the model of Ukhayḍir has been followed.[70]

In addition there are six fragments of brackets with a triple volute design (fig.54; pl.29f), and one fragment has been illustrated with an outside corner.[71] The volutes themselves have a palm-trunk pattern, paralleled in Sasanian and Umayyad stuccowork. The brackets have widths varying between 0.33m and 0.54m, but all appear to project 0.40m. This projection is greater than the projection of the buttresses. Almagro offered two solutions: that there was an overhang running the full length of the south facade, and a small return along the east and west facades; or that the projection was limited to the area of the south door and its adjoining buttresses.[72]

It is naturally difficult to find parallels for the upper parts of the building, and to find explanations for the use of these brackets. One possibility is a *machicoulis* corbelled out over the entrance, as is found in the Umayyad period at Qaṣr al-Ḥayr al-Sharqī,[73] but that solution is excluded by the existence of too many fragments, and an outside corner. The use of corbels to support stone roofing slabs is also common in the basalt architecture of the Ḥawrān, but there is no evidence here that stone slab roofing is part of the building's design. Very probably the recess of the south door was arched over, although it is not certain whether the facade of this arch was flush with the buttresses, or recessed. It seems most likely that Almagro's second suggestion is correct, and a projection was intended to emphasize the main door.

The idea of an emphasis to the main south door is also supported by recalling that there is evidence from the inside that the design of the door was changed in the course of the construction; the obvious motive would be an enhancement, in the course of construction and at the instruction of the patron, of the visual impression of the south door. There are also two curved architectural fragments (F/2–3), which might have belonged to a great roundel over the south door, similar to the round window from Khirbat al-Mafjar.[74] However there is insufficient information to judge how it might have looked.

There are also cornice blocks, with dentils, a bead-and-reel moulding, and a sloping panel carved with two registers of unlinked half-palmettes, which appear to belong to the exterior (C/4–11: fig.54, pl.29c). The reason for the assignation to the exterior is that one block (C/5: pl.29d) is a *vertical* corner, and this would be impossible in the interior. However, its placing on the exterior is also a problem: it must belong to a raised facade surrounding an arch, similar to a later Islamic *īwān* facade. Such a use seems contradictory to the idea of a projecting element supported by brackets over the south door. This contradiction can only be resolved by proposing a chronological succession in the south door – that one design was replaced by another – a point already suggested by the change in the masonry inside the door. Alternatively, the raised facade may have belonged to the north door.[75]

Only part of one stepped merlon survives (fig.56). The steps are steeply angled, and it is carved with a half-palmette scroll on both sides.[76] In spite of the solitary survival, it seems most likely that both the interior and exterior facades were finished off with a line of merlons. The low level of survival might be explained by noting that such merlons are the first elements to disappear.[77]

The effects of the building are concentrated on the interior, and this is highly ornamented (figs 38–40). In the centre is a space 10.3m square. The four facades are symmetrical, with tiers of niches flanking an arched opening. The panels of the facades are covered with relief carving from the top of the plain dado to the cornice. Whether this decoration was painted or not is impossible to say; the excavator, Bartoccini, did find traces of red paint.[78] But such painting might equally well have been a product of later occupation.

The arms of the cross were simpler than the interior facades. Their decoration consists of a single register of niches and two mouldings, contrasted with the plain stonework of the semi-dome or tunnel vault. But there is also additional architectural detail: the tall arched doorways, the string-line raised in a square pattern over them, and the 'squinches'.

However, there is a question crucial to the reconstruction of this central part of the building: was this space, which today is open, ever roofed? Although many have thought the centre of the building was intended to be open,[79] some more recent opinion has considered that the building would make more sense if the centre had in fact been roofed. Gaube thought there might have been a wooden dome.[80] Almagro considers the possibility that the building was open, or had a wooden dome, but prefers the idea that the building had a stone dome on squinches, lit by three windows on each side.[81]

The available evidence is summed up in a photograph taken by Brünnow and von Domaszewski in 1898, when the cornice was still largely in position (pl.16; cf. pls 17b, 20a). There is no visible evidence of a roofing system for the central space.

The possibility of a wooden roof in the original construction, a roof which might have been either domical or pyramidal in shape, cannot be evaluated, or excluded, as there is no evidence either for or against the suggestion. However, there was probably a later wooden roof (see above).

In the case of a stone dome, there are substantial objections. There is clear evidence that there was no transition to a dome, by means of a pendentive, squinch or other device, up to the height of the cornice, that is, the top of the building as it survived into modern times. No suitable fragments of a dome or windows have been found; and a dome whose transition only began above the surviving cornice level would have been disproportionately high – in Almagro's reconstruction it is 21m above floor level, twice the height of the building as it now stands (10.4m).[82]

The third possibility, that the centre was an open court, is consistent with the negative evidence. But there is also positive evidence that points in the same direction.

The decoration is carved entirely in stone; if the central area were an interior, one would have expected some carved stone mouldings, but much of the decoration would have been in a more delicate medium: painted plaster or stucco. Carved stone decoration is intended to resist the effects of the weather, and the choice of material would suggest that the building was intended to be open.

The beam holes visible in the facade are discussed above as a secondary feature. If the holes were intended for scaffolding (although this is unlikely as no further holes appear lower down on the facade), the building could have been originally either open or roofed. If, as is more likely, these beams were intended for a wooden roof, or to support an awning, then obviously no roof existed at the time that this later roof was erected.

Thirdly, the parallels of the arms and their court facades are those of *īwāns* and their external facades. The east and west arms with their semi-domes are closest in appearance to the side *īwān*s of the Bāb al-'Āmma at Sāmarrā', which also have a semi-dome on squinches above a shallow rectangular space, and rectangular buttresses at the mouth of the *īwāns*.[83] This is a closer parallel than the semi-domed apses of the Byzantine churches of Jordan, or the *exedrae* of the Bath Hall at Khirbat al-Mafjar.[84]

The rectangular buttresses also appear at the Tāq-i Kisrā (fig.72). The north and south arms have the typical tunnel vault of the early *īwān*, and closely resemble the indubitable *īwān* of the North Building in this palace. The use of *īwāns*, vaulted or semi-domed open-fronted halls, was in fact spread throughout the palace, as will be seen below.

Tiers of niches framing an arch are also typical of an external, not an internal facade, in the Partho-Sasanian and Early Islamic architectural traditions.[85] Individually the facades were correctly described by Hayter Lewis as resembling those of the Tāq-i Kisrā at Ctesiphon, but the effect is miniaturized, with only three tiers of niches in place of six (fig.72).[86]

These facades at 'Ammān fit well into the known sequence of early external *īwān* facades. The facade of the Tāq-i Kisrā can be described as a descendent of the facade of the Parthian palace of Assur, as reconstructed in the Staatliche Museen in Berlin,[87] and 'Ammān follows in that series. In another example we have of this kind of tiered niching framing an arch, from a 10th–11th century house in Sistan, it is again an external facade.[88]

The centre of the building, then, was likely to have been an open court. Such a conclusion is open to the objection that the open centre would make the hall unusable in the cold Jordanian winter. This objection is a utilitarian one, based upon the commonsense demands of practical architecture. It is argued elsewhere in this study that artistic imagery played an important role in the design of the palace. The explanation would seem to be that the demands of artistic imagery in architecture can result in a building that is difficult to use, a point which many people today have experience of. The unsuitability of the building in the winter would be a good reason for the wooden roof that seems to have been added later.

ix. Stylistic Analysis of the Architecture

The technique of construction is purely local. The use of ashlar masonry, particularly in the vaults and semi-domes, and lime mortar, are what one would expect of an Ammonite architect and masons. Yet the resulting building is very hard to parallel in Levantine architecture. The paradox of the building is one of local construction, but alien appearance.

The setting out of the plan is geometrically similar to the cross-in-square basilica, a type with which the architect at 'Ammān was presumably familiar. An example relatively close in space and time is the audience hall of al-Mundhir ibn Jabala at Ruṣāfa, dated to the late 6th century AD.[89] This relationship apparently formed the basis of Creswell's theory about this 'Ammān building, which 'bears such a close resemblance' to Ruṣāfa, and 'lacks merely an apse'.[90] But Creswell was wrong in failing to notice that the two southern side-rooms here are incorporated into the cross, instead of being added to it, as they would be in a basilica.

Moreover, the similarity in the setting-out of the plan, although it plays a part, is deceptive; for the effects of the resulting buildings at Ruṣāfa and 'Ammān are quite different, thanks to the arrangement of the cross. At 'Ammān each of the arms is an independent entity, for they do not connect with one another except through the central court, and only the southern arm connects with side-rooms. Moreover, at 'Ammān it is the wall-faces that lie on the drawn-out lines of the cross, rather than the centre points of the piers, as at Ruṣāfa. Ultimately one cannot deny that there is some influence of the cross-in-square basilica on the ground-plan, but it may not be a direct effect.

The idea that this building has a four-*īwān* plan has also been suggested by a number of scholars, particularly those familiar with Iranian architecture: van Berchem, Creswell, Herzfeld, Fehervari, and Warren.[91] It is true that four identical facades frame four equally sized spaces, such that the quadruple effect of the interior must have come over quite strongly to an onlooker.

But it would be equally wrong to consider the building as simply a four-*īwān* plan. Buildings have been found with a four-*īwān* layout predating or contemporary with 'Ammān (figs 58–9), at Assur,[92] Nippur,[93] the site of al-Ma'āriḍ IV at Ctesiphon,[94] Kūfa,[95] Tulūl al-Shu'ayba,[96] and Bishapur (the audience hall).[97] All of these are in Iraq, except Bishapur, which is in Iran. Keall argues that Iraq was the original home of the four-*īwān* layout in the Parthian period.[98] All but Bishapur consist of a court with four *īwāns* integrated into a larger complex, and the smallest of them is considerably larger in ground area than 'Ammān (fig.59). In any case the four-*īwān* plan in this period was little different from one-, two-, and three-*īwān* arrangements, though it could well have had a greater reputation because of its symmetry.

'Ammān, by contrast, is constricted within its external rectangle. One might argue then that 'Ammān is a version of the audience hall at Bishapur, which is contained within an external square (fig.58). There are two difficulties with this proposition. Firstly, the excavator, Ghirshman, reconstructs the central space at Bishapur with a dome, thus proposing that it is a large *chahār tāq*, and not a four-*īwān* plan. (This reconstruction is disputed by Godard on the grounds that the central space, 23m square, is too large for a dome.[99] In any case the only reliable information provided by Bishapur is its ground plan, as the walls are only preserved to a height of about two metres.) Secondly, Bishapur is too far distant in time from 'Ammān (3rd century AD), and one would have to hypothesize a continuing tradition of later but similar buildings, about which nothing is known, to provide a link. However, it is possible that the audience hall at Bishapur was still standing in the Umayyad period: the adjacent triple *īwān* was redecorated with stuccoes late in the Sasanian period.[100] In either case the evidence as it stands is inadequate to make an argument of influence convincing.

One can suggest that we have the same situation here as with the counterfeit 'squinches', that is, that the building is a representation of a four-*īwān* plan by an architect who did not know how they were normally set out. At this point the relationship to the cross-in-square basilica needs to be reintroduced; if an architect versed in the Levantine tradition, and thus familiar with the cross-in-square basilica, had been asked by his patron to build a four-*īwān* plan, the resulting building might well have looked like the Reception Hall at 'Ammān.

b. The Buildings of the First Enclosure

The first enclosure, in as far as it has been excavated, seems to have been filled with a single complex, whose buildings on the east side all bond, and by design are connected with the largely unexcavated buildings on the west side.

There is a tripartite division of the enclosure on the north-south axis, with divisions on the east side of 26, 24 and 25m. This appears to be reflected on the west side.

i. Court 1 (pls 15b, 30)

Court 1 is a near square courtyard (26.1 × 24.2m) located on the north side of the Reception Hall. The surfacing is partly the paving blocks of the *temenos*, and partly an earth surface, which was probably stiffened with *huwwar* (chalk gravel). There is no evidence to indicate that there was ever a colonnade; rather it seems to have been a small plain blank-walled courtyard.

On the north side a gateway 2.2m wide, closable by a gate, led through into the columned street.

At a subsequent date to the construction, a rectagular room was added in the northeast corner, with an L-shaped seat adjacent to it. There are also traces to indicate that the west half of the court was also built over at a later date.

Court 1 was obviously laid out at the same time as the Reception Hall, whose external dimensions it exactly reflects.

ii. The Columned Street (fig.60; pls 30a, 32a)

A columned street 50.6m long connects Court 1 with the gate in the north wall of the first enclosure, and leads to the second enclosure. This street is 9.8m wide, with a distance of 4.75m between kerbs. The kerbs have a double step and vary between 0.22 and 0.45m wide. There were thirteen columns on each side, of which two on the east side are now missing (pl.32a). There is evidence of restoration by the Italian Mission. The columns are 0.4m in diameter, with plain block bases 0.63m square. Although the columns are consistent in size, the stone dressing technique is different from that of the kerbs: the kerbs were shaped with a plain tool, but the columns were dressed with a toothed adze or chisel. For this reason it may be thought that they are reused from elsewhere.

The columns carried an arcade, the sockets for which can be seen in the north wall of the enclosure. The evidence of these sockets indicates that the columns were 3.4m high, including base and capital; the underside of the arches would have been 1.7m higher, or 4.95m from the street level. The arcade was probably covered by a wooden roof: there is just enough evidence from the highest surviving section of side wall, outside Room 40, to indicate that there was no barrel vault.

At the north end the street rose through five steps to go through the gateway, and of these only three now survive.[101] On each side of the gate two of the podiums were cut down and transformed into seats with arm rests of the typical Early Islamic quarter-circle form. The paving of the street is the original Roman paving, with a drain at its north end emptying into a cistern opposite the doorway to Building 4.

iii. The East Side (pls 30b, 31a)

CONSTRUCTION. Construction is of the second type commonly found in the work of this period at the Qal'a, that is, mortared rubble walling. This type of walling in places has, and in others does not have, a rubble foundation. For the majority of the walling in this enclosure, founded as it was on Roman paving and the like, foundations were not built. But in either case a bed of *terra rossa* was laid for levelling.

The walling itself varies between 0.96 and 1.06m wide, and is of coursed, often roughly squared rubble, limestone and flint, bonded with the same lime mortar that was used in the Reception Hall. Roman architectural fragments are often used in the first course: column bases have been inserted in the west wall of the columned street. The surface of the wall is smoothed by an unusually large number of small fragments, which have been used both to wedge the larger blocks and fill in spaces.

The surfaces were then plastered with the same mortar, and stippled with wedge-shaped keying impressions, and/or studded with pieces of soft chalk or lime. In no place was a second layer of fine plaster added, and the keying impressions seem to have been used merely to variegate the surface. Plastering is found principally on areas of rubble construction in the palace; where ashlar masonry is used, the masonry is intended to be seen.

As far as can be judged the floors were of earth; there is no evidence of anything else, and this impression is confirmed by the excavation of similar buildings in Area C and the Museum site.

The walls survive to a height that varies between one course and about five metres. One can only deduce the type of roofing by implication; one contemporary room in Area B has the springing of a tunnel vault (Room D, Building D), and the rooms in these buildings of Area B have the rectangular or square shape required for such a vault (fig.145), without concern for an even width of wall. An irregularly-shaped room is not easy to tolerate where a simple tunnel vault is being used. The west wall of Building 4 in the palace displays a similar feature: the inside face is stepped in plan from room to room, to provide a perfectly rectangular room shape. Moreover an additional buttress was added to the north wall of Tower A to provide a springing for such a vault.

BUILDING 6 (fig.61). This building is the best preserved, although the west side was demolished in 1976: the area of the gate has had to be reconstructed from photographs, with a consequent loss of accuracy in measurement.[102] The building measures 26 × 29.6m

There is a single entrance from Court 1 to the west, and a central court with rooms on three sides, except for the intrusion of Tower A in the southeast corner; this tower bonds with the building.

There are three rooms in the west range, four on the south and four on the east. The ranges are 5.34–6.0m deep (measured internally), and the rooms vary between 3.9 and 4.5m wide, with the exception of 610, 2.4m wide, which is apparently a latrine. However, two rooms, 65 and 67, are wider, 5.4 and 5.9m respectively. Both these are open-fronted, and may therefore be described as *īwāns*.

In Room 60 there is an arched alcove, with a second smaller alcove set at right angles to it; the shape of the arches is rough, but approximately semi-elliptical. Across the front of the smaller alcove is a line of stones making a basin, but no sign of drainage can be seen. Although the author earlier concluded that this Room 60 was the latrine,[103] and not 610, the Spanish mission, by clearing the room, has shown that it was most probably a staircase – a spiral without a central pier, but with the stairs supported on arches.[104] Nevertheless, it remains an open question whether there was a second storey: the stair might have simply given access to the roof space.

There is one cistern, in Room 65, fed by a drain running down from the roof: the horizontal part of the drain survives. The lining is of two layers, a base of grey lime mortar, and a facing of impervious white cement with red chips. A second drain can be seen on the facade between Rooms 68 and 69.

The arcade is apparently a later addition (Period 4), for the style of construction is completely different. The arcade consists of round piers 0.8m in diameter with a square base, constructed of small rubble stones and gypsum, as opposed to lime mortar (pl.32b). Two piers of the arcade now survive, but nine were originally excavated. Two piers were added in the mouth of *īwān* 67, and possibly in that of *īwān* 65; this feature is also found in *īwān* 55. One can suggest two possible explanations of these rather curious additional piers:

1. The extra-wide vaults of the *īwāns* had been weakened in some way, for example by the earthquake of 130/747, and needed strengthening.
2. That when the arcade was built, it was roofed with a barrel vault, and this would need to be carried past the high open front of the *īwān* (fig.62).

At a later date (Period 5), subdivisions of rough rubble walling were put into Rooms 64 to 68. It is particularly to be noted that the open fronts of *īwāns* 65 and 67 were closed off.

BUILDING 5 (fig.63). Measuring 25 × 33.4m, this building reproduces an almost identical plan to Building 6, with the exception that only two ranges of rooms now survive in place of three, but the existence of a third is demonstrated by the arcade of rubble piers. The west range was never found by the Italians, and must have been demolished in the course of the building's lifetime.[105]

The east range is 5.3m deep, and the south 6.25m deep; the room widths vary between 3.8 and 4.8m, and there is an *īwān* 5.8m wide at Room 55, with a probable second *īwān* at Room 51. The arcade, of which nine piers survive, and the two piers in *īwān* 55, are identical to those of Building 6. A narrow corridor on the east side gives access to the Roman rooms incorporated into the complex.

BUILDING 4 (fig.35). As excavated in 1927 this building seems to have been well-preserved,[106] but the remains were demolished in the course of the Italian excavations, and it is very difficult to reconstruct the plan. However, it is clear that the general arrangements were the same. The building measured 25 × 35m. The west wall on the street has bonds for three walls, an entrance and a staircase of the same kind as 60 at Room 40. Two rubble pier bases indicate an arcade, and there are traces of a corridor along the east side for access to the east rooms.

iv. The West Side

In the unexcavated area to the west of Court 1 and the columned street, fragmentary evidence is to be seen of the nature of the plan. To the west of Court 1, two rooms of a building (Building 7) are partly exposed in various cuts (Rooms 70 and 72). It is evident from the collapse mounds, and the air photograph from the First World War (pl.2a), that this was also a courtyard building similar to those on the east side. Spanish excavations have recently been conducted in this building (1989), and a correct plan may be expected in the future.

The west facade of the columned street contains three entrances, respectively from south to north, 2.0m, 1.6m and 1.8m wide. Seven walls can be detected bonding with this facade. From the surface it can be seen that the southern entrance is for a corridor that leads over to the far western area of the enclosure.

It seems evident from the air photography that the evidence represents two further residential buildings in this area (Buildings 8 and 9). Thus the west side of the street and Court 1 would be roughly symmetrical with the east side.

There is, then, space for further buildings before the west wall. It is apparent from Plate 2, that the long east-west walls dividing buildings 7, 8, and 9 continued as far as the western platform wall. The remaining space was thus divided into three areas. It is uncertain whether these spaces contained formal courtyard buildings, or were open yards. There are some wall sections belonging to rooms exposed on the north side of Tower C.

c. The Buildings of the Second Enclosure

In the second enclosure there is a further group of buildings erected over the remains of the Roman period. Although these buildings have no direct stratigraphic connection with the remainder of the palace, the constructional technique, dimensions and architectural decoration are closely similar to the foregoing. The visible remains constitute the parts of more than one building, and probably represent three – Buildings 2, 3 and the North Building.

The division is marked on the one hand by a corridor 1.5m wide between Buildings 2 and 3, and on the other by a series of three straight joints between Building 2 and the North Building, through which the plastering of Building 2 continues. Apparently the North Building was added later.

On the west side there seems to have been one further courtyard building, lined with rooms along the west and north walls.

i. Buildings 2 and 3 (fig.35)

The remains of Buildings 2 and 3 consist of a row of rooms 5.7m deep and varying between 3.3 and 3.8m wide, facing east, with a dividing corridor that has been turned into an L-shaped passage by the later addition of the North Building. The surviving range of rooms must have faced onto a pair of courtyards with additional ranges of rooms on the north, south and east sides, but the remains have been eroded away by collapse down the hill, and other factors.

Construction in these buildings differs only slightly from those in the first enclosure; these have a single-course foundation of ashlars. It was noted earlier that what has been taken to be a Roman stylobate on the south side is most probably an example of this foundation.

When the area was first excavated, the west wall of Building 3 extended as far as the gate leading to the columned street, and slightly narrowed the passage.[107] The main entrance of this building was an axial one on the west side (Room 32). The entrance to Building 2 must have lain somewhere along the corridor. North of this passage are the only two rooms of the building to survive, but traces of the foundation work continue as the north wall of the platform, thus excluding the possibility of a further passage.

ii. The North Building (figs 64–8; pls 33–6)
The building as it stands today survives with walls that vary in height between 1.4 and 7.6m, but all forms of roofing have fallen. When the author's survey was conducted, only the east side-rooms, and the court in front, had been excavated by the Italians.[108] Subsequently, in 1979, the main rooms were excavated by the Spanish Mission.[109]

CONSTRUCTION. The style of this building is similar to those already discussed: mortared rubble walling with lime plaster still adhering in places. In the one place where the foundation is visible, ashlar blocks are used to support the facade wall. The facade wall and the two main chambers have a facing of ashlar blocks; these were presumably not plastered.

DESCRIPTION. The building faces onto a small court, 24 × 10m (Court 2). The west side of this court is lined with rooms facing onto it. A bond exists at the north-west corner of the court, and, if this range is homogeneous, then it was also part of the main building. In the northeast corner a reused column base *in situ* lines up with an engaged pier on the facade of the building. The most likely run of this colonnade would be along the east side of the court. The excavations of the Spanish mission demonstrated that there was a colonnade on the west side also.[110]

The main chambers consist of a vaulted hall with a cruciform room behind. The front hall measures 9.6 × 6.8m, and the west wall survives to the springing of a barrel vault. The vault is constructed of ashlars, like those of the Reception Hall. The vault is stilted by three courses above a double string-line. If the vault were round the inside height would be 9.8m, if it were a two-centre pointed vault, like those of the Reception Hall, then the height would have been 10m. The hall is open-fronted, but the open end is strengthened with a shallow rectangular buttress (1.25 × 0.20m). Thus this is also an *īwān*.

The Spanish excavations brought to light a rough cobbled floor, almost certainly the sub-stratum of a finer surfacing, probably of mosaic. In addition they exposed the base of double pilasters, in the technique of rubble and gypsum mortar similar to the secondary piers of Buildings 4–6 (pl.36d). These were placed against the rectangular buttresses at the entrance to the *īwān*, and are clearly secondary, although Almagro concludes that they are original.[111]

The *īwān* was divided from the cruciform chamber by a wall with a single doorway. The cruciform chamber is not aligned straight onto the *īwān*; there is a distortion of approximately two degrees. The interior is a square of 7.3m with four recesses of 4.75 × 1.6m, presumably arched in their original form. Each of these recesses contains a doorway. The west wall of this chamber and that of the *īwān* have complete arched doorways 4.6m high. The corner buttresses of the chamber are enormously thick, with the exception of the one in the southwest corner, which contains a vaulted latrine. The shape of the room is a typical one for a dome chamber, but there is no evidence surviving of the transition to a dome. Almagro suggests that the dome was supported on squinches similar to those of the Reception Hall.[112] While in principle such an arrangement of squinches is quite within the bounds of possibility, the squinches of the Reception Hall are decorative rather than functional, and it is equally possible that when the builders of the North Building came to construct the dome, they may have used the local traditions of the pendentive, for ease of construction.

In the course of the Spanish excavations, remnants of a mosaic were found on the west side of the room (for a depiction, see Olávarri 1985, figs 28–9). The mosaic has a cable border and interlace patterns paralleled at al-Qasṭal.[113] In addition there was a square structure in the centre of the room that is not easy to explain, but was possibly a pool.

On each side of the *īwān*, there are side-rooms which connect with the hall and the court in front (N1: 4.8 × 9.8m; N8: 6.4 × 9.4m). On the east side, at least, where there has been excavation, two more rooms flank the dome chamber (N2: 4.9 × 6.6m; N3: 3.4 × 6.6m). On the west side of this chamber the arrangement is not at all clear. On the north side the remains are eroded by the collapse of the upper parts of the platform wall. But it is possible to conclude that the building extended as far as the platform wall, for the west wall of Room N4 can be traced that far. In fact four wall-lines for N4 can be traced (4.5 × 6.0m). Therefore there must have been two rooms on this side. If the west side were similar then the space behind the dome chamber (N5: 10.0 × 12.3m) would form a small court.

RECONSTRUCTION OF THE FACADE AND DECORATION. No architectural decoration remains *in situ*, but a number of pieces survive in the rubble (for catalogue, see Appendix A; pls 35–6). The fragments divide into two groups, one from inside the *īwān*, and the second from Court 2. It is probable therefore that decoration was in two places: on the back wall of the *īwān*, and on the facade.

From inside – or probably inside – the *īwān*, five fragments have been recovered. There are two niche-head blocks: NB/3, of which only the left half survives, has a single line of denticulated moulding around the arch, and in the spandrel panels a pair of round-lobed rosettes flanking a miniature niche (pl.35c). On the underside of the arch there is an apparently decorative slot. NB/4 is larger, but again there is a single line of denticulation and two rosettes in the spandrel panels (pl.35d). In addition there is a block with a right-angle corner in a half-round moulding (NB/5: pl.35e), a block with the half-round moulding and an engaged colonnette (NB/2: pl.35b), and a niche back panel with a slot (NB/1: pl.35a). Almagro, surely correctly, reconstructs these blocks to suggest three niches on the rear wall of the *īwān* over the door.[114] The half-round moulding ran in a raised pattern over the niches. Almagro's drawing indicates that the back panel of the larger central niche was carved with half-palmettes.[115] The niche back panel with a slot (NB/1) fits with the block with engaged colonnette (NB/2), and evidently belongs to one of the side niches. Conder, on his visits to the site in 1881–2, also recorded a niche base with a slot (fig.66). Evidently the side niches resembled the niches in Room 32 at Ukhayḍir, which have a vertical arrow-slit decoration, a motif of considerable antiquity in Iranian decoration.[116]

The reconstruction of the exterior facade has less certainty. The first issue is whether there was a raised facade over the *īwān* arch, on the pattern of later Islamic *īwān* facades, or whether the facade was of one height. In the author's first essay of reconstruction of the building (fig.67),[117] and in Almagro's reconstruction,[118] it was assumed that there was a raised facade over the *īwān*; these depictions followed Reuther's reconstruction of the *īwān* facade at Ukhayḍir.[119] However Reuther appears to have been wrong; while it is certainly true that the *īwān* vault at Ukhayḍir was higher than the surrounding roof level, there is clear evidence that a facade with two registers of blind niches, now found only on the north side of the Court of Honour at Ukhayḍir, certainly existed on two more sides, and presumably also on the fourth.[120] The *īwān* at Ukhayḍir was thus framed by two registers of niches, not one as presented by Reuther.[121]

The admittedly very limited evidence for *īwān* facades in the period up to Samarra' in the 3rd/9th century includes no example of a raised section of facade over the *īwān*. The earliest *īwān* facade known is that from the Parthian palace at Assur, reconstructed in the Staatliche Museen in Berlin. In addition to the 6th-century Tāq-i Kisrā at Ctesiphon, there is also a recently excavated *graffito* of an *īwān* facade from an Early 'Abbāsid house at Ctesiphon (fig.72).[122] The *graffito* is not necessarily a drawing of the Tāq-i Kisrā, but perhaps represented what an *īwān* facade normally looked like: there is a full height facade over a round-arched *īwān*, flanked by two engaged piers, and finished with a line of merlons. The Bab al-'Āmma at Sāmarrā' also has a full-height facade.[123]

If the facade here followed the normal practice of the period, then it had a single-height facade, approximately 10.3m high (fig.68), topped by a line of merlons, of which one has been found (NB/21: pl.36c).[124] The bottom half of this facade was probably left plain: it is broken by two doorways, and there is no indication of blind niches in the surviving height of the wall.

Of the architectural blocks that probably come from the facade, the commonest type (six examples) is a block with two engaged pilasters, and a slightly recessed rectangular panel with a vertical slot (NB/6–12: pl.35f; fig.66). Although Almagro reconstructed this as a panel dividing two niches, this is unlikely as the sides of the blocks are left rough.[125] Rather, these blocks more likely formed a frieze on their own; in one of the variations of circular medallion friezes at Qaṣr Kharāna, each medallion is flanked by a pair of miniature engaged pilasters, with a similar effect.[126]

There are two examples of niche heads with denticulation around the arch, and one has a vine stem with two bunches of grapes in the spandrel panel (NB/19: pl.36a). In addition there are three examples of blocks of double pairs of engaged pilasters. We can deduce therefore that there was also a frieze of niches.

The normal arrangement of such a frieze in the Sasanian architectural tradition is of a single line below the top of the facade, a formulation used both by our first reconstruction, and by Almagro. However, both the number and variety of blocks, and the height of the facade, suggest that the arrangement was more elaborate. The blocks with a pair of engaged pilasters and a slot suit a frieze at the top of the facade. The placement of the niches lacks certainty. One possible solution, presented in fig.68, is that three niches were placed over each of the side doors, an arrangement which can be paralleled at the later Main Palace at Lashkarī Bāzār.[127]

LATER HISTORY. Two further periods of work on the building may be noted:

1. There are fragments of fallen arches in Rooms N2 and N8, made from small rubble stones and gypsum mortar (pl.36f).[128] In a similar technique, the doorway between Room N2 and the L-shaped passage leading to Building 2 was rebuilt with a lower lintel (pl.36e). In addition one may quote the Spanish Archaeological Mission's find of rubble and mortar double engaged piers in the entrance of the *īwān*. These were clearly a later addition.
2. The *īwān* opening was blocked with reused ashlar masonry. The doorway of N2 mentioned above was also blocked. And there is a partition wall in N2 (Period 5). The Spanish excavations found later occupation up to the Ayyūbid or Mamlūk periods inside the *īwān* and dome chamber.[129]

The work described in (1) implies that at least in Period 4

the side-rooms were not vaulted, but arched. This extensive work on the upper parts of the building and the entrance to the *īwān* is in a technique (Period 4) that elsewhere in the palace is an early modification. The building may never have been finished in its original form, or could have collapsed, perhaps in the earthquake of 130/747–8.

DISCUSSION. In 1889 Conder described this building as 'of the same kind' as the Reception Hall.[130] The evidence available today confirms this early impression, especially in the field of architectural detail: round-arched doorways, ashlar vaulting with a double string-line, the rectangular strengthening buttress at the south of the *īwān*, and niches with plain colonnettes, are all to be found in the first building.

The plan of the building is, however, quite different. Nevertheless, it is a version of a well-known Eastern type: an *īwān* with a dome chamber, a plan widely known in the Sasanian and Early Islamic periods in Iraq and Iran. At Kish,[131] Tepe Hissar (Damghan),[132] Kūfa (fig.69),[133] and Tulūl al-Ukhayḍir (fig.70),[134] the vault is supported on piers; the 'Ammān example is more reminiscent of the Tāq-i Kisrā (fig.72), or the 'Abbāsid *īwāns* at Ukhayḍir,[135] and Bab al-'Āmma at Sāmarrā'.[136]

The eastern associations of the plan also appear in the decoration: niches with plain colonnettes and a vertical slot occur at Ukhayḍir.[137] Nevertheless, here again we see a local type of construction – ashlar masonry and an ashlar vault. The latrine type is also local, and is paralleled at Umm al-Jimāl.[138] Thus the same paradox appears in this building as in the Reception Hall: an eastern appearance, but local practice in the construction. However, here there is actually an example of decoration in the Roman-Byzantine tradition: the mosaic.

d. Sequence and Dating of the Palace

The structural evidence of the palace and post-palace periods in the double enclosure may usefully be broken down into three basic periods.

i. Original Construction of the Palace (Period 3; fig.35)

The various buildings of the complex, the Reception Hall, the structures of the first enclosure, and those of the second enclosure, must have been erected within a short space of time, and according to a single plan.

It is true that these groups do not bond with one another. The Reception Hall does not bond with the structures of the first enclosure. There is no surviving connection between the structures of the first enclosure and those of the second, while the North Building is demonstrably an addition to Buildings 2 and 3.

Nevertheless, it is most probable that they represent a single unit, for stylistically they are almost identical, and that style is quite distinctive among the many periods of building to be found at the Qal'a. It appears again in the Umayyad buildings of Areas B, C, and the Museum site. Moreover, as we noted, the Reception Hall and the buildings of the first enclosure have an inter-relationship of plan in the dimensions of Court 1. In addition, the layout has clearly been designed, and this organized design is one that can be compared with other sites.

Therefore the significance of the lack of bonding lies in either short-term delays in the execution of the project, or the use of different building crews. In the case of the buildings of the second enclosure, there is the additional possibility of a change of plan, but the organized character of the plan argues for an initial overall concept.

The Reception Hall was built first, then the buildings of the first enclosure, possibly at the same time as Buildings 2 and 3; lastly the North Building was added. The similarity of the North Building to the Reception Hall shows that it is not likely that this sequence spread over a long period of time. The less elaborate construction and decoration of the North Building might suggest that the project was running out of money, and it certainly indicates that the public audience hall was more important.

So from the point of view of dating, the whole complex may be regarded as contemporary. The author's survey recovered two sherds of Umayyad red-painted ware, closely comparable with that of the earthquake destruction deposit of Area C (figs 131–3) and the Museum site,[139] from the mortar of the west wall of Building 4, together with a number of coarse red ware sherds of indeterminate Roman, Byzantine or Umayyad date.[140] Two more red-painted sherds, covered with traces of mortar, were found loose on the roof of the Reception Hall. The excavations of Almagro and Olávarri excavated an Umayyad post-reform *fils* from construction levels on the east side of the Reception Hall.[141] In addition they report the find of Umayyad pottery in the staircase of this building. The *terminus post quem* for the date therefore must lie in the Umayyad period, and quite late in that period, as sherds of red-painted ware were found in the construction.[142]

The solution of the problem of a *terminus ante quem* for the date depends on the evidence of destruction for the buildings related stratigraphically to the palace, excavated in Area C and the Museum Site. The question of the dating of this destruction is considered elsewhere in this volume, but the evidence points to the earthquake of 130/747–8.

There is also the evidence of architectural style: the use of broad, slightly pointed tunnel vaults is comparable to the nearby Qaṣr Mshattā and Qaṣr Ṭūba, and the same shape appears again at the Early 'Abbāsid Ukhayḍir, built after the Revolution of 132/750.

All these points would suggest a date in the middle of the 2nd/8th century, before the 'Abbāsid Revolution in 132/750. Grabar makes the interesting speculation that Mshattā and 'Ammān might belong to the early 'Abbāsid period, that is, the second half of the 2nd/8th century, because of the relationship of plan between Mshattā and al-Ukhayḍir.[143] While from a stylistic point of view such a redating, of about forty years, would be possible, the *terminus ante* is dependent on the earthquake evidence of Area C.

It is most likely, then, that the palace was built in the latter part of the Umayyad period, in the twenty years between the accession of Hishām ibn 'Abd al-Malik in 105/724, and the death of Walīd ibn Yazīd in 126/744, which precipitated the Third Civil War.

ii. Reconstruction (Period 4)

There is a second constructional style to be found in the palace: Buildings 4, 5 and 6 have arcades of rubble and gypsum mortar piers, including a pair of piers in the entrances of *īwāns* 55 and 67, possibly also in 65. In addition there are fallen arches in this technique in Rooms N2 and N8 of the North Building; part of a wall of N2 has also been rebuilt like this. Furthermore there are rubble and mortar double engaged piers in the entrance of the *īwān* of the North Building: they are clearly a later addition.

The piers with square bases (pl.32b) are straightforward versions of the piers used in Sasanian and Early Islamic Iraq and Iran, built of either brick, or rubble stones, and utilizing the strength of gypsum mortar. Roughly contemporary examples in brick are at Kūfa,[144] Tārīk Khāne (Damghān),[145] and Tulūl al-Ukhayḍir.[146] Small rubble stones could be used in place of brick, as at Ukhayḍir.[147] This precise type of rubble-and-mortar pier is unusual in Jordan.

In Jordan the only parallel is the engaged piers at Qaṣr al-Kharāna.[148] The use of gypsum mortar is alien to Roman and post-Roman Jordan, where lime mortar is most common for stone construction. One might suggest that in this case the work was actually carried out by eastern craftsmen, probably from Iraq or Iran.

The piers in the residential buildings may have replaced an earlier colonnade, or represent a completion of an unfinished scheme. The fallen arches in the North Building represent either the completion of an unfinished building or the repair of one that had been damaged, as for example in an earthquake. It is not really possible to prove which of these interpretations is correct. But it is certainly true that the North Building is sited on a high section of the Roman platform, and would have been exceptionally vulnerable to the shaking effect of an earthquake. It will appear most likely from the discussion of earthquake damage at the Qal'a (Chapter 11), that it was in fact the earthquake of 129–30/747–8 that led to the need for restoration in the North Building.

However, it is clear that the reconstruction work is closely associated with the original building plan and use of the palace, and thus should be close to it in date. The work in each instance predates the Period 5 subdivisions of the rooms. If the work is a response to earthquake damage, it probably postdates the Revolution of 132/750, and belongs to the Early 'Abbāsid period.

iii. Continued Occupation (Period 5; fig.73)

The palace was subsequently divided: the Reception Hall was turned into a self-contained building by the blocking of the north door, and the cutting of a passage from the cross into the northeast room. It was probably in the course of this work that the Reception Hall was roofed over. Rooms in all the buildings were subdivided into small compartments, with no further evidence of monumental rebuilding. The evidence from surface observation does not permit a sequencing of these events; one can only remark upon the surface pottery. 'Abbāsid and Fāṭimid sherds, covering the period up to the 5th/11th century, have been seen by the author. There is also evidence for Ayyubid and/or Mamlūk occupation.

The end of the complex's use as a palace must be earlier than this date; for al-Muqaddasī's account of 'Ammān (*c*.375/985) does not recognize the existence of an Islamic palace at the site. The majority of the Period 5 structures therefore simply represent residential occupation.

Carved Stone Decoration

1. GENERAL DESCRIPTION AND LAYOUT

The flat panels of all three registers of niches and the cornice in the Reception Hall are decorated in carved relief. The areas of decoration are extensive, but limited to defined areas of the building; the ornamented effect was offset by large areas of plain stonework, especially the vaults and dadoes.

An unusually high proportion of the decoration is preserved *in situ*, and it is possible to form an estimate of both its original extent, and the proportion that has survived. If the cornices, whose dimensions cannot now be calculated, are excluded, there were originally 414 decorated panels. Of these, 205 are now decipherable, or are destroyed but were recorded in photographs, that is, 49.52% of the original decoration scheme.[149] This proportion compares only with the Qubbat al-Sakhra, Quṣayr 'Amra and Qaṣr al-Kharāna as a quantifiable record of an Umayyad building's decoration.[150]

Nevertheless, much of the stonework is very worn and the original pattern can only be deciphered with difficulty. This was not so at the end of the last century, when early photographs (e.g. pl.16) show the decoration to have been well preserved. The deterioration has been caused by two factors: firstly, the loss of the third register of niches, and secondly, air pollution stemming from the growing urbanization of 'Ammān. The east-side facades are also much more heavily worn than those on the west side: it is likely that differential wear has resulted from the prevailing westerly wind and its concomitant storms.

The carving is executed in low relief on flat panels. The work is fairly coarse, but the fineness of the delineation does vary, and from this it is possible to deduce that there were several hands at work. In part of the carving use is made of angled surfaces, but elsewhere pattern is delineated by relief line, either rounded or squared. In quality the carving nowhere reaches the standards of the finest carving of the Graeco-Roman tradition in the Levant, even in its latter-day form, such as Byzantine work at Jarash, or Umayyad work at Mshattā or Khirbat al-Mafjar.

The range of decoration is fairly limited, and does not include human or animal figures. It consists of foliage, geometrical patterns and medallions. These patterns are then mixed indiscriminately, forming a medley, so that no panel appears to bear a relationship to its neighbour. A few patterns only occur once, but the majority recur. And in some cases the same pattern is repeated with small variations.

For this reason the discussion will be based on the patterns, rather than the sequence of niches, a catalogue of which will be found in Appendix A, and which is illustrated in plates 21–29. The niches of Register 1 have been numbered in order from 1 to 106, starting at the right-hand side of the south door and running anti-clockwise (fig.44).[151]

In each niche there are three types of block: a block of engaged columns, lettered C (40 × 105cm); a niche back-panel, lettered B (29 × 105cm); and a niche head block bearing the representation of an arch, lettered A (69 × 58cm; fig.45). The spandrel panel above the arch is lettered Aa, and the horseshoe shape inside the arch which forms the head of the niche back-panel is lettered Ab. Panels Ab and B are both intended to form parts of the niche back; they are often the same and are always related. If a B panel has a number of separate elements in it, any individual element is designated by an extra number that runs from the bottom of the panel upwards. Thus a typical panel could be described as 59/B, and as panel 59/B is a scroll the third element from the bottom would be described as 59/B/3.

The situation is different in Register 2. Each of the eight niches is designated by its position: facade first, side of *īwān* second – for example, SW means south facade, west niche, and WS means west facade, south niche. In Register 2 the entire niche back-panel is called panel D. There is also a spandrel panel, designated panel F; and lastly a narrow border panel, designated E, is found at the outer corners of the court facades at this level (fig.50). As in Register 1, an extra figure is added to the designation to describe individual elements within a panel, if they exist, running from bottom to top in cases of a single vertical line, and from bottom left round to bottom right in the case of a double series, e.g. the third roundel up from the left in the D panel of niche WS would be described as WS/D/3.

The twenty-four niches of Register 3 exist now only as fragments. However, it proved possible to decipher nine of the niches from older photographs, and these have been included in the catalogue. The panels from Register 3 can also be described when necessary as Aa, Ab and B panels. The fallen fragments from standard niches have been numbered with a prefix (SN), as it not always certain that they belonged to Register 3. Six of the fallen fragments may be the same as those from Register 3 visible in the photographs.

Single block niches, probably from the exterior, are similar in style to the main registers, with an engaged colonnette on each side of a niche with a flat back-panel; the decoration is found on the back-panel. The arch of the niche has a single line of denticulated moulding. The niches have been numbered with a prefix (SB) (fig.55).

The cornice blocks have dentils and a bead-and-reel moulding, and a sloping panel with pattern decoration; the blocks have been numbered with a prefix (C).

There are two further fragments with pattern decoration, which perhaps belonged to a roundel, and these have been numbered with the prefix 'F'.

For the purposes of this discussion, the patterns encountered will be classified into four basic groups:

a. Half-Palmettes
b. 'Oak' Leaves and Vines
c. Stylized Patterns
d. Rosettes, Roundels and Medallions

2. ANALYSIS OF MOTIVES

a. Half-Palmettes

Half-palmettes are the most widespread decorative motif, found in one form or another on 60 decipherable panels, and may possibly be recognized on five more, that is, 37.5%. The leaf is lobed, growing from a stem on one side; it has one pointed lobe, turned outwards at the tip, and from two to six rounded lobes. The form is called by Balustraitis and Hamilton a 'half-palmette'.[152] Acanthus forms, as found in the later classical period,[153] and their descendants in the Umayyad period,[154] seem to be completely missing from this building; the half-palmette is used in their place. While the two are undoubtedly similar, and used for similar purposes, it is clear that what is used here is not acanthus. The pointed and rounded lobes, and the position of the stem, point to an origin in Sasanian decoration, where the half-palmette is found in stuccoes from Tepe Hissar, Damghān,[155] Chal Tarkhan,[156] Ctesiphon,[157] and Babylon.[158] Introduced to Syria in the Umayyad period, it is found in stucco at Qaṣr al-Kharāna,[159] in stone and stucco at Mafjar,[160] in stucco at Qaṣr al-Ḥayr al-Gharbī,[161] and in stone at Muwaqqar.[162] Further afield it occurs at Qayrawān,[163] while in Iraq the tradition continues in the Islamic period in stucco at al-Ḥīra,[164] at Tulūl al-Ukhayḍir,[165] and in stone at Wāsiṭ.[166] In pottery it occurs on a number of white glaze vessels of 'Samarra' ware, with blue decoration and polychrome lustre painting,[167] but in stucco it only occurs in the abstract Style C form at Sāmarrā' itself.[168] The half-palmette is in fact so common in Early Islamic decoration that it would be impossible to quote all the occurrences of the motif.

Opposed Half-Palmettes (fig. 47.1–3)

In the arch spandrel panels of Register 1 (Aa panels) the most common form is a pair of opposed half-palmettes springing from the spandrels of the arch (Niches 56, 69, 76, 77: pls 23–5). In Register 3 when the Aa panel is almost eliminated by a reduction in the height of the block, this pattern is found on all surviving blocks (SN/1, 2, 3, 5, 6, 7, 9, 12: pl.28). The basic pattern may be modified by the addition of a central tear-drop (Niches 79, 91: pl.25) or a bead border (13: fig.47.3; pl.21). A second variation of this type is four half-palmettes with a central tear-drop (Niches 25, 86: fig.47.2; pls 22, 25). The parallels to these arrangements are from Nizāmābād, a half-palmette placed in a spandrel with a bead border to the arch,[169] and Mafjar.[170]

An alternative way of using this space is a scroll of half-palmettes (Niche 97) or a border of unlinked half-palmettes radiating from the arch (95): both these types are related to patterns in other spaces discussed below.

Split-Palmette Flowers

The niche back-panels (Ab and B) also use the half-palmette extensively. The horseshoe space in the top block (Ab) in fifteen examples (12, 25, 27, 29, 52, 68, 80, 91, 3/22, SN/2, SN/8, SN/9, SN/11, SN/16, SN/18: figs 48.13, 16; pls 21–5) with a variety of B panels, employs a pair of half-palmettes forming a plant head. Although some versions of this are more rudimentary than others, the more developed examples have 'oak' leaves emerging from between the half-palmettes, while at the base of the motif there is a complete leaf placed vertically and two more placed horizontally. This pattern is also found as the filler of a roundel (WS/D/6, WN/D/7: fig.52; pl.27), while a much expanded version occurs as the head of these two panels (WS/D, WN/D). In the latter two panels four small half-palmettes have been added to help fill out the panel.

A closely related scheme has a pair of half-palmettes framing a central bud (C/1, 2: fig.54.1–2; pl.29), which is either round or pointed. In this case the half-palmettes are more outward opening.

This form with a bud is also found miniaturized, placed horizontally with the half-palmettes turned outwards, and repeated three times in an Aa panel (22/Aa: fig.47.4; pl.21). The first form is also repeated three times vertically in a B panel (25/B: fig.48.13; pl.22). There is a divider of 'oak' leaves between each item.

Only the form with a bud can be paralleled: it is

found reversed in Sasanian stuccoes at Chal Tarkhan,[171] in stone on column drums from Wāsiṭ,[172] and in a stucco roundel at Mafjar.[173] In a wider setting it is found in wood on the *minbar* at Qayrawān,[174] in stucco at al-Ḥīra,[175] and again in a stylized form at Sāmarrā'.[176] This range of comparative material suggests that we are here dealing with a form of split palmette. Split palmettes perhaps more often have their framing leaves facing outwards, as in 22/Aa.[177]

Such an origin might explain the 'oak' leaves that peep out between the half-palmettes. Perhaps the closest parallel for this motif is a pier sheathing from Tepe Hissar with a repeating pattern of two opposed half-palmettes, springing from a trefoil base.[178] In 'Ammān the trefoil is replaced by one vertical and two horizontal 'oak' leaves.

Straight Stem with Half-Palmettes

The body of the niche recesses (B Panel) that have split-palmette heads vary. An example was referred to above of the head pattern being repeated three more times (25/B), but a straight stem placed centrally in the B panel is more common.

The stem is planted in a ground represented by three semi-circles – a motif which is widely used on this and other B panels, occurring in fourteen places in Register 1, three blocks of Register 3, and one single-block niche: 1/27, 32, 34, 40, 52, 54, 58, 59, 61, 73, 75, 80, 85, 86, 87; SN/22, SN/26, SN/27, SB/1. It even appears in field patterns that do not require a ground. This ground may be compared with two panels at Chal Tarkhan.[179]

The stem is straight and sprouts three pairs of half-palmettes, each with seven lobes, either pointing upwards (27, 52: fig.48.14; pls 22–23), or drooping (1/91, 3/22, SN/1, SN/3, SN/22: fig. 48.15; pl.25). An identical type of panel appears in stucco in the niches of the facade at Qaṣr al-Kharāna.[180]

In the two D panels from Register 2 (WS and WN: fig. 52, pl.27), the stem resembles a chain link, and is flanked by pairs of rosettes and roundels: seven pairs in WS and eight in WN. These are represented as 'leaves' by a link to the stem, and they are in fact also linked to one another. Trefoils are then used as fillers between the roundels.

Half-Palmette Borders and their Expansions

HALF-PALMETTE SCROLL (figs 47.5–6; 49.2, 53.2). In a very similar pattern to the foregoing, the straight stem in the B panel becomes a scroll with five half-palmettes placed alternately each side of the stem (34/B: partly destroyed, 56/Ab, 58/B: pls 22–3), and in this form the half-palmette is also found with the tips of the lobes doubled (84: fig.49.2; pl.37). The same pattern is recognizable, though inevitably distorted, in an Aa panel (97: fig.47.5; pl.26), where the scroll stem grows from one spandrel to the other.

These varieties appear to be an enlarged version of a border that is found in the vertical narrow E panels of Register 2 (SW/E, WN/E, EN/E: fig. 53.2; pl.27), where the pattern is a clear half-palmette scroll border. This half-palmette scroll appears again in a miniaturized form in two Aa panels forming a rectangular frieze (21, 75: fig.47.6; pls 21, 24). The panel has a border of hearts, and the spandrels are filled with further half-palmettes.

The half-palmette scroll was popular in stucco-work, being found in all the published Sasanian stuccoes.[181] In the Umayyad period we find it in the Levant at Mafjar, as a motif in both stone and stucco,[182] and in Iraq at Tulūl al-Ukhayḍir.[183] In the 'Abbāsid period it is found at the palace excavated at Raqqa in the early 1950s,[184] and at Sāmarrā',[185] while on a less securely datable piece it appears on a lobed dish in the Hermitage.[186]

UNLINKED HALF-PALMETTES. A second form of border is constituted from two rows of unlinked half-palmettes pointing upwards, and this is found on eight cornice blocks (C/4–11: pl.29). In 95/Aa such a row is developed into a curving band around the top of the arch. Although part of this stone has been recut, in the space left by the curving band in the surviving top right-hand corner there is a second row of half-palmettes added. It is on the basis of this second row that one may suggest that the pattern is a development of that found on the cornices.

This particular arrangement of unlinked items appears on a stone capital from Muwaqqar,[187] and on a Sasanian stucco frieze from Ctesiphon.[188]

Half-Palmette Flowers

The half-palmette was also formulated into two varieties of complex groups to form flowers.

THREE OR FOUR HALF-PALMETTES (figs 48.3–4, 49.16, 53.7–8). Three or four half-palmettes may be joined at a boss to form a single flower. These flowers are found in an enlarged format on the spandrels of Register 2, WS/F and WN/F, where they have been distorted to fit the spandrel shape (fig.53.7; pl.27) – and in a smaller form combined with rosettes in Register 1 (50/Aa, 52/Aa: fig.48.3–4; pl.23).

In the first of these latter two examples, the flower has the spandrel space, as in the panels of Register 2, while in the second the flower is miniaturized and drawn between two rosettes. It also occurs as the filler of a scroll (59/B/2: fig.49.16; pl.24). At other sites half-palmettes are more usually joined in threes, e.g.

Mafjar,[189] and Chal Tarkhan,[190] or the white glaze plate referred to earlier.[191] However, a flower of four half-palmettes is known from a polychrome lustre vessel in the collection of the Kuwait National Museum.[192]

EIGHT HALF-PALMETTES (fig.48.6). The most elaborate composition of half-palmettes is a flower of eight stems emerging in a cross formation from a boss, with the half-palmette turned inwards from the stem. The result is similar to a rose (77/Ab, SN/5, SN/33). A flower constructed on similar principles, but with a different appearance, occurs in the stuccoes of the bath porch at Mafjar.[193]

b. 'Oak' Leaves and Vines

These forms occur less frequently than the foregoing and are found in only eight and five instances respectively.

'Oak' Leaves (figs 47.9, 49.3–4, 51–53)

This foliage form has a small oval leaf growing from a thin central stem. In the Aa panels two stems are found, one springing from each spandrel with leaves on either side (78, 93: pls 25-6). Among the niche back-panels we have six examples of the Ab panel (32, 75, 78, 93, SN/7, SN/21), all of which have a spray of leaves, but of B panels there are only two: Niche 32 appears to have a curling central stem and leaves springing from a ground of three semi-circles (fig.49.3; pl.22). But Niche 40 is different, and has a straight stem springing from a similar ground. The leaves sprouting symmetrically are interspersed with seed pods which split into two at the end. This B panel also has an Ab panel that is difficult to decipher, but appears to differ from the leaf spray (fig.49.4; pl.23).

In Register 2 a quadrilobe medallion of panel NE/D uses this form for a tree to fill the frame, and in WS/D/10 three 'oak' leaves are the filler for a roundel.

The closest published parallels are from Chal Tarkhan, where Thompson describes them as 'oak leaves'.[194] That site has identical forms for the roundel and the curving stem panel, while other fragments have similar leaf forms and twin-lobed seeds, described as 'acorns' by Thompson.[195] A very similar straight stem with 'oak' leaves and 'acorns' has been found on a stucco fragment found at Babylon.[196] These comparisons suggest that further material is also relevant, e.g. from Tepe Mill,[197] Mafjar,[198] where leaf sprays occur, and from Kish where the leaf occurs in a more stylized form, being rounded, but in the company of twin-lobed acorns.[199]

Vines

Vines are formed of bunches of grapes hanging from stems, but with the single exception of the composite tree of SW/D, vine leaves are not depicted. In the one example of an Aa panel there is a curling vine growing from one spandrel to the other, bearing three bunches of grapes: the bunches are depicted as irregular ovals (98/Aa: fig.47.8; pl.26). In the two examples of an Ab panel (30, 92: fig.49.5; pls 22, 26), there is also a curling vine with two bunches. But the one example of a B panel (80/B: fig.49.6; pl.25) has an Ab panel with a split-palmette head, and consists of a straight central stem with a spiral vine and bunches of grapes. A more straightforward example does exist as a fragment: this has a curling vine developing from a ground of three semi-circles and bearing bunches of grapes only (SN/26: fig.49.5).

Comparative material on vine decorations is vast, spread as they are throughout the areas of Hellenistic culture. In the vicinity of 'Ammān a curling vine on the pediment of the facade of the Byzantine Cave of the Seven Sleepers may be noted, but this is rather sparser in its bunches.[200] Vine decorations in the basalt region are also comparable.[201] There is a spiral vine around a central stem in the Temple of Dushare at Sī'.[202]

Equally, vines are a feature of Sasanian stuccowork; the Sasanian examples also tend to lack vine leaves.[203] Even though not forming as high a proportion of the ornamentation as in Roman work, they are found at Chal Tarkhan,[204] Kish,[205] and Ctesiphon.[206]

The D panel of niche SW is related to both the foregoing types. This has been described as a tree of life.[207] If, however, we consider its content, it may be described as a composite tree with alternating branches with the 'oak' leaf form and 'acorns', and vines with bunches of grapes. A composite tree with alternating half-palmettes, 'oak'-leaves, and a pomegranate, is also found on one of the single-block niches (SB/1: pl.28f, fig.53). The composite tree with differing foliage and flower forms is also a Sasanian tradition, as at Ctesiphon.[208]

c. Stylized Patterns

Stylized Leaf Bands

Stylized leaf forms are found in three kinds of bands: one is a band of sharply pointed leaves, radiating from the archivolt (24/Aa: fig.47.10; pl.22). Because the flat-topped shape of the Aa panel does not readily lend itself to curved bands of this sort, two small spaces are left in the upper corners.

At Mafjar the same band is used with a curved top to the archivolt. In Umayyad Iraq, this band occurs at Shu'ayba,[209] in Syria at Ruṣāfa,[210] and in the Sasanian period at Kish.[211]

A second band with round-topped leaves, curving

at the base, is found in a similar curve with half-palmettes and trefoils in the upper corners (77/Aa: fig.47.12; pl.25), in a large rectangular frieze (SW/F: fig 53.8; pl.27), and in a smaller version with a border of hearts (7/Aa: fig.47.11; pl.21). Comparable bands with round-topped leaves may be found at Ruṣāfa,[212] and Qaṣr al-Ḥayr al-Gharbī.[213]

Another form of curved band on the archivolt is an upturned heart alternating with thistle heads, and linked by curved loops (84/Aa, 90/Aa: fig.47.13; pl.25). This band with a rosette replacing the heart is found at Ctesiphon;[214] and that comparative example shows us that this band is related to a wide range of bands with different ornaments joined by looped links. For example a plaque from Chal Tarkhan alternates rosettes and trefoils.[215] The Khāsakī *miḥrāb* in the Iraq Museum, Baghdad, has an archivolt frieze of palmettes and lotus buds.[216] Also, at Mafjar, a similar band of palmettes occurs on a balustrade.[217]

Trefoils

Trefoils are represented in a similar fashion to the European fleur-de-lis, with one central pointed leaf and two spreading to the sides. Here the side leaves are more often like rounded lobes. The trefoil does not apparently occur in Roman and Byzantine Levantine art, with the exception of Khirbat al-Bayḍā', which has been thought Ghassānid , i.e. Late Byzantine.[218] Nevertheless, it occurs widely in ornament of the Sasanian tradition, and possibly from that source appears in the Levant in the Umayyad period.

TREFOIL ARRANGEMENTS. On its own the trefoil is used as a filler, like the heart-shaped floret and half-palmette – filling up spandrels (22/Aa, 77/Aa, 90/Aa: figs 47.12, 13; pls 21, 25), and dividing rosettes (WS/D, WN/F: figs 52.1, 53.7; pl.27). More elaborately, four trefoils are used to form a diagonal cross pointing at a larger fifth, between two rosettes (48/Aa: fig.48.5; pl.22). In two panels related to this, trefoils are used in a band radiating from the arch (68/Aa, 74/Aa: fig.47.14; pl.24; cf. also F/3). Further uses on their own include two vertical rows in a niche back-panel (102/B: pl.26), and, as a derivative of that, a single row forming half such a panel, while the other half is a row of quatrefoils (87/B: fig.49.8; pl.25). One single-block niche, of which only the upper part survives, has a single large trefoil placed vertically, possibly the top element of a vertical line of trefoils (SB/3).

TREFOIL AND DIAMOND GRID. The trefoil is used as a filler for a variety of grids that form infinitely extensible patterns. The trefoil is placed vertically in a diamond with a double outline, while the diamonds repeat in a grid form (22/Ab, SN/4, SN/19, SN/34: fig.48.7; pls 21, 28).

This form occurs at Chal Tarkhan; two examples from that site have downturned outer leaves, while a third has the lobed trefoil found at 'Ammān.[219] Trefoils in diamond grids also occur at Tepe Hissar,[220] and in a panel from Nizāmābād.[221]

TREFOIL AND SQUARE GRID. An alternative to the diamond grid is a grid of squares, with the trefoils placed vertically (79/B, SE/D, SN/27: fig.49.7; pls 25, 27). In the case of a square grid, the squares have only a single outline. This version cannot be precisely paralleled, but a square grid is found with human figures as early as Qal'eh-i Yazdigird (2nd-3rd centuries AD), and also with a filler of quatrefoils.[222] The square grid with quatrefoils appears again at Chal Tarkhan.[223]

Square or rectangular frames are used again for another form of grid in which the trefoil is placed diagonally pointing to the upper right (87/Aa, 92/Aa: fig.47.15; pls 25–6), or alternately to the upper and lower right (SE/E: fig.53.3; pl.27). Whereas the other grids are used for field patterns, this form is only used in linear developments, either vertically in the E panel, or horizontally in the Aa panel as a rectangular frieze. In other words it is a border form. A very similar diagonal trefoil border occurs in the *dīwān* at Mafjar,[224] on window frames at Qaṣr al-Ḥayr al-Gharbī,[225] and at Ḥammām al-Sarakh.[226]

Quatrefoils and Pierced Beads

The diamond grid with a pierced bead replacing the trefoil filler may be detectable in two worn panels (6/Aa, 85/Aa: pls 21, 25), although this interpretation is not certain; such a pattern occurs at Ctesiphon.[227] But the pierced bead is more generally associated with quatrefoils without a grid.

Quatrefoils and pierced beads occur as a single vertical column shared with a column of trefoils in a B panel (87/B: fig.49.8; pl.25), and similarly as a vertical border in two E panels (NE/E, NW/E: fig.53; pl.27). There are also examples as a field pattern on an Aa panel (36Aa: fig.48.1; pl.22) as well as on niche back-panels (ES/D, 3/8, SN/6, SN/31: pls 27–8).

In Sasanian stuccowork this pattern is one of compass-drawn interlocking circles in which the pierced bead marks the centre of the circle.[228] The 'Ammān examples are not based on compass drawn circles: in one case the field is compressed in the vertical dimension, elongating the circles horizontally (48/Ab: fig.48.8, pl.23), and in a second the vertical to horizontal proportion varies from the top of the panel to the bottom (ES/D). Nevertheless, the 'Ammān examples do closely follow the appearance of the Sasanian stuccoes.

In a related form this pattern is a favourite one for mosaics in the Levant, occurring in fourteen panels from Antioch,[229] and one panel from Jarash.[230] In Byzantine mosaics from Palestine the circles may be dislocated by the invasion of other elements.[231] At Mafjar a similar dislocated version in mosaic has a diamond grid of quatrefoils.[232] In these cases the pattern is presented on a larger scale than at 'Ammān, and the centre point, if there is one, is a square or diamond.

In Sasanian work there are two alternative ways of treating the quatrefoil: either the quatrefoil is the filling of a square frame, the square often being part of a grid, as discussed above. Or, when the square is absent, interlocking circles can form a grid of quatrefoils, as in an example from Kish discussed by Balustraitis.[233] The interpretation as a quatrefoil is still valid, because the meeting point of four leaves retains a boss, while the circle centre is also given one. At Chal Tarkhan both forms occur, but in the latter the circles have become dominant with the disappearance of the quatrefoil boss,[234] cf. also Ctesiphon[235] and Nizāmābād.[236]

At Mafjar Hamilton analyses this form as a straightforward series of overlapping circles with pierced beads.[237] The scheme thus also resembles the pierced bead in a diamond grid, but with curved lines; and this is an alternative analysis of the 'Ammān pattern.

The 'Braid' Border and its Expansion

The last type of extensible field pattern to be considered is a field of overlapping arcs amounting to a quarter-circle usually, but sometimes up to three-quarters of a circle. Each of the overlapping arcs is then composed of a series of concentric lines. It is found in both compass-drawn and hand-drawn versions, and is common on both Aa panels (8, 20, 29, 30, 66, 94, 96, 100, 101: fig. 48.2; pls 21–26), and B panels (23, 60, 81, 3/24, SN/29: fig.49.9; pls 22, 24–25). It is also found as a field pattern at al-Qasṭal.[238]

Apparently it is an expansion of a border, seen at 'Ammān in an E panel (WS/E: fig.53.5; pl.27), which is comparable with one from Chal Tarkhan.[239] This link shows us that we are concerned with a field development of a common border pattern, which is found in flat versions, but also as a half-round moulding. This is classified by Thompson as a 'braid' pattern, but also described as a palm-trunk pattern.[240]

In the half-round form it occurs as an archivolt moulding in Sasanian stuccoes, and has variations with straight lines in place of curves, and with pierced beads in spaces. This last version approaches the pierced bead and diamond grid pattern discussed above. These Sasanian versions probably derive from the patterned colonnettes of mud-brick Sumerian and Babylonian architecture.[241]

In the Islamic period it appears in both half-round and flat versions at Mafjar,[242] at Sāmarrā',[243]and in wood panels from the Aqṣā Mosque.[244]

Alternative uses of similar fields may be seen in Sasano-Islamic metalwork, where this pattern is used to represent water on a silver dish,[245] and in another it represents the ground.[246] No example of this pattern occurs in the Levant before the Umayyad period, but a motif of overlapping half-circles, scale-like in appearance, but without the concentric arcs, is a standard feature in mosaic.[247]

d. Rosettes, Roundels and Medallions

Forms

In addition to the field developments of the last group, geometrical shapes also formed outlines for fillers of various types. While the majority of outlines are round, other more complex shapes do occur, and this range extends from simple rosettes and flowers, with and without circles, to roundels with other fillers, and finally to other forms of outline.

ROSETTES. The simple rosette at 'Ammān has a boss and rounded petals raised in outline, numbering between six and twelve, with a surround of a single or a double circle (e.g. SN/35), or a bead border (SN/12, SN/13). In a secondary form the petal tips are given a doubled outline (WS/D/12: fig.52; pl.27).

A second rosette form has four spike petals (e.g. 48/Aa: fig.48.5; pl.23), or in one case six (SN/24: fig.49.13), divided by pairs of rounded petals, which might be interpreted as heart-shaped florets. A derivative has no circle (94/Ab: fig.48.10; pl.26). The resulting flower may then be elongated in the vertical direction to fit a B panel (54/B: fig.49.12; pl.23).

A third rosette has spike petals with a recessed boss (95/Ab: fig. 48.11; pl.26), or a protruding one (26/B, NW/F: pls 22, 27). A version with no circle may be detectable in two worn panels (66, 99/Ab: pls 24, 26). There is also an example with a bead border (SN/32).

Rosettes are an ancient and general ornamental form in the Near East. Nevertheless, it is interesting to note that the three types displayed here are all included in the much wider variety found at the contemporary Khirbat al-Mafjar.[248] Also the three rosette types are included among the four found at Chal Tarkhan, another instance of the remarkable similarities between 'Ammān and this North Iranian site. The other type at Chal Tarkhan has flatter, pointed petals, pierced with holes.[249]

If we consider the comparative material for the rosette types on an individual level, of the three the most distinctive is the type with four spike petals. This is clearly of eastern origin for it occurs in the same form on the archivolt moulding of the *īwān* at Tāq-i Bustān,[250] and on a Sasano-Islamic silver dish,[251] in addition to Chal Tarkhan.

With the other two varieties of rosette less certainty is possible. The spike-petalled rosette occurs on a stucco fragment from Bishapur with a double circle,[252] at Tepe Hissar,[253] Ctesiphon,[254] and Nizāmābād.[255] Equally something similar to the spike-petalled rosette occurs on a sarcophagus from Palestine, and this also encloses an inner rosette of the round-petalled variety.[256]

Round-petalled rosettes are common in the southern Levantine area: they occur locally at 'Araq al-Amīr in the Hellenistic period,[257] and later quite similarly in an unpublished stone panel, at present in the Cathedral at Jarash. This type of rosette is carved in relief with a flat petal delineated by its exterior shape. A version of this rosette in lower relief appears at Khirbat al-Bayḍā',[258] and the same type in mosaic, quite similar in appearance to the 'Ammān rosettes, is used as a border to the Barāda panel in the Umayyad Mosque of Damascus.[259] Round-petal rosettes with a raised outline and sunken centre to each petal also appear elsewhere in the eastern tradition, known at Qal'eh-i Yazdigird, where the round-petalled rosette is analysed as a rosette of four heart-shaped florets.[260] This resolution also occurs at Chal Tarkhan in both the Main and Subsidiary Palaces.

ROUNDELS WITH PALMETTES. The same double circle that encloses the rosettes, encloses other forms as well. Among these are three kinds of palmette. One consists entirely of round-lobed shoots, and is found both in an oval form and as a roundel (73/B, 83/B, SN/30: fig.49.15; pls 24–5). In this oval form especially, though it may be derivative of the roundel, it resembles the Greek palmette, but is also known in the contemporary stuccoes of Mafjar,[261] and in the Sasanian stuccoes of Ctesiphon.[262]

The second type has six rounded lobes and three pointed ones, and only occurs in the 'roundel trees' of Niches WS and WN (WS/D/3, 8, 13; WN/D/2: fig.52, pl.27). This pointed palmette is a straightforward borrowing from the stucco groups described for other patterns: it occurs on a frieze panel at Kish,[263] and Ctesiphon,[264] as the filler of a diamond grid at Tepe Hissar,[265] and at al-Qasṭal.[266]

The third kind of palmette is split and has an 'oak' leaf form inserted between the two half-palmettes, which face outwards (WS/D/7, 10; WN/D/8, 14: fig. 52; pl.27). A comparative type appears in a moulding at Tepe Hissar.[267]

OTHER ROUNDELS. Aside from the palmette roundels, there are a number of other patterns found in the 'roundel trees' of the west side in Register 2. One type encloses a spiral of foliage (WS/D/1, 4; WN/D/2: fig.52; pl.27), and this filler is also found in the scroll of 59/B (fig.49.16; pl.24). This appears to be a rather coarse version of what Hamilton calls a 'bracken-tip spiral', found in miniature as a border at Mafjar,[268] at Nizāmābād,[269] and at Chal Tarkhan.[270] These roundels also include one with three 'oak' leaves, discussed earlier, and another with the split-palmette head (WS/D/2, 6, 14; WN/D/7: fig.52).

Composition of Rosettes and Roundels

In composition rosettes and roundels are most commonly employed in panels of five, with the spaces filled by heart-shaped florets, half-palmettes, and trefoils. Such panels might be placed horizontally over a niche arch, e.g. WN/F with round-lobed rosettes (fig.53.7; pl.27), or NW/F with spike-petalled rosettes; alternatively they are placed vertically as a niche back-panel, e.g. round-lobed: 61/B, 86/B, 3/20, SN/35 (fig.49.10; pls 24–5); spike and round-lobed: SN/24; spike-petalled: 26/B, 3/11 (pl.22); mixed: SN/32.

The same is implied where only the top rosette survives in an Ab panel (13, 20, 28, 55, 57, 66, 95, 3/2: fig.48.11). A second alternative is also possible here – three items on the B panel in place of four (54, 73, 83: fig.49.12; pls 23–5). This is the explanation of why the circle of the roundel turns into an oval, or the item is elongated.

A third, extraordinary development, which illustrates very well the way in which patterns were varied to fit different spaces, is the apparent enlargement of the same scheme that is detectable on the badly worn D panel of niche NW (fig.51; pl.27). On this there appear to have been five roundels, each approximately 0.8m in diameter, as opposed to the normal 0.26m. The contents of these roundels appear to have been complex and various: NW/D/4 resembles a spike-petalled rosette, while NW/D/1 has a scroll inside the border. The central three roundels have a bead border. Probably they resembled some of the round stucco plaques found in Umayyad and Sasanian decoration, for example at Qaṣr al-Kharāna,[271] Qaṣr al-Ḥayr al-Gharbī,[272] Ctesiphon,[273] Bishapur,[274] and Kūfa.[275]

At the other end of the scale, a narrow vertical field of twelve miniature six-lobed rosettes is also found (21/Ab-B; fig.49.11; pl.21). As this fills only the central third of a B-field, it is expanded with a zigzag border on each side, with fillers of heart-shaped florets in the triangular spaces.[276]

The linear formation is retained in both these variations. It may be that, as in the case of the half-palmette scroll and the braid pattern, this linear arrangement of rosettes is an expansion of a rosette border. Although we do not have here an example of a rosette border, that is, a rosette border in the E panel, rosette borders are found in the mosaic from the Umayyad Mosque in Damascus discussed above, and in stucco at Chal Tarkhan[277] and Ctesiphon.[278] In a Levantine context such a rosette border would be linked together by a cable outline – cf. Khirbat al-Bayḍā',[279] and Mafjar[280] – or a scroll, cf. Mafjar.[281] But with the exception of the scroll of 59/B, rosette scrolls or cables do not occur in 'Ammān.[282]

The shape of the space on Aa panels does not suit rosettes, and these are only employed in composition with other elements. In two cases the round-petalled rosette is combined with the flower of four half-palmettes (50, 52: fig.48.3–4; pl.23), and in a third two rosettes with four spike petals flank a pattern of trefoils (48Aa: fig.48.5; pl.23).

The last form of composition of roundels and rosettes is the 'roundel trees' of Register 2 (WS/D and WN/D: fig.52; pl.27); here two vertical lines of roundels flank a central stem, to which they are linked by branches (and to each other). The composition is topped by a split-palmette head.

Other Frames and Medallions

If circles could be used as frames, so could other shapes: a diamond interwoven into a cable occurs in three Ab panels (70, 74, 90: fig.48.12; pls 23–5). This diamond is delineated by two lines, and has a filling of two half-palmettes. In a second form (SN/17, SN/23: fig.49.14) the diamond is composed of a pierced bead border, and the filler is a round-petalled rosette. A further form of interlaced diamonds forms an eight-pointed star, delineated by a bead border (SN/10).

A scroll of the kind so commonly found in Roman and Byzantine art in the Levant occurs only at 59/B: it grows out of a ground of three semi-circles, and encloses a palmette,[283] a flower of four half-palmettes, a 'bracken-tip' spiral, and a fourth indecipherable element.

The most distinctive of the geometrical shapes is a medallion, repeated four times on NE/D (fig.51; pl.27), which has four semi-circular lobes added to a squat cross shape. This medallion recalls one in mosaic in the Dome of the Rock,[284] a stucco panel from the Bath Hall at Khirbat al-Mafjar,[285] and a further example in stucco at al-Ḥīra.[286] The fillers of the comparative examples all differ from those of 'Ammān. The fillers of only two (NE/D/2 and 4) can now be deciphered, but they are better preserved in the sketches drawn by Mauss for Dieulafoy.[287] Medallion 4 at the top contains a tree with a triangular root and 'oak' leaf forms. In Medallion 3 only a reversed triangle marking the base of a tree is visible today, but it is indicated by Mauss to have been the same as Medallion 2 below. Medallion 2 has a tree with the same triangular base, and a stem indicated by three lines, from which a pair of half-palmettes droop down. An 'oak' leaf, and a third half-palmette are visible on the left of the medallion. Mauss reconstructs the pattern as a composite tree of half-palmettes and 'oak' leaves. Of the filler of Medallion 1 only a few 'oak' leaves are to be seen. The triangle base, three-line depiction of a stem, and the drooping half-palmettes are paralleled on a frieze of trees from Umm al-Za'ātir, Ctesiphon.[288]

In only one case is the imagery of the niche itself used – one Ab and B panel with three round-headed niches placed vertically, each with a bead border to the arch. This panel is unfortunately now lost (3/19).

In fact the range of outlines recorded from 'Ammān is small. At other sites a much greater variety is to be seen: hexagons and trilobe arches at Qaṣr al-Ḥayr al-Gharbī;[289] octagons and six-lobed roundels at Mshattā.[290]

3. DISCUSSION OF THE DECORATION

From the analysis above it is clear that the range of pattern employed on the building is quite limited: half-palmettes, 'oak' leaves, vines, trefoils, quatrefoils, the braid border, rosettes and a series of roundels and medallions comprise the entire stock of pattern. However, because 205 panels have survived, there is evidence for a wide variety of different ways in which that basic stock has been employed.

The way that pattern is developed is dictated by the shapes of the spaces to be filled. There are three varieties of space: a rectangular niche back-panel with a round head comes in two sizes, 0.25 × 1.27m in Register 1, and 0.79 × 3.31m in Register 2 (Ab, B and D). The archivolt panel in the two registers has a generous space above the top of the arch, 0.67m wide in Register 1 and 1.67m wide in Register 2. In Register 3 this panel is eliminated by a reduction in the height of the A block. The third form of panel (E) is a narrow vertical panel, 4.03 × 0.20m. Of these, the E panel is unusual in location, but is a good shape for a border pattern. The B panel is small for a well worked out pattern, but the D panel is larger and suitable for trees. The most awkward panel to use is the archivolt panel (Aa and F). The most satisfactory solution appears in Register 2, where there is more space. Invariably here the ornament is a rectangular frieze surmounting two independent spandrel ornaments. In the Aa panels this solution has been adopted in only six cases. In spite of the fact that there is already an archivolt moulding of dog-tooth pattern, in four instances a second curved band has been added (24, 68, 74, 95), leaving small triangular spaces in the upper corners. In the others the entire space is filled with one pattern, e.g. two half-palmettes growing out of the spandrels, or an overall field of the braid pattern.

To fill the spaces thus available the craftsman had a basic range of patterns – patterns which, one can deduce from the parallels, were common elsewhere. These patterns were fitted to the available spaces by a series of simple processes. One useful form already present in the sources was the infinitely extensible field pattern, e.g. quatrefoils and pierced beads. This was applied to all shapes of panel.

A second method was to expand a border pattern to cover a field. This seems to be clearly the case with the half-palmette scroll and the braid pattern, but it may also be the case with the rosette border.

Once a pattern was arrived at for one location it was simply enlarged or reduced for another location, with little alteration. The B panel of five rosettes was enlarged to fit the D panel and miniaturized for another B panel without changing the basic pattern. Register 2 has been affected by this particularly, for all the D panels except two are derivatives of Register 1 panels: EN/D is indecipherable, and the composite tree of SW/D is reflected in a niche from the exterior that is decorated with a composite tree (SB/1: fig.54.4; pl.28f).

In principle, the scheme of any one panel is unrelated to adjacent panels, but in practice it is the Register 1 panels, which seem to have been carved before installation, that best illustrate the point: only in one case do several variations on the same theme occur in close proximity – in Niches 48, 50 and 52 a rosette is placed in an Aa panel and related to trefoils and half-palmettes. In Register 2, carved after erection, there is a progression: in the D panels of SE and ES there are two field patterns, while in NE and NW there are two types of medallion in a vertical arrangement, with the same quatrefoil E panel. NW and WN have the same F panel of a horizontal frieze of rosettes. WN and WS have the same roundel trees in variant versions, while SW has a different sort of tree but the same F panel as WS.

The sources of the decorative tradition employed in the building are to be derived from the comparative material. For the period before the Arab Conquest remarkably little comparative material can be traced in the literature on decoration in the Levant,[291] and what can be traced is not related closely. The principal elements relevant to this point are vines, rosettes, the round-lobed palmette, and the field of quatrefoils, or interlocking circles, although these are treated differently in mosaic work.

In the Umayyad period the picture is different, and a number of sites have comparative forms: the Qubbat al-Sakhra, the Umayyad Mosque in Damascus, Qaṣr al-Kharāna, Muwaqqar, Qasṭal, and Qaṣr al-Ḥayr al-Gharbī. Of Umayyad sites in the Levant, however, by far the most important comparative material comes from Khirbat al-Mafjar. All the basic forms occur there, and half of all variations. These patterns occur among the carved stone and painted work, but chiefly among the stucco of that site, although the ornamentation from Mafjar is much more varied and innovative. Mafjar is located close to ʿAmmān, and is a contemporary building. One might assume then that both palaces were to some extent the product of the same experience. Hamilton concludes, in his discussion of the stuccoes, that they are the product of a Mesopotamian building tradition, but executed by Syrian hands.[292]

Precisely the same group of Iraqi and Iranian stucco-decorated sites that Hamilton found most similar to Mafjar can also be compared with ʿAmmān. These sites between them – Kish, Ctesiphon, Tepe Hissar (Damghān), to which one may add Chal Tarkhan, Tepe Mill and Nizāmābād – have all the basic patterns of ʿAmmān, and nevertheless form a homogeneous group, indicating a common building tradition.

These are all palaces or houses of the middle to late Sasanian period, with some spill over into the Islamic period. The palace of Kish is now attributed to the reign of Bahrām Gūr (420–438),[293] while Tepe Hissar probably also belongs to the 5th century.[294] The houses in Ctesiphon in the mounds of Umm al-Zaʿātir and al-Maʿāriḍ (fig.59) may probably be dated to the 6th century AD.[295] The Main Palace at Chal Tarkhan is dated also to the Late Sasanian period, with reoccupation and new construction in the Subsidiary Palace in the Early Islamic period.[296] The resemblance of the Chal Tarkhan stuccoes is very close, and especial notice should be taken of the roundel with three 'oak' leaves, the curving stem with 'oak' leaves and the flat form of the braid border, all of which point clearly to a close relationship. As Chal Tarkhan is geographically distant, the relationship is likely to be chronological; perhaps Chal Tarkhan is very late in the Sasanian period, or even to be dated after the Arab Conquest.[297]

This Sasanian stucco tradition continues into the Umayyad period. In Iraq similar stuccoes are to be seen at Shuʿayba, and Tulūl al-Ukhayḍir. However, the style seems to have been on the wane, for we find very different stuccoes at al-Ḥīra, Qaṣr al-Ḥayr al-Sharqī,[298] Raqqa,[299] and Sāmarrāʾ.[300]

The greater part of this decorative tradition was expressed in stucco, either moulded or carved, but there is some evidence for it in stone at Ṭāq-i Bustān, and column drums from the Great Mosque at Wāsiṭ, though the treatments are somewhat different. There is also evidence for comparable motives in metalwork.

The tradition was then imported into the Levant during the Umayyad period, and mixed with the local Byzantine tradition in stone-carving and stucco-work. But at 'Ammān there is very little of the Byzantine tradition, and two of the most common Graeco-Roman motives, the vine-leaf (save one example, the exception which proves the rule) and the acanthus, are completely missing, while what there is, is only that which is also found in the Sasanian and post-Sasanian (i.e. Umayyad) tradition. In other words, there is much evidence for the hypothesis that the source of pattern for these decorations is simply the tradition of the territories of the Sasanian empire, virtually to the exclusion of the local traditions of ornament. This position is in sharp contrast to the contemporary architecture of nearby Qaṣr Mshattā, and Khirbat al-Mafjar, where a combination of motives of local and Sasanian descent appear.

Moreover a series of patterns were being used that were basically intended for stucco-work. Although a good many of the patterns are also found in other media, the range found in this building is very close to that in contemporary stucco-work: the extensive comparisons to the stuccoes of Mafjar and Chal Tarkhan point to this. Part of the reason lies in the way that the stone was cut. For example, the half-palmettes have the 45° angled facets used in the contemporary carving of stucco, rather than the flat curly treatment used at Muwaqqar;[301] and this similarity of treatment is also true of vines, 'oak' leaves, quatrefoils, rosettes, the 'braid border' pattern, and, to a lesser extent, of the trefoils.

The adoption of an alien tradition could have occurred in two possible ways: craftsmen from the eastern territories of the Caliphate may have carried out the work, or perhaps supervised it; or it could have been executed by local masons using some form of pattern book.

The case for eastern craftsmen having been employed rests upon the character of the motives alone. Yet it is true that the work has been carried out in a way rather foreign to the eastern tradition from which it is drawn. For example, the mason was not familiar with the geometrical origins of the quatrefoil and pierced bead pattern in over-lapping circles, for there are examples where the circle is lengthened into an oval (ES/D, 48Ab: fig.48.8). All the comparative examples in stucco are drawn out with circles, and one might expect a craftsman brought up with the tradition to follow it. One might also regard the use of the 'braid border' pattern (figs 48.2; 49.9), the half-palmette scroll (figs 47.5; 49.2), and linear arrangements of rosettes (fig.49.10), all normally border patterns, as unusual choices for a field pattern.

In the case of a pattern book, the selection of a decorative style must have been a deliberate act on the part of the patron, for no mason would have completely ignored his own tradition unless he had been specifically ordered to do so. A deliberate choice on the part of the patron might also be true of the first possibility, but not necessarily so.

The evidence is not conclusive, but it is rather more probable than not that the work was carried out by local craftsmen, or at least craftsmen of the Roman tradition, because of the awkward and unsophisticated approach to the Sasanian decorative tradition; and it seems very probable that the patron had a specific desire for an oriental scheme of decoration, in addition to the other orientalizing features of the palace.

At any rate it is significant that only half the eastern tradition was adopted, and figural relief was ignored. This must be deliberate, as a concession to Muslim sentiment in an urban public audience hall.

Interpretation

1. THE PALACE IN CONTEXT

By the Umayyad period the sites of the pagan temples, located as they were in central positions in the Roman cities of the Levant, were available as sites for development. The majority of Roman temples fell into disuse, or were actually destroyed, in the last years of the 4th century and the early years of the 5th.[302] In some cases, as at Ba'albakk[303] and Damascus, churches were built in these enclosures, although this was not always the case; at Jarash the complex of churches is built next to the *temenos* of the Temple of Artemis, not in it. The Muslims had no reservations about the use of these ready-made sites, where the masonry of the earlier building would in itself provide for the new.

Other sites where this sort of development occurred are the Umayyad Mosque in Damascus, built in the *temenos* of the Temple of Jupiter Damascenus,[304] and the building of the Qubbat al-Sakhra and the Aqṣā Mosque on the site of Herod's Temple in Jerusalem.[305] In Damascus and Jerusalem the new constructions were mosques, continuing the tradition of sanctity; but 'Ammān is a palace.

The palace built in the Roman enclosure at 'Ammān is quite a large complex (15,600 sq.m.). Only two known palaces of the Umayyad period are larger in area: the *dār al-imāra* of Kūfa (26,000 sq.m.),[306] and Mshattā (21,600 sq.m.).[307]

By the time that the palace was constructed in the second quarter of the 2nd/8th century the tradition of Umayyad palace building had been developing for some time,[308] and it clearly belongs to the group of later Umayyad palaces. One may quote, as rough contemporaries, the palaces at Khirbat al-Mafjar (before 125/743),[309] Mshattā (*c.*126/744), Qaṣr Ṭūba (*c.*126/744),[310] Ḥammām al-Sarakh,[311] and the Large Enclosure of Qaṣr al-Ḥayr al-Sharqī (110/728–9),[312] all of which, like 'Ammān, have examples of the two-centre pointed arch or vault. If one were to disregard this criterion, one might add the Umayyad palace at Ruṣāfa,[313] Qaṣr al-Ḥayr al-Gharbī,[314] and the Small Enclosure at Qaṣr al-Ḥayr al-Sharqī,[315]where either round arches are present or no arches are known.

The only close parallel of the layout is the rather later Abbasid Ukhayḍir, in western Iraq, dated by Creswell to the years following 159/775-6 (fig.77).[316] Ukhayḍir has a fortified square outer enclosure, measuring 169 × 174m, and a rectangular inner enclosure, 81 × 112m, which contains the principal accommodation. The gatehouse block of this enclosure has two further storeys, and there are two annexes, one inside and one outside the main outer enclosure. The total area of accommodation, *c.*14,500 sq.m., is similar to 'Ammān. The central block has an enclosed tunnel-vaulted hall at the entrance, and an *īwān* and dome chamber arrangement facing it across a rectangular court. There are four residential units, each with two *īwān*s, surrounding the halls, and two further units in the upper storeys.

Nevertheless, 'Ammān and Ukhayḍir are very different buildings, Ukhayḍir being a rubble and mortar construction, clearly to be placed in a continuing tradition of Mesopotamian architecture. The common elements are: the enclosed hall at the entrance, an *īwān* and dome chamber at the far end of the layout, and the employment of residential units around their own courtyards, although these are different in plan.

One can project this parallel further by recalling the similarity of the plan of the unfinished palace at Qaṣr Mshattā (125–6/743–4) to Ukhayḍir. At Mshattā there is a columned basilical hall and triconch reception room facing onto a central courtyard (fig.76). The gate block was insufficiently finished for one to be quite certain of its arrangements.[317] However, as one entered the gate, one passed into a passageway or closed hall, then into a square area, which may have been planned to be open, and then into the main courtyard. In the Qaṣr al-Dhahab, al-Manṣūr's palace in the Round City of Baghdad (141–145/762–6), it is reported that there was at the back an *īwān* measuring 30 × 20 cubits (15.5 × 10.3m), and a domed audience room 20 × 20 cubits (10.3m square).[318] This description matches the situation in Mshattā, 'Ammān, and Ukhayḍir, and the palace may have been similar in design;[319] at Baghdad, however, there was also a second storey audience room. All these buildings are closely grouped in date around the middle of the 2nd/8th century, and it seems that at this time there was a trend towards designing palaces with a closed hall at the entrance, and an *īwān* and dome chamber at the far end. This pattern is not found again at Sāmarrā' in the major palaces, but can be seen in grand houses or small palaces: Houses nos 1 and 3 in the Shāri' al-A'ẓam, dated to the construction of al-Mutawakkiliyya in 245–7/859–61.[320]

Most Early Islamic palaces known, up to Sāmarrā', subdivided their residential accommodation into groups of rooms that were relatively independent units. In the Umayyad *quṣūr* on the pattern of a fort the accommodation sub-units would appear to correspond with what Creswell has called the 'Syrian *bayt*', that is, a large room or small hall flanked by four or more smaller rooms (fig.75).[321] This pattern is also found in the palace and houses of 'Anjar (fig.169): two such units are to be seen in a house near the south gate. In 'Ammān the '*bayts*' seem to have developed into full-sized houses around their own courtyards, with two *īwān*s and a number of additional rooms.

In the Large Enclosure at Qaṣr al-Ḥayr al-Sharqī, houses round their own courtyards are also to be seen, but the foundation inscription describes the enclosure as a *madīna*, not a *qaṣr*; the Small Enclosure has the 'Syrian *bayt*' (fig.170).

In Abbasid Iraq, Ukhayḍir has residential units of a courtyard with two *īwān*s, each described by Creswell as a 'Persian *bayt*' (fig.77).[322] At Sāmarrā' the palaces included within the enclosures of Iṣṭabulāt, Balkuwārā (fig.78), and the Ja'farī palace of al-Mutawakkil[323] have accommodation in the form of house units, as do subsections of the palace of al-Mu'taṣim (*Dār al-Khilāfa* or *Jawsaq al-Khāqānī*) at Sāmarrā'.[324]

The prevalence of this form of subdivision in early Islamic palaces suggests that it was a reflection of social structure. In Iraq, at least, dividing palace accommodation into house units was not new to the Islamic period: the 6th-century palace at Qaṣr-i Shīrīn has units of a single *īwān* and courtyard (fig.74).[325]

The Reception Hall and the North Building represent the halls of the palace. The Reception Hall stood at the entrance, and seems also to have been the principal gate. Access to the remainder of the palace, including the North Building, was obtained through it and along the columned street. This would seem to be archaeological evidence of the Islamic notion of *majlis al-'āmm* and *majlis al-khāṣṣ*, public and private audience.[326]

Elsewhere in the Umayyad period archaeological evidence of such a distinction is only known in the Bath Hall at Khirbat al-Mafjar, where a small richly decorated side-room is attached to the main hall. The public character of the southern building as an audience hall is emphasized by the lack of figural decoration in an ornate building, surely a reflection of public iconoclastic sentiment among the Muslims.

The Reception Hall, standing at the entrance, is the centre-piece of the palace, built first, with the finest materials and decoration. A governor's palace requires a substantial audience hall, for petitions and other business, preferably placed near the entrance for public access (as in the Byzantine governor's palace at Apollonia[327]).

In the pre-modern Middle East the public were often expected to wait at the gate of the palace, but 'gate' could also mean the court itself. Under the Sasanians the mint name *baba*' (the Aramaic word for 'gate') is usually interpreted as the mint of the Sasanian royal court.[328] The *Fihrist* of Ibn al-Nadīm quotes an explanation by Ibn al-Muqaffaʿ of the Persian dialect of *darī*: 'those at the gate of the King used to speak it', i.e. it was the court language.[329] Most often, of course, one waited at the gate for an opportunity to see someone, as Khālid al-Qasrī met a young man looking for an opportunity at Hishām's gate in 105/724.[330] For this kind of activity one would not expect architectural provision, though, as in many periods, seats were sometimes provided in the entrances to Umayyad palaces.[331]

2. PERSIANIZING IMAGERY

a. Archaeological Evidence

The design of the palace includes features of both the Roman-Byzantine and the Sasanian architectural traditions.

The Roman elements relate, on the whole, to local building practices. The construction throughout is either of limestone ashlars, or of limestone and flint rubble masonry, with a combination of the two in one wall being a noticeable feature. The whole is cemented with a lime mortar mixed with ash. The arches, vaults and semi-domes are of ashlars, not rubble or brick. A columned street connects the two halls. The setting out of the plan of the Reception Hall appears to be similar to that of a cross-in-square basilica.

On the other hand the eastern elements, which might be described as deriving from the Iraqi or Iranian architectural traditions, relate to the external appearance of the palace. These elements are of two kinds: those in the plan and those in the architectural decoration.

Of the former, the Reception Hall appears to be intended as some version of the four-*īwān* plan, although it is not easy to parallel directly. The North Building is a classic example of the *īwān* and dome chamber plan, widely paralleled in Sasanian and Early Islamic eastern architecture. *Īwāns* are also found in the residential units of the palace. In the decoration there are 'squinches' for the transition to the semi-dome, single and double string-lines at the base of the vault, rectangular buttresses at the mouth of the *īwāns*, three registers of blind arcaded niches resembling the Tāq-i Kisrā, blind arrow-slots in the North Building, and a decoration scheme derived from eastern, mainly stucco, resources.

It is important to notice how much has been done in this ʿAmmān building for purely visual effect. In addition to the facades, which are a pure copy of the eastern type, we have noted that the 'squinches' are ornamental, employing the Sasanian elliptical arch which occurs nowhere in the structural arches. There is also an ornamental string-line and the employment of square buttresses at the mouth of each *īwān* after the manner of the Tāq-i Kisrā or the Bab al-ʿĀmma at Sāmarrā'. The exterior, an almost square block with buttresses, could also be viewed in this light. The fact that much of the work executed on the building was ornamental suggests that what we are confronted with is not so much the importation of building techniques from the East, but a deliberate attempt to create the impression of a very 'Persian' building.

The appearance of Persian-style features is quite common in Umayyad architecture of the Levant, and in other aspects of the culture, and has been widely commented on.

Persian-style architecture does occur in Jordan, an area of the Levant with no close natural links with Mesopotamia, and there has been substantial scholarly discussion to explain this phenomenon. Qaṣr Mshattā, Qaṣr Ṭūba, and Qaṣr Kharāna, quite apart from ʿAmmān, all display Persian features. One, perhaps simplistic, explanation of the style of buildings of this period is the suggestion that the Persian features are actual evidence of Persian authorship.

Mshattā, for example, 'has made more ink flow than any other (monument) in Syria',[332] and, although it is now known to be Umayyad, the different attributions discussed earlier this century involved both the Sasanians, in the course of the invasion of Syria by Khusraw Parvīz in AD 614–28, and the Lakhmids, the Arab clients of the Sasanians in al-Ḥīra.[333] Qaṣr Kharāna has also been attributed to the Sasanian invasion.[334] It has also been suggested that a pair of column bases drilled with holes and found in the Hippodrome at Jarash were, in fact, Sasanian polo posts.[335]

However, in the present state of knowledge, there is no conclusive evidence that the Sasanians built anything at all during their fourteen-year occupation of Syria; these datings are the products of 'attribution', not of evidence.

Secondly, a case has been made that the Umayyads, particularly in court life, followed Sasanian ways. Grabar's unpublished thesis concluded that Umayyad ceremonial was based on Sasanian practices.[336] Ettinghausen's study of the Bath Hall of Khirbat al-Mafjar was interested in showing that the hall was intended for Sasanian-style ceremonies, a proposition strongly rejected by the site's excavator, Hamilton.[337]

One might divide the archaeological evidence of forms with eastern parallels into four different types of phenomenon:

i. Import of Movable Artifacts

A hoard of Sasanian, Arab-Sasanian and Umayyad *dirhams*, many of eastern mint, found in Damascus, has been published by al-'Ūsh.[338] In addition, occasional sherds with soft yellow fabric and opaque blue-green glaze have been recovered from Umayyad and earlier deposits in the excavations of Qal'at 'Ammān (a total of three sherds in five seasons of excavations). Part of a blue-green glazed jar of probable Late Sasanian date was recovered by the excavations of Zayadine, Najjar and Greene on the Lower Terrace, from Byzantine-Umayyad levels.[339] No doubt these represent evidence of imports from Iraq. Some predated the Conquest. Apart from these there are no parallels between Umayyad pottery from the Qal'a and Iraqi types from the Umayyad period, although the Umayyad pottery of Iraq is hardly well known.[340] Excavators of reliably dated Umayyad deposits at other sites in Jordan and Palestine have not so far reported evidence of pottery with similar eastern parallels. As matters stand, there is relatively little evidence for this category, though more will no doubt emerge in the future.

ii. Conscription of Workmen

Conscription of workmen and craftsmen from other provinces of the Caliphate for building projects was a widespread practice. The practice is known particularly from the rebuilding of the Mosque of the Prophet in Madīna in 88–90/707–9, when according to Balādhurī, Rūmīs and Copts were brought in for the work but in Ṭabarī and other versions workmen and materials were demanded of the Byzantine emperor.[341] Ibn al-Zubayr is also stated in the *Kitāb al-Aghānī* to have employed Persian craftsmen in rebuilding the Ka'ba in 65/684.[342]

Archaeological evidence is to be found at Qaṣr Kharāna, if we assume here that Kharāna is of Umayyad date, as now seems fairly certain.[343] The technique of construction is alien to Jordanian practice: the rubble masonry is built in lifts of *c.*0.5m, and is mortared with a gypsum, not a lime, mortar. Engaged colonnettes and base plaster are included in the mortaring. This technique is comparable with Ukhayḍir. The decoration is all derived from Sasanian styles.[344] These points suggest that the builders came from Iraq, and were working in their own tradition.

Nevertheless, the plan is more typical of the Umayyad *quṣūr* of the Levant: it does not use *īwān* architecture, but the Syrian '*bayt*', while the doors have lintels and stilted, round relieving arches in the Syrian style.[345]

Kharāna thus represents precisely the reverse situation to that in 'Ammān: Kharāna has alien construction and local design, while 'Ammān has local construction and alien design.

iii. Import of Technique and Motif

According to Hamilton, the use of carved stucco in late Umayyad architectural decoration, at Khirbat al-Mafjar and Qaṣr al-Ḥayr al-Gharbī, can be regarded as the product of Syrian craftsmen who learnt from Iraqi masters.[346] The sites of Qaṣr al-Ḥallabāt[347] and Ruṣāfa[348] could be added to the list of sites with late Umayyad stuccoes.

The non-figural and animal repertoire and style in Umayyad Syrian stucco-work has many points of comparison with contemporary Iraqi stuccoes at Tulūl al-Ukhayḍir[349] and Shu'ayba,[350] and late Sasanian stuccoes at Ctesiphon,[351] Chal Tarkhan[352] and Damghan,[353] but the human figures do not (excepting figures in Persian dress).

The adoption of motives only, appears in the mosaics of the Qubbat al-Sakhra,[354] Muwaqqar (half-palmettes),[355] the facade of Mshattā (gryphons, palmette and bead borders),[356] Qaṣr Ṭūba,[357] and al-Qasṭal (palmettes and braid border).[358] Use of the baked-brick vault at Qaṣr al-Ḥayr al-Sharqī, Mshattā, and Qaṣr Ṭūba may have a Mesopotamian origin.[359]

In these examples either technique or decorative motives would appear to have been taken up by Syrians in the construction trade, as part of the cultural interchange of the Umayyad period that followed the abolition of the border between Syria and Iraq at the time of the Conquest.

iv. Deliberate Persianizing Styles

There are several examples where a conscious attempt

appears to have been made to give a Persian appearance. One can note particularly the stucco figure of the prince from the gate of the Bath Hall at Khirbat al-Mafjar. The figure is dressed in a long Persian coat edged with a border of pierced beads, and baggy trousers.[360] Hamilton sees the stuccoes as made by Syrian craftsmen.[361] A similar figure from Qaṣr al-Ḥayr al-Gharbī, also probably placed over the entrance, is dressed in another variety of Persian coat.[362] In both these cases the prince deliberately presents himself in Persian costume. Elsewhere at Mafjar the figures are dressed in various styles of costume, including Persian.[363] At Qaṣral-Ḥayr al-Gharbī there is also a pair of floor-paintings, one suggested to be in Byzantine, and the other in Persian style.[364] In this case the pairing illustrates a deliberate contrast between eastern and western styles.

There is no evidence to indicate that any of these examples were executed by Iraqi or Iranian craftsmen, and this is an important point in showing that a Persian appearance was desired. These examples would be evidence of a fashion for things Persian among the Umayyad elite.

If we attempt to place 'Ammān in one of these categories, we may note that no evidence has been identified, from the construction of the palace, or from the remainder of the Umayyad citadel, to suggest that the builders were other than local people. There is positive evidence that some at least were from the city. The construction of the Umayyad fortifications is remarkably similar to the Roman wall, while the latrine type of the North Building is a local one. And many other features are consistent with the idea of local craftsmen.

One might however speculate on the possibility of imported workmen on the grounds that the construction of the Qal'a was a big project. In the Late Umayyad period, there was an enormous quantity of construction activity in the area of 'Ammān, and there may have been a shortage of skilled labour.

Nevertheless, where a deliberate image is appropriate, that is, in the ground-plan of the two halls, their architectural detail and decoration, the parallels are entirely with the architecture and decoration of the Sasanian and post-Sasanian tradition. There are several features where this point comes over strongly. 'Ammān is so far the only unambiguous use of *īwān* architecture in Umayyad buildings of the Levant, *īwān*s being found in both halls, and the residential units, but not in the houses of the residential settlement (fig.166).

Secondly, the relief decoration of the Reception Hall: it is unusual to find that the motives can be attributed almost entirely to eastern, mainly stucco, resources. Even the commonest of Roman-Byzantine motives, the acanthus, is missing, while another common Roman motif, the vine, is done in the Sasanian, not the local, style.

At the Umayyad sites of the Qubbat al-Sakhra, Qaṣr al-Hallabat, Qaṣr al-Ḥayr al-Gharbī, Khirbat al-Mafjar and Qaṣr Mshattā, all having extensive decorations, a mix of Roman and Sasanian derived motives is to be found; this situation was obviously common in Umayyad Syria. It is difficult to believe that the craftsmen at 'Ammān would have used a pure eastern scheme of decoration without instruction from the patron.

One may speculate that it was precisely because of a shortage of skilled labour, and the fact that the best architects were reserved for the Caliph's projects, that we find a more simple and less well-integrated approach to Persian themes of decoration than is to be found at, say, Mafjar or Mshattā. This simpler approach, of course, makes the evidence easier to analyse.

Lastly, the question of the so-called 'squinches' is important: the outline of a typically Sasanian squinch has been carved on the masonry, but structurally the transition to the semi-dome is not a squinch at all, but a gradual rounding of the masonry. It was obviously the image of a Persian squinch that was required, but the craftsmen did not know how to build the real thing.

One could suggest other points where something similar may have happened, but the picture is not so clear-cut. It was proposed earlier that a cross-in-square seems to be used to depict a four-*īwān* plan in the Reception Hall; the result is a rather impractical main hall, open to the winter. In the decoration, motives normally found in stucco are here carved in stone.

The obvious conclusion is that Persian imagery was important to the patron, but the craftsmen available were not fully conversant with the appropriate techniques. The craftsmen produced the right impression where image was important, but in the remainder of the citadel worked in their normal fashion. The fact that the palace is not such a fine piece of architecture as Khirbat al-Mafjar or Mshattā helps to make this point clear. The palace could be described as the equivalent in architectural terms of the prince in Persian costume from the Bath Hall at Mafjar.

b. Literary Evidence

Before turning to the literary evidence that might provide an explanation of a Persianizing phenomenon, there are several preliminary points to be made.

As rulers of the Caliphate – administrators, soldiers, and recipients of provincial tax revenues – the Arabs of Umayyad Syria were in a better position to remain close to the cultural traditions that they entered Islam with than were Arabs who settled elsewhere. The cultural assimilation which it is now agreed that the Arabs in Iran underwent, did not necessarily apply in Syria. Furthermore, Syria, though part of the Near Eastern cultural sphere, had been under Hellenistic influence for 900 years, since the conquest of Alexander the Great.

Nevertheless, in the long term a revival of Persian culture under Islam was inevitable. The Sasanian empire, one of the major empires of its time, and itself heir to the traditions of the Mesopotamian empires, had been completely absorbed into the territories of the Caliphate. A culture of that kind could not be totally extinguished, and later on, of course, Iranian culture came to have a dominant position in the Islamic world. By the 3rd/9th and 4th/10th centuries Iranian successor states were already laying claim to a revival of Persian kingship.[365] But the Umayyad period saw only the very beginnings of this process.

The extent to which Persianizing did take place can be assessed under four different headings: the circumstances of the court circles, the Syrian governors and soldiers who went to the East, the contacts of the construction industry, as they appear in the archaeological evidence, and trade. It is not possible to deal here with the question of trade, as the appropriate primary investigation of what evidence that there might be has never been made, though the earlier discussion of eastern imported artifacts suggests that the evidence is limited.

Considerable numbers of Syrians went to the East as governors and soldiers. The governor of Iraq was usually a Syrian from the time of al-Ḥajjāj ibn Yūsuf onwards (75/694), and there was a Syrian garrison at Wāsiṭ. There were Syrians in the army of Khurāsān.[366]

Some of the Syrians who went to the East stayed there, but some must have returned to Syria. Two figures who played a part in the history of the Balqā' at the end of the Umayyad period had seen service in the East and returned: Yūsuf ibn 'Umar al-Thaqafī, governor of Iraq and its dependencies (120/738–126/744), maintained a house in the Balqā', which he fled back to on his dismissal, and Ḥabīb ibn Murra al-Marrī, who may have been in Khurāsān, rebelled against the 'Abbāsids in 132/750.[367] The Arabs of the 'Abbāsid Khurāsāniyya, recruited from long-term residents of Khurāsān, spoke Persian,[368] and may have taken up other Persian habits;[369] similarly, governors and officials who returned to Syria may have received a more lim-ited degree of Persian acculturation.

Banī Umayya themselves were in a different situation: relatively few were appointed to the East. From the time of 'Abd al-Malik onwards only Bishr ibn Marwān[370] and Maslama ibn 'Abd al-Malik (102/720)[371] were governors of Iraq. Rather, the court circles were faced with a transition from a form of state that resembled a tribal chieftainship in the time of Mu'āwiya, to a sophisticated Near Eastern state – a transition that was finally completed by the 'Abbāsids. It was inevitable that some of the accoutrements of state should have derived from the traditions of Sasanian kingship, heir as it was to a long tradition of Near Eastern monarchy, and that these borrowings should be accompanied by additional fashionable trivia. But in fact the evidence is not so extensive as one might imagine.

The key figure among the Umayyads is the Caliph Walīd ibn Yazīd (125/743–126/744), who was accounted a libertine, and might have been expected to take to extremes any Persianizing tendency at the Umayyad court.[372] Apart from the archaeological evidence – particularly Khirbat al-Mafjar, assuming that it is correctly attributed to Walīd[373] – the record is, however, slim. While Walīd, according to the 4th/10th century *Kitāb al-Aghānī*, lived a life of ostentatious luxury, the only specifically Persian traits are said to be the occasional Persian phrase, for example *Haft hafteh*[374] and the wearing of the *qalansuwa ṭawīla*.[375] Yet Walīd was renowned for his connoisseurship and composition of poetry, his years spent in the desert, his devotion to hunting, parties and drinking, and his entertainment of pilgrims returning from the *Ḥajj* at Zīzā': in all these activities he seems to have taken to extremes what one might have expected of a sophisticated Arab gentleman.

The record of his predecessor, Hishām ibn 'Abd al-Malik (105/724–125/743), is similar, if more sober. Gibb observes that Hisham had an interest in the methods of administration of empire.[376] Mas'ūdī claims to have seen a translation made for Hishām of the histories of the Kings of Persia – presumably a version of the Persian national epic that resulted in the *Shāhnāmeh* of Firdawsī – and other Persian books.[377] This was balanced by a translation of the supposed epistles of Aristotle to Alexander.[378]

But on another occasion the poet Ismaīl ibn Yāsār, who prided himself on his Persian descent, was thrown into a fountain and banished to the Ḥijāz, for reciting verses which praised the Persians;[379] a second version attributes the punishment to Walīd ibn Yazīd.[380] The successor of Walīd, Yazīd ibn Walīd (126/744), whose mother had a Sasanian genealogy, composed a couplet which appears in his obituary in Ṭabarī: 'I am the son of Kisrā, and my father is Marwān; Caesar is one grandfather, and the other Khāqān'. Note that there is no accented claim to Sasanian descent, but rather one of a cosmopolitan quality.[381] The tone is rather similar to the painting of the Six Kings at Quṣayr 'Amra.[382] The Sasanians were only one among the fore-runners of the Umayyads.

Lastly, the role of 'Abd al-Ḥamīd ibn Yaḥyā is

important. 'Abd al-Ḥamīd, the chief secretary *(kātib)* of Marwān ibn Muḥammad, the last Umayyad Caliph (126/744 – 132/750), was a *mawlā*, and probably a native of al-Anbār in Iraq.[383] 'Abd al-Ḥamīd extracted from the Persian tongue the modes of secretarial composition which he illustrated and transposed into the Arabic tongue',[384] and might have been expected to be a Persianizing influence on the Umayyads. Of his six surviving epistles, the *risāla* to the *kuttāb* opens with the statement that men are divided into classes, a remark reminiscent of the hierarchical structure of Sasanian society, and continues with a series of maxims on secretaryship that have been described by Gibb as related to those of the Iranian *dibhers*.[385] But the *risāla* to 'Abdallah, the son of Marwān ibn Muḥammad, composed for the occasion of his departure on campaign against Ḍaḥḥāk ibn Qays al-Shaybānī, but dated a year later (129/746–7), and the only contemporary account of Umayyad princely behaviour, has no reminiscences of Sasanian kingship, but is a straightforward account of personal behaviour, choice and treatment of the retinue, and dwells on behaviour in the *majlis* (the audience). The second half of the *risāla* is devoted to military organization and tactics, and this section has a flavour of Romano-Byzantine military manuals. The Umayyads themselves were probably less interested in the traditions of the Sasanian empire than their secretaries.

The impression left by the literary evidence, as by the majority of the archaeological evidence, is that the Umayyads borrowed from the Sasanian, and the Roman-Byzantine traditions, equally. In the case of the literary evidence one must remember that Persianizing literature, and the translations from the Pahlevī which were produced early in the 'Abbāsid period, have nearly all failed to survive,[386] but the surviving epistles of 'Abd al-Ḥamīd ibn Yaḥyā are a good indicator of attitudes. It is in fact archaeological evidence, the stucco statues in Persian costume from Khirbat al-Mafjar and Qaṣr al-Ḥayr al-Gharbī, and the 'Ammān palace, that are sug gestive of more deliberate Persianizing fashions. Nevertheless, it is clear from this limited evidence that Persianizing was only an incipient phenomenon, preparatory to the much greater influence of Iran upon Islam in later times.

8

THE FORTIFICATIONS

by Jason Wood

The existence of a prominent, isolated and steep-sided hill provided the first settlers of 'Ammān with a strong, natural defensive position. Consequently, as part of the sequence of occupation and development of 'Ammān the Citadel has borne witness to a long history of fortification.

The earliest defences identified belong to the end of the Middle Bronze Age. In 1969, sondages excavated by Dornemann, immediately north of the Northern Temple platform of the Upper Citadel, revealed the intersecting stone foundations of two Middle Bronze Age walls laid directly on a ledge in the bedrock. The acute angle between these walls led Dornemann to suggest the likelihood of a fort or gateway at this point,[1] though the solution favoured by Zayadine of a junction between a lower city wall and a citadel fortification cannot be ruled out.[2] Some further evidence indicates that the Middle Bronze Age defences in this area were curved, and lay partly within the line of the west platform wall of the Northern Temple.[3] Recent excavations by Humbert have also revealed traces of a Middle Bronze Age wall immediately outside the line of the south wall of the Lower Citadel.[4] If this wall belonged to the same circuit as that excavated further north, then its discovery gives some idea of the size of the defended area at this date.

Dornemann also identified two phases of a curved Iron Age wall lying beyond the line of the Middle Bronze Age wall outside the northwest corner of the Northern Temple platform. Excavations in 1969 indicated that a Phase 1 buttressed wall was built either directly on bedrock, or cut into or built up against the Middle Bronze Age defences. The addition, in Phase 2, of a wall built at right-angles to the curtain might be part of an external projecting tower or gateway, or might possibly be evidence for a casemated fortification.[5] A further stretch of Iron Age wall was located by Zayadine during excavations in 1968 and 1972–3 outside the southeast corner of the Lower Citadel.[6] If this wall was linked to that identified further north, then this might be evidence for a slightly increased fortified area in the Iron Age. It was in this period, in the 10th century BC, that 'Ammān was besieged by David.[7]

Two phases of a Hellenistic wall were identified by Zayadine in his excavations outside the southeast corner of the Lower Citadel.[8] In addition, a possible tower of Early Roman date, which, if correctly interpreted, would have formed part of the Hellenistic circuit, is discussed below in Chapter 10. Elsewhere, all that can be said is that the Hellenistic fortification probably lay outside the line of the later walls, although Dornemann believes that some of the lowest courses of the west platform wall of the Northern Temple are of pre-Roman construction.[9] It would have been the Hellenistic wall that came under attack in *c.*218 BC when the Citadel was besieged by the Seleucid, Antiochus III.

Parts of the system of fortifications which form the present wall-line were visible to the early visitors and survey expeditions. By general agreement the 'Acropolis' was attributed to the Roman period, including the fortifications.[10] Butler recognized some medieval rebuilding in the south wall, but described the northern section (which is actually the platform of the Northern Temple) as 'one of the finest examples of ancient fortifications in existence'.[11] Textual evidence also implies the existence of Roman defences. As has already been remarked upon in Chapter 5, Ammianus Marcellinus, writing *c.* AD 380, said that Philadelphia, Bostra and Gerasa were 'large and well-fortified with walls'.[12] Until recently, therefore, a Roman date for the extant Citadel fortifications has been the accepted opinion.[13]

In 1976, excavations across the line of the west wall in Area C indicated an Umayyad date for the wall's construction.[14] This was an important discovery as no other urban fortifications of this period are known. The suggestion of an Umayyad fortification wall also helps explain a *qasīda* of the Umayyad poet al-Aḥwas al-Anṣārī (d.86/705), which refers to *Ḥiṣn 'Ammān*, that is, 'the fort (or castle) of 'Ammān '.[15] In 1979, the well-preserved plan of a Roman gate in the south wall was uncovered. It appeared to have belonged to the *temenos* of the so-called Temple of Hercules. An assessment of the *temenos* was essential to an improved understanding of the sequence of the fortifications, and in 1981 the area was further examined by clearance and excavation.[16] Work that year also involved detailed architectural analysis of the visible remains of the entire fortification wall circuit and incorporated structures, together with the production of survey drawings of most of the surviving wall elevations and sections based largely on rectified photography.[17] The results of the excavations and the information gained from the architectural survey form the basis of the present study.

LAYOUT AND SEQUENCE OF THE FORTIFICATIONS

The fortifications surround two sections of the tripartite division of the L-shaped plateau known as the Jabal al-Qal'a, that is, the Upper and Lower Terraces of the Citadel, but not the easternmost arm now occupied by houses. The total circuit is approximately 1680m. In addition, there is a cross-wall, 144.50m long, dividing the two terraces.

The fortifications were divided, for the purposes of analysis, into 26 sectors of curtain wall, which differ in line and/or construction. Eleven towers (including gate-towers) and three gates could be identified or implied from constructional features. The scheme is presented in fig.79. Sectors are numbered anti-clockwise around the circuit, starting from the southeast corner of the Northern Temple enclosure. Towers and gates are identified alphabetically, the towers (with the exception of Tower B) being labelled anti-clockwise, but separately around the Upper and Lower Terraces. Where long sectors are sub-divided by towers or numbered buttresses, individual stretches of curtain wall are distinguished by adding to the sector number the suffix a, b, c, etc.

In view of the complexities of the wall circuit, the fortifications will be described in order by sector, gate and tower, including, where applicable, the evidence for local structural sequence and archaeological dating. An overall sequence and dating will then be offered. Finally, the character of the fortifications will be compared to other sites in the Near and Middle East in an attempt to assess their place in the development of Roman and Islamic fortification. A catalogue of reused architectural fragments found in the walls is also appended (Appendix B).

Although it is possible that one or more periods of construction have escaped notice, it is proposed that the following sequence can account for the present-day condition of the walls:

Period 1 *(Roman pre-fortification)*: The platform and double enclosure of the Northern Temple, and other Roman structures of the 1st and 2nd century AD, all of which pre-date the fortifications.

Period 2 *(Roman Wall)*: The *temenos* of the Temple of Hercules and a Roman curtain wall, which were built together at a point between AD 161 and 166, or a little later.

Period 3 *(Umayyad Wall)*: A new Umayyad fortification wall, incorporating sections of Roman date (Periods 1 and 2), built at the same time as the Umayyad palace, *c.*117/735 (plus or minus ten years).

Period 4 *('Abbāsid restoration)*: Restoration of the Umayyad wall in the early 'Abbāsid period, probably following the earthquake of 130/747–8.

Period 5 *('Abbāsid destruction)*: Destruction of the Umayyad wall during the 'Abbāsid period at some date in the 3rd/9th century.

Period 6 *(Ayyūbid Tower)*: Erection of Tower B as an Ayyūbid watch-tower at the beginning of the 7th/13th century.

Description

1. PLATFORM AND TEMENOS OF THE NORTHERN TEMPLE (UPPER CITADEL)

Tower A (fig.81, pls 31a, 37)

This interesting structure in the southeast corner of the double enclosure was probably excavated by the Italian Mission in the 1930s.[18]

PERIOD 1 (ROMAN PRE-FORTIFICATION): TEMENOS CORNER ?TOWER. The building is an approximate square of 8.25 × 7.90m. The east and south walls are 0.9m wide, of plain-dressed limestone ashlars, and belong to the respective sections of the *temenos* enclosure. The north wall has nine courses of smaller ashlars averaging 0.95 × 0.62 × 0.70m and stands to a height of 4.75m. In the wall is a doorway 1.76m high and 1.05m wide, with a relieving arch of three voussoirs above a flat stone lintel. In the east wall there are three springers, 0.60m wide, for transverse arches to carry a roof or second floor. Assuming that the structure in this first period had similar dimensions as in the later period, this roof or second floor would have stood at a height of *c.*6.5m above the enclosure surface. While it is possible that the structure was simply a corner room of the *temenos*, its similarity to Tower C at the southwest corner, apparently in origin a corner tower of the *temenos*, would suggest that it too was a tower and had had more than one storey. The ground floor was subsequently divided into two by the addition of a wooden floor, whose joist holes are visible in the east wall.

PERIOD 3 (UMAYYAD WALL): FORTIFICATION TOWER. The Period 1 structure was rebuilt with a new west wall, 1.1m thick, of larger ashlars. This wall bonds with Building 6 of the Umayyad palace. A fill of earth and masonry blocks was put into the base of the tower, and a paving of limestone flags and grey lime mortar was laid at least 3.3m higher than the former enclosure surface, at about the same level as the earlier joist holes. The doorway in the north wall, though open today, was presumably blocked, and an additional width of walling built onto the north side, probably to carry the vault of Room 67 (Building 6). It would seem that the Period 1 structure was in a ruinous or dangerous condition when it was rebuilt. The rebuilding occurred at the same time as the construction of the Umayyad palace, but there is no direct communication with the palace, and the rebuilding is best interpreted as being for a wall-tower.

Sector 1 (pl.38a)

Length 80m. The inside face has been excavated, while the external facade is only partially cleared.

PERIOD 1 (ROMAN PRE-FORTIFICATION): TEMENOS WALL. A 0.9m wide wall forming the east side of the southern enclosure. The wall is built of smooth-dressed limestone ashlars with dimensions of 1.30 × 0.65 × 0.35m and 0.55 × 0.50 × 0.90m The inside face survives to a maximum height of 2.45m, and is composed of six alternating courses of headers and stretchers. The headers penetrate the full width of the wall, while the stretcher courses are two blocks thick. Traces of what is probably part of a buttress survive at the external corner with Sector 2.

Sector 2 (pl.38b)

Length 14.5m. The external face is partly buried below spoil from the excavations of the Italian Mission.

PERIOD 1 (ROMAN PRE-FORTIFICATION): PLATFORM AND TEMENOS WALL. The wall is visible to a maximum height of 4.8m, of which the upper three surviving courses belong to the superstructure of the northeast angle of the southern enclosure. This upper part of the wall is 1.5m thick and built of smooth-dressed ashlars. The remainder is of rusticated ashlars 0.80 × 0.60 x ?m and belongs to the platform on which this part of the *temenos* wall was built. A photograph taken by Garstang of the re-entrant angle in the 1920s, before the dumping of excavation spoil, shows a doorway in the face of the platform wall, presumably a postern (pl.38b).[19] The exterior corner with Sector 1 is strengthened with a buttress 8.85m long, projecting 0.45m. Although there is no evidence for anything other than a room (E5) inside this corner,[20] one may speculate that it was the site of a tower similar to Tower A.

Sector 3

Length *c.*52m. A section of wall almost entirely covered by spoil from the excavations of the Italian Mission.

PERIOD 1 (ROMAN PRE-FORTIFICATION): PLATFORM AND TEMENOS WALL. At the southern end of the wall, close to the return of Sector 2, are seven courses of ashlars with dimensions 1.05 × 0.60 × 0.55m, surviving to a maximum height of 1.9m. The wall forms the east side of the northern enclosure.

Sector 4 (pl.39)

Length 101m. The accumulation of deposits against the

external facade was cleared down to bedrock by the Department of Antiquities in 1968, permitting a view of the full height of the surviving wall. The base of the eastern end, however, is partly obscured by earth and rubble derived from modern road construction.[21]

PERIOD 1 (ROMAN PRE-FORTIFICATION): PLATFORM WALL. The north side of the northern enclosure, 1.85m wide. The wall was founded directly on bedrock and straddles the convex profile which the bedrock displays at this point. The wall thus attained its greatest height at each end. Of the surviving courses, 22 are visible to a height of 13.5m at the east end, 10 to a height of 5.5m in the centre, and 23 to about 13.8m at the west end. Much of the facade is constructed of rusticated ashlars laid in header/stretcher fashion with dimensions of 0.65 × 0.45–0.62 × 0.95m, the largest blocks being 1.30–1.50 × 0.62 × ?m. The wall has a pronounced batter, each course being recessed *c.*50mm from the one below, while the blocks themselves are cut with drafted margins, 60–80mm wide, the embossed part of the face projecting by the same dimensions. The upper courses of the wall have largely fallen away, exposing core-work behind. However, in some places at the top of the surviving facade, there appear to be up to five courses of vertical, smooth-dressed ashlars, characteristic of *opus quadratum* construction. The height of these courses is either 0.5 or 0.7m. No traces of mortar or clay could be found in the joints between any of the masonry blocks. The corners of the wall at both ends are strengthened with buttresses; the eastern buttress base being 10.2 × 0.6m, the western 10.95 × 1m. The western buttress is placed square to the line of Sector 5 and has a pronounced batter with an angle of 80–85°. It is likely that these two buttresses carried towers similar to Tower A, but no evidence survives on the ground today.[22]

PERIOD 3 (UMAYYAD WALL): FORTIFICATION WALL. There are traces of grey lime plaster pointing within the joints of the Period 1 masonry. The same plaster was used in the construction of the Umayyad palace.

Sector 5 (pl.40a)

Length 57.3m. The outside line of the wall has been cleared to its base, partly exposing its foundation.[23]

PERIOD 1 (ROMAN PRE-FORTIFICATION): PLATFORM WALL. The wall forms part of the western perimeter of the double enclosure. A foundation of small fragments of flint rubble (0.15 × 0.15 × ?m), set in brown earth, is visible in places to a depth of 0.6m. The superstructure is 1.9m or more wide, and displays the same constructional features as Sector 4, being built mostly of rusticated limestone ashlars with dimensions of 0.80–1.05 × 0.60 × ?m and 1.15 × 0.37 × ?m. Above the battered facade, there appear to be a few courses of vertical *opus quadratum* masonry. The exterior corner with Sector 4 is strengthened with a buttress which measures 10.9 × 1.3m at its base and survives to a maximum height of 13.8m. A photograph taken in the 1870s shows a possible Period 1 wall outside the line of Sector 5, which may have supported a staircase leading up to a supposed western gate to the double enclosure, in the position now occupied by part of Sector 6.[24]

PERIOD 4 ('ABBĀSID RESTORATION): REVETMENT. Two short stretches of a sloping glacis-like revetment survive to a maximum height of 3.5m; they are each 0.6m wide and slope at an angle of 80°. There is an offset ledge 0.2m wide above a stepped base 0.4m high. The revetment is constructed of small limestone and flint rubble, heavily snecked with smaller stones and set in *terra rossa*. The face is coated with a grey lime plaster, studded with pieces of chalk.

Sector 6 (fig.34)

Length 32.5m, but only visible for 13.7m. The southern end of the wall is concealed below steps built *c.*1958, but since semi-demolished and denuded of their masonry facing.[25]

PERIOD 3 (UMAYYAD WALL): FORTIFICATION WALL. Sector 5 ends in a vertical straight joint. Of Sector 6, a maximum of seven courses survive to a height of 3.1m. The wall-face is constructed of uneven limestone blocks, probably reused ashlars, and snecked with small stones. The blocks are of various sizes (1.05 × 0.60 × ?m and 0.50 × 0.37 × ?m) and form a facade, 0.9m deep, fronting a rubble core. On the south side of the modern steps, there is a projecting buttress that measures 2.5 × 1m. Sector 6 is certainly a later insert on the line of the western perimeter wall of the double enclosure, and probably covers the site of a Period 1 gateway to the southern enclosure.

Sector 7 (pl.40b)

Length 41.75m.[26]

PERIOD 1 (ROMAN PRE-FORTIFICATION): TEMENOS WALL. A wall of smooth-dressed ashlar masonry, with a maximum of nine courses visible, standing to a height of 5.3m. The ashlars are well laid in alternating horizontal courses of headers and stretchers, as in Sector 1. The blocks are of large dimension (1.40 × 0.65 × 0.45m and 1 × 0.60 × ?m) and form a facade, 0.8m deep, fronting a rubble core.

PERIOD 3 (UMAYYAD WALL): FORTIFICATION WALL. Traces of grey lime plaster are found on the face of the Period 1 wall.

Gate A (figs 82–3; pl.41)

The gate was partially excavated by the Italian Mission in 1933.[27] In addition, the outside line has since been cleared well below the original external surfaces of the gate. The gate consists of a single passageway flanked by two towers of different periods, Towers C and D, described below.[28]

PERIOD 3 (UMAYYAD WALL): FORTIFICATION GATE STRUCTURE. The structure of the gate arch is bonded into the fourth course of the rebuilt south wall of Tower C. The gate itself has a single passage- way 2.3m wide, set back 2.6m from the tower facades. It is built of rather irregular soft limestone blocks and provided with door-jambs which survive about one metre above the threshold. A foundation of rubble and *terra rossa* is visible to a depth of 0.8m. Just outside the threshold, a contemporary surface was detected at a level 1.2m above the proposed original Period 1 external surface.

Tower C

PERIOD 1 (ROMAN PRE-FORTIFICATION): TEMENOS CORNER TOWER. Tower C is a square tower at the southwest corner of the double enclosure. The tower measures 8.55 × 8.40m and projects 0.7m from Sector 7, with which it bonds. The facade or west wall is 1.65m wide, while the remaining walls vary between 0.9 and 1.25m in thickness. The walls are constructed of plain-dressed limestone ashlars (1.37 × 0.65 × ?m and 0.62 × 0.42 × ?m), but the two lowest courses of the facade are of rusticated masonry. The facade is visible for a height of ten courses (*c*.5.4m). Above the fourth course there is an offset ledge, 0.3m wide, found only at the southwest corner. The original external surface was probably at this level. In the rear or east wall there is a doorway and two of the original three springers, 0.6m wide, for transverse arches to carry a roof or second floor across an internal room. Within the room are traces of a secondary partition wall.

PERIOD 3 (UMAYYAD WALL): FORTIFICATION GATE-TOWER. It is apparent from an examination of the surviving masonry that the south wall of Tower C was given a new facing at the time when the gate structure itself was built. Much of this refacing on the west side has collapsed.

Tower D

PERIOD 3 (UMAYYAD WALL): FORTIFICATION GATE-TOWER. Tower D is bonded with the gate structure and appears to be contemporary. The tower, most of the rear line of which is unexcavated, may be an approximate square measuring 6.1 × 5.5m, or a trapezoid, if the line of the south wall, as appears from its projection (1.85m), was built square to Sector 8. A foundation of large rubble and *terra rossa* is visible. Above this, five courses of the facade survive to a height of 2.6m. The facade is composed of dressed limestone blocks (1.27 × 0.50 × ?m and 0.65 × 0.55 × ?m), of which two and a half courses originally lay below the Period 3 ground surface.

2. THE WEST WALL (UPPER CITADEL)

Sector 8 (figs 84–5; pls 42–44a)

Length 115.5m. A straight wall linking Tower D of Gate A with Tower E. The external face has been cleared along its entire length, with the exception of a spoil dump from building operations in the centre. The wall was excavated on both sides in 1976 and 1978 (Area C, Trenches C0, C1, C10 and C11).[29]

PERIOD 2: CURTAIN WALL. At the northern end of the sector (8a), traces of a wall of regular soft limestone blocks (0.70 × 0.35 × ?m) are visible in the core of the later Period 3 wall. In Period 3, this earlier curtain was presumably a denuded stump and was refaced with less regular blocks. In Area C, the sector shows evidence for only one period of curtain-wall building, that of the later Period 3.

PERIOD 3 (UMAYYAD WALL): FORTIFICATION WALL. In Area C (fig.86), a 3.8m length of the inner foundations was exposed to a depth of 2.4m. A foundation trench had been cut into a levelling fill (Stratum VI), but without demolishing earlier Stratum VIII walls, which project into the trench. The trench was packed with *terra rossa* and random rubble of hard and soft limestone, with some flint. The largest fragments (0.50 × 0.20 × ?m) tended to be concentrated towards the base of the foundations, where the stones appeared to be more compacted and to have less *terra rossa* in between. The foundation of the exterior facade at this point comprised a free-standing wall of rubble, although ashlars of the facade also extend to two courses below their contemporary ground surface. This foundation is 1.5m deep; the difference being made up by a higher contemporary ground surface on the inside. The wall thus acted as a buttress to the levelling fill. Both types of foundation clearly belong to the same project of construction. Elsewhere, a short stretch of foundation is exposed below the external facade to the north of Tower E (8f). It is visible for a length of seven metres and to a maximum depth of 0.6m, and consists of closely packed rubble (mostly flint of various sizes) with some *terra rossa*.

The wall superstructure in Area C is four metres wide. The internal face, which is exposed only in Area

C, consists of an unmortared rubble wall containing four courses of limestone and flint fragments (averaging 0.35 × 0.20 × 0.23) with an unusually large number of snecking stones (pl.44a). There are traces of grey lime plaster studded with pieces of chalk. An offset, 0.3m wide, occurs *c.*0.75m above a contemporary floor surface (Stratum V). The exterior facade of Sector 8 survives to a maximum height of 2.5m, the number of courses visible above the later Period 4 revetment varying between three and six. The facade is built of a mixture of different sizes and styles of limestone blocks, varying widely between one stretch of wall and the next. Some blocks with architectural mouldings are obviously reused, and flint is also employed as facing material in 8c, 8d and 8e. The horizontality of the courses was maintained between blocks of different sizes by using snecking stones. The more regular well-dressed masonry blocks in 8e and 8f required less snecking. The dimensions of these regular blocks (0.65 × 0.40 × 0.40m – though some are as long as 1.15m) suggests the possibility that they are reused facing material from the destroyed Period 2 curtain wall. All of the blocks of the exterior facade are laid without mortar, but there are traces, particularly in 8e and 8f, of grey lime plaster pointing in the joints. Both faces of the wall superstructure front a compact rubble core, the external facade being a maximum of two blocks (1.2m) thick in Area C. The core consists mainly of undressed limestone, together with some architectural fragments, set in *terra rossa*, but it also contains a higher preponderance of flint than the facings.

There are five rectangular buttresses on the exterior facade, on average 14.54m apart, 6m long and projecting 0.77m from the wall-face (pl.43b). They are all bonded into the wall to an average depth of 0.35m, and display a markedly similar style of construction to that of the curtain.

PERIOD 4 ('ABBĀSID RESTORATION): REBUILT BUTTRESSES AND REVETMENT. The first two Period 3 buttresses adjacent to Gate A were rebuilt with a new sloping facade (*c.*70°) and a stepped base (0.60–0.65m high). Buttress 1 (fig.87; pl.42a) measures 8.60 × 1.75–2.10m, while Buttress 2 (fig.88; pl.42b) is slightly smaller at 8.35 × 1.8–1.9m. Each has a foundation of compact flint rubble, capped by an offset 0.1m wide. The sloping facades, of which six courses survive, are built of soft limestone and flint rubble, snecked with small stones and fragments of tile. Dressed soft limestone blocks (0.60 × 0.30 × 0.28m and 0.60 × 0.55 × 0.50m) strengthen the corners of the bases. There are traces of a grey lime plaster coating.

Subsequent to the rebuild of the two buttresses was the addition of a sloping revetment to the front face of the curtain wall (and also Buttress 4). This is best preserved in 8b and 8e, and survives to a maximum height of 1.25m and an average width of 0.68m. The revetment has a curved profile, with an angle varying between 50° and 80°. Its appearance is similar to that of the rebuilt buttresses in that it is constructed of snecked flint and limestone rubble (averaging 0.30 × 0.20 × ?m) packed with *terra rossa*. There are also surviving areas of a grey lime plaster coating.

PERIOD 5: DESTRUCTION. In Area C, the wall of a house (Stratum IVb) was built over the inner face of the Period 3 fortification wall, with the implication that the curtain wall had collapsed to its present height by the time the house was built (fig.86).

ARCHAEOLOGICAL DATING. In Area C (figs 86, 89) the construction of the fortification wall (Period 3) is clearly contemporary with the levelling and buildings of Stratum V–VI, which can be dated to the Umayyad period. Period 2 is earlier, but not datable here; it is not certain how it related to the evidence (Stratum VIII) of Byzantine buildings running underneath the Umayyad wall. The subsequent rebuilding of buttresses and provision of revetment (Period 4) is also not dated here, though both constructions share the same external surface as the Umayyad wall. Stratum IVb (Period 5) is dated to the 'Abbāsid/Fāṭimid period (3rd/9th–4th/10th centuries).

Tower E (fig.157; pl.77)

The tower is set askew from the lines of Sectors 8 and 9, from which it projects 0.7m and 3.6m respectively. It was partially excavated in 1977–8 as part of Area D. The inner wall of the tower is concealed by later phases of domestic architecture.[30]

PERIOD 3 (UMAYYAD WALL): FORTIFICATION TOWER. The tower is an approximate square of 6 × ?5.8m, and only survives to its ground-level course, except in the south-east corner where rubble masonry stands to a height of a further one metre. The west and south facades, outside the line of Sector 9, are faced with large limestone ashlars, which, like Tower D, continue for at least two courses below their contemporary ground surface. The remainder of the construction is of unshaped rubble masonry. The west wall, 1.9m wide, is broader than the south wall, which is only one metre wide. On the latter are traces of grey lime plaster studded with pieces of chalk. A section of earth flooring was found within the walls, suggesting that the tower had an internal room. Tower E makes a straight joint with both Sectors 8 and 9 and appears to have been erected prior to the curtain. Nevertheless, the design shows that they are contemporary. The tower wall facing towards Sector 8 (at least,

what can be seen of it) is a rough rubble wall. The south wall has two sorts of facade: a rubble wall butting against Sector 9 and an ashlar facing for the external facade. The tower must, therefore, be Period 3 in origin.
PERIOD 5: DESTRUCTION. The collapse down to Tower E's present height took place before a house was built over it (see Sector 9 description).

Sector 9 (fig.84; pl.44b)

Length 106m. A straight wall linking Tower E with Tower F at the southwest corner of the Citadel. The northern end of the sector was excavated in Area D (fig.157).[31]
PERIOD 3 (UMAYYAD WALL): FORTIFICATION WALL. The construction of the curtain is similar to that of Sector 8, though narrower, being only 2.6m wide. Excavation in Area D revealed a foundation of rubble and *terra rossa*, and an inside face of rubble walling. The exterior facade, a maximum of two blocks (1.2m or more) deep, fronts a core of rubble and *terra rossa*. The facade survives to a maximum height of 2.6m, and is built of a mixture of soft limestone blocks of different sizes, with some flint. Certain blocks are evidently reused, such as those in 9c and 9e whose standard dimensions (0.70 × 0.37 × 0.40m and 0.40 × 0.35 × 0.57m) indicate the possible reuse of facing material from a destroyed Period 2 curtain wall. The horizontality of the courses is maintained by snecking stones, especially in 9b and 9c, while in 9c and 9d, three flat-stone levelling/bonding courses are interspersed with larger header/stretcher type facing. The facade is coated with grey lime plaster, which is well preserved in 9a and 9c.

At least four, and probably five, rectangular buttresses are bonded into the exterior wall-face to an average depth of 0.32m. The buttresses are, on average, 4.95m long and 13.4m apart, with projections varying between 0.2 and 0.7m. As in Sector 8, the appearance of each buttress is generally similar to that of neighbouring stretches of curtain. For instance, Buttress 3 (fig.90) maintains the use of flat-stone levelling/bonding courses that are present in the curtain either side, and also displays a slight offset 50mm wide, which continues through into 9d. Adjacent to Tower E a drain of rectangular cross-section, 0.3 × 0.4m, is built through the wall.
PERIOD 4 ('ABBĀSID RESTORATION): REBUILT BUTTRESS AND REVETMENT. Buttress 1 was rebuilt in a fashion corresponding to the rebuilt buttresses of Sector 8, although here the remains survive only to a height of one metre. Three courses of the new sloping facade (75°) and a stepped base 0.65m high are visible, above a flint rubble foundation, offset by 0.15m. The superstructure is of snecked soft limestone and flint rubble, with a dressed limestone block (0.70 × 0.20 × 0.15m) to strengthen the corner of the base. The buttress measures 7.5 × 1.8–1.9m and was coated with grey lime plaster. Investigation revealed no trace of the original Period 3 buttress face behind, and it may be presumed that the rebuilding was a restoration after a complete collapse.

As in Sector 8, the sloping revetment was added subsequent to the buttress rebuilding. The revetment was built against the curtain and Buttresses 3, 4 and 5, and displays the characteristic curved profile with a varying incline of 60–65°. It is constructed of snecked flint and limestone rubble (averaging 0.30 × 0.15 × 0.15m) set in *terra rossa* and coated with grey lime plaster. In Sector 9 it attains a maximum height of 1.10m and an average width of 0.79m. At the exit point of the drain adjacent to Tower E, an extension channel was built into the structure of the revetment.
PERIOD 5: DESTRUCTION. Excavations in Area D (fig. 157) showed that a building had been added to the rear face of the Period 3 fortification wall and that the drain adjacent to Tower E had been redirected. The wall was the destroyed or collapsed down to its surviving height before a house with three major phases of construction was erected over the wall and Tower E.
ARCHAEOLOGICAL DATING. Pottery from the make-up of the earliest form of the Period 5 house, although scant, is suggested to date to the end of the 3rd/9th century. It follows that the destruction of the fortification wall took place in the 'Abbāsid period in the 3rd/9th century, or possibly at the end of the 2nd/8th.

Tower F

Unexcavated foundation platform at the southwest corner of the Citadel.
PERIOD 3 (UMAYYAD WALL): FORTIFICATION TOWER. Only the west side of the foundation platform is visible, with a measurable length of 5.8m projecting 1.4m from the face of Sector 9. Three courses of large soft limestone blocks can be seen, the largest being 1.10 × 0.20 × 0.55m.

3. THE SOUTH WALL (UPPER CITADEL)

Gate B

No remains survive. Exact position of gate uncertain.
PERIOD 3 (UMAYYAD WALL): FORTIFICATION GATE. The known alignment of a Period 3 street is good evidence for the existence of a gate in the southwest corner of the Citadel at the extreme western end of Sector 10. However, the street may have had a predecessor on the same

alignment and, therefore, it is possible that such a gate owed its origin to an earlier period.

Sector 10

Length uncertain.

PERIOD 3 (UMAYYAD WALL): FORTIFICATION WALL. A length of only 2.5m of the external facing, standing to a maximum height of 1.5m, is exposed, but a section through the wall is visible, four metres or more wide. Two courses of the facade survive above a foundation offset 0.2m wide. The facing material is composed of soft limestone blocks, the largest being 1.15 × 1.05 × 0.30m. Included in a number of fallen facing blocks is a reused architectural fragment from a large Corinthian-style building, though this is probably not from the Temple of Hercules. The facade, 0.5m deep, fronts a core of random limestone and flint rubble packed with *terra rossa*. The internal face also appears to be constructed of rubble set in *terra rossa*.

Sector 11 (fig.91; pl.45)

Length 12.4m or more. The facade has been partially cleared and in 1981 a sondage was made outside, and an excavation (Trench E21) made inside, the wall-line (figs.92–3). It is not known where the joint with Sector 10 is located, and the facade is continuous with Sector 12.

PERIOD 2: TEMENOS WALL. Part of the south *temenos* wall of the Temple of Hercules, discussed further in the description of Sector 12. In Trench E21, part of the base course of the internal face of the wall superstructure was found, with block dimensions of 0.62 × 0.30+ × 1.20m. The wall superstructure was 3.2m wide, while the foundation on the inside is 0.6m wider and has a built-rubble facade. The core is of random rubble with a brown clay packing. The internal foundation bonds with that of a wall leading to the north, possibly the west *temenos* wall. To the west of this return, the foundation narrows to 3.1m wide. Part of what is probably the external foundation of the south temenos wall is seen at the base of the Sector 11 facade, projecting 0.4–0.7m from the wall-line. It consists of at least one course of limestone headers (0.50 × 0.35 × 0.45m+) and is visible for a length of 6.75m. At its west end, the course was found to lie on compact rubble set in brown clay. The *temenos* foundation at this point was evidently much lower than that on the inside, so as to take account of the natural sloping ground.

PERIOD 3 (UMAYYAD WALL): FORTIFICATION WALL. The Period 2 wall had been largely destroyed down to its foundation by the time that a new Period 3 foundation was laid on top of the remains. The new foundation was narrower, being 2.5m wide, and composed of flint and limestone rubble set in *terra rossa*. The external facade is one block thick and survives to a maximum height of 2.7m. It is made up of five courses of soft limestone ashlars (0.90 × 0.60 × 0.35m) laid alternately in header/stretcher technique. There is a slight offset 0.13m wide, below the uppermost surviving course. The facing and new core behind evidently contain some reused Period 2 material, including four column shafts. There are slight traces of grey lime plaster on some of the lower courses. The external facade is founded *c.*3m below the excavated internal foundation in Trench E21. Clearly, as with the Period 2 wall, the external surface was much lower than the internal.

PERIOD ?4: ?REVETMENT. Several large undressed limestone blocks were found at the base of the west end of the exposed part of Sector 11 and were removed during excavation of the sondage. The blocks were obviously later than the Period 3 wall, but their purpose is obscure, unless they formed part of the lowest course of a sloping revetment.

Sector 12 (figs 84, 91; pl.48)

Length 110m. The wall, which deviates slightly from a straight alignment at the position of Tower B (described below), completes the line of the southern perimeter of the Upper Citadel. The facade has been cleared along its entire length to a level well below the original external surface, so that considerable parts of the foundations are now visible. Excavations were made in 1979 on either side of Tower B (Trenches E1 and E2) and adjacent to Gate C (Trenches E3 and E5).

PERIOD 1 (ROMAN PRE-FORTIFICATION): PRE-WALL STRUCTURES. A number of rubble-built walls (0.8–1m wide) are visible at different angles at the base of the clearance. These appear to relate to the occupation levels encountered in Trench E3 (see Gate C description).

PERIOD 2: TEMENOS WALL. The south wall of the *temenos* of the Temple of Hercules. As in Sector 11, the wall is 3.2m wide and founded internally on a free-standing rubble wall up to 0.6m wider than the superstructure. This foundation was excavated to its base, which lies at a depth of 2.4m in Trench E5 (fig.95). The external foundation partly overlies the Period 1 structures and is visible to a depth of 1.20 and 0.55m in 12b and 12c respectively. The inside face of the superstructure has a base course of large limestone ashlars, 1.20 × 0.60 × 0.30m. Above this, both facades are built in header/stretcher fashion using smaller soft limestone ashlars of standard dimensions, 0.70 × 0.35 × 0.40m (external) and 0.60 × 0.40 × 0.30m (internal). Both facades are 0.9–1m deep and front a core of limestone and flint rubble (0.45 × 0.35 × ?m and 0.30 × 0.15 × ?m) packed with small stones and brown clay.

PERIOD 3 (UMAYYAD WALL): FORTIFICATION WALL. In Sector 11, a new wall had been built on the foundations of the Period 2 wall. In Sector 12, the Period 2 wall was simply refaced, no doubt because it was still standing to a considerable height. The external facade was cut back to a depth of at least one block (0.5–0.6m), some headers of the Period 2 facing being cut through and their remaining parts left *in situ* (fig.95). A foundation for the new facade was then put in, up to 2.8m deep in Trench E3. In most places the new foundation starts from a lower level than that of the Period 2 wall, and sometimes overlies Period 1 structures. The foundation offset has an average width of 0.38m and maintains a fairly constant level, except at both ends of the sector where the foundations are stepped down slightly to take account of the natural slope. The foundation material consists mainly of limestone rubble and some flint (averaging 0.45 × 0.32 × 0.38m) packed with small stones, brown earth and *terra rossa*. Some dressed masonry is reused in parts of the foundation; the masonry in 12a would appear to have originated from the cutting back of the Period 2 wall.

The new facade survives to a maximum height of 3.15m and is composed largely of reused limestone ashlars (averaging 0.54 × 0.36 × 0.35m+) and architectural fragments from the Period 2 Temple of Hercules. The courses vary in height and are occasionally snecked with small stones and finished with a pointing of grey lime plaster. The depth of the new facing is always one block (on average 0.57m) and no attempt was made to bond it with the Period 2 work. Any gaps which were left were filled with rubble and *terra rossa*.

Three rectangular buttresses were provided on the external facade, with average dimensions of 6.08 × 0.52m. They were not deeply bonded, but like the curtain were supported on substantial foundations. As with the buttresses elsewhere, all resemble closely the appearance of their neighbouring stretch of curtain. There was very likely a fourth buttress between Buttresses 1 and 2, behind Tower B. A wider section of wall at 12d probably indicates an internal projection; possibly infill for a collapsed area of Period 2 wall or the site of steps to a rampart walk.

PERIOD 4 ('ABBĀSID RESTORATION): REBUILT BUTTRESS. The western buttress (Buttress 1) was rebuilt. Only the core of limestone and flint rubble and abundant *terra rossa* survives, with a stepped base 0.5m high that doubtless supported a sloping facade – as in Sectors 8 and 9. Just enough remains to suggest that the buttress measured 6.85+ × 2.65m.

Tower B (South Tower: fig.94; pls 46–7)

Excavations were made in 1979 inside the tower (Trench E4).

PERIOD 6: WATCH-TOWER. By the time that Tower B was built over the top of Sector 12, the combination of the Period 2 *temenos* and Period 3 fortification wall had collapsed down to its present height, and the external ground surface had dropped significantly. The tower is a rectangle measuring 9.45 × 7.55m, set slightly askew to the line of Sector 12, from which it projects. A door in the rear or north wall leads to a single interior room, 4.8 × 3.1m, which may have been vaulted. A staircase in the thickness of the north wall led to the roof. There is a single arrow slit in each of the west, south and east faces. The arrow slits are set into rectangular recesses and have flat tops, but any arch over the recesses has disappeared. The south facade still appears to stand to its original height of 8.1m, and rests on a single course of reused column shafts, which in turn rest upon bedrock. The north wall is no longer complete, especially in the area of the doorway. However, in 1881 the Palestine Exploration Fund Survey found the tower intact, the door having a flat stone lintel with a *tabula ansata* in relief below a segmental relieving arch of five voussoirs.[32]

The tower is constructed throughout of reused limestone ashlars of varying dimension, the largest block measuring 2.70 × 1.25 × 0.70m. Many of the blocks on the west, south and east faces have narrow drafted margins, while the interiors and north wall are built wholly of plain-dressed masonry. All four walls have a rubble core and are mortared with hard white gritty cement. There are at least thirteen reused and recut architectural fragments in the wall-faces, mostly originating from the Period 2 Temple of Hercules. In particular, the south face has two large column drums placed symmetrically. These are wedged in position with triangular stones, carefully purpose-cut with drafted margins. The original floor excavated in Trench E4 is of rough uneven rubble. Later, a second earth floor packed with limestone blocks was laid *c.*0.3m higher. The tower intermittently remained in use for a long time, possibly up until the First World War.

ARCHAEOLOGICAL DATING. Conder believed Tower B was Byzantine, but it is clear from the structural sequence of the underlying walls that this cannot be correct.[33] An Ayyubid *fils* minted in Damascus was found in an ash patch overlying the rocky and uneven first floor of the interior, and thus between the two known floors (Appendix D: no.11). As the ash patch could not have been deposited very long after the construction of the tower, this bronze provides us with a *terminus post quem* date for Period 6 in the late 6th/12th or early 7th/13th century. We have no clear *terminus ante quem*; nevertheless, the large size of the masonry makes it unlikely that the tower is late Mamlūk or Ottoman. Rather, one might suggest that it is in fact Ayyūbid.

Gate C and Sector 13 (fig.97; pls 49–51)

Gate C is located at the southeast corner of the Upper Citadel and was probably the main entrance to the *temenos* of the Temple of Hercules. Sector 13 is a corner of masonry visible below the southwest corner of the gate. (The remains outside the west and south sides of Gate C have been denuded except for this surviving corner of masonry.) From here, the ground falls away steeply to the Lower City. Before excavation, the gate appeared only to be a block of masonry projecting from the wall-line, and Conder thought it to be a tower (fig.4).[34] Butler, however, appreciated that it was a gate, linked with the Propylaeon in the Lower City (figs 5,120).[35] The gate was excavated in 1979 and 1981 (Trenches E6, E8, E9 and E11). Sondages, both outside (Trench E3) and inside (Trench E5) the wall-line immediately to the west were also excavated. The southeast corner of the *temenos* was examined in Trench E10.

PERIOD 1 (ROMAN PRE-FORTIFICATION): PRE-WALL AND PRE-GATE STRUCTURES. In Trench E3, part of a structure with four floor surfaces was excavated. In the northwest corner of the sondage, this building was overlain by a further wall pre-dating the Period 2 *temenos* (fig.96).

GATE C: PERIOD 1 (ROMAN PRE-FORTIFICATION): PLASTERED WALL PLATFORM. Gate C was mounted directly on top of an earlier structure, which it used as a foundation. This structure was apparently a rectangle measuring 13.3 × 13.6–16.0m (the north wall was not found), built partly of rubble and partly of cut limestone. Five courses of limestone blocks laid lengthways (1.20 × 0.40 × ?m) are visible at the southwest corner (pl.50a). The facade was coated with a white lime plaster. The structure is believed to be a platform, but no conclusive evidence as to its purpose was found. It is possible that it was an earlier version of Gate C.

GATE C: PERIOD 2: TEMENOS GATE. The gate consists of a rectangular exterior set at an angle of 70° to the line of the *temenos* wall. There is a threshold, 4.1m wide, with six bolt holes (Trench E11) (pl.50b). The interior of the gate is semi-circular and leads up to a stylobate (Trench E8). Most of the surviving masonry is of the gate foundations. Only in the southeast corner does one course of the superstructure still remain above the level of the threshold. Up to two courses of the foundation are visible, with the large limestone blocks (0.60 × 0.40 × 1.25m) displaying their shorter face outwards. The blocks of the superstructure are smaller, being 0.43 × 0.30 × 0.70m. The stylobate is a linear podium, 16m long, of well-dressed limestone blocks built on a heavy foundation of rusticated masonry (Trench E6). It narrows from 2m wide at its western end to 1.2m wide at its eastern. In the semi-circle, traces of a paving of cut limestone and cobbles were found adjacent to the main threshold, and two blocks of limestone were provided for a rough step up onto the stylobate. However, over most of the area there are surfacings of *huwwar* or chalk gravel. Mounds of *huwwar* were also found over the latest surface; perhaps prepared for laying but never actually used.

On the east side of the gate, a second smaller threshold, 1.45m wide, opens into a side room which has an earth floor firmed up with cobbles (Trench E9). The outer line of the room has been eroded; presumably it continued the facade of the gate to join Sector 25, the east wall of the *temenos* (Trench E10).

SECTOR 13: PERIOD 2: TEMENOS GATE LANDING-SUPPORT. The western elevation is visible in three places, the most substantial stretch being at the southwest angle, where it survives for a length of 5.25m and to a maximum height of 2.20m (nine courses). There is the slight trace within the facing of an offset 40mm wide. The southern elevation is 8.7m long and 2.1m high (eight courses). The width of the wall is uncertain, though the backs of possible internal facing stones are visible near the southwest angle. The facing material is wholly of limestone blocks of regular size (0.60 × 0.37 × 0.40m). The facade is 0.5–0.6m deep and fronts a core of limestone and flint rubble. A number of courses of rubble masonry and earth fill were found added to the west wall of the Period 1 plastered wall platform and are possibly part of Sector 13.

Because of the difficulties of excavation, it was not possible to prove that the Sector 13 wall was contemporary with the *temenos* gate (it may be later). However, the masonry is of a similar size and style to that of the Period 2 south *temenos* wall. Moreover, some sort of structure on this line would surely have been necessary to support a landing outside the gate.

GATE C: PERIOD 3 (UMAYYAD WALL): FORTIFICATION GATE (FIGS 97–8). The Period 2 gate was rebuilt with the addition of a curved foundation of medium rubble, *terra rossa*, grey soil and patches of mortar. This foundation was 2.5m wide and up to 1.6m deep, and followed the line of the semi-circular wall on the west side and part of the line on the east (Trench E8). In all probability, the Period 2 curved wall of the semi-circle was still standing, and the foundation was for a 2.5m wall intended to strengthen it. The northern end of the new wall on the west side extends beyond the line of the Period 2 stylobate to form a buttress projecting 0.65m (Trenches E5 and E6). A secondary threshold, 1.4m wide, behind the main Period 2 threshold, may also belong to this rebuild. Although it lacked a provable relationship with the new foundation (because of denudation of the deposits), it is well-placed to be linked with it. It would appear, therefore, that the form of the gate changed from an enclosed structure with a wide passageway to an open semi-circular bastion with a small postern.

ARCHAEOLOGICAL DATING OF PERIODS 1–3. The Period 1 pre-wall and pre-gate structures excavated in Trench E3 represent an occupation of approximately the 1st century AD, dated by a Nabataean coin of Aretas and Shagilat (9BC – AD 40) from the second floor level (Floor 32). A conclusive dating of the plastered wall platform was prevented by the interference caused by the later construction of Sector 13. However, it was evident that the building was either contemporary with or post-dated the E3 occupation, and therefore is probably datable to the 1st century AD.

Excavation inside the line of the Period 2 south *temenos* wall in Trench E5 penetrated the fills that backed onto the wall and Gate C itself (fig.95). These earth fills were homogeneous and apparently constituted the levelling fill of the *temenos* courtyard. The fills were put in after the building of the *temenos* wall and the stylobate of the gate. The gate and *temenos* would appear, therefore, to be contemporary. Dornemann, in an unpublished excavation on the site of the steps of the Temple of Hercules, encountered a jumbled fill of earth and limestone masonry, also representing the levelling fill of the courtyard. While it cannot be proved conclusively that the fills belong to the same period of construction, it seems most probable that the *temenos* was built for the present temple, and may be dated by its inscription to AD 161–166.[36]

A floor deposit of sherds in the side-room of Gate C indicates an abandonment, possibly in the 3rd or 4th century AD. Part of the top course of the stylobate was also robbed out, and the consequent robber trench contained sherds of three Late Byzantine ribbed cooking pots. While these two pieces of evidence suggest the termination of maintenance of the Period 2 structure in the Byzantine period, passage through the gate may well have continued. The Period 3 rebuilt gate is clearly Umayyad, from sherds of red-painted ware found in the curved foundation.

SECTOR 13: PERIOD 4 ('ABBĀSID RESTORATION): REVETMENT. The sloping revetment was added to both sides of the southwest corner.[37] On the west it survives to a maximum height of 2.15m and width of 1.30m; on the south to a height of 2.05m and width of 1.50m. The south side has a stepped base with an offset ledge 0.15m wide. Both stretches exhibit a profile of 75–80° and are built of flint and limestone rubble of larger than average dimensions (0.40 × 0.30 × 0.30m+). A probable additional section of steeper incline (80–85°) runs from the southeast corner of Gate C. This revets not a wall, but a mass of rubble. By this period, therefore, the gate may have been entirely blocked off.

GATE C: PERIOD ?5: DESTRUCTION. A wall was built askew to the line of the back of the Period 3 gate. It contained some reused fallen Period 2 masonry and overlay the east end of the stylobate (Trenches E8 and E10). The wall's function and date are indeterminate (fig.97).

4. THE SOUTH WALL (LOWER CITADEL)

Sector 14

Sector 14 has a total length of 70m. However, it is an apparently heterogeneous wall, with two different kinds of construction visible. The description is therefore divided into two parts, starting at the western end.

Sector 14A (fig.100; pl.52a)

The wall makes a straight joint with the east *temenos* wall of the Temple of Hercules (Sector 25). Approximately 20m east of this return, a modern track cut for the approach to a house on the slope below Gate C has exposed a cross-section at a point where the wall stands to a height of 3.8m. In 1981, the section was cleaned and a sondage (1.5m square) was excavated against the facade (Trench E14).

PERIOD 1 (ROMAN PRE-FORTIFICATION): PRE-WALL BUILDING. The external wall of a building had clearly been reused to form the inside face of the later curtain. The wall is 1.34m thick, with a doorway one metre wide. The construction is of unmortared rubble, with cut stone door-jambs. Outside the door, part of a surface of paving stones and cobbles, very similar to the paving in Gate C, was preserved under the rubble fill of Period 2.

PERIOD 2: CURTAIN WALL. Only a foundation for the facade was necessary as the inside face was formed out of the pre-existing Period 1 wall. The foundation filled a narrow vertically sided trench, and consisted of a free-standing rubble wall 1.42m deep and not more than 2.4m wide, packed with grey-brown clay. The wall superstructure (excluding Period 1) is 3.4m wide. The facade has a base course of large limestone blocks (0.60 × 0.60 × 1.20m) and above this a facing, two blocks thick, of smaller dry-laid limestone blocks averaging 0.34 × 0.34 × 0.70m. The core is of undressed limestone set in grey-brown earth, presumably the deteriorated remnants of a clay similar to that used in the foundation.

ARCHAEOLOGICAL DATING OF PERIODS 1 AND 2 The style

of the Period 1 construction and a few sherds from above the paving suggest a Roman date. Deposits predating the Period 2 foundation were excavated in the sondage. They closely resemble the *temenos* fills encountered near Gate C, and pottery from them may be tentatively dated to the 1st – 2nd centuries. Following the construction of the Period 2 curtain, a dump of pottery and organic materials accumulated against the outside face of the wall. The pottery is comparable with, or slightly later than, that recovered from a 3rd-century tomb in 'Ammān excavated by Harding.[38] The construction, therefore, may well be related to that of the *temenos* (AD 161–180).

PERIOD 3 (UMAYYAD WALL): FORTIFICATION WALL. The face of the Period 2 wall was cut back down to the third course above the foundation, and a new facade of less regular limestone blocks was added. The new facade does not bond with the Period 2 structure and the joints are pointed with grey lime plaster. The work presumably belongs to the same construction project as the refacing of Sector 12.

PERIOD 4 ('ABBĀSID RESTORATION): REVETMENT. A sloping revetment with curved profile was added to the Period 3 fortification. It is 2.4m wide at its base and preserved to a height of *c*.2.6m. The construction is of medium rubble, but packed with brown earth rather than the more usual *terra rossa*. The face of the revetment is coated with grey lime plaster studded with lumps of chalk.

Sector 14B

In the eastern part of Sector 14 the construction appears to be different.

PERIOD 3 (UMAYYAD WALL): FORTIFICATION WALL. A foundation, visible at one point only, consists of limestone and flint rubble (averaging 0.30 × 0.25 × 0.30m), together with some reused dressed masonry, packed with *terra rossa* and small stones. Of the superstructure, a maximum of six courses survive to a height of 2.85m. The facade contains some limestone blocks (averaging 0.80 × 0.50 × 0.50m), but also a considerable amount of undressed limestone and flint. The coursework is bad, uneven and not horizontal, the facing depth varying between 0.6–0.9m. Over a distance of *c*.27m, the facing material has fallen away to reveal a core made up of nine courses of large boulders (averaging 0.80 × 0.50 × 0.60m), with smaller stones in between.

PERIOD 4 ('ABBĀSID RESTORATION): REVETMENT. A section of revetment is visible for a distance of c. 8m west of Gate D, with a maximum height of 1.8m and width of *c*.2m. Its incline is not greater than 45°, and the construction is of limestone and flint rubble of fairly large dimensions (0.60 × 0.50 × ?m). There may have been a stepped base.

Gate D (pl.52b)

Unexcavated. The gate covers an area of 18.6 × ?7.1m and lies askew to the line of the wall. It has a single passageway flanked by two towers, Towers J and K.

PERIOD 3 (UMAYYAD WALL): FORTIFICATION GATE STRUCTURE. The threshold is recessed to a maximum of 3m between the towers and the door-jambs survive two courses high. Behind the threshold, the passageway is 4.35m wide and 4m deep, and is stepped.

Tower J

PERIOD 3 (UMAYYAD WALL): FORTIFICATION GATE-TOWER. The tower projects ?0.6m from Sector 14B and has a frontage of 4.85m. Five to six courses of dressed limestone blocks (averaging 0.90 × 0.40 × 0.50m) survive to a height of 2.45m. The facing is two blocks deep (1.30m) and there are traces of grey lime plaster.

Tower K

PERIOD 3 (UMAYYAD WALL): FORTIFICATION GATE-TOWER. The tower projects 0.95m from Sector 15 and has a frontage of 5.8m. Three courses of well-laid dressed limestone blocks (1.10 × 0.50 × 0.65m) survive to a height of 1.3m. The facing is one or two blocks deep (1.35m) built in header/stretcher fashion.

Sector 15 (fig.107; pl.53a)

Length 18.85m. The exterior facade is cleared well below the original external surface so that the foundation courses are now exposed. The internal face remains buried.

PERIOD 3 (UMAYYAD WALL): FORTIFICATION WALL. The foundation is partly laid on what appears to be an earlier rubble-faced wall and is visible to a depth of 1.9m. It consists of large limestone and flint rubble masonry (averaging 0.60 × 0.40 × 0.30m+) with a packing of small stones and brown earth. The width of the foundation offset varies between 0.30 and 0.66m, being widest at the eastern end.

The wall superstructure survives to a maximum height of 2.3m, with an estimated width of *c*.3.55m. The facade has five surviving courses of snecked limestone and flint material. The first two courses consist of undressed small rubble with fragments of dressed stone (averaging 0.40 × 0.30 × ?m). Larger reused blocks (averaging 1 × 0.60 × 0.43m) appear further up and front the core to a varying depth of between 0.43 and 0.85 (one or two blocks). The core is of random limestone and flint rubble, but no *terra rossa* is visible. A drain, with a rectangular cross-section of 0.4 × 0.6m, can be traced for a length of one metre, three courses above the foundation offset at the eastern end of the wall, close to Sector 16. The drain is doubtless to prevent excess water from winter rains pooling behind the wall, and its position thus marks the level of the original internal ground surface.

Sector 16 (figs 84, 101, 107; pls 53b, 54a)

Length 24.2m. The wall is built slightly askew to the line of Sector 15. The outside face is cleared well below the top of the foundations, while the inside face is only visible at the eastern end, at the junction with Sector 17. At this point, a cross-section through the wall was exposed in a breach (blocked in 1981).

PERIOD 3 (UMAYYAD WALL): FORTIFICATION WALL. The foundation is visible to a depth of 2.2m. It consists of two snecked courses of roughly dressed blocks (averaging 0.70 × 0.57 × 0.45m), which also contain some reused architectural fragments, laid above random small limestone and flint rubble (averaging 0.25 × 0.10 × 0.15m) set in brown earth. There is a foundation offset, 0.25m or more wide, equivalent in height to that of Sector 15, and widest at its western end.

The wall superstructure is 2.57m wide. The external facade survives to a maximum height of 5.1m and displays ten courses of regular, well-dressed limestone blocks (averaging 1.0 × 0.57 × 0.40m) laid in header/stretcher fashion. The facing depth varies between 0.30 and 1.05m. There is an offset ledge 0.30–0.35m wide, three courses above the top of the foundation. Sitting upon this ledge and bonded into the face of the wall are three rectangular buttresses. On average, the buttresses are 3.88m long and 6.30m apart, projecting 0.20–0.23m. The internal face, of which seven courses survive, is a wall of rubble (averaging 0.50 × 0.45 × 0.65m) with many small snecking stones. The whole face is mortared with a grey lime mortar, similar in quality to the grey lime plaster found elsewhere. The core is of mortared small limestone and flint rubble (averaging 0.20 × 0.10 × 0.15m), together with some larger fragments (averaging 0.35 × 0.20 × 0.15m). The core was laid in broad courses, with distinct lift lines in the mortar marking the stages in construction (fig.101).

PERIOD 4 (ʿABBĀSID RESTORATION): REBUILT BUTTRESS AND REVETMENT. The two lowest courses of Buttress 2 were rebuilt using small fragments of limestone and flint, following a partial subsidence in this area. There are also traces of a sloping revetment 1.3m high, visible for a short stretch (1.4m), built up from the level of the foundation offset against the wall-face below Buttress 2.

Sector 17 (figs 84, 107; pls 53b–55a)

Length 26.55m. The wall is built slightly askew to the line of Sector 16, but parallel to Sector 15. The outside face has been cleared to a level below the original external surface, and the inside face is partly visible at the western end. Sections through the wall were visible at either end, but that to the west was blocked-off in 1981.

PERIOD 3 (UMAYYAD WALL): FORTIFICATION WALL. The foundation is visible to a depth of 0.75m and consists of one or two courses of roughly dressed limestone and flint blocks (averaging 0.70 × 0.50 × 0.40m+) packed with small stones and grey lime mortar. The top of the foundation offset is 0.3m wide and its position lies four courses below that of Sector 16.

The superstructure of the wall is three metres wide. The external facade displays a maximum of sixteen courses (8.25m high) of neatly dressed limestone blocks laid in header/stretcher fashion (1.10 × 0.60 × 0.37m and 0.90 × 0.55 × 0.65m). Eight courses above the foundation, there is an offset ledge 0.55–0.60m wide, level with, but wider than, the offset ledge of Sector 16. Sitting on the ledge and bonded into the face of the wall is a single buttress, 6.24m long and projecting 0.55m. Sector 17 is unique in that dressed limestone blocks are used in the construction of the internal facade and core of the wall (fig.103). The inside face contains more stretcher blocks than the external facade (averaging 1 × 0.45 × 0.55m) and also retains some traces of grey lime plaster coating, which is studded with pieces of chalk. Within the core, some wedging stones and grey lime mortar fill spaces between the blocks. The sector also includes an unusually high number of reused architectural fragments (pl.55a). At least fourteen are visible in the core of the wall and others lie fallen nearby. It might be that the sector marks the reuse *in toto* of a Roman monumental building – presumably one located somewhere in the Lower Citadel area. This would certainly help explain why dressed blocks are found in the wall core and inside face.

The offset ledges of Sectors 16 and 17 are approximately level with the drain at the eastern end of Sector 15. This offset probably marks the level of the original internal ground surface. The plain walls below the offset, therefore, are simply terrace walling for the hill. The use of unusually fine masonry and mortaring in these two sectors might suggest that this part of the hill was particularly unstable at the time the wall was built.

Sector 18 (figs 84, 107; pl.55b)

Length 68.3m. The wall is built slightly askew to the line of Sector 17. The outside face has been cleared and the inside face is visible at the surface. Part of the facing bulges outwards and there are collapsed sections between the two surviving buttresses and at the east end near the junction with Sector 19.

PERIOD 3 (UMAYYAD WALL): FORTIFICATION WALL. The wall superstructure is *c.*4m wide and survives to a maximum height of 3.8m. The external facade is of unevenly coursed limestone and flint rubble (0.70 × 0.50 × 0.45m and 0.50 × 0.40 × 0.40m) with many snecking stones. Some material is evidently reused and the facing depth is 0.65m. There are traces of a brown lime plaster coating stippled with wedge-shaped impressions. Two buttresses, loosely bonded to the exterior facade, lie 13.9m apart. They measure 5.90 × 0.65–1m and 7 × 0.65–0.70m respectively. The internal face, to judge from the one course visible, is similar to the external. The core is of random rubble (averaging 0.25 × 0.15 × 0.15m) packed with brown earth and flint chips.

The contrast with the fine ashlar masonry of Sectors 16 and 17 is quite striking. The poor construction might be explained in part by the observation that the facade of Sector 18, as it stands, is terrace walling, and thus equivalent to the lower courses of Sectors 16 and 17. Traces of the upper facade of the fortification wall reappear in Sector 19.

Sector 19 (pl.56a)

Length 90m or more. Sector 19 forms a straight wall between the end of Sector 18 and Tower L at the southeast corner of the Citadel. The external face has not been cleared, but is visible in places. The inside line of the wall was excavated by Zayadine in Area A (Lower Terrace) in 1968 and 1972–3. Further excavations and clearance work have recently been conducted by Humbert, immediately west of Area A.[39]

PERIOD 2: CURTAIN WALL. Three courses of well-dressed soft limestone blocks (0.70 × 0.37 × 0.40m) are visible where the external facing of the later Period 3 wall has fallen away. These may be remnants of the earlier curtain wall cut back to receive the later facade.[40]

PERIOD 3 (UMAYYAD WALL): FORTIFICATION WALL. An 8.4m length of the foundation of the inside face was excavated in Area A. It was built of snecked limestone rubble and flint, similar to the materials used in Sector 8, and set in a foundation trench 1–1.5m wide and 2.5m deep, with large boulders at the bottom. The wall superstructure is 3.25m wide. The inside face is a snecked rubble wall standing two courses high (0.9m) and one block deep (0.8m) on an offset ledge 0.25m wide. Again, the style is very similar to the Sector 8 wall excavated in Area C. The exterior facade is also a rubble wall. Five courses survive to a maximum height of 2.4m. The facing is composed of limestone and flint blocks (0.50 × 0.45 × 0.50m and 0.70 × 0.45 × 0.40m) and varies in depth between 0.5m and metre. One buttress is bonded to the external face, being 6.15m long and projecting 0.65–0.70m. The wall core is of random rubble and earth.

ARCHAEOLOGICAL DATING. Zayadine dates the section of excavated Period 3 wall to the 3rd/9th century, on the basis of an 'Abbāsid *fils* of Damascus (162/778–79).[41] This was the latest coin found in Locus 2, a subsurface debris deposit exposed all over the excavated area, but which had been cut by levels associated with the building of the wall. The stratigraphy is not clear from the published section and this later dating need not stand against the better evidence from Area C.

Tower L (pl.56b)

A projection of masonry suggests that there may have been a tower at the southeast corner of the Citadel.

PERIOD 3 (UMAYYAD WALL): FORTIFICATION TOWER. Four courses of good quality limestone blocks (averaging 0.75 × 0.50 × 0.60m) survive to a maximum height of 1.9m. There are traces of a grey lime plaster coating.

PERIOD 4 ('ABBĀSID RESTORATION): REVETMENT. A section of sloping revetment, 1.7m wide, is visible against the east side of the tower. It is constructed of limestone and flint rubble (averaging 0.40 × 0.30 × ?m) and inclined at 80°.

5. THE EAST AND NORTH WALLS (LOWER CITADEL)

Sector 20

Length *c.*99m. The east wall of the Lower Citadel. The wall is exposed at two points only, and is cut by a modern road towards its northern end.

PERIOD 2: CURTAIN WALL. Some regular soft limestone blocks (0.70 × 0.37 × 0.40m) are visible, and might belong to the external face of a wall cut back and refaced in Period 3.

PERIOD 3 (UMAYYAD WALL): FORTIFICATION WALL. Three courses of the external facade survive. The facing material is reused limestone and flint (averaging 0.40 × 0.30 × 0.25m+) and is of inferior quality to that used in Tower L. Traces of a possible south corner of a buttress are visible near where the road cuts through the wall. At this point there is also a length of what is probably an internal face of rubble masonry, with a core of rubble and brown earth. The internal face and core could equally well belong to the Period 2 curtain.

PERIOD 4 ('ABBĀSID RESTORATION): REVETMENT. A sloping revetment is visible at two places, surviving to a maximum height of 1.2m and to a width of 0.65–1m. It is constructed of limestone and flint rubble (averaging 0.25 × 0.20 × ?m) and inclined at 50–55°.

Sector 21

Length *c*.289m. The wall on the north side of the Lower Citadel is now entirely concealed by a modern road.
PERIOD ?3: FORTIFICATION WALL. A section of this wall was probably excavated by the Italian Mission before 1933, revealing a rubble inner face, but the published photographs are not clear (cf. pl.11).[42]

Sector 22 (fig.104; pl.57)

Length 60m. The curving wall of Sector 22 is visible on the surface, and a cross-section is exposed at the eastern end, where it is cut by a modern road (fig.104).
PERIOD 2: CURTAIN WALL. A 3.2m wide wall, whose inner face is constructed of snecked limestone and flint rubble of medium size (averaging 0.55 × 0.33 × 0.40m). The face, 0.35m deep, fronts a core of rubble packed with brown earth. Eight courses of the external facade are visible to a height of 2.9m. The facing is composed of soft limestone blocks with standard dimensions of 0.70 × 0.37 × 0.40m, and is two blocks (1.1m) deep.
PERIOD 3 (UMAYYAD WALL): FORTIFICATION WALL. Above the third course, the Period 2 facade was cut back and refaced with small limestone and flint rubble (averaging 0.40 × 0.15 × 0.25m), with a little filling of *terra rossa*. Both the external and internal faces were coated with grey lime plaster studded with pieces of chalk. Further west, the wall has an external facade of limestone blocks (averaging 0.90 × 0.55 × 0.30m) laid in header/stretcher fashion. The facing is one block thick and fronts a mortared rubble core. Three rectangular buttresses appear to belong to this period. They are, on average, 4.48m long and 14.22m apart, with projections of 0.62m.
PERIOD 4 ('ABBĀSID RESTORATION): REVETMENT. A sloping revetment of small limestone and flint rubble (averaging 0.25 × 0.15 × 0.15m), cemented with grey lime mortar, was added to the exterior wall-face. The revetment is founded on material dumped against the Period 2 wall and is level with the base of the Period 3 refacing. The construction is 1.9m high and 1.7m wide and was mortared instead of being packed with *terra rossa*, presumably to give additional strength in a weak area.

Tower H

The Palestine Exploration Fund Special Survey plan of 1881 records a square or rectangular tower at the junction of Sectors 22, 23 and 26.[43] Masonry belonging to the tower is visible in early photographs.[44] Today the spot is occupied by a modern army bunker.
PERIOD 3 (UMAYYAD WALL): FORTIFICATION TOWER. Dimensions unknown. The tower facade was flush with the line of the wall, and so Tower H was probably one of the standard Period 3 wall-towers.

6. THE EAST AND NORTHEAST WALLS (UPPER CITADEL)

Sector 23

Length 134m. Part of the wall was excavated by Zayadine in Area A (Upper Terrace) in 1975 and 1977, but has not been published.
PERIOD 3 (UMAYYAD WALL): FORTIFICATION WALL. The wall superstructure is 3.8m wide. The external facade is composed of large well-laid limestone blocks (averaging 0.65 × 0.32+ × 1.20m), while the internal face is of heavily snecked flint rubble with some dressed limestone fragments (0.30 × 0.25 × ?m and 0.60 × 0.25 × 0.25m). Both faces are one block deep (0.55–1.20m) and front a core of compact limestone and flint rubble set in brown earth. Within the excavated area, a drain is visible for a length of 2.8m running through the middle of a buttress, projecting 0.6–0.7m from the external wall-face. The drain is constructed of dressed limestone blocks and presents a rectangular cross-section to the internal face with dimensions of 0.60 × 0.45m.
ARCHAEOLOGICAL DATING. According to Zayadine, the Period 3 wall is dated to the 6th century, but it is not apparent what evidence this conclusion is based upon.[45]
PERIOD 4 ('ABBĀSID RESTORATION): REVETMENT. The sloping revetment survives to a height of 0.85m, to a width of 0.80m, and at an incline of 55–60°. The construction is of snecked limestone and flint rubble (averaging 0.30 × 0.15 × 0.15m) coated with grey lime plaster. To the north of the Period 3 buttress, the revetment has a stepped base and there is no trace of the Period 3 wall-face behind it. Presumably there was a rebuild in this area.

Sector 24

Length *c*.21m. Uncleared.
PERIOD 3 (UMAYYAD WALL): FORTIFICATION WALL. Two external courses of rough-dressed limestone blocks (averaging 0.90 × 0.60 × 0.55m) are visible at the western end of the sector, adjacent to Tower A.

7. THE CROSS-WALL (BETWEEN UPPER AND LOWER CITADELS)

Sector 25 and Tower G

Sector 25

Length 81.5m. The outside face of Sector 25 south of Tower G was examined by Dornemann in an unpublished excavation in 1969.[46] The trench was dug to test Conder's supposition that column drums visible in the surface formed part of a gate between the Upper and Lower Citadel.[47] Dornemann did not find a gate, and so the location of the gate between the two terraces remains unknown. In 1979 and 1981, both sides of the wall were excavated (Trenches E10, E13 and E17) in the course of the excavation of Gate C and Tower G.

PERIOD 2: TEMENOS WALL. East of Gate C, the south *temenos* wall of the Temple of Hercules returns north (Trench E10) to form the east side of the *temenos*. The surviving wall is 0.9m wide and built of dressed limestone blocks (averaging 1.22 × ? × 0.35m), two blocks thick (fig.97). No trace of the Period 2 wall was recovered at the northern end of the sector in the vicinity of Tower G, although part of a Roman mortared foundation was found at right-angles to the wall-line (fig.105).

PERIOD 3 (UMAYYAD WALL): FORTIFICATION WALL. At the northern end of the sector, part of a 1.2m wide wall is evident. It was built of reused limestone blocks, including architectural fragments from the Period 2 Temple of Hercules, laid dry without any foundation. The most striking feature of the wall is the incorporation of at least seven column drums, the largest being 1.5m diameter × 2m. These were set vertically and were thus wider than the wall itself. As discovered by Dornemann, Conder's supposed gate is actually column drums reused in a later wall. On the north side of Tower G, the 1.2m-wide wall makes a turn to the west to link up with Sector 26. At the southern end of Sector 25, any superimposed fortification wall has been eroded.

ARCHAEOLOGICAL DATING. The evidence from Trenches E13 and E17 is similar to that discovered by Dornemann – namely that Umayyad pottery may be found down to the base of the Period 3 wall. There was no evidence of earlier rubbish dumps along the base, such as were found in Sector 14A; rather, the stratigraphy changed directly from Roman deposits to Umayyad deposits. It seems likely, therefore, that the northern end of the sector is Umayyad in date.

Tower G (fig.105; pl.58)

The inside of the tower was excavated in 1979 and 1981 (Trench E7).

PERIOD 3 (UMAYYAD WALL): FORTIFICATION TOWER. Tower G projects from the eastern facade of Sector 25 and is clearly an addition to the wall, being linked by a straight joint. The tower is 5.8m square, without reference to the dimensions of the curtain wall behind. The south and north walls of the tower are 0.90–1.05m thick, while the east wall is 1.3m wide. The walls are laid on a built rubble foundation. The superstructure is of reused dressed limestone masonry for the facade (0.80 × 0.60 × ?m and 1.20 × 0.40 × ?m), and rubble walling for the inside face (averaging 0.30 × 0.20 × ?m). The walls are all mortared and display patches of grey lime plaster on their faces, mostly in the form of pointing of the joints. In the northwest corner of the tower, a doorway one metre wide, opening from outside the defended area of the Upper Citadel, led to an internal room with an earth floor. The springers (0.50m wide) survive for a central east-west transverse arch. The arch may be reckoned to have supported another floor *c.*3m higher.

ARCHAEOLOGICAL DATING. The terminus post quem dating for Tower G is the Umayyad date of Sector 25, while a terminus ante quem is provided by a dump of Umayyad pottery against the north wall of the tower, sealed by a later Ayyūbid surface. Thus we are limited to an Umayyad construction (Period 3) or one of the period of the revetment (Period 4). The similarity of Tower G to Tower E, which pre-dates the revetment, would suggest that the former choice is the more likely. The tower was presumably added to Sector 25 as an after-thought.

Sector 26

Length 63m. No part of this wall has been cleared, but its line may be followed. A cut created by a modern road allows a view of the cross-section at its southern end.

PERIOD 2: CURTAIN WALL. The east exterior facade is of dressed limestone (1 × 0.40 × 0.55m), two blocks (1.15m) thick. The inside face of limestone rubble (averaging 0.50 × 0.35 × 0.55m) is one block (0.55m) deep, fronting a core of limestone and flint fragments packed with brown earth. There are no traces of grey lime plaster on either face.

Discussion of the Main Features and Their Sequence

The sequence and features outlined so far describe a wall circuit with either one or two building periods at each point. The evidence suggests that the first of these is Roman (Period 2), the second Umayyad (Period 3). There are also additional elements, namely the pre-wall structures like the Northern Temple (Period 1); the contemporary Roman-period Temple of Hercules (Period 2); the post-Umayyad buttress rebuilds and revetment (Period 4); and Tower B (Period 6). Zayadine has produced variant datings for what would appear to be sections of the Period 3 wall: he initially assigned Sector 19 to the 3rd/9th century, and then to the Byzantine period, and he dated Sector 23 to the 6th century AD.[48] Although it is always possible that periods of building have been missed, evidence of construction at other points that could be interpreted as supporting Zayadine's datings was not found. It is proposed, therefore, that the nature of the surviving remains can be explained by the six periods of development outlined below.

Period 1: The Platform and Temenos of the Northern Temple

With one exception, Sectors 1–7 and Towers A and C belong to the independent construction of the double enclosure of the Northern Temple. The exception is Sector 6, which is an insert of Period 3 date that probably marks the site of a Period 1 western gate. Sectors 2–5 represent the platform wall and Sectors 1–3 and 7 are parts of the *temenos* superstructure. An important point to note is that Sector 1 is only 0.9m wide. Although in later arrangements of the wall circuit the wall must have formed part of the defences, it does not appear to have been built as a fortification wall. It has to be concluded, therefore, that at the time Sectors 1–5 and 7 were erected, they were not designed as a fortification, but simply as an imposing perimeter wall for the Northern Temple. The Roman curtain wall (Period 2), further south and east, must be later in date, and so seems to have incorporated the temple perimeter wall of Period 1 into its circuit. A dating of the Northern Temple to the early or middle 2nd century has been proposed elsewhere in this volume.

Period 2: The Temenos of the Temple of Hercules and the Roman Curtain Wall

Gate C, the contemporary Period 2 walls of Sectors 12 and 13, and the underlying parts of Sectors 11 and 25, all appear to belong to the *temenos* of the Temple of Hercules, representing its southern and eastern sides. The southeast and possibly southwest corners of the *temenos* have been located (Trenches E10 and E21), and give a length of 119m for the south *temenos* wall. Although the east *temenos* wall is only 0.9m wide, the same width as the enclosure wall of the Northern Temple, the south wall (Sectors 11 and 12) is 3.2m wide, and appears to have been designed as part of the curtain wall circuit.

Gate C is presumably the principal gate of the Temple of Hercules, approached from the Lower City by a stairway from the Propylaeon. The gate's rectangular exterior and semi-circular interior is unusual, but we have no direct evidence of the appearance of the superstructure other than this. However, the later addition of a curved foundation for a Period 3 wall behind the Period 2 semi-circular internal face, would tend to imply that the rectangular exterior may have been a plinth for a semi-circular superstructure. If the superstructure had been rectangular, such a curved strengthening wall would not have been appropriate; rather, an attempt would have been made to restore the gate in a rectangular form. In any case, a rectangular plinth was forced upon the builders by the shape of the Period 1 plastered wall platform underneath. It may be concluded, therefore, that originally the gate had a semi-circular superstructure, with a single passageway, resting on a rectangular plinth (fig.106).

A suggested reconstruction of the portico on the inside face of the gate can be derived from traces of wear on the stylobate and the position of chisel marks indicating where structures were fitted onto the flat surface. The fitting mark of one column base, 1.05m × 1m, is recognizable, and a second matching column probably sat upon the section of stylobate that was subsequently robbed out. At the western end of the stylobate, one apparently original block belonging to a side wall survived mortared onto the surface. Wear marks suggest that side walls projected 1.7m on the west and 1.15m on the east, over the surface of the stylobate and flush with its back face. These side walls presumably carried pilasters. A column shaft and entablature fragment found collapsed and/or later reused inside the gate probably derive from the portico structure (fig.97). Tiling recovered from the gate suggests that the semicircular area had originally been covered by a beam and tile roof. Although there is a possibility that the tile roof was limited to the side-room, the provision of a two-column portico indicates the likelihood that the whole gate was roofed in tile.

Outside the gate, there should have been a landing. This was presumably supported by a wall on the line of the Sector 13 wall, or, in all probability, by that wall itself. The line of Sector 13 diverges from the facade of the gate and would permit a stairway six metres wide to lead down to the east from the landing. If this is the case, then a winding, rather than a straight stairway must have led down to the Lower City. No trace, however, is visible today on the surface of the slope.

As regards the Roman curtain wall, one stretch has been conclusively identified in Sector 14A, to the east of the *temenos*. It is dated on stratigraphic grounds to between the 1st and 4th centuries AD. Its style of construction – the rubble foundation wall, regular limestone masonry of the facade, and brown clay packing – is almost identical to the south *temenos* wall of Sector 12. Both were also later given a new Period 3 facade. Sector 12 is 3.2m wide. The width of Sector 14A, however, is greater, being 3.4m, but this is no doubt atypical as the wall was built reusing a pre-existing Period 1 structure as its internal face. Other sectors where regular limestone blocks appear behind a Period 3 facade are the northern half of Sector 8 and Sectors 19, 20 and 22. These walls are not in themselves dated, but Sectors 19 and 22 are both *c*.3.2m wide with a rubble core packed with brown earth, presumably the deteriorated remnants of a clay. The internal face of Sector 22 is a rubble wall.

It could be suggested, therefore, that the main characteristics of the Period 2 Roman curtain wall are as follows: a width of 3.2m; an external facade of regular limestone blocks laid in header/stretcher fashion (average dimensions 0.70 × 0.36 × 0.39m); an inner face of rubble (average dimensions 0.52 × 0.34 × 0.47m); and a rubble core packed with brown clay (Table 6). Exceptions to these characteristics are found in the walls of the *temenos* and the cross-wall; Sector 12 (dressed inner face), Sector 25 (narrow wall, dressed inner face and no packing) and Sector 26 (larger than average external facade blocks).

The total list of areas with Period 2 walling *in situ* – Sectors 8, 11, and 12, Gate C and Sectors 13, 14A, 19, 20, 22, 25 and 26 – shows that the Roman wall followed approximately the same line as the later Period 3 wall. Apart from the *temenos* walls and Gate C, nothing is known about the architectural features of the Roman wall. There is no evidence for buttresses and none of the gates (apart from Gate C), or any of the towers, can at present be attributed with confidence to its construction. In the absence of identifiable defensive elements, it might be concluded that we are dealing with no more than an extensive perimeter curtain wall surrounding the Citadel, rather than a fortification in the true sense of the word. However, there are a number of reasons for concluding that the Period 2 curtain does belong to a fortification wall, and that we are simply lacking the evidence for the gates and towers. Firstly, Ammianus Marcellinus' text describes Philadelphia as 'well-fortified'.[49] There is no substantial evidence for, and, indeed, quite clear evidence in certain places against, any other Roman fortification wall round the whole city. Secondly, the wall-width of 3.2m is too wide for buttressing, terracing or perimeter walling. It is the kind of width one would require for resisting ramming and other forms of assault. Finally, in the Period 2 *temenos* wall of the Temple of Hercules, the differentiation of width between the south wall (3.2m) and the east wall (0.9m) is very distinctive. There must have been a particular reason for this deliberate differentiation, and that must have been defence.

When the Northern Temple was built some time in the 2nd century, the Roman wall of Period 2 was not in existence. However, by the time the Temple of Hercules was built, between AD 161–166, it was already either in existence or planned.[50] Sector 14A is butted against the east *temenos* wall (Sector 25). While it is possible that a recently built curtain wall was cut through to insert the *temenos*, the similarity of style suggests that the curtain belongs to the same construction scheme as the *temenos*, and was built at the same time as the temple or a little later.

By the time that the Period 3 Umayyad wall was built, the Roman construction of Period 2 was in a ruinous state. Tower A, Sectors 1 and 7, Tower C, Sector 12, Gate C and Sectors 13, 14A, 22 and 26 were still standing to a substantial, though not necessarily full, height. However, in Sector 11 the wall was reduced to its foundation before reconstruction, while in Sector 8 (Area C) and under Tower G the Roman wall could not be detected at all. This is almost certainly the case in Sectors 14B–18, where a total collapse of the earlier curtain had presumably occurred. It is not clear when all this destruction took place. It ought to post-date Ammianus Marcellinus' description of Philadelphia in the late 4th century AD as 'well-fortified'.[51] However, there are a few indications that the ruin of the walls may have happened as early as the 4th century: a building in Area C in the vicinity of the wall-line partly collapsed down the hill, leaving a 4th-century abandonment deposit (figs 122–3);[52] a 4th-century abandonment deposit and 6th-century robbing occur in Gate C; and late Roman tombs are present in Area A (Lower Terrace) immediately inside the line of Sector 19, suggesting that the Roman wall in this area was possibly given over to a cemetery.[53] This evidence would agree with Hadidi's interpretation of abandonment and destruction in the Lower City area of the forum, theatre and odeum, attributed to the earthquake of AD 363.[54] The implication would be that the Citadel in the Byzantine period was unfortified. This is a possibility, but it is not proven.

Period 3: The Umayyad Fortification Wall

In the places where there was enough evidence about the Periods 1 and 2 Roman walls to detect rebuilds, only one major period of rebuild to the walls themselves was observed. Equally, where Roman walls were not detected, there appears to be only one recognizable period of construction, ignoring for the moment the restoration work associated with Period 4. It would thus appear that in Period 3, we are dealing with a single new wall which varied in its constructional style. The disparities in construction can perhaps be explained by the different methods adopted by the wall builders to overcome various topographical irregularities, by the use and reuse of certain pre-existing structures, and by the different materials that came to hand.

Where substantial Roman structures still stood, these were reworked. Tower A of Period 1 was remodelled in a new form and parts of the Period 1 external facade of the double enclosure of the Northern Temple were restored with grey lime plaster. In Tower C of Period 1 and Sectors 8 (northern half), 11, 12, 14A, 19, 20 and 22 of Period 2, the Roman facings were cut back by one block and a new facade added, which does not bond with the earlier facade. The masonry used in these refacings is diverse, ranging from well-dressed limestone blocks in Tower C, reused soft limestone blocks and architectural fragments in Sectors 11 and 12, to small rubble masonry in Sector 22. In Sector 11 (Trench E21), the refacing was associated with a new wall built on top of the earlier one. No doubt elsewhere the refacings were connected with rebuilding the upper parts of the wall, which have now disappeared.

There were also many new stretches of walling, some abutting one another end to end. Sectors 6, 8 (Area C), 9, 10, 14B, 15, 16, 17, 18 and 23 all seem to be new walls without the characteristic refacing discussed above. The pattern of walling tended to produce a wall 2.65m or 3.90m wide, with facings coated in grey or brown lime plaster. The wall foundation and core are usually packed with *terra rossa*, though brown earth (clay) and grey lime mortar were also employed (Table 7). In general, the construction method is broadly similar to the Period 2 curtain, though *terra rossa* and lime plaster and mortar are never found in the Roman wall. There is some evidence that the 2.65m (narrow wall) and 3.9m (broad wall) sectors alternated, suggesting that the wall was built by particular construction gangs who worked their way around the circuit. However, the picture is confused by the inclusion of the pre-existing remains of the Roman wall, and by the incomplete exposure today of the wall-line. The exception to this pattern is Sector 25, which is only 1.2m wide. This was probably due to the fact that it formed part of the cross-wall within the main line of the fortification circuit, and was not deemed sufficiently important to merit similar treatment.

The exterior of the Umayyad wall is marked by a series of shallow, regularly spaced rectangular buttresses. On average, the broad wall has buttresses 6.15m long, projecting 0.75m, while the narrow wall has buttresses 4.68m long and projecting 0.36m. Where the 3.2m-wide Period 2 wall was refaced, buttresses were also provided. In Sectors 12 and 19, the size of these buttresses largely resembles those of the broad wall, while in Sector 22 the lengths of the buttresses seem a closer match to those found on the narrow wall. The projection of the Sector 22 buttresses, however, is much greater (on average 0.62m) than would be expected, no doubt to provide additional strength in a weak area (Table 7).

Where new gates were built, they had square towers flanking a single passageway. Gate A belongs to this period and it is probable that the similar, but unexcavated, Gate D does also. Gate C was rebuilt as an open semi-circular bastion with a small postern. A suggested reconstruction of its plan is shown in fig. 107. Nothing is known of the supposed Gate B in Sector 10, or of the location of the gate in the cross-wall. Presumably, there must have been other gates and towers around the circuit which have now disappeared.

Of the ten known towers (including gate-towers) thought to belong to Period 3, the two largest (Towers A and C) seem to have been originally corner towers of the Period 1 *temenos* of the Northern Temple which were subsequently rebuilt in the Umayyad period. Excluding the gate-towers (Towers D, J and K), the five remaining curtain wall towers, as far as can be judged, were of standard dimensions, approximating to a square of 5.8m. They were built into the wall at changes in its alignment, with only a limited projection, on average 1.9m (Table 8). Tower H, though now disappeared, seems to have matched this pattern. Tower G, the only truly projecting tower, is an exception because it was added slightly later, presumably to strengthen the cross-wall curtain. The towers which have been excavated (Towers E and G) are quite similar to one another, having thickened facade walls, ashlar masonry only as a facing, and internal earth-floored rooms. Four towers (Towers D, E, F and G) can be definitely related to the Period 3 wall construction; the dating of the other four is less certain. There is some evidence to suggest that Towers D and E were erected prior to the contemporary curtain wall or facade (Sector 8) that connects them.

The highest surviving sections of Period 3 walling above the contemporary internal ground surfaces are 4m (Sector 17) and 3.8m (Sector 14A). It is not known how high the wall originally was or whether the height, in view of the variation in wall thickness, was constant. One section of the Period 1 south *temenos* wall of the Northern Temple stands to a height of 6.1m, and the original arched ceiling of the contemporary Tower A would have been *c.*6.5m high; presumably all of the *temenos* wall was at least this height. This information does not provide direct evidence of how high the fortification wall was, but it does have some bearing on the heights of the towers. Tower A (rebuilt *temenos* corner) and Tower G (standard 5.8m square), although of different origins and dimensions, offer similar evidence regarding the nature of their elevations. Both towers had a higher floor at *c.*3–3.3m above the internal ground surface. In the case of Tower A the ground storey was filled, but in Tower G there was a room. In both, this higher floor must have been intended for an internal room. However, towers which do not project only make sense if they have additional height above the curtain wall and, therefore, at least one storey above the level of the rampart walk. Because of the height of the south *temenos* wall, Tower A must have had a further room, and so stood at least three stories high. Assuming that the floors were 3–3.3m apart, and that the parapet was approximately two metres high, Tower A probably stood 11–12m tall. As circuit towers that have been built together are commonly of the same height, the limited-projection curtain towers, gate-towers, and Tower G probably had three rooms as well. It is worth noting here that a stylized depiction of the city of Philadelphia, including its fortifications, has been recently discovered on a church mosaic excavated at Umm al-Raṣāṣ in central Jordan.[55] The mosaic, which dates from *c.*756 in the ʿAbbāsid period, appears to show four projecting square towers, two of which flank a single gate-passage. Although one has always to be wary of stereotyped imagery, it is interesting, nevertheless, to note that the towers are depicted as having three stories.

Positive dating evidence from the majority of the wall circuit confirms that Period 3 is Umayyad. Sector 8 in Area C is clearly contemporary with the Umayyad buildings of Stratum V. Tower E and Sector 9 appear to be contemporary with Sector 8. The rebuild of Gate C and Sector 25 and the construction of Tower G are all dated by Umayyad pottery. The redesign of Tower A is bonded to the Umayyad palace and shows that the fortification wall is part of the same scheme of development, i.e. 105/724–126/744.

Period 4: The Early ʿAbbāsid Restoration

Four buttresses were rebuilt with a sloping facade and a stepped base in Sectors 8, 9 and 12. On average they are 7.82m or more long, with a projection of 1.98m (Table 9). The rebuilding of the buttresses preceded the addition of the glacis-like revetment, but it seems probable from the appearance of the stepped base in the revetment of Sectors 5, 13, ?14B and 23, that it belonged to the same project of restoration. The sloping revetment is visible at many points around the wall (Sectors 5, 8, 9, ?11, 13, 14 and 16, Tower L and Sectors 20, 22 and 23) and may well have been built around the entire circuit. Its average width is *c.*1.2m (Table 9).

Where the base of the revetment can be seen, it shares the same external ground surface as the Period 3 Umayyad wall, and has a similar method of construction, namely rubble packed with *terra rossa*, brown earth or grey lime mortar, and coated with grey lime plaster. It was therefore added soon after the Umayyad wall was built. In the case of one rebuilt buttress (Sector 9, Buttress 1), rebuilding can be shown to be a restoration of an original buttress that had completely collapsed. In Sector 8, Buttress 2 displays a broken bonding stone at the junction with the wall-face (fig.88) and further subsidence can be seen in 8b and 8e (fig.85). In Sector 16, Buttress 2 has undergone partial restoration following subsidence (fig.101), and part of the original wall-face behind the revetment of Sector 23 has gone, indicating a rebuild at this point also. In Sector 13, the use of the revetment to buttress a mass of rubble on the line of the original Period 2 stairway is similar evidence of patching up.

The revetment is obviously a response to damage to the Umayyad wall. It is apparent from excavations conducted on the Citadel that Umayyad houses suffered severely from an earthquake in 129–30/747–8 (see below, Chapter 11). The damage to the fortifications could also be a result of that earthquake and, if so, the rebuilt buttresses and revetment are probably an early ʿAbbāsid restoration. Where the revetment is not a direct response to damage, it may have been intended to firm up the base of the wall against future subsidence or earthquakes.

Period 5: The ʿAbbāsid Destruction

The evidence from Tower E and the adjacent stretch of Sector 9 in Area D indicates that the restored walls did not survive for more than a century. By that time the tower, wall and revetment had been razed to the ground and covered by a house built in the ʿAbbāsid period (fig.157). In the present state of knowledge, it is difficult to date this event more precisely than the late 3rd/9th–early 4th/10th centuries. At the same period in Area C, the wall of another house was built over the inner face of Sector 8 (fig.89).

Period 6: The Ayyūbid Watch-Tower

Tower B is a solitary addition to the Citadel of the Ayyūbid period. As such it must have served as a watch-tower to oversee the town. If the dating to the Ayyūbid period is correct, that is, to the end of the 6th/12th or the first half of the 7th/13th century, then one might link the construction of the tower with the period of castle building that followed the Battle of Hattīn (583/1187). In an era of castle building, the fact that only a watch-tower was built on a site which would have been ideal for a castle is an eloquent testimony to the decline of 'Ammān's importance.

Comparative Evidence

The following is a short attempt to assess the place of the 'Ammān Citadel fortifications in the development of Roman and Islamic defensive architecture from the 1st to 7th/13th centuries. Comparative evidence is drawn from a variety of sites and should go some way towards a better understanding of the numerous fortification traditions prevalent in the Near and Middle East during these periods.

1. Roman and Early Byzantine

Although dating and building sequences on certain sites still require refinement, there seems little doubt that urban wall circuits of the early Roman period followed the Greek Hellenistic tradition of a stone curtain, with regular, projecting towers, usually square, as exemplified at the Parthian cities of Dura (Syria)[56] and Hatra (Iraq),[57] and Nabataean Petra (Jordan).[58] Roman military defences, displaying square plans with projecting square towers, similarly betray earlier origins, as exhibited at the Hellenistic fort at Jabal Sartaba (Jordan),[59] and several Nabataean forts in the Province of Arabia, namely the Lower Fort at Maḥaṭṭat al-Ḥajj, Khirbat al-Fityān and Khirbat al-Qirāna (Jordan), and Hazeva (Palestine).[60]

The original Roman city wall at Palmyra (Syria) is dated to the first half of the 1st century AD,[61] and the curtain, close-set square towers and original gates at Jerash (Jordan) to the second half of the century, probably *c.*AD 75.[62] However, the epigraphic evidence on which the latter date is based is only circumstantial, and a late Roman date for the curtain and towers has now been put forward following the results of recent excavations.[63]

Securely attested fortifications of the 2nd century are relatively few. Evidence is too insubstantial to support the Parker theory that the forts of the *Limes Arabicus* are contemporary with Trajan's rebuild of the *Via Nova*,[64] or Johnson's suggestion that certain forts date originally to the Antonine period.[65] It is more likely, as Lander proposes, that the Syrian troops during the 2nd century were billeted in the towns or occupied pre-existing Nabataean military sites. The exception would appear to be the fortress at Udhruḥ (Jordan), where excavations suggest a Trajanic date for the initial building phase of the enclosure wall.[66] Apart from the Roman curtain wall at 'Ammān, the only other known 2nd-century urban circuit in Arabia is that at Umm al-Jimāl. Here, epigraphic evidence suggesting an AD 177–180 construction date[67] has been confirmed by excavation.[68]

Firm evidence for Severan fortifications in the East is also lacking. Some small forts or (?) customs posts appear to have been built or expanded in the northern sector of the *Limes Arabicus* in Jordan, namely Qaṣr al-'Uwaynid,[69] Qaṣr al-Ḥallabāt,[70] and Qaṣr al-Usaykhin.[71] Several other Jordanian sites belonging to the central and southern sectors of the *limes*, which might have housed the larger, epigraphically attested, auxiliary units, are suggested by Lander as possible Severan foundations.[72] These include Da'jāniya, the Upper Fort at Maḥaṭṭat al-Ḥajj, al-Quwayra, Qaṣr al-Kithāra and Qaṣr al-Thurayyā, as well as the Syrian fort at al-Diyātha (Diyate). Further afield, the fort at 'Ayn Sinu II (Iraq), which formed part of Severus' Mesopotamian frontier, displays the first use in the Roman East of projecting, rounded towers, as well as the traditional square variety.[73] The second city wall at Palmyra (Syria) possibly also belongs to this late 2nd/early 3rd-century period.[74]

A major strengthening of the *Limes Arabicus* appears to have taken place *c.*AD 300.[75] New military forts, both large and small, are attested epigraphically and archaeologically. The large Jordanian legionary fortresses at al-Lajjūn,[76] and Udhruḥ,[77] together with the site at al-Dumayr in Syria,[78] display projecting, U-shaped interval towers and circular, three-quarter round/fan-shaped angle towers.[79] U-shaped towers are characteristic of the late Roman period, and close parallels can be found with fortifications on the Lower Danube and Mesopotamian frontiers.[80] Eastern examples include the small fort at Pagnik (Turkey), the town walls at Dibsī Faraj (Syria),[81] the Diocletianic inner wall at Palmyra (Syria),[82] and the early 4th-century town defences at Singara (Iraq).[83]

Other late Roman forts, commonly found in Jordan, are of the so-called *quadriburgia* plan – small, rectangular structures with square, projecting towers. Examples include Dayr al-Kahf, Qaṣr Bshayr, Qaṣr al-Azraq and Khirbat ez-Zona.[84] Mention should be made here of the existence in Saudi Arabia of the fortified sites at Taymā[85] and Qaryat al-Faw.[86] Both are built of stone and are commonly believed to date to the early centuries AD. The similarity between them and the Roman *quadriburgia* fort plan is particularly marked.

The use of both square and U-shaped interval towers and circular, three-quarter round angle towers continued into the early Byzantine period. Examples of early 6th-century foundations and/or restorations include the cites of Dara and Theodosiopolis (Erzerum) in Turkey, and the important Syrian strategic sites of Sergiopolis (Ruṣāfa), Zenobia (Ḥalabiyya) and Circesium (Buṣayra).[87] In North Africa, early Byzantine foundations tend to follow a 'text book' rectangular plan with rectangular, projecting towers at the corners and, on large circuits, at intervals along the sides. U-shaped towers are unattested and circular, three-quarter round angle towers only occur on town walls, as at Bagai (Algeria).[88]

2. Sasanian

Limited evidence suggests that Sasanian fortifications in Iraq and Iran from the early 3rd century onwards were quite distinctive in character and markedly different from the contemporary late Roman and early Byzantine defences.[89] The 3rd-century city walls at Ctesiphon (Iraq) had massive, rounded projecting towers; as far as is known, U-shaped or, more commonly, semi-circular towers were exclusively used in Sasanian fort walls, such as those at the Iranian sites of Bishapur,[90] 4th-century Sīrāf,[91] 6th-century Tureng Tepe,[92] and late 6th/early 7th-century Qaṣr-i Shīrīn.[93]

3. Umayyad and 'Abbāsid

During the late 1st/7th to early 2nd/8th centuries under the Umayyads, several former Roman and Byzantine frontier forts were re-occupied as fortified residences; the clearest example in Jordan is Qaṣr al-Ḥallabāt (see Table 4). There was also new construction following the pattern of a fort. These Umayyad buildings consist essentially of a square enclosure with a central courtyard, defended by semi-circular interval, and circular, three-quarter round angle, buttresses or buttress-like towers. For the list of buildings, see Table 4.

The larger sites at 'Anjar (Lebanon) and Qaṣr al-Ḥayr al-Sharqī also follow the tradition of half-round towers. At 'Anjar the walls are strengthened at regular intervals by projecting U-shaped solid towers with hollow three-quarter round angle towers (fig.169). At Qaṣr al-Ḥayr the half-round tower is used, solid in the lower section, but with a room at the level of the rampart walk (fig.170).

In the late 2nd/8th century, the Umayyad palace plan continued to be used, as exemplified at the large early 'Abbāsid site at Ukhayḍir (fig.77).[94] Similarly, there are solid U-shaped interval towers, and larger hollow hollow round corner towers, at the near contemporary sites of Raqqa,[95] and the Octagon at Qādisiyya.[96] One may connect both these plans with the Round City of Baghdad.[97]

Further afield, there are two sites of mid-3rd/9th century date where square towers and buttresses occur, at Aghlabid Sousse (Tunisia) and 'Abbāsid Anavarza (Turkey). The city walls of Sousse are much rebuilt. The exterior is characterized by regular, square, projecting towers and, on one wall at least, by long, rectangular buttresses.[98] Anavarza ('Ayn Zarba) in Cilicia was one of the principal fortified cities of the *thughūr*, the early Islamic frontier against Byzantium. Hellenkemper's work at the site has distinguished three wall-lines, of which one is an early 'Abbāsid, mid-3rd/9th century fortification, and another a Ḥamdānid wall of the mid-4th/10th century.[99] The 'Abbāsid, wall is characterized by external, rectangular buttresses and two square, projecting gate-towers; no other towers are visible. The Hamdanid wall displays regular, projecting square towers.

4. Fāṭimid and Ayyūbid

The characteristics of Fāṭimid defensive architecture are well illustrated in the walls of Cairo. The late 5th/11th-century city wall displays a majority of square, projecting towers, together with some U-shaped examples. The citadel walls, built almost a century later, similarly exhibit the combined use of square, semi-circular and three-quarter round towers.[100]

During the Ayyūbid period following the Battle of Ḥaṭṭīn (583/1187), castles with square towers were built or rebuilt at the Jordanian sites at Azraq, Salṭ,[101] 'Ajlūn (Qal'at al-Rabaḍ),[102] and at Pilgrim's Castle, Athlīt in Palestine.[103] The Ayyūbid city walls at Aleppo and Damascus (Syria), Jerusalem (Palestine) and Cairo

(Egypt) all remain in part. Even more striking are the citadels of Aleppo,[104] Cairo,[105] and Bosra (Syria) – where the citadel grew up round the Roman theatre.[106]

5. Discussion

As discussed above, the major tradition of urban and military fortification in the eastern Roman Empire and early Byzantine world was a wall provided with regular, projecting, square towers. However, from the 3rd century onwards, there appears to be an almost simultaneous adoption of the use of round-fronted towers (either U-shaped or three-quarter round) in Sasanian Mesopotamia and on a number of late Roman sites on the eastern frontiers.[107] Smaller, round-fronted buttresses or buttress-like towers (mostly semi-circular or three-quarter round) are a characteristic of new construction in the Umayyad period, and their architecture reflects both Roman and Sasanian influences.[108] However, the main architectural tradition of the ʿAbbāsid Caliphate in Iraq was little influenced by the Roman tradition, and uses the half-round buttress and tower universally. Nevertheless the square-tower tradition did survive, as seen at Anavarza and Sousse, and continued into the Fāṭimid and Ayyūbid periods.

The Umayyad fortification wall at ʿAmmān Citadel, with its occasional square towers and rectangular buttresses, is clearly different in character from the dominant contemporary tradition of regular, semi-circular and three-quarter round buttresses and buttress-like towers. Although the Qalʿa of the Umayyad period was, in function, similar to the other new settlements of the period discussed in chapter 11, the tradition of fortification those settlements represented was ignored in favour of one related to urban fortification.

It is evident that the Umayyad wall of ʿAmmān is derived from an inherited tradition of urban fortification of the Hellenistic and east Roman worlds, that is, of a wall provided with regular, projecting, square towers. At ʿAmmān, this tradition has become transformed into the use of regular rectangular buttresses and square towers at changes in the line of the wall. Similar combinations of towers and buttresses occur at the 3rd/9th century walls at Sousse and Anavarza, although the dimensions of their buttresses are different from ʿAmmān.

One can identify, therefore, at ʿAmmān, Sousse and Anavarza, a continuing variant of the Hellenistic tradition of square towers, alongside the more widespread early Islamic tradition of Syrian and Mesopotamian round-fronted towers and/or buttresses. One might also propose a trend in urban fortification during the 2nd/8th and 3rd/9th centuries, towards a reduction in the numbers of full towers and their replacement by buttresses or solid towers. Such a development would mirror the parallel trend in the Umayyad *quṣūr*, where in only a relatively few cases are the semi-circular buttresses real towers.

Although new city walls are known from textual sources to have been built at a number of places in the Umayyad period,[109] ʿAmmān Citadel is the only example so far known from the archaeological record of Umayyad fortification work that could be described as belonging to the tradition of city defences. Furthermore, the revetment and rebuilt buttresses, although physically unimpressive, are one of the few examples in Jordan of ʿAbbāsid constructional activity of a remotely monumental kind. The early Islamic defences at ʿAmmān, therefore, provide an important link between the fortification traditions of Rome, Byzantium and medieval Islam.

9

THE TEMPLE OF HERCULES: A REASSESSMENT

by Julian M. C. Bowsher

The temple is situated on the southern part of the upper terrace. The remains measure some 43 by 27 metres, and reach a height of 840 metres above sea level. It is the first monument to be seen as one ascends the Citadel from the east, to the left of the road, just below the Jordan Archaeological Museum. It dominates the southern part of the Citadel today, as it must have done in antiquity.

Impressive though the remains seem, it must be remembered that the temple itself has fared badly over the years. What is left is only a fraction of its former magnificence, the vast proportion of it having been destroyed or removed. Moreover, the temple was just the centrepiece within a complex that covered over eight and a half thousand square metres.

Ever since it was first described at the beginning of the last century, the temple has excited much interest and speculation. As a result of this interest it has been tentatively identified, and become popularly known, as the Temple of Hercules.

Despite its importance, the temple complex as a whole has never been fully discussed – the Italian excavations of the 1930s not having been finally published. There has been piecemeal work on the temple since the 1930s, but recent work on the *temenos* walls, discussed in detail by Wood in this volume, has provided an opportunity to assess the whole complex afresh. There is no attempt here to offer a detailed architectural analysis, but a discussion and description based on a synthesis of all available information, old and new. Such architectural and historical conclusions will only be tested by future archaeological investigations within the area.

HISTORIOGRAPHY

1. Surveys

In early 1806 'Ammān attracted the attention of Ulrich Jasper Seetzen.[1] After a description of the remains in the valley, Seetzen reported that even more ruins were to be seen on the hill to the northwest. Principally, there were some enormous Corinthian columns fallen, it seemed to him, from a rotunda, which nevertheless must have been very imposing. He was also impressed by the beautiful red and white 'marble' they that were made of.

In 1812 John Lewis Burckhardt produced the first plan of 'Ammān.[2] Figure *n* on his map is described as: 'traces of a large temple; several of its broken columns are lying on the ground, they are the largest I saw at Amman, some of them being three foot and a half in diameter, their capitals are of the Corinthian order.' Thus our first identification of the monument is as a temple.

Four years after Burckhardt's journey, James Silk Buckingham was even more impressed by 'the ruins of a magnificent edifice, too much destroyed for any plan of it to be taken, but showing, by its broken fragments, evident marks of its former grandeur. The pedestals of the pillars that formed a colonnade along its eastern front, were still standing in their original positions, and many fine Corinthian capitals were scattered near them. The shafts were of a greater diameter than the length of my musket, or at least five foot. They were composed of several pieces raised one above the other, having a square hole in the centre of each piece for the reception of a central iron rod, by which the whole were kept together.' He then went on to describe the letters noted on the bases of the drums concluding that they were for the 'guidance of the workmen in uniting them'. Farther on he found 'a fine Corinthian architrave of a doorway, apparently belonging to the ruined temple last described, but now partly buried in the earth....'[3] Buckingham was the first to note on this stone the dedicatory inscription of the temple, but he failed to offer any interpretation.[4]

In 1826 Léon de Laborde noted that crowning the heights of the Citadel was a temple of large dimensions.[5] This he deduced from the diameter of the columns being not less than five feet.

Four years later George Robinson was also to ascribe the great size of this temple to the three and a half feet diameter of the columns and capitals 'lying prostrate in the area'.[6] H. B. Tristram saw in 1864 'one group of six enormous columns, of which the bases only are standing, while the prostrate shafts are five feet in diameter.'[7]

In 1863 however, F. de Saulcy had made a number of interesting observations.[8] He noted that it was generally the 'basements' of the temple which had survived. The entrance had consisted of a 'stylobate' from which had fallen, evidently as a result of an earthquake, two enormous columns still lying as they fell. Indeed it was probably columns like these which now adorned the facade of the 'great square tower'.[9] He also described fragments of 'cornice', three quarters buried, decorated with fascia, an olive scroll and palmettes, carrying an inscription.

In the spring of 1871 the Reverend A. E. Northey travelled across the Jordan to visit sites noted by Tristram. Arriving on the citadel at 'Ammān he noted 'a colossal temple' whose 'columns were of an immense size'. He reproduced the plan drawn up by Warren with the temple (labelled 'M') marked as a plain rectangle (fig.3).[10]

The American Selah Merrill, in 'Ammān in 1875, had no doubts about the 'magnificent temple on the hill to the north'.[11] It was, he decided, 'fifty feet wide by one hundred and sixty feet long. It had four columns on each end, and eight on each side. The columns were forty five feet high ... and ... six feet in diameter', whilst the capitals were of 'rich Corinthian work'. 'Around the entire building there appears to have extended an architrave, which was three foot wide, and under a portion of it, at least, was a Greek inscription beautifully carved in two lines, the single letters being six inches in length. The stones composing this architrave were badly broken when the building fell, and some of them are covered in the earth, while others, half buried, project from the ground.' Merrill was also the first to publish a reconstructed plan of the temple (fig.108).

Laurence Oliphant described the 'magnificent edifice' succinctly: 'The foundations of this temple were about eighty by forty yards, and its facade was composed of four colossal columns the pedestals of which are still standing while the columns themselves measure about five feet in diameter, are prostrate at their base.'[12]

Captain Conder of the Royal Engineers visited 'Ammān for the Palestine Exploration Fund in 1881 (figs 4, 109, pl.61a).[13] Of the temple he was the first to realise that 'The western part ... has entirely disappeared' and that 'Only the foundation of the pronaos or porch remains, and scattered fragments of a huge cornice. The pillars have fallen, and only the bases remain, four on the east and one on the north, and another on the south side of the porch. They stand on a wall ten feet high, which is 52 feet north and south, by 23′7″ east and west. The shafts lying on the ground are 4′6″ in diameter; and battered capitals of the Corinthian order were also lying on the ground. The building must have been a very large one, as the pillars exceed in diameter any others in Amman.' He later notes 'The cornices or epistylia are 3 ft high, and bear Greek inscriptions.' Conder produced a restored scale plan of the pronaos (fig.109), and a profile of one of the pillar bases.

Much is owed to Howard Crosby Butler, the American archaeologist, for our knowledge of Roman and later architecture in the area.[14] He noted the position of the temple and considered it 'prostyle, tetrastyle, with one column on the return on either side; the antae consisted of half columns' (fig.110). At the time he thought the ruins proved this, for they showed the 'entire front wall of the podium is in situ together with seven metres of the north wall of the podium, adjoining the front wall. Upon these walls stand the massive bases of the two middle columns of the pronaos, and the base of the column on the return on the north side.' The bases of two half-columns and drums of others lay nearby, including the south eastern column 'practically intact ... having fallen in perfect order from base to capital. Sections of the heavy cap moulding of the podium are to be found on all sides. Blocks of the architrave are visible on the surface', whilst 'bits of carved frieze and cornice built into ... the south wall' were similar to fragments from the Temple of Zeus at Jerash. Butler also noted that the bases were unusual in having 'large square pulvinated blocks below their regular plinths'. As to the building itself, he realised that the 'structure of the parotids was gone' and the 'Cella with part of the podium beneath has entirely disappeared', although he hoped that 'excavations might reveal the foundations'. Lastly he gave some measurements. The height of the podium exclusive of the base moulding was 2.7m. Fragments of column aggregated to 9.3m in height. The capitals were in two sections, the lower 0.70m high, the upper 0.85m high, and 1.6m wide at the top. The architrave, one metre high, was tri-fasciaed, separated by bead-and-reel mouldings seven centimetres wide. Butler's reconstruction, based on Vitruvius and the Jerash example, has remained until recently the most popular conception of what the temple was like. He was also the first to draw detailed plans and elevations of the monument as it appeared (fig.110a–g).

The scale of the remains can be detected in an aerial photograph of 1918 (pl.2a), when they were probably in much the same condition as when Seetzen saw them in 1806.[15] All the descriptions were influenced by the temple's (incomplete) size, and referred to it as enormous, magnificent, colossal and large, although early measurements vary; Merrill imagined the dimensions to have been 50′ × 160′ (15 × 49m), Oliphant 40 × 80 yds (36 × 73m), Conder 52′ × 23′ 7″(*c*.15.8 × 7.2m). But apart from an increasing sophistication in description and analysis it appears that there had been changes to the monument. Tristram saw six column bases, Oliphant four, Conder six and Butler three. Given that Conder's drawing is clearly a reconstruction, it seems that the number of surviving bases did decline. The diameter of the columns likewise seems to have been thought to vary, between 3′ 6″, 4′ 6″, 5′ and 6′, with five foot the average. Recent measurements have ranged from 1.3m (4′ 3″) and 1.4m (4′ 7″) to around 1.6m. (5′ 3″), the last being the most common, although the shafts taper. None have been found of 6′ (1.83m).

2. Excavations and Recent Research

Such was the state of the temple when it attracted the attention of the Italian archaeological team directed by Renato Bartoccini in 1930. Despite a number of articles, his team's work was never satisfactorily published, indeed many of their plans and drawings, by the architect Carlo Ceschi, have only recently emerged.[16] Bartoccini's declared intention was to clear the monument completely, including the removal of fallen architectural elements and later deposits, but little description of a methodology emerged.[17] The remains were soon stripped and for the first time the entire temple plan emerged and was accurately recorded.

In 1968 a 'modest joint excavation' in the area of the temple was carried out by the American Center for Oriental Research, the University of Jordan and the Department of Antiquities. Trench I (area v) was adjacent to the surviving eastern end, trench III (iv) was at the southwest corner of the temple. A further trench (vi) was opened up some fifty metres further east, south of Tower G on the east wall. Bedrock was reached in all areas and a promising amount of information about the temple was uncovered.[18]

Following these excavations of the 1960s, Fakharani published in 1975 a detailed study of the building; this revisionist study sees the building as a library, and not a temple.[19]

In 1979 and 1981 Alastair Northedge conducted investigations into the Citadel fortifications. This included a series of excavations along the southern and eastern portions of what turned out to be the *temenos* enclosure around the temple. For the first time, a detailed architectural documentation and a stratigraphic analysis has provided important evidence for the layout and chronology of the area, and a basis for this chapter.[20]

After the first draft of this paper was written, a new programme of work on the temple was begun in July 1990. The project, conducted jointly by the American Center of Oriental Research and the Jordanian Department of Antiquities, included widespread excavations in the *temenos* of the temple, and a scheme of restoration for the temple itself. At the time of writing, publication of the results was not available, but we would like to thank those responsible for the project for advance information on their findings.[21]

TOPOGRAPHY

Although the natural topography of the Citadel is not fully understood, the height of the bedrock does seem to have varied considerably.[22] The temple itself was built on a spur of rock which sloped down to the east and south.

Occupation or construction in the area prior to the erection of the temple is difficult to elucidate, because the temple itself was built directly on the bedrock. The Italian assertion of an earlier Ammonite High Place within the temple, has been dismissed after further examination.[23] What does exist is a Bronze Age tomb,[24] and cisterns of Iron Age date cut into the rock in and around the temple.[25] There was Hellenistic activity associated with the remodelling of these cisterns, and dump deposits of similar date (for an unknown purpose) were encountered to the east and north of the temple.[26] Fakharani recorded two 'Graeco-Roman' tombs ten metres north of the temple, which, he suggests, predate the complex. But given their position within the acropolis, indeed the *temenos*, it is more likely that they reflect a use of the area after the complex was abandoned.[27] There is, therefore, no evidence for any construction on the site antedating the existing remains. At present it is still fair to agree with the assumption of Harding that the Romans had swept away all earlier remains to make room for a new town-planning scheme. In the area of the temple they left the spur of bedrock as a base on which to build, but filled in the lower surrounding parts.

THE TEMPLE (fig.111; pls 61b, 62–3)

The foundations of the temple lie directly on and around the bedrock; however, given the slope of the bedrock down to the east, there is a difference in the coursing. Much of the southern part was revealed by the

Italian expedition. These lower courses consist of roughly rusticated white limestone blocks measuring, on average, 1.50 × 0.40 × 0.60m, each stepping out further than the course on top. Bartoccini believed this masonry to have belonged to a Hellenistic building on top of which the Romans had built their temple.[28] A sounding dug by Fakharani and Dornemann at the eastern end revealed twelve internal courses rising from the bedrock.[29] The four lowest courses are regularly laid headers and stretchers with thin layers of mortar. The upper foundation courses here were distinctly less regular. This difference in coursing led Fakharani to consider that, although the larger rusticated blocks were contemporary foundations, these lower levels at the eastern end were associated with an earlier structure dating to the late Hellenistic/early Roman period.[30] Zayadine noted that the uppermost foundation level at the western end projects out of alignment, and suggested again that this indicated the remains of an earlier structure, thereby giving credence to the Bartoccini theory.[31]

The top of the uppermost foundation blocks therefore, is where Fakharani recognized the Roman ground level, at a height of 836.43 metres above sea level.[32] The superstructure is composed of finely dressed blocks of pinkish limestone, averaging 0.95 × 0.90 × 0.60m, a quality of stone that impressed Seetzen. All that remains of the podium is one plain course superimposed by a base moulding (fig.112; pl.62b).[33] Recessed above this are two further plain courses (of similar dimensions), surviving only on the northern side. The original height of the podium will have been that level on which the column plinths survive at the eastern end (pl.62a). Fragments of the cap moulding found in the vicinity (fig.113; pl.63a) measure 0.69m, allowing room for two further courses above the base moulding.[34] The full height of the podium, from the *temenos* surface to the temple floor, is therefore four metres,[35] similar in style and dimension to the podium of the temple of Artemis at Jerash.

As noted above, the podium survives to its full height at the eastern end, where there are fragments of four squarish pulvinated plinths, three along the front, with one set behind the northernmost one (pl.62a).[36] Excepting the southern plinth, they are all surmounted by Attic column bases (fig.114; pl.63b). These constitute the highest point of the remains. The full height of the column shafts is a little over ten metres (pl.63f).[37] The shafts also taper from a diameter of 1.55m. at the base to 1.15m. at the top; they are plain, but have a slight *entasis*. Many of the column drums are inscribed with numbers related to their construction.[38] The capitals (fig.115), although much weathered, are free Corinthian without *cauliculi*, the abacus is decorated with floral motifs which descend in between the *helices*.[39] They were mostly made in two blocks, occasionally one, and are 1.46m high.

The architrave is one metre high with three fascia separated by elongated bead and reel mouldings, a *cyma recta* decorated with palmettes and a plain fillet (pl.63g). The soffit is decorated with a garland motif three leaves wide (fig.116).[40] Four blocks of the architrave found inscribed with the dedication aggregate to a length of 9.84m.[41] To date, however, no fragments of frieze or cornice have been positively identified. A cornice fragment reused in a nearby wall would appear to come from the temple entablature, and other fragments have been found recently.[42]

The floor would have been level across the building, and it is clear that, along with the superstructure, almost all of the podium core above the bedrock shelf has disappeared. The cistern was filled with earth, and other cavities with masonry. The large unworked boulder at the eastern end, Bartoccini's 'Sacred Rock', merely forms part of the podium core, being below the level of the floor.[43]

The foundations of the east wall of the *cella* appear ten metres behind the front colonnade, and are about 17m long. There are also traces of the central doorway, with an aperture of 2.7m, paralleled by the central intercolumniation of the facade. These foundations continue along the southern side for a certain distance, whilst the line of the north wall of the *cella* can be made out in the bedrock. The return at the north-west corner is similarly marked, showing the length of the *cella* to be about 25m.

From the moment that the Italian expedition uncovered and published the full extent of the podium, some 43 by 27 metres, a temple peripteral and hexastyle in plan should have been recognized. However, Ceschi produced a tetrastyle restoration that was similar to Butler's (fig.110g).[44] Fakharani, following the tetrastyle restoration, postulated eleven (or thirteen) columns along each side, basing himself on the preferred option of Vitruvius.[45] Later restorations proposed a peripteral and hexastyle plan.[46] The recent work on the temple, however, has again suggested a tetrastyle prostyle plan.[47]

There was clearly one column on the return either side of the central opening, and it can be seen that the intercolumniation of the facade is not only the same as that on its return to the north, but appears to be that of the *pteroma* also. This intercolumniation is just over the diameter of three columns, regarded as dangerously wide by Vitruvius.[48] This measurement does not provide for a number of exactly equidistantly spaced peristyle columns, and it is possible that there may have been some shortening of intercolumnar spacing along the sides. The discovery of engaged column fragments[49] reveal that the *cella* walls projected as *antae*, but whether they included internal stairways, as seen on many other eastern temples, is unknown. There was perhaps also an *adyton* at the back of the *cella*, but no evidence remains.[50] The reconstruction by Ceschi reveals a series of pilasters against the outer wall of the *cella*,[51] but this appears to be hypothetical. The shape of the temple would have been more solid than beautiful.

Parotids, projecting from the eastern end of the podium, would have enclosed steps down to the surface of the *temenos*. This structure has entirely disappeared with no trace, at present, of its extent.

It is evident that the podium was built for a hexastyle peripteral temple. If the temple as finally constructed was a tetrastyle prostyle building, it would appear that the scale of the building was reduced in the course of construction – that is, a smaller temple was built on a large podium. However the remains of the superstructure of the temple are relatively fragmentary, and the clearest evidence about the form of the building comes from the podium.

THE TEMENOS

It is certain that a temple of these proportions would be placed within a *temenos* (enclosure) in order to enhance its grandeur. The *temenos* itself also formed a sacred precinct, as was common in sanctuaries of this period. Aerial photographs hint at such an area, revealing a rectangle around the temple with one entrance to the south east (fig.164; pl.11). Bartoccini noted that levelled ground to the south of the temple was probably associated with a gate,[52] as Butler had earlier realized that the Propylaeon below was linked with a gate in the *temenos* wall, as an access to the temple.[53] A *temenos* had certainly therefore been postulated,[54] but it was the British excavations of 1979 that finally established its form. Within the *temenos*, in front of the temple, there would probably have been an altar, although there are no surviving traces of such, owing to much of the area being occupied by later Islamic graves.

The south wall of the *temenos* also formed a stretch of the southern curtain wall. This was built on a foundation of rusticated blocks, the superstructure being 3.2m wide. A small stretch of the inner face was found in 1981 at the western end, the blocks were laid header and stretcher, and measured an average of 0.60 × 0.30 × 1.20m. The southeast corner is clearly defined in the curtain wall line, and from here a narrower eastern wall is visible for a short stretch running north, before being obscured by the later fortification wall of Sector 25. However, excavations around Tower G revealed no further trace of it, perhaps because of robbing activity. This east wall was 0.9m wide, and its blocks were an average of 1.22 × ? × 0.35m. The western wall of the *temenos* was not visible on the surface but excavations in trench E21 revealed a foundation line two metres wide bonded into the south wall (fig.92). The southern width of the *temenos* was thus probably 119m, although the possibility remains that this bond does not represent the southwest corner of the *temenos*, but rather the wall of a room attached to the south wall.[55] The line of the northern wall has been conjectured from the westwards return in Sector 25 of the wall next to Tower G, or about 15m north of the temple. Similar, in fact, to the 14m distance between the temple and the west wall. This conjectured wall would be largely under the modern road.[56]

These enclosure walls, then, were clearly solid, and define an area roughly 119 metres by 73 metres. The discovery of a stretch of stylobate to the west of the temple indicates that there was also an inner colonnade.[57] The stylobate is one metre wide, and the projected line of the western enclosure wall shows the distance between them to have been three metres. Excavations in the southeast corner (trenches E5, E6 and E10) failed to pick up remains of the colonnade, but it may well yet be found in this area.

Surviving on this stretch of stylobate on the west side are two plinths with superimposed column bases cut from single blocks, two metres apart. The pedestals, of squat dimensions, have a narrow flat dado, whilst the bases have the same Attic proportions as those from the temple (fig.117; pl.63c). Some column shaft fragments from this colonnade have recently been identified and reassembled, giving a height 'close to five metres'.[58] A number of capitals, 0.62m high, also survive. These are free Corinthian with two rows of abacus leaves visible, and a single rosette in the abacus (fig.118; pl.63d).

Also present are a number of mutilated architrave blocks, 0.69m high, in remaining details similar to those of the temple (fig.119). These fragments have usually been associated with the temple, without, however, any discussion of their exact provenance.[59] Although this architrave is slightly taller than the capital, it can be proposed that these fragments come from the *temenos* colonnade. There are no other suitable candidates for this element, and neither do there appear to be any remaining fragments of frieze or cornice.[60]

Despite the similarity between the architectural details of the colonnade and the temple, the reduced proportions are not constant, and the full height of the colonnade remains uncertain. The roof of the portico itself was almost certainly tiled, and sloped down into the *temenos*.

As noted above, the ground surface associated with

the temple (on its southern side) was 836.43m above sea level; the level of the stylobate to the west is a mere two centimetres higher. The threshold of Gate C, however, is at the height of 835.30m. Excavations against the south wall corroborate the suggestion of a widespread remodelling of the area. From at least three metres below the level of the threshold there are substantial fill layers of second century date, and a series of *huwwar* (rammed chalk) surfaces, abutting and therefore post-dating the wall (fig.95). There is no trace of any stone paving in the *temenos* itself, only in the gateway, perhaps on account of the area involved. The first surface is at a height of 834.75m against the wall, but it then slopes down a little to the north. The level of the superstructure of the south wall above its foundations at its western end is at about 835.80m. Thus the level of the gate threshold is a little over a metre lower than the surface next to the temple, some 25m to the north. The surface however, is a metre and a half lower than the temple. Although there may have been architectural reasons for the differences in level in this gate area, the surface of the *temenos*, being of chalk, was obviously susceptible to wear, as shown by the resurfacing seen in section. However, Roman levels immediately west of Tower G are just over 835.00, which indicate a gradual slope southwards and eastwards.[61]

Unfortunately the excavated sequence of the gate cannot be checked against the temple area owing to a lack of published stratigraphy. But the excavations of 1968 obviously penetrated through post-construction, and perhaps post-destruction, dump levels in front of the *pronaos*. These rubble layers did produce 'pottery sherds and coins ... mixed together and belonging to Roman, Byzantine and later periods'.[62]

Only one gate into the *temenos* has been found to date, Gate C in the southeast corner. Before Butler's work, it was regarded as a tower, but excavations in 1979 and 1981 confirmed and elucidated its function. The gate took the form of a rectangular structure projecting at an angle of 55° from the wall. Flush with the line of the wall, there was an opening, revealed by scars on the surviving slabs, of 10.6m. There is also the scar of a column base plinth. From these marks one can reconstruct the plan of it as having pilasters or half columns at the edges, with two columns either side of a central passageway (fig.106; pls 49–50).[63] The space between the pilaster and column bases exactly parallels that between the colonnade plinths in front, at two metres. The central opening of about 4.4m was probably also paralleled in the colonnade. The projecting structure of the gate enclosed a semi-circular area, with a gate threshold at its apex to the south. The nature of the external facade is unclear, although its plan would probably not allow for any monumentality of design either on the inside or the outside. The plan of the whole structure is curious and reminiscent of military gateways. However it may have been dictated by an earlier form: traces of a 1st century AD structure underneath Gate C might also be the remains of a gate.[64]

Conder thought that he had detected a gate in the line of the east wall,[65] but excavations in 1968 disproved this.[66] There appeared to be some Roman occupation further east on the lower terrace,[67] and there may well have been an entrance somewhere in the east wall whose traces have disappeared. Foundations of Roman date, not earlier than the *temenos*, uncovered in excavations on the west side of Tower G, are as yet of an unknown function (fig.105).

It is also possible that there may have been another gate in the northeast corner of the *temenos*, opposite Gate C. This follows the suggestion that the line of an Islamic road passing through Area B lies on the alignment of an earlier Roman road (figs 145–6, 164–5).[68] A gate in this position would certainly make sense in that it entered the *temenos* well in front of the temple. For the same reason it is unlikely that there was a gate on the west or rear wall. Indeed, there is no present archaeological information for this south-western part of the citadel in the Roman period.

Finally it should be noted that there must have been a way down from Gate C to the monumental Propylaeon on the lower slopes of the citadel hill: the two structures were aligned in strict axiality. However the notion of a straight stairway is unlikely because of the extreme gradient of the slope in this area, which could not have been negotiated by elderly or infirm inhabitants of Roman Philadelphia, while the evidence of the support wall of Gate C (Sector 13: figs 97, 106; pl.51b) also suggests that the path made a turn to the east outside the gate. The route reproduced (fig.164), therefore, is based on more sympathetic contours.

Many earlier writers considered the Propylaeon as a temple in its own right until Butler recognised its connection with Gate C (fig.120; pl.64).[69] Although the remains are no longer extant, it appears to have consisted, in the main, of a facade with one large central opening and two smaller flanking ones, with free standing columns in front matching engaged elements of the facade (fig.120a). The facade measured 25m across, whilst its original height may have been nearly 12m (fig.120c–d). There were gabled niches above the side doors with, probably, a pediment over the whole facade. Butler's restoration presents two different possibilities for the pediment (fig. 120c & d), one reconstructed according to the Propylaeon at Jerash, and the second with an arched pediment, after a photograph. It is evident that the reconstruction with an arched pediment is the correct one (pl.64b).[70]

The pilaster capitals were Corinthian and appeared to have a rosette within the abacus. A tri-fasciaed architrave supported a frieze of a floral scroll and a modillion cornice, all of similar proportions. To judge by the photographs, the decoration appears compatible with a mid-2nd century date.

THE SITING AND LAYOUT OF THE COMPLEX

We know that the Iron Age and Hellenistic cities were centred on the Citadel hill, but that during the Roman period settlement expanded to the valley west and principally to the south. Although the position of the temple complex may indeed be associated with earlier developments, we can, at present, only judge it by the known date of the Roman period.

However it seems that the builders followed the Hellenistic tradition of placing the whole temple complex on a height.[71] Butler noted that it was not on the highest part of the citadel, that being a little to the north.[72] The Temple of Hercules was obviously one of the most important shrines of Roman Philadelphia, and its position on the southern part of the citadel ensured its dominance not only of the acropolis but of the Roman city below.

Although it is the only surviving temple building definitely attested from classical 'Ammān, the proposed site of the Northern Temple discussed elsewhere in this volume suggests that as with many Roman cities of the East, Philadelphia seems to have had two major temples. From a study of the wall sequence around the citadel it is clear that the development discussed here was a little later than that of the northern court. The similarity of decorative elements from that area does, however, suggest a contemporary date.[73] It may also be possible to show that the planning of the northern court took account of what was happening (or about to happen) to the south. The road which runs across the outer court is out of alignment with the rest of the complex but is angled towards Gate C at the southern end of the citadel. Likewise, the possible Roman road across the centre of the citadel is similarly oriented (hence the suggested gateway).

It is most likely that the temple was planned and built at the same time as its *temenos*. It can be seen already that the south, west and east walls, as well as Gate C, are contemporary. The method of construction of the walls; a dressed limestone header and stretcher superstructure resting on a thicker alignment of rusticated blocks of limestone, parallels the construction of the temple. Fills against the southern wall dating to the second century reflect a levelling almost certainly associated with the southwards slope of the bedrock. Although the two developments cannot be linked stratigraphically, the fill details are not incompatible and the surface levels are within an acceptable range. Moreover, architectural details from the *temenos* and the temple are very similar, and are all cut from the same hard grey limestone.

That there might have been difficulties associated with such an ambitious scheme are suggested by the divergence of opinion on the final plan of the temple. A solution to these problems may be sought in a change of plan during construction. Structural, or more likely, financial constraints may well have resulted in a modification of the original conception. A similar fate may also have befallen the southeast gateway (Gate C), where only a rough block was placed for the step up onto the inner stylobate.

The temple itself faces east after the Greek tradition.[74] But it was not axially proportioned within the *temenos*, being further west (space must be left for the parotids and an altar) and north of centre. As it stands, the temple is parallel to the southern wall and quite probably was also parallel to the western wall, but if the later wall of Sector 25 is a true reflection of the earlier *temenos* walls then the eastern and northern walls were slightly out of true. The (one surviving) gateway has no axial relationship with the temple, its position being dictated by the topography and earlier developments.

Sanctuary (and town) planning in the east in the second century was increasingly 'Baroque', involving monumentality and excessive axiality.[75] A supreme example of this new design is seen in the Artemis complex at Jarash, the propylaeon of which, at least, is dated to a decade earlier than the 'Ammān temple.[76] The temple of Hercules did not have the gracefulness associated with a feminine deity, being more squat and simple in design and possessing monumental proportions, nor did its *temenos* have the sophistication of a double enclosure. One would suggest, therefore, that this complex was of a more conservative plan than neighbouring examples.[77] This may be a reflection of previous developments or contemporary restrictions on the citadel, as well as of the topography.

DATE

Nobody has ever suggested that the temple as it stands is anything but Roman; the architectural details alone confirm this. A complex such as this would have taken some years to complete, but a *terminus post quem* can be taken from the dedication recorded in the fragmentary inscription from the *pronaos* facade. This has long been assigned to the reign of Marcus Aurelius, but it has now been refined, not only to the joint reign of Marcus and Lucius Verus, but to the governorship of Publius Iulius Geminius Marcianus, datable to 161–166 AD.[78] It is noteworthy that the Temple of Zeus in Jerash, amongst other buildings within the province, was also dedicated under the governorship of Marcianus.[79]

ATTRIBUTION

The predominant position of the temple makes it the most important religious structure in Philadelphia. The association with Hercules rests largely on the predominance of Heracles in the Philadelphian pantheon; at least, as reflected by his appearance on coins of the city.[80] The Ptolemies responsible for the founding of (classical) 'Ammān also proclaimed Heracles as a divine ancestor,[81] although Philadelphian Heracles was clearly associated with Tyrian Melqart.[82] However it is the association of Heracles/Melqart with an earlier Ammonite deity that has attracted the identification of the temple.[83]

Biblical references depict the chief god of Iron Age Rabbath Ammon as Milcom or Molech/Moloch. A 9th century BC reused inscription found in 1961 just outside the line of the walls at the southwest corner of the citadel confirmed the presence of Milcom.[84] This was generally taken to have referred to a temple of Milcom on the citadel, and an architectural layout for it has recently been proposed.[85]

One should note that it has been suggested that the Citadel also contained temples dedicated to Ishtar or Hathor.[86] The only evidence offered to illustrate previous worship on the site was the now rejected view of Bartoccini's that the boulder underneath the *pronaos* floor was an Ammonite sacred rock.[87]

Fakharani had argued that a Roman temple would not necessarily be associated with pre-classical gods,[88] but I showed that this was precisely the case in a number of examples.[89] Thus Oliphant's suggestion over a hundred years ago that there may have been a previous temple dedicated to 'the sun or to Hercules ... associated with Baal or Moloch' was quite plausible.[90] Milcom/Moloch would have been worshipped throughout Ammonitis, and a later identification with Hercules is perhaps reflected in the general popularity of the latter throughout the region in the Roman period.[91]

Coins of Philadelphia, unlike many other cities in the area, reveal no architectural representations, but show instead a 'car' of Heracles, which carries a portable shrine associated perhaps with cultic processions.[92] It has been suggested that this was a temple of 'Jupiter Zeus'.[93] Zeus was important in the area, being associated with temples on 'High Places';[94] moreover, he also had solar affinities.[95]

Fragments of a colossal statue found in the vicinity of the temple have not been satisfactorily identified, although it is likely to have been the cult statue from the temple itself.[96] Measurements of the surviving left hand (pl.63h) indicate a standing figure of over 12 metres, but a seated figure of just over nine metres would be more likely. A marble head of Tyche from nearby may have been associated with this temple, but is more likely to have been associated with a subsidiary shrine.[97]

The dedicatory inscription describes the temple as an *ieron* (sanctuary), and a newly disovered fragment of this dedication calls the temple an *eortasma* (festival place). This new fragment also suggests that this temple was indeed the Heracleion.[98]

An inscription, found at the beginning of this century, recorded that one Martas, son of Diogenes, built the Heracleion, and that this was gratefully recognized by the community. Martas was the *gymnasiarch* of Philadelphia, but it is not certain whether he built the temple as part of his public – and perhaps religious – duties, or as an expression of private benevolence.[99]

The remodelling of the whole Citadel was likely to have been a civic enterprise, although public funds were clearly supplemented by donations, including those of Martas, who 'built' the temple, and Doseos, who donated columns.[100] However, an Imperial sanction would have been given by the provincial governor.[101]

THE FINAL YEARS

The temple was evidently an important asset to the city of Philadelphia, and quite possibly the object of veneration for a wide area. Indeed, it is suggested that the complex was the venue for the annual festival of Hercules.[102] However little is know of its history and maintenance. There is only evidence that the *temenos* was resurfaced on at least three occasions. The eventual destruction of the temple is much more apparent.

De Saulcy's conclusion that it had been turned into a church in the 4th century was based on a misinterpretation of the inscription and has no archaeological corroboration.[103] Conversely, Conder assumed that it had been 'destroyed by the Christians of the Byzantine period'.[104] Indeed, the eventual demise of the complex may well have been associated with a change of religious affinities. The side-room of Gate C had been abandoned in the fourth century,[105] and by the early fifth century the *temenos* colonnade was being used as a source of building material for the nearby church.[106] There was clearly a partial collapse of the complex, associated perhaps with the earthquake of 363 AD.[107]

The immediate fate of the temple is unknown, but it must have been a sufficiently large ruin in the Byzantine and Umayyad periods for it not to have been built over. By the latter period, however, it was being thoroughly looted for building material. Harding reported reused Roman blocks in Umayyad buildings on the site of the Museum, whilst a number of fragments are found in the later walls.[108] After much looting, the final collapse of the remains seems to have come in the earthquake of 129–30/747–8.[109]

CONCLUSION

The history of ʿAmmān and the topography of the citadel suggest that there might have been religious structures of an early date here. At present however there is no evidence for any structural or pseudo-structural feature of a sacred nature on the southern part of the citadel which antedates the present remains.

The present remains comprise a temple set within a *temenos*. The temple, of which very little survives, was built on a spur of bedrock, and was at least originally planned as hexastyle peripteral. The *temenos* courtyard comprised an outer solid wall with an internal colonnade, and a gate in the southeast corner which was connected with a Propylaeon in the lower city. The temple and *temenos* are almost certainly contemporary and were built as part of a remodelling of the entire citadel in the mid second century AD.

The temple was dedicated to a supreme deity, almost certainly Hercules. It was clearly one of the most important religious sanctuaries of Roman ʿAmmān, and is indeed the only one where the actual building survives at all.

10

THE EXCAVATIONS IN AREAS B, C, AND D

by Alastair Northedge

The rescue excavations conducted by Mrs C-M. Bennett between 1975 and 1979 on behalf of the Department of Antiquities were located in three areas of the hexagonal area of the Upper Citadel: Areas B, C, and D, identified on fig.28. Area B is located in the centre of the hexagonal area, nearly at the highest part of the hill, and rather to the north of the peak of the limestone bedrock. Area C was effectively a cross-section of the western slope of the hill, west from the area of the present National Archaeological Museum. Area D was placed over a change in the line of the fortification wall, 30m south of Area C.

The three areas can be described in general terms as having uncovered samples of the residential settlement of the Citadel, while Areas C and D also brought to light information about the fortifications of the site.[1] No monumental architecture was identified.

The stratigraphic sequence recovered may be summarized as belonging to eleven strata between Middle Bronze and the Ayyūbid period (see list on p.12). However, this long list conceals a heavy preponderance of remains between Strata VIII (Byzantine) and III (Fāṭimid). Extensive deposits dating to before the 2nd century AD were only found outside the fortification wall in Area C, and post-Fāṭimid occupation was lightly scattered.

Although the sequence recovered in each area closely reflected the others, different parts of the sequence, with different emphases, were found in each area. To give the clearest idea of the development, the areas are discussed in the order: Area C, Area B, and Area D. The various buildings and occupation levels were distinguished by upper-case (Umayyad) and lower-case (Byzantine) letters of the alphabet, or numerals Fāṭimid).

Area C

Area C (figs 121–143; pls 65–71), excavated between 1976 and 1978, was composed of two parallel lines of 5m squares laid out on the west slope of the Qalʿa, extending from close to the Jordan Archaeological Museum to as far as the fortification wall, and a short distance down the slope outside the wall. This gave a total length of 65m, with a breadth of 12m including baulks (pl.66).[2] The total area excavated was 777 square metres. The southern line of trenches was numbered C30, C0, C1–8, and the northern C10–18. In addition three further 5m squares were dug to the north of this double line (C25–6 and C36).

The discussion is divided into the area outside the fortification wall, and the area inside the wall, each of which produced markedly different results.

Excavations outside the fortification wall

Three trenches were dug outside the line of the fortification wall. C0, excavated in 1976, and C30, excavated in 1977–8, continued the southern line of trenches from inside the wall-line. C10, excavated in 1978, continued the northern line of trenches.

The outside face of the wall had been cleared in the past,[3] and the area landscaped by the planting of a line of trees. As a result of this clearance, the surface is flat for a distance of ten metres out from the wall-line, and then slopes steeply down to a road which feeds from Jabal Ḥusayn along the west side of the Qalʿa.

The sequence recovered in this area can broadly be described as:

1. A small deposit of Middle Bronze Age material (C0).
2. First-century BC/AD structures (C30).
3. An early Byzantine house (C0/10).
4. Later undated walls intended to terrace the face of the hill (C30).

1. Middle Bronze Age Remains

At the base of the deposits excavated outside the fortification wall, in C0, a small deposit of Middle Bronze Age pottery was excavated, including a red-painted jug with snake handle, the semi-complete condition of which indicated that the deposit had not been disturbed.[4] The deposit consisted of a thin layer of ash indicating a surface, and was recovered from adjacent to a wall that may have been a section of the Middle Bronze Age fortification wall. However it was impossible to confirm this identification, because there were a number of stone walls and foundations in close proximity. Only the east face of the wall survived, the west face having been removed by the insertion of a wall of the following period.

The Middle Bronze Age wall of the Citadel has been identified in two other locations: at the north end of the Citadel, by Dornemann, and in the southeast area of the Lower Citadel, by Humbert.[5] These finds suggest that the Middle Bronze Age wall should be located in about the area of Co, in relation to the later fortification wall.

2. First-century BC/AD Remains (figs 121, 142; pl.65a)

To the west of the Middle Bronze Age remains a structure surviving to a height of two metres was built, apparently 4.9 metres square with walls 0.7–0.9m thick, although the south wall was not recovered owing to the overburden of later walls. The structure has a central pier measuring 1.2 × 1.4m. The whole was built of small rubble stones with mud mortar, and some mud plastering.[6] The fill between the walls was uniform, and it is possible that the structure was deliberately filled up in order to support a superstructure.

West of this structure, there was a further solid square block of stonework measuring 2.2 × 1.5m, and a wall. Around this block there was a dump deposit containing pottery of the first centuries BC and AD, including Eastern Sigillata A and B, mixed in with Iron Age pottery.

It was concluded that the square structure with the central pier was possibly the base of a tower of the Hellenistic-Early Roman fortification wall. Although one might have thought a structure of this shape would have been a spiral staircase, there was no evidence of steps or a ramp, though these might once have existed at a higher level.

3. Byzantine remains (figs 122–3; pl.65b–c)

Although in the western part of the area, the earlier remains were only covered by mixed material collapsed down the slope, in the eastern part there were substantial Byzantine remains. As elsewhere in the excavations, there were no remains dating from the 2nd–3rd centuries AD.

On the north side in Co/10 the eastern half of a building of rubble masonry with a plaster floor was excavated; it was at least 7.5m long, and was divided by a cross-wall. In the south and cross-walls there were doorways, and in the east wall there was a niche measuring 0.75 × 0.35m. In the southeast corner of the inner room a stone-lined basin was excavated. The building had been built up against a further wall on the east side, and there was evidence of a further structure on the south side of the area. Outside the south door a quarter-circular stone platform carried the remains of a bread oven. A two-handled ribbed cooking pot of a type datable to the period between the mid-3rd and early 4th centuries AD was sunk into the earth surface adjacent (fig.123.6).

The western half of the building was eroded by a collapse down the hillside, and the plaster floor was broken off. There was an abandonment deposit of pottery on the floor, of types datable to the period between the mid/late 4th century and the early 5th century (fig.123). The abandonment deposit on the floor, and the buckling in the plaster floor, strongly suggest that the collapse was the cause of its abandonment. The building may well have been destroyed by the earthquake of AD 363 (see Chapter 11).

4. Later Remains

The Early Byzantine period was the last substantial period of occupation outside the wall. At a later date the face of the hill was buttressed with terrace walls, but it was not possible to date these satisfactorily (pl.65c). Immediately under the surface there were whitish striated layers, which possibly represent material tread into this area during the construction of the fortification wall.

Excavations inside the fortification wall

The area excavated inside the fortification ultimately consisted of a rectangle of 5m squares, with three further squares to the north at the eastern end (pl.66).

The limestone bedrock of the hill was probably reached at only one point, and the earliest phase discussed was built upon it. Penetration to bedrock here, and elsewhere, was hindered by the loose nature of the deposits, especially those of the Stratum VI fills, which made work dangerous. The limited area of bedrock which it was possible to expose made a firm conclusion impossible.

The deposits excavated can be divided into three main periods:

1. A Byzantine and Early Umayyad residential

settlement.
2. The covering of the Byzantine settlement by a levelling fill, and a pattern of buildings belonging to the Umayyad Citadel.
3. An early medieval residential settlement of the 'Abbāsid and Fāṭimid periods built upon, and partly reoccupying, the destroyed remains of the Umayyad buildings.

1. Byzantine and Early Umayyad Remains: Strata VII and VIII (fig.124)

Access to pre-Stratum V occupation was gained in five distinct and separate areas. Three buildings were partially exposed, and fragments from two others:

Building (a) in Trench C1 (figs 124, 142; pl.67a)
The east, north and south walls survive of a square or rectangular room, over which the foundations of Sector 8 of the fortification wall run. The north-south measurement is 4m, and the walling is preserved, buried in the later fill, to a height of 2.1m. There is a doorway in the east side, 1.1m wide. The building was constructed of dry-laid rubble masonry 0.8m wide, with cut stone door-frames, and an earth floor. Further wall stubs on the south side indicate that this room belonged to a larger structure.

The floor surface was approximately one metre higher than that of the Early Byzantine building outside the fortification wall.

Building (b) and Passageway in Trench C2 (figs 125, 143; pl.67b)
Excavation of the Stratum VI building-fill in trench C2 revealed the facade of a building with two doorways, surviving to a height of 1.8m. The construction was of worn ashlars, finished with lime plaster.

Both doorways had fittings for wooden doors. The northern door led into a room whose dimensions could not be determined. The southern door led into a small arched alcove, measuring 1.0 × 1.3m. The arch was found standing 1.8m high (pl.67b). The alcove was probably a booth for a shop, or a small workshop of an individual craftsman.

The two doorways give the impression of opening onto a street or alley with earth surfaces. The street was a minimum of three metres wide.

Building (c) in Trench C4 and C15 (fig.124)
Penetration of the Stratum V surfaces in trench C4 exposed a square room with a threshold facing north, measuring 5.2 × 5.0m. Only the threshold course and the foundations have survived; there was no interior floor remaining. It was evidently part of a larger building, for a further bonded wall continued to the south. In addition, to the north of the structure there were two areas of a mosaic floor of white tesserae. Although two separate areas were excavated, they were clearly parts of a single mosaic measuring three metres north to south. On the west side of the square room there was a further room with a well-laid plaster floor.

Although this building was much denuded by the later Stratum V, it seems to have been a fairly substantial house.

Building (d) Fragments
Further fragments of building were also found in penetrations through the Umayyad floors in C6 and C8.

Dating
Excavations through these Stratum VII–VIII floors were only made in two places: in the probable passageway in front of building (b), and into the make-up below building (d).

The *terminus post quem* of the Byzantine settlement in this area was clearly indicated by the 3rd–4th century date of the building outside the wall in C0–10, although it was not possible to establish a foundation date for the buildings inside the wall.

From the last floor deposit of the passageway in trench C2 a *follis* was recovered (Appendix D: no.1) which appears to be a copy or a forgery of a type of Constans II (641–668). This evidence of occupation after the Arab conquest (Stratum VII) is also supported by the lack of silting on the floors of buildings (a) and (b), and in C6 and C8, before the laying of the fills that comprise Stratum VI.[7] While silting might have indicated an abandonment, the clean deposition of fills suggests that this settlement continued in occupation until the building operations associated with the construction of the Umayyad citadel commenced.

2. The Umayyad Citadel: Strata V and VI (figs 126–33; pls 66, 68–70)

Levelling Fill: Stratum VI (figs 142–3)
Strata VII and VIII are divided from the next occupation deposits of Stratum V by a considerable volume of fill. These fills were found wherever penetration was made through the floor levels of Stratum V on the inside of the fortification wall. In composition the fills vary from soil and clays to mixed soil and building rubble, to almost pure building rubble. In no place is the material well-compacted.

Stratum VI varies in depth from 2.2m, adjacent to the fortification wall (fig.142), to approximately 0.2m in

C15. Under Building B the fill steps up and a depth of two metres is again found in C6, reducing to 0.75m in C8. That is, the fill levelled the site into rough steps.

A large content of building rubble will impede compaction of the fill. Although nothing is known about what methods were used to compact the levelling fills – perhaps some kind of roller – a rubble content in which the blocks touched one another would make it impossible to stabilize the fill. Without doubt it was the loose character of the fill that made this area vulnerable to an earthquake.

There is every reason to suppose that these fills were deliberately laid. The pottery is a mix of Byzantine and Umayyad from top to bottom, though with concentrations of pottery from one period or another in different places, as is to be expected where various sources of fill material were used. There is no sign of occupational activity or silting. And a drain was laid in the fill in C2 without any sign of a foundation trench.

Buildings: Stratum V (fig.126)

The structures built on top of the fill consist firstly of the fortification wall (Sector 8). The foundations of the Sector 8 wall are trench-built into the fill on the inside,[8] and the wall is connected with the Stratum V surface (fig.142). Inside the fortification wall there appear to be two large buildings, A and B, divided by a street, three metres wide, which runs north-south approximately parallel to the fortification wall (pl.68a).

BUILDING A (FIG.127) Building A is the more damaged of the two, being overlaid by Stratum III houses at its western end, and its plan is not clear. The maximum demonstrable east-west dimension is 19m, but it is possible that the building extended as far as the fortification wall. There was an entrance onto the street in C5. The southern side of the excavated area merely has a surface of this stratum sloping up from the fortification wall to the gate on the street, in two segments divided by a short flight of steps; presumably this was an open yard. The surface was not continuously traceable; in C2 (fig.143) it disappeared, although the loose rubble fill beneath was clear. It is possible that movement in the loose fill broke up the surface.

On the north side three rooms were identified, respectively 2.5, 2.3, and 3.2m wide. The lengths of these rooms were not clear, but the southern two rooms were at least 6.5m long and could have been up to 17.5m long. These have the long, narrow shape typical of a storeroom. However, we should not necessarily interpret the whole building as a store-house, for a combination of similar long, narrow rooms and open yards is found in residential buildings at the contemporary Large Enclosure at Qaṣr al-Ḥayr al-Sharqī.[9]

BUILDING B (FIG.128) Building B was also large: a frontage of 18m was uncovered on its western side (pl.68a). By comparison with the building on the Museum site (fig.161), it can be seen that what has been excavated is most of one house (Rooms A–C, E–H), plus one room from another (Room D). Bearing in mind that the whole of the structure is bonded, it is apparent that the building is a residential block containing more than one house unit.

The house appears to have had rooms surrounding a courtyard at J, although neither the southern wall nor the main door were excavated. But one may suggest that door opened onto a street to the east which is visible on the surface.

The courtyard is 8.6m wide. There is a cistern in the courtyard, with a surround that went through two phases (figs 128, 130; pl.69b). In the second a plastered basin linked to the cistern was blocked off. The cistern may have been a reuse of an earlier one, for a second mouth-stone is to be seen 2.25m down.

Rooms A (4.1 × 5.1m), B (4.0 × 5.1m), and F (3.6 × 4.2m or more) can be identified as residential from their destruction deposits (figs 131–3). Room B, in addition to smashed vessels on the floor, also had a small hearth in the northeast corner (pl.68b). The reception room was probably at G (5.8 × 5.1m), on the analogy of the Museum site. The adjacent Room E (4.2 × 6.2m) has a pair of interconnected basins, one square and open (1.2 × 1.0m), and the second deep and round (0.5m diameter; fig.129, pl.70a). The arrangement is obviously intended for the collection of liquid pressed from some material in the upper basin. It is not certain what was being pressed. Room C (3.5 × 5.7m) has three rough stone bins, and was obviously a storeroom (pl.69a).

Construction Techniques

The buildings have the unified constructional technique, which is widely seen elsewhere on the Qal'a, and is an identifier of Stratum V construction. The walling is of limestone rubble masonry with a standard thickness of 1.0m, with a range of variation from 0.95 to 1.07m. However, the two faces of the wall are sometimes not parallel, although straight and flat. Small stones are used to wedge the larger masonry firmly, and are also used to smooth the surface ready for plastering.

The walling is mortared with large quantities of a lime mortar containing ash. The walls are then plastered with the same material, the surface of which studded with small pieces of chalk, and stippled with wedge-shaped keying impressions.

The foundation work is varied. Three types were observed: (a) free-standing built foundations identical to the upper walls; (b) free-standing foundations of small stones; and (c) trench built foundations of rubble and *terra rossa*.[10]

No evidence survives of roofing techniques, but in B area the generally similar Building D was barrel-vaulted. The rooms have the rectangular shape necessary for barrel-vaulting, even at the expense of regular thickness in the walls.[11] The buildings were apparently single-storey, for no evidence was recovered here or, with a single exception (fig.161), elsewhere, of a second storey or of staircases to the roof.

Flooring varies around the theme of tamped earth. Courtyards and storerooms (Building B, Room C; the yard surfaces of Building A; the street) have plain earth surfaces. In Building B, Rooms B and F have carefully packed surfaces, Room A has a thin coating of lime, while Room D, possibly a reception room, has a laid clay floor.

Dating

The latest coins from Area C are Umayyad post-reform *fulūs*, with the exception of two coins stratigraphically associated with Stratum III. In particular Umayyad *fulūs* came from sealed locations in the fill below Room F of Building B, and from between two floors of Room A (Appendix D: nos 2, 4–6).

Destruction

Apart from a rebuild to the cistern at J, and a second floor in Room A, there is little evidence of change and development in the buildings of Stratum V; but there was a destruction.

Building A was so extensively destroyed that only a limited area could be reused in the following periods. However, there was little destruction evidence; a deposit of ash in C1–2 (fig.143), up to 0.75m deep, need not have been related to the destruction. However Building B has clear evidence of violent destruction in the same period that it was erected. Rooms A, B, E and F all collapsed on their contents (figs 131–3). In addition, a skeleton was found on the stone threshold of Room B: the outflung position of both arms, and the left leg, still articulated, suggest that this individual was a victim of the collapse of the house (pl.70b).

In the absence of any evidence for fire or military activity, the sudden collapse of the buildings may have been due to an earthquake. The loose fills beneath the buildings would have increased the effects of the shock.

The majority of Building B was not occupied again – a situation which led to the preservation of its destruction level. Rooms G and H were reoccupied and sub-divided in Stratum IVb/III. Room A had a later floor of uncertain date, and a built tomb containing two infant burials.

3. Continued Occupation: Strata IVb–III (fig.134)

During the period represented by Stratum IVb/III the area was occupied by rubble-built houses, and the Stratum V buildings discussed above were reinhabited. All the new construction is in rubble walling, some rather rough and built without foundations. Building 1, Room 4 has a trace of mud-plaster.

Two streets appear to have crossed the area in a north-south direction. Firstly, the Umayyad street referred to above continued to be used; there is evidence of a continuous build-up of surfaces, and the abandoned remains of Building B were buttressed to prevent their collapse into the street (fig.143). Secondly, there was a new alley, 1.5m wide, running approximately parallel 11m to the west.

There are four building complexes identified.

Building 1 (figs 135–7, 142–3; pl.70c)

Building 1 is a housing complex at the west end, in trenches C1–2 and C11–12. It probably constitutes one house, and measures 13.2 × 10.9m or more. There are two main phases:

PHASE 1 Three rooms – Rooms 1 (2.8 × 2.7m), 2 (2.7 × 2.6m), and 3/4 (? × 5.8m) – were built together with an east wall (of Room 6) facing onto the alley, constituting a house with a courtyard. Room 3/4 is larger, and appears to be the reception room. Its roof was supported by a reused column. Room 2 has a stone paving and the bases of two bread ovens *(tābūn)* on its east side. A hard tamped-earth level under the Phase 2 rooms was probably the courtyard surface of the Phase 1 building.

PHASE 2 The building was extended by the addition of Rooms 5–8. Room 5 measures 2.4 × 4.3m; Room 6: 4.0 × 2.3m; Room 7: 3.0 × 3.8m; Room 8: ? × 3.8m. In this period there seems to have been a courtyard in the centre of the building. The reception room (3/4 of Phase 1) was divided in two rooms – 3 and 4. These two rooms continued to be residential, to judge by the destruction deposit on the floors (figs 137), which is the only destruction deposit found in this building. There was a bench (Ar. *maṣṭaba*) in Room 5. In Room 6 there was a hearth, and single-course stone partitions that might have been socles for low mud walls.

There are second phase floors in the Phase 1 rooms, raised 0.25–0.40m higher and composed of soft earth. The Phase 1 construction is carefully built, but the quality of the walling is rough in Phase 2. The building gives the impression of being an early version of the later traditional Islamic houses of Jordan, and was the only semi-complete plan of new construction, as opposed to re-use of Umayyad buildings, recovered from Stratum IVb–III.

Building 2: Trenches C13–15 (figs 138–9)

The Stratum V storerooms of Building A were turned into a self-contained structure with a door opening onto the alley to the west. The southern long room of the Umayyad building had a new outer wall with doorway built on the west side, and three further partitions. It is not certain whether partitions of this period excavated in the middle Umayyad room represented an independent building or not.

Building 3: Trenches C4–5 (figs 140–1)

A one-room structure divided by a partition wall (5.4 × 2.6m), and with a door facing west, was built on top of the east end of Building A. A wall stub suggested that there may have been further rooms to the south of the excavation area. There was an open yard on the west side, with a boundary wall to the western alley. Adjacent to this there was a stone-lined pit, possibly for grain storage. The room excavated was clearly residential in purpose, to judge from the destruction deposit on the floor (fig.141), and there were three successive earth floors.

Building 4 (pl.71b)

In Building B only Rooms G and H were reoccupied, though the infant burial in Room A mentioned above may have been connected with this period. Both rooms were divided in half, and the walls repaired, to create a four-roomed structure (although it is uncertain whether the building thus constituted extended beyond the area excavated). The largest room (5.2 × 3.5m) was given a new earth floor, reinforced with a stone foundation; this room may have been a reception room, but no destruction deposit was found. The adjacent room to the east had a hearth in the southwest corner, and benches (Ar. *maṣṭaba*) on the south and east sides.[12]

Dating

Building 1 has two phases. Phase 1 postdates the final destruction of the fortifications, and is best dated by a Stratum IVb cooking pot, half of which was found lying on the earliest floor of Room 3/4 – the room which was divided at a later date. The second phase was terminated by the Stratum III destruction (fig.137).

In addition a Fāṭimid *dīnār* of al-Ḥākim, unworn, dated 407/1016–7, was found as part of a cache also containing silver bells and rings, under a stone below the base of a wall of Room 6, but above the Phase 1 surface (Appendix D: no.9). The deposition of the cache occurred during the lifetime of the building; therefore the destruction is later, but the foundation of the building may very well be earlier than the mint date.

The street experienced continuous build-up from Stratum V to Stratum III. House 3, adjacent to it, had three floors, terminating in the Stratum III destruction (fig.141). In the latest floor was found a Fāṭimid *dirham* (Appendix D: no.10) of al-Ẓāhir (411/1021–427/1036). The destruction of the building again postdates the mint date, and its construction was probably, but not necessarily, earlier.

These houses, therefore, were most probably occupied during the 4th/10th and 5th/11th centuries. There was no reoccupation during Stratum IIb or later; this is probably to be attributed to the complete collapse of the buildings during the Stratum III destruction.

Area B

Area B (figs 144–56; pls 72–76) consists of an irregular area of excavation in the centre of the upper terrace of the Qalʿa, measuring at its greatest extent 44 × 36m.[13] It was excavated by Mrs Bennett for the Department of Antiquities in 1975, 1976, 1977, 1978 and 1979. The area was originally opened to explore the damage done by an excavation for foundations of a building for the Royal Jordanian army (pl.72b; see fig.144 for location). This cut is an approximate rectangle measuring 12 × 23m, and it has removed the archaeological strata down to bedrock. However, the bedrock is uneven, and archaeological deposits have been left in pockets. The proposed building was never erected.[14] The total area of the excavation, including the military cut, was 967 square metres.

The sequence begins with isolated pre-Stratum VIII deposits: a pocket of Early-Middle Bronze material in the bedrock; a small area containing Iron Age deposits; and some Roman deposits. The first overall stratum is Stratum VIII (Byzantine), comprising domestic architecture spread over the whole area. Stratum VIII is succeeded by overall Stratum V construction (Umayyad Citadel); these buildings then continued in occupation, and were subjected to repairs and modifications, through Strata IVb and III (ʿAbbāsid-Fāṭimid), up to Stratum IIb (Ayyūbid). There are also traces of later occupation, but these proved to be undatable.

1. Pre-Byzantine Occupation

The earliest trace of occupation was a pocket of EB-MB material in the bedrock in trench B5 in the southwest corner of the army excavation.[15] There was also a deposit of Iron Age II pottery associated with a wall in the base of the excavation in B30.1. Adjacent to this there was a cave filled with animal bone, but it did not prove possible to date the bone with associated artefacts.[16]

In trench B23, an area above the limestone bedrock of the hill proved to contain undisturbed deposits of the 1st century AD.

In all these cases the deposits proved to be discontinuous areas of material, which predated the Roman construction of the temples in the 2nd century AD. The earliest dates associated with the succeeding stratum can be placed in the 3rd–4th centuries AD.

2. Byzantine and Early Umayyad Strata VII and VIII (fig.144)

Access to the stratum below the Stratum V buildings was gained via small, mainly separated, penetrations in trenches B19, B20, B23, B25, B26, B40, B43 and B53. In addition, the Stratum VI levelling fills of the Umayyad period were thinner than in Area C, and consequently the covered Byzantine buildings were not preserved to so great a height.

In trench B40 a neatly constructed set of steps, of cut limestone blocks, was excavated, leading down onto a stone cobbled surface, which was later covered with a secondary earth surface. The steps were aligned with the later Stratum V street, and lay some 2.5m west of that street's line. It seemed likely that the Stratum V street lay on the same line as an earlier street, and this was to some extent confirmed by the alignment of the Byzantine Church to such a street further south. The line runs from the south gate of the *temenos* of the Northern Temple, later replaced by the Umayyad Reception Hall, to the north side of the *temenos* of the Temple of Hercules, opposite to Gate C. By reason of this alignment, it has been proposed elsewhere in this volume that there was also a north gate to the *temenos* of the Temple of Hercules.[17]

Excavation along the line of the Stratum V street further north in trench B43 revealed street levels down to bedrock (fig.146). Below the adjacent Stratum V building levels there were up to seven surfaces, plastered in areas; these can be assumed to belong to the earlier street. Nevertheless, Umayyad pottery continued to be found down to floor 10. There is no doubt that the Stratum VIII settlement continued to be occupied, at least in part during the earlier part of the Umayyad period (Stratum VII).

In addition, the orientation of the Stratum VIII walls is remarkably similar to that of the following Stratum V. In the east of Area B the construction is oriented north-northwest to south-southeast, and in the west of the area north-northeast to south-southwest. In Stratum V the structures were laid out in this manner because they lay between two radial streets diverging from the Reception Hall. It is quite possible, therefore, that this Stratum V reconstruction followed an already existing pattern of radial streets.

Building (e)

At least in Stratum VIII, the street was not as straight as it was later to be, and perhaps had been originally. In trenches B42–3 the facade of a building was uncovered which seems to have protruded into the west side of the street to a distance of 1.8m. It includes a doorway, and is later than the two earliest street levels. The stratigraphy depicted in fig.146 would suggest that it had been built in the earlier part of the Umayyad period.

The doorway led into a stone-paved area in trench B19, and on the north side parts of two rooms were excavated in B19–25 (Room 1: ? × 3m, earth floor; Room 2: dimensions unknown, stone paving). The associated walls still stand *c.*0.5m high.

Building (f) (pls 73a–b)

The second Stratum VIII complex about which anything is known is a group of four rooms in B20 and B23. The principal room, excavated in the centre of the group and measuring ? × 3.2m, has a fine lime plaster floor with a plastered basin measuring 0.8 × 0.6m set into it, and a central column with five drums, presumably to support the roof. The room to the north measures 2.2m wide.

In many parts of the area two phases of Stratum VIII construction were noted, although in no place did it prove possible to date these phases closely. Nevertheless, deposits were identified whose latest pottery dated to the 3rd–4th centuries AD, while in others the latest pottery was of the 6th century. It is evident that the settlement began to develop in the 3rd–4th centuries on bedrock, and continued through into the Umayyad period.

Mrs Bennett felt there was evidence of abandonment in both buildings (e) and (f). In building (f) there was evidence of weathering on the column, which suggested that the building had been roofless for some time;[18] and in building (e) there was evidence of squatter occupation in B19.[19] Nevertheless, in trench B25 the Umayyad levelling fills of Stratum VI were deposited cleanly on the stone-paved floor of Stratum VIII, which was clear of rubbish or silting. It would seem likely that we are observing here evidence of contraction of settlement and partial abandonment in the earlier part of the Umayyad period.

3. The Umayyad Citadel and Later Occupation (Umayyad Citadel: Strata V and VI; Later Occupation: Strata IVb–IIb (figs 145, 156)

As in Area C, the following period saw a complete reconstruction of the area, with some of the Stratum VIII buildings covered with a levelling fill, and others almost completely removed. However, in Area B the buildings of Stratum V were not destroyed and largely built over in the following period, as happened in Area C; rather, the buildings continued in occupation and were modified over time. There is only one exception, discussed below. For this reason, in this area the later occupation is discussed together with the original construction.

Levelling Fill (Stratum VI)

The Stratum VIII floors are divided from the subsequent Stratum V Building C by fills that are less substantial than in Area C (between 0.5m and 1m in thickness). The penetration in Room B of Building C (B25.1) found mixed Umayyad and Byzantine pottery (V and VIII) down to the stone-paved floor of Stratum VIII. Buildings D and E are built on bedrock.

Buildings and Later Occupation (Stratum V and IVb–IIb)

The Stratum V remains in B Area appear to consist of a street, limited evidence of a second street, and parts of five buildings: Buildings C, D, E, F, and G. Building C is probably structurally continuous with Building D, but the excavation did not uncover the connection.

STREETS A length of 45m of a straight street, five metres wide, was revealed in Area B. It was walled on both sides with the stone walls of the adjacent buildings. In trenches B42 and B43 the build-up of the street surfaces was examined, and it was apparent that the surfaces consisted of packed earth with patches of plaster and pebbles. In the course of the life of the street its surface rose 0.5m above the level of the adjacent building foundation, and it seems to have continued in use until Stratum III (fig.146).

The street was aligned from the north door of the Reception Hall, straight past the site of the Byzantine church to the east end of the *temenos* of the Temple of Hercules, and it would have been possible to descend to the east end of the lower city through Gate C, as rebuilt in the Umayyad period.

There is apparent evidence of a second street, 3.7m wide, in the south side of the military excavation, dividing Buildings D and E. As it did not continue through to the north of Area B, nor meet an east-west street, it may be that it turned in a right-angle to the west on the north side of Building E, or, perhaps more likely, that it was a blind alley which gave access only to the buildings.

BUILDING F Building F is a fragment of building revealed in the extreme north of the excavation area in trenches B60 and B61. Its principal feature is a wall running west from the street and terminating in a square block of masonry 1.8m square. In addition there is one wall bonded, and running north. It seems there was no continuation of the street wall here in the original period, and thus the street widened.

The north and west walls of Building C are built up against the Building F wall, and are evidently an addition, though to judge from their style of construction they are of the same period. Whatever original plan of Building F was intended, it was not completed, for the square block of masonry serves no purpose.

Later occupation: The street wall from the south was extended to create a room. In this room there are benches on the south and east sides, and a bread oven in the southeast corner. There is a further wall in the northwest corner, but the excavation was too limited to explain this. On the west side of the north-south wall, the area was divided into two rooms, 2m × 3.5m, and ? × 1.5m, with a doorway between. The divide wall included two column sections. In the western room there was also a door to the south, blocked up, and a stone bin. The pottery indicated that occupation had continued through to Stratum III, and then ceased.

BUILDING C (FIGS 147–52; PLS 74A–B) The limits of the building are known on all four sides: on the east it fronts onto the street, and on the west, the walls of Rooms D and E appear to have been built into a contemporary rise in the ground, for these walls are single-faced. To the south it seems that the building shared a wall with Building D, but this area has been damaged by the military excavation. On the north side the delineation is a matter of interpretation. The north wall of what one might attribute to Building C is built up against a wall of a further residential unit of separate but similar construction (Building F). The plan is irregular, but the maximum dimensions are 24 × 16m.

On the west side all the walls are single-faced, suggesting that the building was built into a rise in the ground.

The building appears to consist of two separate residential units bonded together. The unit on the north side (unit 1) was nearly completely cleared. It had a door to the street opening into a courtyard that measured

5.3 × 5.7m. Two rooms opened from the south side of the courtyard: Room A measured 3.3 × 5.4m, and Room E, 3.3 × 4.2m.

The southern unit (unit 2) has three further rooms. Room B measured 3.3 × 4.0m; Room C: 3.9 × 3.5m; Room D: 4.5 × 4.9m. Room C opens into Room D, which opens to the south into a further room now mostly destroyed. No doorway was satisfactorily established for Room B, and the southern part of the unit was removed by the military excavation. However it seems likely that this unit was on a larger scale, and was perhaps akin to the house units of Area C and the Museum site.

The building has been set out in an extraordinary fashion. While all the rooms are roughly square or rectangular, the alignment of one room to another is irregular, with no attempt to maintain a constant thickness for the walls. The same phenomenon occurs to a lesser extent in Building B. The diverging alignment of the rooms was probably dictated by the street pattern of the area.

One may suggest that the preservation of properly square or rectangular rooms on an irregularly shaped site was important for the easy construction of barrel vaults. Two parallel walls are an essential minimum.

The exception in the method of roofing seems to be Room D: here there are the remains of a pier, which must have carried an arch across the room.

Later occupation: There is no clear evidence of early destruction in the building, as was found in Area C; however there is evidence of a refacing of the walls relatively early in the building's life.

In the northern residential unit there was clear evidence of the sequence of occupation. In the northwest corner of the courtyard there was a platform with a bread oven (*tābūn*), of the latest period of occupation (pl.74b). However, the trenches exposing this courtyard (B27–8) were only dug down to the latest floor levels.

Inside Room A excavations continued down to the Stratum VIII levels. The Stratum V earth floor of the room was low, exposing some of the wall foundations, a situation also observed in Building B of Stratum V in Area C (fig. 148). This floor then had a hearth and a pit cut into it (B26.1.24). Both were characterized by early IVb pottery (fig. 149). Later accumulations at the south end of the room also had IVb pottery, including *sgraffiato* wares. In Stratum III a new threshold stone was added with new higher floors, as well as a further pit to the left of the door (fig.150), and a platform at the south end, which was paved on one side. The room was abandoned finally during this period, and an abandonment deposit was left on the floor (fig.151).

However, in the southwest corner of the courtyard, and Room E, occupation continued into the Ayyūbid or early Mamlūk periods. At the south end of Room E, a bread oven was built and a partition wall, and there was a deposit of early Pseudo-prehistoric ware (fig.152).[20]

BUILDING D (FIGS 153–5) Building D can also be described as a block building, probably again containing two units. Only the central part of the building was fully excavated. To the north the probable limits of the building were partly destroyed by the military basin, and partly not excavated. The limits on east and west were clear, though those walls diverge at an angle of 20°. But to the south it was evident that the building continued further than the excavation area. The dimensions of the building east and west were 17.3m (median figure), and the north-south dimension, as far as could be seen, was 17.6m.

The building is divided into two units by an east-west wall without doorways. On the north side of the divide wall, unit 1 appears to consist of six rooms in the original construction. Room A measures 4.3 × 3.1m; Room B: 2.3 × 3.3m; Room B1: 2.25 × 3.4m; Room G: 1.8 × 3.4m; Room F: 3.0 × 3.4m; and Room H: ? × 2.0m.

The remnant of an east-west boundary wall, which probably separated this unit from Building C, can be seen ten metres north of the divide wall. The northwest quarter of the unit, west of Room H, was likely to be the courtyard. Cut into the bedrock in this courtyard area there is a cistern, which may well have been first excavated at an earlier date, and reused in this period. There are two plastered water-collecting drains, one leading from a vertical drain on the facade of Room B1, and the second running south from Building C (pl.74c).

On the south side of the divide wall, unit 2 of the building has three rooms. Room C measures 4.5 × 4.7m; Room D: 4.7 × 4.9m; and Room E: 4.9 × 4.0m. Room D has a doorway to the south, where there may have been a courtyard. The doorways of the other two rooms are not known, but Room E must have opened into Room D, and the heavily rebuilt divide wall conceals the opening.

Rooms B and D preserve the springing of barrel vaults. The construction is similar to Stratum V/VI in Area C, but the Stratum VI fill is missing, except in Room E, for nearly the whole building is built on bedrock.

Later occupation: In unit 1, the evidence for later occupation was patchy because of the removal of deposits by the military excavation. In Room B1 there was a secondary Stratum III floor. In Rooms G and F there was an extensive rebuild, with the a new doorway between the two rooms, and a new north wall for Room F (pl.75a). In addition there was a bread oven on a platform on the south side of Room G. This occupation ended in Stratum III, probably as a result of the destruction during that period.

Unit 2 provided information for Rooms E and D. In Room E there was a further floor for Stratum III. The room seems to have been included in the Stratum III destruction, and a lamp was recovered from the latest floor. The room was then abandoned.

Room D (fig.154) was entirely excavated down to the second IIb floor (Ayyūbid), but only the western half was taken down to the original floors. The earliest occupation consisted of two earth floors closely superimposed. Two circles of stones, related to both these floors, represent some kind of installation, but the purpose of this is not known. On the upper floor there is an abandonment deposit of IVb pottery (fig.155). The succeeding deposit is of a clean, brown organic soil mixed with small rocks. This may be interpreted as silting up from abandonment, or possibly as a deposit from use as a byre. An earth floor with Stratum III pottery, much broken up with rocks, was superimposed upon this, and included a hearth cut down into it, indicating a resumption of occupation.

A further possible period of abandonment ensued, and then three earth floors were laid down, with IIb pottery (pl.76b).

During this period, the east wall, which had probably originally contained a doorway leading into the adjacent Room E, was rebuilt in a rough rubble technique. As the barrel vault whose springing is evident in the west wall also rested on this wall, it is evident that the vault had fallen by this time. The room was perhaps roofed by timbers. The collapse of the vault had perhaps been caused by the Stratum III destruction.

The south wall was also rebuilt and the doorway to the south was given a new threshold stone; at the end the doorway was blocked up. Outside the door two buttresses seem to have been added to support the wall.

In the lowest of the IIb floors was a pit in which iron-smelting had been carried out. The 'puddle' technique was used, in which ore and fuel are mixed together and fired. The molten iron collects on the surface as a puddle. A brief comment on the slags by R. F. Tylecote confirms this assessment.[21]

During this period there was a platform or bench *(maṣṭaba)* against the east wall, and the partition visible in fig.154 may have buttressed a further platform. In addition there were two stone bins adjacent to the south door. As only small quantities of Ayyūbid pottery were recovered from the room, it is possible that there was no human habitation in the IIb period, and that it was only used as a workroom.

BUILDING E Building E is only visible as the stumps of two walls 2.9m apart, surviving to a height of 1.75m, together with associated floors, exposed in the south section of the military cut. The construction is of the type described for Stratum V in Area C.

Building E is divided from Building D by a street 3.7m wide.

BUILDING G (PL.76A) On the east side of the street, one room was excavated of a building attached to the wall of the street, measuring ? × 4.8m. There was a doorway to the east, and a stone paving over the northern part of the floor. As no further walls were attached to the street wall further to the north, it was concluded that the northern part of the east side had been an open yard. The air photograph of the Citadel taken during the First World War (pl.2a) confirms that there was little evidence of building debris visible on the surface to the east of Area B.[22]

Dating

Building C is dated to the Umayyad period by the find of Umayyad red-painted pottery and by a post-reform *fils* (Appendix D: no.3) in its Stratum VI levelling fill.

Building D has few finds from its construction levels, as it is built on bedrock, but an Umayyad dating is suggested by its construction and sequence of occupation.

The beginning of these two sequences is fixed by the construction of Stratum V. In the case of Room D, Building D, the termination is also approximately fixed by a group of six bronze coins found together between the two latest IIb floors.

There are three bronzes of the Ayyūbid al-Malik al-ʿĀdil (d. 615/1218), and one of Saladin, with a decipherable date of 587/1190–1 or 589/1193 (Appendix D; nos 12–17). On the remaining two bronzes only the name of the ʿAbbāsid Caliph al-Nāṣir li-Dīn Allah (575/1180–622/1225) can be read.

The deposition of this homogeneous hoard could not have postdated the death of al-Nāṣir by more than a few years.

Bearing in mind the addition of one later floor, we may suggest that occupation terminated not later than the middle of the 7th/13th century. Apart from these terminal points, we have only the pottery sequence, datable from elsewhere on the site. One other room in Area B, Room E of Building C also had IIb occupation (fig.152). The three trenches of Area D (figs 157–160; pls. 77–8)

Area D

were laid out over and inside the line of the fortification wall, 30m south of Area C, and excavated in 1977–8 by Mrs Bennett for the Department of Antiquities.[23] Excavation was not pursued to bedrock, and study was limited to the fortification wall and its succeeding phases. The sequence of the area consisted broadly of modern remains overlying domestic architecture, of which four, or possibly five, major constructional phases were recognized. These overlie the abandoned fortification wall, which has two main phases. The architectural characteristics of the fortifications are dealt with in Chapter 8; this section is concerned with sequence. Briefly, the fortification architecture is a square tower, 5.6 × 5.7m (Tower E), linking two straight sections of wall (Sectors 8 and 9; fig.157). In the second phase the first buttress on the wall south of Area D (Sector 9, Buttress 1) was rebuilt with a sloping face, and a battered revetment was added to the outside of the wall. By the time that the succeeding phases of house construction appeared – with the exception of Phase 1a – the wall had been abandoned, and had collapsed down to its present height of between one and four courses above the contemporary ground-level.

The phases of house construction are (fig.157):

Phase 1a

A wall was built, attached to the southeast corner of the tower, and perpendicular to Sector 9 of the wall. It is 0.8m wide, of carefully constructed rubble with a built foundation. It presumably belonged to a building attached to the rear of, or built over, the fortification wall. It has at least one associated floor. A drain of the fortification period adjacent to the tower was blocked off and re-directed parallel to this wall. The evidence does not allow us to be certain that this structure postdated the abandonment of the fortifications; the fortifications were probably still standing at this time. It is not linked stratigraphically with Phase lb.

Phase 1b

This consists of a building over the north half of the tower, with walls 0.8m thick, built of rubble and reused ashlars. The revealed area includes a corridor with doorways to the south and east, and a room overlying part of the fortification wall in Sector 8.

Phase 2

The 1a and 1b buildings were linked by new rooms on the east side. The 1a wall was rebuilt, and a room was added on its south side (fig.159b) (D3.4). In the southeast corner of this room is a plastered basin (0.4 × 0.5m) installed over the foundations of the fortification wall, the wall itself having disappeared at this point. This drain was connected through a short plastered drain to a cistern (fig.158). The construction of this phase is similarly built of rubble, but with the foundations omitted.

Phase 3

In this phase the plastered basin and cistern of Phase 2 were abandoned, and a new room added, extending over the southern half of the tower and outside the line of the fortifications. This phase of the room has two major earth floors. A second floor in the Phase 2 room may be contemporary with this phase.

Phase 4

The Phase 3 room was reduced in size by means of a new south wall. There is one associated floor level, and some pottery in a destruction deposit. One may speculate that the reduction was prompted by the collapse of part of the Phase 3 room into the Phase 2 cistern that it was built over, or down the side of the hill. The east side rooms of Phase 2 have deposits of this period, but poor surfaces and a large build-up of deposits suggest a semi-abandonment.

Dating

A number of coins were recovered from this area, but all appeared to be residual, and none were Islamic. The fortification wall, dated to the Umayyad period by its link to Area C, provides a fixed point. In Chapter 8 the rebuild of the fortifications is argued to have postdated the ʿAbbāsid Revolution, but the remainder of the sequence can only be dated by pottery.

Phases 2 and 3 are associated with Stratum IVb pottery (fig.160). The pottery associated with Phase 2 was very scant, but included a bowl with painted polychrome glaze designs, and a sherd of splashed ware with green and dark manganese purple-brown colourants on an opaque white glaze. While certain types of splash glaze – green on opaque white glaze and drip splash – are found at Sāmarrāʾ in the 3rd/9th century, the traditional type of splash glaze, a transparent lead glaze over a white slip, seems to be connected with the introduction of *sgraffiato* in the first part of the 4th/10th century.[24] The pottery evidence here is consistent with the earlier phase of splashed ware, and so one would probably place the construction of Phase 2 at about the end of the 3rd/9th century, or the beginning of the 4th/10th century.

The occupation deposit of Phase 3 included a sherd of a glazed bowl with a straight flaring rim, which might be of late 4th/10th century or early 5th/11th century date; at any rate, it predates the Stratum III pottery.[25]

The occupation of Phase 4 is associated with Stratum III pottery and is presumably contemporary with Stratum III in Area C. This area also has an abandonment deposit (fig.161).

We may conclude, then, that Area D has a continuous sequence of occupation from the building of the fortification wall (Stratum V) up until a final abandonment at about the same time as Area C.

11

THE DEVELOPMENT OF THE CITADEL

by Alastair Northedge

Archaeological Topography of the Citadel

1. THE UPPER TERRACE

Up to the time of writing there have been six areas excavated within the bounds of this terrace. Areas B, C and D of the excavations of Mrs C-M. Bennett, described in Chapter 10, were placed respectively in the centre of the terrace behind the museum, on the western slope stretching from the museum to the fortification wall, and over a tower (E) to the south of Area C. Area A, excavated by Dr Fawzi Zayadine in 1975–7, is placed in the northeast corner next to the circular cistern. Rescue excavations on the site of the present Jordan Archaeological Museum were conducted by G. L. Harding in 1949 (Museum Site). Lastly, the site of the Byzantine Church was first excavated by the Italian Mission in 1938, and subsequently re-excavated by Dr Fawzi Zayadine in 1977.

The results of these other excavations, and the standing structures of the area, are summarized here for the benefit of the reader.

Excavations of G.L. Harding on the Museum Site (fig.161)

Rescue excavations on the site of the present Jordan Archaeological Museum were conducted by G. L. Harding in 1949.[1] A cruciform area was opened up, measuring 23 × 26m, and approximating to the shape of the museum. The final stratum was excavated to its floor levels, and sondages sunk below, which revealed 'only a jumbled, comparatively sterile layer'.[2]

This final stratum consisted of a series of rooms, possibly belonging to one building, but forming more than one unit. The majority of one unit, a house from its finds, and parts of three others were excavated; of these three, those on the north and south were only touched upon.

1. The main house measured 18.4 × *c.*20m, and consisted of a courtyard (H), with an outside entrance in the unexcavated area to the west, surrounded by rooms on the west, north and east sides. Room D, on the north side, had a doorway two metres wide, and may have been the reception room. Rooms C and E open from it, to form a *'bayt'*, which may be compared with the Syrian 'proto-*bayts*' at Khirbat al-Bayḍā'.[3] Room P may have been a latrine. There was a raised stone platform in the courtyard; and a cistern in Room J, to which plastered drains in the corners of the courtyard brought water from the roofs. Harding thought the cistern was a reuse of an earlier one.

2. The house on the east, of which only a limited part was excavated, was of finer construction (Rooms K, L and M). A large quantity of plain white tesserae in Room K suggested to Harding that an upper storey had existed here with a mosaic floor. Further evidence of an upper storey is to be found in Rooms L and M: piers for arches to support the roof were excavated. These piers stood above complete arches carrying a ground floor over a basement.[4]

Harding dated these houses to the Umayyad period on the basis of a single Umayyad coin from the floor of Room J.

The main house is obviously a parallel to the Stratum V Building B of Area C. The construction is identical to that described for Stratum V, while the plan is a mirror image (fig.166), and the buildings are mounted on the equivalent of the Stratum VI fill ('the jumbled, comparatively sterile layer').

In addition, the main house at least was destroyed suddenly, creating a destruction deposit of Umayyad artefacts in Rooms C-G, J and N.[5] It may be suggested therefore that the building suffered the same kind of destruction. However, by contrast with the sequence in the excavation areas discussed in Chapter 10, there is no trace of occupation later than the Umayyad period.

Excavations in Area A of Dr Fawzi Zayadine

Dr Fawzi Zayadine of the Department of Antiquities

excavated Area A in 1975, 1977 and 1979, on the east side of the upper terrace. Dr Zayadine's sequence, which has been published,[6] is as follows:

1. EBIA (Proto-urban) plastered bank and associated deposits.
2. Widespread Hellenistic and Early Roman remains.
3. A Byzantine domestic settlement, including an oil press.
4. An Umayyad pavement running up to rooms built on the inside of the fortification wall. In particular, the pavement links with an open circular cistern, discussed below.

One can comment that, as was to be expected on the eastern side of the hill, the height of the bedrock of the hill is lower in this area, and earlier remains were well preserved. In parallel with the excavations of Areas B and C, there was a substantial Byzantine settlement. And after an open area in the Umayyad period, there was no further occupation.

Citadel Church (fig.162; pl.79)
Northeast of the Temple of Hercules, a small basilica was excavated by the Italian Archaeological Mission, and re-excavated by Dr Zayadine in 1977.[7]

The original construction is a basilica measuring 20.3 × 12.3m, not perfectly rectangular, but trapezoidal, with the north and south walls not parallel. The apse is external, with a square exterior. There are doors to the north, west and south, and there is a colonnade outside the west door. Adjoining the north side is an additional corridor, off which open several rooms. The clerestory was carried on reused columns. The floors are paved, and the nave has a mosaic floor. It is not certain that this mosaic is part of the original construction. The design is an abstract one of overlapping circles, and it is patched with repairs. Zayadine concludes that the church is of 5th-century date, and that the mosaic floor may be a 6th-century addition.

A sacristy was added on the south side of the apse, and a second room on the north, which does not appear to have a door into the church. According to Zayadine, pottery found above the latest floor dates a use of these rooms to the Umayyad period. In addition, Umayyad coins and pottery date a plaster floor laid outside the west door.

In spite of a lack of certainty in the dating of the church, the general picture remains clear: it is a fifth or a sixth century church, repaired, reused – though not necessarily for ecclesiastical purposes – and possibly rebuilt in the Umayyad period, but abandoned during that time.

It would seem logical that the abandonment took place before the construction of the Umayyad Citadel at the end of the period, for it is unlikely that a Christian religious building would have been allowed to stand in the midst of a new Islamic development.

The Circular Cistern (fig.163; pl.80)
The cistern, placed in the northeast corner of the hexagon, is almost a perfect circle 17.5m in diameter.[8] Although it was partly cleared by the Italian Archaeological Mission, there is still rubble in the base.[9] The cistern has a present maximum depth of six metres. It is almost entirely a built structure, except for a short section on the north-west, where it is cut into the bedrock. The surround wall was excavated by Dr Zayadine in Area A, and found to be 2–2.5m in width, built mainly of ashlars, but with column drums and capitals on the inner face. The outer wall is of rubble masonry.

The whole is bonded with the lime mortar of the Stratum V buildings. No traces of the plastering survive.

On the west side, steps descend into the cistern over the distance of precisely a quarter-circle. The cistern was fed by two channels on the north and west sides. The present depth from the inverts of the feeder channels, presumably the maximum fill level, is 4.5m. With this depth the cistern had a capacity of approximately 1020 cubic metres of water.

DATING AND DISCUSSION. The cistern is dated to the Umayyad period and to Stratum V by its link with the Umayyad paving of Area A, by the fact that it cuts through Byzantine houses, and by the similarity of its construction to the Stratum V technique.

Despite the superficial similarity of this cistern's architecture to a pair of early Islamic cisterns, the slightly later circular Aghlabid cisterns at Qayrawān,[10] its architectural tradition is more properly related to the contemporary, rectangular open cistern at al-Muwaqqar.[11] This is in itself related to local rectangular cisterns of Roman date, e.g. at al-Jīza (Zīzā'), and at Umm al-Jimāl. An Umayyad cistern has also been found at al-Qasṭal.[12] The water-tanks of the Darb Zubayda, dated to the Early 'Abbāsid period, are either circular or rectangular.[13]

The South Side of the Upper Terrace
To the south of the Archaeological Museum, the most prominent feature is the 2nd-century Temple of Hercules, discussed in Chapter 9.

To the east, the area of the Temple *temenos* has been overlaid by a recent cemetery, dating probably to the late 19th and early 20th centuries.

To the west of the temple, but overlying part of the *temenos*, a portion of a rectangular building has been cleared, showing typical Stratum V construction (fig.165).

It seems likely that this was a further building connected with those excavated by Harding on the Museum site.

To the north of the temple, on the rise to the east of the museum, a number of walls, including a street-line, and caves in the bedrock, have been cleared. There is no dating evidence, but some of the walls have the mortar of Stratum V, and have been included in the overall plan of the Umayyad Citadel (fig.165).

2. THE LOWER TERRACE

There have been six excavation areas within the walls:

Excavations of the Italian Mission

An area in the northeast corner dug by the Italian Mission in the 1930s, now covered by a tarmac road.[14] The location is visible in pl.11. As Bartoccini called this 'David's City', the finds were presumably of the Iron Age.[15]

Joint Excavations of ACOR and the University of Jordan (1969)

Four squares dug by Dornemann *c.*1969, adjacent to Gate D. The excavation is unpublished, but a brief report exists in the Registration Centre of the Department of Antiquities.[16] A Roman house was found.

Area A

Area A, adjacent to the Sector 19 wall on the south side, was excavated and published by Dr Zayadine.[17] Two periods of Iron Age II occupation were recovered. Apart from the fortification wall, no occupation was found later than a cemetery of the 3rd century ad. Excavations have recently been resumed in a joint project of the Department of Antiquities and the École Biblique.[18] The principal published discovery so far of these new excavations is a section of the Middle Bronze Age wall.

Area B

Area B was also dug by Dr Zayadine; it is located in the southeast corner of the lower terrace. The work is unpublished, but brief references indicate that an Iron Age and a Hellenistic city wall were found.[19]

Rescue Excavations of 1987

Rescue excavations were conducted by Zayadine, Najjar, and Greene in the centre of the Lower Terrace in 1987, on the proposed site of a school.[20] The main structure revealed was a rectangular hall (9.25 × 4.02m), adjoined north and south by rooms. There was an apse at the east end, and over the main part of the hall a floor of white and coloured mosaic. In the centre of the floor there was a circular medallion, and to the west a further T-shaped medallion depicting a standing man in the posture of an *orante*. Occupation of both the Byzantine and Umayyad periods was found. Two further rooms were excavated to the north, and three rooms and a corridor to the south.

Although the excavators do not accept the possibility that the hall was a church, it would seem to an outside commentator that it was in fact a Byzantine chapel, and possibly part of a small monastic foundation, if one takes into consideration the additional rooms. The hall has the correct orientation, and a raised platform for the altar, though no altar rail or screen.

The project also excavated a deep sounding to the west of the main excavation. At the base of the sounding an occupation dating to the Early Bronze IB period was recovered. This was succeeded by a deposit of Middle Bronze Age IIB/C, and a large deposit of Iron Age II. The Iron Age occupation was followed by reconstruction in the later Hellenistic period (2nd century BC), and a fill of the Early Roman period (1st century AD). The latest occupation was a series of plaster floors laid down in the Byzantine and Umayyad periods, though it did not prove possible to relate them to structures.

One might suppose that the evidence of Byzantine-Umayyad occupation here is similar to that of the church of the Upper Terrace, that is, that a building of Byzantine date was occupied into the Umayyad period, but could have been abandoned or demolished in the course of the latter period.

The Overall Sequence of the Citadel

By collation of the analyses area by area so far, it is possible to reach a rough depiction of the sequence of development of the Citadel over the period of its history, though this picture will inevitably be subject to revision and change as excavation work at the Citadel continues.

In the Upper Citadel, extensive remains predating the Roman reconstruction of the Citadel in the 2nd century AD seem in general to be well preserved mainly around the edges of the hill, and in areas where the bedrock of the hill is low. On the Lower Terrace, the work of Dr Zayadine and the École Biblique in Area A, and of Zayadine, Najjar and Greene, indicate that there may be pre-classical remains over much of the terrace.[21] Surface reconnaissance of the easternmost limb of the hill, now covered by houses, indicates pottery of at least the Iron Age and Early Roman periods.[22] Nevertheless, because of the overburden of later remains, it seems inevitable that it will never be possible to recover a detailed picture of the pre-classical city.

1. Hellenistic and Early Roman Remains

The first period about which anything substantial is known is the late Hellenistic and Early Roman periods, extending from the 2nd century BC up till the reconstruction of the Citadel in the 2nd century AD. There is scattered evidence of the earlier part of this period. Zayadine, Najjar and Greene found structural evidence of the 2nd century BC.[23] Dr Zayadine excavated part of the Hellenistic wall in the southeast corner of the Lower Terrace.

It is not certain whether this was part of the same wall as that for which the excavations in Area C proposed a square tower. It is quite likely that the same fortification wall continued in use from the Hellenistic period through to the 1st century AD, and our dating evidence only came from the latest floor levels and above. At any rate, there is evidence that the pre-2nd century AD wall lay somewhat further down the hill than the later fortification line.[24]

Of the plan inside the walls in the 1st century, it is evident that there was housing on the south side of the Citadel, and a platform of 1st-century date underlying the Roman Gate C (the 'plastered wall building', see Chapter 8). Possibly this was the platform for a building, such as a small temple, but it might have been for a gate into an earlier temple on the site of the Temple of Hercules (though, as indicated in Chapter 9, there is no positive evidence of such a temple). Dr Zayadine also excavated a long monumental wall of the 1st century running east-west in Area A (Upper Citadel), but the purpose of this wall was not identified.[25]

2. The Clearance and Reconstruction of the Upper Citadel: 2nd century AD (fig. 164)

It is evident that from the foundation of settlement on the Citadel, until the 2nd century AD, layers of settlement probably developed superimposed on one another in the fashion widely found on Near Eastern city sites, interrupted only by intermittent earthquakes, as a result of which a certain proportion of the remains must have collapsed down the steep slopes which surround the Qal'a.

However it is clear that there was a severe interruption in the development during the 2nd century AD. Harding was the first to think, based on his long experience of Jordanian archaeology, that the Romans had cleared away much of the ancient tell. He noted 'the finding of sherds of the Early and Middle Bronze Ages, Iron Age and Hellenistic period mixed up with Roman sherds in deep cuttings made on the slopes of the Citadel Hill'.[26] In the author's experience, sherds from tip lines on the slopes are indeed nearly all earlier than the 2nd century AD.

To match this evidence, it is clear from the excavations in Areas A, B, and C that the Hexagon area of the Upper Citadel had been levelled as part of a monumental operation, for the Byzantine urban settlement was either founded directly on bedrock, or on 1st-century remains.[27] As the appearance of the Byzantine settlement could not have brought this about, it must have occurred earlier, and be connected with the Roman monumental construction on the Citadel.

In the course of the Roman monumental reconstruction, two major complexes were constructed, a new fortification wall was built, and there was at least one minor building. The first complex to be built was the so-called Northern Temple. The details of what is known of the layout have been described in Chapter 7, and the intention here is to integrate this information in the overall layout of the Citadel. The complex was built on a very substantial platform, and may have included one or two temples, while there were gates descending to the west, and on the south side. The evidence is that, while its details suggest a 2nd-century date, the east wall shows that it predated the Roman fortification wall and the Temple of Hercules, for it does not take into account any fortifications.

At a slightly later date, now identified as between 161 and 166 AD, the Temple of Hercules was added (Chapter 9). This had a rectangular colonnaded *temenos*, and a gate leading down to the Lower City at Gate C. From the gate, a staircase led down to the Lower City; although we cannot finally prove it, because of the danger of excavation, the staircase seems not to have been straight, as suggested by the alignment of the gate and the Propylaeon, but must have zigzagged down the hill. The Propylaeon was located on the main colonnaded street of the Lower City. As indicated by Bowsher's study, there may well have been a second gate on the north side of the *temenos*, for passage from the Temple of Hercules to the Northern Temple.

The evidence seems certain that the Roman period of the fortifications was approximately contemporary with the Temple, for the southern wall of the *temenos* and Gate C are part of the fortification wall. We have little evidence about the wall, aside from the character of the curtain wall: we have no details of towers or gates apart from Gate C. However the line is clear, surrounding the upper two terraces of the Citadel, and it is also evident that it was intended to act as the defence of Roman Philadelphia, for no other city walls have been identified.

There must have been at least one further building, whose precise location is not known: Sector 17 of the fortification wall was constructed in the Umayyad period from the masonry of apparently one Roman building, including architectural fragments, which was probably of 2nd-century date. It is possible that this was a temple of Tyche, for the excavations of Zayadine, Najjar, and Greene identified an inscription to the goddess on a reused marble block, which they suggest may have been a statue base. The block was incorporated in the Byzantine-Umayyad phase about 75m from Sector 17. The building would probably have stood on the western part of the Lower Citadel, close to the Temple of Hercules.

It also seems significant that the excavations in the three areas recovered no 2nd-century buildings in the area between the two temple complexes. With the reservation that this is an *argumentum e silentio*, it appears to be the case that the upper terrace was cleared for the monumental construction, levelling it to bedrock in the centre of the area and leaving 1st-century deposits intact on the fringes of the summit; but apart from the monumental buildings we know about, the area seems to have been left empty. Nevertheless, the later street pattern seems related to the known gateways of the Roman buildings, and it may be that streets were laid out. One can only speculate on the reasons for the empty space, but the obvious hypothesis is that a more extensive programme of construction was envisaged in the 2nd century than ever proved possible to put into effect: the familiar story of a grand building project running out of money.

Our understanding of the Lower Terrace in this period is less certain. Zayadine does not make a specific case for 2nd-century occupation; a slightly later occupation of the 3rd century is mentioned.[28]

3. The Byzantine Suburb and the Earlier Umayyad Period

In this period the upper terrace developed a settlement, with construction in Areas A, B and C. In addition there was construction in the enclosure of the Northern Temple. The Citadel Church should also be linked to this settlement. The lower terrace excavation at Area A only produced Byzantine coins;[29] but there was also a building complex, possibly a chapel, excavated by Zayadine, Najjar, and Greene. This was an residential settlement that developed organically with no imposed plan, and with one church, and possibly a second, as the only public buildings so far located.

Projecting back the evidence of the Umayyad period indicates that in this period also there was a radial street pattern, diverging from the south gate of the Northern Temple. The street for which there is substantial Byzantine evidence ran from the south gate in a south-south-easterly direction past the Byzantine Church to the suggested north gate of the Temple of Hercules, or to Gate C. There is no direct evidence for the existence of a second street running south-southwest from the south gate of the Northern Temple to the southwest corner of the Citadel. Nevertheless the alignments of the Byzantine buildings match quite closely the line of the buildings of the Umayyad period citadel.

The pottery evidence suggests that the settlement began to appear in the 3rd or early 4th century, that is, 100–150 years after the construction of the Temple of Hercules. At least one building appears to have been destroyed in an earthquake, which is most likely to be identified with that of AD 363.[30] The Temple of Hercules itself may have collapsed in this earthquake. The survival of one collapsed column lying on the ground in complete order suggests that the temple collapsed naturally, and then was denuded of masonry in the Byzantine and Umayyad periods. At least one capital, and probably at least one whole column, in the Byzantine Church come from the *temenos* of the Temple of Hercules. The east room of Gate C had an abandonment deposit of about the 4th century.

Where possible to detect, there were two Byzantine phases in the settlement, the minimum one would expect of a settlement that lasted from the 3rd–4th centuries till the 7th–8th centuries.

There is considerable evidence that at least in parts the Byzantine settlement continued in occupation after the Islamic conquests, and into the earlier part of the Umayyad period (Stratum VII). At one point we may be certain of the continuity: a *follis* type of Constans II (641–68), or a copy thereof, in the last surface adjacent to Building (b) of Stratum VIII, Area C, cannot have been deposited before the Conquest. There were also indications of Umayyad pottery in the street surfaces of Area B predating the construction of the Umayyad Citadel, and the possibility that Building (e) in Area B had only been constructed after the Conquest. Umayyad pottery is already found in the construction fills of the Umayyad Citadel (Stratum VI). Also the Stratum VI fills were deposited cleanly on the stone threshold of Building (b), Area C, and the stone paving of B19/25. There would have been considerable silting if the buildings had been abandoned for a century.

Nevertheless there were also indications of abandonment, which suggest a partial contraction of settlement. On the whole it seems more likely that at least part of the settlement was still in occupation when the Umayyad Citadel was built.

In the Byzantine Church, Zayadine notes Umayyad pottery in above-floor deposits in rooms on the north side of the church, and in the two side-rooms, which are in themselves later additions.[31] These last two rooms produced reconstructable pottery, which might be construed as an abandonment deposit. Later strata in its area have been eroded. Reasoning, however, indicates that it is unlikely that a church would be maintained in the midst of an Islamic development. The Umayyad occupation of the church should belong to Stratum VII, and the church was probably abandoned before or at the time of the Umayyad Stratum V/VI construction. The same situation was probably also true of the Byzantine-Umayyad complex excavated by Zayadine, Najjar and Greene in 1987, especially if, as suggested, it was an ecclesiastical foundation.

4. The Umayyad Citadel (fig.165)

With Strata VI and V a radical reworking of the plan is to be observed. New construction appeared everywhere. This seems to represent a single, planned unit – an Umayyad citadel.[32] The elements that make up this citadel are: the palace, laid out in the double enclosure at the north end; the rebuild of the fortification circuit; the open cistern; and the Stratum V buildings of Areas B, C, and the Museum site.

The dating of these individual elements separately to the Umayyad period has been discussed earlier. It remains to show that they formed part of a single monumental construction project.

Attention was first alerted to this possibility by the regular layout of the Umayyad buildings of Area C, but it soon became obvious that there is a unified building technique shared by all the construction assigned to Stratum V. While there is nothing markedly unusual for 'Ammān, or Jordan in general, about the elements of this technique – lime mortar with ash, plastering studded with chalk, and rubble walling – the similarity of work is distinctive.[33]

The Stratum VI fills, on which the Stratum V construction rests, are visible in Areas B, C and the Museum site. Had there been an unplanned organic development of these areas, then no fills, or small ones, would have been the practice. It is evident from Area C that large areas were filled and levelled at one time.

In Area C the Stratum VI fills are contemporary with the construction of Sector 8 of the Umayyad fortification wall, and the wall was intended partly as a terrace wall to edge the fill. The foundations of Sector 8 on the inside are trench-built into the fill on the inside, but are a free-standing wall on the outside. The Umayyad period of work on the fortifications can also be shown to be contemporary with the palace by the bond of Tower A to Palace Building 6.

Stratum V in Area C then must be contemporary with the palace. At the same time the house of this stratum in Area C has almost identical architecture and finds as the Museum site (fig.166). Stratum V in Area B cannot be directly connected stratigraphically, but seems to belong to the same plan.

In addition to the general dating to the Umayyad period established by coins and pottery from the excavations, one can only refine the dating by means of the place of the palace in the sequence of Umayyad architecture. As suggested earlier, the broad slightly pointed tunnel vaults cannot be seen as earlier than about the reign of Hishām ibn 'Abd al-Malik (105/724–125/743). Equally, the vast construction project cannot be seen as postdating the 'Abbāsid revolution of 132/750, when the resources of the Caliphate were diverted to Iraq, for the later events of destruction and reconstruction also have to be fitted in. It follows that the *terminus ante* should be the beginning of the Third Civil War in 126/744. The median date is 117/735. This is about right, for even given the Umayyads' ability to provide large gangs of workmen, stone construction takes time. The relatively complete state of the result indicates that a number of years had been spent on the work.

5. The Town-Planning of the Umayyad Citadel (fig.165)

Two terraces of the hill were enclosed within the fortification wall, leaving the easternmost terrace outside. This produced two enclosures, but so far no evidence has emerged of habitation on the lower terrace. This may therefore have been an 'outer bailey'; or perhaps it was intended to be built over, though it never actually was. The settlement, then, was limited to the upper terrace. The central focus was the palace (which occupies a third of the upper terrace) and, particularly, its public audience hall. The remaining two-thirds of the terrace was partly occupied by buildings.

In this area four streets have been identified. The street of Area C ran parallel to Sector 8 of the fortification wall, bounding a building strip 25m wide, and is itself three metres wide; the straight line of the street is clearly visible on plate 2a. A street to the east of Area C is partly visible in the surface, but is also derived from the necessity for a street on the west side of the buildings of the Museum site, and the alignment of Building B in Area C. This had a different alignment, appearing to lead from the Reception Hall of the palace to the southwest corner of the Qal'a, where there may have been a gate leading down to the area of the Congregational Mosque. On the south side of Area B a street is visible in section between Buildings D and E: this appears to run parallel to that in Area C, and is 4.1m wide. Fourthly, a 45m length of a street five metres wide runs on the east side of Area B, apparently from the Reception Hall towards Gate C and the east end of the lower town.

It is certain that the Umayyad Citadel did not possess a rectangular grid of streets. Perhaps this was not to be expected on an irregular hill-top site. If the lines have been extrapolated correctly, then the basic pattern was radial, diverging from the Reception Hall.

The alignments, however, converge not on the south door of the hall, but on the north door, the site of the Roman gate of the double enclosure. This radial pattern is reminiscent of the depiction of the street pattern of Jerusalem in the Mādabā mosaic.[34] In addition, the convergence on the site of the north door of the Reception Hall, the location of the Roman gate, rather than its actual south main entrance, and the alignment of the church with the eastern street, led to the suggestion mentioned earlier that these Umayyad streets may have been laid out, at least partly, on the lines of an earlier, Romano-Byzantine, street pattern.[35] If this is the case, then these lines would necessarily go back to the 2nd-3rd centuries AD, when the temples were functioning, and probably stem from the period of the reconstruction of the Citadel in the 2nd century.

In addition to the rather irregular street pattern, the building pattern was also irregular. The enclosure was not completely filled. Although there was extensive construction on the west side (Area C) and in the central area (Area B, Museum site), Area A had an open pavement. In retrospect, the actual area of construction can be recognized from the lie of debris visible in plate 2a, and corresponds to the area marked 'ruins (heaps of stones)' in Conder's Special Survey map of 1881 (fig.4), while a similar picture is presented by the 1863 plan by Gélis and published by de Saulcy (fig.2). The approximate area of this settlement was 20,400 square metres.

There was apparently little at the southern end of the upper terrace, where the ruins of the Temple of Hercules still stood. It was earlier suggested that this may have collapsed, and at least became delapidated before the Umayyad period. The building served as a stone quarry for the builders of the Umayyad wall. But it was not built over, and there is relatively little evidence of Islamic occupation in its vicinity.

All the Umayyad buildings of the settlement except Building A can reasonably be identified as houses, built as multi-unit blocks (fig.166). Of the units whose plans are sufficiently complete, one (Museum site) has rooms on three sides of a courtyard, a latrine (P), and a reception suite (C, D, and E) that resembles a 'Syrian *bayt*' of the Umayyad *quṣūr* (fig.75), and is directly paralleled by the 'Proto-*bayts*' at Khirbat al-Bayḍā'. The Building B house appears to be a mirror image of the Museum site. Both seem to be simplified forms of the residential buildings of the palace.

Harding's excavation described part of a house as 'more ambitious architecturally' on the east side of the main house on the Museum site, and further houses as 'of inferior construction' to the north and south of it.[36] At the lower end of the scale, unit 1 of Building C of Area B consists of two rooms and a courtyard, which opens onto the street (fig.166). Although this might be regarded as too small to be a house unit, it is in fact paralleled directly by two sub-units of House no.4 in Mudaqq al-Ṭabl at Sāmarrā'.[37]

It is evident that the project included the construction of separate courtyard house units of a variety of sizes, ranging from two rooms and a courtyard, to seven rooms, a latrine and a courtyard, up to the residential units of the palace, of which Building 6 has ten rooms, latrine, staircase and courtyard.

There was one further distinctive square building identifiable in plate 2a, to the north of the present site of the Museum, and now covered by one of the Museum buildings, which may have been Umayyad, to judge by its alignment with the western radial street, but it is not possible to be certain of its purpose.

6. The Destruction of the Citadel: the Earthquake of 129–30/747–8 (fig.167)

Two areas, Building B of Area C and the Museum site, show distinct evidence of a destruction shortly after they were built. In both cases the buildings collapsed on their contents. Further confirmation of the violence comes from the skeleton on a threshold of Building B, lying in an impossible position for a burial (pl.70b). Evidence of damage might also be seen in the restorations, discussed in the next section, that were subsequently made to the fortification wall and the palace, particularly the North Building. But the damage was not universal: the buildings of Area B show no sign of interruption in their occupation. The Reception Hall continued to stand.

There seem to be two options to explain the cause of the destruction: (i) an earthquake and (ii) a sack. The possibility of a sack resultant upon an attack on the Qal'a does not carry conviction: there is insufficient evidence of fire. However, 'Abdallah ibn 'Alī is reported to have sent an army to subdue the Balqā' in 132/750.

The use of earthquakes as an explanation of destruction is not one to be taken lightly. There are two important problems: firstly, reasonable certainty that the evidence of destruction visible represents an earthquake; and secondly, dating the evidence to a particular shock known from textual sources.

Here the evidence available matches the expected results of a severe earthquake and is further supported by the partial nature of the destruction (for a distribution map of the destruction, see fig.167). The areas which appear to have suffered most damage (Area C, the Museum site, the fortification wall, and the North Building), are all built on fills of greater or lesser stability. Structures which were little damaged, the Reception Hall and Area B, are built directly on bedrock, or close to it. Alluvial valley fills increase the effects of seismic activity.[38] So, too, with constructional fills.

We have two earthquakes to choose from, one on 18th January between 746 and 749, and a second on 9th March, ten years later.[39] But there is little doubt from literary sources that the first was of much greater intensity:

> A great earthquake in Palestine, Jordan and all Syria, 18th January at the fourth hour [that is, 11 am] ... innumerable myriads died; churches and monasteries were ruined, especially in the desert of the Holy City.[40]

The archaeological parallels for the destruction at 'Ammān are extensive, and by general consensus they have been attributed to this earthquake. In Jerusalem the Aqṣā mosque was damaged,[41] and the Umayyad complex on the south side of the Ḥaram was completely destroyed.[42] At Jericho the unfinished palace at Khirbat al-Mafjar was partly destroyed, but continued in occupation; the Bath Hall was also destroyed.[43] At Tabaqat Faḥl (Pella) an extensive earthquake destruction level in a residential area,[44] and the final destruction of the West Church, are attributed to this earthquake, while a distinctive report has been published on the find of camel skeletons apparently killed in this earthquake.[45] The monastery of the Memorial of Moses at Mt Nebo may also have evidence of a destruction of this period.[46] Umm al-Jimāl apparently suffered damage at this time, and was subsequently abandoned.[47]

The earthquake and the 'Abbāsid revolution, which culminated in 132/750, virtually coincided. Although the course and background of the revolution have in recent years been well charted, from the increasing resentment of the secularity of Umayyad rule to the self-destruction of the Umayyad power base in Syria in the Third Civil War, it is also true that the widespread devastation of much of the southern part of Bilād al-Shām visible in the archaeological evidence, an event which took place in the middle of the winter, must also have lowered the capabilities of the Umayyad armies when it came to the battle on the Zāb in that year.

7. The Restoration of the Citadel in the Early 'Abbāsid Period

There are two important pieces of evidence which suggest that the Qal'a was restored after the earthquake damage.

The first of these is the addition of the sloping buttresses and revetment to the Umayyad wall circuit. This work was evidently a restoration of the fortifications; for example, in rebuilt Buttress 1 of Sector 9 there was no good wall face behind the addition, and the original buttress must have collapsed.

The second is the Period 4 construction in the palace: in this phase colonnades were added in Buildings 4, 5 and 6, using round piers of rubble and gypsum mortar, and in the North Building rubble and gypsum mortar engaged columns were added at the mouth of the *īwān*, while the side-room N2 was reroofed with a transverse arch of the same construction.

There is no direct evidence that both these items belong to the same project of restoration, nor is it necessary for us that they should do. They are both modifications that clearly postdate the Umayyad construction. Over a period, or at one time, the Qal'a was being restored in a modest fashion. Some areas of the residential settlement, however, remained derelict.

There would not have been time to undertake the restoration outlined above before the revolution. Rather, the reconstruction was perhaps the work of one or more of the early 'Abbāsid governors of the Balqā'. We know the names of two: Muḥammad ibn 'Ubaydallah under al-Manṣūr (158/774) and Ṣāliḥ ibn Sulaymān under al-Rashīd (180/796). Either of these Easterners could have introduced the oriental rubble and gypsum mortar technique of Period 4 in the palace. The use of this technique is consistent with the work of the entourage of a governor who came from Iraq or further east. However, Muḥammad ibn 'Ubaydallah is only known to have been in the Balqā' for a year. Ṣāliḥ ibn Sulaymān was a supporter of Ja'far ibn Yaḥyā al-Barmakī, who was sent to Syria to bring peace to the country. Ja'far was a member of the famous family of *wazīrs*, who originated from Balkh, but built up their power base in Iraq, and fell from power in 187/803.

The parallelism between the events of the 129–30/747–8 earthquake and restoration here, and at the Ḥaram in Jerusalem, another site with Umayyad construction built on a platform and other fills, is quite striking. The Qubbat al-Sakhra, built on the bedrock, of course, continued to stand. The Umayyad complex south of the Haram, built on fills over Byzantine houses, was completely demolished and not rebuilt.[48] The Aqṣā (*al-mughaṭṭā*) was destroyed 'except for the part around the *miḥrāb*'.[49]

The restoration of the Aqṣā was in a more modest form of construction, like 'Ammān; the colonnades were supported on lofty piers (*asāṭīn mushayyada*), in place of the former marble columns (*a'midat al-rukhām*).[50]

Muqaddasī's explanation of this more modest restoration could also parallel 'Ammān:

> When the news (of the earthquake) reached the Caliph, he was told that the treasury of the Muslims was not adequate to restore (the mosque) to what it had been before. So he wrote to the amirs of the provinces and the other commanders, that each one of them should build a colonnade. And they built it firmer and more substantial than it had been before.[51]

The date of Manṣūr's work on the Aqṣā is given by Pseudo-Dionysius as the year before work was begun on Raqqa, that is, 771, although he misunderstands the work as a conversion of Solomon's Temple into a mosque.[52] This was some 24 years after the earthquake of 130/747–8, a very long time for the rebuilding of a major sanctuary after an earthquake, and gives an idea of how long it might have taken before the less important Qal'a at 'Ammān was restored.

8. The Early Islamic Settlement

Following this restoration the next event appears to have been the final collapse or destruction of the fortifications. They had collapsed in Areas C and D down to their present level by house Phase 1b of Area D, which is the time of the construction of a building over Tower E. Our only information on dating comes from this: Phase 1b is characterized by Stratum IVb pottery, including early polychrome glazed wares.

One might tentatively suggest that the collapse occurred before the end of the 3rd/9th century. But we know nothing of the causes. The walls might have been razed, perhaps in connection with a revolt, such as that of Sa'īd ibn Khālid al-'Uthmānī al-Fudaynī under al-Ma'mūn (198/813–218/833). Alternatively, the destruction might have been the product of a further earthquake. There was an earthquake of confused date in the Damascus region in the period 230–3/845–7, which might have been strongly felt at 'Ammān, considering the vulnerability of the Qal'a to earthquake effect (demonstrated in the earthquake of 129–30/747–8).[53] At any rate, the walls were never restored.

Occupation at the Qal'a continued in three main periods, distinguished by their ceramic horizons. In the main the pattern of the Umayyad settlement was retained – occupation in the palace and its immediate vicinity, the northern and western areas of the upper terrace (Areas B, C, and D, but not Area A). As far as our evidence goes, the street lines of the Umayyad period continued to be used up to Stratum III, even when the Umayyad buildings were no longer occupied.

To generalize from the Area analysis, one may say that in places Umayyad buildings continued to be occupied (Areas B and C), and in others new buildings were erected (Areas C and D). The palace was converted into a small-scale occupation. The whole appears to represent an urban settlement.

Stratum IVb (3rd/9th–4th/10th centuries) is represented in Areas B, C, D, and the palace. In this period are found the first constructions over the top of the fortification wall, in Areas C and D.

Unfortunately there are no coins to date this stratum. However, characteristic Stratum IVb pottery is an early introduction, for it appears on or connected with earth floors that must be Umayyad in date or shortly postdate the 'Abbāsid Revolution (132/750). Polychrome glazed ware appears in the course of this stratum, but not necessarily at the beginning of it. Local polychrome, splashed and early *sgraffiato* wares are all found associated with it. This stratum can only be broadly assigned to the 3rd/9th and 4th/10th centuries.

In Stratum III (5th/11th century) the settlement expanded but remained essentially a continuation of the IVb period. Area C was widely reoccupied, and traces of occupation are found in all areas of the upper terrace except Area A. This stratum is associated with two Fāṭimid coins, both of the early 5th/11th century.

9. The Stratum III Destruction: A further earthquake

At the end of this period there was a further widespread abandonment, with deposits of pottery on floors in Areas B, C, and D. Areas C and D were not occupied again. Although the buildings in the three areas, and even within each area, are not clearly stratigraphically linked, there is enough similarity in the pottery to suggest that the abandonment occurred at the same time in all the rooms whose contents are illustrated (figs 137, 141, 151). In the case of Room 4 of Building 1 in Area C, the sherds of one cooking pot were found high up in the tumble, suggesting that the pot had fallen from a high niche in the course of the collapse of the building. This building, at least, collapsed on its contents; a collapse of the vault in Room D, Building D, at this period was also indicated by the necessity to rebuild the east wall before further occupation in Stratum IIb. It was more difficult to be certain elsewhere, for the poor quality of construction did not leave the distinctive traces found from the Umayyad earthquake.

Nevertheless the traces that were found, and the widespread nature of the abandonment, suggest quite strongly that the cause was a further earthquake. If, because of the loose Stratum VI fills, many of the areas of the Qal'a were vulnerable to earthquake in 129–30/747–8, the same areas would only be more vulnerable a second time, through the build-up of occupation deposits over the centuries.

The effects of this second earthquake, if it was an earthquake, seem to have been different from the first, for destruction deposits of pottery were excavated from every building of the stratum excavated in Areas B, C, and D, with the exception of the limited reoccupation of Umayyad Building B in Area C. In particular it is to be noted that the buildings of Area B, which had escaped lightly in 129–30/747–8, were affected by this event. It is known that the character of seismic waves can vary according to the distance of the affected site from the epicentre of the shock, and the depth of the epicentre below the earth's crust. No human or animal remains trapped in the collapse were found, and it is possible that a fore-shock had given warning.

This destruction seems to have terminated general occupation in Areas B, C, and D. The abandonment was not in itself, of course, the product of the earthquake, but resulted from the inhabitants being unable to rebuild their property, and is a reflection of the economic and political circumstances of the times.

Dating this earthquake is more difficult than dating that of 129–30/747–8. It must postdate the latest Fāṭimid coin found, a minting of al-Ẓahir, thus postdating his accession year, 411/1021, as it is undated. The position is complicated by the rarity of late Fāṭimid mintings.[54] It should predate the Ayyūbid period and the introduction of Pseudo-prehistoric ware. Furthermore, it must have been a severe earthquake to cause such widespread destruction.

The earthquakes of this period which might have affected 'Ammān were:

Severe Earthquakes

(a) 10th Muḥarram 425/5th December 1033. Ramla, Jerusalem (the wall and the Aqṣā Mosque were damaged), Gaza, Tiberias.[55]

(b) 11th Jumāda I, 460/18th March 1068. Palestine and northern Hijāz: Ramla, Jerusalem (Qubbat al-Sakhra damaged), al-Madina, Wādī Ṣafra, Khaybar, Badr, Yanbū', Wādī al-Qurā, Taymā, Ayla ('Aqaba).[56]

(c) 20th May 1202. Reported over an area from Anatolia to Egypt, and from Sicily to Iraq. The epicentre seems to have been in northern Palestine, Lebanon and south-central Syria.[57]

Distant or Less Severe Earthquakes

(d) 500/24th December 1105. Jerusalem, reported in Crusader sources, not mentioned in Islamic sources.[58]

(e) 565/29th June 1170. Severe in Syria at Damascus, Homs, Hama Aleppo, Ba'albakk. Strong in Palestine at Caesaraea.[59]

Of these options, the distant or less severe earthquakes described were probably insufficient to cause extensive damage at 'Ammān, but the three severe earthquakes are possibilities, if their dates are consistent with the evidence from 'Ammān.

The earthquake of 425/1033 is an attractive option, as the excavators of Tiberias date a destruction and abandonment to this earthquake.[60] But for 'Ammān there are two problems:

(i) that the *dirham* of al-Ẓahir found in the floor of Area C, Building 3, and minted at the earliest in 411/1020–1, is worn, and that wear would have had to occur in 14 years, although it is within the bounds of possibility that heavy usage could have brought about a degree of wear in that time.

(ii) The pottery is largely paralleled by Crusader and Middle Islamic pottery of the 6th/12th century, and even the 7th/13th century. Although the pottery sequence of the 5th/11th century is hardly well known, it is questionable whether one could date the pottery of the destruction into the first half of that century. Pottery dating in the 'Abbāsid and Fāṭimid periods is made difficult by a general lack of coins of the period found in excavations; nevertheless, the number of different pottery phases which require to be fitted into the period mean that any one phase is unlikely to be in error by more than fifty years.[61]

There is a pottery phase at the Qal'a which ought to be fitted into the late 4th/10th and early 5th/11th centuries, for example, pottery excavated by the Spanish Archaeological Mission, including splashed wares with straight flaring rims.[62] But splashed wares with straight flaring rims did not appear in the Stratum III destruction, which was evidently later, but rather in earlier occupation in Area D.

The effects of the earthquake of 460/1068 were concentrated in Palestine and the northern Hijāz, on either side of the Balqā', and the epicentre has been suggested to have lain in the northern Red Sea, while there may even have been a second associated earthquake in Palestine.[63] The same problem of ceramic dating applies also, but to a lesser degree, to this earthquake, but it is a more likely candidate.

The earthquake of 20th May 1202 is within the bounds of possibility, but is not likely. The Stratum III destruction occurred before the introduction of Pseudo-prehistoric ware, which is characteristic of the following Stratum IIb. Although no archaeological evidence is yet available to date the introduction of Pseudo-prehistoric ware, it is generally connected in its early phase with the Ayyūbid period and the early 7th/13th century; no specific evidence has yet been recovered connecting it with the 6th/12th century. The early 7th/13th century date connected with Stratum IIb at the Qalʿa (see below) makes it difficult to suggest that a complete ceramic change occurred in only 25 years.

It seems most likely that the earthquake of 460/1068 was the cause of the Stratum III destruction. A certain degree of support is lent to this conclusion by the fact that at Jerusalem in this earthquake it was the Qubbat al-Sakhra, built on bedrock, that was damaged, and not – as was more usual – the Aqṣā mosque. This parallels our own evidence that the buildings of Area B, also built on the bedrock, were affected, although they had previously escaped. One might suppose that the wavelength and amplitude of the seismic waves were somewhat different from what they had been in 747–8.

Nevertheless an attribution to the earthquake of 460/1068 should be regarded with caution. The identification and dating of the pottery sequence for the 5th/11th and 6th/12th centuries have not yet been securely established. The evidence that it was an earthquake is by no means as clear as for 129–30/747–8, although such evidence would probably emerge from further excavation. And lastly, we have seen no trace of the two most serious earthquakes of the period – 1033 and 1202. From the point of view of the pottery dating, the destruction might have taken place at any time in the second half of the 5th/11th century, or the first half of the 6th/12th century.

10. Stratum IIb: 7th/13th Century (Ayyūbid)

With the IIb settlement there is a completely new ceramic tradition, with no carry-over from previous periods. It may also be that there is an occupational gap, representing the majority of the 6th/12th century: the only detailed sequence available (Room D of Building D) suggests such a gap. The settlement is much smaller than in Stratum III: two rooms only in Area B, and Ayyūbid-Mamlūk occupation from the North Building of the palace.[64] In addition, Tower B was built to watch over the city.

The settlement essentially postdates the Battle of Ḥaṭṭīn (583/1187). It is dated by the group of Ayyūbid coppers from Room D, Building D, which were deposited not much later than the death of al-Nāṣir in 622/1225. The occupation of Room D could not have lasted longer than the middle of the 7th/13th century. We do not know if this date applied to the remainder of the Qalʿa; occupation probably petered out rather slowly, with clear literary evidence of occupation in the city in the 8th/14th century.

The Parallels of the Umayyad Citadel

The Umayyad Citadel may be summarized as consisting of the following elements: a fortified enclosure of the hill, a palace, and a settlement inside the walls, which includes accommodation in house units, together with some evidence of other forms of building (fig.165).

As first suggested by Gaube,[65] the palace should be a *dār al-imāra*, the 'Government House', where official business was conducted, but also the governor's palace. There was an *ʿāmil* of the Balqāʾ, and the existence of the congregational mosque, and the Umayyad mint, indicate that the main residence was in ʿAmmān; but there is no name among the known governors of the Balqāʾ to whom the construction could be attributed. All the known names cited in Table 3 are too early for the archaeological dating of the complex. Nevertheless, the grandiose scale suggests that the unknown governor had access to substantial funds, probably rather more than the size of the governorate would justify. As Table 3 indicates, it was possible for a member of Banī Umayya to be *ʿāmil* of the Balqāʾ, and perhaps this was what happened again: a wealthy Umayyad with access to funds through family connections was given an unproblematic governorate. Certainly the proportionately large size of the palace would support such a conclusion.

It could not have been the first *dār al-imāra* of ʿAmmān, for the palace was only built late in the Umayyad Caliphate, and there is substantial historical evidence of Umayyad activity in ʿAmmān at an earlier date. If, as seems likely from architectural style, the congregational mosque predates the palace, it is possible that an early Umayyad government building lay in its vicinity. The Umayyad palace of the Qalʿa would then represent a replacement of earlier arrangements.

However there is also the fortified enclosure and residential settlement to consider. The whole gives the impression of being a fortress, perhaps an early version of a medieval Islamic citadel, as for example the great medieval citadels of Aleppo, Damascus and Jerusalem. While a direct comparison would be anachronistic, there must be an element of truth in this, and it is true that 'Ammān was defended by a citadel, not by city walls, in the Roman period.

The most significant difference from these later structures lay in the substantial area of residential accommodation. At the end of the Umayyad period, at least, there was a garrison in the Balqā', called *jund al-Balqā'*.[66] The only known activity of this *jund* was the arrest of the 'Abbāsid Ibrahīm al-Imam at Ḥumayma in 132/750; the governor of Damascus, al-Walīd ibn Mu'āwiya, was instructed by Marwān ibn Muḥammad to write to his *'āmil* in the Balqā' to send cavalry to Ḥumayma for the arrest.[67] It seems most probable that these were the people accommodated in the residential settlement.

There are a number of parallels to this designed arrangement of palace and residential settlement in the Early Islamic period. From the Umayyad period there is archaeological evidence from 'Anjar and Qaṣr al-Ḥayr al-Sharqī, and now possibly 'Aqaba and Madīnat al-Fār. Although different in being built on a hill, 'Ammān could be considered part of a larger group of contemporary sites, in terms of function..

In addition to these Umayyad sites where such a layout appears to exist, Grabar has also concluded that the Umayyad complex excavated in Jerusalem to the south of the Aqsā mosque might be included within a group of quasi-urban settlements comparable with Qaṣr al-Ḥayr al-Sharqī. However, this Umayyad complex in Jerusalem does not meet the criterion of a residential settlement, and it seemed inappropriate to include it.[68]

1. 'Anjar (fig. 169)

'Anjar,[69] located in the Biqā' valley in Lebanon, is a fortified, almost square, enclosure, 310 × 370m, with four colonnaded streets meeting at a central tetrapylon. The streets are lined with Roman-style shop units, and the enclosure includes a main palace, a mosque, two subsidiary palaces, of which only one was built above foundation level, and two baths. The remaining buildings excavated are built in sub-rectangular blocks. Nearly all of these are divided into house units around courtyards. The most recent report notes that the excavation of the site by the Lebanese Department of Antiquities is almost complete, and that there were substantial areas within the enclosure that were never built up.[70]

Not much archaeological evidence has been published to substantiate the dating of 'Anjar, although there are Umayyad graffiti.[71] Nevertheless, although suggestions have continued to be made that it is Roman,[72] it is clear enough that it is Umayyad. It is a one-period site with little evidence of rebuilding, the plan incorporates a mosque, and the houses include the so-called 'Syrian *bayt*'.[73] The design of the fortifications also finds parallels in the 2nd/8th century: the combination of solid round-fronted interval towers and hollow corner towers is certainly reflected at the Octagon at Qādisiyya (before 180/796), and possibly at Raqqa (155/772).

'Anjar has been associated with the early name of 'Ayn al-Jarr, at which Egyptian workmen are known from the Aphrodito papyri to have worked.[74] An anonymous Syriac chronicle of the 9th century AD, whose sources can be followed back to about 750 AD, says that Walīd ibn 'Abd al-Malik built a 'city' called 'In Gero.[75] Theophanes' version, under Anno Mundi 6202 (AD 711), is that 'Abbās ibn al-Walīd began to build *Garis* in the territory of Heliopolis (Ba'albakk).[76] Inscriptions at a nearby quarry at Kamed date work to 96/714–15, in the reign of Walīd ibn 'Abd al-Malik.[77]

Of the two traditions concerning the builder, Walīd and his son 'Abbās, the latter is more likely, in that it is more specific, the *lectio difficilior*: the Kamed inscriptions also refer to work in the reign of Walīd, not to work by that Caliph. The Islamic Arabic sources, which one might expect to report major activities of a Caliph, and which do report the construction activities of other Umayyad Caliphs, are silent on the subject of 'Anjar.

'Abbās was a soldier, a general in the Byzantine campaigns working with Maslama ibn 'Abd al-Malik.[78] He was governor of Hims, and had a long association with that city, where he had a house, and where he seems to have lived towards the end of his life.[79]

It is evident that the plan of 'Anjar resembles that of a Roman legionary *castrum*, particularly the Jordanian *castra* at Lajjūn and Udhruḥ[80] though there were also similar Roman civilian settlements. However, the accommodation in Roman *castra* differed from 'Anjar in being composed of lines of single rooms, perhaps to be described as barracks. In the Roman army, soldiers were single until retirement. By contrast, the soldiers of the Caliphate were often married men, as we see at Sāmarrā', where al-Mu'taṣim purchased girls for the Turks to marry.[81]

At the time that 'Abbās ibn al-Walīd began the construction of 'Anjar, he was at the height of his military career. According to Theophanes, the foundation was one year after the conquest of Tuwāna, a campaign in which he co-operated, as he usually did, with Maslama ibn 'Abd al-Malik.[82] His last known campaign, again with Maslama, was against Yazīd ibn al-Muhallab in Iraq in 102/720.[83] The logical requirement at this period of his career would be for accommodation for his own *jund* – his personal troops, as it were. It must be stressed that, when viewed from the perspective of the evidence of the site itself, and the historical references, this interpretation is not a certainty.

2. Qaṣr al-Ḥayr al-Sharqī (fig.170)

Qaṣr al-Ḥayr al-Sharqī[84] is located some 100 km northeast of Palmyra, and some 60 km southwest of Ruṣāfa, on a road from Palmyra to the Euphrates. The site, excavated by Grabar in the 1960s, is composed of two enclosures, a bath, a settlement of unexcavated mud-brick buildings dated to the Umayyad period, and a large walled area, perhaps a *ḥayr* or enclosure. The Small Enclosure (*c.*66 metres square) is a version of the typical Umayyad square fort-like castle, built of ashlar masonry and fired brick. The Large Enclosure is similar to, but smaller than, ʿAnjar (*c.*163 metres square), and has different internal arrangements: a large central court, a mosque, seven courtyard houses, open yards in the corners and a service unit, in which a press was found. One of the courtyard houses (Sector VI on the west side of the mosque) is more elaborately constructed than the others, with early ʿAbbāsid stucco decorations, but no larger in overall dimensions. Apart from the outer wall and mosque, which are built of ashlar masonry and some fired brick, construction is of mud-brick above a base course of stone.

An inscription seen by Rousseau in the mosque identifies the Large Enclosure as a *madīna*, a 'city', built by the people of Ḥimṣ in 110/728–9.

Grabar's interpretation of the site is that the Small Enclosure is a *khān* or caravanserai rather than a *qaṣr*, and he bases his view on the geographical location of Qaṣr al-Ḥayr on a major route from central Syria to the Euphrates, and the lack of decoration in the building.[85] He describes the Large Enclosure as a quasi-urban settlement, and it is clear that he uses the expression 'quasi-urban' because of the inscription which calls the Large Enclosure a *madīna*. The more elaborate Sector VI house is called by Grabar the *dār al-imāra*.[86]

This interpretation of Qaṣr al-Ḥayr al-Sharqī is not entirely satisfactory; the principal objection is that there is no obvious palatial residence, which is a strong feature of all our other sites. The Sector VI house is more nearly the equivalent of a larger house. The interior arrangements of the Small Enclosure are also undoubtedly of finer construction, ashlar masonry and fired brick, than those of the Large Enclosure, whose buildings, excepting the mosque, are of mud-brick.

Lack of decoration is not a serious objection; one can only agree with Grabar that the Umayyads had a penchant for highly decorated *quṣūr*, but quantity of decoration can hardly be a criterion for deciding whether a building was a *qaṣr* or not. There might be many reasons why a building was little decorated: the personal preferences of the patron, the craft tradition of the builders, who might or might not have been closely supervised by the patron, a failure to complete the original programme of construction, lack of money, and, finally, subsequent removal or disappearance of decorations that had once been in existence.

Unfortunately no samples were excavated of the mud-brick settlement, which on the basis of surface sherding was said to be Umayyad. So the full spectrum of the settlement at Qaṣr al-Ḥayr al-Sharqī remains unclear.

It may be suggested, however, that the Small Enclosure was in fact the *qaṣr*, because of its higher quality of construction, and the Large Enclosure the residential settlement, but the combination has become divorced into two separate enclosures, whereas in our other sites these are combined. The term *madīna*, known from the foundation inscription, would apply particularly to the residential settlement.

There is more than one way to explain how this division might have occurred. One is that the two are not exactly contemporary. The *qaṣr* could have been built first, and the *madīna* (the Large Enclosure) added a few years later, when there was more money available, or there was an increased demand for accommodation. The vaults of the Small Enclosure are of a semi-circular form, while the mosque of the Large Enclosure has two-centre pointed arches. Normally in the architectural history of Islam one thinks of a chronological development from the round arch to the pointed, and Qaṣr al-Ḥayr was built at the time when the two-centre pointed arch was being first introduced.[87]

But it is not a strong argument; at this time there must have been craftsmen who worked in the pointed arch tradition, but also others who still preferred round arches. There are examples, including the Large Enclosure of Qaṣr al-Ḥayr, where both round and pointed arches have been used in the same building.

An alternative explanation might be that the two are in fact part of the same scheme of development, but the tradition of building and living in castles, a strong Umayyad tradition of which there are many examples, suggested to the patron that his own personal residence should be in this form, and separate from the remainder of his people.

3. ʿAqaba

Excavations of the Oriental Institute, Chicago, have recently begun at the site of the early medieval settlement at ʻAqaba, under the direction of D. Whitcomb.[88] These excavations have revealed a stone-built quadrilateral enclosure with hollow round-fronted towers and one square tower, approximately 165 x 140m. There appears originally to have been a cross of streets, meeting at a possible tetrapylon; however, substantial later occupation in the ʻAbbāsid and Fāṭimid periods has made difficult any extensive clearing of the original plan.

Whitcomb interprets the site to have been founded in the middle of the 7th century, possibly as a settlement of the *mawālī* of the Caliph ʻUthmān ibn ʻAffān (23/644–35/656). While this dating was mainly based on historical sources, the earliest pottery recovered is reported to be of the 7th century.[89]

However, this interpretation has been criticized in a book review by Knauf and Brooker.[90] They suggest that the original foundation was the legionary camp of the *Legio X Fretensis*, which is known to have been located at ʻAqaba in the 4th century AD, and that the Islamic occupation is a secondary urban settlement developed on the site of the camp, a phenomenon which is known to have happened at the *castrum* of Udhruḥ. Regrettably, the high water-table has made impossible an extensive investigation of the foundation levels of the original construction.

At any rate, the round-fronted towers have good parallels in the fourth-century *castra* at Udhruḥ and Lajjūn, but no parallels in later Umayyad architecture. Parallels with Roman practice are to be expected in an Islamic structure as early as the middle of the 7th century. However, both 7th-century pottery and the parallels of the architecture are compatible with a 4th-century dating as well as one in the 7th century, while it seems likely that there was a legionary *castrum* located somewhere in the vicinity.

At the time of writing it seems that the dating is not finally proven. If it is Islamic, then one would wish to suggest that it be dated rather later, not before the beginning of the 2nd/8th century.

4. Madīnat al-Fār

German-Syrian excavations have recently begun at the site of Madīnat al-Fār on the Balīkh in Syria.[91] The site includes a rectangular palace and large walled settlement, although the plan of neither is yet clear. The palace is a square of about 300m, and the settlement measures approximately 900m by 1500m.

An identification has been proposed with the Umayyad settlement of Ḥiṣn Maslama, the residence of Maslama ibn ʻAbd al-Malik. Ḥiṣn Maslama certainly should be located in this area, and there are no alternative historical identifications. However, the sondages of 1987 and 1989 recovered only ʻAbbāsid pottery down to virgin soil, and the size is comparable to the constructions of ʻAbbāsid Iraq.

5. Discussion

Leaving aside ʻAqaba and Madīnat al-Fār as still uncertain examples, one can say that the three sites of ʻAnjar, Qaṣr al-Ḥayr al-Sharqī, and Qalʻat ʻAmmān are all relatively small settlements with prominent palaces; they are walled, and include a relatively small number of courtyard houses, together with other service buildings of various kinds – storehouses, open enclosures, cisterns, and what Grabar called at Qaṣr al-Ḥayr al-Sharqī an ʻindustrial area', which included an olive press.

It is not surprising that elements of the architectural tradition of the legionary *castra* appear in two of the three sites, while the irregular site of ʻAmmān was fortified in the tradition of Roman urban fortification. However, the issue of architectural tradition is not important; there was no alternative in post-Roman Syria.

There is a clear relationship with the Umayyad castles (*qaṣr*, pl. *quṣūr*). In the case of Qaṣr al-Ḥayr al-Sharqī, the site seems to be an expansion of a *qaṣr*, and it is sited in a typical desert location. It is also possible to imagine that settlements such as are found in a designed layout here, could also have existed in an irregular unfortified form. In the past it was thought that the settlement surrounding the *qaṣr* at Jebel Seis, as planned by Sauvaget,[92] was an example, but it now seems that the settlement had a longer history, stretching back into the Byzantine period. However one might also quote the extramural settlement of the Umayyad period at Ruṣāfa, the survey of which is not yet published.[93] The Umayyad settlement at Ruṣāfa was built as a Caliph's residence by Hishām ibn ʻAbd al-Malik (105/724–125/743), and appears to include four castle-like buildings, and about thirty others, scattered over the landscape.[94]

There is a surviving account of the foundation of such a site, that of al-Ramla, the plan of which is no longer visible:

> Al-Walīd ibn ʻAbd al-Malik appointed Sulaymān ibn ʻAbd al-Malik governor of *jund Filasṭīn*, and he [Sulaymān] settled in Ludd. Then he founded the city of al-Ramla *(madīnat al-Ramla)*, and made it a *miṣr (maṣṣarahā)*. The first that was built of it was his palace *(qaṣr)* and the house known as *Dār al-Sabbāghīn* (House of the Dyers), and he placed a cistern centrally in the house. Then he marked out a plan for the mosque, and built it, but he succeeded to the Caliphate before its completion; then there was later construction in it during his caliphate.

> Then 'Umar ibn 'Abd al-'Azīz completed it, and reduced the original plan. ... When Sulaymān had built for himself, he gave permission to the people for construction, and they built; and he dug for the people of al-Ramla their canal which is called Barada, and he dug wells ...[95]

While the construction of one of the archaeological sites discussed can well be recognized in this description, there are points to be noted. Firstly, that it was planned and begun before Sulaymān became Caliph (96/715–99/717), and thus is evidence of building activity among the Umayyad elite, rather than that of the Caliph. Secondly, the extent of construction was later reduced, as is also found in the archaeological sites, and thirdly, people were responsible for building their own houses.

It was suggested above that the settlements of two of the three sites, 'Anjar and 'Ammān, might have included the accommodation of military units. While this is quite likely, there is no clear archaeological evidence, or specific historical evidence, that this was so. It is certain that the majority of the Umayyad army of Syria was not accommodated in such specially built settlements, but rather spread through the cities and villages of Syria.

At the time of the Islamic Conquests and afterwards, the armies were constituted of the male population of the Arab tribes, led by the tribal *ashrāf*, with some exceptions. By the late Umayyad period, the armies were organized in irregularly-sized units under *quwwād*, or commanders. The number of men commanded by a *qā'id* varied; examples are known of 400,[96] or 1000.[97] The late Umayyad army of Syria continued to be largely recruited by tribe.[98]

There were also separate regiments of *mawālī*. The names are known of the Waḍḍāḥiyya,[99] the Qīqāniyya,[100] the Ṣaḥṣaḥiyya, the Dāliqiyya, and the Rāshidiyya.[101] The Dhakwāniyya were a *mawlā* regiment of Sulaymān ibn Hishām and numbered 3000.[102] The Dhakwāniyya were in effect the private army of Sulaymān ibn Hishām.

Other late Umayyad leaders also acquired private retinues which could, if necessary, be mobilized for war. These accounts mention *ahl al-bayt*, the household, *qawm*, people of the same tribe, and *mawālī*. In 102/720 Yazīd ibn al-Muhallab fought in rebellion, with *aṣḥābihi wa-mawālīhi wa-nās min qawmihi*, his companions, *mawālī*, and some of his *qawm*.[103] In 126/744 'Abbās ibn Walīd prepared to fight with 150 of his sons and *mawālī*.[104] Hurayth ibn Abī al-Jahm collected his *mawālī* and companions, about thirty armed men.[105] Sulaymān ibn Hishām joined the Khawārij of Ḍaḥḥak ibn Qays with his household, *ahl al-bayt*, and *mawālī*, numbering more than 3000.[106] Abū al-Ward, when rebelling against the 'Abbāsids in 132/750, took to war 500 of *ahl baytihi wa-qawmihi*.[107]

It has been commented that there was apparently little difference in status between such a personal following and the *jund*.[108] Thābit ibn Nu'aym al-Judhāmī gathered his *qawm* and his *jund* in rebellion in 127/745.[109] 'Abd al-'Azīz ibn Hārūn refused the governorship of Iraq, because he had no *jund*.[110]

While these details and historical interpretation are not new to scholarship,[111] the significant issue is that it is clear that the archaeological evidence reflects such a military and social order of leaders and personal followings. The numbers of the *jund*s and *mawālī* mentioned vary between 150 and 3000. The varying sizes of the followings noted above would explain why these Umayyad settlements are of different dimensions. The personal nature of the relationship between leader and follower would explain why it was that such a settlement came to be built at the isolated desert site of Qaṣr al-Ḥayr al-Sharqī; it was a personal responsibility for an *amīr* or *qā'id* to provide accommodation, and he was presumably free to choose the location. The broad spread of locations reflects the character of Arab settlement in Syria during the Umayyad period. The Caliph Hishām built his residence at Ruṣāfa; the settlements of the military and other leaders were not there, but in other parts of Syria and Jazīra.

Evidently one of the social features of Umayyad Syria was the development of personal followings by leading figures of the period, especially towards the end of the Umayyad Caliphate, with little differentation between military and civilian followings. Apparently here at 'Ammān, it was the governor of the Balqā' – who appears to have been a man of wealth, to judge by the size of the palace – and his following was paid by the state as the garrison of the Balqā'. The fact that the settlement is built on a hill and looks like a citadel is not very important. Rather it was a miniature version of Ramla, and the equivalent of a number of other Umayyad settlements, such as at 'Anjar and Qaṣr al-Ḥayr al-Sharqī. In effect Umayyad Syria was dotted with small settlements, and the caliph could have a larger but similar settlement, such as that of Hishām at Ruṣāfa. By contrast in Iraq these settlements were agglomerated into cities, as at Baghdāḍ and Sāmarrā.[112] When the unusual social structure of Umayyad Syria dissolved, in the half-century after 'Abbāsid Revolution in 132/750, the need for these settlements disappeared. Some, as 'Anjar and Qaṣr al-Ḥayr al-Shaqī were abandoned – the latter by about 860. 'Ammān, although rebuilt in the second half of the 2nd/8th century, eventually transmitted itself into a suburb of the city.

TABLES

Table 1. Towns and Administrative Districts of al-Balqā' in the 3rd/9th century according to the Arab Geographers (fig. 10)

Jund	*Modern name*	*Classical name*	*Ibn Khurdādhbih p. 77*	*al-Balādhurī pp. 116, 126*	*al-Ya'qūbī pp. 326–7*	*Population (after al-Ya'qūbī)*
Urdunn	Tabaqat Faḥl	Pella	Faḥl	Faḥl	Faḥl	
	Jarash	Gerasa	Jarash	Jarash	Jarash	Mix of Arabs and
	Bayt Rās	Capitolias	Bayt Rās	Bayt Rās		'Ajam
	Umm Qays	Gadara	Jadar	Sawād	Sawād	
	Ābil al-Zayt	Abila	Ābil			
Dimashq	al-Balqā'	Philadelphia	Ẓāhir al-Balqā'	al-Balqā'	al-Ẓāhir	Qays and Quraysh
	'Ammān		'Ammān	'Ammān	'Ammān	
	Jericho				Rīḥa	
	al-Rabba	Areopolis	Ma'āb		Ma'āb	
	Mu'ta				Mu'ta	
	al-Ṣāfī	Zoara			Zughar	mixed
	al-Ṭafīla Area		al-Jibāl		al-Jibāl	Ghassān & Balqayn
	Gharandal	Arindela		al-Sharāt wa	'Arandal	
			al-Sharāt	Jibāluhā	al-Sharāt	
	Udhruḥ				Udhruḥ	Mawālī Banī
						Hāshim
	Ḥumayma				Ḥumayma	'Abbāsids

Table 2. Place-names Cited in the Sources as Belonging to the Balqā'

1. Names in agreement with Table 1

'Ammān	
al-Aghdaf	Ṭabarī 2.1795. Identified by Musil with Wādī Ghadaf, site of Qaṣr Ṭūba.
Ḥisbān	Ibn 'Asākir: 53, Abū al-Fidā': 227.
Mādabā	Mas'ūdī: 221.
Māsū,	Ibn 'Asākir: 53. Modern village of same name.
al-Muwaqqar	Yāqūt: 2.687.
al-Qasṭal	Hamadhānī: 1.117.
Ḥarafa	Yāqūt: 3.383, near Ma'āb. Modern Ḥirfa near to al-Qaṣr.
Zīzā'	Yāqūt: 2.966. Modern al-Jīza.

2. Names in conflict with Table 1

Arbad	Ibn 'Asākir: 201, also described as belonging to the *Sawād al-Urdunn*. Modern Irbid, site of death of Yazīd b. 'Abd al-Malik.
al-Jarba	Yāqūt: 2.46. Near to Udhruḥ.
Ma'āb	Ṭabarī: 1.2108. Modern Rabba. Separate *Kūra* in Ibn Khurdādhbih and al-Ya'qūbī.
Ma'ān	Yāqūt: 4.571.
Bāli'a	Yāqūt: 1.479. Probably Bālū' northwest of Rabba.

3. Unidentified names

Biqinnis	Yāqūt: 1.702.
Dayr al-Khiṣyān	Yāqūt: 2.657.
Dhanaba	Yāqūt: 2.724.
Jādiya	Yāqūt: 2.5.
Mashārif al-Balqā'	Ṭabarī: 1.1794 cites as village, probably in error for area name.
al-Ṣawālīk	Ibn al-Athīr: 6.87.
Tanhaj	Yāqūt: 1.882; Ibn 'Asākir: 30.
Yubna	Yāqūt: 1.99, near Mu'ta.

Table 3. Governors of the Balqā'

1. Abān b. Marwān, dates not known, a brother of the Caliph 'Abd al-Malik (Ibn 'Asākir: 6). Also known as a governor of Filasṭīn under 'Abd al-Malik (Crone 1980, p.124).
2. Muḥammad b. 'Umar al-Thaqafī, under 'Abd al-Malik (65/685–86/705). Qaysī, brother of the more famous Yūsuf b. 'Umar, and a relative of al-Ḥajjāj b. Yūsuf (Khalīfa: 394).
3. Ḥārith b. 'Amr al-Ṭā'ī, under 'Umar b. 'Abd al-'Azīz (99/717–101/720). An Umayyad general, later governor of Armenia for Yazīd b. 'Abd al-Malik (Khalīfa: 465; Balādhurī: 206; Ṭabarī: 2.1526, 1532).
4. Muḥammad b. 'Ubaydallah b. Muḥammad b. Sulaymān b. Muḥammad b. 'Abd al-Muṭṭalib b. Rabī'a b. al-Ḥārith, 158/775 under al-Manṣūr (Ṭabarī: 3.416).
5. Ṣāliḥ b. Sulaymān, 180/796, under Hārūn al-Rashīd. An associate of Ja'far b. Yaḥyā al-Barmakī (Ṭabarī: 3.641).
6. Abū Bakr Muḥammad b. Ṭughj al-Ikhshīd, (*c.* 306/ 918–9 to *c.* 316/928). Later founder of the Ikhshīdid dynasty in Egypt (Ibn Khallikān: 5.57–8).
7. Shabīb b. Jarīr al-'Uqalī, to 348/959, under Kāfūr (al-Ḥamdānī: 176).
8. Badr b. Ḥāzim b. 'Alī, *c.* 460/1068. From Āl Jarrāḥ of Ṭayy (Ibn al-Qalānisī: 94).

Note: Under 135/752–3, Ṭabarī (3.84) records Ṣāliḥ b. 'Alī as governor of Filasṭīn and the Balqā'. In the same list 'Abdullah b. 'Alī is given as governor of northern and central Syria. The governorship of Syria had been simply divided in two. Ṣāliḥ b. 'Alī was not a local governor of the Balqā'.

Table 4. Umayyad Quṣūr in Jordan

Distribution in fig.12. Unless otherwise referenced, bibliographies may be found in Creswell 1969

Type/Name	Environment	Comments
1. *Reoccupied Limes Forts*		
Qaṣr al-Azraq	ground-water oasis	Evidence of Umayyad occupation only.[1]
Qaṣr al-Bā'iq	steppe	Umayyad occupation, not certainly a *qaṣr*.[2]
Qaṣr Burqu'	basalt boulder fields with occasional *qā'*s	Umayyad additions to Roman tower; inscription of al-Walīd b. 'Abd al-Malik.[3]
Qaṣr al-Ḥallabāt	cultivable steppe to north	New construction in fort, stuccoes, mosque, houses, enclosure.[4]
Qaṣr al-Ḥammām, Ma'ān	ground-water oasis	Umayyad occupation, not certainly a *qaṣr*.[5]
al-Ḥumayma	sand desert	No certain archaeological evidence of Umayyad occupation, historical identification of residence of 'Abbāsid family during the Umayyad period.[6]
Dayr al-Kahf	steppe/basalt boulder fields	Umayyad occupation, not certainly a *qaṣr*.[7]
2. *New construction in the form of a fort*		
Bayir	*qā'*, centre of drainage basin	Now disappeared. Dating based on architectural evidence, pottery evidence lacking.
Qaṣr Kharāna	desert pavement, thin desert soils	Ink graffito of 92/710–1; Umayyad occupation.[8]
al-Qasṭal	dry-land cultivation	Mosque and cemetery.[9]
Khān al-Zabīb	desert pavement	Possibly Umayyad construction, Umayyad occupation, mosque.[10]
Developed fort forms		
Qaṣr Mshattā	dry steppe, no cultivation	Unfinished.
Qaṣr Ṭūba	desert pavement	Unfinished.
3. *Hall and Bath Buildings*		
Quṣayr 'Amra	desert pavement, wādi	
Ḥammām al-Sarakh	steppe, cultivation	
4. *Palace forms*		
al-Muwaqqar	steppe, dryland cultivation	Plan recorded by Musil; following subsequent destruction the remains have only been minimally excavated.[11]
5. *Unclassified*		
Umm al-Walīd	steppe, dryland cultivation	Umayyad courtyard building, mosque.[12]
Qaṣr Mshāsh	desert pavement	Complex of small buildings.[13]

1. Parker (1976); Kennedy (1982).
2. Parker (1976).
3. Gaube (1974b).
4. Bisheh (1980), Kennedy (1982).
5. Parker (1976).
6. Graf (1979); al-Ya'qūbī: 326.
7. Parker (1976).
8. Jaussen and Savignac (1922); Abbott (1946); Gaube (1977); Urice (1987).
9. Carlier (1989); Carlier and Morin (1987).
10. Parker (1976).
11. Najjar (1989).
12. Bujard et al. (1988).
13. Bisheh (1989); Kennedy (1982).

Table 5. Totals of Decorated Panels in the Reception Hall

	Theoreticals Niche	Panels	Decipherable Panels	Percentage
Register 1	106	318	127	39.9%
Register 2	8	24	19	79.2%
Register 3 (from photographs)	24	72	16	22%
Fallen Standard Blocks			43	
Total	138	414	205	49.52%

Table 6. Period 2 Wall Sectors: Comparative Widths, Facade Masonry

Note: Sector 13 is not included. Dimensions in metres

Sector	Width	Facade Masonry Dimensions Base course (B); External face (E); Internal face (I)	Packing Material
8	?	0.70 × 0.35 × ? (E)	?
11	3.20	0.60 × 0.30+ × 1.20 (B)	brown clay
12	3.20	1.20 × 0.60 × 0.30 (B) 0.70 × 0.35 × 0.40 (E) 0.60 × 0.40 × 0.30 (I)	brown clay
14	3.40	0.60 × 0.60 × 1.20 (B) 0.34 × 0.34 × 0.70 (E)	brown clay
19	3.25	0.70 × 0.37 × 0.40 (E)	?
20	?	0.70 × 0.37 × 0.40 (E)	?
22	3.20	0.70 × 0.37 × 0.40 (E) 0.55 × 0.33 × 0.40 (I)	brown earth
25	0.90	1.05 × ? × 0.35 (E) 1.30 × ? × 0.35 (I)	none
26	3.20	1 × 0.40 × 0.55 (E) 0.50 × 0.35 × 0.55 (I)	brown earth

Table 7. Period 3 Wall Sectors: Comparative Widths, Buttress Dimensions and Packing

Note: Sectors 21 and 24 are not included. Dimensions in metres

Sector	Width	Buttress Dimensions	Packing	Roman	Umayyad
6	?	1. 2.50 × 1	?	—	?
8	4	1. 6.25 × 0.60–0.90 2. 6.10 × 0.80 3. 2.65+ × 1.20 4. 5.80 × 0.65–0.70 5. 5.90 × 0.60–0.70	*terra rossa*	rebuilt/refaced	broad
9	2.60	1. ? 2. 6.10 × 0.65–0.70 3. 4.30 × 0.25–0.35 4. 4.50 × 0.20 5. ? × 0.30	*terra rossa*	—	narrow
10	4+	—	*terra rossa*	—	broad
11	2.50	—	*terra rossa*	rebuilt/refaced	narrow
12	3.20	1. 6.15 × 0.35 2. 6 × 0.60 3. 6.10 × 0.60	*terra rossa*	rebuilt/refaced	as Roman
14A	3.40	—	?	rebuilt/refaced	as Roman
14B	?	—	*terra rossa*	—	?
15	*c.*3.55	—	?	—	broad
16	2.57	1. 3.90 × 0.23 2. 3.95 × 0.23 3. 3.80 × 0.20	mortar	—	narrow
17	3	1. 6.24 × 0.55	mortar	—	narrow
18	*c.*4	1. 5.90 × 0.65–1 2. 7 × 0.65–0.70	brown earth	—	broad
19	3.25	1. 6.15 × 0.65–0.70	brown earth	rebuilt/refaced	as Roman
20	?	1. ?	brown earth	rebuilt/refaced	?
22	3.20	1. 4.20 × 0.50–0.70 2. 4.35 × 0.60–0.70 3. 4.90 × 0.60	*terra rossa* & mortar	rebuilt/refaced	as Roman
23	3.80	1. ? × 0.60–0.70	brown earth	—	broad
25	1.20	—	—	rebuilt/refaced	Exception

Table 8. Period 1 and Period 3 Towers: Comparative Dimensions and Projections

All dimensions in metres

Tower	Dimensions	Projection	Location	Date
A	8.25 × 7.90	none	Curtain	Roman & Umayyad
C	8.55 × 8.40	0.70	Curtain to Gate	Roman & Umayyad
D	6.10 × 5.50	1.85	Gate	Umayyad
E	6 × ?5.80	0.70–3.60	Curtain	Umayyad
F	5.80 × ?	1.40	Curtain	Umayyad
G	5.80 × 5.80	5.80	Curtain	Umayyad
H	?	none	Curtain	Umayyad
J	4.85 × ?7.10	?0.60	Gate	Umayyad
K	5.80 × ?	0.95	Gate	Umayyad
L	?	?	Curtain	Umayyad

Table 9. Period 4: Comparative Rebuilt Buttress and Revetment Dimensions and Packing Materials

Note: Sectors 11 and 16 are not included. All dimensions in metres

Sector or Tower	Buttress Dimensions	Revetment Width	Packing Materials
5		0.60	*terra rossa*
8	1. 8.60 × 1.75–2.10	0.60–0.85	*terra rossa*
	2. 8.35 × 1.80–1.90		
9	1. 7.50 × 1.80–1.90	0.70–0.95	*terra rossa*
12	1. 6.85+ × 2.65	?	*terra rossa*
13		1.30–1.50	?
14		2–2.40	brown earth
L		1.70	?
20		0.65–1	?
22		1.70	mortar
23		0.80	?

Table 10. Comparative Sizes of Umayyad Sites in Ascending Order

Figures in hectares

Site	Total Area	Built-up Area	Palace Area	Percentage of Palace to Built-up Area
ʿAqaba	2.05			
Qaṣr al-Ḥayr	3.0	2.3	0.43	18.5%
Qalʿat ʿAmmān	9.3		1.56	16.7%
ʿAnjar	11.47		0.4	3.5%

APPENDIX A

Catalogue of Niches and Fragments from the Umayyad Palace

Key

No. Niche or fragment number

Panel Panel types: Aa, Ab, B, D, E, F
The placement of these panels is given on fig.45 for Register 1, and fig.50 for Register 2. The placement for Register 3 is the same as for Register 1.

Ill. no. All surviving niches of Registers 1 and 2 are illustrated on plates 21–27 in order. 'Cf.' indicates a comparison with another panel with identical motif.

1. THE RECEPTION HALL

Register 1 (Plates 21–26 illustrate the surviving niches in order).

No.	Panel	Ill. No.	Description
1.	Aa, b		–
	B	fig.49.1	Worn. Central stem with two branches possibly with acorns, above two upward-pointing half-palmettes. Ground of three semi-circles. Bottom third of panel only.
2.	Aa, b		Worn.
	B		–
3.	–		–
4.	–		–
5.	–		–
6.	Aa		Rather worn. Probably a bead border with half-palmette scroll.
	Ab, B		–
7.	Aa	fig.47.11	Rectangular frieze of round-topped stylized leaf form, border of hearts.
	Ab	pl.16, cf. fig.48.1	Quatrefoils and pierced beads. Destroyed: recorded from Brunnow and Domaszewski (1905), abb.838.
	B		–
8.	Aa	pl.16, cf. fig.48.2	field of 'braid border'. Worn: recorded from Brunnow and Domaszewski (1905), abb.838.
	Ab, B		–
9.	Aa	pl.16, cf. fig.47.14	Trefoils radiating from the arch in a curved band. Worn: recorded from Brunnow and Domaszewski (1905), abb.838.
	Ab, B		–
10.	–		–
11.	–		–
12.	Aa	cf. fig.47.3	Opposed half-palmettes with bead border, worn.
	Ab	cf.fig. 48.13	'Split-palmette' head.
	B		–
13.	Aa	fig.47.13	Opposed half-palmettes with bead border.
	Ab		Worn palmette in single circle.
	B		–

No.	Panel	Ill. No.	Description
14.	–		–
15.	–		–
16.	–		–
17.	–		–
18.	–		–
19.	–		–
20.	Aa	cf. fig.48.2	field of 'braid border': right half broken off.
	Ab	cf. fig.48.9	Ten-lobed rosette with round lobes.
	B		–
21.	Aa	cf. fig.47.6	Rectangular frieze of half-palmette scroll; border of hearts; two half-palmettes in spandrel spaces.
	Ab, B	fig.49.11	Central field of 12 six-lobed rosettes, flanked by a zigzag pattern, whose spaces are filled by heart-shaped florets.
22.	Aa	fig.47.4	Three 'split-palmette' heads with lotus bud, placed horizontally; trefoil fillers in the spandrels.
	Ab, B	fig.48.7	Diamond grid with trefoil fillers.
23.	Aa		–
	Ab, B	fig.49.9	field of 'braid border'.
24.	Aa	fig.47.10	Curved band of spike leaves; upper corners indecipherable.
	Ab, B		–
25.	Aa	cf. fig.47.2	Four half-palmettes.
	Ab	fig.48.13	Split-palmette head with 'oak' foliage.
	B		Repeats Ab three times.
26.	Aa		Worn. Two rosettes in the spandrel panels.
	Ab, B	cf. fig.48.11	five 12-lobed rosettes in double circles: spike-lobed with protruding bosses.
27.	Aa		–
	Ab	cf. fig.48.16	Split-palmette head, worn.
	B	cf. fig.48.14	Central stem with six half-palmettes pointing upwards.
28.	Aa		–
	Ab	cf. fig.48.9	Ten-lobed rosette, no circle
	B		–
29.	Aa	cf. fig.48.2	field of 'braid border'.
	Ab	cf. fig.48.16	Split-palmette head.
	B		–
30.	Aa	cf. fig.48.2	field of 'braid border'.
	Ab	fig.49.5	Vine stem with two bunches of grapes.
	B		–
31.	–		–
32.	Aa		–
	Ab, B	fig.49.3	Ground of three semi-circles; curving stem with 'oak' foliage.
33.	–		–
34.	Aa, b		–
	B	cf. fig.49.2	Ground of three semi-circles; half-palmette scroll; only the bottom third survives.
35.	–		–
36.	Aa	fig.48.1	field of quatrefoils and pierced beads.
	Ab		Motif uncertain.
	B		–
37.	Aa	cf. fig.48.5	Two spike-lobed rosettes with trefoils placed diagonally. Similar to 48Aa: destroyed, recorded from Strzygowski (1930), ill.381.
	Ab	cf. fig.48.13	Split-palmette head.
	B		–
38.	–		–
39.	–		–
40.	Aa		–
	Ab		Similar to a split-palmette head, difficult to decipher.
	B	fig.49.4	Central vertical stem with alternating 'oak' leaves and 'acorns'.
41.	Aa		Motif uncertain.
	Ab, B		Cut away for door to Room NE.
42.	–		–

No.	Panel	Ill. No.	Description
43.	–		–
44.	–		–
45.	–		–
46.	–		–
47.	–		–
48.	Aa	fig.48.5	Two rosettes with four spike petals in the corners; four trefoils in the centre pointing at a larger fifth placed vertically.
	Ab	fig.48.8	field of quatrefoils and pierced beads, compressed into horizontal ovals.
49.	–		–
50.	Aa	fig.48.3	Ten-lobed rosette with rounded lobes in a single circle, placed centrally, flanked on the right by a flower of three half-palmettes; left half broken.
	Ab, B		–
51.	–		–
52.	Aa	fig.48.4	Two ten-lobed rosettes with rounded lobes in the corners; a flower of four half-palmettes in the centre.
	Ab	cf. fig.48.16	Split-palmette head.
	B	fig.48.14	Ground of three semi-circles; central stem with probably six half-palmettes pointing upwards: top half not clear.
53.	Aa	cf. fig.47.14	Trefoils radiating from the arch? – badly worn.
	Ab, B		–
54.	Aa		–
	Ab, B	fig.49.12	Three elongated rosettes of four spike lobes without circles; ground of three semi-circles.
55.	Aa	cf. fig.47.10	Curved band of spike leaves, half-palmette in left corner: worn.
	Ab	fig.48.9	13-lobed rosette with round lobes in double circle.
	B		–
56.	Aa	cf. fig.47.1	Opposed half-palmettes.
	Ab		Half-palmette scroll
	B		Replaced by modern panel.
57.	Aa		–
	Ab	cf. fig.48.9	12-lobed rosette in double circle.
	B		Replaced by modern panel.
58.	Aa		–
	Ab, B	cf. fig.49.2	Half-palmette scroll; ground of three semi-circles.
59.	Aa, b		–
	B	fig.49.16	3½ pointed oval frames, forming a scroll, containing: (1) palmette, cf. WS/D/7. (2) flower of four half-palmettes. (3) bracken-tip spiral. (4) ? Ground of three semi-circles, fillers of half-palmettes.
60.	Aa		–
	Ab, B	cf. fig.49.9	'Braid border' field.
61.	Aa, b		–
	B	cf. fig.49.10	Four 13-lobed rosettes with rounded lobes, ground of three semi-circles, fillers of half-palmettes.
62.	–		–
63.	–		–
64.	Aa	cf. fig.47.1	Opposed half-palmettes, badly worn.
	Ab, B		–
65.	Aa	cf. fig.47.1	Opposed half-palmettes, badly worn.
	Ab, B	fig.48.17	five half-palmettes, vertical stem on right.
66.	Aa	fig.48.2	'Braid border' field.
	Ab	cf. fig.48.11	Spike-lobed palmette in double circle.
	B	pl.17b	Two roundels visible. (1) Motif uncertain (2) Spike-lobed rosette. Source: PEF neg. no.OC393.
67.	–		–

No.	Panel	Ill. No.	Description
68.	Aa	fig.47.14	Band of trefoils radiating from arch.
	Ab	cf. fig.48.16	Split-palmette head.
	B		–
69.	Aa	cf. fig.47.1	Opposed half-palmettes.
	Ab		Motif uncertain.
	B		–
70.	Aa	cf. fig.47.1	Opposed half-palmettes? Badly worn.
	Ab	cf. fig.48.12	Diamond frame interlaced with adjacent frame, filler indecipherable: worn.
	B		–
71.	–		–
72.	Aa		–
	Ab	cf. fig.48.9	Ten-lobed rosette with rounded lobes in single circle.
	B		–
73.	Aa		–
	Ab, B	fig.49.15	One round and three oval frames containing palmettes, ground of three semi-circles.
74.	Aa	cf. fig.47.14	Band of trefoils radiating from arch.
	Ab	cf. fig.48.12	Diamond frame, filler indecipherable.
	B		–
75.	Aa	fig.47.6	Rectangular frieze of half-palmette scroll, border of hearts, half-palmettes in spandrels.
	Ab, B	cf. fig.49.3	Curving stem with 'oak' foliage.
76.	Aa	cf. fig.47.1	Opposed half-palmettes.
	Ab, B		Cut away for light-shaft to staircase.
77.	Aa	fig.47.12	Curved band of rounded foliage, two half-palmettes in upper corners, one trefoil: partly defaced.
	Ab	fig.48.6	flower of eight half-palmettes.
	B		–
78.	Aa	cf. fig.47.9	Two stems with 'oak' leaf foliage.
	Ab		Motif uncertain.
	B		–
79.	Aa	cf. fig.47.1	Opposed half-palmettes.
	Ab, B	fig.49.7	field of trefoils in rectangular frames.
80.	Aa		One half-palmette decipherable, badly worn.
	Ab	fig.49.6	Split-palmette head.
	B	fig.49.6	Central vertical stem, with a vine spiralling around it, ground of three semi-circles.
81.	Aa		–
	Ab, B	cf. fig.49.9	field of 'braid border'.
82.	Aa		–
	Ab		Pair of drooping half-palmettes.
	B		–
83.	Aa		–
	Ab, B	fig.49.15	One round, three oval frames containing palmettes.
84.	Aa		Curved band of thistles and lotus buds: only small section preserved.
	Ab, B	fig.49.2	Half-palmette scroll; the lobes have doubled tips.
85.	Aa		Possibly a field of diamonds, each with a filler of a pierced bead, worn.
	Ab, B	cf. fig.48.1	field of quatrefoils and pierced beads.
86.	Aa	fig.47.2	Four opposed half-palmettes with central tear-drop.
	Ab, B	fig.49.10	Five rosettes in double circles, fillers of half-palmettes, ground of three semi-circles.
87.	Aa	fig.47.15	Frieze of four rectangular frames with trefoil fillers pointing diagonally to upper right; four trefoils in the spandrels.
	Ab, B	fig.49.8	Panel divided vertically: to left a column of quatrefoils and pierced beads; to right a vertical row of trefoils.
88.	–		–
89.	–		–
90.	Aa	fig.47.13	Curved band of thistles and hearts, trefoils in the upper corners.
	Ab	fig.48.12	Diamond-shaped frame, interlaced with adjacent frame, filler of small half-palmettes.
	B		–
91.	Aa	fig.47.1	Pair of opposed half-palmettes with central tear-drop.
	Ab	fig.48.16	Split-palmette head.

No.	Panel	Ill. No.	Description
91.	B	fig.48.16	Central stem with pairs of half-palmettes: the top pair droop and the second pair appear to be upward-pointing.
92.	Aa	cf. fig.47.15	Frieze of four rectangular frames with trefoil fillers pointing diagonally to upper right; three trefoils visible in the spandrels.
	Ab	cf. fig.49.5	Vine stem with two bunches of grapes.
	B		–
93.	Aa	fig.47.9	Two stems with 'oak'-leaf foliage.
	Ab	cf. fig.49.3	Stem with 'oak'-leaf foliage.
	B		–
94.	Aa	cf. fig.48.2	Field of 'braid border'.
	Ab	fig.48.10	Rosette with four spike petals and no circle.
	B		–
95.	Aa	fig.47.7	Band of half-palmettes radiating from the arch, second register in upper-right corner: square hole on upper left, broken on lower right.
	Ab	fig.48.11	Spike-lobed rosette in double circle, small half-palmette filler: bottom left broken.
	B		–
96 .	Aa	cf. fig.48.2	Field of 'braid border' pattern.
	Ab, B		–
97.	Aa	fig.47.5	Half-palmette scroll.
	Ab, B		–
98.	Aa	fig.47.8	Vine scroll with bunches of grapes.
	Ab, B		–
99.	Aa		–
	Ab	cf. fig.48.10	Rosette with spike petals and no circle.
	B		–
100.	Aa	cf. fig.48.2	Field of 'braid border' pattern.
	Ab, B		–
101.	Aa	cf. fig.48.2	Field of 'braid border' pattern.
	Ab		Trace of outline on right side.
	B		–
102.	Aa, b		–
	B		Double column of trefoils placed vertically without frames; ground of three semi-circles. Only bottom third survives.
103.	–		–
104.	–		–
105.	–		–
106.	–		–

Register 2

The niches are illustrated in order on plate 27.

No.	Panel	Ill. No.	Description
SE	D	cf. fig.49.7	Overall field of trefoils in square frames.
	E	fig.53.3	Square frames containing trefoils, apparently alternately pointing upper and lower left.
	F		–
ES	D	cf. fig.48.1	field of quatrefoils and pierced beads: uneven drawing of the circles, with some flattened into ovals.
	E	fig.53.6	Oval frames, linked at a boss: each frame contains a reversed palm bud.
	F		–
EN	D		Rectangular frame; contents indecipherable, but includes a round-lobed rosette above a pair of half-palmettes at the top of the panel.
	E	cf. fig.53.2	Half-palmette scroll.
	F		–
NE	D	fig.51.2	Four medallions in the form of a cross with rounded lobes on their tips, arranged in a vertical column: (1) Part of a tree with 'oak'-leaf foliage visible.

No.	Panel	Ill. No.	Description
NE	D		(2) Composite tree: root in the form of a reversed triangle, two drooping half-palmettes, and 'oak'-leaf foliage. (3) Worn, but similar to (2). (4) Tree with root of a reversed triangle and 'oak'-leaf foliage. fillers of trefoils and half-palmettes. Partly recovered from Dieulafoy (1884–9), vol. 2, fig.92.
	E	cf. fig.53.4	Quatrefoils and pierced beads.
	F	pl.17b	Rectangular frieze of five rosettes in circles, possibly spike-lobed. Source: PEF neg. no.556.
NW	D	fig.51.1	Five roundels, arranged vertically, very worn: (1) Part of a scroll. (2) Bead border. (3) Bead border, part of a scroll. (4) Bead border, central circle, spike lobes of a rosette. (5) – Fillers of half-palmettes.
	E	fig.53.4	Quatrefoils and pierced beads.
	F	cf. fig.53.7	Rectangular frieze of spike-lobed rosettes; bead border on arch; spandrel ornament indecipherable. Two beam holes cut into panel.
WN	D	fig.52.2	Roundel Tree: central stem with split-palmette head, and 16 roundels in double-circles: (1) Palmette with three pointed and four rounded lobes. (2) Bracken-tip spiral. (3) – (4) Palmette with pointed and rounded lobes. (5) – (6) Rosette with rounded lobes. (7) Split-palmette flower. (8) Palmette split with an 'oak' leaf or lotus bud. (9) Rosette with rounded lobes. (10) – (11) – (12) Spray of three 'oak', leaves, one only visible. (13) 12-lobed rosette of rounded lobes. (14) Part of a palmette. (15) – (16) Palmette split with an 'oak' leaf or lotus bud.
	E	cf. fig.53.2	Half-palmette scroll.
	F	fig.53.7	Frieze of five 12-lobed rosettes (round lobes), divided by trefoils, and with fillers of small half-palmettes; bead border on arch.
WS	D	fig.52.1	Roundel Tree: central stem with split palmette head, and 14 roundels linked to stem, divided by trefoils: (1) Bracken-tip spiral. (2) Split-palmette flower. (3) Palmette with three pointed and six rounded lobes. (4) Bracken-tip spiral. (5) Rosette of rounded lobes. (6) Split-palmette flower. (7) Palmette split with an 'oak' leaf, or lotus bud. (8) Palmette with three pointed and eight rounded lobes. (9) Rosette of 12 rounded lobes. (10) Palmette split with an 'oak'-leaf or lotus bud. (11) Spray of three 'oak' leaves. (12) Rosette of 12 rounded lobes with double tips. (13) Palmette with three pointed and six rounded lobes. (14) Split-palmette flower.
	E	fig.53.5	Braid border.
	F	pl.20a	Rectangular frieze of foliage and four-petal flowers; two flowers of four half-palmettes in the spandrel spaces. Beam hole cut into the panel.

No.	Panel	Ill. No.	Description
SW	D	fig.53.1, pl.16	Composite tree with central stem, alternating branches with 'oak'-leaves and acorns, with branches with vine leaves and bunches of grapes. Two beam holes. Top of panel destroyed, possibly by bombing in 1918 (Clemen 1919, vol.2, p.178). Source: Brunnow
SW	D		and Domaszewski (1905), abb.838.
	E	fig.53.2	Half-palmette scroll.
	F	fig.53.8, pl.16	Rectangular frieze of stylized round-tipped foliage; two flowers of four half-palmettes in the spandrel spaces. Now destroyed.

Register 3

Note: The niches are numbered from the centre of the south *īwān* in an anti-clockwise direction. No niches now *in situ*. The following are recorded from photographs. Some of the panels were never carved (cf. block SN/20). As far as is known, all Aa panels consist of a half-palmette in each spandrel panel.

No.	Panel	Ill. No.	Description
1.	–		–
2.	Ab	pl.16	Palmette or rosette in circle. Source: Brunnow and Domaszewski (1905), abb.838.
3.	–		–
4.	–		–
5.	–		–
6.	B		Four roundels; only traces of three double circles visible. Source: PEF neg. no.OC381.
7.	–		–
8.	Ab, B	cf. fig.48.8	field of quatrefoils and pierced beads.
9.	–		–
10.	–		–
11.	–		–
12.	–		–
13.	Ab,B		Possibly four rosettes.
14.	Ab,B	pl.17b	Four spike-lobed rosettes in circles. Source: PEF neg. no.OC393.
15.	–		–
16.	–		–
17.	–		–
18.	–		–
19.	Ab,B	pl.20a	Three round-headed niches with bead borders to the arch. (1) One visible 'oak' leaf. (2) ? (3) one visible trefoil. Source: PEF neg. no.OC320.
20.	Ab,B	cf. fig.49.10	five round-lobed rosettes in double-circles.
21.	–		–
22.	Ab	cf. fig.48.16	Split-palmette head
	B	cf. fig.48.15	Half-palmette tree, with central stem.
23.	–		–
24.	Ab,B	pl.16, cf. fig.49.9	field of braid border.

Fallen Standard Niche Fragments

The fragments unreferenced by illustration in this volume or elsewhere are fragments found on site which were apparently excavated in 1977–8 by the Spanish Archaeological Mission, and not published. They are referred to here simply for the sake of completeness.

No.	Panel	Ill. No.	Description
SN/1			Right half of Register 3 niche head.
	Aa		Damaged single half-palmette with five lobes.
	Ab		Half-palmette tree with vertical stem, and two half-palmettes drooping.
SN/2			Upper-left quarter of Register 3 niche head.

No.	Panel	Ill. No.	Description
SN/2	Aa		Single half-palmette with six lobes.
	Ab	cf. fig.48.16	Two half-palmettes from split-palmette head.
SN/3			Left half of Register 3 niche head.
	Aa		Single half-palmette.
	Ab		Half-palmette tree with vertical stem, and two half-palmettes drooping.
SN/4		pl.28a	Fragment from the left side of Register 3 niche head.
	Ab	cf. fig.48.7	Diamond grid with trefoil fillers. Source: Bartoccini (1933), p.14, no.e.
SN/5			Register 3 niche head.
	Aa		Two half-palmettes in the spandrel spaces.
	Ab	cf. fig.48.6	Flower of eight half-palmettes. Source: Bartoccini (1933), p.14, no.f.
SN/6		pl.28b	Register 3 niche head. The block was found whole in the Italian excavations, but only left half survives.
	Aa		Two half-palmettes in the spandrel spaces.
	Ab	cf. fig.48.8	Quatrefoils and pierced beads. The quatrefoils are elongated into ovals. Source: Bartoccini (1933), p.14, no.g.
SN/7		pl.28d	Register 3 niche head, broken on left side.
	Aa		Half-palmette in the right spandrel space.
	Ab	cf. fig.49.3	Curving stem with 'oak'-leaf foliage. Source: Bartoccini (1933), p.14, no.h.
SN/8			Fragment of Register 3 niche head.
	Aa		–
	Ab		Part of half-palmette from split-palmette head.
SN/9			Right half of Register 3 niche head.
	Aa		Part of half-palmette.
	Ab	cf. fig.48.16	Split palmette head.
SN/10			Left half of Register 3 niche head.
	Aa		–
	Ab		Interlaced six-pointed star, with bead borders, and fillers of half-palmettes.
SN/11			Right half of Register 3 niche head.
	Aa		–
	Ab		Single half-palmette from split-palmette head.
SN/12			Right half of register 3 niche head.
	Aa		Single half-palmette.
	Ab		One and a half round-lobed rosettes with bead borders.
SN/13			Fragment of Register 3 niche head.
	Ab		Round-lobed rosette with bead border.
SN/14			Fragment of Register 3 niche head. No decoration visible.
SN/15			Fragment of Register 3 niche head.
	Ab		Part of half-palmette.
SN/16			Fragment of Register 3 niche head.
	Ab	cf. fig.48.16	Part of split-palmette head.
SN/17			Left half of niche head.
	Ab	cf. fig.49.14	Part of interlaced diamond frame with half round-lobed rosette.
SN/18			Left half of niche head.
	Ab	cf. fig.48.16	Part of split-palmette head.
SN/19			Fragment from the left side of niche head.
	Ab	cf. fig.48.7	Diamond grid with trefoil fillers.
SN/20		pl.28c	Left half of niche head. Aa and Ab panels left uncarved.
SN/21			Register 3 niche head, broken on lower left side.
	Aa		Two half-palmettes in the spandrel spaces.
	Ab	cf. fig.49.3	'Oak'-leaf foliage.
SN/22	B	fig.48.15	Central stem with two pairs of half-palmettes drooping; ground of three semi-circles. Lower two-thirds of panel. Source: Bartoccini (1933), p.14, no.k.
SN/23	B	fig.49.14	Two fragments of panel. Interlaced diamond frames with bead borders. fillers of six-lobed rosettes with rounded lobes, and heart-shaped florets. Source: Bartoccini (1933), p.14 , no.l.
SN/24	B	fig.49.13, pl.28e	Top third of panel with rosette of 6 spike petals and 12 rounded lobes in a double circle; divider of a heart-shaped floret. Source: Bartoccini (1933), p.14, no.m.
SN/25	B	cf. fig.53.6	Top half of panel with one and a half oval frames, containing palm buds, and linked by bosses. Three half-palmettes act as fillers. Source: Bartoccini (1933), p.14, no.n.

No.	Panel	Ill. No.	Description
SN/26	B	fig.49.5	Bottom third of panel. Curving stem with a single vine-leaf and four bunches of grapes; ground of three semi-circles. Bartoccini (1933), p.14, no.p.
SN/27	B	cf. fig.49.7	Two fragments with a field of trefoils placed vertically in rectangular frames; ground of three semi-circles. Source: Bartoccini (1933), p.14, no.q.
SN/29	B		Part of B panel. field of 'braid border' pattern.
SN/30	B		Part of B panel. One and a half roundels containing palmettes.
SN/31	B		Part of B panel. field of quatrefoils and pierced beads.
SN/32	B		Part of B panel. Half of one round-lobed rosette with double outline; part of spike-lobed rosette with outline of bead border. filler of small half-palmette.
SN/33	B	cf. fig.48.6	Part of B panel. flower of eight half-palmettes.
SN/34	B		Part of B panel. field of diamonds and trefoils elongated in the horizontal direction.
SN/35	B		Part of B panel. Round-lobed rosette with double outline.
SN/36	B		Part of B panel. Roundel with multiple line x-shaped design.
SN/37	B		Worn roundel with bead border and possibly a round-lobed rosette.

Single Block Niches

No.	Panel	Ill. No.	Description
SB/1		fig.54.4, pl.28f	Lower half of a niche carved from a single block, with two colonnettes flanking a flat back panel. The panel has a composite tree with a zigzag stem with alternating half-palmettes, 'oak'-leaves, and a pomegranate; ground of three semi-circles. h. 62.5cm, w. 44.7cm. Source: Bartoccini (1933), p.14, no.i.
SB/2			Upper half of a niche carved from a single block, with two colonnettes flanking a flat back panel. The panel back has a roundel of four concentric circles. cch.74.5cm, w.62.7cm.
SB/3			Upper half of a niche carved from a single block, with two colonnettes flanking a flat back panel. The panel back has a single vertical trefoil. h.55.7cm, w.50cm.

Cornices

No.	Panel	Ill. No.	Description
C/1		fig.54.1, pl.29a	Row of denticulated moulding above a frieze of split-palmettes with lotus buds; below, a bead-and-reel moulding and dentils. Interior corner. h.38cm, protrusion 15cm. Source: Almagro (1983a), fig.18b.
C/2		fig.54.2, pl.29b	Split-palmette with lotus bud.
C/3			Split-palmette with lotus bud.
C/4		fig.54.3, pl.29c	Two registers of unlinked half-palmettes above a bead-and-reel moulding and dentils.
C/5		cf. fig.54.3, pl.29d	Two registers of unlinked half-palmettes above a bead-and-reel moulding and dentils. Corner of moulding in vertical direction.
C/6		cf. fig.54.3	Two registers of unlinked half-palmettes above a bead-and-reel moulding and dentils. Source: Bartoccini (1933), p.14, no.a. Now lost.
C/7		cf. fig.54.3	Two registers of unlinked half-palmettes above a bead-and-reel moulding and dentils.
C/8		cf. fig.54.3	Two registers of unlinked half-palmettes above a bead-and-reel moulding and dentils. h.38cm, protrusion 27cm. Source: Almagro (1983a), fig.18a.
C/9		cf. fig.54.3	Two registers of unlinked half-palmettes above a bead-and-reel moulding and dentils.
C/10		cf. fig.54.3	Two registers of unlinked half-palmettes above a bead-and-reel moulding and dentils.
C/11		cf. fig.54.3	Two registers of unlinked half-palmettes above a bead-and-reel moulding and dentils.

Brackets

No.	Panel	Ill. No.	Description
B/1			Bracket decorated with three volutes. Broken on right side. w.28cm.
B/2			Bracket decorated with three volutes. w.55cm.
B/3			Bracket decorated with three volutes, broken on left side. w.43cm.
B/4			Part of bracket decorated with three volutes. w.57cm.
B/5			Fragment of bracket decorated with three volutes. w.46cm.
B/6			Bracket decorated with three volutes, and denticulated moulding. w.32cm.
B/7		fig.54.5, pl.29f	Bracket decorated with three volutes, and denticulated moulding. w.54cm, h.34cm, protrusion 40cm. Source: Almagro (1983a), fig.19a.
B/8			Exterior corner block with two brackets, each originally with three volutes. Sources: Bartoccini (1933), p.14 no.c; Almagro (1983a), fig.19b.

Other fragments

No.	Panel	Ill. No.	Description
F/1		fig.56, pl.29e	Fragment of half merlon with two steps, carved with half-palmette scroll on both sides. h.57.6cm, w.27.2cm, t.30.4cm. Source: Almagro (1983a), fig.20, lam 29.c.
F/2			Fragment of roundel with bead-and-reel moulding and two trefoils. h.26.8cm, w.57.3cm.
F/3			Fragment with palm-trunk border moulding and curved interior.

2. ARCHITECTURAL FRAGMENTS FROM THE NORTH BUILDING (fig.66, pls 35–6)

From inside the īwān

No.	Panel	Ill. No.	Description
NB/1		fig.66.1, pl.35a	A rectangular block with a central slot. h.136cm, w.73cm.
NB/2		fig.66.2, pl.35b	A block with an engaged colonnette with a ball-shaped base on the left side, and a central curved panel; cut-out on the rear. h.136cm, w.61cm.

Excavated by the Spanish Archaeological Mission, probably from inside the īwān

No.	Panel	Ill. No.	Description
NB/3		pl.35c	Part of niche head block with arch and slot in underside of arch, dentils around the arch. In the spandrel panel, a central miniature niche, flanked by two round-lobed rosettes. Rounded moulding on the top and left sides. h.45cm, w.56cm.
NB/4		pl.35d	Niche head block broken in two, with round arch, slot in underside of arch, and denticulated moulding around the arch. In the spandrel panel, two round-lobed rosettes, above two half-palmettes. Rounded moulding on the top. The back panel of the arch is badly eroded; according to Almagro (1983a, fig.45) there is a pattern of half-palmettes. h.48cm, w.66cm.
NB/5			Block with half-round moulding similar to NB/3, including right-angled corner. h.30cm, length 80cm.

From Court 2

No.	Panel	Ill. No.	Description
NB/6–12		fig.66.3, pl.35e	Rectangular block with curved panels on the flanks, possibly intended to represent engaged colonnettes. In the centre a vertical slot slightly recessed in a rectangular frame. h.116cm, w.74cm. Six examples.
NB/13–15		fig.66.4, pl.35f	Rectangular block with a pair of engaged plain colonnettes on the face, and on both sides a second pair divided by a slot. h.116cm, w.65cm. Three examples.
NB/16–18			Rectangular block with two engaged plain colonnettes divided by a slot. h.120cm, w.38cm. Three examples.

Excavated by the Spanish Archaeological Mission, probably from Court 2

No.	Panel	Ill. No.	Description
NB/19		pl.36a	Right side of niche head block, with horseshoe arch, double line of denticulation around the arch, and slot in underside of arch. In the spandrel panel, a vine stem with two bunches of grapes.
NB/20		pl.36b	Block with roundel composed of a central round-lobed rosette, and a concentric outer ring of spike lobes.
NB/21		pl.36c	Fragment from right side of merlon with steeply sloping step, identical to type from Reception Hall. Decorated with one half-palmette.

APPENDIX B

Fortification Wall: Catalogue of Reused Architectural Fragments

Key

No.	Sector No., Tower (T) or Gate (G) / Fragment No.
Location	Specific location
Position	Position
Description	Description and dimensions
	HGLS = hard grey limestone
	SGLS = soft grey limestone
	HPLS = hard pink limestone
	SPLS = soft pink limestone

Dimensions in metres (length × height × depth / diameter × height)

No.	Location	Position	Ill. No.	Description
8.1	8a	fallen		HGLS moulded base block. 0.95 × 0.45 × 0.60.
8.2	8a	fallen		HGLS very simple moulded block. 0.78 × 0.30 × 0.70.
8.3	8e	core		HGLS moulded block. 0.31 × 0.20 × ?
8.4	Butt.5	fallen		SGLS simple architrave. 0.74 × 0.39 × 0.20–0.28.
8.5	8f	core		SGLS smooth, cylindrical column shaft. 0.37 diam. × ?
8.6	8f	core		SPLS smooth, three-quarter round engaged column shaft. 0.40 diam. × ?
9.1	Butt.3	face		SGLS smooth, cylindrical column shaft. 0.45 diam. × ?
10.1		face		SGLS block with slight trace of a simple recessed moulding.
10.2		fallen		SGLS architrave with bead-and-reel decoration. 0.90 × 1.07 × 0.65. One cramp hole at top (? × 0.15 × 0.05).
11.1		face		SGLS smooth, cylindrical column shaft. 0.59 diam. × 1+.
11.2		face		SGLS smooth, cylindrical column shaft. 0.59 diam. × 1+.
11.3		face		SGLS smooth, cylindrical column shaft. 0.59 diam. × 1+.
11.4		face		SGLS smooth, cylindrical column shaft. 0.59 diam. × 1+.
11.5		face		SGLS smooth, cylindrical column shaft. 0.52 diam. × 1+
11.6		face		HGLS block with very simple ridged recession 0.02 deep.
11.7		face		HGLS block with very simple ridged recession 0.02 deep.
11.8		core		SGLS block with recessed rectangular panel. 1.05 × 0.61 × 0.35.
11.9		core		SGLS block with rectangular panel in relief. 0.40 × 0.40+ × 0.26.
11.10		fallen	pl.59a	SGLS architrave with bead-and-reel decoration. 0.62 × 0.69 × 0.42+.
12.1	12a	fdns		HGLS block with rectangular panel in shallow relief. 0.30 × 0.39 × ?
12.2	12a	face		HGLS architrave with bead-and-reel decoration. 0.40 × 0.60 × ?
12.3	12a	face		HGLS block with decorative mouldings in shallow relief. 0.26 × 0.48 × 0.30+.
12.4	12a	face	pl.59b	HGLS bottom drum of Corinthian capital. 0.80-1.40 diam. × 0.85.
12.5	Butt.1	core		HGLS column shaft. 0.58 diam. × 1.30+.

No.	Location	Position	Ill. No.	Description
12.6	Butt.1	core	pl.59e	HGLS stylobate. 1.13 × 0.38 × 0.47.
12.7	12b	fdns		HGLS base with smooth, cylindrical colonnette shaft attached. 0.34–0.49 diam. × 0.48.
12.8	12c	fallen	pl.59f	HGLS block with moulded column base attached. 0.97 × 0.53 × 0.25–0.45. Estimated diam. of column base: 1.69.
12.9	12c	fallen		HGLS smooth, cylindrical column drum. Estimated diam.: 1.60+.
12.10	12d	fdns		HGLS smooth, cylindrical column shaft. 0.64 diam. × ?
12.11	12d	face	pl.59g	HGLS architrave with bead-and-reel decoration and traces of a Greek inscription on upper two fasciae. 1.15 × 0.95 × 0.60–0.66.
12.12	12d	face		HGLS smooth, cylindrical column drum. 0.40 diam. x 0.50.
12.13	12d	fallen		HGLS top drum of Corinthian capital. 1.27 diam. x 0.73. Central cramp hole in underside 0.07 diam.
12.14	Butt.3	core		HGLS architrave with bead-and-reel decoration. 1.75 × 1 × 0.54.
12.15	12e	face		HGLS smooth, cylindrical column shaft. 0.64 diam. × ?
12.16	12e	core		HGLS block with recessed rectangular panel. 1.15 × 0.50+ × 0.42.
12.17	12e	fallen	pl.59h	HGLS cornice. 0.60+ × 0.47 × 0.30+.
12.18	12e	fallen		HGLS stylobate or cornice 1 × 0.44 × 0.30.
TB.1	W.elev.	W.face		HGLS architrave with bead-and-reel decoration. 1.22 × 1.07 × ?
TB.2	W.elev.	E.face		HGLS podium base moulding. 0.56 × 0.84 × 0.14–0.40+.
TB.3	S.elev.	S.face		HGLS column shaft. 0.45 diam. × 1.45.
TB.4	S.elev.	S.face		HGLS column shaft. 0.45 diam. × 1.60.
TB.5	S.elev.	S.face		HGLS column shaft. 0.45 diam. × 1.40.
TB.6	S.elev.	S.face		HGLS column shaft. 0.45 diam. × 0.60.
TB.7	S.elev.	S.face	pl.59c	HGLS architrave with bead-and-reel decoration. 1.67 × 0.75 × 0.65.
TB.8	S.elev.	S.face		HGLS smooth, cylindrical column drum. 1.30 diam. × ?
TB.9	S.elev.	S.face		HGLS smooth, cylindrical column drum. 1.40 diam. × ? Central cramp hole 0.20 × 0.05 set in raised circular boss 0.80 diam.
TB.10	S.elev.	N.face		HGLS block 0.65 × 0.42 × 0.60. Hollowed out to form a trough 0.40 × 0.26 × 0.10.
TB.11	E.elev.	W.face		HGLS podium base moulding.0.58 × 1.20 × 0.14–0.40.
TB.12	E.elev.	W.face	pl.59d	HGLS Corinthian capital. 0.46–0.63 diam. × 0.68.
TB.13	N.elev.	S.face		HGLS moulded cornice.1.10 × 0.44 × 0.60.
GC.1	N.elev.	S.face		HGLS entablature. 3.00 × 0.93 × 0.42–0.57.
14.1		fdns		HGLS smooth, cylindrical column drum. 0.45 diam. × 0.45.
GD.1	Tower J	face		HGLS block with trapezium section. 1.20 × 0.50 × 0.55–0.75.
GD.2		fallen		HGLS smooth, cylindrical column shaft. 0.36 diam. × 0.80. Rectangular cramp hole. 0.12 × 0.05 × 0.035 and square cramp hole 0.03 × 0.03 × ?
15.1		fallen	pl.60a	HGLS pilaster base block. 0.63 × 0.56 × 0.40.
16.1		fdns		HGLS smooth, three-quarter round engaged column shaft. 0.65 diam. × ?
16.2		fdns		HGLS block with acanthus leaf decoration on two sides. 0.56 × 0.38 × ?
16.3		face		HGLS ? volute or block with scroll decoration. 0.55 × 0.52 × 0.39.
16.4		fallen	pl.60b	SGLS pilaster capital with acanthus leaf decoration 0.65 × 0.38 × 0.43
17.1-5				HGLS Corinthian raking cornice fragments with cyma recta, fascia, modillion, cyma reversa, dentil, ovolo and astragal mouldings.
17.1		core		Left side of pediment. 0.62 × 0.615 × 0.835.
17.2		core		Left side of pediment with incised gaming board holes (pl.57a). 0.72 × 0.50 × 0.88.
17.3		core		Left side of pediment. 0.85 × 0.40 × 0.80.
17.4		fallen	pl.60c	Right side of pediment. 0.52 × 0.68 × 0.785.
17.5		fallen		Right side of pediment adjoining. 17.4. 0.47 × 0.335 × 0.92.
17.6–13				HGLS Corinthian cornice fragments with cyma recta, fascia, modillion, cyma reversa, dentil, ovolo and astragal mouldings
17.6		core		Corner block. 0.65 × 0.50 × 0.55 Cramp hole in underside 0.03 diam.
17.7		core		0.90 × 0.47 × 0.80.
17.8		core		0.60 × 0.32 × 1.32.
17.9		core		Mouldings slightly larger and angled. 0.50 × 0.27 × 0.72.

No.	Location	Position	Ill. No.	Description
17.10		core		No measurements possible.
17.11		fallen	pl.60d	0.75 × 0.30 × 0.80.
17.12		fallen		0.95 × 0.53 × 0.65.
17.13		fallen		0.65 × 0.30 × 1.30.
17.14–16				HGLS Corinthian architrave fragments with cyma recta and astragal mouldings, bead-and-reel decoration and attached foliated frieze.
17.14		core		0.90 × 0.60 × 0.60 with incised gaming board holes.
17.15		fallen	pl.60e	Corner block with decorated soffit. 1 × 0.60 × 0.44.
17.16		fallen	pl.60f	Corner block with different cyma recta decoration to 17.14 and 17.15 and with plain mouldings to opposite face. Cramp hole at top 0.82 × 0.60 × 0.87.
17.17		fallen		HGLS architrave with plain mouldings as 17.16. 1.17 × 0.57 × 0.45.
17.18		core		HGLS moulded arched cornice block. 0.40 × 0.40 × 1.12.
17.19		core		HGLS block 0.77 × 0.94 × 0.60. With rectangular slot cut into top 0.20 × 0.10.
17.20		core		HPLS column shaft. No measurements possible.
17.21		core		HPLS column shaft. No measurements possible.
17.22		core		HGLS simple moulded block with incised gaming-board holes. 0.70 × 0.15 × 0.90.
17.23		fallen		HGLS block with acanthus leaf decoration. 0.38 × 0.48 × 0.30.
17.24		fallen		HGLS column base and pedestal. 0.45 × 0.44 × 0.45..
18.1	18b	fallen		HGLS stylobate or cornice. 0.37 × 0.34 × 0.60
18.2	18c	face		HPLS smooth, cylindrical column shaft. 0.50 diam. × ?
19.1	Butt. 1	core	pl.60g	HGLS moulded socle. 0.65+ x 0.32 × 0.30–0.60.
20.1		face		HGLS smooth, cylindrical column shaft. 0.60 diam. × 0.70.
25.1–9				HGLS column drums, largest being 1.50 diam. × 2 and one being a top drum 1.20 diam. Greek mason's marks visible on two and cramp holes in some 0.20 × 0.07 × 0.12.
25.1	25a	face		
25.2	25a	face		
25.3	25a	face		
25.4	25a	face		
25.5	25a	face		
25.6	25a	face		
25.7	25a	face		Obscured by Tower G foundations. No measurements possible.
25.8	25a	fallen		
25.9	25a	fallen		
25.10	25a			HGLS architrave with bead-and-reel decoration and Greek inscription on upper two fasciae.
25.11	25a	fallen		HGLS top drum of Corinthian capital. 1.20–1.40 diam. × 0.65.
25.12	25a	fallen	pl.60h	HGLS Corinthian cornice with cyma recta, fascia, modillion and dentil mouldings. 0.72 × 0.57 × 1.26.
25.13	25b	face		HGLS moulded cornice.0.70 × 0.25+ × 0.40+.
25.14	25b	face		HGLS architrave with bead-and-reel decoration. 0.45 × 0.70 × ?
25.15	25b	core		HGLS architrave with bead-and-reel decoration on opposite faces. 0.55 × 0.60 × 0.45.
25.16	25b	core		HGLS block with curved and ridge mouldings. 0.60 × 0.47 × ?
25.17	25b	core		HGLS simple architrave and frieze. 0.21+ × 0.90 × ?
25.18	25b	fallen		HGLS architrave with bead-and-reel decoration. 0.85 × 0.70 × 0.33+.
25.19	25b	fallen		HGLS architrave with bead-and-reel decoration. 0.80 × 0.70 × 0.40.
TG.1	S.elev.	S.face		HGLS rectangular block with roundel decoration. 1.04 × 0.60 × ?

Suggested Provenances

Temple of Hercules

Temple cornice	?25.12
Temple architrave	12.11 (Gatier 1986, 44, insc. D)
	12.14
	TB.1
	TB.7
Temple capitals	12.4
	12.13
	25.11
Temple column drums	12.9
	TB.8
	TB.9
	25.1–9
Temple column base	12.8
Temple podium base moulding	TB.2
	TB.11

Temenos of the Temple of Hercules

Temenos architrave	11.10
	12.2
	25.14
	25.15
	?25.17
	25.18
	25.19
Temenos capital	TB.12

Gate C

Gate stylobate :	12.6
Gate entablature :	GC.1

Unknown building(s) of the Corinthian order (presumably located somewhere in the Lower Citadel area)

Pediment raking cornice	17.1–5
Cornice	17.6–13
	17.18
Architrave and frieze	17.14–17
Pilaster and capital	15.1
	16.4
Column base/pedestal	17.24
Stylobate/cornice	18.1
Socle	19.1

A marble head of Tyche, and a recently discovered reused inscription dedicated to Tyche found in the middle of the Lower Terrace area (Zayadine, Najjar and Greene 1987, p.305), might suggest the presence of a temple or subsidiary shrine of Tyche.

APPENDIX C

The Recording System Used in the Excavations

The recording system used in the rescue excavations of 1975–9 was a modified form of Kenyon's system used at Jericho. The three areas of excavation were lettered B, C, and D.[1]

A grid was not used, rather trenches were placed according to the needs of the excavation. Nevertheless, in Area C two lines of trenches were set out to obtain a section of the west slope of the Upper Terrace. Each trench was numbered with a Roman numeral. The system used major subdivisions of the trench, which were termed 'locus', and were created to recognize divisions of the trench by walls, or field recognition of major new strata. In this report the Roman numerals used for trench numbers are replaced by Arabic numerals, simply for brevity and ease of recognition.

Individual deposits and features were numbered in sequence within the locus, as they were recognized. In addition, walls were named by letters, with a separate letter series for each trench, and there was also a series for archaeological features.

Pottery and other artefacts recovered were assigned to their deposits. In the 1979 season the recording system was modified by the addition of small find numbers issued in the field. After washing, pottery was given a preliminary assessment, and the bodysherds were discarded. The majority of the pottery from the 1975 and 1976 seasons was then taken to Holland to Dr Henk Franken for a technical study, which is to be published in volume II of this publication. The remainder was studied in 'Ammān. Coins were cleaned in the laboratory of the Department of Antiquities.

In the survey and excavations of the fortifications in 1979 and 1981, the trenches were allotted to Area E. Again a grid was not set out, but the trenches were placed according to requirements, as they were widely scattered. In this project the trenches were numbered with Arabic numerals, and the excavation units were given numbers as they were recognized. Locus, wall, and feature numbers were not used. Each bag of pottery was given a number in addition to its assignment to an excavation unit, preceded by the trench number (1979) or the letter 'P' (1981). Small finds were given field numbers according to their basic typology. Pottery was given a preliminary assessment, and then the bodysherds were discarded.

1. Area A was the responsibility of Dr Zayadine.

APPENDIX D

Stratigraphically Significant Coins

The following is a list of coins found in the excavations of the Citadel that offer some help in dating the development. The list is not a catalogue of coins from the excavations. Rather, these are coins that were found in sealed deposits, either the only or the latest coins of a particular deposit, residual coins having been disregarded. They may be regarded as offering *terminus post quem* datings, that is, the deposit could have been laid down at any date after the minting of the coin.

Stratum VII

No.	Reg.no.	Deposit no.	Description of Deposit	Type	References
1.	889	C2.3.27	floor deposit in front of Building (b), Area C	AE. Early Umayyad *fils*, copy of type of Constans II (641–68)	Walker 1956: pl.V Bates 1989

Stratum VI–Levelling Fills

No.	Reg.no.	Deposit no.	Description of Deposit	Type	References
2.	772	C8.1a.9	make-up of Room F, Building B	Umayyad post-reform *fils*	
3.	1065	B26.1.28	Fill under Room A, Building C	Umayyad post-reform *fils*	

Stratum V–Citadel Buildings

No.	Reg.no.	Deposit no.	Description of Deposit	Type	References
4.	520	C6.1.10a	make-up below second floor of Building B, Room A	Umayyad post-reform *fils*, mint possibly Ramla	Walker 1956: no.846
5.	522	C6.1.10	in the second floor of Room A, Building B	Umayyad post-reform *fils*	
6.	736	C8.1a.7	recessed pan in Room F, Building B	Umayyad post-reform *fils*, mint of Damascus	
7.	891	C2.3.7	ash dump in yard of Building A	Umayyad Standing Caliph type of ʻAbd al-Malik, probably mint of ʻAmmān	Walker 1956: no.96 Hadidi 1975: figs 1–2.
8.	890	C2.3.3	occupation deposit in yard of Building A	Umayyad *fils*, no mint or date	

Stratum III

No.	Reg.no.	Deposit no.	Description of Deposit	Type	References
9.	850	C2.2.2	Found with a hoard of silver rings and bells in Building 1	Fāṭimid *dīnār* of al-Ḥākim, dated 407/1016–7	Lane-Poole 1875–90: IV no.73 Bennett 1979a: pl.lxiv
10.	654	C4/5B.9	Last floor of Building 3	Fāṭimid *dirham* of al-Ẓāhir (411/1021–427/1036)	Lane-Poole 1875–90: IX no.123h

Stratum IIB

No.	Reg.no.	Deposit no.	Description of Deposit	Type	References
11.	M4.9	E4.7	in ash patch between first and second floors of Tower B	Ayyūbid bronze of Damascus	S. Shammar pers. comm.
12.	906a	B31.1.22	In make-up of last floor of Room D, Building D	*Fils* of Saladin dated 587/1190–1 or 589/1192–3	Lane-Poole 1897: nos 1334, 1340–1
13.	906b	B31.1.22	As above	Ayyūbid, possibly of Saladin, and Caliph al-Nāṣir li-dīn allah (575/1180-622/1225)	
14.	906c	B31.1.22	As above	Ayyūbid bronze of al-'Ādil, dated 61?/121?, mint of Ḥama?	Lane-Poole 1897: no.1387; Lane-Poole 1875–90: IV no.371 Balog 1980: no.327
15.	906d	B31.1.22	As above	Ayyūbid bronze, of al-'Ādil (592/1196–615/1218)	
16.	906e	B31.1.22	As above	Ayyūbid bronze, possibly of al-Ẓāhir Ghāzī, mint of Aleppo	Balog 1980: nos 670–680
17.	906f	B31.1.22	As above	Ayyūbid bronze, possibly of al-Ẓāhir Ghāzī, mint of Aleppo	Balog 1980: nos 670–680

NOTES

Introduction

1. Northedge (1984).
2. Hübner (1992), *Die Ammoniter. Untersuchungen zur Geschichte, Kultur und Religion eines transjordanischen Volkes im 1. Jahrtausend v.Chr.*
3. The areas discussed below as Areas B and C.
4. The design was produced by Michael Brawne Associates.
5. Zayadine (1977–8).
6. The preliminary reports are to be found in: Bennett, C-M. (1975), 'Excavations at the Citadel, Ammān, 1975', *ADAJ* 20, pp.131–42; Bennett, C-M., and Northedge, A. E. (1977–8), 'Excavations at the Citadel, Ammān, 1976, Second Preliminary Report', *ADAJ* 22, pp.172–9; Bennett, C-M. (1978a), 'Excavations at the Citadel (El-Qal'ah), Ammān, Jordan', *Levant* 10, pp.1–9; Bennett, C-M. (1979a), 'Early Islamic Ammān', *Levant* 11, pp.1–8; Bennett, C-M. (1979b), 'Excavations on the Citadel (al Qal'a), Ammān, 1977', *ADAJ* 23, pp.151–60; Bennett, C-M. (1979c), 'Excavations on the Citadel (al Qal'a), Ammān, 1978', *ADAJ* 23, pp.161–76.
7. Northedge (1977–8, 1979a, 1980).
8. Northedge (1983, 1983–4).
9. Seetzen (1810, 1854).
10. Burckhardt (1822).
11. Buckingham (1821).
12. de Laborde (1837).
13. de Saulcy (1865), pp.240–70.
14. Northey (1872).
15. Conder (1889).
16. Bennett (1978a).
17. Butler (1907–19) pl.1, p.34.
18. de Saulcy (1865), pp.257, 269.
19. See *PEFQS* (1870), pp.284–305. Archives at the Palestine Exploration Fund.
20. MacAdam (1986, pp.234–8, and the references given there). The American Palestine Exploration Society was a short-lived organization, but prints of its photographs were given to the Palestine Exploration Fund and other still-existing archives.
21. Archive at the Palestine Exploration Fund.
22. Gavin (1985). See especially fig.1, p.280.
23. The photograph catalogues of both expeditions were published only recently. For the views of 'Ammān and Ammānitis see MacAdam (1986, p.283 nos 27–39; pp.343–5 nos 701a, 732–7). The archives are to be found at the Department of Art and Archaeology, Princeton University.
24. Kennedy (1982a, p.29) noted 'two aerial mosaics covering Ammān and Salt' which date to the First World War.
25. Copy negative in the Royal Geographical Society, 'Ammān.
26. A number of the photographs survive in the archives of Aerofilms Ltd.
27. Almagro (1980). Other sites included Irbid, Kerak, Petra, 'Aqaba, the Desert Castles and the Mafraq district. An undated aerial photo of 'Ammān (from the Israel Department of Antiquities collection) has been published recently by Segal (1988, fig.6).
28. Zayadine (1977–8).
29. Bartoccini (1930, 1932, 1934, 1935, 1941).
30. Almagro (1983b).
31. Harding (1951a).
32. Harding (1944, 1946, 1950, 1951b, 1951c, 1951d); Harding, Driver and Tufnell (1953); Harding and Isserlin (1953).
33. Hadidi (1974).
34. Dornemann (1970, 1983).
35. Zayadine (1973).
36. Almagro and Almagro (1976,); Almagro and Olávarri (1982 1982, 1983a, 1987); Olávarri-Goicoechea (1985).
37. Zayadine, Najjar and Greene (1987).
38. Zayadine, Humbert and Najjar (1989).

Chapter 1

1. Terminology: 'Levant' will be used to describe the whole complex of Jordan, Palestine, Syria, Lebanon and the Hatay province of Turkey as a geographical phenomenon. Although it must be admitted that the term more properly refers to the coastal zone, it is less clumsy than the alternative 'Syria-Palestine'. 'Syria' means the territory of the present state, but is sometimes used for the medieval Islamic province. 'Southern Levant' means Jordan and Palestine. 'Jordan' means the territory of the present state of the Hashemite Kingdom of Jordan on the East Bank. Note that this is to be distinguished from the *jund al-Urdunn*, whose territory only partly overlapped with modern Jordan (cf. figs 11–12). 'Palestine' describes the geographical entity covered by the present State of Israel, and the occupied territories of the West Bank and Gaza.
2. EI^2 s.v. Balkā'.
3. cf. Hunting Technical Services (1956), p.18.
4. Desert pavement is formed from a soil containing gravel and stones, which has been eroded by wind deflation to

leave an armour of stones, in this case chert, protecting the soil from further erosion. The stones may be faceted by further wind deflation (Hills 1966, p.68). The desert pavement rarely bears vegetation.

5. Called by Quennell the Belqa series (Quennell 1951), although this name has not been followed since.
6. On the basis of vegetation the steppe region might be divided in two: an eastern steppe with Irano-Turanian vegetation, and a western steppe with Mediterranean vegetation.
7. Ibrahim et al. (1976), p.41.
8. Muqaddasī: 175, p.175. The *kunya* of this author, Muḥammad ibn Aḥmad, is transliterated differently by various scholars, either as al-Maqdisī or al-Muqaddasī, the unvowelled Arabic form being the same.
9. Called by Quennell the Ajlun series (Quennell 1951, p.100; Bender 1968, p.188).
10. Ionides (1939), p.279.
11. Conder (1889), pp.52–3.
12. See MacAdam, Chapter 3, for a discussion of the story.
13. Zayadine, Humbert and Najjar (1989).
14. Absolute levels at the Citadel of 'Ammān have been the subject of disagreement. One benchmark was used by the excavations of Mrs C-M. Bennett, and the other British fieldwork; this was measured by 1960s surveys on the roof of the Reception Hall. All the spot heights in this volume relate to this benchmark. However, other projects have used different benchmarks, which differ substantially in their absolute heights.
15. Harding (1967), p.63.

Chapter 2

1. Cf. Conder (1889), pp.19ff.; Harding (1967), pp.61–70; Avi-Yonah and Stern (1978); Weippert (1977), pp.287f.
2. The only complete and final excavation report so far is Almagro Gorbea, A. (1983a), *El Palacio Omeya de Amman* I, *La Arquitectura*, Madrid, and Olávarri-Goicoechea, E. (1985), *El Palacio Omeya* II, *La Arqueologia*, Valencia.
3. Zayadine, F. (1977–8), pp.28, 40, fig.27; Zayadine, Najjar and Greene (1987), p.308; Zayadine, Humbert and Najjar (1989), p.359; Dornemann (1983), p.12; Hanbury-Tenison (1986), *passim.*
4. Conder (1889), pp.20–26; Mackenzie (1911), pp.1–40; Harding (1967), p.63; Hanbury-Tennison (1986), pp.244–6.
5. It has been demonstrated that parts of the vicinity of 'Ammān were settled long before the Chalcolithic Period, cf. the excavations at 'Ayn Ghazāl, or, for example, Rollefson, Kaechele and Kaechele (1982).
6. Cf. most recently Miroschedji (1989).
7. Cf. Zayadine (1979), p.120; Zayadine et al. (1987), pp.306, 308f.; cf. Zayadine (1977–8), pp.28, 40, fig 27; Zayadine, (1986a), p.19; Dornemann (1983), p.12; this volume, Chapters 10 and 11.
8. Zayadine et al. (1989), p.359; Dornemann (1983), p.12; this volume, Chapter 10.
9. Zayadine et al. (1987), p.308. For an overview, see Gerstenblith (1983), *passim*, and most recently the articles by Dever, W. G., Rosen, A. M. and Kochavi, M. in P. de Miroschedji, ed. (1989), *L'Urbanisation de la Palestine à l'âge du Bronze ancien: Bilan et perspectives des recherches actuelles*, Actes du Colloque d'Emmaüs, *BAR*, International Series S 527 I, Oxford, pp.225–46, 247–55, 257–9.
10. Dornemann (1983), p.13; Gerstenblith (1983), p.49.
11. Dajani (1967–8); Hadidi (1982).
12. Cf., for example, Alami (1975), p.19; Helms (1989); Helms and McCreery (1988), pp.319–47; Zayadine (1978); Suleiman (1985).
13. Dornemann (1983), pp.18f.; Zayadine et al. (1987), pp.306, 308; Zayadine et al. (1989), p.359, fig.3f., pl.52: 1; this volume, Chapter 11.
14. Cf., for example, Dajani (1958), pp.400–404; Ward (1966), pp.6–8, pl.19 (Group A); Ma'ayeh (1960b), p.114; Zayadine, (1986a), p.20; Philip (1989), p.436; this volume, Chapters 10 and 11; Cf., for an overview, Boling (1988), pp.28–30.
15. Ward (1966), pp.9–14, pl.19f. (Group B); Bennett and Northedge (1977–8), p.178, pl.101: 2; cf. Bennett (1978a), p.8, fig. 7, pl.vb; Bennett (1979b), p.159; this volume, Chapter 11; Harding and Isserlin (1953); Isserlin (1953); Piccirillo (1978), pp.79–86.
16. Ward (1966), pp.15f., pl.21 (cylinder seal); Dajani (1966b); Dornemann (1983), pp.20–22; Bennett (1979b), p.159; this volume, Chapter 11; Zayadine et al. (1987), p.308. The so-called Airport Temple near Mārkā cannot be examined in detail here, as topographically speaking Mārkā (map ref. 243.153) has nothing to do with 'Ammān, *vide* most recently Hennessy (1989); for a parallel of the square structure at Mārkā, see also the building at Khirbat Umm al-Danānīr in McGovern (1989).
17. For information on Late Bronze Age Ammonitis, cf. also: Kafafi (1977), pp.2–75, 331–53; Dornemann (1983), pp.20–24; Boling (1988), pp.28–30.
18. Cf., for example, Redford (1982); Kafafi (1985). The conclusion of W. Zwickel in Worschech (1990), p.127, note 15, that the toponym *'-y-n* (No.95 of the List of Thutmosis III) is identical with 'Ammān, is speculative.
19. Knauf (1984) and, most recently, Görg (1989), pp.44f.
20. For Late Bronze Saḥāb, cf. especially Ibrahim (1983–4) and (1989).
21. Dornemann, R. H. (1983), pp.31–4; Hadidi (1970a), p.12; Hadidi (1974), pp.83, 85; Zayadine (1973), p.28; Zayadine et al. (1987), p.308; this volume, Chapter 11.
22. Dajani (1966b). Cf. generally Boling (1988), pp.28–30; McGovern (1986). For the Midianite sherd from the Citadel of 'Ammān, cf. Kalsbek and London (1978); Parr (1988); Knauf (1988), pp.15ff.
23. Polybius 5:71, 1–11.
24. Hadidi (1970a), p.12; (1974), pp.83, 85. For an overview see Hadidi (1989).
25. Dornemann (1983), pp.90f., fig.5.9f.; Conder (1889), p.34; Almagro (1983b), pp.608–18, fig.10; Zayadine et al. (1989), pp.357–9, fig.1f; Zayadine (1990).
26. Dornemann (1983), p.90; Zayadine (1986), p.19. Cf. Bartoccini's excavation area on the north side of the Lower Terrace, where he claimed to have found the Davidic city, the proof of which he never published: Bartoccini (1932), p.21; (1941), 'Un decennio di ricerche e di scavi Italiani in Transgiordania', *Bolletino di Reale Istituto d'Archeologia e Storia dell'Arte* 9: Tav. 8, cf. Almagro (1983b), p.607; Hübner (1992c).

27. Cf., on this subject, U. Hübner (1992c), *Die Ammoniter. Untersuchungen zur Geschichte, Kultur und Religion eines transjordanischen Volkes im 1. Jahrtausend v. Chr.*, Chapter V; Hübner (1992a).
28. For all of the following cf. Hübner (1992c), *Die Ammoniter, passim*; also for the problem of the various rectangular and round towers found in the vicinity of 'Ammān, the dating and function of which cannot, however, be dealt with here.
29. Dornemann (1983), pp.18f.; Zayadine (1973), p.17; Zayadine et al. (1989), pp.359–62.
30. Zayadine et al. (1989), pp.359–62; this volume, Chapter 10.
31. Harding, G. L. (1951), Harding (1951c, 1951d); Harding, Driver and Tufnell (1953); Henschel-Simon (1945); Dajani (1966a); (1966c); Ma'ayeh (1960b); Ma'ayeh (1960a); Yassine (1975); Oakeshott (1978), pp.137f., 143–51, 387–93, 410.
32. Zayadine et al. (1987), pp.306, 308f.
33. Abou Assaf (1980), pp.7ff., nos 3, 7, 9–11, 17, 19(?), 21–4; Aufrecht, W. E. (1989), no.73; Zayadine et al. (1989), p.359, pl.51. That these statues were not just the norm in Ammon is shown by the example from Kerak: Hübner (1989b). For the probably Iron Age lion statue from the Citadel of 'Ammān, see Zayadine (1977–8), p.34, pl.16; H. Weippert, (1988), p.668.
34. 'Ammān, Archaeological Museum, no.J 1656. Aufrecht (1989), no.43; Abou Assaf (1980), pp.25–7, no.9; Hübner (1992c), Chapter 1.
35. For the following, cf. Weippert (1987),; Hübner (1992c).
36. For the corpus of Ammonite inscriptions, see Aufrecht (1989), and for a more complete and critical investigation Hübner (1992c), Chapter 1. Cf. also Hübner and Knauf (1992).
37. Aufrecht (1989), nos 38, 40–42, 49. Cf. also Hübner (1989a); Hübner (1992b).
38. Dornemann (1983), p.103, fig. 68, pp.399f.; Aufrecht (1989), no.77.
39. Aufrecht (1989), no.58; Hübner, U. (1992c), Chapter 1.
40. Harding, Driver and Tufnell (1953), pp.59f., pl.6:47.
41. Dajani (1962).
42. Cf. Bennett (1978b).
43. Yassine (1975).
44. 'Amr (1980), pp.51ff., nos 44, 52, 78, 82, 86, etc.
45. Dajani (1966a), pp.41f.; pl.1:1; pl.4:130.
46. Harding (1945), p.74, pl.18:69 (PAM no.41.917).
47. Cf. the parallels from Umm al-Biyāra und Khirbat el-Ghrāre.
48. Cf. Homès-Fredericq (1987); Hübner (1992b).
49. Aufrecht (1989), no.13; Hübner, U. (1992c), *Die Ammoniter*, Chapter 1, no.65.
50. Aufrecht (1989), no.129; Hübner, U. (1992c), Chapter 1, no 88.
51. Joseph., AJ. 10, 9, 7 (§§ 181); cf. Contra Ap. 1, 19f. (§§132, 143). Cf. Zayadine (1986a), p.19; Hübner, U. (1992c), Chapter 3.
52. Cf. Hübner, U. (1992c), Chapter 3; Hübner, U., in Knauf (1989), p.143.
53. Cf. Dornemann (1983), pp.180–82. Attic imports in Ammonitis are known from Khirbat al-Ḥajjār, Khirbat Khalde, Rujm al-Malfūf South, Tell al-'Umeirī, and Umm 'Udhayna.

Chapter 3

1. Bosworth (1974).
2. Stephanus of Byzantium, *Ethnica* s.v. 'Philadelphia (3)'. On the significance of the name *Astartē* see Tcherikover (1961), p.100 and notes 79, 80; his use of the term *polis* regarding *Hellenistic* Philadelphia is anachronistic.
3. *Rabbath, quae hodie a rege Aegupti Ptolemaeo cognomento Philadelpho ... Philadelphia nuncupata est* (*St Jerome*, in *Hiezech.* 25). On various forms of the name see Thomsen (1907), p.113, and especially Abel (1933/8), pp.424–5. In the sixth century AD account of the martyrdom of Saints Zenōn and Zenas (see main text below) the city is described as 'Philadelphia of Arabia ... which in the Law (i.e. the O.T.) is called *Emman* [sic].' Text: *AcS* Iun. vol.v, ch.1.2, p.406; commentary: Milik (1960), p.162 n.32.
4. *PSI* 616.27 (of *c.*258) and Polybius, *Histories* 5.71.4, where the historian *c.*150 is utilizing a third-century source. Polybius likewise ignores the dynastic name 'Berenice' when he makes a contemporary reference to Pella (*Hist.* 5.70.12).
5. For concise accounts of these three cities see Schürer (1979), pp.121–7 [Ptolemais]; 145–8 [Pella]; 142–5 [Scythopolis]. It should be noted that the two Berenices may have been so named as early as the reign of Ptolemy I or as late as the reign of Ptolemy III.
6. *BMC*, 'Phoenicia', p.lxxviii.
7. Will (1985, p.239, n.14) argues that since 'Philadelphia' does not occur in the Zenōn documents the change of name occurred *after* 259.
8. Jones (1971), pp.239–40.
9. E.g. *PCZ* 59003.13 of 259 BC (see the discussion below) and *PSI* 406.13 (undated, but probably of the same year). Hellenistic and later Greek sources use *Ammōn* and *Ammanitis* interchangeably. In the fourth century AD Eusebius (*Onom.* 24.1–2) drew a distinction between the two spellings. 'Ammanitis' is used throughout this paper.
10. Tscherikower (1937), pp.36–8.
11. Bagnall (1976), pp.213–20, especially p.219.
12. *OGIS* 230 (of shortly after 200 BC).
13. Bagnall (1976), pp.18–21.
14. The term *hyparchia* appears in *SB* 8008 (*c.* 261 BC), which was published in 1936. Tcherikover (1961, pp.61–2), correctly incorporated the term, but Jones (1971, p.239) failed to mention it in the text of both his editions (it is acknowledged in n. 19 of that chapter). See more recently Bagnall (1976), pp.14, 18 and n.35.
15. Villeneuve (1988), p.274. The statement of Mazar (1957, p.142) that 'The land [of Ammanitis] was rich in water and fertile soil, which could be cultivated intensively' is exaggerated. Only the Baq'a plain, some 24 sq.km. in area, might fit that description. It lies 20 km north of 'Ammān, just south of the Wādī Zarqā' (biblical Jabbok). See Gatier (1986), p.13.
16. *PCZ* 59003 = *CPJ* 1. The ethnic identity of Sphragis is uncertain; the editors of *CPJ* 1 (see esp. p.120) restored '[Si]donian' in preference to '[Baby]lonian'. Other restorations are possible. Her name is Greek.
17. See the prescient discussion of the term by Enno Littmann (Littmann et al., 1921 p.6) who wrote eight years *before* this

document was unearthed. More recently, see Mazar (1957, p.140), who assumed that Birta superseded an older place-name (Sōr) in the Persian period.

18. Vincent (1920), p.198; Orrieux (1979), p.323.
19. On this, see Mittmann (1970b), pp.202–3, and Mazar (1957), p.141.
20. On this meaning for *baris* see Will (1987), esp. pp.253–4.
21. For earlier archaeological work at the site see Mittmann (1970b), pp.203–4, n.21; the account by P. Lapp in *EAEHL* II (1976), pp.527–31; and the extensive bibliography in Villeneuve (1988), p.285 n.1.
22. Ptolemy, *Geog.* 5.18.
23. Mittmann (1970b), pp.201–6.
24. *PCZ* 59004.6; *P. Lond.* 1930.175.
25. 'There can be no doubt that this [*Sōrabitta*] refers to the Tyrus ... of the Tobiads mentioned by Josephus. The Hebrew name of the place was therefore *Sōr* and its Aramaic name *Bīrthā*; it was the fortress of the land of Tobiah' (Mazar 1957, p.140).
26. Orrieux (1979), pp.324–5; Will (1987), p.254; Villeneuve (1988), pp.263, 278.
27. Good summaries of the Tobiad dynasty are given by Vincent (1920), pp.189–202 and Mazar (1957).
28. The date of this epigraphy has been much disputed, ranging from late sixth to early third century BC; see Villeneuve (1988), p.261, n.8.
29. Dentzer et al. (1982, p.207) have suggested that the site was an 'animal breeding centre' from which Tobias shipped prize specialities to Egypt.
30. That phrase, perhaps equivalent to 'Ammanitis', appears in *CPJ* 2d (259 BC); see also 1 Macc. 5:13.
31. Orrieux (1979), p.326, n.11.
32. Tcherikover (1972), pp.97–8.
33. Mittmann (1970b), p.207 and notes 41–2.
34. The full descriptive name *Rbt bny ʿmwn* (literally 'Rabbat [i.e. principal city] of the sons of 'Ammōn') occurs as such only twice, in Deut. 3:11 and Ezek. 21:20. On the usage and meaning of the phrase *bny ʿmwn*, see Block (1984).
35. Since the document concerned is an official record of a transaction, the fact that 'Philadelphia' is not used almost certainly means that the dynastic name had not yet been bestowed. Portions of a massive walled structure, perhaps the 'Birta' itself, have recently been found on the Lower Terrace of the Citadel. The excavators date its initial construction to the Late Iron II period, and suggest some renovations in the Early Hellenistic Era. Silver and bronze coins of Ptolemy II Philadelphus (285–246 BC), the first of that king found in 'Ammān, were discovered in associated structures. See Zayadine et al. (1989, pp.362–3), and for a narrative account and detailed discussion of the entire siege episode see Zayadine (1990).
36. Mlaker (1943), p.39 [the 'Ammonite']; p.36 [the 'Moabite']. See also Graf (1983), pp.564–5, and *IDB* I.113.
37. For numerous other examples see the 'General Index' under several rubrics for 'slave' (e.g. *sōma*, *sōmation*, *paidion*, *paidiskē*, etc.) in Pestman (1981).
38. Tscherikower (1937), pp.16–20.
39. Rostovtzeff (1922), pp.167–8. For a discussion of the types of animals (horses, asses, etc.) bred for racing or domestic use see Hauben (1984).
40. Harper (1928), pp.13–16.
41. Hadidi (1970b). No contemporary architectural remains have been found.
42. See Chapter 5 for a discussion of which sections of wall might have been vulnerable.
43. Diodorus Siculus 19.94.1 ff.
44. *PSI* 406.21–22.
45. On these see Starcky (1985), pp.167–8 (provenance unknown; Damascus museum, 3rd century BC), and Starcky (1966), p.930 (from Bostra, 2nd century BC).
46. *AJ* 12.4.11. Doubts about that identification are noted in *IDB* I, p.113.
47. For Jason's previous refuge in Ammanitis, see 2 Macc. 4:26–7.
48. See the comments in Habicht (1976, p.225, n.8b), and the account in Kasher (1988, pp.21–4).
49. See the discussion in Goldstein (1976, pp.296–7), and the detailed account in Bar-Kochva (1989, pp.508–15). There is no evidence to support the latter's assertion (p.515) that Timotheus was 'the Seleucid *stratēgos* in Galaaditis'. The debate about the identity and role of Timotheus was best summarized more than fifty years ago by Johannes Regner (*RE* VI AII [1937] cols 1330–1).
50. Also Butler (1907–19), pl.I, p.33, n.1, and Goldstein (1983), pp.393–4. Avi Yonah (1966, p.179) is less certain.
51. Strabo notes (*Geog.* 16.2.20) that South Arabian *merchants* (not just their *merchandise*) were at the mercy of bandits who raided the Ḥawrān from their strongholds in Trachonitis. That situation obtained until direct Roman intervention in 64/63 BC. This is interesting for a number of reasons. It indicates clearly that the Nabataeans did not control the area, and implies that such trade by-passed Philadelphia. Moreover, as Isaac (1989, p.242) points out, Strabo is our only witness for a direct commercial link between Arabia Felix and the Ḥawrān in the late Hellenistic period.
52. Josephus, *BJ* 1.60; *AJ* 13.235.
53. Zenōn is a common enough Greek name, but Clermont-Ganneau (*RAO* I.5) demonstrated that Greek names beginning with *Zēn-* or *Dio-* could be used to render Semitic *Baʿal* (or Zeus). Cf. also Wüthnow (1930, p.50) and Sourdel (1952, pp.20–21).
54. Robert (1960), p.489, n. 2; *LSJ* s.v. *kotylea*.
55. *CIS* II 214 (AD 39/40) is the tomb inscription (Nabataean) of 'Matiyū the '*strtg*' (*stratēgos*), son of '*WPRNS* (*Euphronus*) the *hyprk*' (*eparchos*). In this case father and son are clearly associated with the military. See also *CIS* II 201 (AD 8/9), which attests a *klyrk*' (*chiliarchos*) with dual names, Nabataean (Hunaynu) and Greek (*HPSTYWN* = *Hephaistion*). Starcky (1971, especially p.157) gives several examples from epigraphy of Nabataean military officers whose fathers have Greek names transliterated into Nabataean, e.g. *CIS* II 234 (*DMSPS* = *Damasippus*).
56. Gerasa: *BJ* 1.4.8; Gadara and Amathus: *AJ* 13.13.3; *BJ* 1.4.2.
57. Josephus, *AJ* 13.13; *BJ* 1.4.
58. *BJ* 1.128–9. Josephus' use of 'Philadelphia' here is consistent with his preference for that term rather than 'Rabbatammana'.
59. *BJ* 1.128–9.
60. Jones (1971, p.455, n.39; p.462, n.64) with reference to Josephus and Syncellus.

61. Neither Gadara nor Abila of the Peraea is to be confused with cities of the same name belonging to the Decapolis. Gadara has long been identified with Tell Jadūr near modern Salṭ. The location of Abila is still disputed in spite of Avi-Yonah's (1966, p.96) identification of it with Khirbat Kifrayn.
62. Graf (1986); Gatier (1988).
63. Hadidi (1974, p.85) notes the 'discovery of Nabataean sherds and coins of the first century AD' in the forum area.
64. 'Hellenistic' pottery and coins were found mixed with Iron Age sherds beneath the Roman level of the forum. The coins were exclusively Seleucid. See Hadidi (1974), p.85.
65. Villeneuve (1988), p.279. Results are based on surface surveys only.
66. Strabo, *Geography* 16.2.40.
67. Villeneuve (1988), pp.280–2.
68. Gatier (1986) includes the epigraphy from Quwaysma and Rajīb; that from Zarqā' will appear in *IJ*, vol. 5.
69. Avi Yonah (1966, p.177) tried to establish the eastern border of Philadelphia's territory on the basis of milestone distances computed from Philadelphia or Bostra along the Roman road. Road distances were calculated north to south until AD 181, thereafter south to north. Milestone distances to or from any city have nothing to do with territorial limits.
70. On the formation of the Peraea and the location of Zia see de Vaux (1941), pp.39–44.
71. Josephus, *AJ* 14.4.4.
72. Schürer (1979), p.156, n.381.
73. Thus the view of Rey-Coquais (1982), p.7.
74. Parker (1975).
75. Isaac (1981), republishing *IGR* 1.824.
76. Graf (1986), pp.789–90.
77. Gatier (1988), pp.161–3.
78. Will (1985), p.238.
79. Will (1985), p.240; Rey-Coquais (1982), p.9.
80. The most recent comprehensive account of Gadara is Weber (1989). No structure or inscription earlier than the late first century AD has so far been found. One may note that a native of Gadara named 'Diodorus the son of Heliodorus' was buried somewhere in Italy in the mid-second century AD. His tombstone (see *SEG* 30, 1980, no.1801) proclaims his city as 'Gadara of the Syrian Decapolis' a half-century *after* that institution ceased to exist. See, most recently, Gatier (1990), pp.204–5, no.1.
81. *BJ* 3.9.7. A new Greek inscription from Scythopolis (*SEG* 37 (1987) no.1531), of Severan date, proclaims that city to be 'among the Greek *poleis* of Coele-Syria', the latter term presumably a substitute for 'Decapolis'. See Gatier (1990), pp.205–6, no.2.
82. Gatier (1982), p.10 and box A, p.11. The date is AD 22/23.
83. Spijkerman (1978), pp.128–9.
84. Spijkerman (1978), pp.128–9. Herakles and Athena are depicted on coins of 64/63.
85. Braemer (1987, especially p.529) notes an occupational gap at Jarash between the 7th–2nd centuries BC. Either an early Hellenistic foundation lay elsewhere than the *tell*, or a settlement of that date did not exist. A preliminary study of Roman sculpture from the Decapolis cities has been published by Thomas Weber (1990).
86. See, for example, Bietenhard (1977), p.232. Again the exception is Gadara, which had been destroyed by the Hasmonaeans. Pompey rebuilt the city for his Gadarene freedman, Demetrius. The Hellenization process in early Roman Palestine has been surveyed recently by Martin Hengel (1989).
87. Isaac (1981).
88. Isaac (1981), pp.71–2. A parallel arrangement involving the administration of Trachonitis and Auranitis may be noted. Numerous epigraphic references (of the later Antonine period) attest centurions, acting as military attachés under the aegis of the Syrian governor, overseeing projects or honoured by villagers. See MacAdam (1986, pp.54–7). The enhanced status of the Decapolis would have required a higher-ranking official, such as the equestrian attested.
89. Josephus, *AJ* 15.7.3; *BJ* 1.20.3.
90. *AJ* 17.11.4.
91. Josephus, *BJ* 2.13.2. Concerning the problem of which Abila is meant, see Schürer (1979), p.137, n.265.
92. Villeneuve (1988), pp.280–2.
93. *CIL* 3.13483a (= *ILS* 9168).
94. Wüthnow (1930), p.96, s.v. Rabbēlos, Rabēlos; cf. the onomastic index in Sartre (1985), pp.230–1, s.v. Rabibēlos.
95. Tacitus, *Histories*, 2.83.
96. Bowersock (1973).
97. This information was communicated by J. Seigne, 'Jarash romaine et byzantine: développement urbain d'une ville provinciale', read at the Fourth Conference on the History and Archaeology of Jordan, Lyons, France, May–June 1989.
98. Gatier (1986, p.53) notes only the parallels from Gerasa. For municipal offices at Canatha, see *Wadd.* 2216; 2339 (councillors), *Wadd.* 2341 (*proedros*) and *Wadd.* 2330 (*agoranomos*).
99. *IJ* 2.60, 2.61 from Ḥisbān; *IJ* 2.74 from a ruined monastery near Mt Nebo. All are Christian.
100. A good summary and specific examples are given by Gatier (1986, p.24). The calculation of the Pompeian Era is reviewed by Rey-Coquais (1981, pp.25–7).
101. *IJ* 2.53. The inscription commemorates the rebuilding of the church, presumably following the great earthquake of AD 717. That eliminates all but the Pompeian era in calculating the date.
102. The fundamental study of the city's (and the region's) coinage is Spijkerman (1978, esp. pp.242–57). Fr Spijkerman's division of Philadelphia's coinage into the now archaic classifications of 'quasi-autonomous' and 'colonial' is misleading.
103. See, for example, Spijkerman (1978), pp.244–5, nos 4 ('year 441') and 5 ('year 442'). Spijkerman offered no comment except a question mark before each year-number. Both readings are impossible. In no.5 the unit number is more probably a *stigma* (6) than a *beta* (2). The possibility exists that both nos 4 and 5 were tooled, so that their dates should read 146 of the Pompeian era, i.e. AD 83/84. The same year, but a variant reading, was suggested by Hill, *BMC Arabia*, no.37.1.
104. Gatier (1986, p.53) draws attention to the marble head of Philadelphia's Tychē found during construction of the Archaeological Museum on the Citadel.

105. Spijkerman (1978), pp.244–5, no.2; pp.246–7 nos 7, 9, 10.
106. Coins: Spijkerman (1978), e.g. pp.246–7, nos 11, 12; inscriptions: *IJ* 2.23 (AD 189/90); see also *IJ* 2.24, undated but probably mid-second century.
107. Rey-Coquais (1981), pp.27–31.
108. Rey-Coquais (1981), pp.27–31. That view is accepted by Bowersock (1988, pp.51–2) and rejected by Gatier (1986, p.48).
109. Bowersock (1983, pp.79–89) summarizes the circumstances of the creation of Provincia Arabia.
110. Bowersock (1983), pp.90–2.
111. Spijkerman (1978), pp.256–7, nos 44–7.
112. I am grateful to Dr Donald S. Whitcomb, Oriental Institute, University of Chicago, for this information.
113. Butler (1910), p.xiv; Bauzou (1988), p.294.
114. Bauzou (1988), p.294. Low mileage figures (e.g. II) on milestones found just north of Philadelphia may refer to this branch road only. They are not, as Avi Yonah (1966, p.177) maintained, connected with Philadelphia's territorial limits.
115. Bowersock (1983, p.167, n.10) discusses the various editions of the Peutinger Map, including the facsimile edition published in 1976. Segments 9 and 10 of the map show the road from 'Aqaba to Bostra and beyond.
116. Bowersock (1983), p.174.
117. MacAdam (1986), pp.29,33 (see map, fig.6).
118. Gatier (1986), p.55.
119. Jaussen and Savignac (1909).
120. Gatier (1986), p.181.
121. Olávarri (1980). Independent publications announced the recent discovery of a Greek metrical inscription from an underground tomb complex at Rajīb, six kilometres south-east of 'Ammān. It attests for the first time the cult of Zeus-Demeter east of the Jordan. Associated evidence dates the inscription to the mid-second century AD. See Campagano (1988), Gatier and Vérilhac (1989).
122. *Dialogue with Trypho* 119 (*PG* 6.752).
123. *Ethnica* s.v. 'Amanon'.
124. Bowersock (1983), pp.142–7.
125. *Onom.* s.v. 'Amman' and 'Ammōn'.
126. Dunand (1931).
127. Parker (1986), pp.32–4.
128. Piccirillo (1985).
129. Homès-Fredericq and Hennessy (1986) and (1989).
130. Homès-Fredericq (1986); Miller (1979).
131. The result of five campaigns between 1968–76 were summarized in Boraas and Geraty (1978).
132. The best summary of the work done is Villeneuve (1988). For a description of the area surveyed see Villeneuve (1988), pp.264–74.
133. Ibach (1978), p.212 and Table 1.
134. Younker et al. (1990) summarize the 1989 season. The 1984 season was reported in *AUSS* 23 (1985, pp.85–110) and that of 1987 in Geraty et al. (1988).
135. Geraty et al. (1988), p.229.
136. Villeneuve (1988), p.282.
137. E.g. for southern Edom (Wādī Ḥasā area) see MacDonald (1981); for the Jordanian Ḥawrān and adjacent areas see King (1982, 1983).
138. On the transitional period in Jordan see most recently Schick (1987, 1988).
139. Bietenhard (1977), pp.255–6.
140. Bruce (1975), p.23.
141. The interested reader may review the standard theories on the topic via a superb short essay entitled 'Tradition and Form in the Acts of the Christian Martyrs' in Musurillo (1972, pp.l–lvii).
142. *In Arabia acommemoratio plurimorum sanctorum martyrum qui sub Galerio Maximiano imperatore saevissime caesi sunt* (Propylaeum ad Acta Sanctorum [Decembris], p.72); on the *synodus* see *AcS* Nov. vol. II, pp.408, 410.
143. Peeters (1926). The Georgian text is presented with a Latin translation and notes on pp.88–101.
144. Peeters (1926, pp.86–7) has identified the town, called *Pede* in the Georgian text, as Pella. Pella was never part of Roman or Byzantine Arabia, and therefore outside the jurisdiction of that province's governor. Milik's (1960, p.165, n.42) conjecture that Pede transliterates Greek *pedion* ('plain') is implausible.
145. Peeters (1926), p.84.
146. *AcS* Iun. vol.v, pp.405–11, on p.406; Peeters (1926), p.84, n.2.
147. *AcS* Iun. vol.v., ch.1; cf. Moore (1964), p.3. The excerpt is from the preface (*Commentarius Praevius*), p.405.
148. Milik (1960, pp.162–3, n.39) has identified a specific military term in this document that argues for its authenticity.
149. *AcS* Iun. vol.v, ch.14. Milik (1960, p.162, n.33) believes the reference (*hippikon* in the Greek text) is to 'la place forte de la caserne de cavalerie'.
150. Moore (1964), pp.4, 25.
151. The initial publication was inevitably limited to those scholars reading Georgian. Milik (1960, pp.166–70) made no attempt to summarize the narrative. Garitte (1961), with introduction, résumé, Georgian text and Latin translation, plus commentary, is now the definitive publication.
152. Garitte (1961), p.429. The name of St Elianus was later associated with a small, columned basilica in Philadelphia, identified as such by the Survey of Eastern Palestine in 1881. See Conder (1889), p.56, with Bagatti (1973), pp.271–2.
153. Garitte (1961), pp.418, 421, 430. The description fits the 'oval forum' at Gerasa better than any known feature of Roman Philadelphia.
154. Garitte (1961), p.442.
155. Khouri (1988), p.16.
156. Khouri (1988), pp.37–8.
157. Khouri (1988), pp.31–2.
158. Khouri (1988), pp.33–5.
159. Mhaisen (1976).
160. *IJ* 2.56. The numeral indicating hundreds is missing.
161. Khouri (1988), p.26.
162. Zayadine (1982b).
163. Piccirillo (1982).
164. Gatier (1986), pp.66–7.
165. Gatier (1986), Appendix following p.201.
166. Gatier (1986), Appendix [= *PL* 87.153–64].
167. Piccirillo (1987b).
168. Wilkinson (1977) and Hunt (1982).
169. One may consult with profit Wilkinson's (1977, pp.148–78) 'Gazetteer' of the biblical sites.

170. A full bibliography of the map's publications can be found in Gatier (1986, pp.148–9). Handy facsimiles of the map, with Greek and English captions respectively, are presented in Wilkinson (1977) as endpieces. For a recent critique of the map and its significance see Donceel-Voûte (1988), who prefers a date in the early 7th century. Her argument (which is not convincing) focuses on the religious turmoil subsequent to the creation of the patriarchate of Jerusalem (mid-fifth century) and the prominence of Transjordanian bishoprics on the map itself.
171. Piccirillo and Attiyah (1986) with black and white photos only (plates LXX–LXXVII). Almost the entire volume of *Biblical Archaeology* 51 (1988) is devoted to aspects of the new mosaics, accompanied by splendid colour photographs. On its religious, social and artistic significance, see in particular Schick (1988), Piccirillo (1988) and Wilkin (1988).
172. For a dissenting opinion on this identification, see Elitzur (1989).
173. There is a good photograph of this Tychē in Moore (1964, opposite p.16).
174. The most recent discussion of Malchus is that of Shahid (1989, pp.59–113, *passim*); this does not supersede the masterly article by Baldwin (1977). See also Blockley (1981, pp.71–85, 124–7; 1983, pp.402–62), and the additional bibliography given in Shahid (1989, p.59, nn.2, 3). The entry in *PLRE* II (p.73) is quite inadequate.
175. Shahid (1989), pp.61–2.
176. Baldwin (1977, p.92) placed Philadelphia in 'Palestine'. Even if he meant the Byzantine province of Palaestina (Tertia), it did not include central Jordan.
177. Baldwin (1977), p.104.
178. The meanings of 'sophist' and 'rhetor' underwent modification from the classical period through Byzantine times. When applied to Malchus, they might mean 'teacher' and 'lawyer', respectively. See the discussion in Baldwin (1977), pp.91–2, n.4a.
179. Blockley (1981), p.90.
180. Baldwin (1977, pp.94–6) summarizes the issue.
181. Blockley (1981), p.77.
182. *FHG* IV,pp.112–13; *Excerpta Historica issu imp. Constantini Porphyrogeniti Confecta* (whence *Excerpta de Legationibus*), vol.1.1, pp.568–9. Shahid (1989, pp.112–13) has reproduced the Greek text of the latter. Frag. 1 is also reproduced in Greek, with an English translation and commentary, in Blockley (1983, pp.404–7).
183. 'Amorkesos' in Greek has been taken to transliterate the Arabic *Imru' al-Qays*, but Shahid (1989, pp.61–3) suggests that *'Amr ibn Kays* is also possible. His decision to use the Greek spelling throughout his discussion is judicious indeed. Baldwin (1977, pp.101, 103) refers to Amorkesos as a 'Persian'.
184. This incident is summarized well by Sartre (1982, pp.154–5).
185. E.g. '... its loss is to be deplored both as an invaluable source and as a superior work of historiography' (Blockley, 1981, p.85); 'All in all, Malchus was a readable and effective stylist ... The surviving fragments make one wish for more. That cannot be said of all late Greek historians' (Baldwin, 1977, p.107).

Chapter 4

1. Ghawanma, Y. (1979), *'Ammān, ḥadāratuhā wa-tārīkhuhā*, 'Ammān.
2. The basis of this judgement is the size of the mosque in the Umayyad period, on which see chapter 6.
3. Deschamps 1933, 1939.
4. Mas'ūdī, *Tanbīh*: 186. The notion of *malik* (king) is to be seen purely within the context of Arab tribal society, and does not necessarily imply a territorial power. In the Nemara inscription of AD 328 individual Arab tribes appear to have had *maliks* (Kropp in Caubet 1990), who were thus the equivalent of a tribal *shaykh*.
5. Ḥamza al-Iṣfahānī: 1.115–7.
6. al-Balādhurī: 129.
7. al-Ṭabarī: 1.2136–58; al-Balādhurī: 123.
8. al-Balādhurī: 113. The translation is that of Hitti.
9. The word *jund* (army) signifying a military district or grouping, and thus related to the Umayyad armies, is not the only word used; others are: *kūra* (Ibn Khurdādhbih), *arḍ* (al-Ṭabarī: 1.1794), *'amal* (al-Ṭabarī: 3.1342), and *iqlīm* (Ibn Khurdādhbih: 77).
   It has been argued by Shahid that the name *jund*, and the boundaries of the original four *ajnād*, derived from an otherwise unknown reorganization of the Syrian provinces by Heraclius *circa* 628 'in the aftermath of the Sasanian occupation' into military/administrative *themata*, on the pattern of the *themata* of Anatolia (Shahid 1986).
10. al-Iṣṭakhrī: 56.
11. al-Muqaddasī: 154.
12. EI[2] s.v. Balkā'.
13. al-Ṭabarī: 1.2108.
14. al-Ṭabarī: 2.1975, 3.25–6.
15. al-Ṭabarī: 2.1841–2.
16. The main literature on the mint of 'Ammān is: Nassar 1946, Walker 1956, Hadidi 1975, Bates 1989, Nabrawi 1989.
17. Bates 1989: 218–9.
18. Hadidi 1975.
19. Walker (1956), pp.274–5, nos 905–7.
20. Nabrawi 1989: 20, no.8.
21. The only other Umayyad mint-site currently known in Jordan is Jarash, see Naghawi 1989, Bates 1989: 223–4.
22. Lane-Poole 1875–90: II no.206, II no.212, IX no.260.
23. Parr 1965, 1986. Artefactual evidence of the Byzantine period at Petra is common (cf. Hammond 1975), though little accompanied by monumental building; in particular there is only one church, a reuse of the Urn Tomb (Harding 1967: 132).
24. See Smith 1973, Smith 1989, and McNicoll et al. 1982, for occupation of churches and a continuing domestic settlement terminated by the earthquake of 130/747–8.
25. See Wagner-Lux et al. (1979, 1980), Weber (1989) for evidence of occupation. Also Mershen and Knauf (1988).
26. Kraeling et al. 1938; Zayadine 1986b, 1989; Khouri 1986.
27. Andrews University excavations 1968–76. Sauer 1973 gives a preliminary account of the pottery and coins, and an impression of the kind of occupation encountered from the Umayyad period.
28. Mare 1986.
29. Lenzen and Knauf 1987; Lenzen 1990; McQuitty 1986.

30. The Church of the Virgin may postdate the Conquest: for discussion and bibliography see Piccirillo 1980. Excavation of the Salayta district church encountered Umayyad pottery (*ADAJ* 17: 77–80).
31. Smith 1989.
32. Gawlikowski 1986.
33. Published by 'Ayda Naghawi, *ADAJ* 26: pp.20–2 (Ar. sect.).
34. The small mosque discovered in Jarash could have been either the main mosque of the town, or a small mosque of a residential quarter. That such a small mosque could be the main mosque of a town is suggested at 'Āna, where a small Umayyad mosque was replaced by a full-sized *jāmi'* in the 'Abbāsid period (Northedge, Bamber and Roaf 1988: fig.6).
35. Mittmann 1970a.
36. Ibrahim, Sauer and Yassine 1976.
37. Waterhouse and Ibach 1975; Ibach 1987.
38. Miller 1979.
39. Macdonald 1980, 1981.
40. 1:100,000 Palestine/South Levant, dated 1945–7, used by Mittmann. Increase since that date would probably make the figures of comparable scale.
41. Ibach 1987: 202–5.
42. This is only intended to make a tentative point. The problems of assessing the value of surface surveys for settlement history are ignored here; see Adams 1981 for a recent discussion.
43. Ṭabarī: 2.1122–3.
44. Balādhurī: 144.
45. Conrad 1986.
46. For example, the Caliph Hishām 'oppressed men with excessive taxes and levies of money' (Michael the Syrian: 2.490).
47. The most recent treatment of the fragmentary information on the Umayyad taxation system in Syria is Rebstock 1989.
48. Adams 1965: 99; 1981: 63.
49. E.g. Helms 1990.
50. Sauvaget 1939c, 1967.
51. For example, Qaṣr al-Ḥallabāt (Bisheh 1980, 1985).
52. Sauvaget 1967.
53. Grabar (1963a) adds that many of these agricultural estates must have been economically ill-judged, as most were abandoned after the 'Abbāsid Revolution.
54. Agapius of Manbij: 359.
55. The main example of Umayyad practice in agricultural investment explained in detail in the texts is the canal at Bālis on the Euphrates, Nahr Maslama, referred to by Agapius as a work of Hishām. Maslama ibn 'Abd al-Malik made an agreement with Bālis and its surrounding villages for a canal from the Euphrates to irrigate previously rain-fed lands, which had been paying *'ushr*. One third of the produce was payable to Maslama, on top of *'ushr* for the government. The arrangement was heritable, and passed after the revolution into the hands of the 'Abbāsid family (Balādhurī: 151). See also Nahr Sa'īd, and al-Hanī wal-Marī (Balādhurī: 179–80).

The financial prospects of a conversion from dry-land farming to irrigation are good; the desert edge which is the site of most of the Umayyad *quṣūr* of Jordan however has no substantial irrigation prospects – for distribution of Umayyad *quṣūr*, see fig. 13 (FAO 1970; Aresvik 1976).

56. Balādhurī: 129.
57. Yāqūt: 4.687.
58. Ibn 'Asākir: 67.
59. Ṭabarī: 2.1795, 2.1754, 2.1743.
60. Ṭabarī: 2.1776.
61. Ṭabarī: 2.1841–2.
62. Yāqūt: s.v. Tanhaj. The location of this village is unknown.
63. The extensive anecdotal information in the 4th/10th century *Kitāb al-Aghānī* of al-Iṣfahānī on the luxurious lifestyle of the Umayyads has been treated by Hillenbrand (1982), and more recently by Hamilton (1988). Much of this material may be exaggerated for the sake of a good story, or perhaps represents the activities of a few extreme individuals, such as the libertine Caliph al-Walīd ibn Yazīd (125/743–126/744). For a more sober and more contemporary account of Umayyad princely life, see 'Abd al-Ḥamīd ibn Yaḥyā, *Risāla 'an Marwān ilā ibnihi 'Abdallah*.
64. Ṭabarī: 2.1834.
65. Aphrodito Papyri nos 1403, 1414, 1435 (Bell 1928) are demands from Qurra ibn Sharīk to the Prefect of Aphrodito for money to pay for labourers and skilled workmen working on the Mosque and palace in Jerusalem.
66. In return for his payment, Yūsuf ibn 'Umar proposed to take possession of the person of Khālid, with the opportunity to extort what he could (Ṭabarī: 2.1778–80). The issue was the recovery of Khālid al-Qaṣrī's profits of office, which were presumably larger than the offer.
67. Part of the money went to the importation of materials and craftsmen from other parts of the Middle East for the building construction.
68. In al-Jazīra, for example, the Christian tribe of Banī Taghlib were taxed on only double the level of the *sadaqa* of Muslim Arabs (Balādhurī: 183).
69. The latest summary of the situation of churches during the Umayyad period is Schick 1987, currently in the course of publication.
70. Whitcomb 1989.
71. Schick 1987, 1988.
72. Piccirillo and Attiyah 1986; Piccirillo 1987a, 1988.
73. Ṭabarī: 3.52.
74. Ṭabarī: 3.48.
75. Ibn 'Asākir: 70.
76. Ṭabarī: 3.53; Madelung 1986.
77. Ibn 'Asākir: 130.
78. Ibn al-Athīr: 6.87; Ṭabarī: 3.639.
79. Balādhurī: 144.
80. Kirkbride 1951.
81. Ibn 'Asākir: 53; Grabar 1963b.
82. The last revolt in the name of the Umayyads was that of Abū Ḥarb al-Mubarqa' in Filasṭīn and Urdunn in 227/842 (Ṭabarī: 3.1319ff.)
83. Theophanes: 484, 487, 499. See also Schick 1990.
84. Muqaddasī: 168.
85. Ṭabarī: 3.416.
86. Ṭabarī: 3.1342.
87. Ibn Khallikān: 5.57–8.
88. Maqrīzī, *Itti'āẓ*: 1.260.
89. Ibn Ḥawqal: 173.
90. Sourdel (1980), p.166.
91. Kennedy, H. (1986), pp.287–292.

92. al-Ḥamdānī: 176.
93. von Oppenheim 1939: 350–75; Hayari 1977.
94. Ibn al-Qalānisī: 94; Hayari 1977: 53.
95. The most extreme proponent of this view was Sauer (1973, 1982, 1986).
96. Walmesley 1990; Whitcomb 1990.
97. Ibrahim et al. 1976: 61.
98. Ibach 1987: 202–5.
99. Villeneuve 1988: 282.
100. Falkner 1990.
101. Walmesley 1986, 1990.
102. Najjar 1989.
103. Whitcomb 1988a.
104. Prawer 1962: 247.
105. Ibn al-Qalānisī: 158–9.
106. Ibn al-Qalānisī: 164, 174.
107. Deschamps 1933, 1939; Mayer 1987.
108. Deschamps 1933: 46.
109. Abū Shāma: 1.2.464.
110. Ibn al-Athīr: 11.330; Ghawanma 1979: 236, quoting the manuscript of al-ʿImād al-Kātib al-Iṣfahānī.
111. Humphreys 1977: 63.
112. Ibn Shaddād: 83-5.
113. Ibn Shaddād: 86-91.
114. Dimashqī: 272, 292.
115. Maqrīzī, *Sulūk*: 1.665: *niyābat al-salṭana bil-Ṣalt wal-Balqā'* (678/1279).
116. EI²: s.v. Balkā'.
117. Maqrīzī, *Sulūk*: 3.30. Ghawanma (1979: 145) questions the verb *ʿammara* 'to build, develop', and amends the word *madīna* in the expression *madīnat ʿAmmān* ('the city of ʿAmmān') to read *madrasa*: Sarghatmish built a *madrasa* at ʿAmmān. However *ʿammara* can also mean 'restore'. In the texts ʿAmmān apparently continued to be called *madīna* ('city'), even when it was only a small village.
118. Hütteroth and Abdulfattah 1977.
119. The most recent study of the *Darb al-Ḥajj* and its Ottoman forts is Petersen 1989.
120. The accepted date for the refounding of ʿAmmān is 1878. However there are no signs of Circassian habitation in the photographs taken by the Palestine Exploration Fund in October 1881 (pls 2b, 6a, 14a, 61a), nor are the Circassians mentioned by Conder (1889: 34ff.). Perhaps the actual establishment of the settlement was somewhat later than the official date.

Chapter 5

1. Zayadine (1973), pp.25–7; Zayadine, Najjar and Greene (1987), p.309.
2. See Chapter 10.
3. Zayadine (1977–8), pp.27–8.
4. DoA (1975), p.12.
5. See Chapter 3.
6. Conder (1889), p.34; Zayadine, Humbert and Najjar (1989).
7. Butler (1907–19), pl.I, pp.34–62; Hadidi (1974, 1978); cf. also Conder (1889), pp.29–53.
8. Conder (1889).
9. Bagatti (1973), p.263. Cf. MacAdam in Chapter 3.
10. '*ingentes murorum firmitate cautissimas*', Ammianus XIV.8.3.
11 Cf. Wood in Chapter 8.
12. Butler only visited ʿAmmān after the growth of the Circassian settlement had destroyed the evidence.
13 See Bowsher in Chapter 9.
14. Zayadine (1969); Rey–Coquais (1981).
15. Many of the encroaching modern buildings have been recently cleared by the Department of Antiquities.
16. *IJ* 2.12.
17. *IJ* 2.17.
18. Butler (1907–19), pl.I, p.59.
19 Conder (1889), pp.41–52.
20. Zayadine (1973), pp.22–5.
21. Conder (1889), pp 47–51.
22. Harding (1950, 1951b); Dana (1970); Zayadine (1981).
23. Conder (1889), p.42; Laborde (1837), no.176.
24. Conder (1889), p.172.
25. Conder (1889), p.43–4.
26. Khairy (1979); Conder (1889), pp.47–8.
27. Conder (1889), p.48. Palestine Exploration Fund photograph no.550 shows a clear mausoleum building on Jabal Ashrafiyya (pl.5a in this volume).
28. Dana (1970).
29. Conder (1889), pp.47–8.
30. Zayadine (1973), pp.22–5.
31. Broshi (1980), p.5.
32. Conder (1889), pp.54–6; Butler (1907–19), pl.I pp.59–61; Bagatti (1973), pp.265–71.
33. Conder (1889), p.53.
34. Conder (1889), p.56; Bagatti (1973), pp.271–2.
35. Conder (1889), p.56; Milik (1960), pp.167–9; Bagatti (1973), pp.272–7.
36. Milik (1960).
37. Kraeling (1938), pp.254–5.
38. Hadidi (1974), pl.XXV.F.
39. Muqaddasī: 175; repeated in Yāqūt: 3.719.
40. The masculine pronoun apparently refers to the mosque, but another reference to the same comparison (Muqaddasī: 71) shows that it is ʿAmmān's location in the bottom of a wadi that is being referred to.
41. Zayadine (1973), p.22.
42. Conder (1889), p.59.
43. Conder (1889), p.59.
44. Adams (1965), p.98; Northedge (1987).

Chapter 6

1. *Wa-lahu jāmiʿ Ẓarīf bi-ṭaraf al-sūq mufasfas al-ṣaḥn*, Muqaddasī: 175. The clause following this sentence '*wa-qad qulnā innahu shabiha Makka*', has been taken to describe the mosque also; and in the Leiden text the pronoun is correct. However, the statement refers to the position of ʿAmmān and Makka in a wadi (see Miquel's translation, sect. 186).
2. Conder (1889), pp.57–9.
3. Photographs nos OC317, entitled 'Amman: Tower and Arches', 546, 'General view from west', and 548 'General view looking east', in the Palestine Exploration Fund archive.
4. Butler (1907–19), pl.I, pp.60–1.

5. Creswell Archive, Ashmolean Museum: Transjordan nos 68–9.
6. Capt. Creswell, *Archaeological Reports*, Occupied Enemy Territory Administration, 1920, p.20. Courtesy of Dr Christine Kessler.
7. Garstang Collection (housed at the Palestine Exploration Fund), nos.G180, G183.
8. The Philby photographs are housed in the Middle East Centre, St Anthony's College, Oxford: No. Phil/Misc. 1, 'Amir Abdullah laying foundation stone of new mosque, July 2, 1922; Nos. 3131–6/PJ2898–2902, six photographs showing the demolition of the old mosque and the completion of the new.
9. Littmann (1949), no.2.
10. Van Berchem (1922), nos 10 and 15.
11. Van Berchem (1922), no.19.
12. *EI*[2] s.v. *kā'id.*
13. Monroe (1973), p.129.
14. American Palestine Exploration Society, no.94.
15. The left-hand round arch is visible in PEF photograph OC317 (pl.8a); the right-hand doorway in American Palestine Exploration Society, no.94 (pl.4).
16. Northedge (1989).
17. Aalund, Meinecke and Muqdad (1990), p.27.
18. Butler (1907–19), pl.1, p.61.
19. The straight joint of the stonework can be seen in the background of plate 10a.
20. Examples of mosques where an aisle has been added to widen the prayer hall are common, for example Ḥarrān (Creswell 1969, Allen 1986). The mosque of 'Āna is an example of a prayer hall reduced in width from three to two transverse aisles (Northedge, Bamber and Roaf 1988, fig.6).
21. Sack (1990).
22. Creswell (1969), pp.198–201.
23. Creswell (1969), fig.578.
24. Hellenkemper (1976), p.380; Gough (1952), pp.98, 103–7.
25. Rice (1952).
26. The latest discussion of the mosque of Ḥarrān, including drawings from D. S. Rice's unpublished work, is to be found in Allen (1986).
27. Northedge (1989).
28. When the present mosque was built, the *qibla* was recalculated by Philby. A poet of 'Ammān celebrated this event (Monroe 1973, p.129):

    Our prince, like the moon which
    enlightens the east and the west,
    Abandoned the qibla of Omar,
    because he thought Philby's the best.

29. Creswell (1969), fig.24.
30. Creswell (1969), pls 79–80.
31. Creswell (1969), fig.559.
32. Creswell (19690, figs 88, 92 and 96.
33. Butler (1907–19), pl.4, ills 248, 281–6.
34. Butler (1929).
35. Butler (1929).
36. Cf. Chapter 7.
37. Creswell (1969), p.492.
38. Van Berchem (1922), pp.87–90.
39. Van Berchem (1922), pp.101–3.
40. Creswell (1969), fig.540.
41. Grabar et al. (1978), fig.27D.
42. Aalund, Meinecke and Muqdad (1990, pp.24–30) argue for a later date in the 12th century for the Jāmi' al-'Umarī.
43. Creswell (1969), fig.561.
44. Creswell (1969), fig.537.
45. Creswell (1940), pp.31–8.
46. Whitehouse (1980).
47. Creswell (1940), pp.45–8, fig.33.
48. Creswell (1940), pp.171–96.
49. Ghirshman (1947–8), Rougeule (1984).
50. Al-Shafi'i proposed that an absolute figure of one square metre was required by each adult for prayer, to be calculated including the structural and circulation areas of the mosque (*al-'Imāra al-'Arabiyya*, pp.497–8). If this were the case, then the mosque, as first built in the Umayyad period, would have accommodated a maximum of about 2,200; however, it would be unwise to place too much reliance on the figure.
51. Ṭabarī 3.467.

Notes To Chapter 7

1. Northedge (1977–8, 1980).
2. Almagro (1983a); Olávarri (1985).
3. For a review of A. Almagro (1983a), *El Palacio Omeya de Amman*, by this author, see *BSOAS* 50 (1987), pp.553–5. This author would like to record his indebtedness for the information on measurements in the above volume, which made possible the reconstruction of the exterior of the Reception Hall in fig.39.
4. Butler (1907–19), pl.1, pp.41–3.
5. Conder (1889), p.63.
6. Almagro (1983b) has published many of the unpublished drawings of the Italian Mission; however, regrettably he omitted the drawings of this area, on the grounds that they had been superseded by his own work.
7. Bartoccini (1934).
8. Almagro's original interpretation can be read in Almagro and Almagro (1976).
9. Dornemann (1970), pp.50, 233; Dornemann (1983), fig.5.
10. Almagro (1983a), p.121, fig.29.
11. Bartoccini (1933), tav. 4.12.
12. Almagro (1983a), pp.123–4, figs 30–1.
13. Olávarri-Goicoechea (1985), fig.4.
14. Butler (1907–19), pl.1, pp.41–3, ill.26.
15. Bartoccini (1934).
16. Zayadine (1969), pp.34ff.
17. Segal (1975), pp.iii, vi; Segal (1988).
18. Butler (1907–19), pl.6.
19. Gatier (1986), pp.48–9, no.24.
20. Butler (1907–19), pl.1, p.43.
21. Almagro (1983a, p.59) interprets the overall plan rather differently, in that he supposes that there was a further enclosure wall to the south of the Reception Hall. The basis of this idea is a substantial east–west wall excavated by Dr Fawzi Zayadine in Area A. However this wall is dated by Dr Zayadine to the Early Roman period. It seems more likely that the outer enclosure of the palace was in fact the contemporary Umayyad fortification wall.

22. Cf. also Almagro (1983a), Lám. 1.b., for an air photograph of 1939.
23. The Spanish Archaeological Mission began excavations in Building 7 in 1989.
24. Almagro places the mosque on the west side of the Reception Hall (Almagro 1983a, fig.2). There is a modern mosque belonging to the army and police on this site, but there is no other evidence known to the author which would substantiate this placement.
25. Creswell (1940), p.113; Almagro and Olávarri (1982), p.307; Almagro (1983a), p.60. The layout of the Umayyad buildings may well have been influenced by the pattern of the Roman complex, when a gate probably stood on the site of the Reception Hall.
26. Clemen (1919), vol. 2, p.178.
27. Sources of information on the Reception Hall not otherwise mentioned in this section: C. R. Conder, *PEFQS* (1882), pp.100–2; Conder (1882), *Heth and Moab*, pp.157–9; Thomsen, *The Land and the Book*, vol. 3, pp.617–9; Phene Spiers, *Architecture East and West*, pp.83–8; Gayet, *L'Art Persan*, pp.112–6; Riegl, *Altorientalische Teppiche*, pp.138–9; Kondakov, *Arkheologicheskoe Puteshostvie po Sirii i Palestiniye*, pp.127–35; Schulz and Strzygowski (1904), pp.350–3; van Berchem, *Journal des Savants* (1905), pp.475–6; Strzygowski, *Die Persische Trompenkuppel*, p.10, *Asiens Bildende Kunst*, pp.107–9, 198, *Ancien Art Chrétien de Syrie*, p.109; Clemen (1919), vol. 2, p.178; Harding (1967), p.67.
28. Buckingham (1821), pp.68–9.
29. Tristram (1865), pp.548–9.
30. Northey (1872), p.67.
31. Lewis (1882), pp.113–5.
32. Dieulafoy (1884–9), pp.100–4.
33. Warren (1977).
34. Godard (1951).
35. Brunnow and Domaszewski (1905), vol. 2, p.216.
36. Butler (1907–19), pl.1, ill.26.
37. *EI*[1] s.v. Architecture.
38. Creswell (1940), pp.113–14.
39. Almagro and Almargo (1976).
40. Almagro and Olávarri (1982); Almagro (1983a).
41. Rivoira (1918), pp.119–20.
42. Diez (1915), p.28.
43. Bell (1909), p.140.
44. Herzfeld (1942), p.14.
45. Gaube (1977).
46. Iṣṭakhrī, p.259; Creswell (1940), pp.3–4.
47. Toueir (1982).
48. Bartoccini (1933), p.13.
49. Olávarri (1985), Lám. 7.
50. Warren (1977), p.52.
51. Hamilton (1959), fig.48.
52. Creswell (1940), p.114.
53. Jones and Michell (1972).
54. The *tesserae* of a mosaic are stuck into a bed of fine mortar, and this is laid over a make-up of *terra rossa* (field inspection of mosaics at Mt Nebo). A floor of paving stones at Ḥammām al-Sarakh has the same foundation of fine mortar.
55. Conder (1889), pp.60–1; Bartoccini (1933), tav. VII.20.
56. This doorway now no longer exists; it was filled up in the course of the conservation work carried out by the Spanish Archaeological Mission.
57. Traces of mortar can be seen adhering to the walls inside the entrance to the staircase.
58. Merrill (1881), p.264.
59. Hamilton (1946b).
60. Hamilton (1959), p.40.
61. Carlier and Morin (1987).
62. Roaf (1978).
63. Abel (1926); Chen (1980). Much of the western Roman empire used the Attic foot of 29.6 cm; it may be that Abel's measurement represents a version of the Attic foot.
64. Roaf (1978). The discussion here is deliberately imprecise in identifying an exact length of unit, for there was undoubtedly variability within a range.
The 51.5–52.5cm cubit is the same as that used in 'Abbāsid Iraq (see Northedge 1990a for more detail).
65. Almagro (1983a, pp.88–91) proposed a scheme based upon a cubit of about 50 cm. The complexities and odd numbers produced by this scheme place a question mark over its correctness.
66. On the west facade the upper masonry has been rebuilt, and has cut off the central buttress.
67. Almagro (1983a), figs.9–10.
68. Almagro and Olávarri (1982), fig.5; Almagro (1983a), p.83.
69. Gaube (1977), taf. 5c; Urice (1987), fig.116.
70. The niches average 52 cm wide, which is approximately equivalent to one cubit. The facades between the buttresses measure 5.3 and 5.4m in width, probably a little over ten cubits.
71. Almagro (1983a), fig.19, Bartoccini (1933), p.14, no.c, tav. viii.
72. Almagro (1983a), figs 9–10.
73. Grabar et al. (1978), figs 16D, 26D.
74. Hamilton (1959), pl.12.5.
75. One block of this type of cornice was found outside the north door; this suggests that the north facade did have this type of cornice.
76. For similar merlons in stucco with a half-palmette scroll, see Hamilton (1959), fig.129.
77. Only two merlons were recovered from the excavations of the Great Mosque of Siraf, a building maintained for public use for a much longer period (Whitehouse 1980).
78. Bartoccini (1933), p.13.
79. E.g. Buckingham (1821), pp.68–9; Conder (1889), p.61; Creswell (1940), pp.113–14.
80. Gaube (1977), pp.56f.
81. Almagro and Olávarri (1982), pp.310–11; Almagro (1983a), p.86, cf. especially fig.13. Although Almagro's text allows for a variety of possibilities, only the solution of a stone dome is presented graphically, in seven drawings.
82. Almagro and Olávarri (1982), fig.9.
83. Creswell (1940), pp.233–5.
84. Hamilton (1959), fig.48.
85. In later Islamic architecture a four-*īwān* plan could have a covered central space.
86. Pope and Ackerman (1938), fig.155.
87. Andrae and Lenzen (1933).
88. Fischer (1974), vol. 2, pp.109–10.
89. Spanner and Guyer (1926), pp.42–4; Sauvaget (1939b), pp.115–20.
90. Creswell (1940), p.114.

91. Creswell (1940), p.113; Fehérvári (1974); van Berchem in *EI*[1] s.v. Architecture; Herzfeld (1942), p.14; Warren (1977).
92. Andrae and Lenzen (1933), pp.25–54, pls 9–11.
93. Knudstad (1968), pp.95–106.
94. Kröger (1982), p.93.
95. Mustafa (1956).
96. Majhul (1972).
97. Ghirshman (1938), pp.15–17; Ghirshman (1956).
98. Keall (1974), p.130.
99. Godard (1965), p.282 n.2; cf. also Herrmann (1977), p.103; Keall (1974), p.129.
100. Kröger (1982), p.195.
101. Bartoccini (1934), p.277, ill.5.
102. The plan was confirmed by Spanish excavation.
103. Northedge (1980), p.146.
104. Almagro and Olávarri (1982), fig.3; Almagro (1983a), figs 38–9.
105. The layout of the west range has been recently rebuilt by the Spanish Archaeological Mission. It is not known whether they had excavation evidence for the positions of the walls.
106. Bartoccini (1930), p.20, pl.4.1.
107. Bartoccini (1934), p.277, ill.4.
108. Northedge (1977–8), pp.9–10; Northedge (1980), pp.148–52.
109. Almagro and Olávarri (1982), pp.312–15; Almagro (1983a), pp.153–68; Olávarri (1985).
110. Almagro also supposed that there was a colonnade along the south side of the court (Almagro 1983a, pl.4). At present there is no evidence for this.
111. Almagro (1983a), pp.156–8, fig.43.
112. Almagro (1983a), fig.46.
113. Carlier (1989), ills 10–11.
114. Almagro (1983a), fig.44.
115. Almagro (1983a), fig.45. The pattern of half-palmettes is not evident on the actual block, as it is to be seen today.
116. Creswell (1940), figs 49–50. Arrow-slit decoration can be found as far back as the Median site of Nūsh-i Jān.
117. Northedge (1980).
118. Almagro (1983a), fig.43.
119. Reuther (1912).
120. There is a bond in the masonry, indicating the existence of a raised facade along the long sides of the court.
121. The *īwān* facades at Ukhayḍir, incidentally, thus looked more like the interior facades of the Reception Hall at 'Ammān than was previously thought.
122. 'Abd al-Khāliq (1985–6), p.122.
123. The Bāb al-'Āmma was probably originally a two-storey structure.
124. The merlon found is identical to the single example from the Reception Hall. A further type of fragment from the North Building area (NB/16–8: three examples), with two engaged colonnettes, is again identical to block C from Registers 1 and 3 of the Reception Hall; the blocks may have migrated from that building. The merlon may also actually belong to the Reception Hall.
125. Almagro (1983a), fig.43.
126. Urice (1987), fig.137.
127. Schlumberger (1978), pl.56a.
128. These arches disappeared in the course of the Spanish excavations.
129. Olávarri (1985), fig.53.
130. Conder (1889), p.63.
131. Moorey (1978), pp.134–7.
132. Schmidt (1937), pp.327–50.
133. Mustafa (1956).
134. Finster and Schmidt (1976), pp.57–150.
135. Creswell (1940), pp.66–7.
136. Creswell (1940), pp.232–5.
137. Creswell (1940), figs 49–50.
138. Butler (1907–19), pl.3, ills. 141, 147, 152, 167, 178.
139. Harding (1951a), fig.3.
140. Northedge (1980), p.152.
141. Olávarri (1985), p.17, fig.11.
142. Although no clear date for the introduction of red-painted ware has been established, it is clear that there are also earlier phases of Umayyad pottery. The only other Umayyad *quṣūr* known to the author in which red-painted ware is found related to the period of construction, rather than occupation, are Mshattā and Ṭūba, both accepted as belonging to the end of the period.
143. Grabar (1987).
144. Mustafa (1956), fig.1.
145. Creswell (1940), p.98.
146. Finster and Schmidt (1976), taf.28a.
147. Creswell (1940), pl.15d, 16a.
148. Jaussen and Savignac (1922), pls xxvi.3, xxxi, xxxiii–iv; Urice (1987), *passim*.
149. There may be some overlap between the panels recorded from photographs in Register 3, and the fallen blocks still in existence. The maximum possible overlap is six.
150. The scheme of the sparsely decorated Qaṣr Kharāna could be described as nearly complete, although the north side was not finished (Urice 1987). At Quṣayr 'Amra, famous for the complete preservation of its frescoes, nothing has in fact survived below the height and reach of a man. In the Qubbat al-Sakhra, the original exterior decoration has disappeared, and substantial parts of the interior decoration have been reworked. At Khirbat al-Mafjar and at Qaṣr al-Ḥayr al-Gharbī probably quite a high proportion of the stucco decoration has survived, but it is not possible to quantify it. At Mshattā the building is too unfinished to be sure how much decoration was intended. One can suggest therefore that a higher proportion only survives at Quṣayr 'Amra and Qaṣr al-Kharāna.
151. The same numbering system is employed as in Gaube's study of the Hall: this is intended to facilitate comparison (Gaube 1977). However, the lettering of the panels is different, as more detail appeared to be necessary.
152. Pope and Ackerman (1938), pp.613f.; Hamilton (1959), p.165.
153. cf. Butler (1907–19), *passim* for local acanthus styles. Note especially pl.6, ill.336, Temple of Dushare at Sī'.
154. E.g. Hamilton (1959), pl.xx.i; Hamilton (1946a), fig.7; Bisheh (1989), taf.61.
155. Schmidt (1937), pls 72, 73, 75, 78.
156. Thompson (1976), pp.76–8.
157. Kröger (1982), *passim*.
158. Kröger (1982), taf.77.2c.
159. Gaube (1977), taf. 5c; Urice (1987), fig.116.
160. Khirbat al-Mafjar (Hamilton 1959): stone – figs 85, 87, 89; stucco – figs 122, 126j, 176b–c, pl.xiv.4, xx.1.

161. Damascus Museum; Schlumberger (1939b).
162. Hamilton (1946a), fig.10.
163. Creswell (1940), pls 87–9.
164. Talbot-Rice (1934), fig.12.
165. Finster and Schmidt (1976), taf. 32–5.
166. Safar (1945), pls xv–i.
167. E.g. Lane (1947), pl.8.
168. Herzfeld (1923), Orn. 30 and 273.
169. Kröger (1982), p.262.
170. Hamilton (1959), pl.xi.6.
171. Thompson (1976), pl.xii.2.
172. Safar (1945), fig.xv–i.
173. Hamilton (1959), fig.126.j.
174. Creswell (1940), pl.89c.
175. Talbot-Rice (1934), fig.12.
176. Herzfeld (1923), Orn. 273.
177. cf. Hamilton (1959), figs 89, 111, 147; Thompson (1976), pl.xii.2, 3; Kröger (1982), Abb. 137, where it is called a pomegranate motif.
178. Schmidt (1937), pl.72.
179. Thompson (1976), pl.xii.3, xviii.3.
180. Gaube (1977), taf. 5c; Urice (1987), fig.116.
181. Chal Tarkhan (Thompson 1976, pl.xvi), Tepe Hissar (Schmidt 1937, pl.lxxviii). Kish (Pope and Ackerman 1938, fig.194b), Ctesiphon (Kröger 1982, nos 74, 232–3).
182. Hamilton (1959), fig.89 bis, 176b and c; pl.xiv.4, xx.1.
183. Finster and Schmidt (1976), Abb. 8.
184. Abd ul-Haqq and Salibi (1951), ill.10.
185. Herzfeld (1923), Orn. 36.
186. Pope and Ackerman (1938), fig.257a.
187. Hamilton (1946a), fig.6.
188. Kröger (1982), no.185.
189. Hamilton (1959), fig.122.
190. Thompson (1976), pl.xi.2.
191. Cf. note 167.
192. Jenkins (1982), p.22
193. Hamilton (1959), pl.xxxiii.
194. Thompson (1976), 74f.
195. Thompson (1976), pls xiii.3, 6, xviii.5, xix.7.
196. Kröger (1982), taf.77.1.
197. Kröger (1982), taf.96.3, 97.1.
198. Hamilton (1959), pl.xliii.1., xix.4.
199. Pope and Ackerman (1938), fig.184a.
200. Brunnow and Domaszewski (1905), vol. 2, p.202, Abb. 795.
201. Cf. Butler (1907–19), pls 3–7, especially vine ornamentation at al-Umtaiyeh (ill.68), Subheh (ill.90), and Damit al-ʻAlya (ill.376).
202. Butler (1907–19), pl.6., ill.326–7, 327.
203. Leaves in vine ornament are found in Parthian stucco, e.g. Qalʻeh-i Yazdigird (Keall et al. 1980, fig.6). Equally in early ʻAbbāsid stuccoes, vine leaves are a dominant part of the ornament.
204. Thompson (1976), pls x.3–4, xxiv.
205. Pope and Ackerman (1938), fig.193b–c.
206. Kröger (1982), no.130.
207. E.g. Strzygowski (1930), p.109.
208. Cf. Kröger (1982), no.134.
209. Majhul (1972), pp.243–6, ill.5.
210. Otto-Dorn (1957), Abb. 10.
211. Pope and Ackerman (1938), fig.188f.
212. Otto-Dorn (1957), Abb. 1–2.
213. Creswell (1969), fig.89c.
214. Kröger (1982), nos 50, 160.
215. Thompson (1976), pl.iv.3.
216. Creswell (1940), pl.1.
217. Hamilton (1959), pl.lxv.
218. Gaube (1974a), taf. x.7.
219. Thompson (1976), pp.67f., pl xii.1, xiv.8, xvii.4.
220. Schmidt (1937), pl.lxxvii.
221. Kröger (1982), nos 232–3, 245.
222. Keall et al. (1980), fig.18.
223. Thompson (1976), pl.xiv.
224. Hamilton (1959), fig.148.
225. On exhibition in the Damascus Museum.
226. Bisheh (1989), taf.62a.
227. Kröger (1982), nos 2, 61.
228. Pope and Ackerman (1938), fig.182.
229. Levi (1948), pls.ii.b–c, ix.a, xciii, xcv.a, xcvii, xcvii.e, xcviii.f, c, ci, cii, cxx.a, cxx.i, cxxxiii.d.
230. Kraeling (1938), pl.lxii.
231. Avi Yonah (1981), p.288, type J5.
232. Hamilton (1959), pl.lxxxi.
233. Pope and Ackerman (1938), fig. 182a.
234. Thompson (1976), p.79, pl.xiv.1, 2, xvii.2.
235. Kröger (1982), nos 50, 215.
236. Kröger (1982), no.246.
237. Hamilton (1959), p.214, fig.162.
238. Gaube (1977), taf. 7h.
239. Thompson (1976), pl.xiii.6.
240. Thompson (1976), pp.83–6.
241. E.g. Lloyd (1978), fig.19.
242. Hamilton (1959), figs 170, 176.
243. Herzfeld (1923), orn.169, 245.
244. Hamilton (1949), pl.i, liv, lvii.
245. Pope and Ackerman (1938), pl.232.
246. Pope and Ackerman (1938), fig.310.
247. Kraeling et al. (1938), pl.lxxx.h; Avi Yonah (1981), p.288, type J3; Hamilton (1959), pl.xc.
248. Khirbat al-Mafjar (Hamilton 1959): Round-lobed rosettes: stucco – fig.120, pls.xxxix.3, xliii.2, liii.1, lx; stone – pl.xviii. Rosettes with four spike petals: stucco – fig.126a; painted – fig.182, 256, pl.xiii.1. Rosettes with spike petals: stucco – fig.126a; painted – fig.128.1–2, pl.xxxi–iii, xxxix.1.
249. Chal Tarkhan (Thompson 1976): Main Palace – pl.xiii.3 and 5, xiv.10, 11, 13, xx.1; Subsidiary Palace: pl.xvii.3 and 5, xviii.2.
250. Pope and Ackerman (1938), pl.146b.
251. Pope and Ackerman (1938), pl.204.
252. Ghirshman (1938), pl.xiv.2.
253. Schmidt (1937), pl.lxxix.
254. Kröger (1982), no.160.
255. Kröger (1982), no.240.
256. Avi Yonah (1981), pl.17.2.
257. Butler (1907–19), Div. II Sect. A pl.1, ill.5.3.
258. Gaube (1974a), pp.82–4, taf. vii.
259. Creswell (1969), pl.54b.
260. Keall et al. (1980), fig. 18.1.
261. Hamilton (1959), pl.xliii.2.
262. Kröger (1982), nos 110, 164.
263. Pope and Ackerman (1938), fig.186, 188a.

264. Kröger (1982), nos 87–8.
265. Schmidt (1937), pl.lxxii.
266. Gaube (1977), taf. 7c.
267. Schmidt (1937), pl.lxxv.
268. Hamilton (1959), fig.166, 176.h; pls xxx, xxxv.7.
269. Kröger (1982), nos 234–40.
270. Thompson (1976), pl.xii.2, xv.4, xvi.3.
271. Gaube (1977), abb. 9; Urice (1987), figs 136 and 140.
272. Facade: Damascus Museum.
273. Kröger (1982), nos 7, 110.
274. Kröger (1982), taf. 91.2–6.
275. Mustafa (1954), fig.7.
276. Related to this arrangement, the Ab panels of SN/12 and SN/13, which might originally have been part of the same block, have half-rosettes flanking the top rosette, suggesting an alternative method of flanking a line of smaller rosettes. However, the surviving fragments are too small for a confident conclusion.
277. Thompson (1976), pls.xxii.1, xxiv.1.
278. Kröger (1982), no.160.
279. Gaube (1974a), taf.vii.
280. Hamilton (1959), pl.lxviii.
281. Hamilton (1959), pl.lx.
282. Gaube (1977), abb. 2 shows a rosette scroll at Niche 61, but this is inaccurately drawn.
283. cf. Pope and Ackerman (1938), pl.171c.
284. Creswell (1969), fig.331.
285. Hamilton (1959), figs 131–2, pls.xxxi–iii.
286. Talbot-Rice (1934), fig. 3.
287. Dieulafoy (1884–9), p.5, fig.92.
288. Kröger (1982), no.71.
289. Damascus Museum.
290. Creswell (1969), pls.119–136.
291. The main sources of comparison for local Graeco-Roman ornament are: Levi (1948), *Antioch Mosaic Pavements*; Avi Yonah (1981), *Art in Ancient Palestine*, containing his earlier series of articles: *Mosaic Pavements in Palestine*, and *Oriental Elements in Palestinian Art*; Butler (1913–19), *Publications of the Princeton Archaeological Expedition to Syria*.
292. Hamilton (1959), pp.156f.
293. Moorey (1978), p.136.
294. Schmidt (1937), pp.387f.; Moorey (1978), pp.139–40.
295. Kröger (1982), pp.255ff.
296. Thompson (1976), Chapter 2.
297. Kröger (1982), pp.201, 256, 263.
298. Early 'Abbāsid stuccoes added to the Umayyad construction in Sector 6 of the Large Enclosure (Grabar et al. 1978, figs 139, 142).
299. 'Abd al-Haqq and Salibi (1951).
300. Herzfeld (1923); DGA (1940).
301. Hamilton (1946a), fig.6.
302. Brown (1971), p.104.
303. Krencker et al. (1923), pp.130–50.
304. Creswell (1969), pp.156–65.
305. Creswell (1969), pp.65–131, 373–80.
306. Mustafa (1956).
307. Creswell (1969), pp.578–606.
308. The earliest known Umayyad palace in Syria is reported to have been the Qubbat al-Khaḍrā' of Mu'āwiya in Damascus, between 23/644 and 35/656 (Creswell 1969, pp.40–1). The earliest archaeological evidence of Umayyad 'palatial' construction appears to be Qaṣr al-Kharāna (Urice 1987; Abbott 1946).
309. Hamilton (1959).
310. Creswell (1969), pp.607–13.
311. Creswell (1969), pp.498–502.
312. Grabar et al. (1978), Chapter 3.
313. Otto-Dorn (1957).
314. Schlumberger (1939, 1986).
315. Grabar et al. (1978), Chapter 2.
316. Creswell (1940), pp.49–98. See this source for other bibliography.
317. The gate block at Mshattā seems not to have been built above two courses, and one cannot say how it might have been finished.
318. Lassner (1970), p.53.
319. *Pace* Creswell's view that the plan had four *īwāns*.
320. For House no.1, see 'Abd al-Fattah (1984). A partial plan of House no.3 appears in Hanīn (1985–6).
321. Creswell (1969), pp.515–18.
322. Creswell (1969), p.518. It is evident that while Creswell's 'Syrian *bayt*' corresponds to a complete residential unit, the concept of the 'Persian *bayt*' does not. A residential unit in Iraq always included a courtyard.
323. Herzfeld (1948), Luftbildaufnahme I; Northedge (1990b).
324. Creswell (1940), fig.194. The use of the name 'Jawsaq al-Khāqānī' as an overall term for the main caliphal palace complex at Sāmarrā' by Herzfeld and Creswell is almost certainly erroneous, see the author's forthcoming *Historical Topography of Sāmarrā'*.
325. Pope and Ackerman (1938), figs 153–4.
326. Cf. *Aghānī*: 4.81.
327. Goodchild (1960).
328. Paruck (1924), p.144.
329. Ibn al-Nadīm: 24.
330. Ṭabarī: 2.1468–9.
331. Seats at the entrance are known at Khirbat al-Mafjar (Hamilton 1959, pl.iii), and Qaṣr al-Ḥayr al-Gharbī (Creswell 1969, pl.86c), apart from 'Ammān itself. Similar seats in the entrance with quarter-circular arm-rests are to be seen at Sāmarrā' in the excavated House no.1 in *Shāri' al-A'ẓam* ('Abd al-Fattah 1984).
332. van Berchem quoted by Creswell (1969), p.423.
333. Creswell (1969), pp.622–36.
334. Creswell (1969), pp.447–8; Warren (1977).
335. Kraeling (1938), pp.68, 86.
336. Grabar (1954a).
337. Ettinghausen (1972).
338. al-'Ush (1972).
339. Zayadine, Najjar and Greene (1987), p.304.
340. The best description of Umayyad pottery from Iraq is based on material from Tulūl al-Ukhayḍir (Finster and Schmidt 1976). A further short discussion may be found in Northedge, Bamber and Roaf (1988), pp.77–82.
341. Balādhurī: 6–7; Ṭabarī: 2.1194; Creswell (1969), pp.231–9.
342. *Kitāb al-Aghānī*: 3.85.
343. Gaube (1977); Grabar et al. (1978), p.31; Urice (1987).
344. Gaube (1977), Abb. 9–11, taf. 5c; Urice (1987).
345. Creswell (1969), fig.565.
346. Hamilton (1953).

347. Bisheh (1980).
348. Otto-Dorn (1957).
349. Finster and Schmidt (1976).
350. Majhul (1972).
351. Kröger (1982).
352. Thompson (1976).
353. Schmidt (1937).
354. Creswell (1969), p.322.
355. Hamilton (1946a).
356. Creswell (1969), pl.120–36.
357. Creswell (1969), pl.138.
358. Gaube (1977), taf. 7; Carlier (1989), ill.8.
359. Creswell (1969), p.544.
360. Hamilton (1959), pp.228–32, pl.lv.1, 5.
361. Hamilton (1959), p.157.
362. Creswell (1969), pl.86d.
363. E.g. Hamilton (1959), pl.xxxvi.6–7.
364. Schlumberger (1946–8), p.93.
365. Stern (1971); Busse (1973); Bosworth (1973).
366. Crone (1980), pp.43–4, Appendices III–IV.
367. Crone (1980), App. IV no.58; Ṭabarī: 2.1529, 3.52.
368. Ṭabarī: 3.16, 51, 64, 65.
369. Wellhausen (1927), pp.493–4.
370. *EI*[2]: s.v. Bishr ibn Marwān.
371. *EI*[2]: s.v. Maslama ibn 'Abd al-Malik.
372. Derenk (1974); Hillenbrand (1982).
373. Hamilton (1969).
374. Mas'ūdī, *Murūj*: 6.12.
375. Grabar (1954a), pp.339–41; Ettinghausen (1972), pp.30–33; Hillenbrand (1982), p.12.
376. Gibb (1962), p.63.
377. Mas'ūdī, *Tanbīh*: 106.
378. Ibn al-Nadīm: 117.
379. *Aghānī*: 4.125.
380. *Aghānī*: 4.121.
381. Ṭabarī 2.1874.
382. Grabar (1954b).
383. *EI*[2]: s.v. 'Abd al-Ḥamīd ibn Yaḥyā.
384. al-'Askarī, *Dīwān al-Ma'ānī*: 2.89, quoted in *EI*[2]: s.v. 'Abd al-Ḥamīd ibn Yaḥyā.
385. Jahshiyārī: 74–78; *EI*[2]: s.v. 'Abd al-Ḥamīd ibn Yaḥyā.
386. Gibb (1962), p.65.

Chapter 8

1. Dornemann (1983), p.19.
2. DoA (1975), pp.13–14.
3. Dornemann (1983), pp.89, 93.
4. Information supplied by F. Zayadine, 1989.
5. Dornemann (1983), pp.91–3.
6. Zayadine (1973), p.17.
7. 2 Samuel:10–12.
8. Zayadine (1973), p.17.
9. Dornemann (1983), p.93.
10. Conder (1889), pp.29ff.
11. Butler (1907), p.37.
12. *'ingentes murorum firmitate cautissimas'*, Ammianus Marcellinus XIV. 8. 13.
13. E.g. Zayadine (1973); Hadidi (1978), p.216.
14. Bennett and Northedge (1977–8).
15. Al-Aḥwas al-Anṣarī, *Dīwān*, no.91.
16. Preliminary results of this work and a summary discussion of the fortification sequence were first published by Northedge (1983).
17. For a description of the techniques of rectified photography see Dallas (1980). Elevation drawings of the Northern Temple platform walls were not attempted, as certain of these had already been photogrammetrically surveyed by the Spanish Mission, see Almagro (1983a), pls 5–7.
18. Tower A was certainly cleared by November 1943. See Almagro (1983a), p.121, pl.31a [Room III].
19. Northedge (1980), p.138.
20. Almagro (1983a), p.58 [Room XI].
21. Almagro (1983a), pp.53–4, pl.7.
22. The plan of the Northern Temple enclosure published by Butler shows towers in these positions (fig.30).
23. Almagro (1983a), pp.54–5, pl.5.
24. PEF photograph no.551.
25. Almagro (1983a), p.55, pl.5.
26. Almagro (1983a), p.55, pl.6.
27. Bartoccini (1934), pp.275–8.
28. Almagro (1983a, pp.55, 58) believes the gate-towers to be contemporary Roman structures (i.e. Period 1) and that Gate A was only reused, not built, by the Umayyads (Period 3).
29. Preliminary results of these excavations were first published by Bennett and Northedge (1977–8) and Bennett (1979b).
30. Preliminary results of the excavations were first published by Northedge (1979b).
31. Northedge (1979b).
32. Conder (1889), pp.33–4. The tower appears in the background of PEF photographs no.546 and no.548, taken in 1881 and 1882 respectively. See pl.2b in this volume
33. Conder (1889), pp.33–4.
34. Special Survey Plan of Amman, 1881 (Conder 1889).
35. Butler (1907–19), pl.1, pp.34, 45.
36. Dornemann (1969); Gatier (1986), p.44, no.18.
37. The revetment has recently been prone to collapse.
38. Harding (1950).
39. Zayadine (1973), pp.21–2; Zayadine, Humbert and Najjar (1989).
40. This hypothesis has been confirmed in Zayadine and Humbert's excavations (Zayadine, Humbert and Najjar 1989).
41. Zayadine (1973), pp.21–2.
42. Bartoccini (1934), p.278.
43. Conder (1889).
44. E.g. Butler (1907), ill.25.
45. Zayadine pers. comm. (1977).
46. Dornemann (1969).
47. Conder (1889), p.31.
48. Zayadine (1973), p.22, and pers. comm. (1977); Zayadine, Humbert and Najjar (1989).
49. Ammianus Marcellinus XIV. 8. 13.
50. The temple dedication inscription has long been assigned to the reign of Marcus Aurelius (AD 161–180) but it has now been refined, not only to the co-emperorship of Marcus Aurelius and Lucius Verus (AD 161–169) (Littmann et al. 1921, inscr. 4) but to the governorship of Publius Iulius Geminius Marcianus, datable to AD 161–166 (Gatier 1986,

p.44, no.18). See Bowsher in Chapter 9.
51. Ammianus Marcellinus XIV. 8. 13.
52. See Chapter 10.
53. Zayadine (1973), p.25.
54. Hadidi (1974), p.79; Russell (1980); Amiran (1950–51), p.225.
55. Piccirillo (1988).
56. Von Gerkan (1939), p.61.
57. Reuther (1938), p.573.
58. Parr (1965), pp.255–6.
59. Smith (1982), pp.331–2.
60. Lander (1984), pp.17–18.
61. Gawlikowski (1974), p.236.
62. Kraeling et al.(1938), pp.41–2.
63. Seigne (1986), pp.55, 59.
64. Parker (1979), pp.219–22.
65. Johnson (1983), p.29.
66. Killick (1983), p.112, and pers. comm. (1983). The controversial dating is re-stated, with reservations, in Killick (1986). The towers at Udhruḥ must represent secondary construction as they do not bond with the curtain (Parker 1986, p.98).
67. Littmann et al. (1921), p.131, inscr. 232.
68. De Vries (1982), p.111; (1986).
69. Kennedy (1982), pp.113–21; Lander (1984), pp.136–8.
70. Bisheh (1980), pp.61–2; Kennedy (1982), pp.17–53; Lander (1984), pp.138–9.
71. Kennedy (1982), pp.107–13.
72. Lander (1984), pp.144–7.
73. Oates (1968), pp.85–6.
74. M. Gawlikowski, pers. comm. (1983).
75. The hypothesis was first suggested by Parker (1976), following surface sherd collection at a number of sites, and is now largely confirmed by recent research. For a detailed discussion of the evidence, see Parker (1986, pp.135–43). A cautionary note has, however, been sounded by Graf (1978, p.13), regarding the pottery dates on which Parker's work is based. The evidence could relate to earlier construction efforts in the late 3rd century, such as those which presumably accompanied Aurelian's reorganization of the frontier after 273, or the new work erected by the Illyrian emperors.
76. De Vries (1987).
77. Killick (1983, 1986).
78. Lander (1984), pp.223, 227.
79. Lander's Category B fan-shaped towers (Lander 1984, p.248).
80. Parker (1985), p.13.
81. Harper (1977).
82. Gawlikowski (1974), p.231.
83. Oates (1968), pp.100, 103.
84. Sites such as these are conveniently illustrated by Kennedy (1982, p.76), and the evidence is summarized in Parker (1986).
85. Bawden et al. (1980), p.162.
86. Al-Ansary (1982), p.34.
87. See Mango (1976). Foundations and/or restorations are mainly the work of Justinian, though some fortifications may belong to the slightly earlier reign of Anastasius (Karnapp 1976, pp.51–3; Croke and Crow 1983).
88. Pringle (1981), pp.140, 157–8.
89. Reuther (1938), p.573.
90. Ghirshman (1954), p.322.
91. Whitehouse (1974), pp.7–8.
92. Boucharlat (1977), p.329.
93. Stern (1946), p.85.
94. Creswell (1940), pp.50–100; (1958), pp.192–203.
95. Creswell (1940), pp.39–45; Khalaf (1985).
96. Northedge and Falkner (1987).
97. Creswell (1940), pp.10–14.
98. Creswell (1940), pp.271–3. Creswell does not consider the buttresses original, but they may well have belonged to the Aghlabid construction. Another probable Aghlabid site where square towers dominate is that at Sfax, also in Tunisia (Marçais 1954, pp.35–6).
99. Hellenkemper (1976), pp.191–201, 380; Hellenkemper (1990).
100. Briggs (1924), pp.72–3.
101. Ibn Shaddād: 83–5.
102. Ibn Shaddād: 86–91; Johns (1932).
103. Johns (1931).
104. Saouaf (1958).
105. Creswell (1952), pp.122–3.
106. Abel (1956); Aalund et al. (1990).
107. Reasons for the appearance of round-fronted towers are debatable. De Vries' suggestion that the Romans may have learned from earlier Parthian fortifications (De Vries 1987, p.350) has to be set against Lander's cautionary observation that the builders of sites such as Ain Sinu II were legionaries trained in the West, with perhaps more experience of experimentation with fortification design (Lander 1984, p.135).
108. It was Creswell's view that Umayyad palace architecture adopted the square fort plan tradition of Rome and early Byzantium, the Umayyad caliphs having been influenced by their re-occupation of *limes* forts (Creswell 1952, pp.90–91). Stern took the argument one stage further, acknowledging that the shapes and dimensions of the palaces followed those of Roman and early Byzantine forts, but stressing that the use of small, round-fronted, buttress-like towers was derived from Sasanian models (Stern 1946, p.85). The similarity between the Umayyad palaces and Sasanian forts is striking. A further proposal is that round-fronted towers may have been elements transmitted from Iran in the pre-Islamic period via the semi-nomadic Arab Ghassanids (Scerrato 1976, p.26).
109. Amongst the new garrison cities (*amṣār*) of Iraq, Wāsiṭ was fortified, but Kūfa and Baṣra were not defended until the 'Abbāsid period (Ṭabarī 2, 1905). Mosul was fortified in the Umayyad period (al-Balādhurī: 332; Diwachi 1947).

Chapter 9

1. Seetzen (1854) p.397. Although Seetzen was the 'discoverer' of many sites in the region, his full accounts were not published until half a century later.
2. Burckhardt 1822: 359. Burckhardt's plan appears opposite p.357.
3. Buckingham 1821: 70f.
4. Gatier 1986: 44, no.18, frag. C.
5. Laborde 1837: 99.
6. Robinson 1837: 175.
7. Tristram 1865: 548.
8. De Saulcy 1865: 246. De Saulcy's plan, opposite p.244,

shows a rectangular building with three columns at the eastern end.

9. That is, fragments TB.8 and TB.9, Appendix B.
10. Northey 1872: 67. Warren himself made little mention of the temple (*PEFQS* 1868: 295).
11. Merrill 1881: 264.
12. Oliphant 1880: 261.
13. Conder 1889: 31f.
14. Butler (1907–19) pl.1 pp.39f.
15. Note also the photographs published by Butler (1907–19, p.40, ill.25), and Bartoccini, pre-excavation, looking north-east (1938, tav. 1, no.1).
16. Bartoccini (1932, 1938); Almagro (1983b).
17. Work in progress can be seen in Bartoccini 1932: 17, Tav. 1, fig.1; p.20, Tav. IV, fig.1.
18. The archaeological results were never published, although a report by Dornemann exists in the Department of Antiquities Registration Centre, from which some extracts were published by him in 1983. Fakharani however, published a most detailed architectural description with a comprehensive plan in 1975. A 'final report' of the excavations was still expected in 1978 (Hadidi 1978: fn. 28).
19. Fakharani 1975.
20. Preliminary reports were published by Northedge in 1983, with some further details in his unpublished doctoral thesis of 1984. The plan reproduced here is by architect Richard Brotherton, and the architectural drawings by Judith MacKenzie. Further references here are to Wood, this volume, Chapter 8.
21. This work was begun under the direction of R. H. Dornemann and Khair Yassine, subsequently continued by Muhammad Najjar and (the late) Kenneth W. Russell. At the time of writing, only a note of this work has been published in *ACOR Newsletter* no.5 (November 1991): 1–3. I am grateful to Dr Russell, and project architect Chryssanthos Kanellopoulos, for supplying me with details of their findings.
22. Harding 1951a: 7; Bennett 1975: 137; Fakharani 1975: 534.
23. Bartoccini imagined channels, recesses and steps cut into it (1932: 21; 1938: 104). See also Zayadine 1973: 19, and Fakharani 1975: 549.
24. M. Najjar, forthcoming in *ADAJ* vol. 36 (1991).
25. Bartoccini notes two cisterns outside the temple walls and one in the cella (1932: 21). The latter and one to the east are discussed by Fakharani (1975: 534, nn.13 and 14), and Dornemann (1983: 105). It is noted that the builders of the Temple of Artemis in Jerash also had to fill in earlier cisterns (Bitti 1986: 191).
26. Dornemann 1983: 105.
27. Fakharani 1975: 584. It is a pity that there is no further chronological refinement. A Late Roman infant burial was recorded from the lower, eastern terrace (Zayadine 1973: 25).
28. Bartoccini 1932: 16. Fine rusticated masonry was used by the Romans for the exterior of the Nymphaeum in the lower city, and for the platform of the Northern Temple.
29. Fakharani 1975: 538.
30. Fakharani 1975: 553. He cites a number of parallels without noting that they are from exteriors, not the core.
31. Zayadine 1982: 23. The lack of stratigraphic recording by Bartoccini and Fakharani has hampered any chronological refinement. I know of no mortar analysis either.
32. Fakharani 1975: 536. This height was recorded by Northedge in 1981 but there is a discrepancy of about ten metres between this height (used throughout this report) and those recorded by Fakharani on his Plan I. See also Chapter 1, note 14.
33. Cf. fragments TB.2 and TB.11 in Appendix B; Butler 1919: ill.24 C, thought they were cap mouldings, possibly referring to loose fragments, whilst Ceschi refers to them as socles – Almagro (1983b: n.15, fig.6). The 'frammento architettonico', also on fig.6, is not recognizable.
34. Despite the absence of any decoration Ceschi thought it part of the crowning cornice – Almagro (1983b: n.15, fig.7).
35. First defined and illustrated (unscaled) by Fakharani 1975: 543. There are many fragments of this moulding in the vicinity. An alternative, of which there is only a single example, block 12.17 (Appendix B), does not have the same flow of line.
36. Cf. Butler (1907–19), pl.1, ill.24B; Ceschi (Almagro 1983b: fig.4).
37. The remains of a fallen column to the southeast were measured by Butler as 9.3m (1907–19), pl.1, p.41. A reconstructed facade by Ceschi gives it as about a metre taller (Almagro 1983b: fig. 9). A figure of 'slightly higher than 10m' has recently been calculated by Kanellopoulos, although details remain to be determined (Kanellopoulos pers. comm.). Certainly all of the individual elements vary in dimension, often due to weathering and movement, cf. Butler's measurements.
38. Gatier 1986: 45, no.22. Cf. Buckingham 1821, *supra*.
39. Cf. Ceschi (Almagro 1983b: fig.4), and fragments 12.4 lower, 12.13 upper, 25.11 upper in Appendix B. Lyttleton notes this style as of Hellenistic origin (1974: 47, 58). It was common in the Roman period, similar but not exact parallels are found in Jerash, cf. Kraeling 1938: fig. XVI.
40. Cf. Butler (1907–19), pl.1, ill.24.D; Ceschi (Almagro 1983b: fig.7), 'architrave del Pronao'. Cf. reused blocks 12.11 (inscr. D), 12.14, TB.1, TB.7, 25.10, in Appendix B. A block of similar dimensions, but with a different beading and cut from a different stone, was found at the western end of the Citadel, reused block 10.2.
41. Gatier 1986: 44, block A – 1.45m; B – 2.9m; C – 4.49; D – 1m.
42. Fragment 25.12, a fine Corinthian cornice with modillions, reminiscent of western, rather than Hellenistic decoration (Murray 1917: 5). Bagatti noted a reused cornice block in the church (1973: 278). Also the recent project has found more blocks (Kanellopoulos pers. comm.).
43. The rock can be seen in section (Almagro 1983b: figs 2, 3, related to the plan published by Bartoccini 1938: Tav. V, fig. 7, which was apparently unknown to Almagro). Bartoccini realised the rock was below the floor level, but suggested that by keeping it within the temple the Romans were respecting its sanctity (1938: 105, 108).
44. Almagro 1983b: fig.1; Butler (1907–19), pl.1, ill.24.F.
45. Fakharani 1975: 546; Vitruvius, *De Architectura Libri X*, III.4.3. Fakharani's eventual rejection of a peripteros was based largely on the lack of sufficient fragments of column, capital, etc., in the vicinity (1975: 546). However, as the remains of the temple were subsequently robbed, a negative argument does not have a very great value.

46. A plan of the Citadel by Susan Balderstone, based on the work and observations of Alastair Northedge, published in *ADAJ* 22 (1977–1978): 21 and 174, and *ADAJ* 23 (1979): 162, shows the temple as peripteral, as does the plan published by Zayadine 1982a: 20, 24, fig.21.
47. These views are partly based on the problem of the length of the podium, the existence of the column *in antis*, and evidence of the existence, dismantling or collapse, and robbing, of only six columns, plus two more *in antis* (Russell and Kanellopoulos pers. comm.). Russell and Kanellopoulos have also considered the possibility of an amphitetra style design, that is, a four-column portico on both front and rear.
48. Vitruvius, III.3.4, There are, in fact, very few Vitruvian 'rules' that were adopted by the builders of this temple. The wider central intercolumniation may even have necessitated an arcuated lintel, as seems to have been the case with the Propylaeon (on which see below).
49. The bases were noted by Butler (1907–19), pl.1, p.40, whilst the column fragments are illustrated by Almagro 1983b: fig.5. These engaged columns are confusingly referred to by Bartoccini 1932: 16 as *pilastro*. I am grateful to the late Dr Russell for pointing this out.
50. An adyton would also add strength to the structure (Murray 1917: 17). Fakharani's restoration includes an apse projecting from the *cella* at the west end. This was based on the discovery of an east-west 'wall' discovered within the bedrock (Fakharani 1975: 540, 547), but this does not appear to be clearly defined in his photograph (1975: fig.16 or Plan I). I suggest that it merely represents filling of the rock. He also proposes, with no discernible evidence, an internal colonnade (1975: 547, 542), utilizing what appear to be the base plinths from the *temenos* colonnade. It is largely these architectural misinterpretations that seem to have led Fakharani to suggest that the building might have been a library.
51. It is not known where pilaster fragments were found by the Italian Mission, but their shape on the reconstruction plan (Almagro 1983b: fig.1), differs from that of the individual pilaster drawing (Almagro 1983b: fig.5). Moreover the aggregate of heights for the shafts of the engaged column and the pilaster is 7.63m., at variance, therefore, with the column height.
52. Bartoccini 1932: 21.
53. Butler (1907–19), pl.1, pp.43ff.
54. Although Bagatti had noted that there were reused elements in the Byzantine church (Bagatti 1973: 278f.), it was Zayadine who later associated them with a *temenos* of the Hercules temple (Zayadine 1977–8: 36).
55. Further details are found in Wood, this volume Chapter 8: south wall, Sectors 11 and 12; east wall, Sector 25 and Tower G.
56. Dornemann noted 'Hellenistic and Roman tipped fills' revealed by the construction cut for the road, but made no mention of a wall (Dornemann 1983: 105).
57. The date of this discovery is unknown but it was presumably after 1968 when Fakharani saw no evidence for a *temenos*.
58. Kanellopoulos pers. comm. A possibly reused column from the nearby church measured only 3.29m (Bagatti 1973: 279).
59. Cf. Ceschi (Almagro 1983b: fig.7) 'architrave minore'. A number of fragments were reused in the walls: Appendix B, fragments 11.10, 12.2, 25.14, 25.15, 25.18, 25.19. If this architrave *had* come from the temple, it may have been from the adyton facade or elsewhere within the *cella*.
60. A mutilated architrave and frieze block 25.17, is a remote possibility.
61. This is based on the height of the 'Roman mortared construction' (see Wood, this volume Chapter 8). Whether this slope was also due to subsequent subsidence is unknown.
62. Dornemann MSS report; Fakharani 1975: 553.
63. An engaged column base fragment, 12.6, found in the southern wall, is of the right dimensions for Gate C, but the Attic scotia details are quite different from the temple *temenos* colonnade bases. Cornice fragment 12.17 (cf. note 33) may also have come from Gate C.
64. On Gate C, see Wood in Chapter 8 of this volume , who also suggests that the earlier structure might have been a small temple.
65. Described as having three entrances with four pillars (Conder 1889: 31).
66. Dornemann MSS report; Fakharani 1975: 549; Northedge 1983: 442.
67. Zayadine 1973: 25, 1987: 309. Note also the number of reused Roman fragments found in the Sector 17 wall in this area (Wood, Chapter 8 of this volume).
68. Northedge, this volume, Chapter 10.
69. E.g. Burckhardt 1822: 359, *k* on his plan; 'a temple … the posterior wall of which only remains, having an entablature, and several niches highly adorned with sculpture.' etc. See photographs taken in 1867 (pl.64B), 1881 (Conder 1889: facing p.32), 1898 (Hadidi 1978: 218, plate XXXIII), and in 1904–5 (Butler 1907–19, pl.1, ill.29); also Butler's analysis of the Propylaeon (1907–19, pl.1, pp.43ff).
70. Examination of Butler's original drawing, preserved in the archives of the Department of Art and Archaeology, University of Princeton, shows that the second reconstruction, labelled 'after Dr. Thomson's photograph', is an addition, stuck over the original. Evidently Butler discovered an older photograph and decided to correct the drawing.
71. Lehmann 1954: 15; note also Vitruvius I.7.1, where the highest site is for 'for those of the gods under whose particular protection the state is thought to rest'.
72. Butler (1907–19) pl.1, p.38.
73. Butler (1907–19) pl.1, p.43.
74. Stillwell 1954: 4.
75. Cf. Lyttleton 1974: 204ff.
76. C. B. Welles, *The Inscriptions*, no.60 in Kraeling et al. 1938.
77. The temple of Zeus at Jerash, of a similar size and date, was built on a traditional site, but its plan attempts to conform to an earlier *temenos*, Kraeling 1938: 18. Double enclosures are seen around the Temple of Jupiter at Damascus, Temple of Jupiter at Ba'albakk, and the Temple of Artemis at Jerash, all of grander design.
78. Gatier 1986: 44, no.18.
79. Welles 1938: no.12. On this man see Sartre 1982: 83, with references.
80. Coins of Philadelphia in Spijkerman 1978: 243ff.
81. On the refounding of the city by Ptolemy II Philadelphos, see MacAdam, this volume, Chapter 3. On Ptolemaic

claims of Heraclean ancestry, cf. e.g. Tarn and Griffith 1966: 51.

82. Cf. e.g. Attridge and Oden 1981: 90, and further references in n.118.
83. This equation has been popular for some time, cf. e.g. Clermont-Ganneau 1906: 150f.
84. Horn 1967: 2.
85. Shea 1991.
86. Noted with references by Amr 1988: 55, who rejects the use of Iron Age sculpted heads from the eastern terrace as temple caryatids.
87. Bartoccini 1932: 16; 1938: 105.
88. Fakharani 1975: 549.
89. Bowsher 1987: 63, concurring with the Hercules identification.
90. Oliphant 1880; Conder (1889, p.32) identified the temple with Hercules on the same basis.
91. See Gatier 1986: 55 for references.
92. Spijkerman 1978: 251, no.21, etc. The portable shrine is perhaps reminiscent of the tabernacle of Milcom (*Amos* 5.26; *Acts* 7.43).
93. Littmann et al. 1921: 11, on slender epigraphic evidence.
94. Bowsher on numismatic representation (1987: 66).
95. Teixidor 1977: 47ff. On p.34f., he notes a suggested triad of Zeus = Baal Shamin, Asteria = Astarte, and Heracles = Melqart.
96. Bartoccini, who gave no satisfactory provenance, suggested it was female (1932: 16), as did Fakharani (1975: 548). Harding thought it to be Hercules (1967: 69), and a male attribution is more likely.
97. Zayadine 1987: 305. There might also have been a temple to Tyche somewhere on the Citadel. There have been attempts to equate her with the Asteria who figures on coins of Philadelphia (Spijkerman 1978: 251, no.24 etc.; cf. Gatier 1986: 53).
98. Cf. Gatier 1986 no.81. Other inscribed fragments (apart from the columns) from the area are Gatier nos 20 and 21. The new fragment was reported in *ACOR Newsletter* no.5 (November 1991). The block is mutilated, and the interpretation is based on restorations.
99. Gatier 1986: 51–4, who suggested that the 'Heracleion' itself was on Jabal Luwaybda, where the inscription was found.
100. Gatier 1986: 45, no.19.
101. On civic works, etc., in eastern Roman cities, see Jones 1979: 236ff. On the civic organization of Roman Philadelphia, see MacAdam in Chapter 3 of this volume.
102. ACOR Newsletter no.5 (November 1991): 3.
103. De Saulcy 1865: 248.
104. Conder 1889: 31.
105. Wood, Chapter 8, this volume.
106. Thus dated by Zayadine 1977–8: 37.
107. See Russell 1980. For damage elsewhere in 'Ammān, see Hadidi 1974: 79.
108. Harding 1951a: 7; Sectors 11, 12, and 25 of the fortifications, see Wood in Chapter 8 of this volume.
109. The excavations of 1990–1 suggest that the *cella*, podium and foundations were robbed in the Umayyad period. Dumping occurred in the robber trenches prior to the collapse of the portico columns and architrave in the earthquake of 129–30/747–8 (Russell pers. comm.).

Chapter 10

1. Information also treated in Chapter 8.
2. The preliminary reports describing Area C are to be found in: Bennett, C-M., and Northedge, A. E. (1977–8), 'Excavations at the Citadel, Amman, 1976, Second Preliminary Report', *ADAJ* 22, pp.172–9; Bennett, C-M. (1978a), 'Excavations at the Citadel (El-Qal'ah), Amman, Jordan', *Levant*, 10, pp.1–9; Bennett, C-M. (1979a), 'Early Islamic Amman', *Levant* 11, pp.1–8; Bennett, C-M. (1979b), 'Excavations on the Citadel (al Qal'a), Amman, 1977', *ADAJ* 23, pp.151–60.
3. Probably in the 1960s.
4. Registration no.633.
5. Dornemann (1970, 1983); Zayadine, Humbert and Najjar (1989).
6. The construction is comparable with a substantial Hellenistic-Early Roman wall excavated by Dr Zayadine in Area A (Zayadine 1977–8, pp.27–8, fig.2).
7. cf. Bennett (1979a), pl.IIIa.
8. For definition of foundation types see note 10 below.
9. Grabar et al. (1978), fig.23D.
10. Free-standing foundations: a foundation built as a free-standing wall. Trench-built foundations: a trench is cut of the same width as the wall, and filled up with rubble stones and mortar (in the Reception Hall) or *terra rossa* (in the fortification wall and these buildings). *Terra rossa*: formed from the decomposition of Ajlun and Belqa limestones; it can form a solid, impermeable mass if wetted and left to harden (Fisher et al. 1966).
11. The phenomenon of regular rectangular rooms, and walls varying in thickness to accommodate the irregularity of the plan, was noted elsewhere in Area B, and in the Umayyad Palace.
12. These structures could also be interpreted as bins, as the fill behind the stone facing wall was soft. However, in our experience compacted earth fills were always found deteriorated into soft, loose material adjacent to stone walls. This phenomenon is probably to be attributed either to water percolation down the wall, during and after the life of the building, or to movement of the wall, for example during earthquakes, or, more probably, to both effects. For this reason it was felt that the placement along the walls was a better indicator that the structures were benches.
13. Preliminary reports on the work in Area B may be found in: Bennett, C-M. (1975), 'Excavations at the Citadel, Amman, 1975', *ADAJ* 20, pp.131–42; Bennett, C-M. (1978a), 'Excavations at the Citadel (El-Qal'ah), Amman, Jordan', *Levant* 10, pp.1–9; Bennett, C-M. (1979a), 'Early Islamic Amman', *Levant* 11, pp.1–8; Bennett, C-M. (1979b), 'Excavations on the Citadel (al Qal'a), Amman, 1977', *ADAJ* 23, pp.151–60; Bennett, C-M. (1979c), 'Excavations on the Citadel (al Qal'a), Amman, 1978', *ADAJ* 23, pp.161–76.
14. The building was said to be for a headquarters building (Bennett 1975, p.132).
15. Bennett (1975), p.137.
16. Bennett (1975), p.141.
17. Cf. Chapter 9.
18. Bennett (1975), p.139.
19. Bennett (1975), p.134.
20. Also known as handmade painted ware, or Ayyūbid-

Mamlūk painted ware.

21. Bennett (1979b), Appendix A.
22. The lie of surface debris in plate 2a should probably be taken as evidence for the Umayyad and later periods, not earlier than the Umayyad reconstruction.
23. The area was supervised by the author. The preliminary reports are appendices by the author to Bennett, C-M. (1979b), 'Excavations on the Citadel (al Qal'a), Amman, 1977', *ADAJ* 23, pp.151–60; Bennett, C-M. (1979c), 'Excavations on the Citadel (al Qal'a), Amman, 1978', *ADAJ* 23, pp.161–76 (=Northedge 1979b).
24. Whitehouse (1979).
25. cf. de Vaux and Stève (1950), pl.A.

Chapter 11

1. Harding (1951a).
2. Harding (1951a), p.7.
3. Gaube (1974a).
4. Harding (1951a), pl.1.5
5. Harding (1951a), figs 2–4; pls III–IV.
6. Zayadine (1977–8).
7. Bibliography: Bartoccini (1939); Bagatti (1973), pp.277–83; Zayadine (1977–8), pp.34–7.
8. Zayadine (1977–8), p.34.
9. Bartoccini (1934), p.275.
10. Creswell (1940), pp.289–90.
11. Hamilton (1946b).
12. Carlier and Morin (1987); Carlier (1989).
13. Rashid (1979).
14. Bartoccini (1934).
15. Hübner (1993) is publishing the Iron Age pottery from the excavation preserved in the Museo Internazionale delle Ceramiche in Faenza.
16. Dornemann (1969).
17. Zayadine (1973).
18. Zayadine, Humbert and Najjar (1989).
19. DoA (1975), p.12.
20. Zayadine, Najjar and Greene (1987). Permission for the proposed school was eventually revoked.
21. Zayadine (1973); Zayadine, Najjar and Greene (1987).
22. Author's reconnaissance (1989).
23. Zayadine, Najjar and Greene (1987), p.309.
24. Excavations in trench E3 in 1979 produced evidence of occupation outside the Roman wall Sector 12. In addition, a number of earlier building walls can be seen projecting from under the Sector 12 wall in the area of Tower B.
25. Zayadine (1977–8), p.28.
26. Harding (1967), p.63.
27. Zayadine (1977–8), p.28.
28. Zayadine (1973).
29. Zayadine (1973), p.22.
30. The building in trench C10. For the earthquake of AD 363 see Russell (1980).
31. Zayadine (1977–8), pp.36–8, 43–4.
32. I have to thank for this suggestion Professor H. Kalayan, who first saw a similarity between the Umayyad buildings of Area C and 'Anjar.
33. Mortar in joints often tends to erode and disappear, and thus it is not always obvious whether a wall is mortared or not. Other buildings of obviously mortared masonry at the Qal'a are Tower B and the Roman enclosures of the temples.
34. Wilkinson (1977); Gatier (1986), pp.148–9; Donceel-Voûte (1988).
35. The preservation of street lines over many centuries is a common phenomenon; for a brief discussion of this topic in a Middle Eastern context, see Northedge, Bamber and Roaf (1988), pp.52–3.
36. Harding (1951a), p.9.
37. Hanin (1985–6), plan 3, Rooms 108–15.
38. Amiran (1952), p.48.
39. Russell (1985), pp.47–9. Russell concludes that the first earthquake, though the year is given differently in various sources, probably took place in AD 748.
40. Theophanes: 422.
41. Creswell (1940), 120.
42. Ben Dov (1971, 1982).
43. Hamilton (1959), p.8.
44. McNicoll et al. (1982).
45. Smith (1973), pp.165–6; Smith (1989).
46. Saller (1941), vol. 2, pls 144, 146, showing Room 89.
47. de Vries (1981), pp.65, 71.
48. Ben Dov (1971, 1982); Yadin (1975).
49. Muqaddasī: 169. According to Jamāl al-Dīn Aḥmad (8th/14th century), the Aqṣā was destroyed twice and rebuilt twice early in the 'Abbāsid period, and this account was accepted by Creswell (Creswell 1940, p.120). Other sources do not support this late account, and it is now generally thought that only one phase of rebuild occurred at the beginning of the 'Abbāsid period (Hamilton 1949, pp.71–3; Creswell 1989, pp.79–82). Al-Muqaddasī says that the earthquake took place 'in the days of the 'Abbāsids'. This is an over-simplification: in fact the earthquake was under the Umayyads, but the restoration took place after the 'Abbāsid revolution (Le Strange 1890, p.92).
50. *Asāṭīn mushayyada* was translated in Creswell's *Early Muslim Architecture* (1940, p.120) as 'built-up piers', implying that the piers were of multiple blocks. A second translation is offered in the recent revised edition of Creswell's *Short Account of Early Muslim Architecture* (Creswell 1989, p.82): 'plastered', from *shīd* 'plaster'. Another common meaning of *mushayyad* is 'lofty, imposing', of buildings. Although Creswell's original translation may not be technically correct, the contrast with marble columns shows that multi-block piers are being referred to.
51. Muqaddasī: 169.
52. Dionysius of Tell Mahre, trans. Chabot, p.108. This text has often been rejected because of its reference to Solomon's temple. However, one would not expect a monk in al-Jazīra to be familiar with the details of Manṣūr's work in Jerusalem, but he would know about the construction of Raqqa, and its date. Ṭabarī and Ibn al-Athīr also mention the visit by Manṣūr to Jerusalem in 154/771, though without mentioning work on the buildings (Ṭabarī: 3.372; Ibn al-Athīr 5.467; Le Strange 1890, p.93). Mas'ūdī (6.212) also mentions a visit by Manṣūr to Jerusalem in 141/758–9.
53. Melville, pers. comm. There was another large earthquake in eastern Anatolia/northern Syria in 245/January 860, but this is likely to have been too far away to have affected 'Ammān.

54. Lowick, pers. comm.
55. Suyūṭī: 18; Creswell (1940), p.121; Amiran (1950–1), p.227.
56. Suyūṭī: 20–1; al-Dhahabī, *Tārīkh al-Islām*: fol. 4b; Ibn al-Qalānisī: 94; Amiran (1950–1), p.227; Ambraseys and Melville (1989).
57. Ambraseys and Melville (1988).
58. Amiran (1950–1), p.227.
59. Amiran (1950–1), p.228.
60. Oren (1971). A cautionary note has to be added that the available report on the excavations is not detailed; the pottery illustrated is similar to that of our Stratum III destruction.
61. On this solution to the dating problems created by lack of coins, see Northedge, Bamber and Roaf (1988, Chapter 5).
62. Olávarri-Goicoechea (1985), figs 22–3; Sauer (1982), fig.6. The pottery is paralleled at Abu Gôsh, where it is dated to the 10th-11th centuries, but not on good evidence (de Vaux and Stève 1950, pl.A). Glazed wares with straight flaring rims and flat ring bases appear to belong to a limited, but not so far well-defined, time range. The form is found among early Fāṭimid lustre wares, though other Fāṭimid lustre wares have out-turned rims. And the same form is found in East Iranian and Central Asian slip-glazed wares in the period AD 950–1050.
63. Melville (1984).
64. Olávarri-Goicoechea (1985), fig.53.
65. Gaube (1977), p.84.
66. Ṭabarī: 2.1841–2.
67. Ṭabarī: 2.1975, 3.25–6.
68. Ben Dov (1982).
69. Creswell (1969), pp.478–81; Sauvaget (1940); Chehab (1963); Chehab (1975, 1978).
70. Chehab (1975, 1978).
71. Ory (1967).
72. Ettinghausen and Grabar (1987), p.390, n.72.
73. Creswell (1969), pp.515–18.
74. Creswell (1969), p.480.
75. Brooks (1898), p.581.
76. Theophanes: 377.
77. Mouterde (1939).
78. *EI*[2]: s.v. al-ʿAbbās ibn al-Walīd.
79. Ṭabarī: 2.1826.
80. Note that Killick interprets Udhruḥ as a civilian settlement (Killick 1983).
81. al-Yaʿqūbī: 263. 'Then he bought slave-girls for them and married them to them.... He arranged standing allowances for the slave-girls of the Turks, and registered their names in the *dīwāns*, and one was not allowed to divorce his wife, nor leave her.' At a later stage in 256/869–70 the Turks demanded that women be removed from the *dīwān* (Ṭabarī: 3.1799).
82. Theophanes: 377.
83. *EI*[2]: s.v. al-ʿAbbās ibn al-Walīd.
84. Grabar et al. (1978); Creswell (1969), pp.522–44.
85. Grabar et al. (1978), p.32.
86. Grabar et al. (1978), p.79.
87. Pointed arches have, of course, been found from earlier dates. The reference here is to the introduction of the pointed arch as a consistent standard architectural style, an introduction which seems to take place from about AD 728 onwards. The late Umayyad buildings have pointed arches and vaults; the early ones do not.
88. Whitcomb (1988a, 1989).
89. Whitcomb (1988a), p.15.
90. Knauf and Brooker (1988).
91. The author is grateful to Dr Claus-Peter Haase and Michael Meinecke for permission to see the unpublished pottery report prepared by Karin Bartl, and to make these remarks. See also Haase (1990).
92. Sauvaget (1939c).
93. The author wishes to thank Dr Dorothée Sack for showing him the survey plan.
94. Two of the buildings were partially excavated by Katherina Otto-Dorn (Otto-Dorn 1957).
95. Balādhurī: 143.
96. Ṭabarī: 2.1892.
97. Ṭabarī: 2.1843, 1877, 1899, 1939.
98. Crone (1980), p.42.
99. Ṭabarī: 2.1268, 1306, 1893.
100. Ṭabarī: 2.1702, 1708.
101. Ṭabarī: 3.2ff.
102. Ṭabarī: 3.1830, 1892, 1897, 1908f., 1913, 1941.
103. Ṭabarī: 2.1403.
104. Ṭabarī: 2.1804.
105. Ṭabarī: 2.1739.
106. Ṭabarī: 2.1941.
107. Ṭabarī: 3.54.
108. Crone (1980).
109. Ṭabarī: 2.1844.
100. Ṭabarī: 2.1836.
111. Shaban (1971), p.154; Crone (1980).
112. The contrast between the settlements of Umayyad Syria and those of ʿAbbāsid Iraq is elaborated in Northedge (forthcoming).

BIBLIOGRAPHY

Modern works are referenced by author and date, according to the Harvard notation, with the references placed in the main text or notes as appropriate. The date reference is given after the author's name in the bibliography. For ancient and medieval works, the usual short form of an author's name is used, but where more than one work of an author is quoted, an abbreviation is used, and this is given after the author's name in the bibliography. In the references in the text, where a particular volume of a multi-volume work is referred to, this is denoted by an Arabic numeral followed by a dot and the relevant page, figure or plate numbers. The same principle has been applied to the volume series of Ṭabarī, *Tārīkh al-Rusul wal-Mulūk;* for example, series III, p.374, is set out 3.374.

Abbreviations

AAAS	*Annales Archéologiques Arabes Syriennes*
AARP	*Art and Archaeology Research Papers*
AASOR	*Annual of the American Schools of Oriental Research*
ÄAT	*Ägypten und altes Testament*
AB	*Analecta Bollandiana*
AcS	*Acta Sanctorum*
ADAJ	*Annual of the Department of Antiquities of Jordan*
AE	*Année Epigraphique*
AfO	*Archiv für Orientforschung*
AI	*Ars Islamica*
AJ	*Antiquities of the Jews*
AJP	*American Journal of Philology*
ANET	*Ancient Near Eastern Texts*, ed. J.B. Pritchard, Princeton 1969
ANRW	*Aufsteig und Niedergang der Römischen Welt*
AO	*Ars Orientalis*
AS	*Ancient Society*
AUSS	*Andrews University Seminary Studies*
BA	*Biblical Archaeologist*
BAR	*British Archaeological Reports*
BASOR	*Bulletin of the American Schools of Oriental Research*
BF	*Byzantinische Forschungen*
BGA	*Bibliotheca Geographorum Arabicorum*
BJ	*Bellum Judaicum*
BMC	British Museum Catalogue (of Coins)
BN	*Biblische Notizen*
BRL	*Biblisches Reallexikon*, 2nd ed., Tübingen 1977
BSOAS	*Bulletin of the School of Oriental and African Studies*
CIL	*Corpus Inscriptionum Latinarum*
CIS	*Corpus Inscriptionum Semiticarum*
CNRS	Centre National de la Recherche Scientifique
CPJ	*Corpus Papyrorum Judaicarum*
CQ	*Classical Quarterly*
DAFI	Délégation Archéologique Française en Iran
DaM	*Damaszener Mitteilungen*
DOP	*Dumbarton Oaks Papers*
EAEHL	*Encyclopedia of Archaeological Excavations in the Holy Land*
EI[1]	*Encyclopaedia of Islam*, 1st Ed., Leiden
EI[2]	*Encyclopaedia of Islam*, 2nd Ed., Leiden 1954–.
HArch	Handbuch der Archäologie
FHG	*Fragmenta Historicorum Graecorum* (ed. C. Müller)
HE	*Historia Ecclesiastica* (Eusebius of Caesarea)
IDB	*Interpreter's Dictionary of the Bible*
IEJ	*Israel Exploration Journal*
IFAPO	Institut Français Archéologique du Proche Orient
IGLS	*Inscriptions Grecques et Latines de la Syrie*
IGR	Inscriptiones Graecae ad Res Romanas Pertinentes
IJ	*Inscriptions de la Jordanie*
ILS	*Inscriptiones Latinae Selectae*
JBL	*Journal of Biblical Literature*
JESHO	*Journal of Economic and Social History of the Orient*
JRS	*Journal of Roman Studies*
JSSEA	*Journal of the Society for the Study of Egyptian Antiquities*
LA	*Liber Annuus*
LSJ	Liddell, Scott and Jones (Greek-English Lexicon)
MB	*Monde de la Bible*
MHA	*Memoria de Historia Antigua*
OGIS	*Orientis Graeci Inscriptiones Selectae*
Onom.	Das Onomastikon der Biblischen Ortsnamen (ed. E. Klostermann)
P Lond	*Papyrus London*
PCZ	*Papyrus Cairo Zenon*
PE	*Praeparatio Evangelica*
PEF	Palestine Exploration Fund
PEFQS	*Palestine Exploration Fund Quarterly Statement*
PEQ	*Palestine Exploration Quarterly*

PG	*Patrologia Graeca* (ed. Migne)
PL	*Patrologia Latina (ed. Migne)*
PLRE	*Prosopography of the Later Roman Empire*
PPUAES	Publications of the Princeton University Archaeological Expeditions to Syria
PSI	*Publicazioni della Società Italiana*
QDAP	*Quarterly of the Department of Antiquities of Palestine*
RAO	*Recueil d'Archéologie Orientale*
RB	*Revue Biblique*
RE	*Realenzyklopädia* (Pauly-Wissowa)
REI	*Répertoire d'Epigraphie Islamique*, Cairo 1931–54
RES	*Répertoire d'Epigraphie Sémitique*
SB	*Sammelbuch (Griechische Urkunden aus Ägypten)*
SDB	*Supplement au Dictionnaire de la Bible*
SH	*Studia Hierosolymitana*
SHAJ	*Studies in the History and Archaeology of Jordan*
Wadd.	W. H. Waddington, *Inscriptions Grecques et Latines de la Syrie*
ZDMG	*Zeitschrift der Deutschen Morgenländischen Gesellschaft*
ZDPV	*Zeitschrift des Deutschen Palästina-Vereins*
ZPE	*Zeitschrift für Papyrologie und Epigraphik*

Ancient Authors

Ammianus Marcellinus, *Res Gestae*, trans. Rolfe, J. C., 3 vols, Loeb Classical Library, 1935–1939.

Diodorus Siculus, *Diodorus of Sicily*, trans. Walton, F. R., Loeb Classical Library, 1957.

Polybius, *Polybius: The Histories*, trans. Paton, W. R., Loeb Classical Library, 1923.

Medieval Works

'Abd al-Ḥamīd b. Yaḥyā, *Risāla 'an Marwān ilā ibnihi 'Abdallah*, no.505 in Safwat, A. Z. (ed.), *Jamharat Rasā'il al-'Arab*, 4 vols, Cairo 1937. See also: Schönig, H. (1985), *Das Sendschreiben des 'Abdalhamid B. Yahya (gest. 132/750) an den Kronprinzen 'Abdallah B. Marwan II. Ein Beitrag zur Kenntnis der frühen arabischen Prosaliteratur*, Stuttgart.

Abū al-Faraj 'Alī b. Ḥusayn al-Iṣfahānī *(Aghānī)*, *Kitāb al-Aghānī*, Cairo 1927–74.

Abū al-Fidā', *Kitāb Taqwīm al-Buldān*, ed. Reinhard and de Slane, Paris 1840.

Abū Shāma, Shihāb al-Dīn 'Abd al-Raḥman b. Isma'īl al-Muqaddasī, *Kitāb al-Rawḍatayn fī Akhbār al-Dawlatayn al-Nūriyya wal-Salāḥiyya*, ed. Muḥammad Ḥilmī Muḥammad, 2 vols, Cairo 1956–62.

Agapius of Manbij, *Kitāb al-'Unwān*, ed. Vasiliev, Paris 1909.

al-Aḥwas al-Anṣārī, *Dīwān*, Beirut.

al-Balādhurī, Aḥmad b. Yaḥyā, *Kitāb Futūḥ al-Buldān*, ed. de Goeje, Leiden 1866.

al-Dhahabī, *Tārīkh al-Islām*, BM. Ms. Or. 50.

al-Dimashqī, Shams al-Dīn Abū 'Abdallah Muḥammad b. Abī Ṭālib al-Anṣārī, *Nukhbat al-Dahr fī 'Ajā'ib al-Birr wal-Baḥr*, 1866. Tr. F. Mehren 1874.

(Pseudo-) Dionysius of Tell Mahre, *Chronique*, ed. and tr. J-B. Chabot, Paris 1985–6.

al-Ḥamdānī, Muḥammad b. 'Abd al-Malik, *Takmilat Tārīkh al-Tabarī*, ed. Albert Yūsuf Kan'ān, Beirut 1961.

Ḥamza al-Isfahānī, *Tārīkh sinī Mulūk al-Arḍ wal-Anbiyā'*, ed. Gottwald, 10 vols, Leipzig 1844–8.

Ibn 'Asākit, 'Alī ibn al-Hasan, *Tārīkh Dimashq*, excerpted by S. Munajjid, *Mu'jam Banī Umayya*, Beirut 1970.

Ibn al-Athīr, 'Izz al-Dīn, *al-Kāmil fī al-Tārīkh*, ed. C. J. Tornberg, 14 vols, Leiden 1866–71.

Ibn al-Jawzī, *Kitāb al-Muntaẓam*, ed. Hyderabad, 1938–41.

Ibn al-Nadīm, Muḥammad b. Isḥāq, *Kitāb al-Fihrist*, ed. and tr. B. Dodge, *The Fihrist of Ibn al-Nadim*, 2 vols, New York 1970.

Ibn al-Qalā nisī, Ḥamza b. Asad, *Dhayl Tārīkh Dimashq*, ed. Amedroz, Beirut 1907.

Ibn Ḥawqal, Muḥammad, *Kitāb al-Masālik wal-Mamālik*, ed. Kramers, *BGA* 2, Leiden 1873.

Ibn Khallikān, *Wafāyāt al-A'yān wa-Anbā' Abnā' al-Zamān*, tr. de Slane, Paris 1842–71.

Ibn Khurdādhbih, 'Ubaydallah b. 'Abdallah, *Kitāb al-Mamālik wal-Masālik*, ed. de Goeje, *BGA* 6, Leiden 1889.

Ibn al-Manẓūr, Jamāl al-Dīn Muḥammad b. Mukram, *Lisān al-'Arab*, Beirut 1955.

Ibn Shaddād, Muḥammad b. Ibrahīm, *al-A'lāq al-Khaṭīra fī Dhikr Umarā' al-Shām wal-Jazīra*, ed. Sami Dahan, Damascus 1963.

al-Iṣṭakhrī, Abū Isḥāq Ibrahīm b. Muḥammad al-Fārisī, *Kitāb al-Masālik wal-Mamālik*, ed. de Goeje, *BGA* 1, Leiden 1870.

al-Jaḥshiyārī, Abū 'Abdallah Muḥammad b. 'Abdūs, *Kitāb al-Wuzarā' wal-Kuttāb*, Cairo 1938.

Khalīfa b. Khayyāṭ, *Tārīkh*, ed. S. Zakkar, 2 vols, Damascus 1967–8.

al-Maqrīzī, Taqī al-Dīn Aḥmad b. 'Alī, *al-Sulūk li-Ma'rifat Duwal al-Mulūk*, ed. Ziada, Cairo 1934–.

al-Maqrīzī, Taqī al-Dīn Aḥmad b. 'Alī, *Itti'āẓ al-Ḥunafā' bi-Akhbār al-Fāṭimiyyīn al-Khulafā'*, vol. 1, ed. Shayyāl, Cairo 1967.

al-Mas'ūdī, Abū al-Ḥasan 'Alī b. al-Ḥusayn, *Kitāb al-Tanbīh wal-Ishrāf*, *BGA* 8, ed. de Goeje, Leiden 1894.

al-Mas'ūdī, Abū al-Ḥasan 'Alī b. al-Ḥusayn, *Murūj al-Dhahab wa-Ma'ādin al-Jawāhīr*, ed. and tr. Barbier de Meynard and P. Courteille, *Les Prairies d'Or*, 9 vols, Paris 1861–77.

Michael the Syrian, *Chronique*, Fr. tr. J-B. Chabot, Paris 1901.

al-Muqaddasī, Muḥammad b. Aḥmad, *Aḥsan al-Taqāsīm fī Ma'rifat al-Aqālīm*, ed. de Goeje, *BGA* 3, Leiden 1906.

Severus b. al-Muqaffa', *History of the Patriarchs of the Coptic Church of Alexandria*, ed. and tr. Evetts, Paris 1904.

al-Suyūṭī, Jalāl al-Dīn, *Kashf al-Silsila 'an Wasf al-Zilzila*, Fr. tr. Nejjar, Rabat 1973–4.

al-Ṭabarī, Muḥammad b. Jarīr, *Tārīkh al-Rusul wal-Mulūk*, ed. de Goeje et al., Leiden 1879–1901.

Theophanes, *Chronographia*, ed. de Boors, Leipzig 1882.

al-Ya'qūbī, Aḥmad b. Abī Ya'qūb b. Wāḍiḥ, *Kitāb al-Buldān*, ed. de Goeje, *BGA* 7, Leiden 1892.

Yāqūt b. 'Abdallah al-Ḥamawī al-Rūmī al-Baghdādī, *Kitāb Mu'jam al-Buldān*, ed. Wüstenfeld, 6 vols, Leipzig 1866–73.

19th-century Travellers and Surveyors

Buckingham, J. S. (1821), *Travels among the Arab Tribes*, London.

Burckhardt, J.L. (1822), *Travels in Syria and the Holy Land*, London.

Conder, C. R. (1882), *Heth and Moab*, London.

Conder, C. R. (1889), *The Survey of Eastern Palestine*: vol. I *The 'Adwan Country*, London.
Conder, C. R. (1896), *Syrian Stone Lore*, London.
de Laborde, L. (1837), *Voyage de la Syrie*, Paris.
Merrill, S. (1881), *East of the Jordan*, London.
Northey, A. E. (1872), 'Expedition to the East of Jordan', *PEFQS* I, pp. 64ff.
Oliphant, L., (1880), *Land of Gilead*, Edinburgh.
Robinson, G. (1837), *Travels in Palestine and Syria*, vol. II, London.
de Saulcy, F. (1865), *Voyage en Terre Sainte*, vol I, Paris.
Seetzen, U. von (1810), *A Brief Account of the Countries adjoining the Lake of Tiberias, the Jordan and the Dead Sea*, Bath.
Seetzen, U. von (1854), *Reisen durch Syrien, Palästina, Phönicien, die Trans-jordan-Lander, Arabia Petraea und Unter-Aegyptien.* vol.I, Berlin.
Tristram, H. B. (1865), *Land of Israel*, London.

Modern Studies

Aalund, F., Meinecke, M., and Muqdad, R. S. (1990), *Islamic Bosra, a brief guide*, Amman.
Abbott, N. (1946), 'The Kasr Kharana Inscription of 92 H (710 AD), a New Reading', *AI* 11–12, pp. 190–5.
'Abd al-Fattāḥ, Nahḍa (1984), 'Mashrū' Iḥyā' madīnatay Sāmarrā' wal-Mutawakkiliyya al-athariyyatayn: Dār raqm (1) wal-shāri' al-a'ẓam fī Sāmarrā', *Sumer* 43, pp.30–49 (Ar. Sect.).
Abd ul-Haqq, S., and Salibi, N. (1951), 'Rapport Préliminaire sur les Campagnes de Fouilles à Raqqa', *AAAS* I, pp. 111–121.
'Abd al-Khāliq, Hanā' (1985–6), 'Natā'ij al-tanqībāt fī Tulūl Jamī'a fī al-Madā'in', *Sumer* 44, pp.111–138 (Ar. Sect.).
Abel, A. (1956), 'La Citadelle Eyyubite de Bosra Eski Cham', *AAAS* 6, pp.93–138.
Abel, F.-M. (1926), 'Inscription Grecque de l'Aqueduc de Jérusalem avec figure du pied Byzantin', *RB* 35, pp.284–95.
Abel, F.-M. (1933; 1938), *Géographie de la Palestine*, 2 vols
al-'Ābidī, M. (1964), 'Ḥafriyāt al-Īṭaliān fī Qal'at 'Ammān', *ADAJ* 8–9, pp.3–8 (Ar. sect.).
Abou Assaf, A. (1980), 'Untersuchungen zur ammonitischen Rundbildkunst', *UF* 12, pp.7–102.
Adams, R. M. (1965), *Land Behind Baghdad*, Chicago.
Adams, R. M. (1981), *Heartland of Cities*, Chicago.
Agrar- und Hydrotechnik (A.H.T.) (1977), *National Water Master Plan of Jordan*. vol. 2, *Main report, Atlas*, Frankfurt, German Agency for Technical Cooperation.
Aharoni, Y. (1979), *The Land of the Bible, a Historical Geography*, London.
Alami, Y. et al. (ed.) (1975), *The History of Amman*, Amman.
Allen, T. (1986), *A Classical Revival in Islamic Architecture*, Wiesbaden.
Almagro, A. and Olávarri, E. (1982), 'A New Umayyad Palace at the Citadel of Amman', pp. 305–22 in Hadidi, A. (ed.), *Studies in the History and Archaeology of Jordan I*, Amman.
Almagro, A. (1980), 'The Photogrammetric Survey of the Citadel of Amman and other Archaeological Sites in Jordan', *ADAJ* 24, pp.111–20.
Almagro, A. (1983a), *El Palacio Omeya de Amman I, La Arquitectura*, Madrid.
Almagro, A. (1983b), 'The Survey of the Roman Monuments of Amman by the Italian Mission in 1930', *ADAJ* 27, pp.607–39.
Almagro, A. (1987), 'Origins and Repercussions of the Architecture of the Umayyad Palace in Amman', *SHAJ* 3, pp.181–192.
Almagro, M. and A. (1976), *The Arab-Spanish Restauration* (sic) *of the 'Umayyad' Palace at the Citadel of Amman*, unpub. report in the Registration Centre of the Dept. of Antiquities, 'Amman.
Ambraseys, N. N., and Melville, C. P. (1988), 'An Analysis of the Eastern Mediterranean Earthquake of 20 May 1202', pp.181ff. in Lee, W. H. K., Meyers, H. and Shimazaki, K. (eds), *Historical Seismograms and Earthquakes of the World.* San Diego, etc.
Ambraseys, N. N., and Melville, C. P. (1989), 'Evidence for Intraplate Earthquakes in Northwest Arabia', *Bulletin of the Seismological Society of America* 79, pp.1279–81.
Amiran, D. H. K. (1950-1), 'A Revised Earthquake Catalogue of Palestine', *IEJ* 1, pp.223–46; (1952) *IEJ* 2, pp.48–65.
Amiran, R. (1969), *Ancient Pottery of the Holy Land*, Jerusalem.
Amr, A. J. (1980), *A Study of the Clay Figurines and Zoomorphic Vessels of Trans-Jordan during the Iron Age, with special Reference to their Symbolism and Function*, Ph.D. thesis (unpubl.), University of London.
Amr, A. J. (1988), 'Four Unique Double-Faced Female Heads from the Amman Citadel', *PEQ* 1988, pp.55–63.
Andrae, W. and Lenzen, H. (1933), *Die Partherstadt Assur*, Leipzig.
al-Ansary, A. R. (1982), *Qaryat al-Faw. A Portrait of pre-Islamic Civilisation in Saudi Arabia*, London.
Aresvik, O. (1976), *The Agricultural Development of Jordan*, New York.
Asīl, Nājī (1947), 'Madīnat al-Mu'taṣim 'alā al-Qāṭūl', *Sumer* 3, pp.160–70 (Ar. sect.).
Attridge, H. W., and Oden, R. A., Jnr. (eds)(1981), *Philo of Byblos, The Phoenician History*, Catholic Biblical Quarterly Monograph Series 9, Washington DC.
Aufrecht, W. E. (1989), *A Corpus of Ammonite Inscriptions* (Ancient Near Eastern Texts and Studies 4), Lewiston/NY – Queenston/Ontario.
Avi-Yonah, M. (1966), *The Holy Land: A Historical Geography*, Grand Rapids.
Avi-Yonah, M. (1981), *Art in Ancient Palestine*, Jerusalem.
Avi-Yonah, M. and Stern, E. (1978), 'Rabbath-Ammon', *EAEHL* 4:987–93.
Bagatti, B. (1973), 'Le Antiche Chiese di Filadelfia-Amman', *Liber Annuus* 23, pp.261–85.
Bagnall, R. S. (1976), *The Administration of the Ptolemaic Possessions Outside Egypt*, Leiden.
Baldwin, B. (1977), 'Malchus of Philadelphia', *DOP* 13, pp.91–107.
Balog, P. (1980), *The Coinage of the Ayyubids*, London.
Bar-Kochva, B. (1989), *Judas Maccabaeus: The Jewish Struggle Against the Seleucids*, Cambridge and New York.
Bartoccini, R. (1941), 'Ricerche e Scoperte della Missione Italiana in Amman', *Bolletino dell' Associazione Internazionale per gli Studi Mediterranei* 1.3, pp.15ff.
Bartoccini, R. (1932), 'Scavi ad Amman della Missione Archeologica Italiana', *Bolletino dell' Associazione Internazionale per gli Studi Mediterranei* 3.2, pp.16ff.
Bartoccini, R. (1933), 'Scavi ad Amman della Missione Archeologica Italiana', *Bolletino dell' Associazione Internazionale per gli Studi Mediterranei* 4.4–5, pp.10ff.
Bartoccini, R. (1934), 'La Terza Campagna di Scavi sull'

Acropoli di Amman', *Bolletino d'Arte del Ministerio dell' Educazione Nazionale* 1934 (Dicembre): 275ff.

Bartoccini, R. (1935), 'La Rocca Sacra degli Ammoniti', *Atti del IV Congresso di Studi Romani,* vol. I. pp.103–8, Rome.

Bartoccini, R. (1939), 'Un Decennio di Ricerche e di Scavi Italiani in Transgiordania', *Bolletino del Reale Instituto di Archeologia e Storia d'Arte* 9, pp.75–84.

Bates, M. L. (1989), 'The Coinage of Syria under the Umayyads', pp. 195–228 in Bakhit, M. A. and Schick, R. (eds), *The History of Bilad al-Sham during the Umayyad Period (Fourth International Conference)*, Amman.

Bauzou, T. (1988), 'Les Voies Romaines entre Damas et Amman', pp.293–300 in P.-L. Gatier et al. (eds), *Géographie Historique au Proche-Orient*, Paris.

Bawden, G., Edens, C. and Miller, R. (1980), 'The Archaeological Resources of Ancient Tayma, Preliminary Investigations at Tayma', *Atlal* 4, pp.69–106.

Bell, G. L. (1909), *Palace and Mosque at Ukhaidir*, Oxford.

Bell, H. I. (1928), *Greek Papyri in the British Museum*, IV, *the Aphrodito Papyri*, London.

Bellamy, J. A. (1988), 'Two Pre-Islamic Inscriptions Revised: Jabal Ramm and Umm al-Jimal', *JAOS* 108, pp.369–78.

Ben Dov, M. (1971), *The Omayyad Structures near the Temple Mount*, Jerusalem.

Ben Dov, M. (1982), *In the Shadow of the Temple*, Jerusalem.

Bender, F. (1968), *Die Geologie von Jordanien*, Berlin and Stuttgart.

Bennett, C-M. (1975), 'Excavations at the Citadel, Amman, 1975', *ADAJ* 20, pp. 131–42.

Bennett, C-M. (1978a), 'Excavations at the Citadel (El-Qal'ah), Amman, Jordan', *Levant* 10, pp.1–9.

Bennett, C-M. (1978b), 'Some Reflections on Neo-Assyrian Influence in Transjordan', pp. 165–71 in: *Archaeology in the Levant. Essays for K. Kenyon*, ed. Moorey, P. R. and Parr, P. J., Warminster, 1978.

Bennett, C-M. (1979a), 'Early Islamic Amman', *Levant* 11, pp.1–8.

Bennett, C-M. (1979b), 'Excavations on the Citadel (al Qal'a), Amman, 1977', *ADAJ* 23, pp.151–60.

Bennett, C-M. (1979c), 'Excavations on the Citadel (al Qal'a), Amman, 1978', *ADAJ* 23, pp.161–76.

Bennett, C-M., and Northedge, A. E. (1977–8), 'Excavations at the Citadel, Amman, 1976, Second Preliminary Report', *ADAJ* 22, pp.172–9.

van Berchem, M. (1922), *Matériaux pour un Corpus Inscriptionum Arabicarum*, Part 2, vol. I: *Jérusalem Ville*, Cairo.

Bietenhard, H. (1977), 'Die syrische Dekapolis von Pompeius bis Traian', *ANRW* II.8, pp.20–61 (cf. *ZDPV* 79 [1963], pp.24–58).

Bisheh, G. (1980), 'Excavations at Qasr al-Hallabat 1979', *ADAJ* 24, pp.69–78.

Bisheh, G. (1985), 'Qasr al-Hallabat: an Umayyad Desert Retreat or Farm Land?', *SHAJ* II, pp.263–5.

Bisheh, G. (1989), 'Hammam al-Sarah in the Light of Recent Excavations', *DaM* 4, pp.225–30.

Bitti, M. C. (1986), '3. The area of the Temple stairway', pp. 189–92 in F. Zayadine (ed), *Jerash Archaeological Project 1981–1983*, vol. I. Amman.

Blankinship, K. Y. (1988), 'The Tribal Factor in the Abbasid Revolution: the Betrayal of the Imam Ibrahim b. Muhammad', *JAOS* 108, pp.589–603.

Block, D. I. (1984), '*Bny 'mwn*: The Sons of Ammon', *AUSS* 22, pp.197–212.

Blockley, R. C. (1981), *The Fragmentary Classicising Historians of the Later Roman Empire: Eunapius, Olympiodorus, Priscus and Malchus,* vol. I, Liverpool.

Blockley, R. C. (1983), *The Fragmentary Classicising Historians of the Later Roman Empire: Eunapius, Olympiodorus, Priscus and Malchus,* vol. II, Liverpool.

Boling, R.G. (1988), *The Early Biblical Community in Transjordan* (The Social World of Biblical Antiquity Series 6), Sheffield.

Boraas, R. S. and Geraty, L. T. (eds) (1978), *Heshbon 1976*, Berrien Springs.

Bosworth, A. B. (1974), 'The Government of Syria under Alexander the Great', *CQ* 24, pp.44–64.

Bosworth, C. E. (1973), 'The Heritage of Rulership in Early Islamic Iran and the search for Dynastic Connections with the Past', *Iran* 11, pp.51–62.

Boucharlat, R. (1977), 'La Forteresse Sassanide de Tureng Tepe', pp.329–42 in Deshayes, J. (ed.), *Le Plateau Iranien et l'Asie Centrale des Origines à la Conquête Islamique – leurs relations à la lumière des documents archéologiques*, Actes du Colloque International No. 567, C.N.R.S., Paris.

Bowersock, G. W. (1973), 'Syria Under Vespasian', *JRS* 63, pp.133–40.

Bowersock, G. W. (1983), *Roman Arabia*, Cambridge.

Bowersock, G. W. (1988), 'The Three Arabias in Ptolemy's Geography', pp. 47–53 in P.-L. Gatier et al. (eds), *Géographie Historique au Proche-Orient,* Paris.

Bowsher, J. M. C. (1987), 'Architecture and Religion in the Decapolis', *PEQ* 1987, pp.62–9.

Braemer, F. (1987), 'Two Campaigns of Excavations on the Ancient Tell of Jerash', *ADAJ* 31, pp.525–9.

Briggs, M.S. (1924), *Muhammedan Architecture in Egypt and Palestine*. Oxford.

Brooks, E. W. (1898), 'A Syriac Chronicle of the year 846', *ZDMG* 51, pp.580–6.

Broshi, M. (1979), 'The Population of Western Palestine in the Roman-Byzantine Period', *BASOR* 236, pp.1–10.

Brown, P. (1971), *The World of Late Antiquity*, London.

Bruce, F. F. (1975), 'Further Thoughts on Paul's Autobiography: Galatians 1:11–2:14', pp. 21–9 in E. Ellis and E. Grasser (1975).

Brunnow, R. E. and von Domaszewski, A. (1905), *Die Provincia Arabia*, 3 vols, Strassburg.

Bujard, J., Haldiman, M-A., and Bonnet, C. (1988), 'Fouilles de la Mission Archéologique Suisse à Umm er-Rasas et Umm al-Walid en 1988', *ADAJ* 32, pp.101–15.

Busse, H. (1973), 'The Revival of Persian Kingship under the Buyids', pp. 47–70 in Richards, D. S. (ed.), *Islamic Civilisation 950–1150*, Oxford.

Butler, H. C. (1910), 'Trajan's Road from Bosra to the Red Sea: The Section between Bosra and Amman', in *PPUAS* Div. III (Greek and Latin Inscriptions in Syria) Sect. A Part 2 (Appendix) vii–xvi.

Butler, H. C. (1907–19), *Publications of the Princeton University Archaeological Expedition to Syria in 1904–5 and 1909*, Div. II, Sect. A., Southern Syria, Leiden.

Butler, H. C. (1929), *Early Churches in Syria, Fourth to Seventh Centuries*, ed. Smith, Princeton.

Campagano, L. S. (1988), 'L'iscrizione metrica greca di

Khirbet er-Rajîb', *LA* 38, pp.253–65.
Carlier, P. (1989), 'Qastal al-Balqa': an Umayyad site in Jordan', pp.104–139 in Bakhit and Schick, eds, *The Fourth International Conference on the History of Bilad al-Sham during the Umayyad period*. Amman.
Carlier, P. and Morin, F. (1987), 'Archaeological Researches at Qastal, second mission, 1985', *ADAJ* 31, pp.221–46.
Caubet, A. (1990), *Aux Sources du Monde Arabe: l'Arabie avant l'Islam,* catalogue of an exhibition at the Institut du Monde Arabe, Paris.
Chehab, H. (1975), 'Les Palais Omeyyades d'Anjar', *Archéologia*, Oct. 1975, no.87, pp.18–24.
Chehab, H. (1978), 'al-Quṣūr al-Umawiyya fī 'Anjar bi-Lubnān', *Sumer* 34, pp.172–80 (Ar. Sect.).
Chehab, M. (1963), 'The Umayyad Palace at 'Anjar', *AO* 5, pp.17–25.
Chen, D. (1980), 'The Design of the Dome of the Rock in Jerusalem', *PEQ* 1980, pp.41–50.
Clemen, P. (1919), *Kunstschutz im Kriege*, 2 vols, Leipzig.
Clermont-Ganneau, C. (1906), 'L'Héracleion de Rabbat-Ammon Philadelphie et la déese Asteria', *RAO* 7, pp.147–55.
Conrad, L. (1986), 'The Plague in Bilad al-Sham in Pre-Islamic Times', pp.143–63 in Bakhit, M. A. and Asfour, M. (eds), *Proceedings of the Symposium on Bilad al-Sham during the Byzantine Period*, Amman, vol. II.
Creswell, K. A. C. (1940), *Early Muslim Architecture*, 1st. Ed., vol. II, Oxford.
Creswell, K. A. C. (1952), 'Fortification in Islam before AD 1250', *Proceedings of the British Academy* 38, pp.89–125.
Creswell, K. A. C. (1969), *Early Muslim Architecture*, 2nd ed., vol. I, pts. I and 2, Oxford.
Creswell, K. A. C. (1989), *A Short Account of Early Muslim Architecture*. Revised and supplemented by J. W. Allan, Aldershot.
Croke, B. and Crow, J. (1983), 'Procopius and Dara', *JRS* 73, pp.143–59.
Crone, P. (1974), *The Mawali in the Umayyad Period*, unpub. PhD thesis, University of London, SOAS.
Crone, P. (1980), *Slaves on Horses*, Cambridge.
Dajani, A. (1958), 'Citadelle d'Amman', *RB* 65, pp.400–402.
Dajani, R. W. (1962), 'A Neo-Babylonian Seal from Amman', *ADAJ* 6–7, pp.124f.
Dajani, R. W. (1966a), 'An Iron-Age Tomb from Amman', *ADAJ* 11, pp.41–47.
Dajani, R. W. (1966b), 'Jabal Nuzha Tomb at Amman', *ADAJ* 11, pp.48–52.
Dajani, R. W. (1966c), 'Amman – Jabal el-Qusur', *ADAJ* 11, pp.103.
Dajani, R. W. (1967–8), 'An EB-MB Burial at Amman', *ADAJ* 12–13, pp.68–9.
Dallas, R. (1980), 'Surveying with a Camera: Rectified Photography', *Architect's Journal*, 20th Feb., pp.395–99.
Dana, S. F. (1970), 'Luweibdeh Roman Tomb', *ADAJ* 15, pp.37–8.
De Vries, B. (1982), 'The Umm el-Jimal Project, 1972–1977', *ADAJ* 26, pp.97–116.
De Vries, B. (1986), 'Umm el-Jimal in the First Three Centuries AD, pp. 227–41 in Freeman, P. and Kennedy, D.L. (eds), *The Defence of the Roman and Byzantine East*, Proceedings of a Colloquium held at the University of Sheffield in April 1986, 2 vols, *BAR* Oxford.
De Vries, B. (1987), 'The Fortifications of el-Lejjun', pp. 311–51 in Parker, S.T. (ed.), *The Roman Frontier in Central Jordan. Interim Report on the Limes Arabicus Project, 1980–1985*, 2 vols, *BAR*, Oxford.
Dennett, D. C. (1939), *Marwan b. Muhammad: the passing of the Umayyad Caliphate*, unpub. PhD thesis, Harvard.
Dennett, D. C. (1950), *Conversion and the Poll-Tax in Early Islam*, Cambridge, Mass.
Dentzer, J.-M. et al. (1982), 'Iraq el Amir: Excavations at the Monumental Gateway', in A. Hadidi (ed.), *SHAJ* I, pp.201–7.
Department of Antiquities (DoA 1975), *The Archaeology of Amman 2000 BC – 750 AD*, catalogue of an exhibition held at the Jordan Intercontinental Hotel, 20–24 November 1975.
Derenk, D. (1974), *Leben und Dichtung des Omaiyadenkhalifen al-Walid ibn Yazid*, Freiburg im Breisgau.
Deschamps, P. (1933), 'Ahamant et el-Habis', *Revue des Études Historiques*.
Deschamps, P. (1939), *Les Chateaux des Croisés en Terre Sainte*, t. II, *La Défense du Royaume de Jérusalem*, Paris.
Dever, W. G. (1989), 'The Collapse of the Urban Early Bronze Age in Palestine – Toward a Systematic Analysis', pp.225–46 in Miroschedji, P. de (ed.), *L'urbanisation de la Palestine à l'âge du Bronze ancien. Bilan et perspectives des recherches actuelles.* Actes du Colloque d'Emmaüs (*BAR*, International Series S 527 II), Oxford.
Dieulafoy, M. (1884–9), *L'art Antique de la Perse*, 2 vols, Paris.
Diez, E. (1915), *Kunst der Islamischen Volker*, Berlin.
Directorate General of Antiquities (DGA 1940), *Hafriyyāt Sāmarrā' 1936–1939*, 2 vols, Baghdad.
Dīwāchī, S. (1947), 'Sūr al-Mawṣil', *Sumer* 3, pp.117–28 (Ar. Sect.).
Donceel-Voûte, P. (1988), 'La Carte de Madaba: Cosmographie, Anachronisme et Propagande', *RB* 95, pp.519–42.
Donner, F. M.(1981), *The Early Islamic Conquests*, Princeton.
Dornemann, R. H. (1969), *Joint Expedition of the University of Jordan, American Center of Oriental Research and Department of Antiquities*, unpublished report, Amman.
Dornemann, R. H. (1970), *The Cultural and Archaeological History of Transjordan in the Bronze and Iron Ages*, unpub. PhD thesis, Chicago.
Dornemann, R. H. (1983), *The Archaeology of the Transjordan in the Bronze and Iron Ages*, Milwaukee.
Dunand, M. (1931), 'La Strata Diocletiana', *RB* 40, pp.227–48.
Elderen, B. van (1970), 'Tell Swafiyeh and Tell Masuh', *Newsletter of ASOR* 9, pp.1–4.
Elitzur, Y. (1989), 'The Identification of Mefa'at in View of the Discoveries at Khirbet Umm er-Resas', *IEJ* 39, pp.267–77.
Ellis, E. and Grasser, E. (eds) (1975), *Jesus und Paulus: Festschrift für Werner Georg Kümmel*, Göttingen.
Ettinghausen, R. (1972), *From Byzantium to Sasanian Iran and the Islamic World*, Leiden.
Ettinghausen, R. and Grabar, O. (1987), *The Art and Architecture of Islam: 650–1250*, London.
Falkner, R. K. (1990), 'Abbasid Pottery in Jordan, with examples from the Amman Citadel and Khirbet Faris', paper given at the Fifth International Conference for the history of Bilad al-Sham, Amman 1990.
el Fakharani, F. (1975), 'The Library of Philadelphia (?), or, The

So-Called Temple on the Citadel Hill in Amman', *Wissenschaftliche Zeitscrift d. Uni. Rostock* XXIV, Gesellschafts-u. Sprachwissenschaftliche Reihe. H.6.: 533–54.
Fehérvári, G. (1974), 'Some Problems of Seljuq art', pp.1–12 in Watson, W. (ed.), *The Art of Iran and Anatolia*, London.
Finster, B. and Schmidt, J. (1976), *Sasanidische und frühislamische Ruinen im Iraq, Baghdader Mitteilungen* 8.
Fischer, K. (1974), *Nimruz*, 2 vols, Bonn.
Fisher, W. B., Atkinson, K., Beaumont, P., Coles, A., Gilchrist-Shirland, D. (1966), *Soil Survey of Wadi Ziqlab, Jordan*, unpub. report, Durham.
Fitzgerald, G. M. (1931), *Beth-Shan Excavations*, I: *the Arab and Byzantine Levels*, Philadelphia.
Food and Agriculture Organisation (FAO) (1970), *Investigation of the Sandstone Aquifers of East Jordan*, based on the work of D. H. Parker, Rome.
Frézouls, E. (1961), 'Recherches sur les Théatres de l'Orient Syrien II', *Syria* 38, pp.54–86.
Fulco, W. J. (1978), 'The Amman Citadel Inscription: a new collation', *BASOR* 230, pp.39–43.
Gabrieli, F. (1935), 'Il Califfato di Hisham', *Mémoires de la Societé Royale d'Archéologie d'Alexandrie* 7.
Garitte, G. (1961), 'La Passion de S. Elien de Philadelphie (Amman)', *AB* 79, pp.412–46.
Gatier, P-L. (1982), 'Inscriptions Grecques et Latines en Jordanie', *MB* 22, pp.10–11.
Gatier, P-L. (1986), *Inscriptions de la Jordanie*, vol 2, IGLS XXI. Paris.
Gatier, P-L. (1988), 'Philadelphie et Gerasa du Royaume Nabatéen à la Province d'Arabie', pp.159–70 in P-L. Gatier et al. (eds), *Géographie Historique au Proche-Orient*, Paris.
Gatier, P-L. (1990), 'Décapole et Coelé-Syrie: Deux Inscriptions Nouvelles', *Syria* 67, pp.204–6.
Gatier, P-L. and Vérilhac, A-M. (1989), 'Les columbes de Déméter à Philadelphie-Amman', *Syria* 66, pp.337–48.
Gaube, H. (1974a), *Hirbet el Baida – Ein Arabischer Palast in Südsyrien*, Beirut.
Gaube, H. (1974b), 'An Examination of the Ruins of Qasr Burqu', *ADAJ* 19, pp.93–100.
Gaube, H. (1977), 'Amman, Harane und Qastal, vier frühislamische Bauwerke in Mitteljordanien', *ZDPV* 93, pp.52–87.
Gaube, H. (1979), 'Die syrischen Wüstenschlösser. Einige wirtschaftliche und politische Gesichstpunkte zu ihrer Entstehung', *ZDPV* 95, pp.182–209.
Gavin, C. (1985), 'Jordan's Environment in Early Photographs', in A. Hadidi (ed.), *SHAJ* II, pp.279–85.
Gawlikowski, M. (1974), 'Les Defenses de Palmyre', *Syria* 51, pp.231–42.
Gawlikowski, M. (1986), 'A Residential Area by the South Decumanus', pp. 107–36 in Zayadine (ed.), *Jerash Archaeological Project* I, 'Amman.
Geraty, L. T. et al. (1988), 'The Joint Madaba Plains Project: A Preliminary Report on the Second Season at Tell el-'Umeiri and Vicinity', *AUSS* 26, pp.217–52.
Von Gerkan, A. (1939), pp.4–61 in Rostovtzeff, M. I., Brown, F.E. and Welles, C.B. (eds), *The Excavations at Dura-Europos – Preliminary Report of the 7th and 8th Seasons of Work, 1933–1934, 1934–1935*, New Haven.
Gerstenblith, P. (1983), *The Levant at the Beginning of the Middle Bronze Age* (*ASOR Diss.Series* 5), Winona Lake/IN.
Gese, H. (1958), 'Ammonitische Grenzfestungen zwischen Wadi es-Sir und Na'ur', *ZDPV* 74, pp.55–64.
Ghawanmeh, Y. (1979), *'Ammān, Ḥaḍāratuhā wa-tārīkhuhā*, Amman.
Ghirshman, R. (1938), 'Les Fouilles de Chapour (Iran), Deuxième Campagne', *Revue des Arts Asiatiques* 12, pp.15–17.
Ghirshman, R. (1947–8), 'Une mosquée de Suse au début de l'Hégire', *Bulletin d'Études Orientales* 12, pp.77–9.
Ghirshman, R. (1954), *Iran from the Earliest Times to the Islamic Conquest*, London.
Ghirshman, R. (1956), *Fouilles de Chapour, Bichapour* II, *Les Mosaïques Sassanides*, Paris.
Gibb, H. A. R. (1962), *Studies on the Civilisation of Islam*, ed. Shaw S. J. and Polk, W. R., London.
Godard A. (1934), 'Le Tari Khana de Damghan', *Gazette de Beaux-Arts*, 6th series, 12, pp.225–35.
Godard, A. (1951), 'L'Origine de la Madrasa à Quatre Iwans', *AI* 15–16, pp.1–10.
Godard, A. (1965), *The Art of Iran*, London.
Goldstein, J. A. (1976), *I Maccabees: A New Translation with Notes and Commentary* (Anchor Bible Series vol. 41.1), New York.
Goldstein, J. A. (1983), *II Maccabees: A New Translation with Notes and Commentary* (Anchor Bible Series vol. 41.2), New York.
Goodchild, R. (1960), 'A Byzantine Palace at Apollonia (Cyrenaica)', *Antiquity* 34, pp.246–58.
Görg, M. (1989), 'Transjordanische Ortsnamen unter Amenophis III.', pp. 40-53 in Görg, M., *Beiträge zur Zeitgeschichte der Anfänge Israels. Dokumente - Materialien - Notizen* (ÄAT 2), Wiesbaden 1989.
Gough, M. (1952), 'Anazarbus', *Anatolian Studies* 2, pp.85–150.
Grabar, O. (1954a), *Ceremonial and Art at the Umayyad Court*, unpub. PhD thesis, Princeton.
Grabar, O. (1954b), 'The Painting of the Six Kings at Qusayr Amrah', *AO* I, pp.185–7.
Grabar, O. (1963a), 'Umayyad Palaces and the Abbasid Revolution', *Studia Islamica* 18, pp.5–18.
Grabar, O. (1963b), 'A Small Episode of Early Abbasid Times and Some Consequences', *Eretz Israel* 7, pp.44–7.
Grabar, O. (1973), *The Formation of Islamic Art*, New Haven.
Grabar, O. (1987), 'The Date and Meaning of Mshatta', *Dumbarton Oaks Papers* 41, pp.243–8.
Grabar, O., Holod, R., Knudstad, J., Trousdale, W. (1978), *City in the Desert: Qasr al-Hayr East*, Cambridge, Mass.
Graf, D. F. (1978), 'Saracens and the Defense of the Arabian Frontier', *BASOR* 229, pp.1–26.
Graf, D. F. (1983), 'Dedanite and Minaean (South Arabian) Inscriptions from the Hisma', *ADAJ* 27, pp.555–69.
Graf, D. F. (1986) 'The Nabataeans and the Decapolis', pp.785–96 in P. Freeman and D. Kennedy (eds), *The Defence of the Roman and Byzantine East* (Oxford, B.A.R.), vol. 2.
Haase, Cl-P. (1990), 'Madinat al-Far/Hisn Maslama – first archaeological soundings at the site, and the history of an Umayyad domain in Abbasid times', paper given at the Fifth International Conference for the history of Bilad al-Sham, 'Amman 1990.
Habicht, C. (1976), *2. Makkabäerbuch* in G. Kümmel (ed.), *Jüdische Schriften aus hellenistisch-römischer Zeit I: Historische und legendarische Erzählungen*, Güttersloh.
Hacker, J. M. (1960), *Modern Amman, a Social Study*, Research

Papers no.3, Dept. of Geography, Durham.
Hadidi, A. (1970a), 'The Pottery of the Roman Forum at Amman', *ADAJ* 15, pp.11–15.
Hadidi, A. (1970b), *The Roman Forum at Amman*, unpub. PhD thesis, University of Missouri, Columbia.
Hadidi, A. (1973a), 'Some Bronze Coins from Amman', *ADAJ* 18, pp.51–4.
Hadidi, A. (1973b), 'A Greek inscribed Altar from Amman', *ADAJ* 18, pp.61–2.
Hadidi, A. (1974), 'The Excavation of the Roman Forum at Amman (Philadelphia) 1964–1967', *ADAJ* 19, pp.71–91.
Hadidi, A. (1975), 'Fulūs Nuḥāsiyya Umawiya min 'Ammā n', *ADAJ* 20, pp.9–14 (Ar. sect.).
Hadidi, A. (1978), 'The Roman Town-Plan of Amman', pp.210–22 in Moorey, P. R. S. and Parr, P. J. (eds), *Archaeology in the Levant*, Warminster.
Hadidi, A. (1982), 'An EB-MB Tomb at Jabal Jofeh in Amman', *ADAJ* 26, pp.283–86.
Hadidi, A. (1987), 'An Ammonite Tomb at Amman', *Levant* 19, pp.101–20.
Hadidi, A. (1989), 'Amman – Roman Forum', pp. 155–166 in: Homès-Fredericq, D. and Hennessy, J.B. (eds), *Archaeology of Jordan* II 1 (Akkadica Suppl. 7), Leuven 1989.
Hamilton, R. W. (1946a), 'Some Eighth-Century Capitals from Al Muwaqqar', *QDAP* 12, pp.63–9.
Hamilton, R. W. (1946b), 'An Eighth-Century Water Gauge at Al Muwaqqar', *QDAP* 12, pp.70-72.
Hamilton, R. W. (1949), *The Structural History of the Aqsa Mosque*, Jerusalem.
Hamilton, R. W. (1953), 'Carved Plaster in Umayyad Architecture', *Iraq* 15, pp.43–55.
Hamilton, R. W. (1959), *Khirbat al Mafjar: An Arabian Mansion in the Jordan Valley*, Oxford.
Hamilton, R. W. (1969), 'Who Built Khirbat al Mafjar?', *Levant* 1, pp.61–7.
Hamilton, R. W. (1988), *Walid and his Friends: an Umayyad Tragedy*. Oxford.
Hammond, P. C. (1975), 'Survey and Excavation at Petra 1973–4', *ADAJ* 20, pp.5–30.
Hanbury-Tenison, J. W. (1986), *The Late Chalcolitic to Early Bronze I Transition in Palestine and Transjordan*, British Archaeological Reports, International Series 311, Oxford.
Ḥanīn, Qāsim Rāḍī (1985–6), 'al-tanqīb wal-ṣiyāna al-athariyya fī dār raqm 4 fī Madaqq al-Ṭabl', *Sumer* 44, pp.158–181 (Ar. Sect.).
Harding, G. L. (1944), 'Two Iron Age Tombs from Amman', *QDAP* 11, pp.67–74; 105–6.
Harding, G. L. (1945), 'Two Iron Age Tombs from Amman', *QDAP* 11, pp.76–74.
Harding, G. L. (1946), 'A Nabatean Tomb at Amman', *QDAP* 12, pp.58–62.
Harding, G. L. (1950), 'Roman Family Tomb on Jebel Jofeh, Amman', *QDAP* 14, pp.81–94.
Harding, G. L. (1951a), 'Excavations on the Citadel of Amman', *ADAJ* 1, pp.7–16.
Harding, G. L. (1951b), 'A Roman Tomb in Amman', *ADAJ* 1, pp.30-33.
Harding, G. L. (1951c), 'Two Iron Age Tombs in Amman', *ADAJ* 1, pp.37–40.
Harding, G. L. (1951d), 'Two Iron Age Tombs from Amman', *QDAP* 11, pp.74–6.
Harding, G. L. (1967), *The Antiquities of Jordan*, 2nd. ed., London.
Harding, G. L. and Isserlin, B. S. J. (1953), 'A Middle Bronze Age Tomb at Amman', pp.14–26 in Harding, G. L. (ed.), *Four Tomb Groups from Jordan* (PEFA 6), London 1953.
Harding, G. L., Driver, G. R. and Tufnell, O. (1953), 'The Tomb of Adoni Nur in Amman', pp. 48–72 in Harding, G. L. (ed.), *Four Tomb Groups from Jordan* (PEFA 6), London 1953.
Harper, G. M. (1928), 'A Study in the Commercial Relations between Egypt and Syria in the Third Century before Christ', *AJP* 49, pp.1–35.
Harper, R. P. (1977), 'Two Excavations on the Euphrates Frontier, 1968–1974: Pagnik Oreni (Eastern Turkey) 1968–1971 and Dibsi Faraj (Northern Syria) 1972–1974', pp.453–60 in Haupt, D. and Horn, H.G. (eds), *Studien zu den Militargrenzen Roms, Vortrage des 10 Internationalen Limeskongresses in der Germania Inferior*, Cologne.
Hauben, H. (1984), "Onagres et Hémionagres' en Trans-jordanie au IIIe Siècle avant J.-C.', *AS* 15, pp.89–111.
Hayari, M. (1977), *al-Imārā al-Ṭā'iyya fī Bilād al-Shām*, Amman.
Hellenkemper, H. (1976), *Burgen der Kreuzritterzeit in der Grafschaft Edessa und im Königreich Kleinarmenien*, Bonn.
Hellenkemper, H. (1990), 'Die Stadtmauern von Anazarbos/'Ayn Zarba', pp. 71–6 in Diem, W. and Falaturi, A. (eds), *XXIV Deutscher Orientalistentag vom 26. bis 30. September 1988 in Köln*, Stuttgart.
Helms, S. and McCreery, D. (1988), 'Rescue Excavations at Umm al-Bighal', The Pottery', *ADAJ* 32, pp.319–47.
Helms, S. (1989), 'A EB IV Pottery Repertoire at Amman', *BASOR* 273, pp.17–36.
Helms, S. W. (1990), *Early Islamic Architecture of the Desert: A Bedouin Station in Eastern Jordan*, Edinburgh.
Hengel, M. (1989), *The 'Hellenization' of Judaea in the First Century after Christ*, Philadelphia.
Hennessy, J. B. (1966), 'Excavation of a Bronze Age Temple at Amman', *PEQ* 1966, pp.155–62.
Hennessy, J. B. (1989), 'Amman Airport', pp.167–78 in Homès-Fredericq, D. and Hennessy, J.B. (ed.), *Archaeology of Jordan* II 1 (Akkadica Suppl. 7), Leuven 1989.
Henschel-Simon, E. (1945), 'Note on the Pottery of the Amman Tombs', *QDAP* 11, pp.75–80.
Herr, L. G. (1976), 'The Amman Airport Excavations 1976', *ADAJ* 21, pp.109–12.
Herrmann, G. (1977), *The Iranian Revival*, Oxford.
Herzfeld, E. (1921), *Mschatta, Hira und Badiya*, Berlin.
Herzfeld, E. (1923), *Der Wandschmuck der Bauten von Samarra und seine Ornamentik, Ausgrabungen von Samarra* I, Berlin.
Herzfeld, E. (1942), 'Damascus: Studies in Architecture II', *AI* 10, pp.13–30.
Herzfeld, E. (1948), *Geschichte der Stadt Samarra*, Ausgrabungen von Samarra VI, Hamburg.
Hill, G. F. (1922), *Catalogue of the Greek Coins of Arabia, Mesopotamia and Persia*, London.
Hillenbrand, R. (1982), 'La Dolce Vita in Early Islamic Syria', *Art History* 5, pp.1–35.
Hills, E. S.(ed.) (1966), *Arid Lands*, London and Paris.
Hinz, W. (1955), *Arabische Masse und Gewichte*, Leiden.
Homès-Fredericq, D. and Hennessy, J. B. (eds) (1986), *Archaeology of Jordan* I.1, *Bibliography and Gazetteer of Sites*.

Leuven.

Homès-Fredericq, D. and Hennessy, J. B., eds (1989), *Archaeology of Jordan* II.1–2, *Field Surveys and Sites*, A-K; L-Z, Leuven.

Homès-Fredericq, D. (1986), 'Prospections Archéologiques en Moab', pp.81–100 in A. Théodoridès et al. (eds), *Archéologie et Philologie dans l'Étude des Civilisations Orientales*. Leuven.

Homès-Fredericq, D. (1987), 'Possible Phoenician Influence in Jordan in the Iron Age', *SHAJ* 3, pp.89–96.

Horn, S. H. (1967), 'The Amman Citadel Inscription', *BASOR* 193, pp.2–13.

Hübner, U. (1989a), 'Fälschungen ammonitischer Siegel', *UF* 21, pp.217–26.

Hübner, U. (1989b), 'Die erste grossformatige Rundplastik aus dem eisenzeitlichen Moab', *UF* 21, pp.227–231.

Hübner, U. (1992a), 'Og von Baschan und sein Bett in Rabbat-Ammon (Deuteronomium 3,11)', *ZAW* 104 (in press).

Hübner, U. (1992b), 'Das ikonographische Repertoire der ammonitischen Siegel und seine Entwicklung', in Keel, O. (ed.), *Die Ikonographie der nordwestsemitischen Stempelsiegel. Studien zu den Stempelsiegeln aus Palästina*, Bd. V (OBO), Fribourg-Göttingen.

Hübner, U. (1992c), *Die Ammoniter. Untersuchungen zur Geschichte, Kultur und Religion eines transjordanischen volkes im 1. Jahrtausend v.Chr.* (ADPV).

Hübner, U. (1993), 'Keramik aus den italienischen Grabungen (1927–1938) in 'Ammān im Museo Internazionale delle Ceramiche in Faenza', *Bolletino del Museo Internazionale delle Ceramiche in Faenza* 79.

Hübner, U. and Knauf, E. A. (1992), Review of Aufrecht, W. E., *A Corpus of Ammonite Inscriptions*, *ZDPV* 108 (forthcoming).

Humphreys, R. S. (1977), *From Saladin to the Mongols*, Albany.

Hunt, E. D. (1982), *Holy Land Pilgrimages in the Later Roman Empire: AD 312-460*, Oxford.

Hunting Technical Services Ltd. (1956), *Report on the Range Classification Survey of the Hashemite Kingdom of Jordan*, London.

Hütteroth, W. D. and Abdulfattah, K. (1977), *Historical Geography of Palestine, Transjordan and Southern Syria in the late 16th century*, Erlangen.

Ibach, R. (1978), 'Expanded Archaeological Survey of the Hesban Region', in Boraas and Gerarty (1978), 201–13 (= *AUSS* 16 [1978], pp.201–13]).

Ibach, R. D. (1987), *Hesban* 5: *Archaeological Survey of the Hesban Region*, Berrien Springs.

Ibrahim, M. M. (1983–1984), 'Saḥāb', *AfO* 29–30, pp.256–60.

Ibrahim, M. M. (1989), 'Sahab', pp. 516–20 in Homès-Fredericq, D. and Hennessy, J.B. (ed.), *Archaeology of Jordan* II 2 (Accadica Suppl. 8), Leuven 1989.

Ibrahim, M., Sauer, J., and Yassin, K. (1976), 'The East Jordan Valley Survey 1975', *BASOR* 222, pp.41–66.

Ionides, M. G. (1939), *Report on the Water Resources of Transjordan and their Development*, London.

Isaac, B. (1981), 'The Decapolis in Syria: A Neglected Inscription', *ZPE* 44, pp.67–74.

Isaac, B. (1989), 'Trade Routes to Arabia and the Roman Presence in the Desert', pp. 241–56 in T. Fahd (ed.), *L'Arabie Préislamique et son Environnement Historique et Culturel*, Leiden.

Isserlin, B. S. J. (1953), 'Notes and Comparisons', pp.19–22 in Harding, G. L. (ed.), *Four Tomb Groups from Jordan* (PEFA 6), London 1953.

Jaussen, A. and Savignac, R. (1909), 'Inscription Grèco-Nabatéen de Zizeh', *RB* 6, pp.587–92.

Jaussen, A. and Savignac, R. (1922), *Mission archéologique en Arabie*, 3 vols, Paris.

Jenkins, M. (1982), *Islamic Art in the Kuwait National Museum*, Kuwait.

Johns, C. N. (1931), 'Excavations at Pilgrims Castle, Athlit', *QDAP* 1, pp.111–29.

Johns, C. N. (1932), 'Medieval 'Ajlun, 1: The Castle', *QDAP* 2, pp.21–33.

Johnson, S. (1983), *Late Roman Fortifications*, London.

Jones, A. H. M. (1971), *The Cities of the Eastern Roman Provinces*, 2nd. ed., Oxford.

Jones, A. H. M. (1979), *The Greek City, from Alexander to Justinian*, Oxford, paperback reprint.

Jones, D. and Michell, G. (1972), 'Squinches and Pendentives: Problems and Definitions', *AARP* 1, pp.9–26.

Kafafi, Z. (1977), *Late Bronze Age Pottery in Jordan (East Bank) 1575–1200 BC*, MA thesis (unpubl.), University of Jordan Amman, Amman 1977.

Kafafi, Z. (1985), 'Egyptian Topographical Lists of the Late Bronze Age on Jordan (East Bank)', *BN* 29, pp.17–22.

Kalsbek, J. and London, G. (1978), 'A Late Second Millennium B.C. Potting Puzzle', *BASOR* 232, pp.47–56.

Karnapp, W. (1976), *Die Stadtmauer von Resafa in Syrien*, Berlin.

Kasher, A. (1988), *Jews, Idumaeans, and Ancient Arabs*, Tübingen.

Keall, E. J. (1974), 'Some Thoughts on the early Eyvan', pp.122–36 in Kouymjian, D. K. (ed.), *Near Eastern Numismatics, Iconography, Epigraphy and History*, Beirut.

Keall, E. J., Leveque, M. A., and Willson, N. (1980), 'Qal'eh-i Yazdigird: Its Architectural Decorations', *Iran* 18, pp.1–42.

Kennedy, D. L. (1982a), 'The Contribution of Aerial Photography to Archaeology in Jordan: with Special Reference to the Roman Period', in A. Hadidi (ed.), *SHAJ* 1, pp.29–36.

Kennedy, D. L. (1982b), *Archaeological Explorations on the Roman Frontier in Northeast Jordan*, *BAR*, Oxford.

Kennedy, H. (1981), *The Early Abbasid Caliphate*, London and Sydney.

Kennedy, H. (1985), 'The Last Century of Byzantine Syria', *BF* 10, pp.141–83.

Kennedy, H. (1986), *The Prophet and the Age of the Caliphates*, London and New York.

Kennedy, H. (1990), 'Nomads and Settled People in Bilad al-Sham in the Fourth/Ninth and Fifth/Tenth Centuries', paper given at the Fifth International Conference for the history of Bilad al-Sham, 'Amman 1990.

Kervran, M. et al (1982), *Excavation of Qal'at al-Bahrain*, part 1, (1977–1979), Bahrain.

Khairy, N. (1979), 'Al-Quweismeh Family Tomb', *PEQ* 1979, pp.51–61.

Khalaf, Murhaf (1985), 'Die 'Abbasidische Stadtmauer von ar-Raqqa/ar-Rafiqa', *DaM* 2, pp.123–31.

Khouri, R. G. (1986), *Jerash: A Frontier City of the Roman East*, London.

Khouri, R. G. (1988), Amman: A Brief Guide to the Antiquities, Amman.

Killick, A. (1983), 'Udruh – The Frontier of an Empire', *Levant* 15, pp.110–131.

Killick, A. C. (1986), 'Udruh – eine antike Statte vor den Toren Petras', in Lindner, M. (ed.), *Petra. Neue Ausgrabungen und*

Entdeckungen, Munich.
King, G. R. D. (1982), 'Preliminary Report on a Survey of Byzantine and Islamic Sites in Jordan (1980)', *ADAJ* 26, pp.85–95.
King, G. R. D. et al. (1983), 'Survey of Byzantine and Islamic Sites in Jordan: Second Season Report (1981)', *ADAJ* 27, pp.385–436.
Kirkbride, A. S. (1951), 'Recent Finds of Arabic Gold Coins', *ADAJ* 1, pp.17–19.
Kister, M. J. (1972), 'Some Reports Concerning Mecca', *JESHO* 15, pp.84–91.
Knauf, E. A. (1984), 'Abel Keramim', *ZDPV* 100, pp.119–21.
Knauf, E. A. (1988), *Midian. Untersuchungen zur Geschichte Palästinas und Nordarabiens am Ende des 2. Jahrtausends v.Chr.* (ADPV), Wiesbaden.
Knauf, E. A. (1989), *Ismael. Untersuchungen zur Geschichte Palästinas und Nordarabiens im 1. Jahrtausend v.Chr.* (ADPV), Wiesbaden.
Knauf, E. A. and Brooker, C. H. (1988), Review of Khouri, R. G. and Whitcomb, D., *Aqaba, Port of Palestine on the China Sea*, *ZDPV* 104, pp.179–81.
Knudstad, J. (1968), 'A Preliminary Report on the 1966–7 Excavations at Nippur', *Sumer* 24, pp.95–106.
Kochavi, M. (1989), 'Urbanization and Re-Urbanization: Early Bronze Age, Middle Bronze Age and the Period In-between Them', pp.257–9 in Miroschedji P. de (ed.), *L'urbanisation de la Palestine à l'âge du Bronze ancien. Bilan et perspectives des recherches actuelles.* Actes du Colloque d'Emmaüs (British Archaeological Reports, International Series S 527 II), Oxford 1989.
Kohl, H. (1925), 'Die Arabische Burg', pp. 41–96 in Wiegand, T., *Baalbek*, Bd. III, Berlin.
Kraeling, C. H. et al. (1938), *Gerasa, City of the Decapolis*, New Haven.
Krencker, D., von Lupke, T., Winnefeld, H. (1923), *Baalbek*, Bd. II, Berlin.
Kröger, J. (1982), *Sasanidische Stuckdekor*, Mainz.
Lammens, H. (1910), 'La Bâdia et la Hira sous les Omaiyades', *Mélanges de la Faculté Orientale* 4, pp.91ff.
Lander, J. (1984), *Roman Stone Fortifications. Variation and Change from the First Century* AD *to the Fourth*, *BAR*, Oxford.
Landes, G. M. (1961), 'The Material Civilisation of the Ammonites', *BA* 24, pp.66–86.
Lane, A. (1947), *Early Islamic Pottery*, London.
Lane-Poole, S. (1875–90), *Catalogue of Oriental Coins in the British Museum*, London.
Lane-Poole, S. (1897), *Catalogue of the Arabic Coins Preserved in the Khedivial Library at Cairo*, London.
Lassner, J. (1970), *The Topography of Baghdad in the Early Middle Ages*, Detroit.
Lassner, J. (1980), *The Shaping of the Abbasid Caliphate*, Princeton.
Lawrence, A. W. (1979), *Aims in Greek Fortification*, Oxford.
Le Strange, G. (1890), *Palestine under the Moslems*, London.
Lehmann, P. H. (1954), 'The Siting of Hellenistic Temples', *Journal of the Society of Architectural Historians* 12, pp.15–20.
Lemaire, A. and Lozachmeur, H. (1987), '*Bîrâh/ birtâ* en araméen', *Syria* 64, pp.261–6.
Lenzen, C. J. (1990), 'Beit Ras Excavations: 1988 and 1989', *Syria* 67, pp.474–6.
Lenzen, C. J., and Knauf, E. A. (1987), 'Beit Ras/Capitolias, A Preliminary Evaluation of the Archaeological and Textual Evidence', *Syria* 64, pp.21–46.
Levi, D. (1948), *Antioch Mosaic Pavements*, 2 vols, Princeton.
Lewis, H. (1882), 'Ancient Buildings at Amman', *PEFQS* 1882, pp.113–15.
Littman, E., Magie, D., and Stuart, D. R. (1921), *Publications of the Princeton Archaeological Exedition to Syria*, Div. III, *Greek and Latin Inscriptions*, Sect. A. pt.1, Leiden.
Littmann, E. (1949), *Publications of the Princeton Archaeological Expedition to Syria*, Div. IV, Sect. D, *Semitic Inscriptions*, Leiden.
Lloyd, S. (1978), *The Archaeology of Mesopotamia*, London.
Lyttleton, M. (1974), *Baroque Architecture in Classical Antiquity*, London.
Ma'ayeh, F. S. (1960a), 'Chronique archéologique', *RB* 67, pp.226–9.
Ma'ayeh, F. S. (1960b), 'Recent Archaeological Discoveries in Jordan', *ADAJ* 4–5, pp.114f.
Ma'ayeh, F. S. (1962), 'Amman', *RB* 69, pp.85f.
MacAdam, H. I. (1986), *Studies in the History of the Roman Province of Arabia*, *BAR*, International Series 297, Oxford
MacDonald, B. (1980), 'The Wadi El Hasa Survey 1979: A Preliminary Report', *ADAJ* 24, pp.169–83.
MacDonald, B. (1981), 'Wadi al-Hesa Survey', *BA* 44, pp.60–1.
MacKenzie, D. (1911), *The Megalithic Monuments of Rabbath Ammon at Amman* (PEFA 1), London 1911, pp.1–40.
Madelung, W. (1986), 'The Sufyani between Tradition and History', *Studia Islamica* 63, pp.5–48.
Majhūl, D. (1972), 'Majmū' at Tulūl al-Shu'ayba', *Sumer* 28, pp.243–6 (Ar. sect.).
Mango, C. (1976), *Byzantine Architecture*, New York.
Marçais, G. (1954), *L'Architecture Musulmane d'Occident*, Paris.
Mare, W. H. (1986), 'Quwailiba: Abila of the Decapolis', *AfO* 33, pp.206–9.
Mayer, H. E. (1987), 'The Crusader Lordship of Kerak and Shaubak, Some Preliminary Remarks', *SHAJ* 3, pp.199–203.
Mazar, B. (1957), 'The Tobiads', *IEJ* 7, pp.137–45; 229–38.
McGovern, P. E. (1986), 'Cultural and Historical Synthesis', pp.335–43 in McGovern, P. E. (ed.), *The Late Bronze and Early Iron Ages of Central Transjordan: The Baq'ah Valley Project, 1977–1981* (University Museum Monograph 65), Philadelphia/PN.
McGovern, P. E. (1989), 'The Baq'ah Valley Project 1987, Khirbet Umm ad-Dananir and al-Qesir', *ADAJ* 33, pp.123–36.
McNicoll, A. et al. (1982), *Pella in Jordan 1: Report of the Joint Sydney University – Wooster College Ohio, Excavations 1979–81*, Canberra.
McQuitty, A. (1986), 'Bait Ras', *AfO* 33, pp.164–6.
Melville, C. P. (1984), 'Sismicité historique de la Mer Rouge septentrionale', IVèmes Rencontres Internationales d'Archéologie et d'Histoire d'Antibes, Tremblements de Terre: Histoire et Archéologie, November 1983.
Mershen, B. and Knauf, E. A. (1988), 'From Gadar to Umm Qais', *ZDPV* 104, pp.128–45.
Mhaisen, M. (1976), 'Jbeyha Church: 1976', *ADAJ* 21, pp.8–22 (Ar. sect).
Milik, J. T. (1960), 'Notes d'Epigraphie et de Topographie Jordaniennes', *LA* 10, pp.147–84.
Miller, J. M. (1979), 'Archaeological Survey of Central Moab

(1978)', *BASOR* 234, pp.43–52.

Miller, K. (1986), *Mappae Arabicae*, ed. H. Gaube, TAVO Beihefte Reihe B nr. 57, 2 vols, Wiesbaden.

Miroschedji, P. de (1989), 'Le processus d'urbanisation en Palestine au Bronze ancien: chronologie et rythmes', pp. 63–79 in Miroschedji, P. de (ed.), *L'urbanisation de la Palestine à l'âge du Bronze ancien. Bilan et perspectives des recherches actuelles.* Actes du Colloque d'Emmaüs (*BAR*, International Series S 527 i), Oxford.

Mittmann, S. (1970a), *Beiträge zur Siedlungs und Territorial-geschichte des Nordlichen Ostjordanlandes*, Wiesbaden.

Mittmann, S. (1970b), 'Zenon im Ostjordanland', pp.201–10 in A. Kuschke and E. Kuschke (eds), *Archäologie und Altes Testament: Festschrift für Kurt Galling*, Tübingen.

Mlaker, K. (1943), *Die Hierodulenlisten von Ma'īn*, Leipzig.

Monroe, E. (1973), *Philby of Arabia*, London.

Moore, E. A. (1964), *Some Soldier Martyrs of the Early Christian Church in East Jordan and Syria*, Beirut.

Moorey, P. R. S. (1978), *Kish Excavations 1923–33*, Oxford.

Morony, M. G. (1984), *Iraq after the Muslim Conquest*, Princeton.

Mouterde, P. (1939), 'Inscriptions en syriaque dialectal à Kamed', *Mélanges de l'Université St. Joseph* 22, pp.73–106.

Murray, S. B. (1917), *Hellenistic Architecture in Syria*, Princeton.

Musil, A. (1907), *Kusejr Amra*, 2 vols, Vienna.

Mustafa, M. A. (1954), 'Taqrīr awwalī 'an al-tanqīb fī al-Kūfa lil-mawsim al-thānī', *Sumer* 10, pp.73–85 (Ar. sect.).

Mustafa, M. A. (1956), 'Taqrīr awwalī 'an al-tanqīb fī al-Kūfa lil-mawsim al-thālith', *Sumer* 12, pp.2–32 (Ar. sect.); tr. Kessler, *Sumer* 19, pp.36–65.

Musurillo, H. ed.(1972), *The Acts of the Christian Martyrs*, Oxford.

al-Nabrāwī, R. M. M. (1989), 'Fulūs 'Ammān wa-Jarash fī ṣadr al-Islām', *Yarmouk Numismatics* 1, pp.11–30.

Naghawi, A. (1989), 'Umayyad Filses minted at Jerash', pp.219–22 in Zayadine, F. (ed.), *Jerash Archaeological Project: 1984–8*, II. IFAPO 18, Paris.

Najjar, M. (1989), 'Abbasid pottery from el-Muwaqqar', *ADAJ* 33, pp.305–22.

Najjār, M., 'Araz, H., and Qusūs, R. (1989), 'Taqrīr awwalī 'an natā'ij al-tanqībāt al-athariyya fī baldat al-Muwaqqar', *ADAJ* 33, pp.5–12 (Ar. Sect.).

Nassar, N. G. (1946), 'The Arabic Mints in Palestine and Transjordan', *QDAP* 13, pp.121–7.

Northedge, A. and Falkner, R. (1987), 'The 1986 Survey Season at Samarra", *Iraq* 49, pp.143–73.

Northedge, A. (1977–8), 'A Survey of Islamic Buildings at Amman', *ADAJ* 22, pp.5–13.

Northedge, A. (1979a), 'The Qasr of Amman', *AARP* 15, pp.22–7.

Northedge, A. (1979b), 'Amman Citadel. Excavations on D Area', 1977–1978, *ADAJ* 23, pp.172–6.

Northedge, A. (1980), 'Survey of the Terrace Area at Amman Citadel', *Levant* 12, pp.135–54.

Northedge, A. (1983), 'The Fortifications of Qal'at Amman', *ADAJ* 27, pp.436–60.

Northedge, A. (1983–4), 'Qal'at Amman 1979–81', *AfO* 29–30, pp.252–5.

Northedge, A. (1984), *Qal'at 'Amman in the Early Islamic Period*, unpublished PhD thesis, London, School of Oriental and African Studies, 2 vols.

Northedge, A. (1987), 'Karkh Fairuz at Samarra', *Mesopotamia* 22, pp.251–64.

Northedge, A. (1988), 'The Typology of Cantonments in the Early Islamic period', unpublished SOAS seminar paper, May 1988.

Northedge, A. (1989), 'The Umayyad Mosque of Amman', pp.140–63 in Bakhit, M. A. and Schick, R. (eds), *The history of Bilad al-Sham during the Umayyad period (Fourth International Conference)*, Amman.

Northedge, A. (1990a), 'The racecourses at Samarra', *BSOAS* 53/1, pp.31–60.

Northedge, A. (1990b), *Samarra, Residenz der 'Abbasidenkalifen*, catalogue of an exhibition at Tübingen, Sept.–Oct. 1990.

Northedge, A. (forthcoming), 'Archaeology and New Urban Settlement in Early Islamic Syria and Iraq', in King, G. R. D. and Cameron A. (eds), *Studies in Late Antiquity and Early Islam* II, *Settlement Patterns in the Byzantine and Early Islamic Near East*, Princeton.

Northedge, A., Bamber, A. and Roaf, M. (1988), *Excavations at 'Ana*, Warminster.

Oakeshott, M. F. (1978), *A Study of the Iron Age II Pottery of East Jordan with Special Reference to Unpublished Material from Edom*, Ph.D. thesis, University of London.

Oates, D. (1968), *Studies in the Ancient History of Northern Iraq*, London.

Olávarri-Goicoechea, E. (1980), 'Altar de Zeus-Ba'alshamin (Procedente de Amman)', *MHA* 4, pp.197–202.

Olávarri-Goicoechea, E. (1985), *El Palacio Omeya de Amman* II, *la Arqueología*, Valencia.

von Oppenheim, M. (1939), *Die Beduinen*, Bd. 1, Leipzig.

Oren, E. D. (1971), 'Early Islamic Material from Ganei Hamat (Tiberias)', *Archaeology* 24, pp.274–7.

Orrieux, C. (1979), 'Les Papyrus de Zénon et la Préhistoire du Mouvement Maccabéen', pp. 321–33 in A. Caquot et al. (eds), *Hellenica et Judaica: Hommage à Valentin Nikiprowetzky*, Leuven and Paris.

Ory, S. (1967), 'Les Graffiti Umayyades de 'Ayn al-Garr', *Bulletin du Musée de Beyrouth* 20, pp.97–148.

Otto-Dorn, K. (1957), 'Grabung in umayyadischen Rusafah', *AO* 2, pp.119–33.

Parker, S. T. (1975), 'The Decapolis Reviewed', *JBL* 94, pp.437–41.

Parker, S. T. (1976), 'Archaeological Survey of the Limes Arabicus, a Preliminary Report', *ADAJ* 21, pp.19–32.

Parker, S. T. (1979), *The Historical Development of the Limes Arabicus.* unpublished dissertation, University of California, Los Angeles.

Parker, S. T. (1985), 'Preliminary Report on the 1982 Season of the Central Limes Arabicus Project', *BASOR*, Suppl. 23, pp.1–34.

Parker, S. T. (1986), *Romans and Saracens; A History of the Arabian Frontier*, Winona Lake.

Parr, P. J. (1965), 'Communication sur une Nouvelle Saison de Fouilles à la Capitale Nabatéenne de Petra, 1964', *RB* 72, pp.253–257.

Parr, P. J. (1986), 'The Last Days of Petra', pp.192–205 in Bakhit, M. A. and Asfour, M. (eds), *Proceedings of the Symposium on Bilad al-Sham during the Byzantine Period*, Amman, vol. II.

Parr, P. J. (1988), 'Pottery of the Late Second Millennium BC from North Arabia and its Historical Implications', pp.72–89 in Potts, D. T. (ed.), *Araby the Blest. Studies in Arabian*

Archaeology, Copenhagen.
Paruck, F. D. J. (1924), *Sasanian Coins*, Bombay.
Peeters, P. (1926), 'La Passion Géorgienne des SS. Théodore, Julien, Eubulus, Malcamon, Mocimus et Salamones', *AB* 44, pp.70-101.
Pestman, P. J. ed. (1981), *A Guide to the Zenon Archive*, Leiden.
Peters, F. E. (1983), 'City planning in Greco-Roman Syria: some new considerations', *DaM* 1, pp.269–77.
Petersen, A. (1989), 'Early Ottoman Forts on the Darb al-Hajj', *Levant* 21, pp.97–118.
Petocz, D. (1987), 'An Early Bronze Age site at Ain Ghazal, Amman', *Levant* 19, pp.27–32.
Pflaum, H-G. (1952), 'La Fortification de la ville de Adraha d'Arabie', *Syria*, 29, pp.307–30.
Philip, G. (1989), *Metal Weapons of the Early and Middle Bronze Ages in Syria-Palestine I–II, BAR*, International Series S 526, 1–2, Oxford.
Piccirillo, M. and Attiyah, T. (1986), 'The Complex of Saint Stephen at Umm er-Rasas – Kastron Mefaa: First Campaign (August, 1986)', *ADAJ* 30, pp.341–51.
Piccirillo, M. (1976), 'New Discoveries on Mt. Nebo', *ADAJ* 21, pp.55–60.
Piccirillo, M. (1978), 'Una Tomba del Bronzo Medio ad Amman?', *LA* 28, pp.73–86.
Piccirillo, M. (1980), 'A Note on the Church of the Virgin at Madaba, Jordan', *ADAJ* 24, pp.151–2.
Piccirillo, M. (1982), 'Il complesso monastico di Zay el-Gharbi e la dicesi di Gadara della Perea', *SH* 3, pp.358–78.
Piccirillo, M. (1985), 'Rural Settlements in Byzantine Jordan', in A. Hadidi (ed.), *SHAJ* II, pp.257–61.
Piccirillo, M. (1987a), 'Le iscrizioni di Um er-Rasas – Kastron Mefaa in Giordania I (1986–7)', *LA* 37, pp.177–239.
Piccirillo, M. (1987b), 'The Jerusalem-Esbus Road and its Sanctuaries in Transjordan', in A. Hadidi (ed.), *SHAJ* III, pp.165–72.
Piccirillo, M. (1988), 'The Mosaics of Um er-Resas in Jordan', *BA* 51, pp.208–13; 222–31.
Poirier, J. P., and Taher, M. A. (1980), 'Historical seismicity in the Near and Middle East, North Africa, and Spain from Arabic Documents (VIIth-XVIIIth century)', *Bulletin of the Seismological Society of America* 70, pp.2185–2201.
Pope, A. U. and Ackerman, P. (eds) (1938), *A Survey of Persian Art*, 4 vols, London.
Prawer, J. (1962), *Histoire du Royaume Latine de Jérusalem*, 2 vols, Paris.
Pringle, D. (1981), *The Defence of Byzantine Africa from Justinian to the Arab Conquest*, BAR, Oxford.
Quennell, A. M. (1951), 'The Geology and Mineral Resources of (Former) Transjordan', *Colonial Geology and Mineral Resources* 2, pp.85–115.
al-Rashid, S. (1979), 'Ancient Water-Tanks on the Haj Route from Iraq to Mecca and their parallels in Other Arab Countries', *Atlal* 3, pp.55–62.
Rebstock, U. (1989), 'Observations on the Diwan al-Kharaj and the Assessment of Taxes in Umayyad Syria', pp. 229–46 in Bakhit, M. A. and Schick, R. (eds), *The history of Bilad al-Sham during the Umayyad period (Fourth International Conference)*, Amman.
Redford, D. (1982), 'A Bronze Age Itinerary in Transjordan (Nos. 89–101 of Thutmose III's List of Asiatic Toponyms)', *JSSEA* 12, pp.55–72.
Reuther, O. (1912), *Ocheidir*, nach Aufnahmen von Mitgliedern der Babylon-Expedition der Deutschen Orient-Gesellschaft dargestellt, Leipzig.
Reuther, O. (1938), 'Sassanian Architecture (A) History', pp.493–578 in Pope and Ackerman (eds), *A Survey of Persian Art from Prehistoric Times to the Present*, London.
Rey-Coquais, J-P. (1981), 'Philadelphie de Coele Syrie', *ADAJ* 25, pp.25–31.
Rey-Coquais, J.-P. (1982), 'Décapole et Province d'Arabie', *MB* 22, pp.7–9.
Rice, D. S. (1952), 'Studies in Medieval Harran I', *Anatolian Studies* 2, pp.36–84.
Rivoira, C. T. (1918), *Moslem Architecture*, Oxford.
Roaf, M. (1978), 'Persepolitan Metrology', *Iran* 16, pp.67–78.
Robert, L. (1960), *Hellenica XI-XII*, Paris.
Rollefson, G., Kaechele, Z. and Kaechele, J. (1982), 'A Burin Site in Umm Utheina District, Jabal Amman', *ADAJ* 26, pp.243–7.
Rosen, A. M. (1989), 'Environmental Change at the End of Early Bronze Age Palestine', pp. 247–55 in Miroschedji P. de (ed.), *L'urbanisation de la Palestine à l'âge du Bronze ancien. Bilan et perspectives des recherches actuelles.* Actes du Colloque d'Emmaüs (*BAR*, International Series S 527 II), Oxford.
Rostovtzeff, M. (1922), *A Large Estate in Egypt in the Third Century* BC, Madison.
Rougeule, A. (1984), 'La Mosquée', in Kervran, M. and Rougeule, A., 'Recherches sur les niveaux islamiques de la Ville des Artisans', *Cahiers de la DAFI* 14, pp.13–40.
Russell, K. W. (1980), 'The Earthquake of May 19, AD 363', *BASOR* 238, pp.47–64.
Russell, K. W. (1985), 'The Earthquake Chronology of Palestine and Northwest Arabia from the 2nd through the mid-8th Century AD', *BASOR* 260, pp.37–59.
Sack, D. (1990), 'The Friday-Mosque at Rusafat Hisham in the Abbasid Period', paper presented to the 5th International Conference for the History of Bilad al-Sham, 'Amman, 1990.
Safar, F. (1945), *Wasit, the Sixth Season's Excavations*, Cairo.
Salibi, K. (1977), *Syria under Islam 634–1097*, Delmar.
Saller, S. J. and Bagatti, B. (1949), *The Town of Nebo*, Jerusalem.
Saller, S. J. (1950), *The Memorial of Moses on Mt. Nebo*, 3 vols, Jerusalem.
Saouaf, S. (1958), *The Citadel of Aleppo*, Aleppo.
Sarre, F. and Herzfeld, E. (1911), *Archäologische Reise im Euphrat- und Tigris-gebiet*, 4 vols, Berlin.
Sartre, M. (1982), *Trois études sur l'Arabie romaine et byzantine.* Collection Latomus 178, Brussels.
Sartre, M. (1985), *Bostra, des origines à l'Islam*, Paris.
Sauer, J. A. (1973), *Heshbon Pottery, 1971.* Berrien Springs.
Sauer, J. A. (1982), 'The Pottery of Jordan in the Early Islamic Periods', pp.329–338 in Hadidi, A. (ed.), *Studies in the History and Archaeology of Jordan* I, Amman.
Sauer, J. A. (1986), 'Umayyad Pottery from Sites in Jordan', pp.301–30 in Geraty, L. T. and Herr, L. G. (eds), *The Archaeology of Jordan and other studies presented to Siegfried H. Horn*, Berrien Springs.
Sauvaget, J. (1939a), 'Remarques sur les Monuments

Omeyyades', *Journal Asiatique* 231, pp.1–59.
Sauvaget, J. (1939b), 'Les Ghassanides et Sergiopolis', *Byzantion* 14, pp.115–30.
Sauvaget, J. (1939c), 'Les Ruines Omeyyades du Djebel Seis', *Syria* 20, pp.239–56.
Sauvaget, J. (1940), 'Les Ruines Omeyyades de 'Andjar', *Bulletin du Musée de Beyrouth* 3, pp.5–11.
Sauvaget, J. (1947), *La mosquée omeyyade de Médine*, Paris.
Sauvaget, J. (1967), 'Chateaux Umayyades de Syrie', *Revue des Études Islamiques* 35, pp.1–52.
Scerrato, U. (1976), *Monuments of Civilisation: Islam*. London.
Schick, R. (1987), *The Fate of the Christians in Palestine during the Byzantine-Umayyad Transition,* Unpublished PhD dissertation, University of Chicago.
Schick, R. (1988), 'Christian Life in Palestine during the Early Islamic Period', *BA* 51, pp.218–21; 239–40.
Schick, R. (1990), 'Christianity in the Patriarchate of Jerusalem in the early Abbasid period AD 750-813', paper given at the Fifth International Conference for the history of Bilad al-Sham, 'Amman 1990.
Schlumberger, D. (1939), 'Les Fouilles de Qasr el-Heir el-Gharbi', *Syria* 20, pp.195–238, 324–373.
Schlumberger, D. (1946–8), 'Deux Fresques Omeyyades', *Syria* 25, pp.86–102.
Schlumberger, D. (1978), *Lashkari Bazar, une résidence royale ghaznévide et ghoride*, vol. IA, *l'Architecture*, Paris.
Schlumberger, D. (1986), *Qasr el-Heir el Gharbi*, Paris, IFAPO vol. cxx.
Schmidt, E. F. (1937), *Excavations at Tepe Hissar, Damghan*, Philadelphia.
Schmidt, J. (1978), 'Qasr-i-Sirin, Feuertempel oder Palast?', *Baghdader Mitteilungen* 9, pp.39–47.
Schulz, B. and Strzygowski, J. (1904), 'Mschatta II', *Jahrbuch des Königlichen Preussischen Kunstsammlungen* 25, pp.350–3.
Schulz, B. (1906), 'Bogenfries und Giebelreihe in der römischen Baukunst', *Jahrbuch des Kaiserlisch Deutschen Archäologischen Instituts* 21, pp.221–30, pls 3–4.
Schürer, E. (1979), *The History of the Jewish People in the Age of Jesus Christ (175 BC-AD 135)*, vol. 2 (revised and edited by G. Vermes et al.), Edinburgh.
Segal, A. (1975), *The Planning of the Cities along the Via Traiana Nova*, 2 vols, Jerusalem.
Segal, A. (1988), *Town Planning and Architecture in Provincia Arabia*, *BAR* International Series 419, Oxford.
Seigne, J. (1986), 'Recherches sur le Sanctuaire de Zeus à Jerash (octobre 1982 – decembre 1983)', pp.29–59 in Zayadine, F. (ed.), *Jerash Archaeological Project, 1981–1983*, Amman.
Shaban, M. A. (1971), *Islamic History* AD *600–750: a new interpretation*, Cambridge.
Shahid, I. (1986), 'The Jund System in Bilad al-Sham: Its Origin', pp.45–52 in Bakhit, M. A. and Asfour, M. (eds), *Proceedings of the Symposium on Bilad al-Sham during the Byzantine Period*, Amman, vol. II.
Shahid, I. (1989), *Byzantium and the Arabs in the Fifth Century*, Washington.
Shea, W. H. (1979), 'Milkom as the Architect of Rabbath-Ammon's Natural Defences in the Amman Citadel Inscription', *PEQ* 1979, pp.17–25.
Shea, W. H. (1991), 'The Architectural Layout of the Amman Citadel Inscription Temple', *PEQ* 1991, pp.62–6.
Smith, R. H. (1973), *Pella of the Decapolis*, Wooster.
Smith, R. H. (1982), 'Preliminary Report on the 1981 Season of the Sydney/Wooster Joint Expedition to Pella (Spring Season)', *ADAJ* 26, pp.323–42.
Smith, R. H. (1989), *Pella of the Decapolis*, vol. 2, Wooster.
Sourdel, D. (1952), *Les Cults du Hauran à l'Époque Romaine,* Paris.
Sourdel, D. (1980), 'La Syrie au temps des premiers califes abbassides (132/750 – 264/878)', *Revue des Études Islamiques* 48, pp.155–75.
Sourdel, D. (1981), 'La fondation umayyade de Ramla', pp.385–97 in *Studien zur Geschichte und Kultur des Vorderen Orients*, Festschrift B. Spuler, ed. Römer H. R. and Noth A., Leiden.
Spanner, H. and Guyer, S. (1926), *Rusafa*, Berlin.
Spijkerman, A. (1978), *The Coins of the Decapolis and Provincia Arabia*, Jerusalem.
Starcky, J. (1966), 'Petra et la Nabatène', *SDB* 7, pp.cols. 886–1017.
Starcky, J. (1971), 'Une Inscription Nabatéenne de l'An 18 d'Arétas IV', pp.151–9 in A. Caquot and M. Philonenko (eds), *Hommages à André Dupont-Sommer,* Paris.
Starcky, J. (1985), 'Les Inscriptions Nabatéennes et l'Histoire de la Syrie Méridionale et du Nord de la Jordanie', pp.167–81 in J.-M. Dentzer (ed.), *Hauran I: Recherches archéologiques sur la Syrie du sud à l'époque hellénistique et romaine*, Part 1, Paris.
Stern, H. (1946), 'Notes sur l'Architecture des Chateaux Omeyyades', *AI* 11–12, pp.72–97.
Stern, H. (1963), 'Recherches sur la mosquée el-Aqsa', *AO* 5, pp.2–48.
Stern, S.M. (1971), 'Ya'qub the Coppersmith and Persian National Sentiment', pp.535–55 in Bosworth, C. E.(ed.), *Iran and Islam*, Edinburgh.
Stillwell, R. (1954), 'The Siting of Greek Temples', *Journal of the Society of Architectural Historians* 12, pp.3–8.
Strassburg, E. (1979), *The Sasanian Influence on Umayyad Art*, unpub. MA dissertation, London, SOAS.
Strzygowski, J. (1930), *Asiens Bildende Kunst,* Augsburg.
Strzygowski, J. (1936), *Ancien Art Chrétien de Syrie,* Paris.
Suleiman, E. (1985), 'An EB/MB Tomb at Tla' el-'Alī', *ADAJ* 29, pp.179ff.
Susa, A., (1948), *Rayy Sāmarrā' fī 'ahd al-Khilāfa al-'Abbāsiyya*, 2 vols, Baghdad.
Talbot Rice, D. (1934), 'The Oxford Excavations at Hira', *AI* 1, pp.51–73.
Tarn, W. and Griffith, G. T. (1966), *Hellenistic Civilisation,* London.
Tcherikover, V.(1961), *Hellenistic Civilization and the Jews,* Philadelphia.
Tcherikover, V. (1972), 'Social Conditions', pp.87–114 in A. Schalit (ed.), *The Hellenistic Age: Political History of Jewish Palestine from 332* BCE *to 67* BCE (The World History of the Jewish People, vol. 6), New Brunswick.
Teixidor, J. (1977), *The Pagan God,* Princeton.
Tell, S. K. (1969), 'Notes on the Archaeology of Amman', *ADAJ* 14, pp.28–33.
Thompson, D. (1976), *Stucco from Chal Tarkhan-Eshqabad near Rayy*, Warminster.
Thomsen, P. (1907), *Loca Sancta,* Halle.
Toueir, Kassem (1982), 'Heraqleh: a unique victory monument of Harun ar-Rashid', *World Archaeology* 14, pp.296–304.

Toueir, Kassem (1985), 'Der Qasr al-Banat in ar-Raqqa, Ausgrabung, Rekonstruktion, und Wiederaufbau (1977–82)', *DaM* 2, pp.297–319.

Tsafrir, Y (1986), 'The Maps used by Theodosius: On the Pilgrim Maps of the Holy Land and Jerusalem in the Sixth Century CE', *DOP* 40, pp.129–45.

Tscherikower, V. (1937), 'Palestine under the Ptolemies: A contribution to the study of the Zenon Papyri', *Mizraim* 4–5, p.36.

Urice, S. (1981), 'The Qasr Kharana Project 1979', *ADAJ* 25, pp.5–20.

Urice, S. K. (1987), *Qasr Kharana in the Transjordan*, Durham NC.

al-'Ush, M. A. (1972), *The Silver Hoard of Damascus*, Damascus.

Vaux, R. de (1938), 'Une Mosaique Byzantine à Ma'in', *RB* 47, pp.227–58.

Vaux, R. de (1941), 'Notes d'Histoire et de Topographie Trans-jordaniennes', *Vivre et Penser* I, pp.16–47 (= *Bible et Orient* [Paris, Les Editions du Cerf], pp.115–49).

Vaux, R. de and Stève, A-M. (1950), *Fouilles à Qaryet el Énab Abu Gôsh*, Paris.

Villeneuve, F. (1984), 'Iraq al-Amir', pp.12–19 in F. Villeneuve (ed.), *Contribution Française à l'Archéologie Jordanienne*, Paris.

Villeneuve, F. (1988), 'Prospection Archéologique et Géographie Historique: La Région d'Iraq al-Amir (Jordanie)', pp.257–88 in P.-L. Gatier et al. (eds), *Géographie Historique au Proche-Orient*, Paris.

Vincent, L. H. (1920), 'La Palestine dans les Papyrus ptolémaïques de Gerza', *RB* 29: 161–202.

Wagner-Lux, U. and Vriezen, K. J. H. (1980), 'A Preliminary Report on the Excavations at Gadara (Umm Qes) in Jordan from 1976 to 1979', *ADAJ* 24, pp.157–62.

Wagner-Lux, U. et al. (1979), 'Bericht über Oberflachenforschung in Gadara (Umm Qes) in Jordanien im Jahre 1974', *ADAJ* 23, pp.31–40.

Walker, J. (1956), *A Catalogue of the Arab-Byzantine and Post-Reform Umaiyad Coins*, London.

Walmsley, A. (1986), 'The Abbasid Occupation in Area XXIX, Preliminary Report on the University of Sydney's seventh season of excavations at Pella (Tabaqat Fahl) in 1985', *ADAJ* 30, pp.182–95.

Walmsley, A. (1987), *The Administrative Structure and Urban Geography of the Jund of Filastin and the Jund of al-Urdunn*, Unpublished PhD thesis, University of Sydney.

Walmsley, A. (1988), 'Pella/Fihl after the Islamic Conquest (AD 635 – *c*.900): A convergence of literary and archaeological evidence', *Mediterranean Archaeology* I, pp.142–59.

Walmsley, A. (1990), 'Architecture and Artefacts from Abbasid Fihl: Implications for the cultural history of Jordan', paper given at the Fifth International Conference for the history of Bilad al-Sham, 'Amman 1990.

Ward, W. A. (1966), 'Scarabs, Seals and Cylinders from Two Tombs at Amman', *ADAJ* 11, pp.5–18.

Warren, J. (1977), 'A Sassanian Attribution for Two Buildings in Jordan', *AARP* 11, pp.49–55.

Warren, J. (1978), 'The Date of the Baghdad Gate at Raqqa', *AARP* 13, pp.22–3.

Waterhouse, S. D. and Ibach, R. (1975), 'The Topographical Survey', in Boraas, R. S. and Horn, S. H., The Third Campaign at Tell Hesban, *Andrews University Seminary Studies* 13, pp.101–247.

Weber, T. (1989), *Umm Qais: Gadara of the Decapolis*, Amman.

Weber, T. (1990), 'A Survey of Roman Sculpture in the Decapolis, Preliminary Report', *ADAJ* 34, pp.351–5.

Weippert, H. (1977), 'Rabbat-Ammon', *BRL*, 258f. in *Biblisches Reallexikon*, 2nd Ed., Tübingen.

Weippert, H. (1987), 'The Relations of the States east of the Jordan with the Mesopotamian Powers during the First Millenium BC', *SHAJ* 3, pp.97–105.

Weippert, H. (1988), *Palästina in vorhellenistischer Zeit*, (HArch, Vorderasien II, 1). Munich.

Welles, C. B. (1938), 'The Inscriptions', pp.354–494 in Kraeling et al. (1938).

Wellhausen, J. (1927), *The Arab Kingdom and its Fall*, tr. M. G. Weir, Calcutta.

Whitcomb, D. (1988a), *Aqaba, 'Port of Palestine on the China Sea'*, Amman.

Whitcomb, D. (1988b), 'Khirbet al-Mafjar Reconsidered: the ceramic evidence', *BASOR* 271, pp.51–67.

Whitcomb, D. (1989), 'Evidence of the Umayyad Period from the Aqaba Excavations,' pp.164–84 in Bakhit, M. A. and Schick, R. (eds), *The History of Bilad al-Sham during the Umayyad period (Fourth International Conference)*, Amman.

Whitcomb, D. (1990), 'Archaeology of the Abbasid Period: the Example of Jordan', *Archéologie Islamique* I, pp.75–85.

Whitehouse, D. (1974), 'Excavations at Siraf: Sixth Interim Report', *Iran* 12, pp.1–30.

Whitehouse, D. (1979), 'Islamic Glazed Pottery in Iraq and the Persian Gulf: the Ninth and Tenth Centuries', *Annali dell' Instituto Orientale di Napoli* 39, pp.45–61.

Whitehouse, D. (1980), *Siraf* III, *The Congregational Mosque and other mosques from the 9th to the 12th centuries*, London.

Wilkin, R. L. (1988), 'Byzantine Palestine: A Christian Holy Land', *BA* 51, pp.214–7; 233–7.

Wilkinson, J. (1977), *Jerusalem Pilgrims before the Crusades*, Warminster.

Will, E. (1985), 'L'Urbanisation de la Jordanie aux époques Héllenistique et Romaine: Conditions Géographiques et Ethniques', in A. Hadidi (ed.), *SHAJ* II, pp.237–41.

Will, E. (1987), 'Qu'est-ce qu'une *baris*?', *Syria* 64, pp.253–9.

Worschech, U. (1990), *Die Beziehungen Moabs zu Israel und Ägypten in der Eisenzeit* (ÄAT 18), Wiesbaden.

Wüthnow, H. (1930), *Die semitischen Menschennamen in griechischen Inschriften und Papyri des vorderen Orients*, Leipzig.

Yadin, Y. (ed.) (1975), *Jerusalem Revealed*, Jerusalem.

Yassine, Kh. N. (1975), 'Anthropoid Coffins from Raghdan Royal Palace Tomb in Amman', *ADAJ* 20, pp.57–68. Also published as pp.33–46 in Yassine, *Archaeology of Jordan: Essays and Reports*, Amman 1988.

Yassine, Kh. N. (1988), 'Ammonite Fortresses, Date and Function', pp.11–31 in Yassine, *Archaeology of Jordan*, Amman.

Yassine, Kh. N. (1988), 'The Dolmens: Construction and Dating Reconsidered', pp.45–54 in Yassine, *Archaeology of Jordan*, Amman.

Younker R. W. et al. (1990), 'The Joint Madaba Plains Project: A Preliminary Report of the 1989 Season, including the Regional Survey and Excavations at El-Dreijat, Tell Jawa, and Tell el-'Umeiri', *AUSS* 28, pp.5–52.

Zayadine, F. (1969), 'A Greek Inscription from the Forum of Amman-Philadelphia, AD 189', *ADAJ* 14, pp.34–5.

Zayadine, F. (1973), 'Recent Excavations on the Citadel of Amman', *ADAJ* 18, pp.17–35.

Zayadine, F. (1977–8), 'Excavations on the Upper Citadel of Amman – Area A (1975–7)', *ADAJ* 22, pp.20–56.

Zayadine, F. (1978), 'An EB-MB Bilobate Tomb at Amman', pp.59–66 in Moorey, P. R. S. and Parr, P. J. (eds), *Archaeology in the Levant*, Warminster.

Zayadine, F. (1979), 'Citadelle d'Amman (1975–1978)', *RB* 86, pp.120–22.

Zayadine, F. (1981), 'Recent Excavations and Restorations of the Department of Antiquities (1979–80)', *ADAJ* 25, pp.341–2.

Zayadine, F. (1982a), 'Amman-Philadelphie', *Le Monde de la Bible* 22, pp.20–27.

Zayadine, F. (1982b), 'A Byzantine Painted Tomb at Jebel el-Jofeh, Amman', *ADAJ* 26, pp.10–12 (Ar. Sect.).

Zayadine, F. (1986a), 'Le pays d'Ammon. La Citadelle d'Amman', *Le Monde de la Bible* 46, pp.17–20.

Zayadine, F. (ed.) (1986b), *Jerash Archaeological Project: 1981–3*, I, 'Amman.

Zayadine, F. (ed.) (1989), *Jerash Archaeological Project: 1984–8*, II, IFAPO 18, Paris.

Zayadine, F. (1990), 'La campagne d'Antiochos III le grand en 219–217 et le siège de Rabbatamana', *RB* 97, pp.68–84.

Zayadine, F., Humbert, J-B., and Najjar, M. (1989), 'The 1988 Excavations on the Citadel of Amman – Lower Terrace, Area A', *ADAJ* 33, pp.357–63.

Zayadine, F., Najjar, M., and Greene, J. A. (1987), 'Recent Excavations on the Citadel of Amman (Lower Terrace), a preliminary report', *ADAJ* 31, pp.299–311.

INDEX

FIGURES

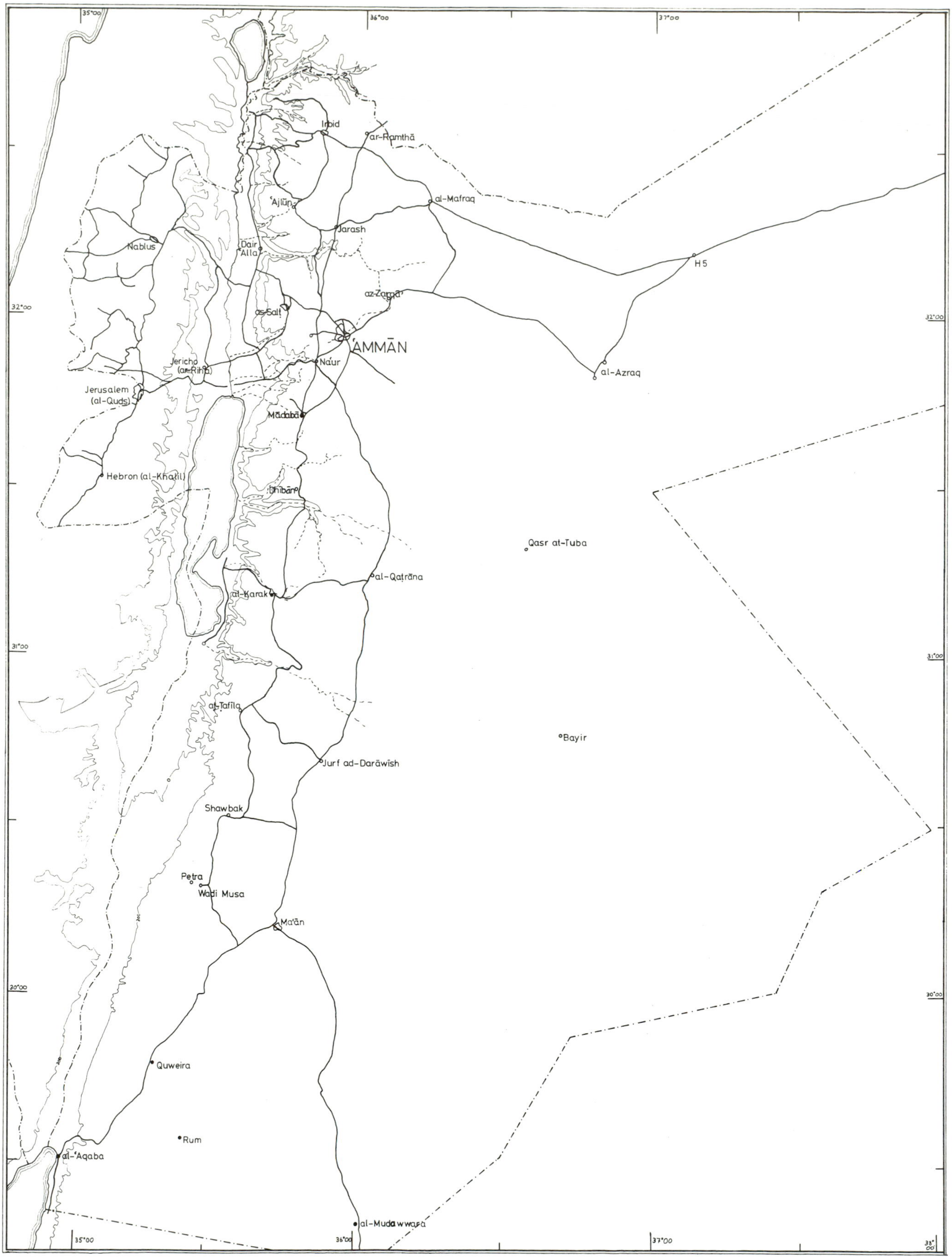

1. Map of Jordan showing position of 'Ammān.

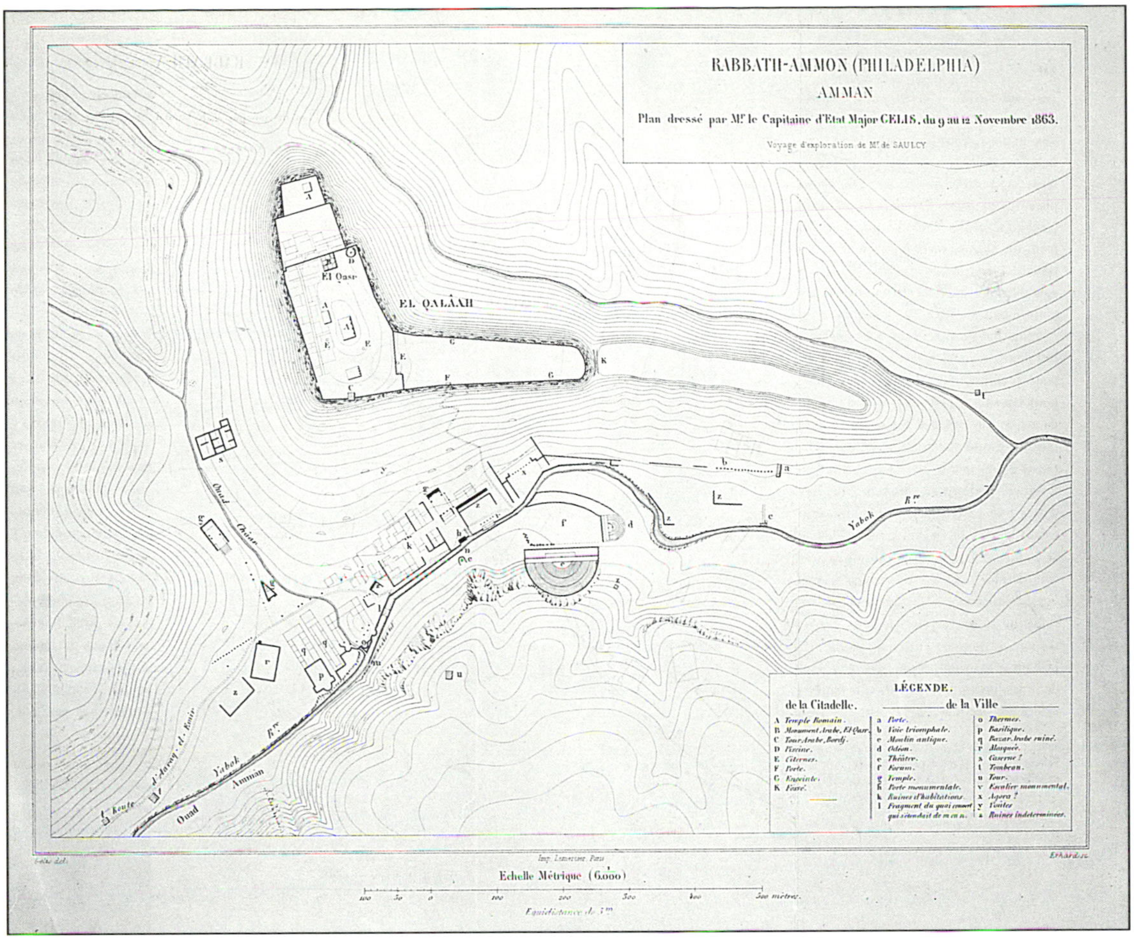

2. Plan of Rabbath-Ammon (Philadelphia) drawn by Capt. d'État Major Gélis, 9th–12th November 1863.

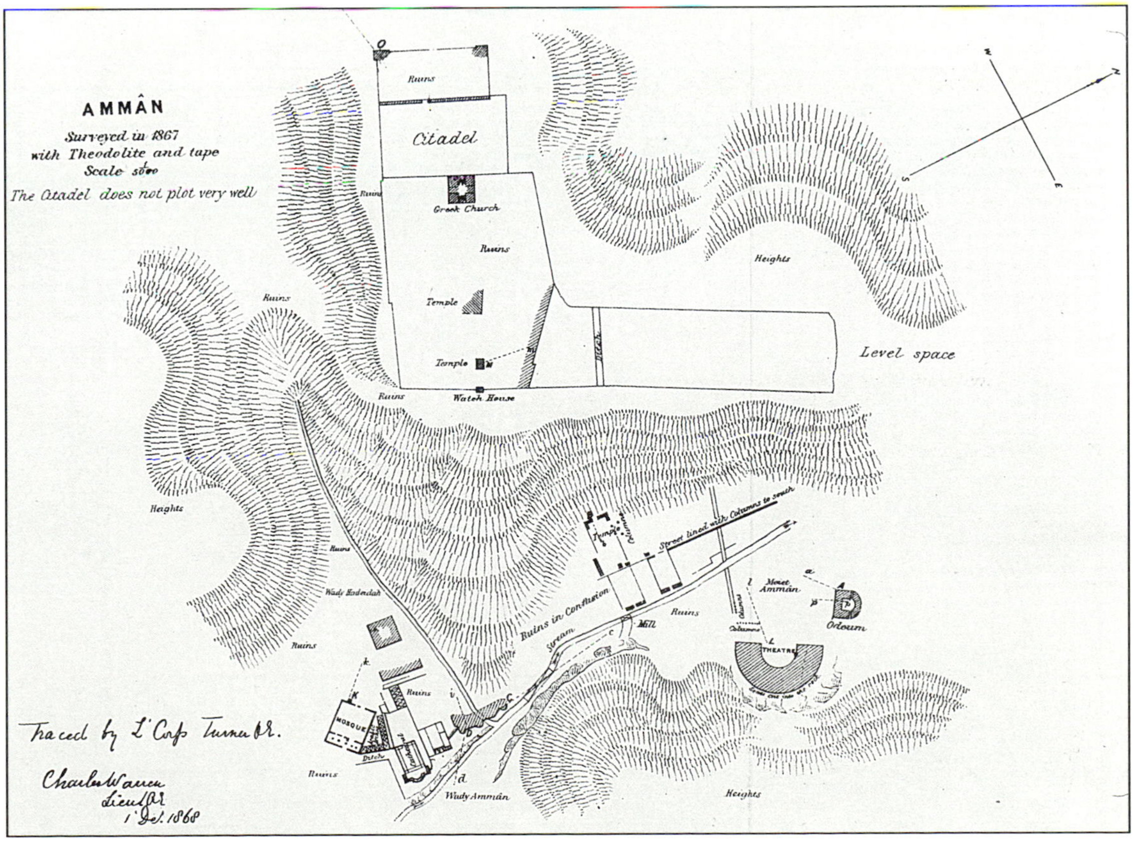

3. Plan of 'Ammān by Lt Charles Warren, July–August 1867.

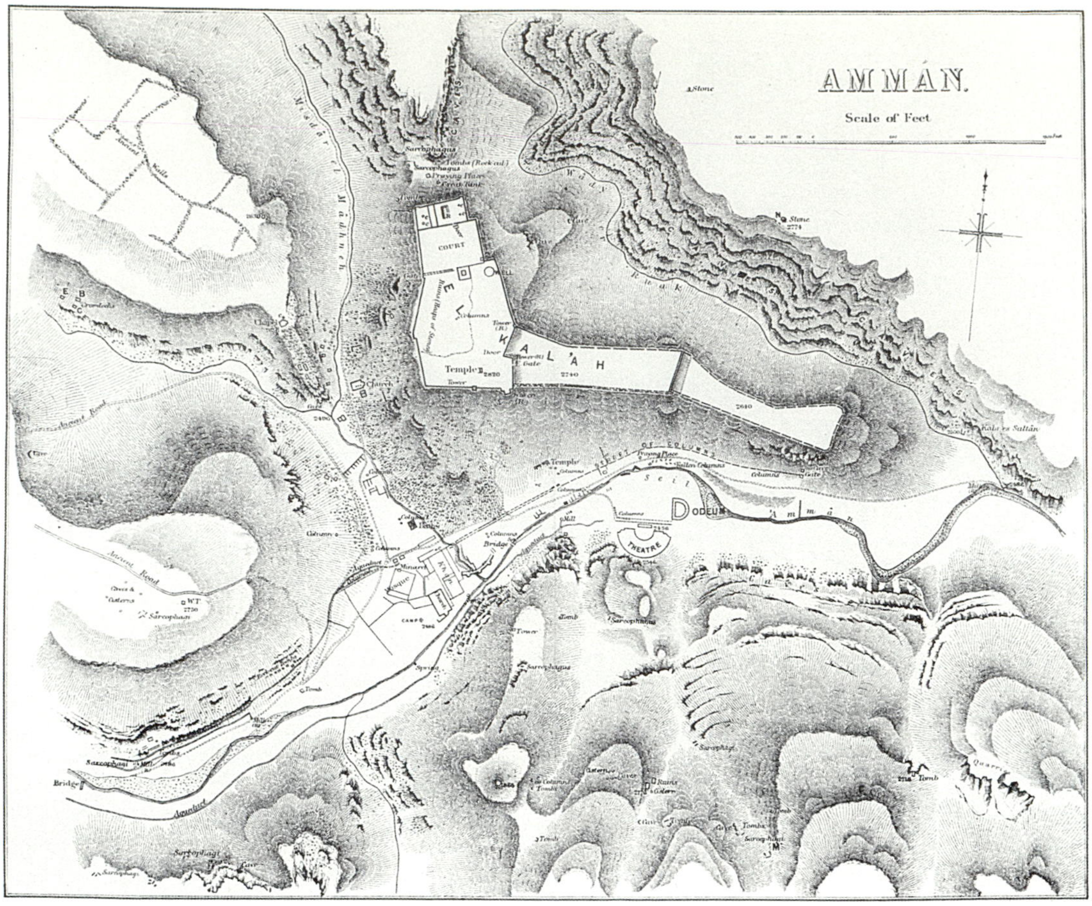

4. The Palestine Exploration Fund Special Survey of 'Ammān, October 1881.

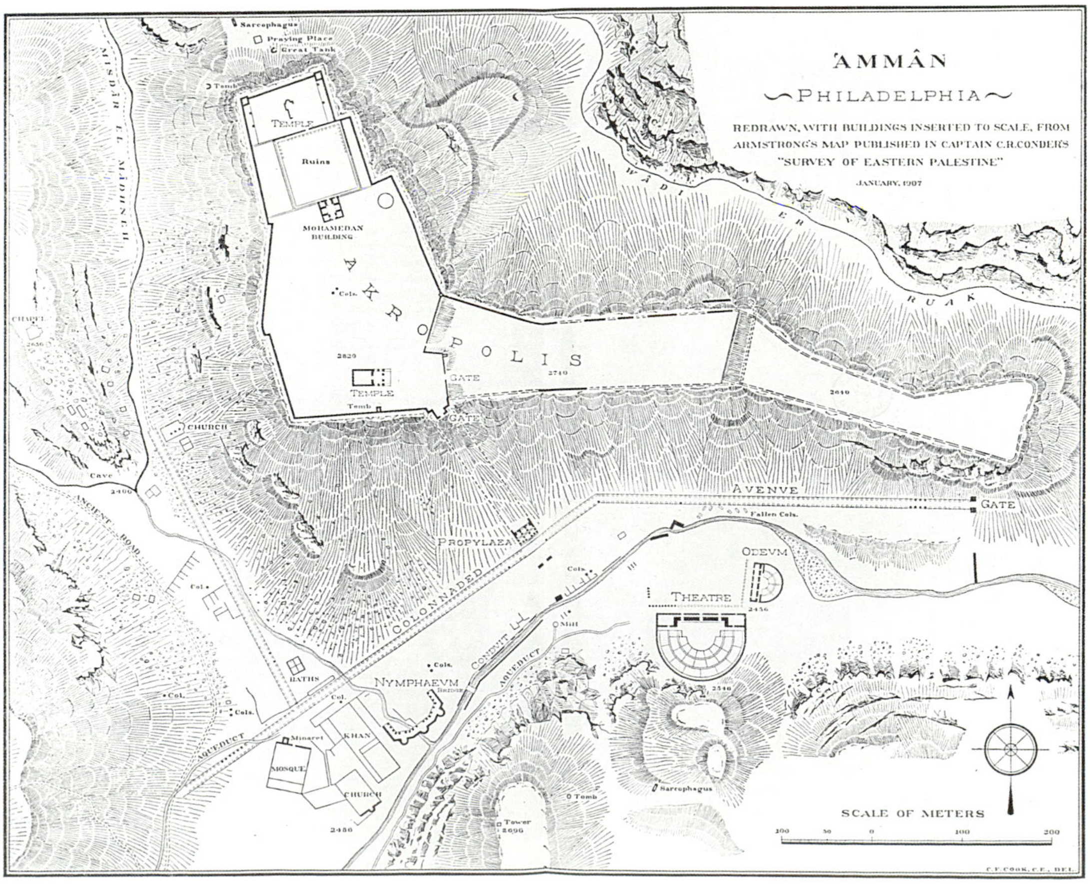

5. Plan of 'Ammān by the Princeton Archaeological Expedition to Syria.

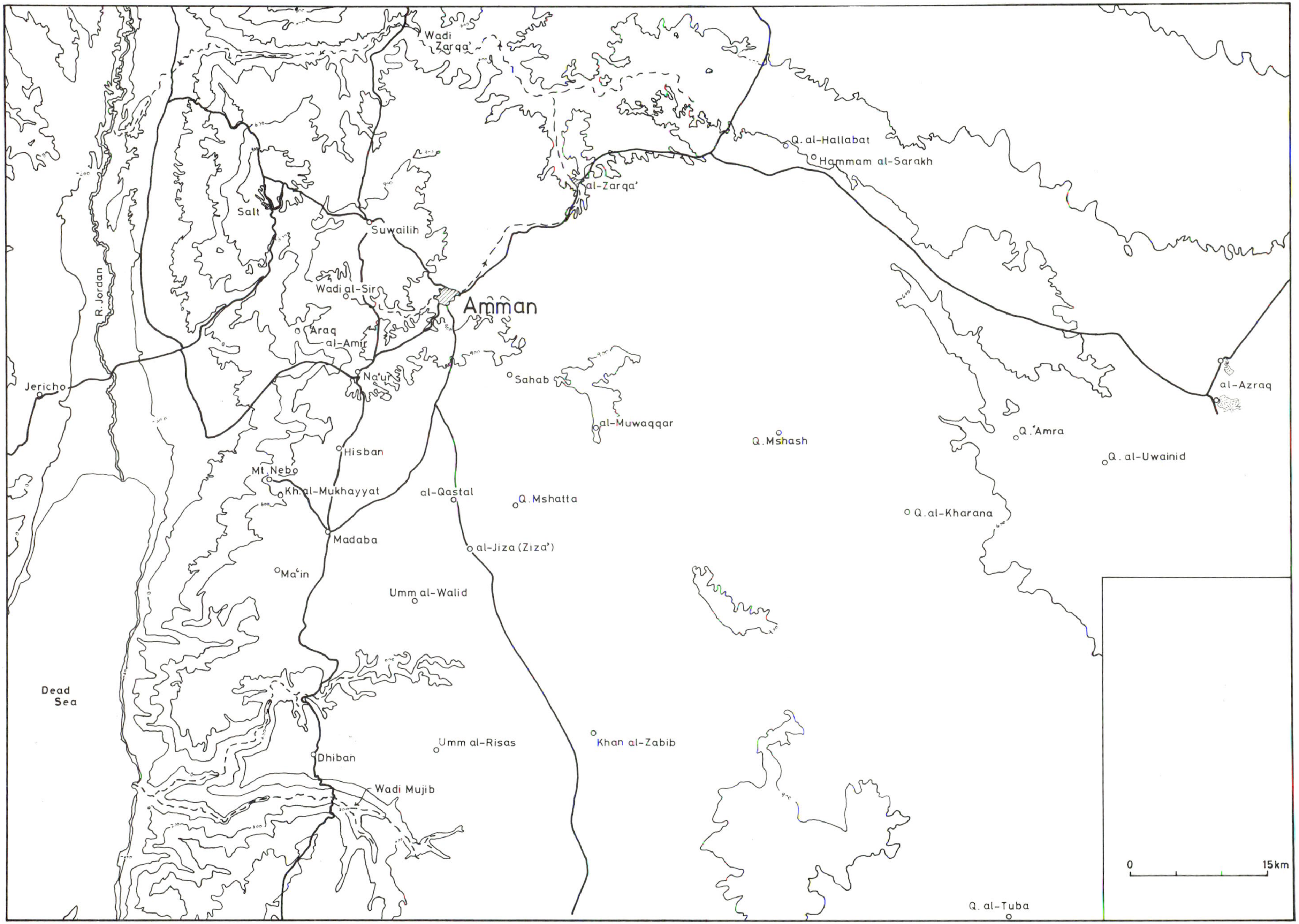

6. Topography of the Balqā', with toponyms around 'Ammān.

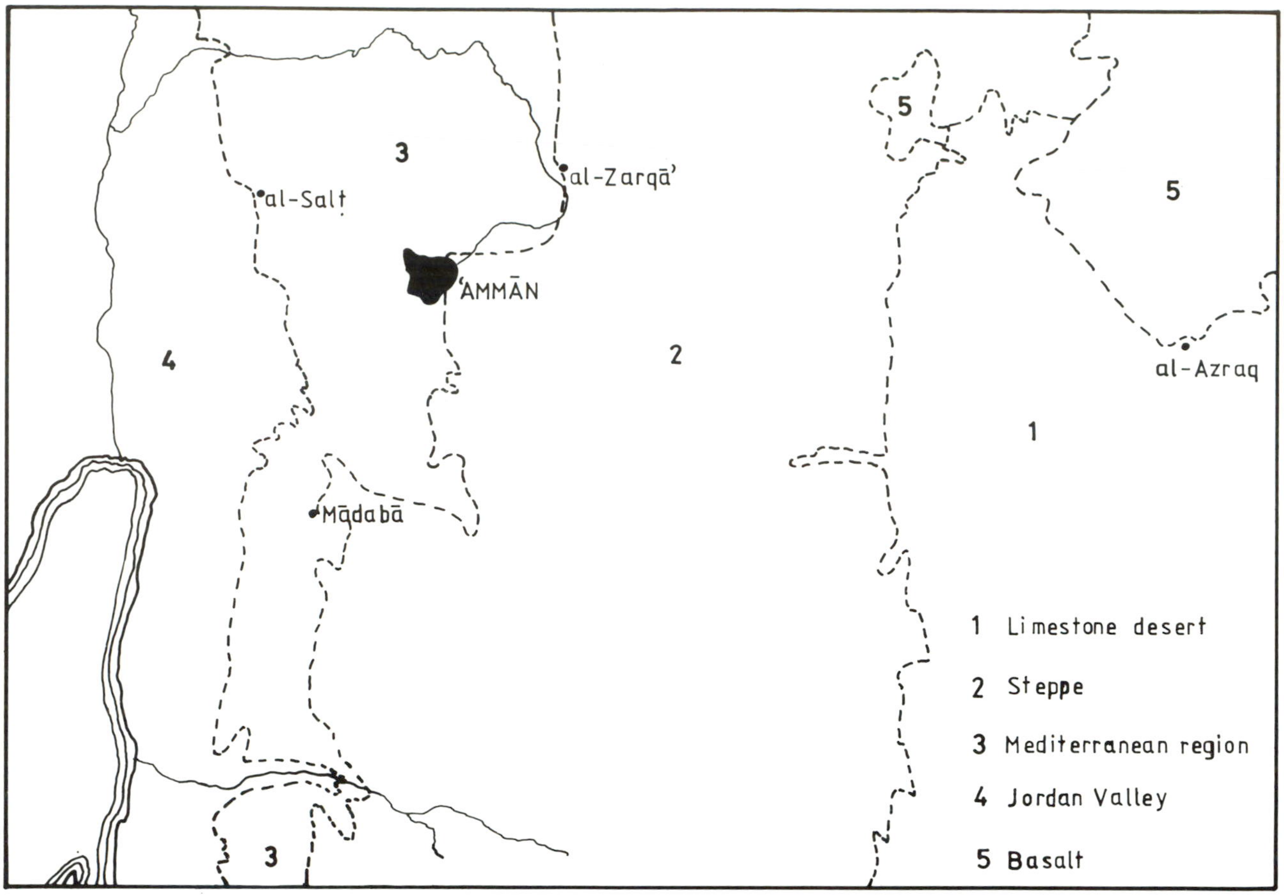

7. Physical divisions of the Balqā': Regions (after Hunting 1956).

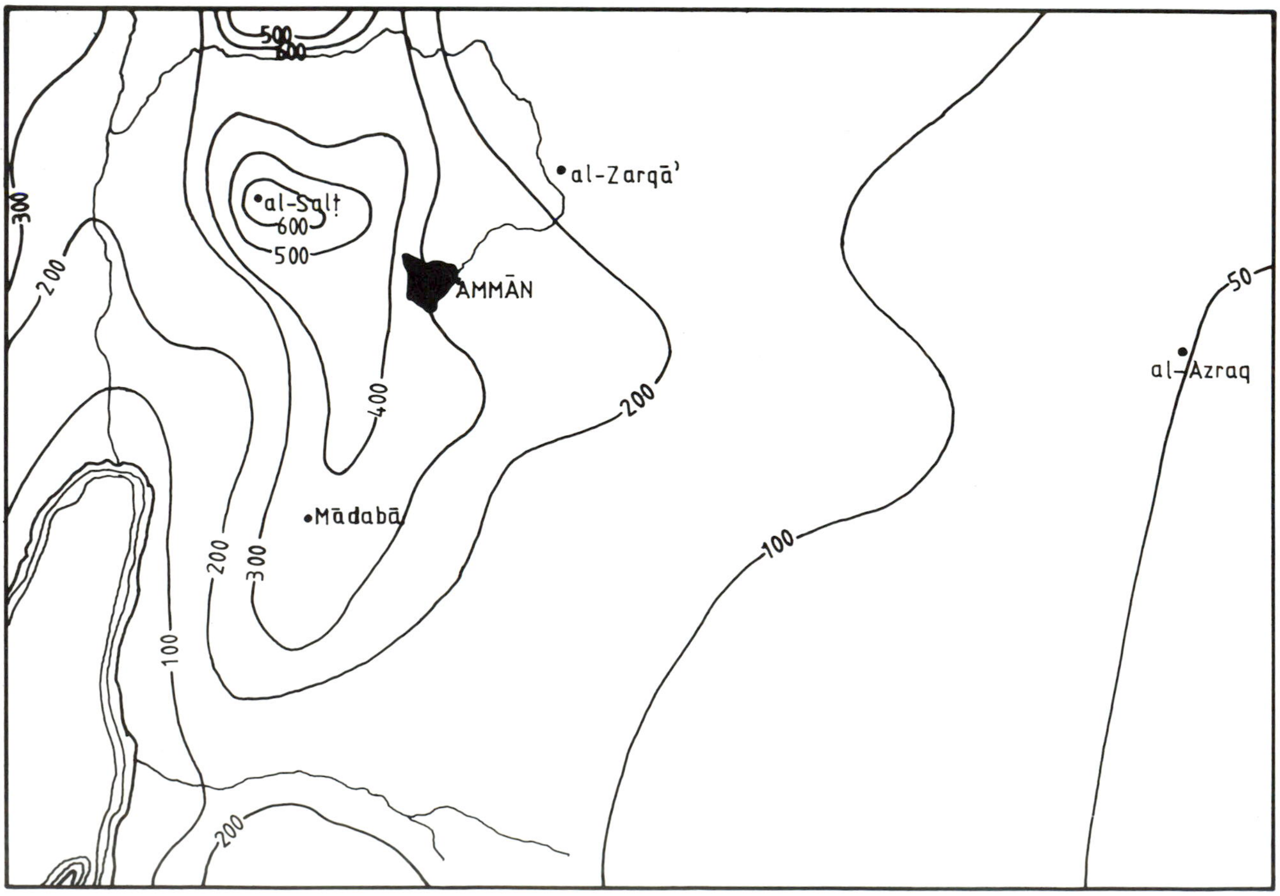

8. Rainfall patterns in the Balqā' 1937–60.

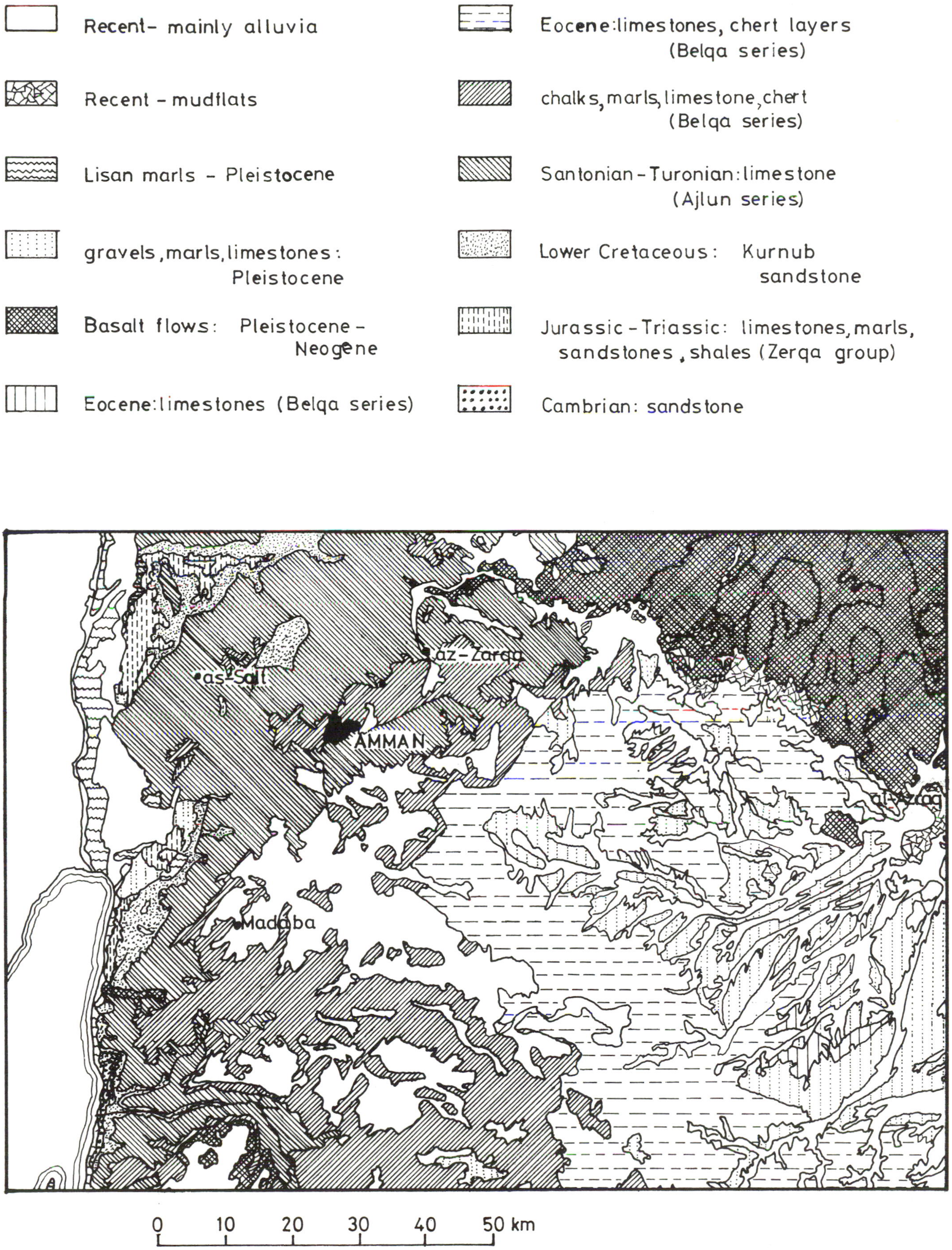
Recent- mainly alluvia
Recent - mudflats
Lisan marls - Pleistocene
gravels, marls, limestones: Pleistocene
Basalt flows: Pleistocene - Neogene
Eocene: limestones (Belqa series)
Eocene: limestones, chert layers (Belqa series)
chalks, marls, limestone, chert (Belqa series)
Santonian - Turonian: limestone (Ajlun series)
Lower Cretaceous: Kurnub sandstone
Jurassic - Triassic: limestones, marls, sandstones, shales (Zerqa group)
Cambrian: sandstone
as-Salt
az-Zarqa
AMMAN
Madaba
0
10
20
30
40
50 km

9. Geological structure of the Balqā'.

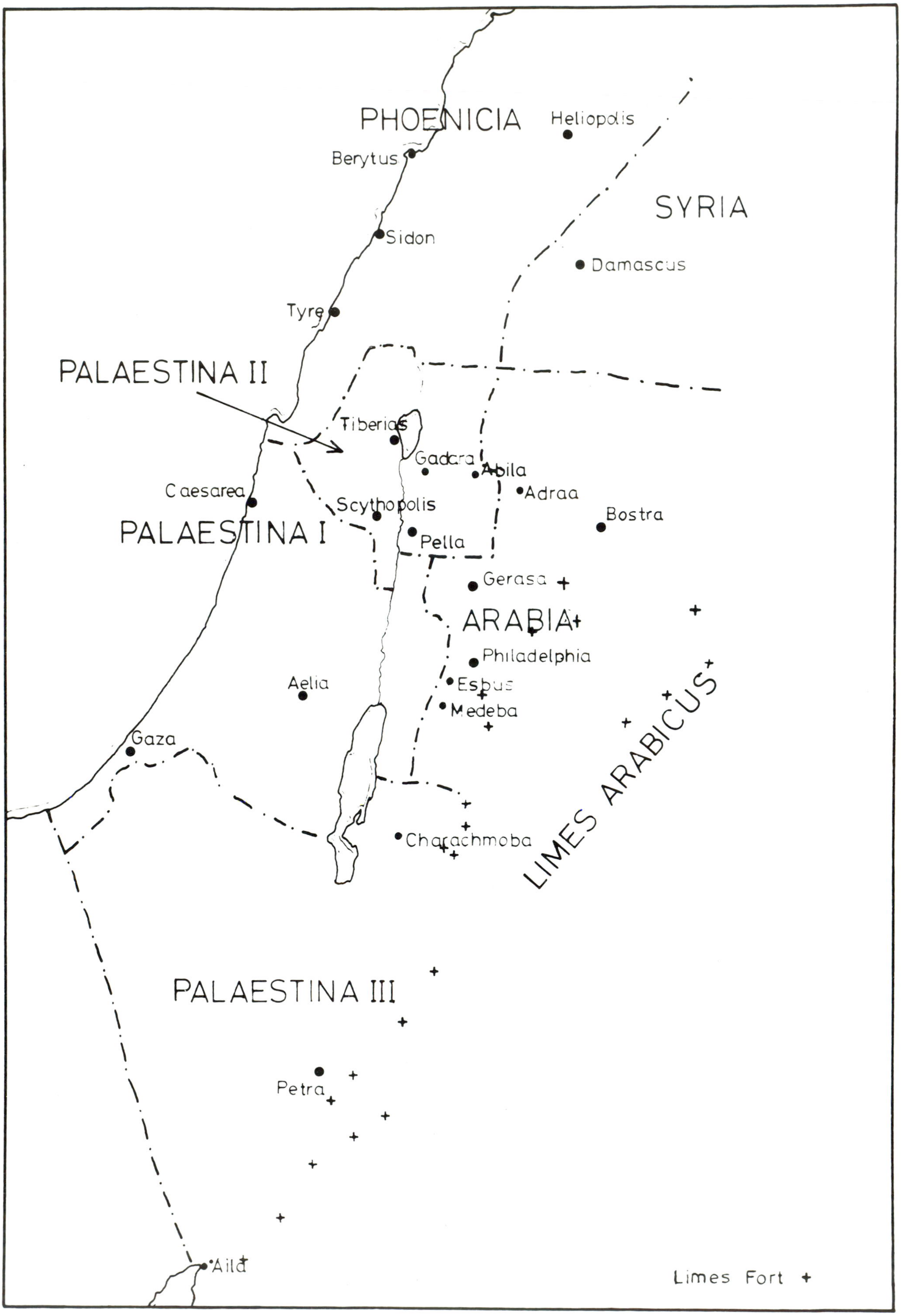

10. The provinces of Palestine and Arabia under the late Roman Empire.

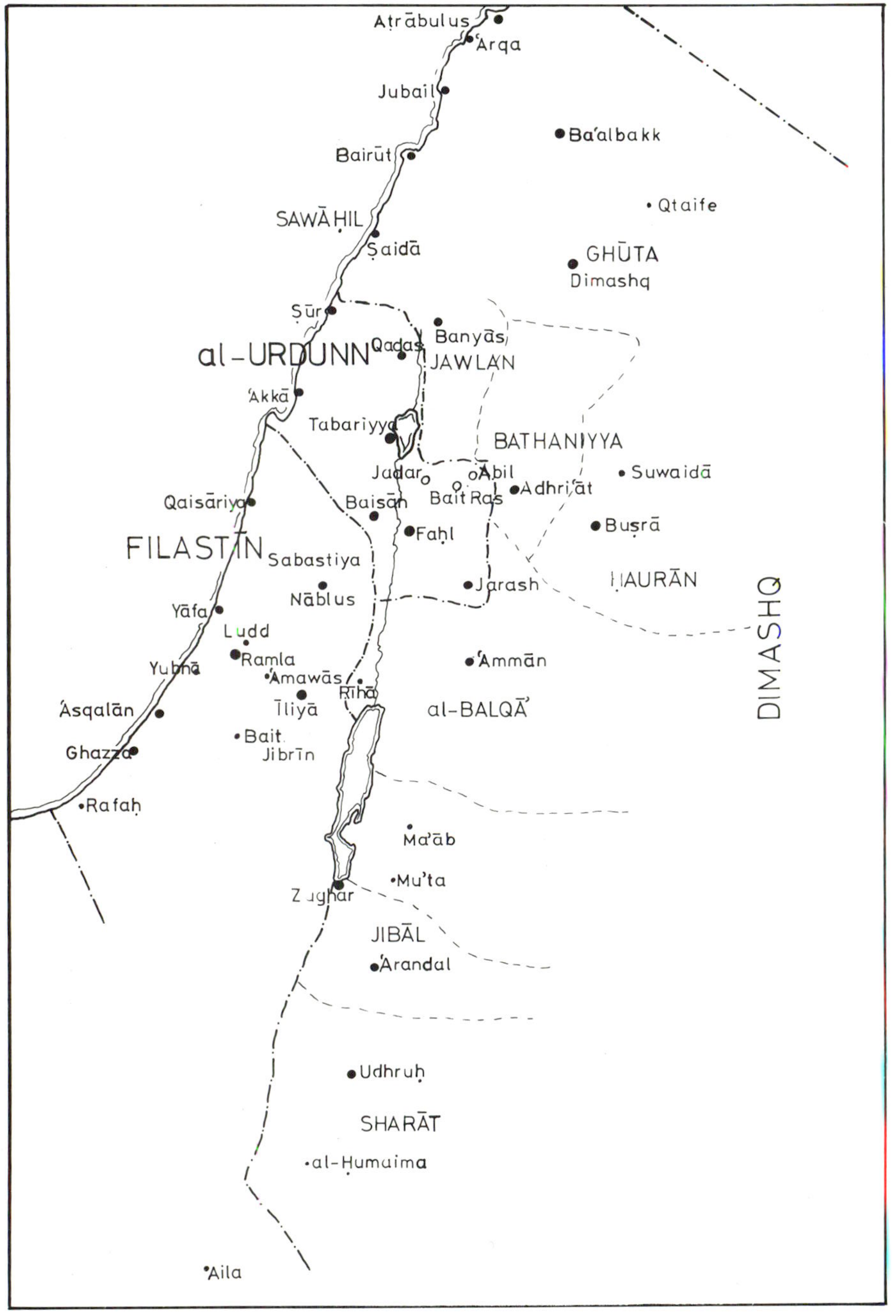

11. Filasṭīn, Urdunn and Dimashq according to al-Yaʿqūbī, *Kitāb al-Buldān* (278/891).

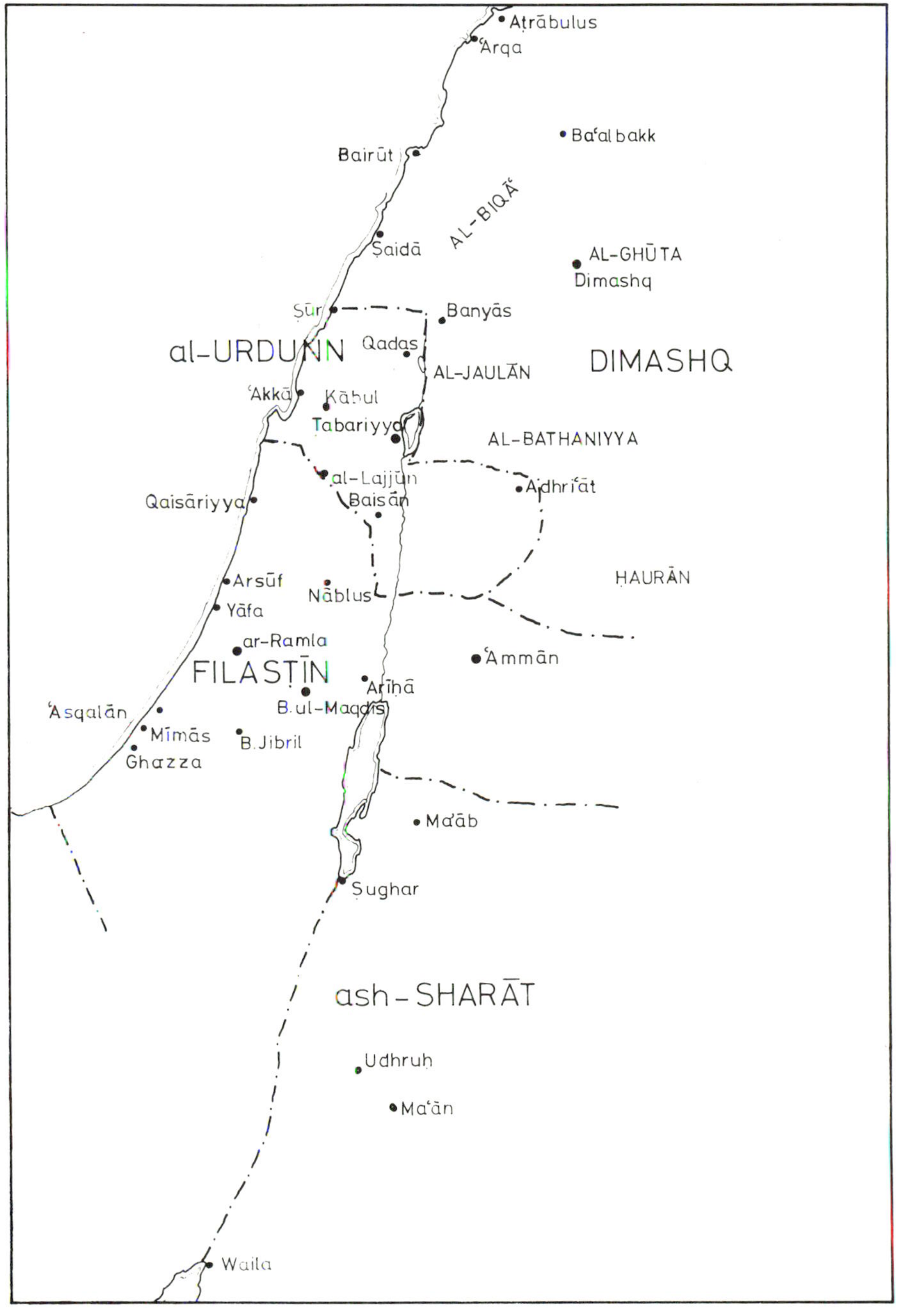

12. Filasṭīn, Urdunn and Dimashq according to al-Muqaddasī, *Aḥsan al-Taqāsīm* (*c.* 375/985).

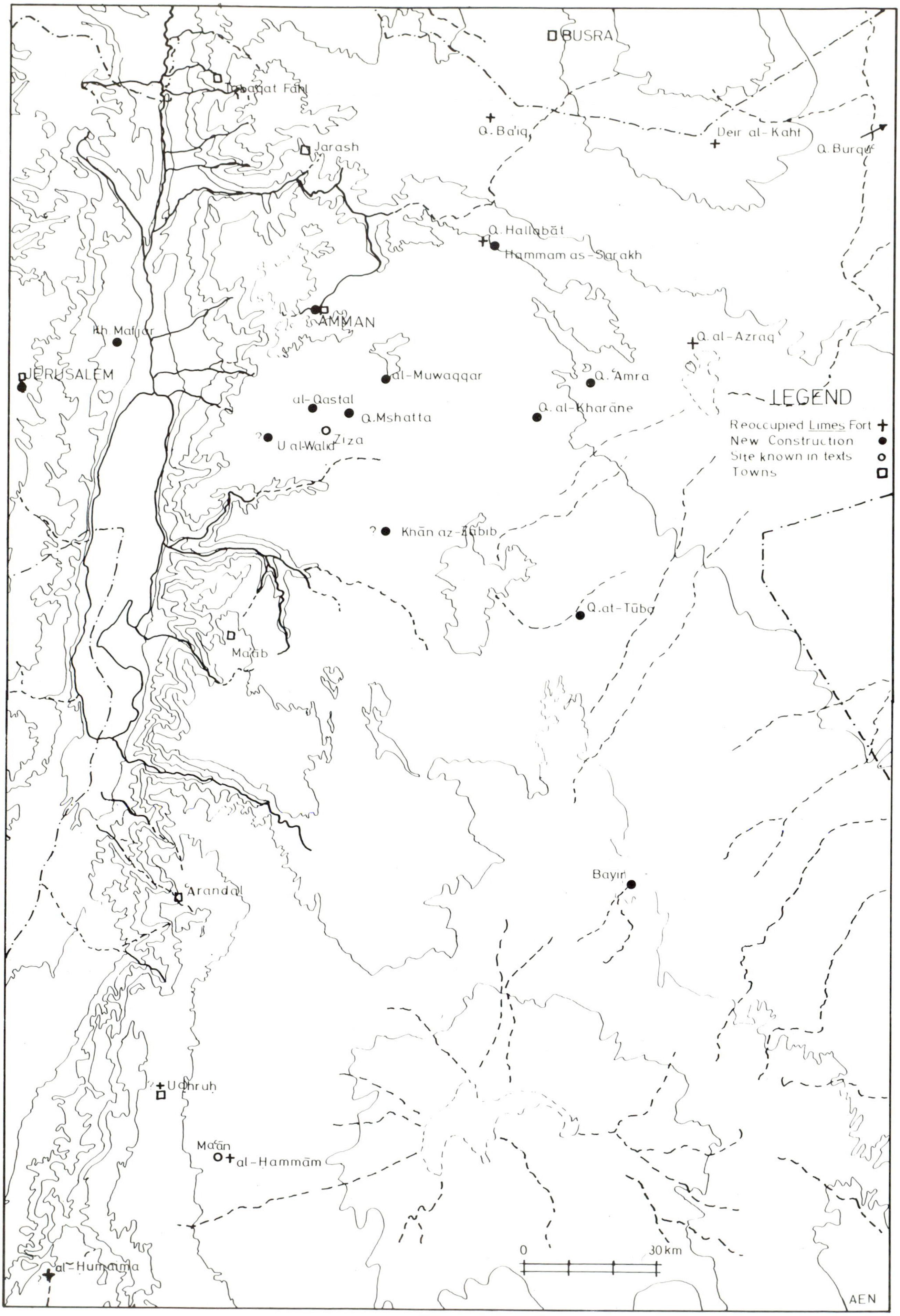

13. Distribution of Umayyad *quṣūr* in Jordan.

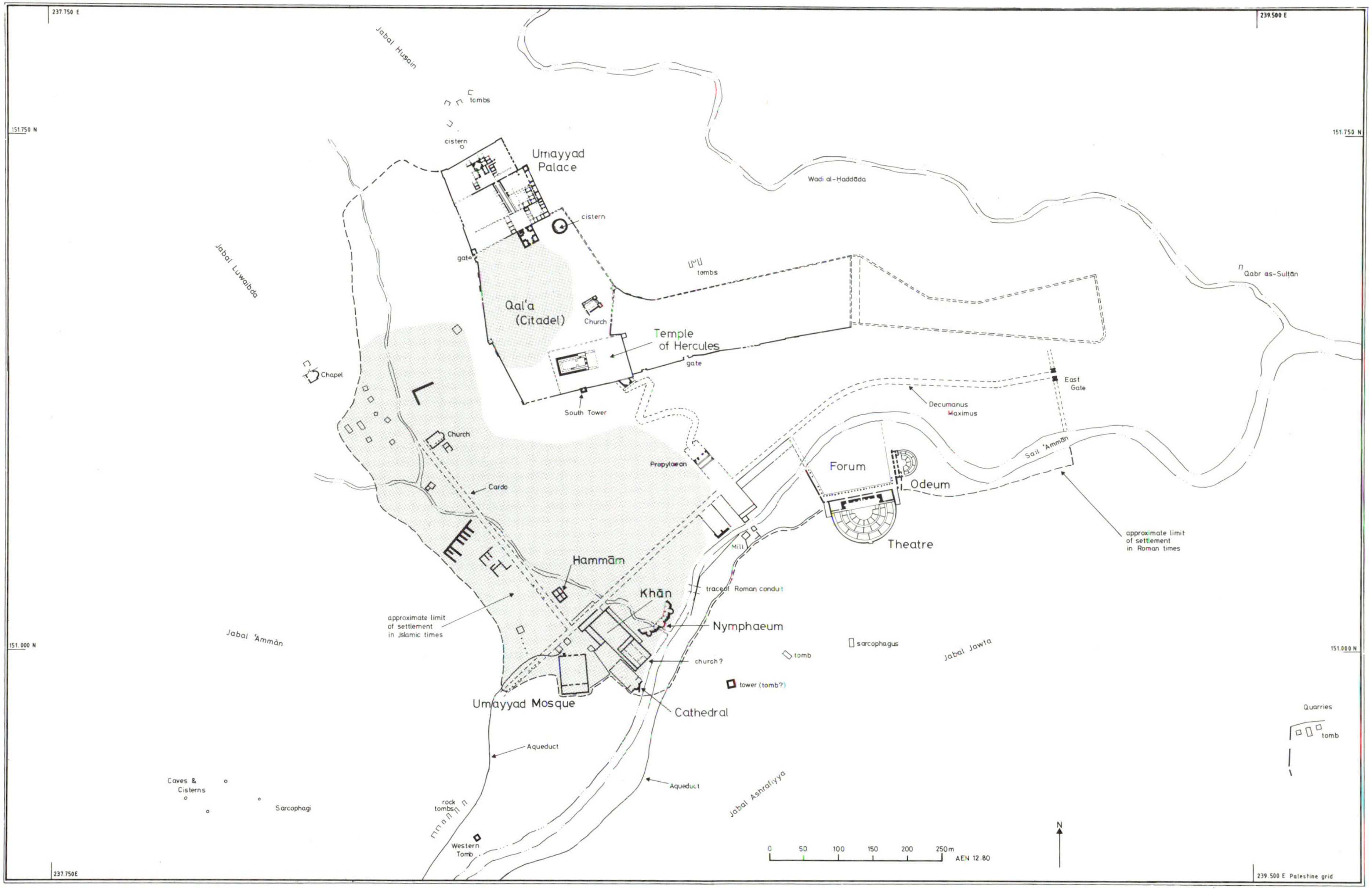

14. Roman and Islamic topography of 'Ammān (1:8000).

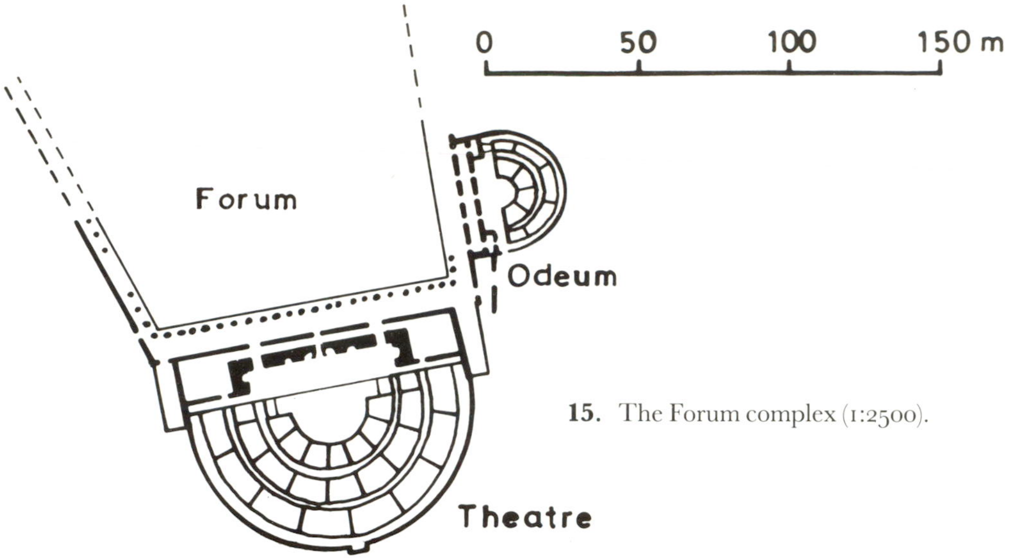

15. The Forum complex (1:2500).

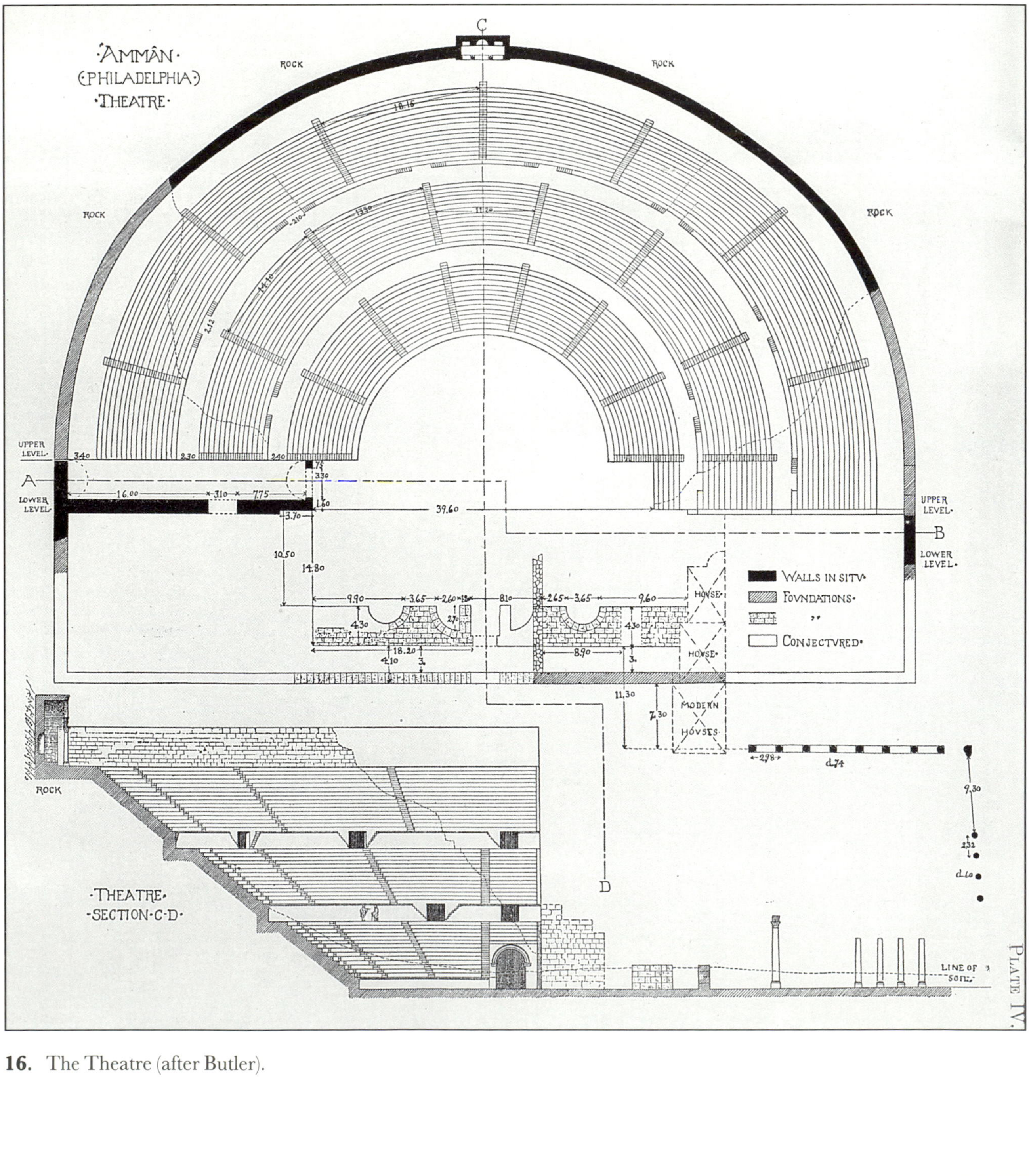

16. The Theatre (after Butler).

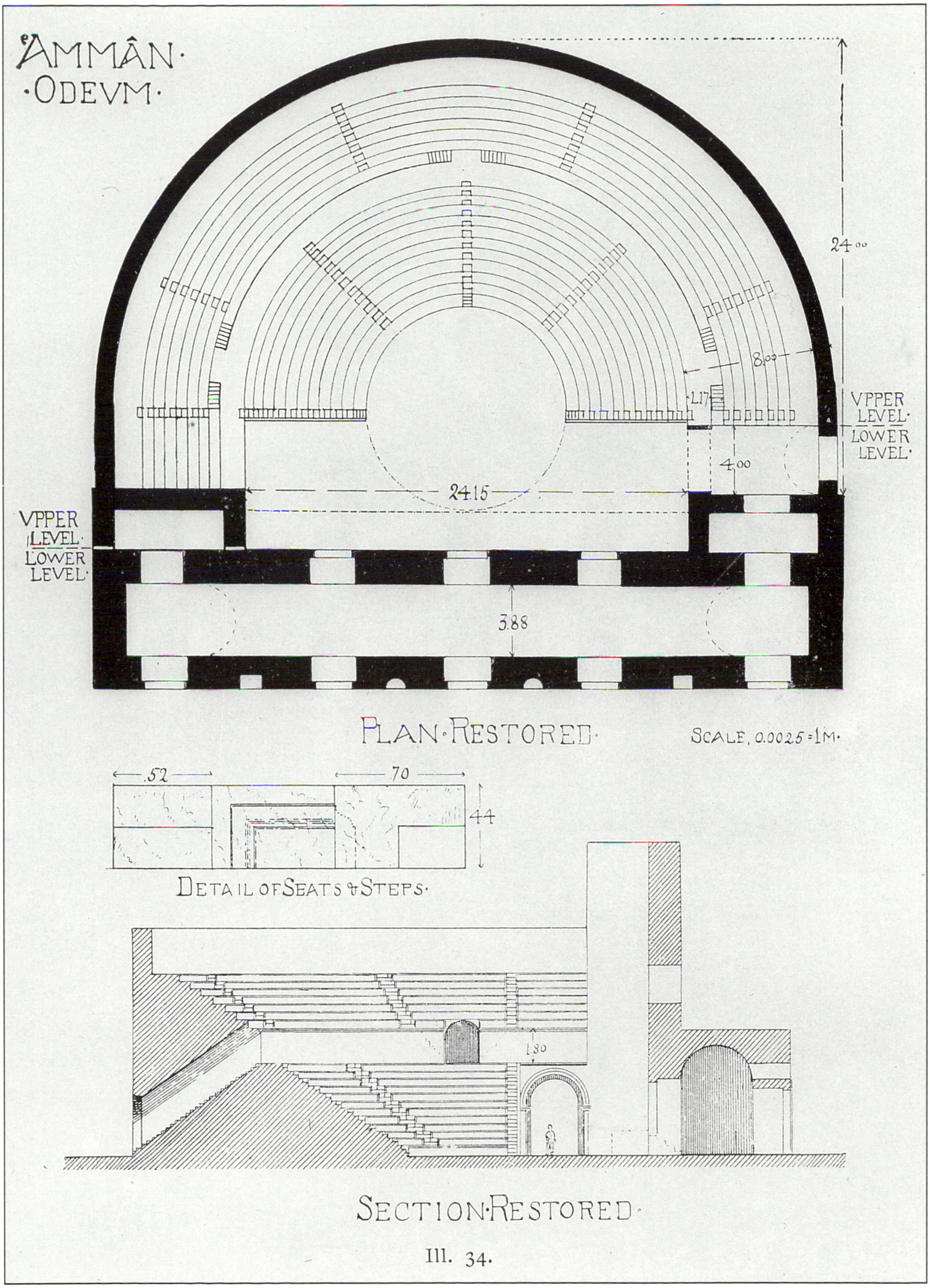

17. The Odeum (after Butler).

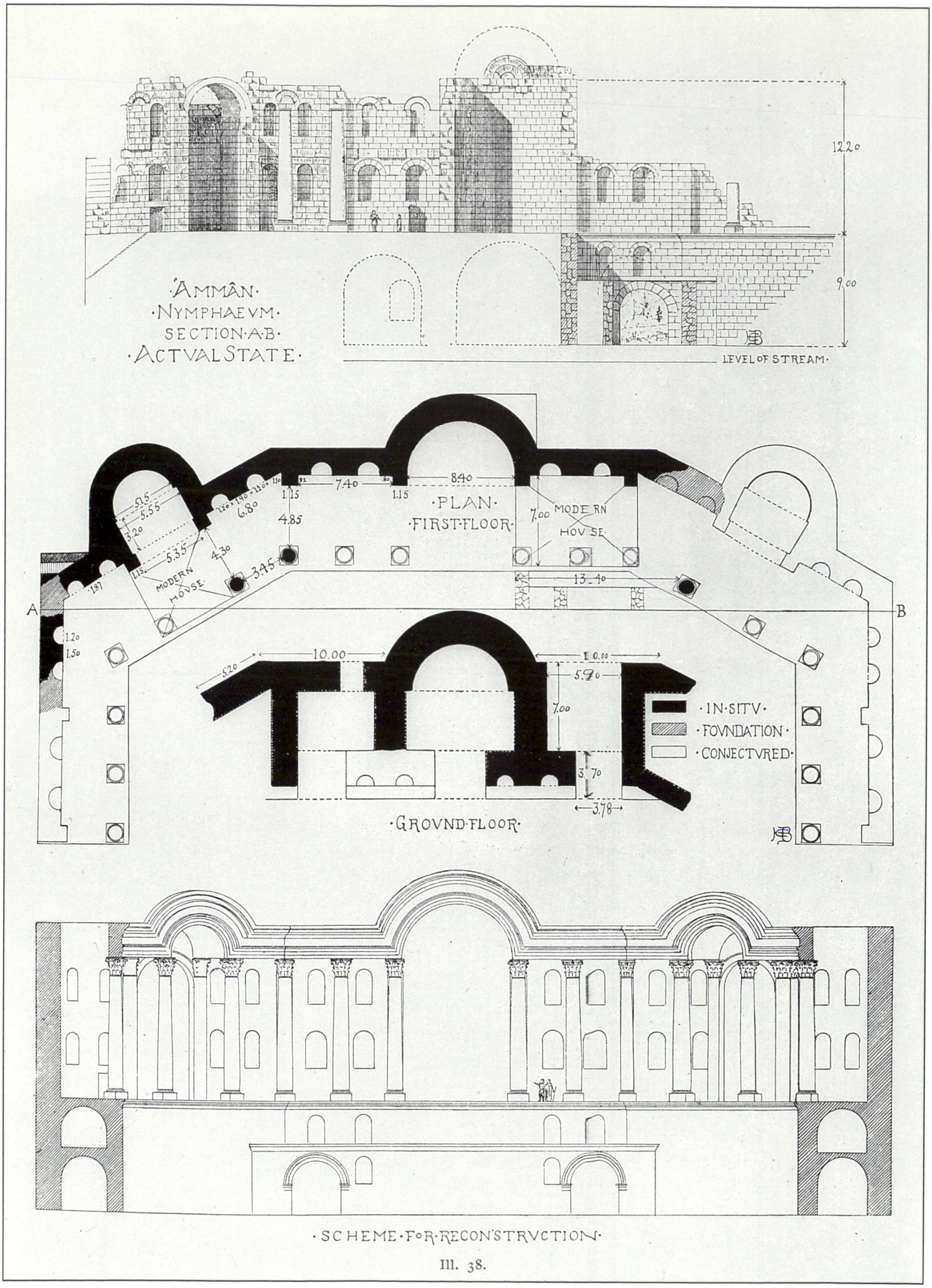

18. The Nymphaeum (after Butler).

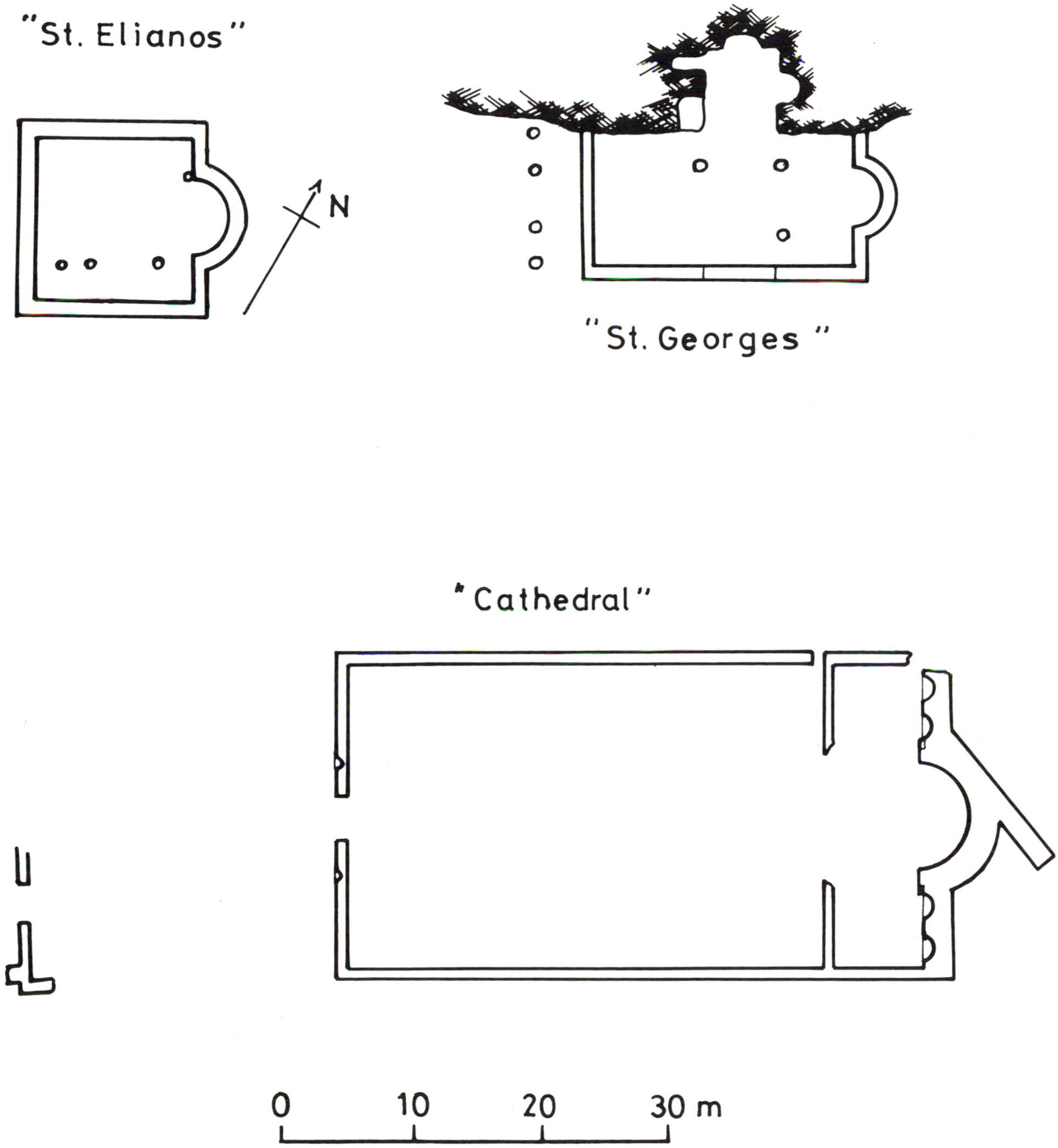

19. Churches of the Lower City (1:450).

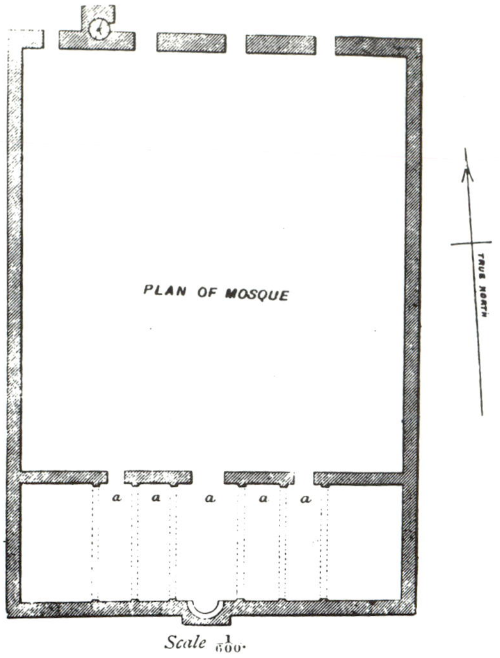

20. The Palestine Exploration Fund plan of the Congregational Mosque (after Conder 1889).

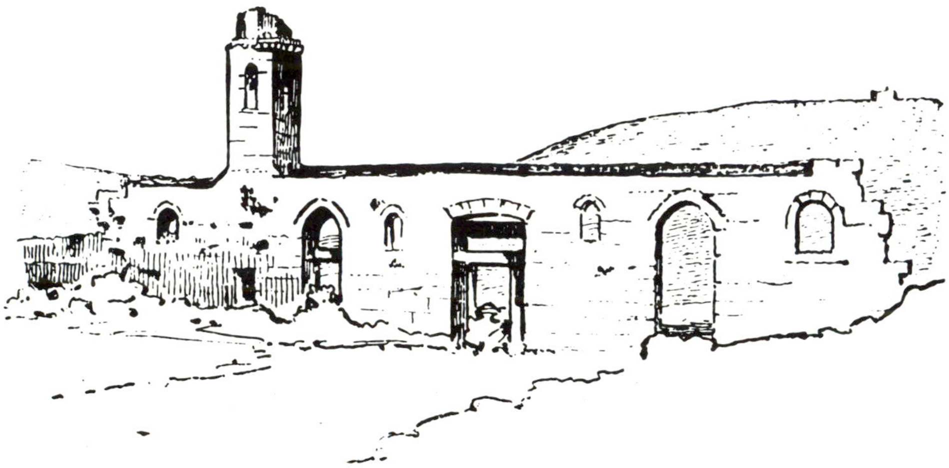

21. Sketch of the north wall of the Umayyad Congregational Mosque (after Conder 1889).

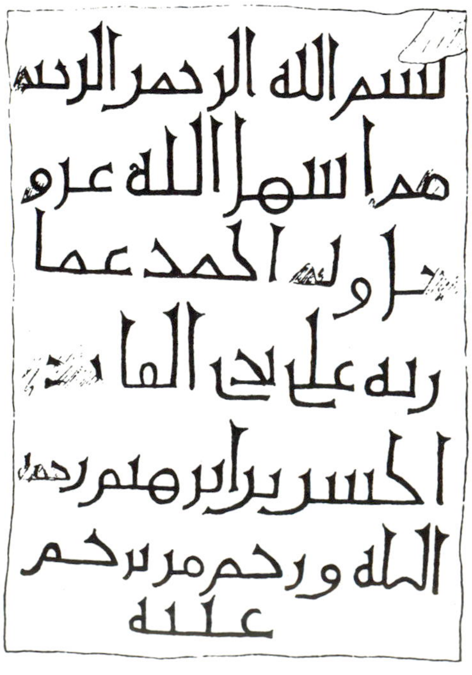

22. Drawing of the Kūfic inscription recovered from the mosque (after Littmann 1949).

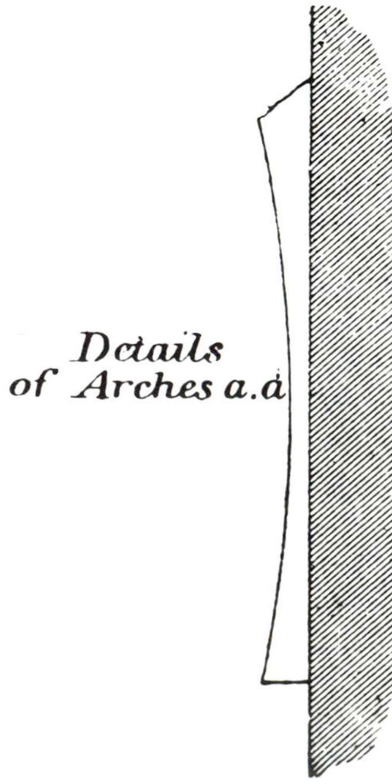

23. Horseshoe arch from the mosque (after Conder 1889).

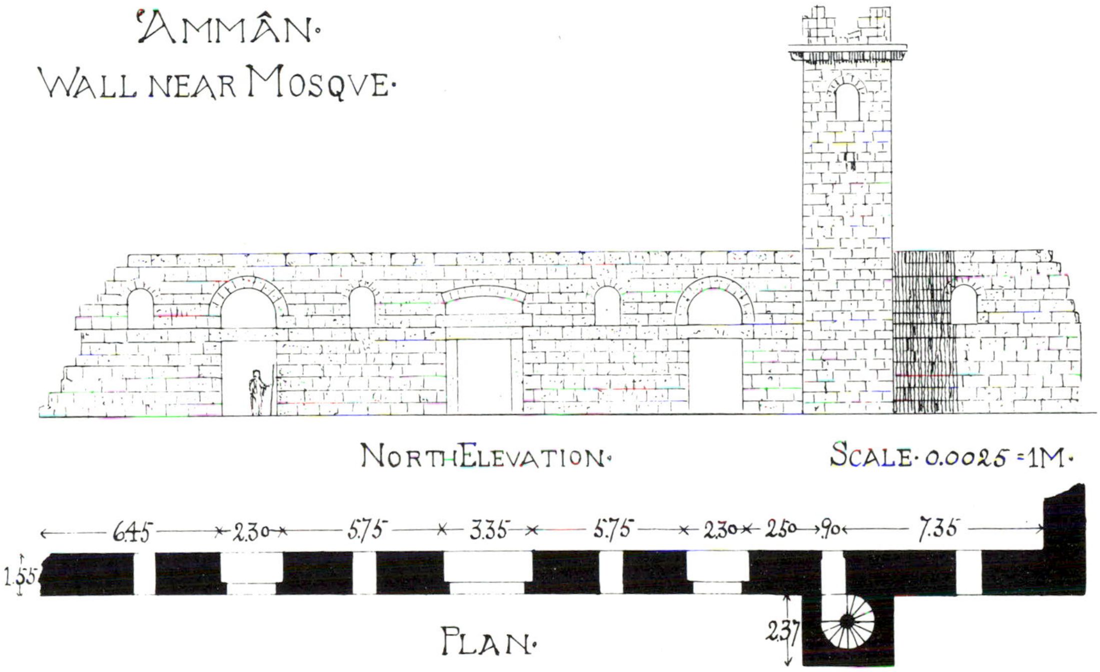

24. Plan and elevation of the north wall of the mosque (after Butler 1913–19).

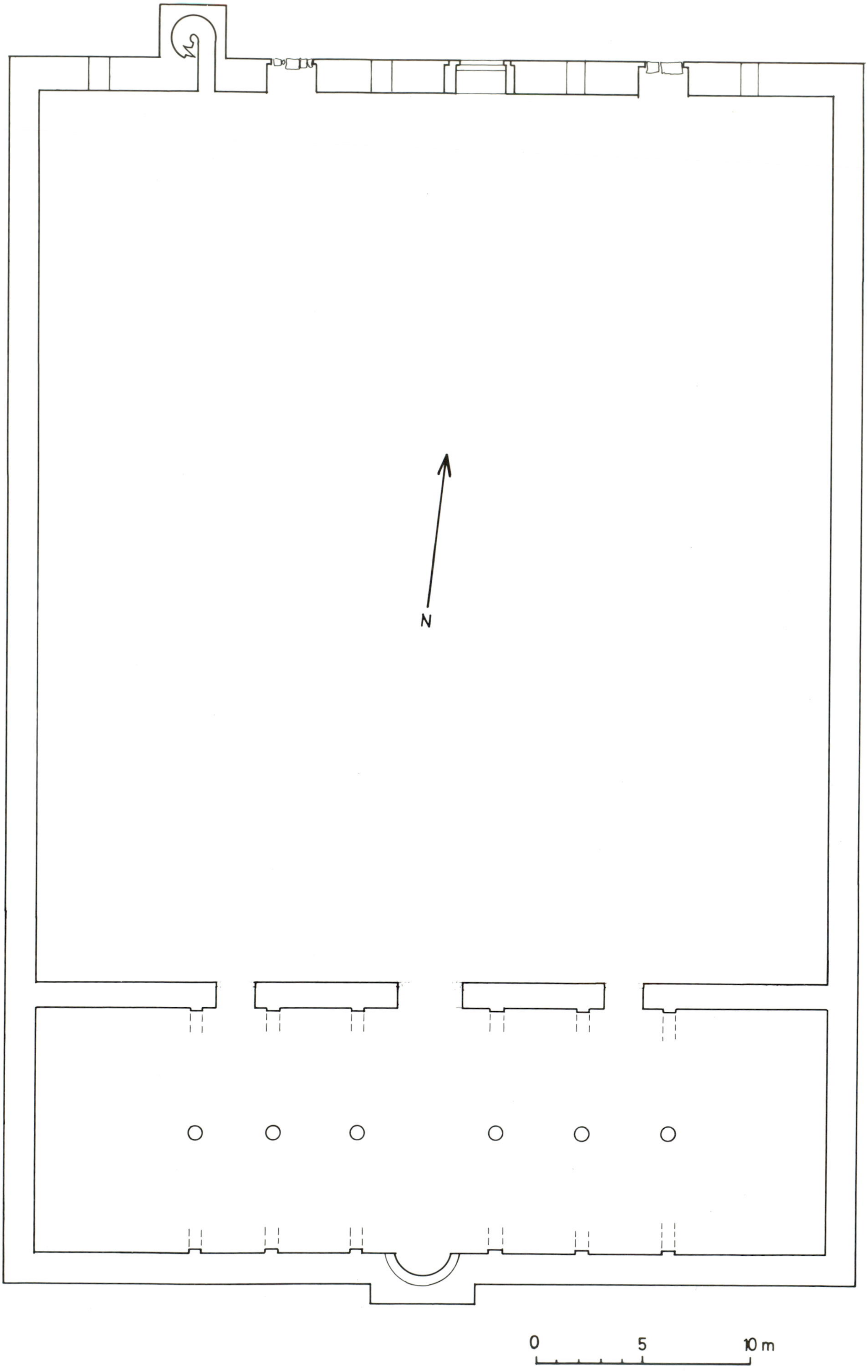

25. Reconstruction of the plan of the remains of the Umayyad Congregational Mosque (after Northey 1872, Conder 1889, and Butler 1913–19)(1:250).

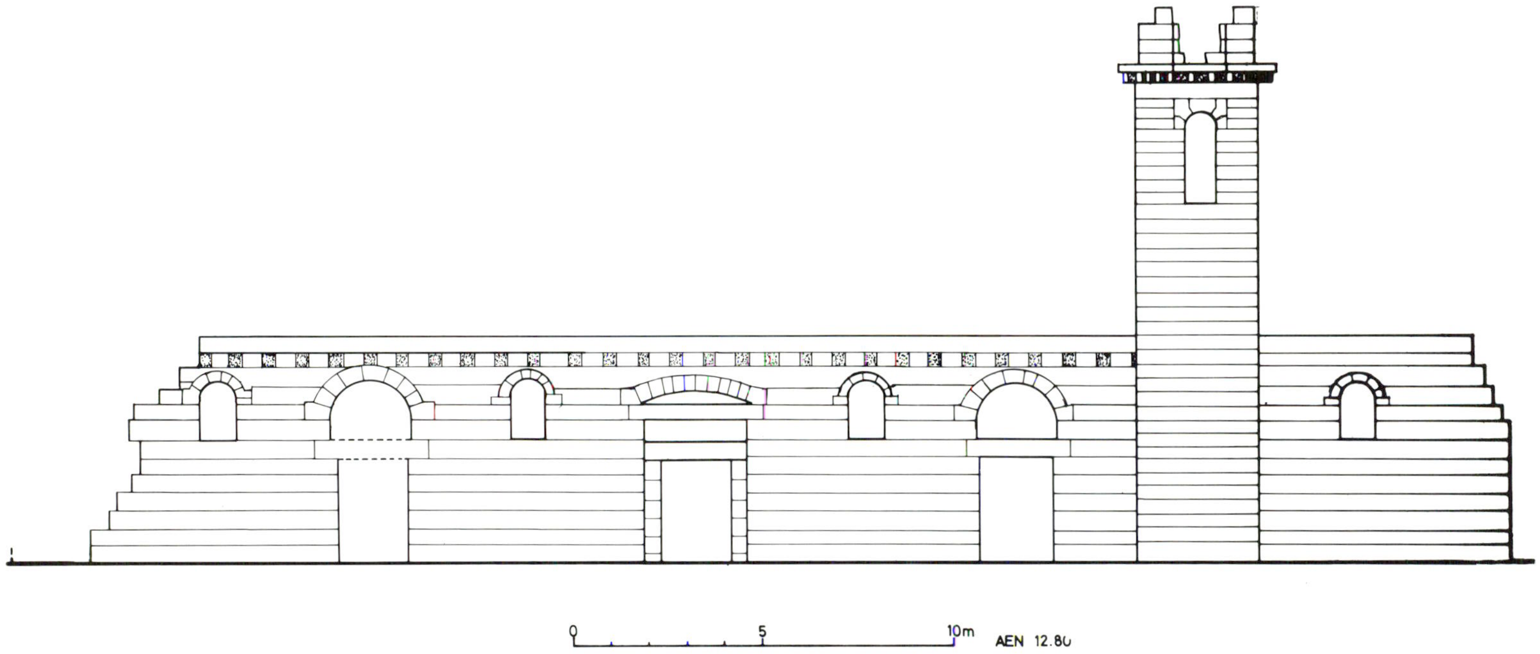

26. Reconstruction of the elevation of the North Wall (after Butler 1913–19) (1:200).

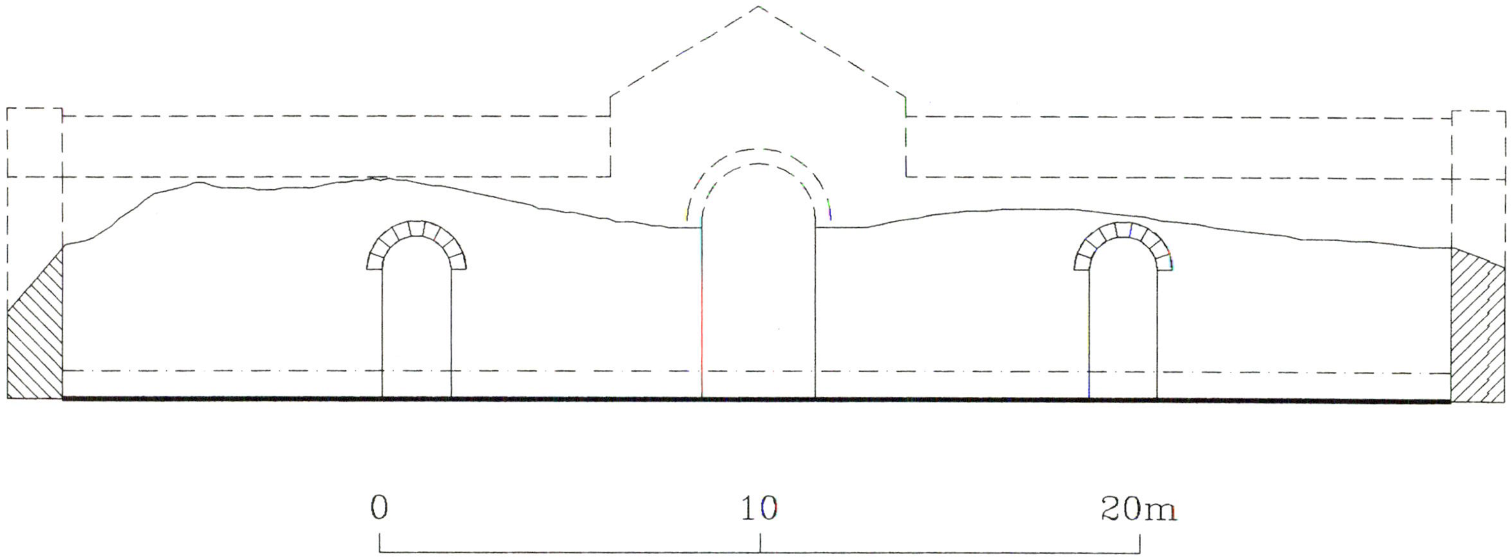

27. Reconstruction of the facade wall of the sanctuary (1:200).

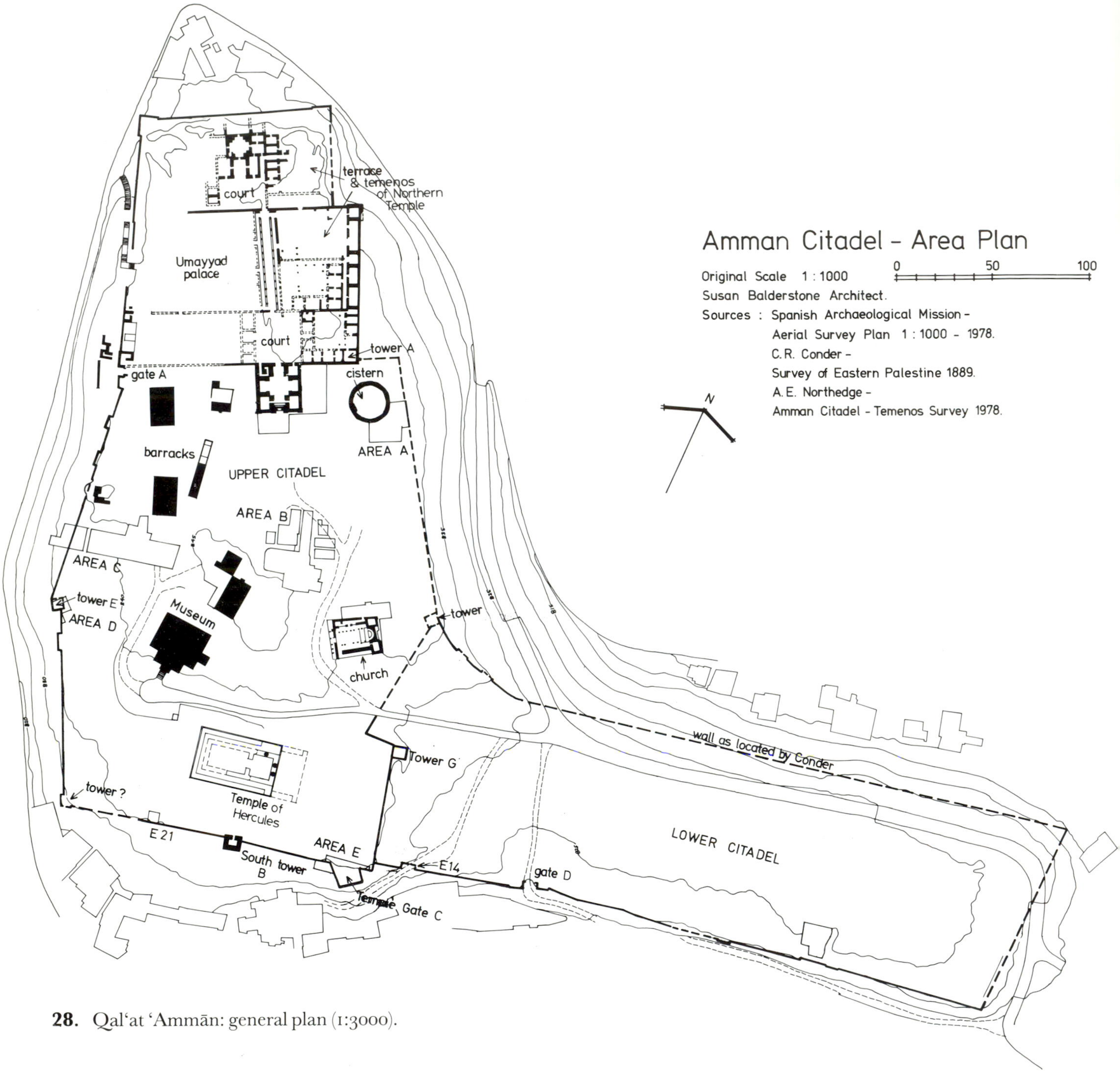
Amman Citadel - Area Plan
Original Scale 1 : 1000
0
50
100
Susan Balderstone Architect.
Sources : Spanish Archaeological Mission -
Aerial Survey Plan 1 : 1000 - 1978.
C.R. Conder -
Survey of Eastern Palestine 1889.
A.E. Northedge -
Amman Citadel - Temenos Survey 1978.
N
terrace & temenos of Northern Temple
court
Umayyad palace
court
tower A
gate A
cistern
barracks
AREA A
UPPER CITADEL
AREA B
AREA C
tower E
AREA D
Museum
tower
church
wall as located by Conder
Tower G
tower ?
Temple of Hercules
E 21
AREA E
South tower B
E14
gate D
LOWER CITADEL
Temple
Gate C

28. Qal'at 'Ammān: general plan (1:3000).

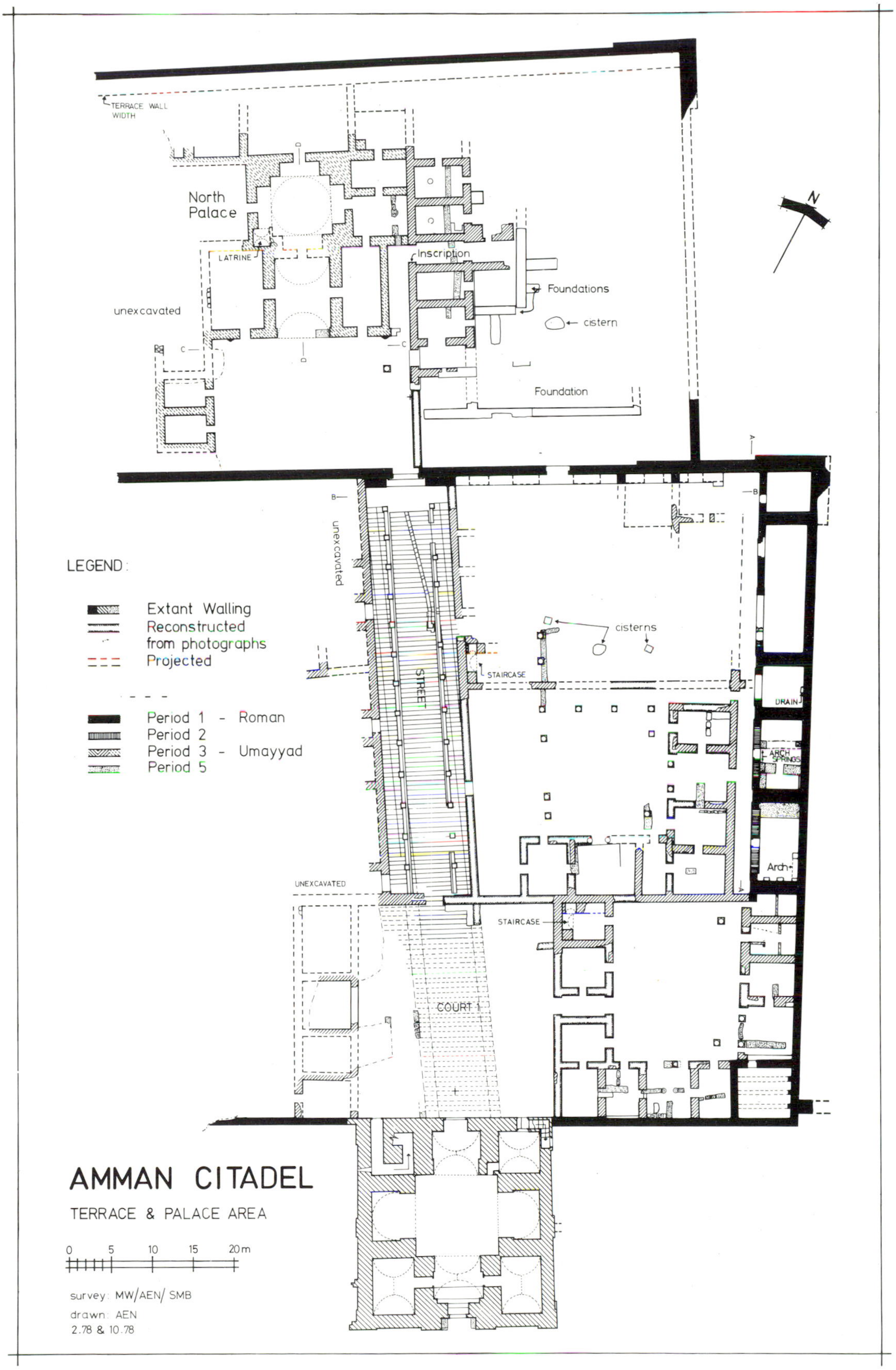

29. The Northern Temple and Palace excavation area (1:650).

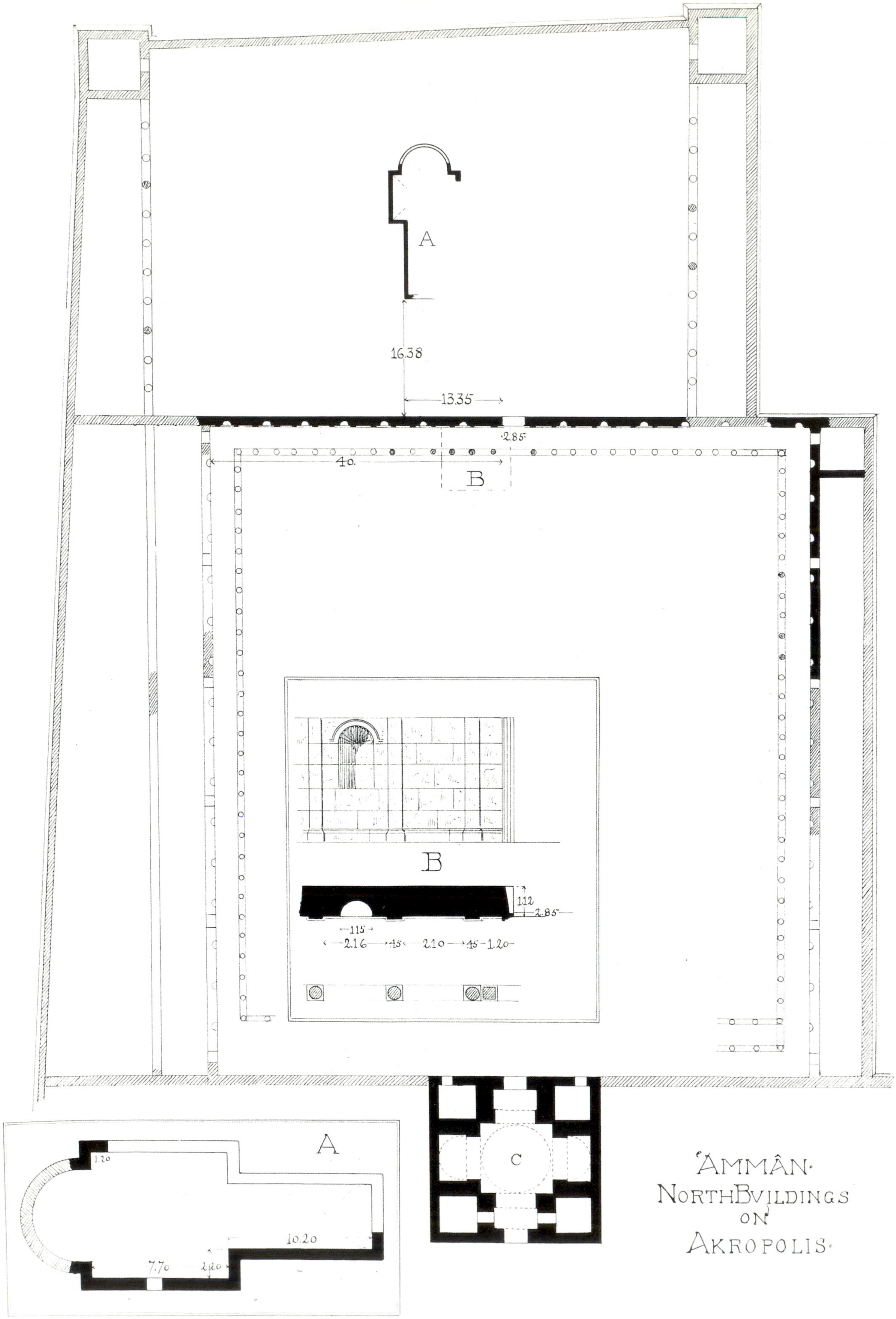

30. The Princeton Archaeological Expedition's plan of the area of the north *temenos*.

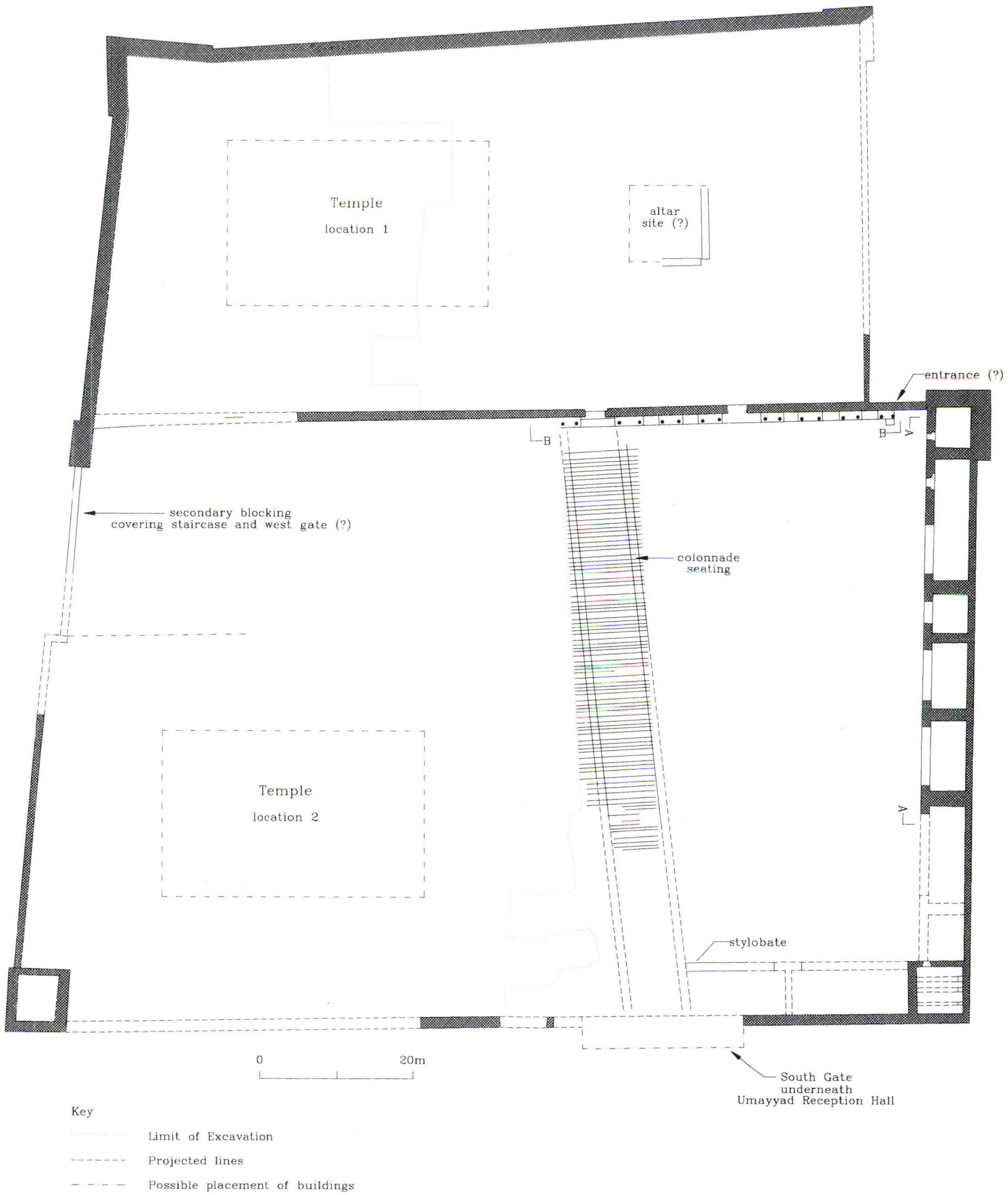

31. The Northern Temple: plan of Roman phase (1:700).

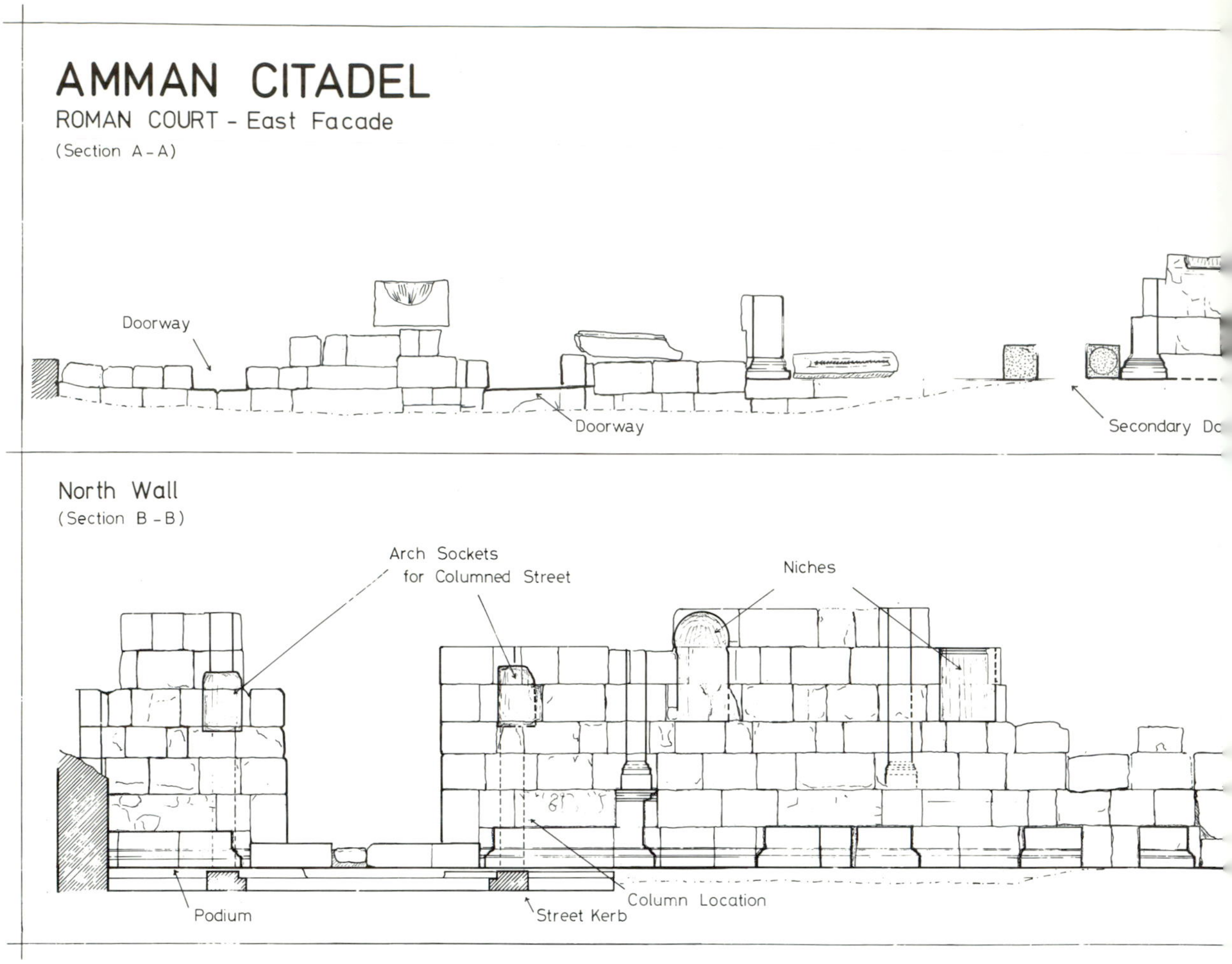

32. Facades of the Roman *temenos* (1:150).

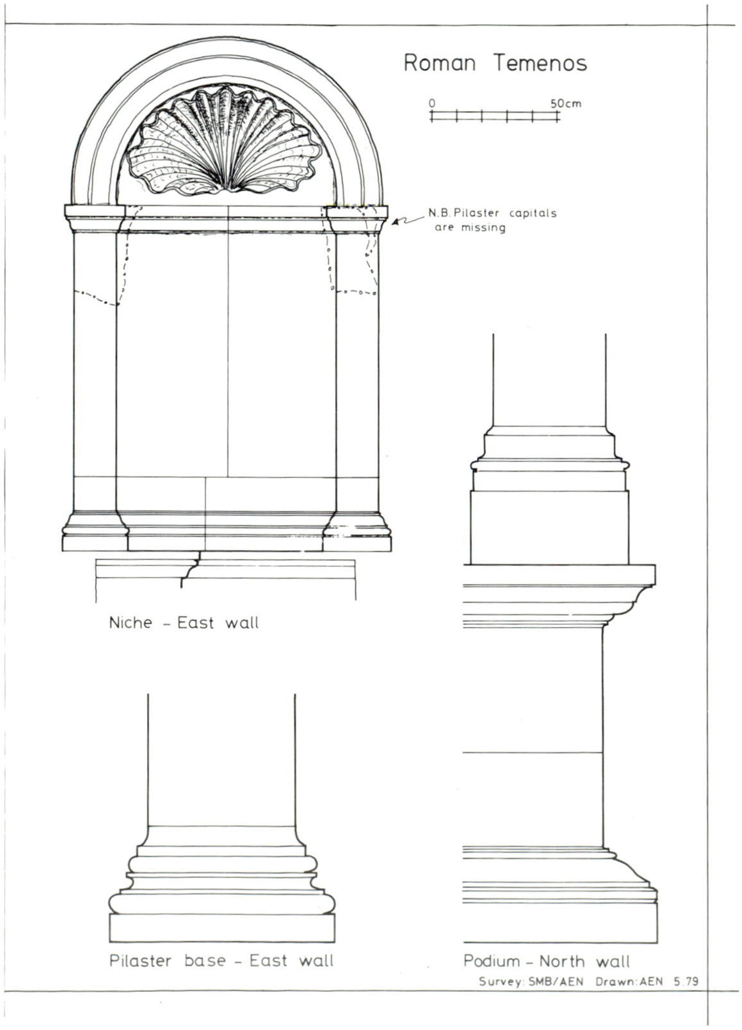

33. Architectural details from the Roman *temenos* (1:30).

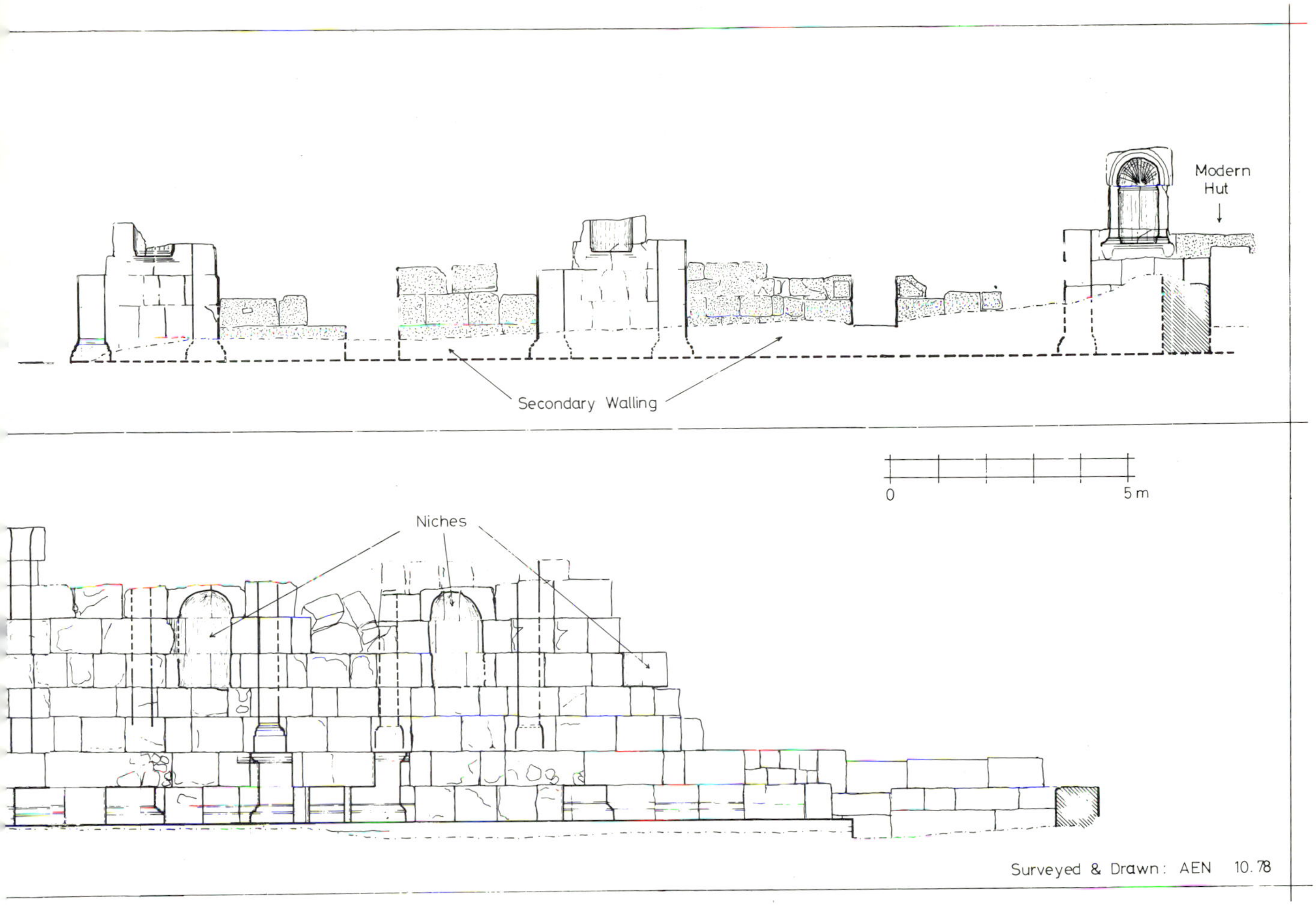

34. Northern Temple, architrave moulding (after Butler 1913–19, ill. 27).

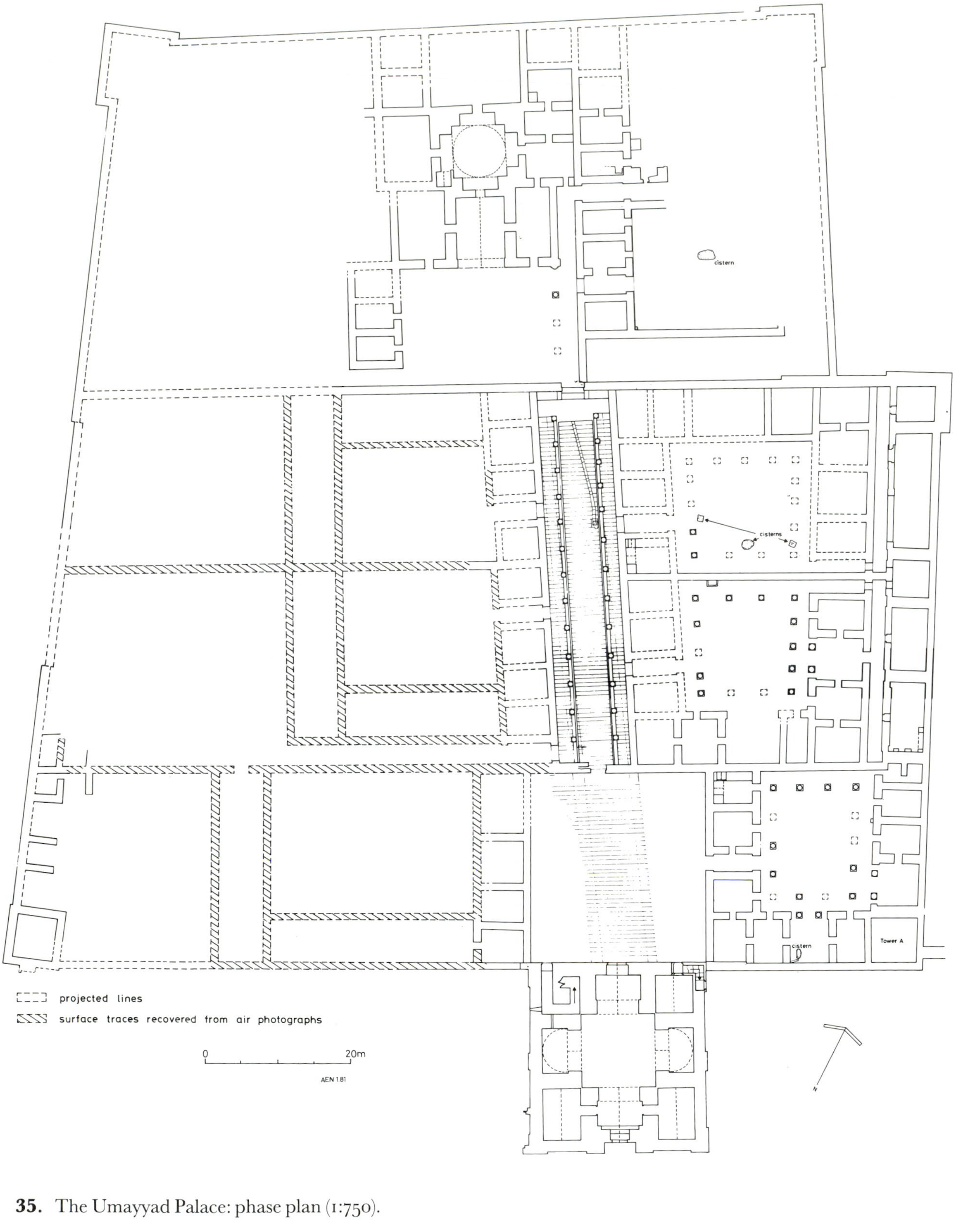

35. The Umayyad Palace: phase plan (1:750).

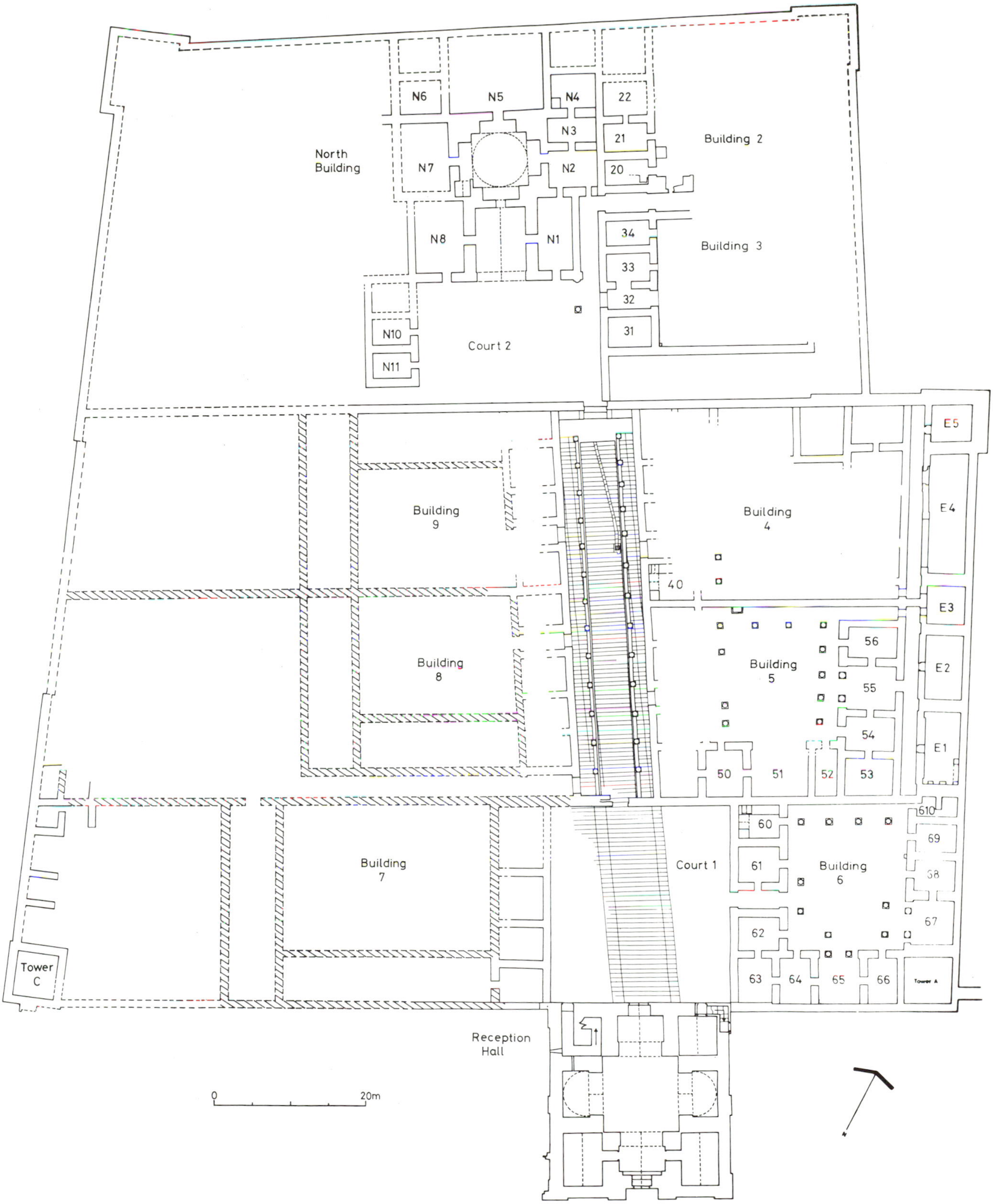

36. Building and room numbers in the Umayyad Palace (1:750).

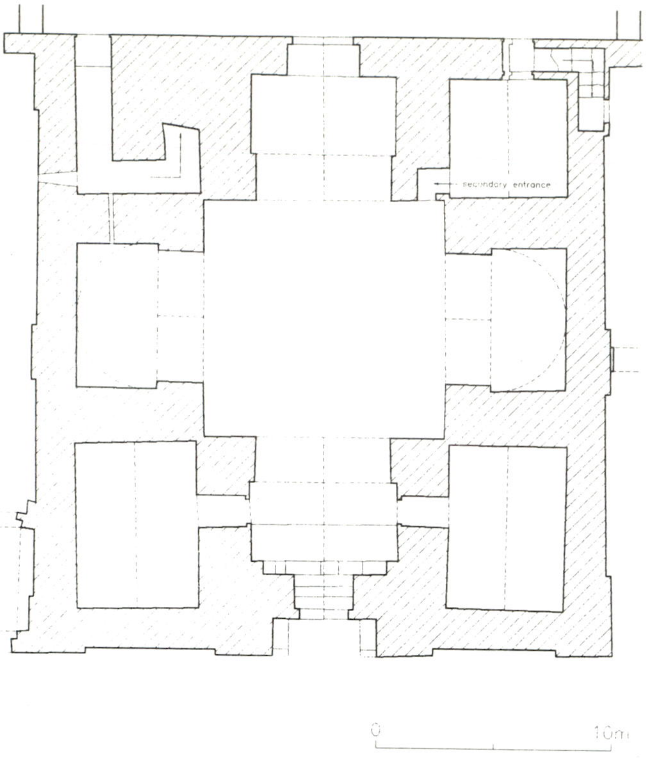

37. Plan of the Reception Hall (1:250).

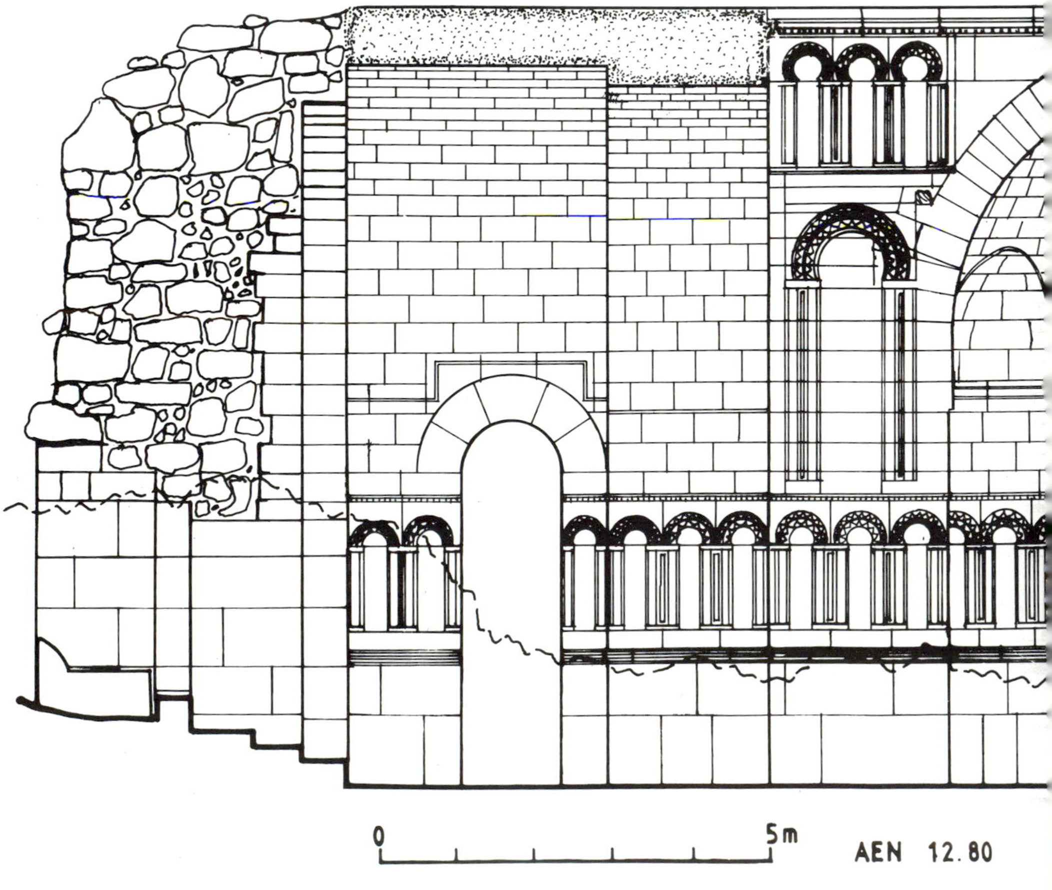

38. The Reception Hall: section looking west (modified from Schulz 1909) (1:100).

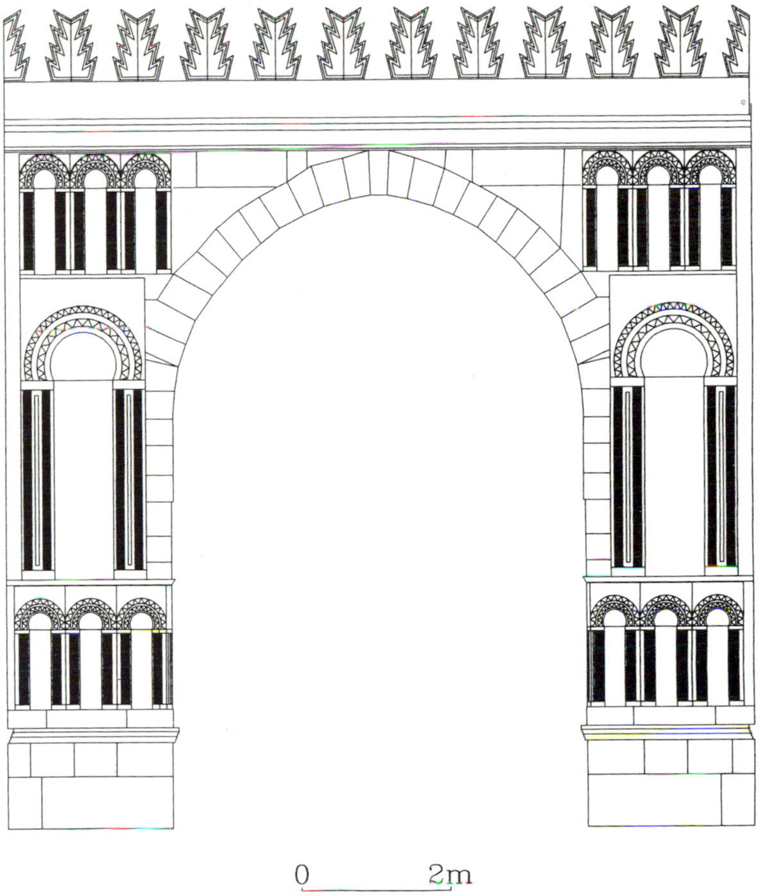

39. Reconstruction of the court facade of the Reception Hall (1:100).

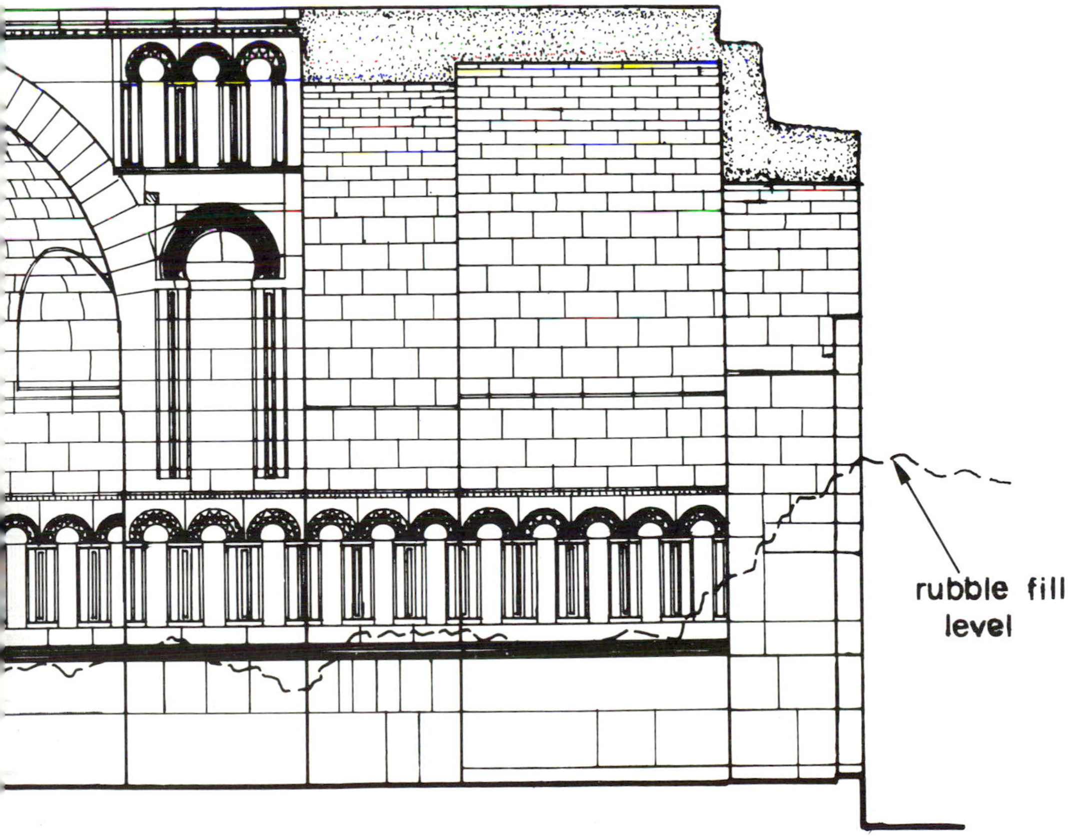

40. Reconstruction of the interior of the Reception Hall (after a photograph).

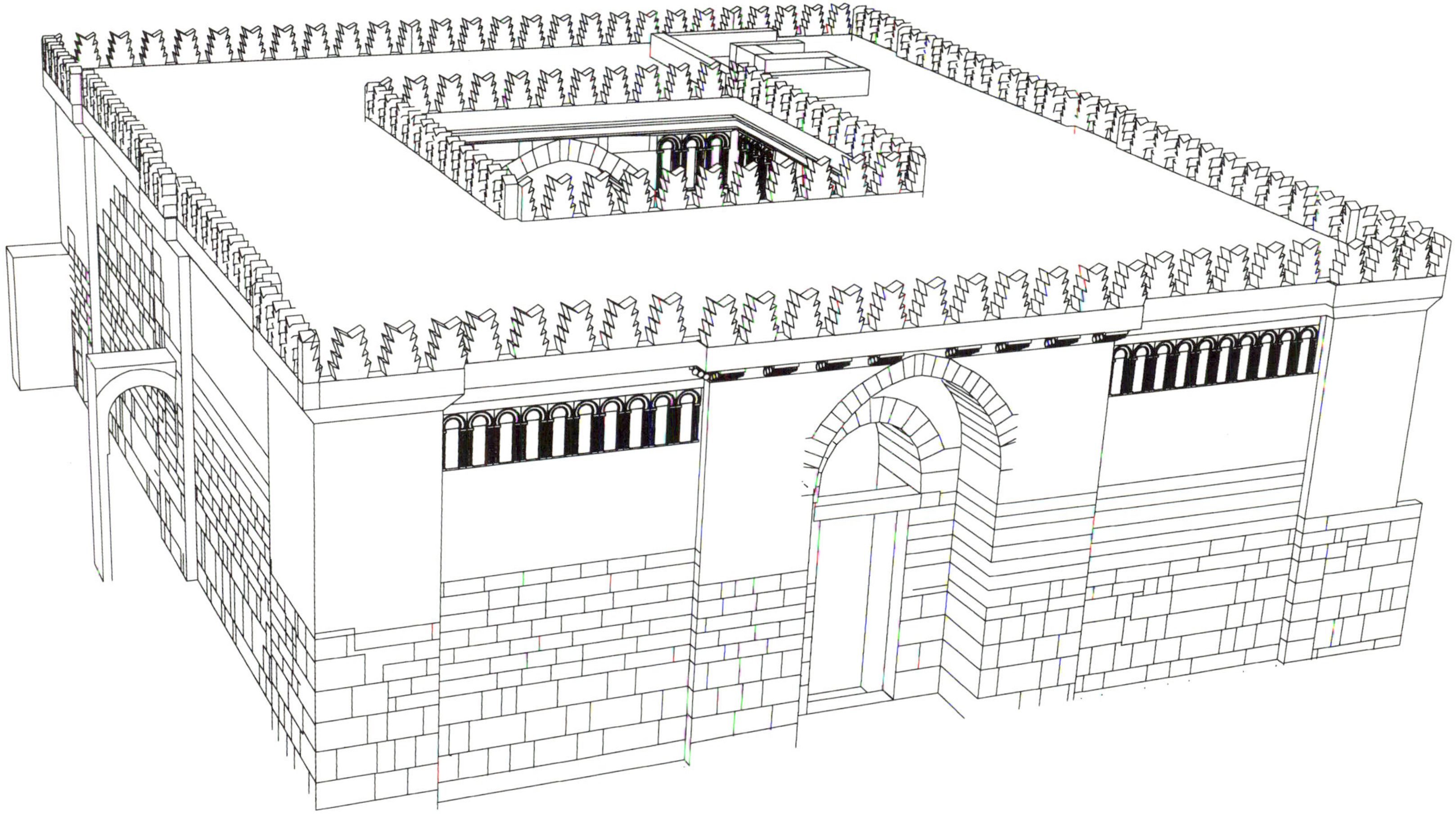

41. Reconstruction of the exterior of the Reception Hall.

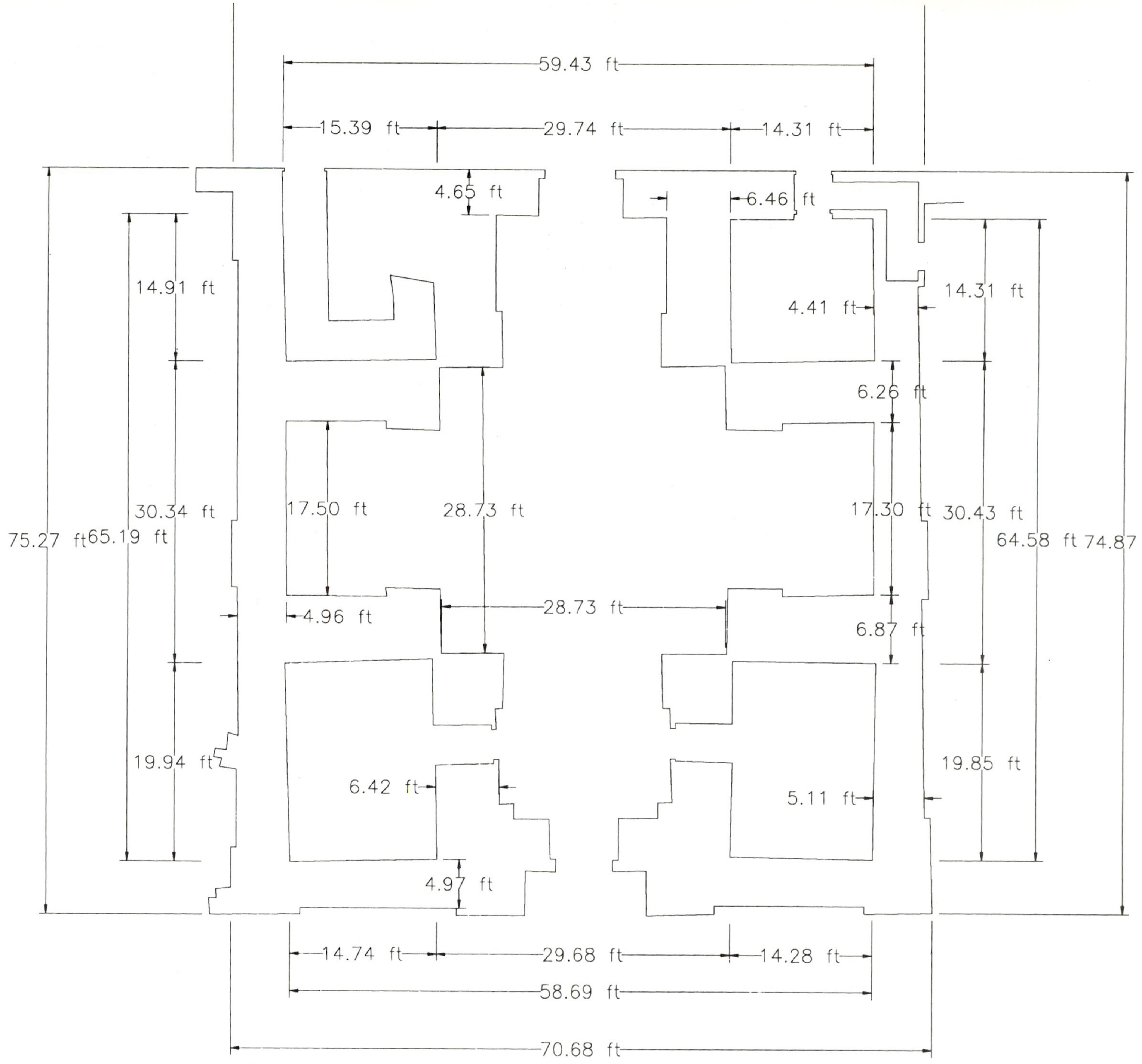

42. Plan of the Reception Hall with measurements according to a foot of 34.8cm (1:175).

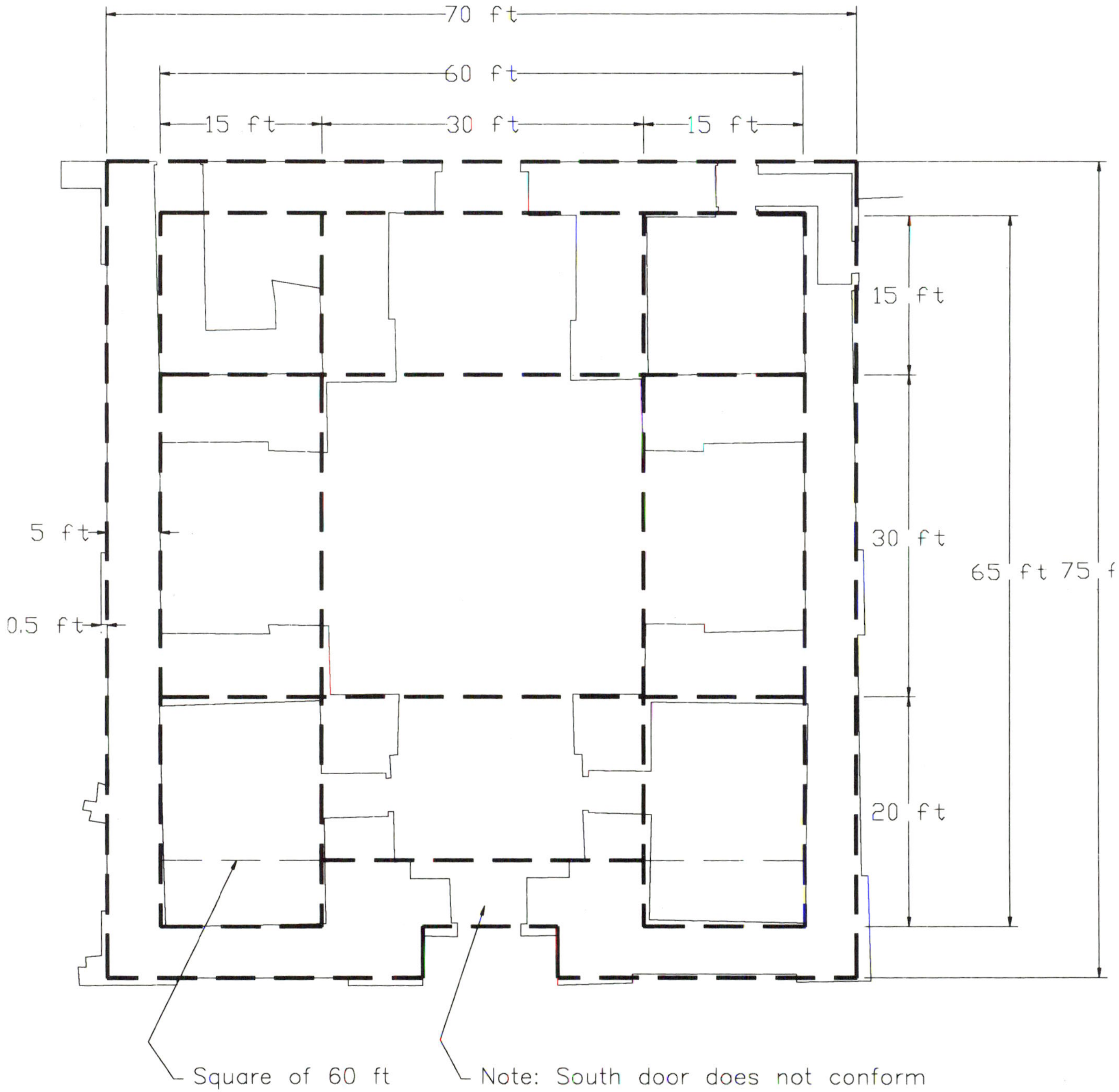

43. Diagram to show the setting out of the Reception Hall, with probable intended measurements according to a foot of 34.8cm (1:175).

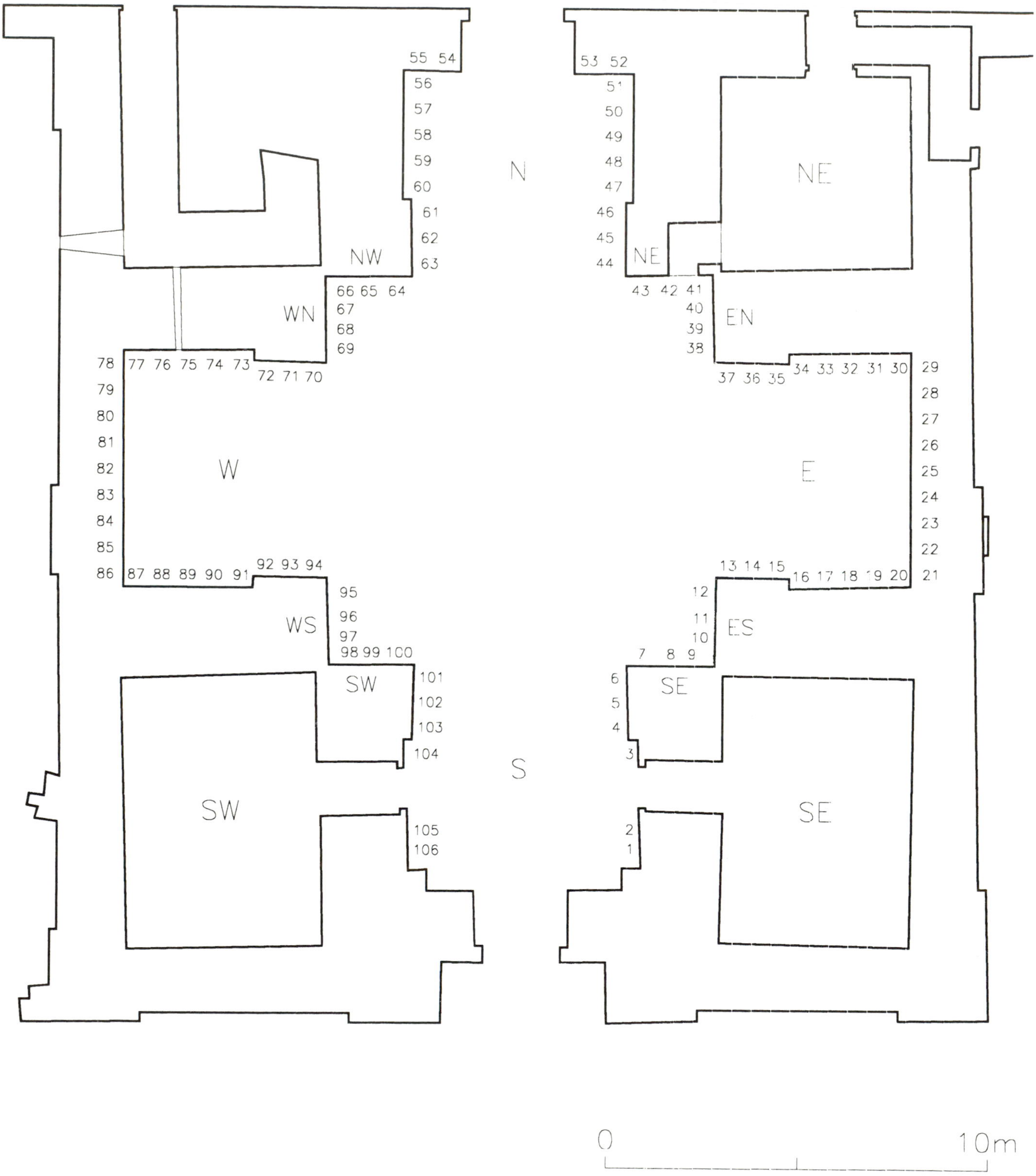

44. Location of Niches in the Reception Hall (1:150).

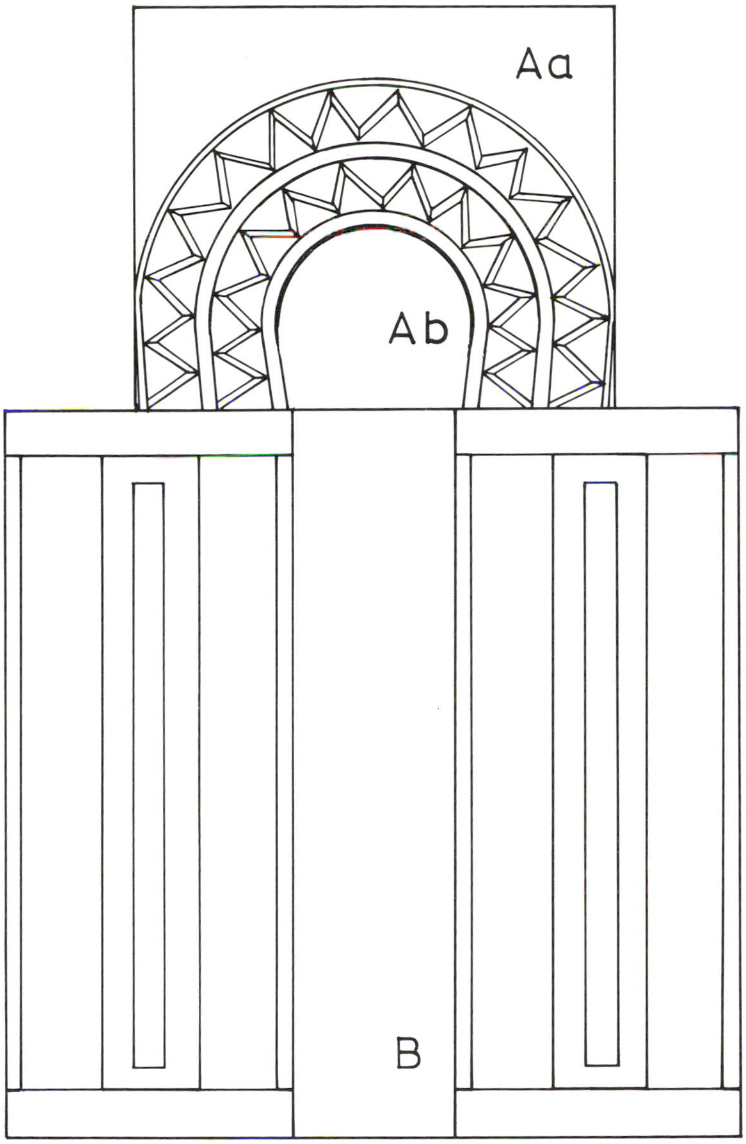

45. Niche of Register 1 in the Reception Hall.

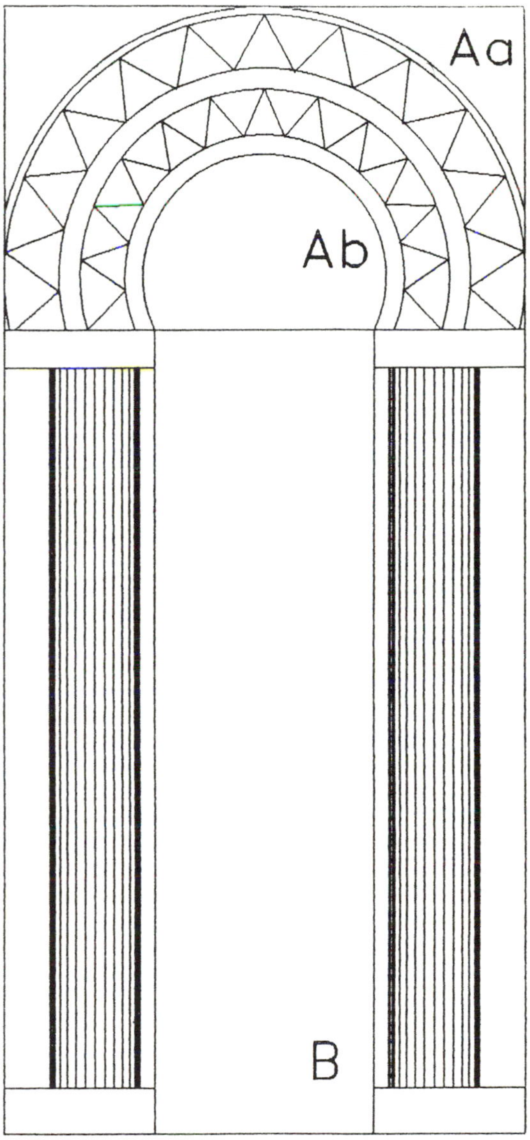

46. Niche of Register 3 in the Reception Hall (1:10).

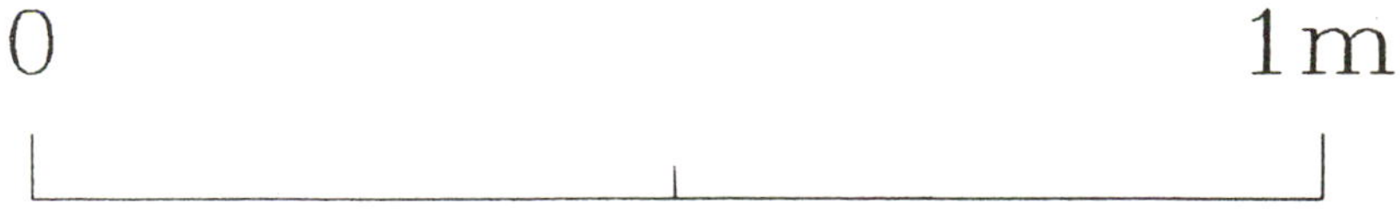

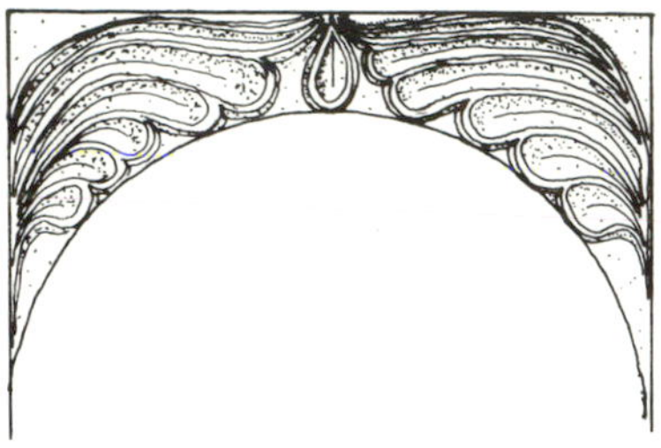

1. 91Aa

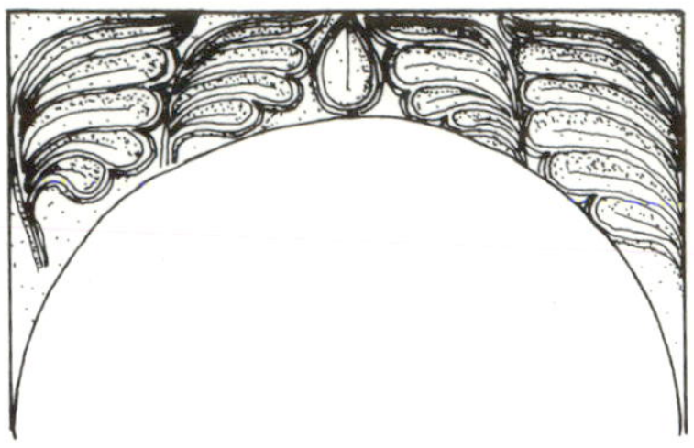

2. 86Aa

3. 13Aa

4. 22Aa

5. 97Aa

6. 75Aa

7. 95Aa

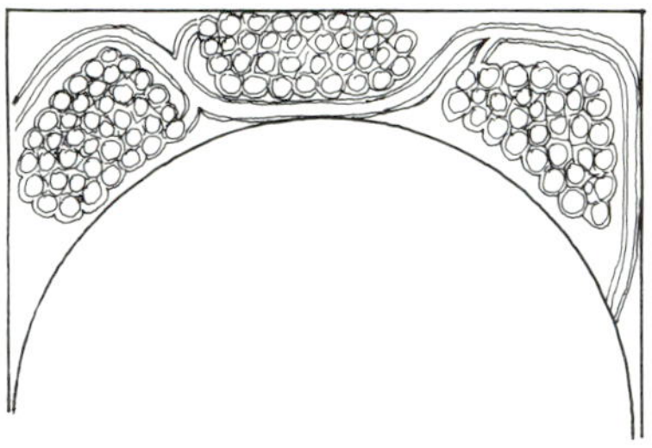

8. 98Aa

9. 93Aa

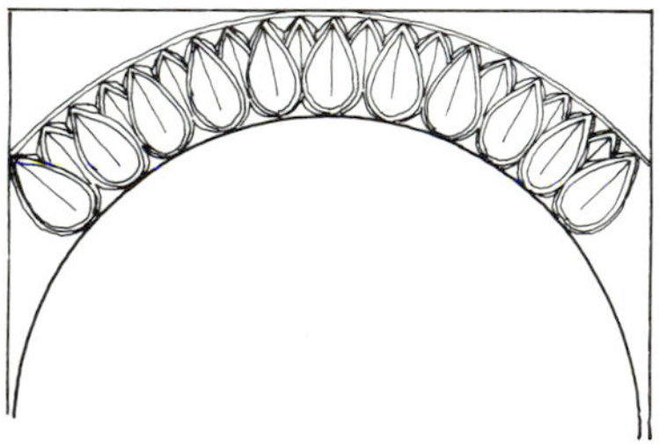

10. 24Aa

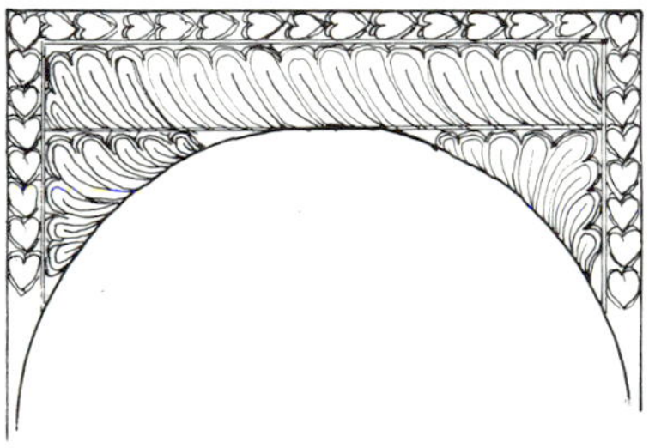

11. 7Aa

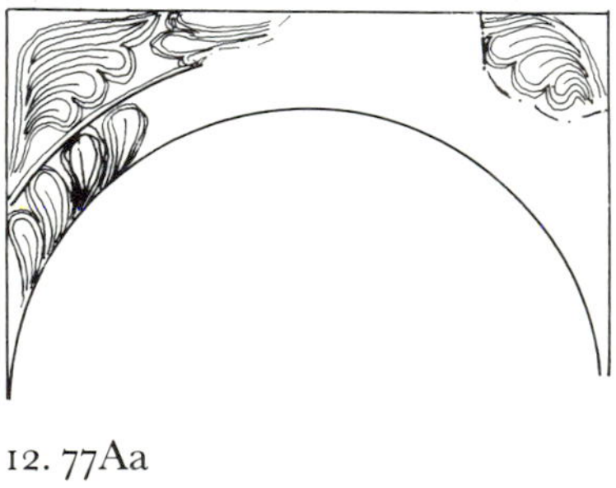

12. 77Aa

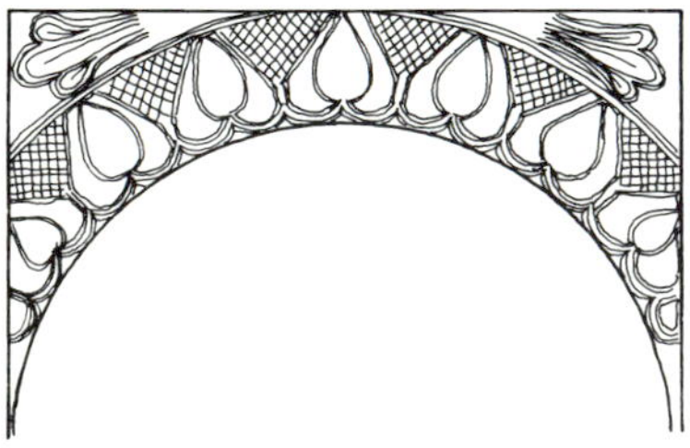

13. 90Aa

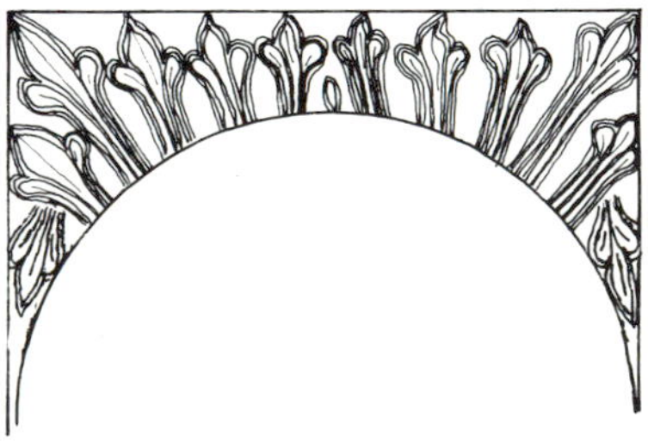

14. 68Aa

15. 87Aa

47. Aa Panels. (1:1.5)

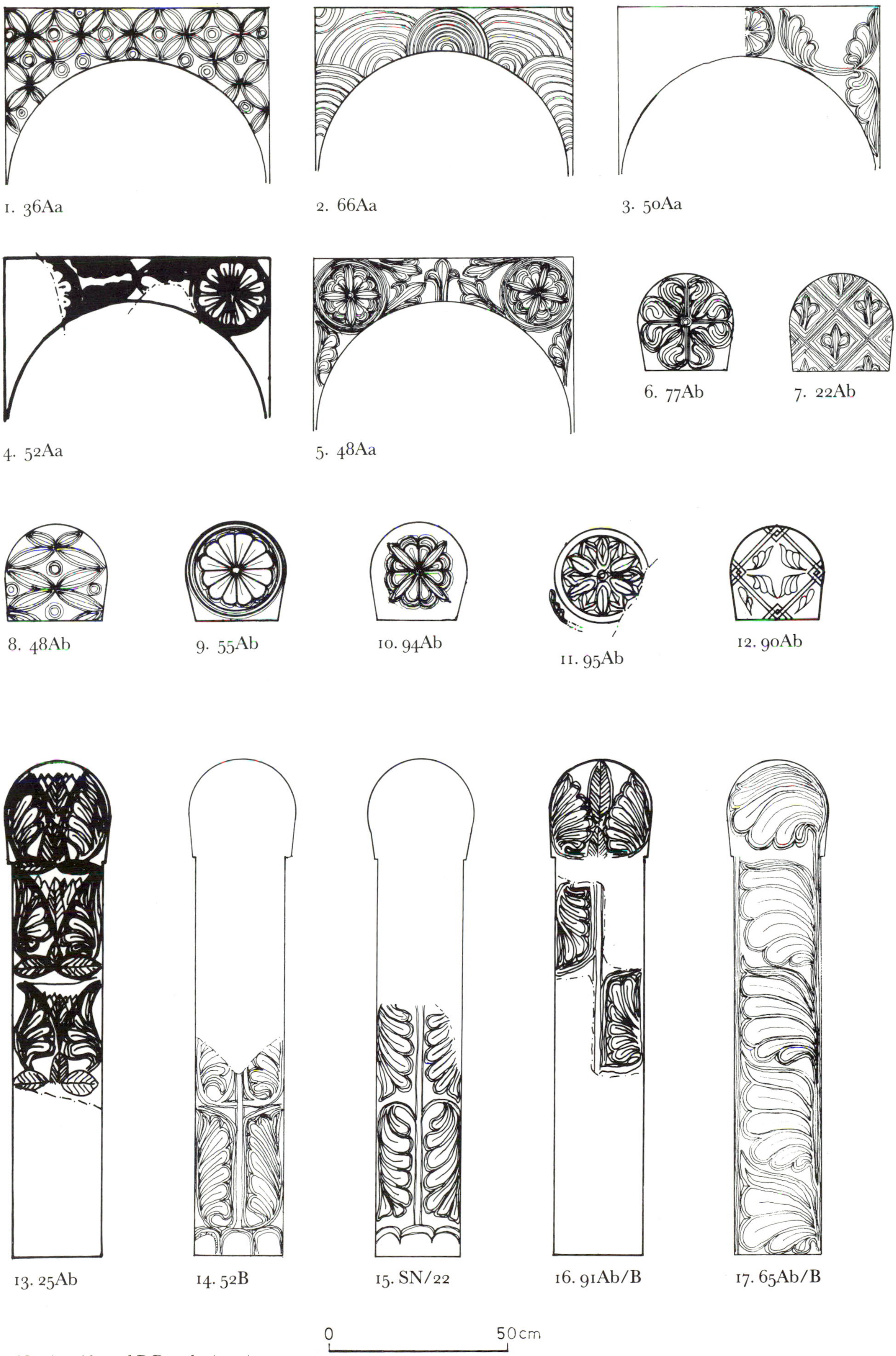

48. Aa, Ab and B Panels. (1:1.5)

1. 1B

2. 84Ab/B

3. 32Ab/B

4. 40B

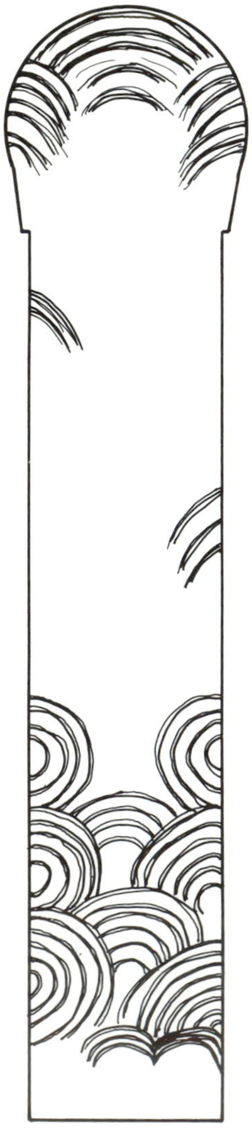

9. 23Ab/B

10. 86Ab/B

11. 21Ab/B

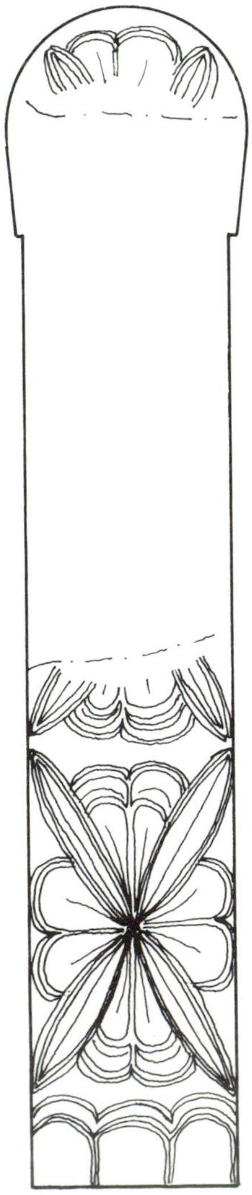

12. 54Ab/B

5. 30Ab, SN/26

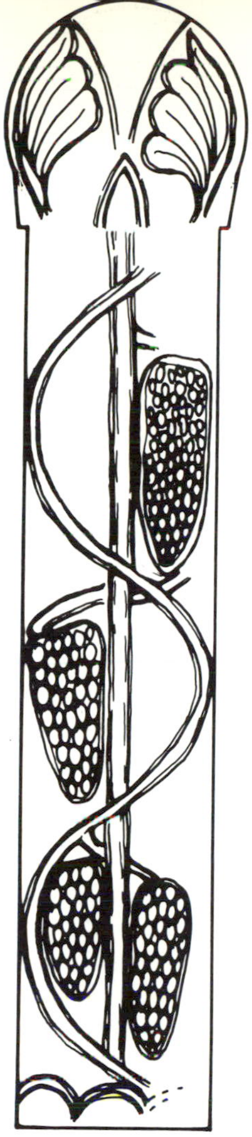

6. 80Ab/B

7. 79B

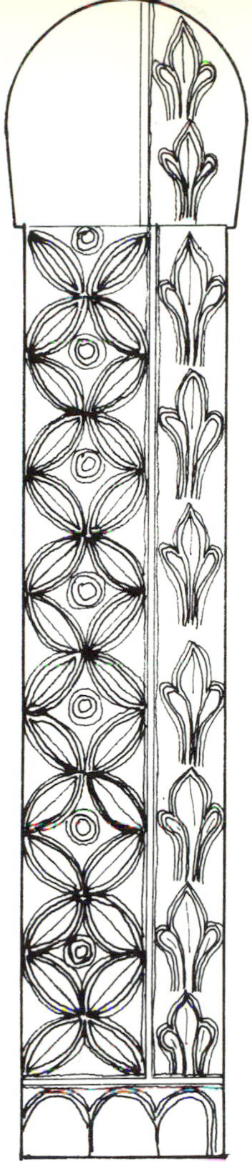

8. 87Ab/B

13. SN/24

14. SN/23

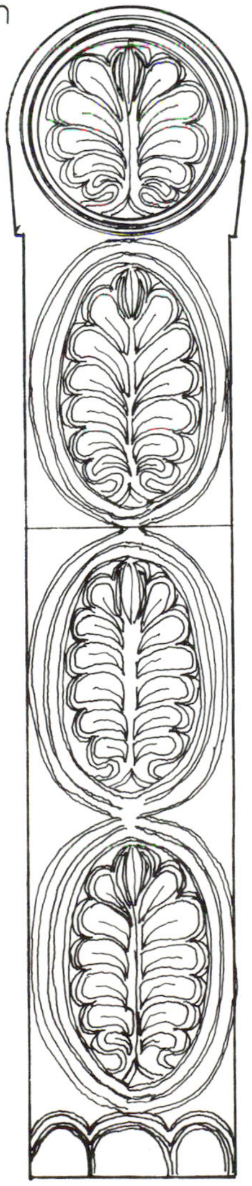

15. 83Ab, 73B

16. 59B

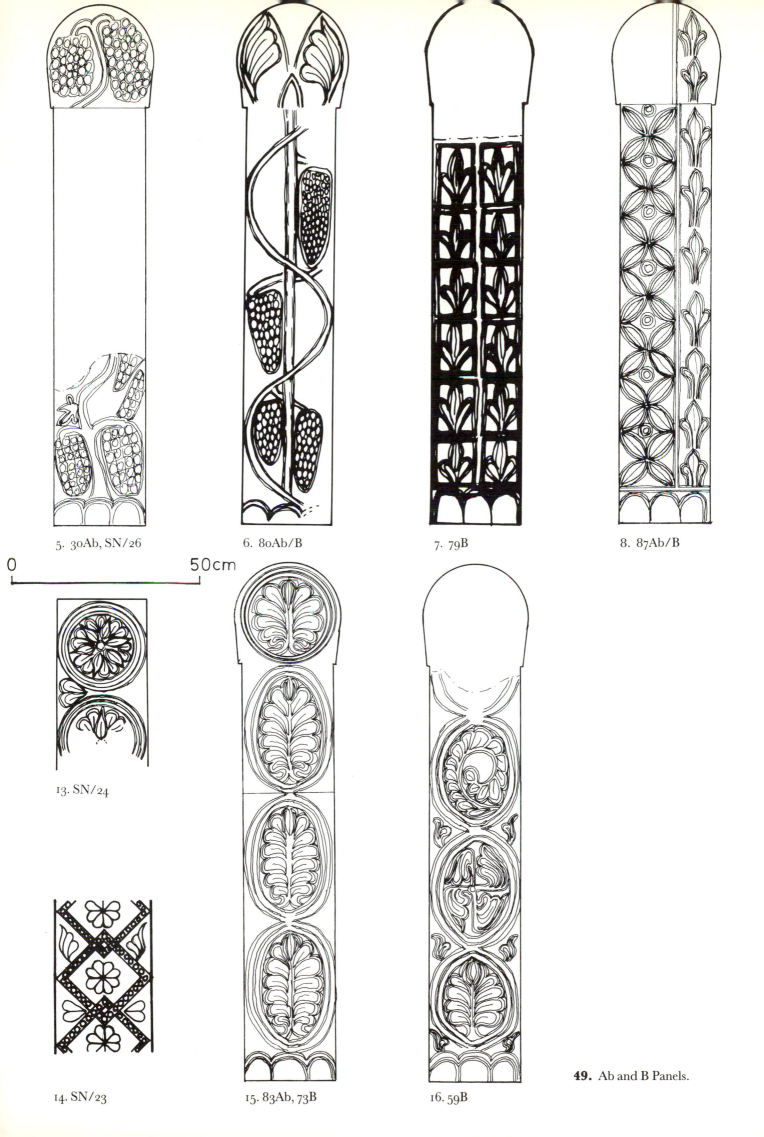

49. Ab and B Panels.

50. Niche of Register 2 in the Reception Hall.

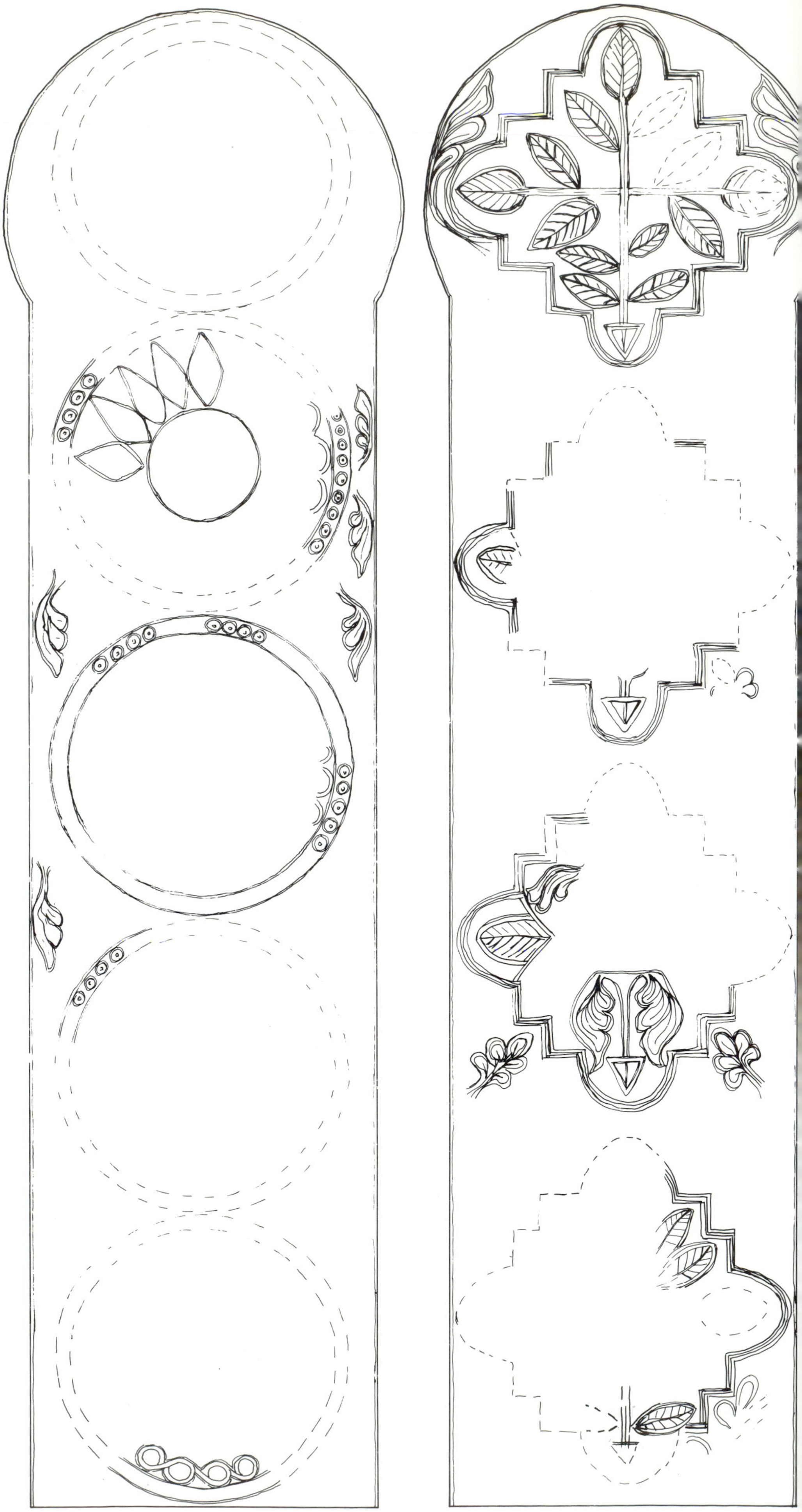

1. NW/D

2. NE/D

51. D Panels.

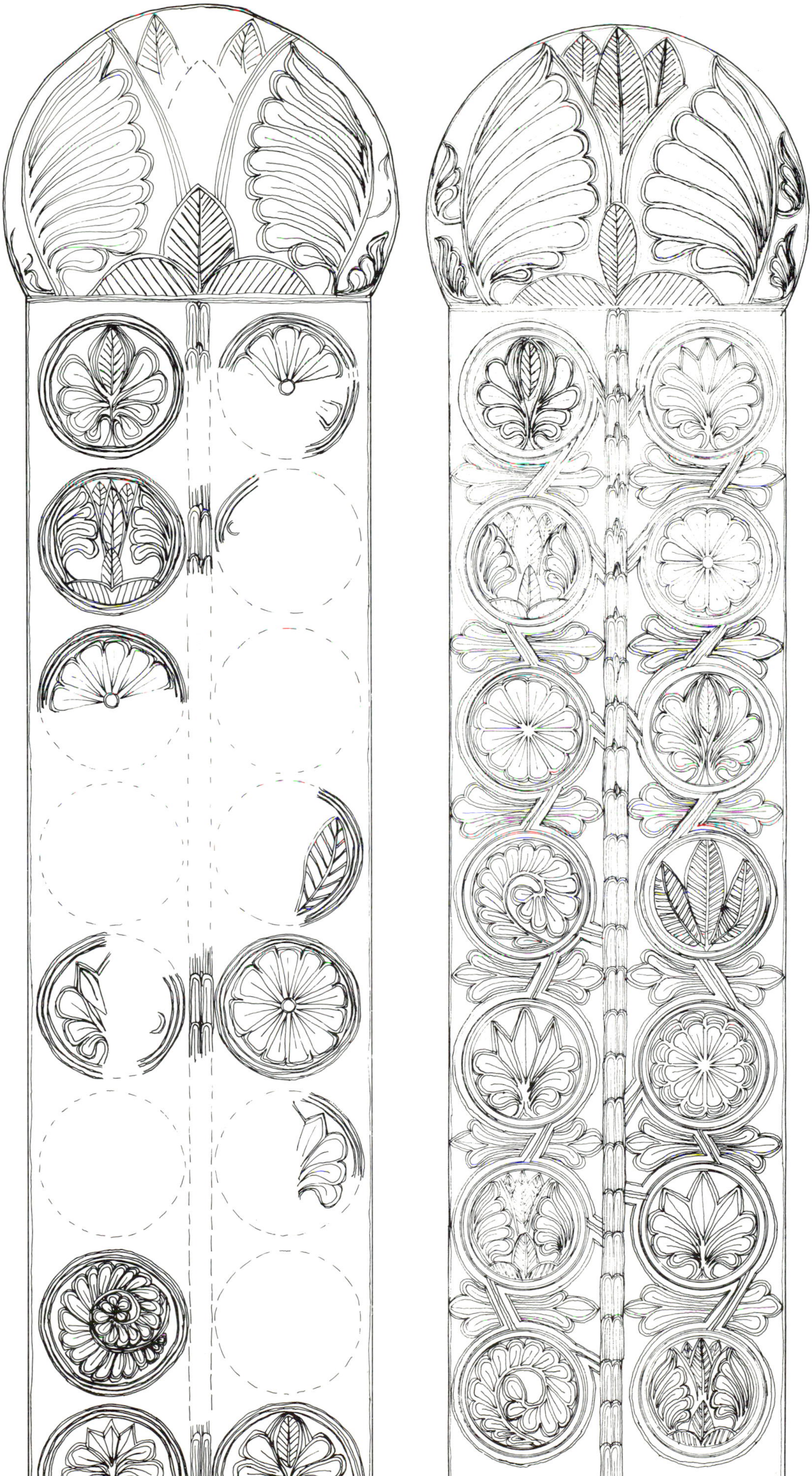

1. WS/D 2. WN/D

52. D Panels.

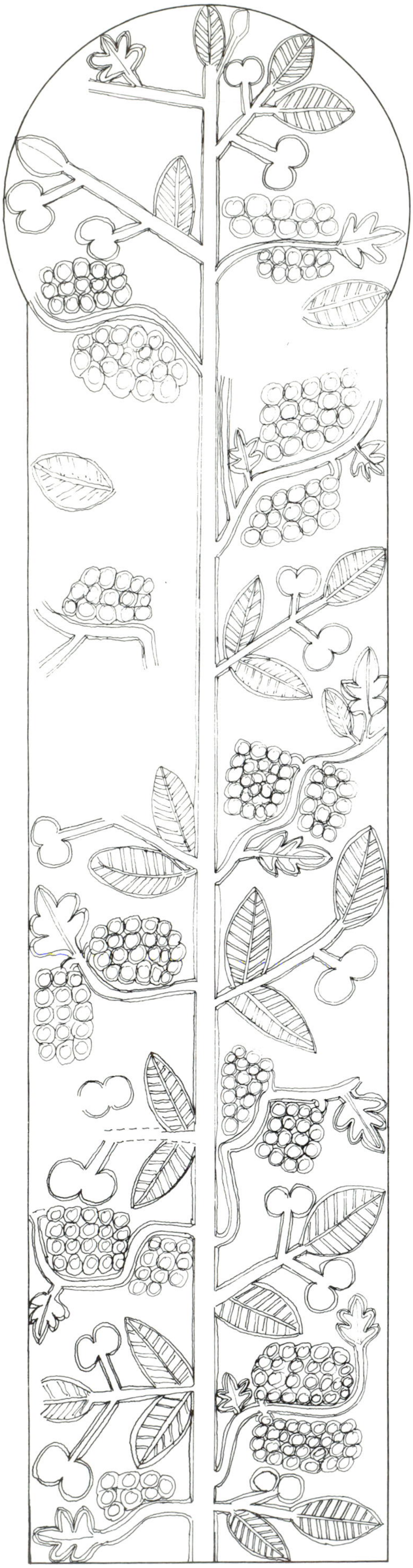

1. SW/D

2. SW/E

3. SE/E

4. NW/E

5. WS/E

6. ES/E

53. D, E and F Panels.

7. WN/F

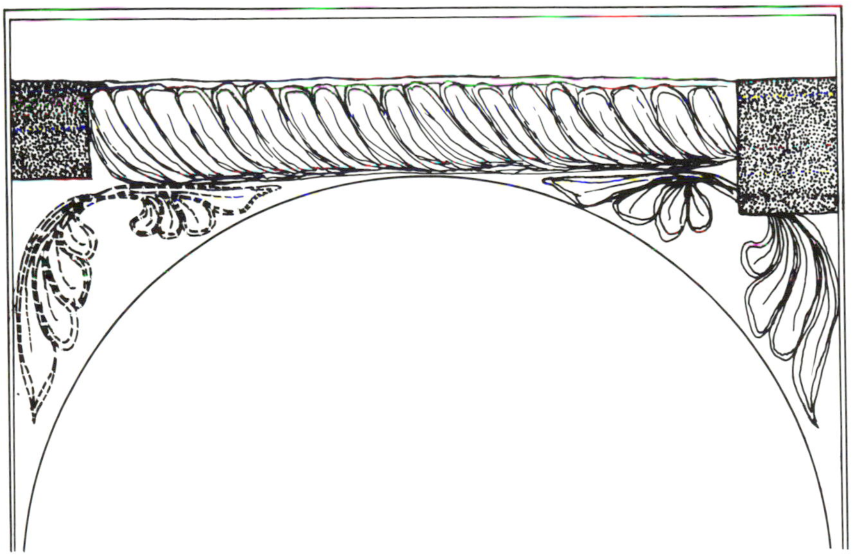

8. SW/F

1. Cornice C/1

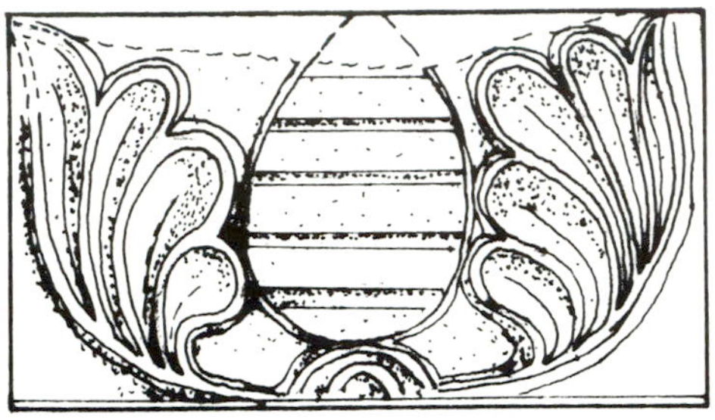

2. Cornice C/2

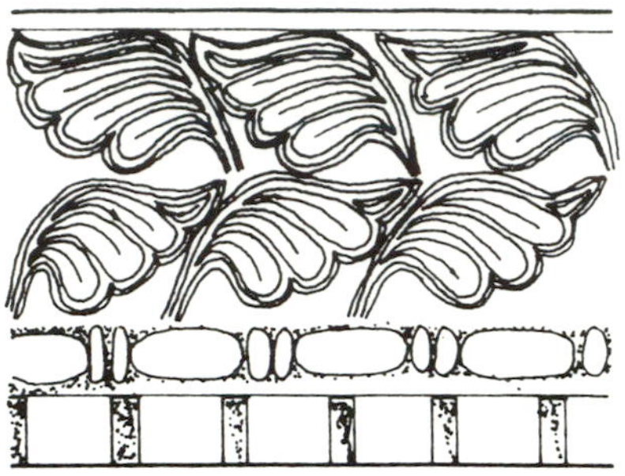

3. Cornice C/4

4. Exterior Niche SB/1

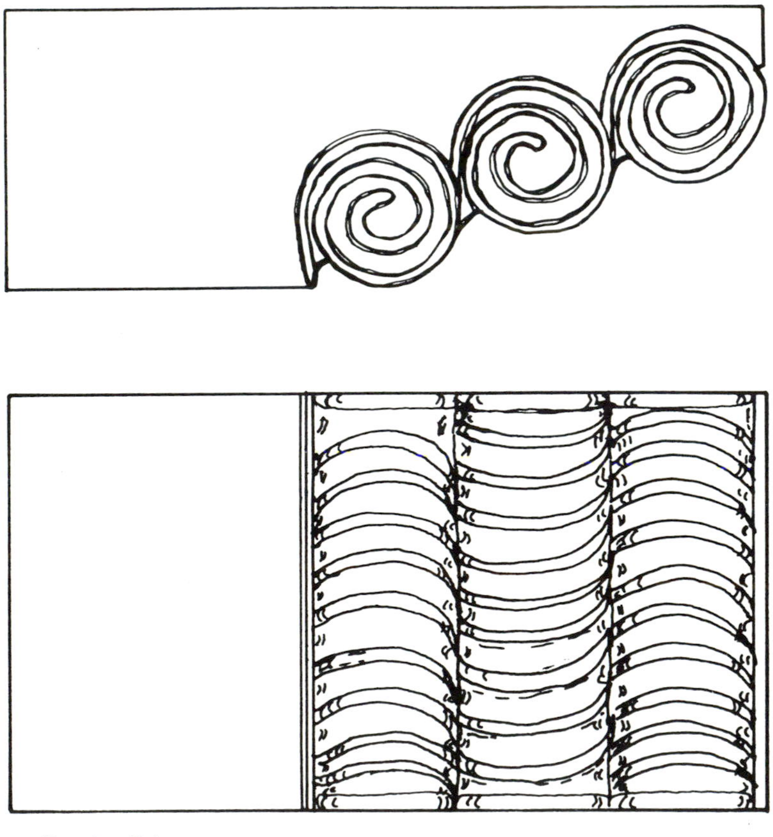

5. Bracket B/7

54. Cornice and Exterior Fragments from the Reception Hall

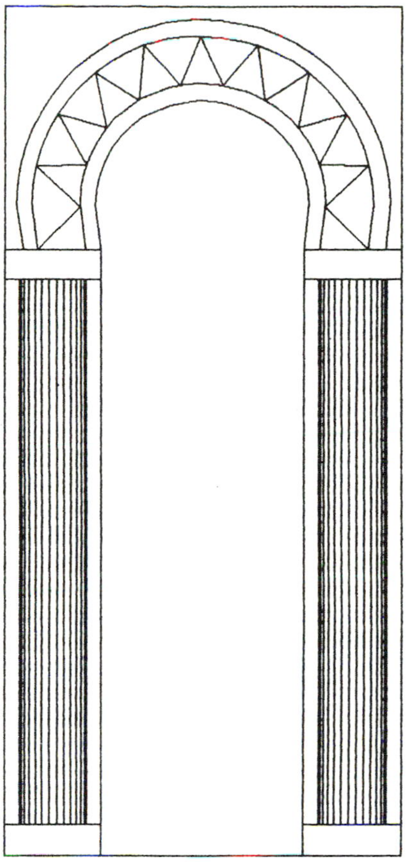

55. Reconstruction of exterior niche from the Reception Hall (1:10).

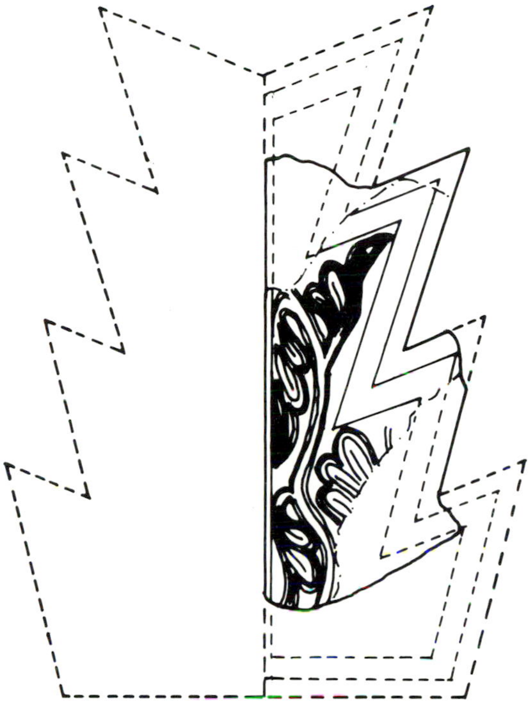

56. Merlon from the Reception Hall (1:10).

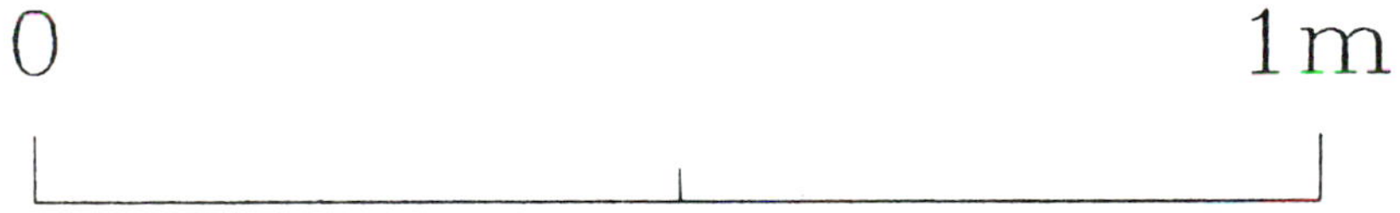

57. Depiction of a Central Asian fortress derived from a silver salver in the Hermitage Museum (after Pope and Ackerman 1938).

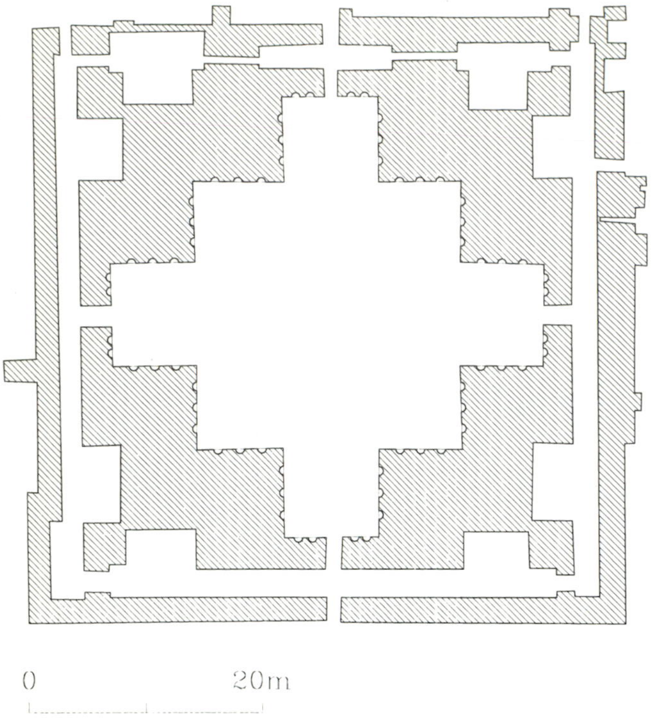

58. Plan of the audience hall at Bīshapūr (1:650).

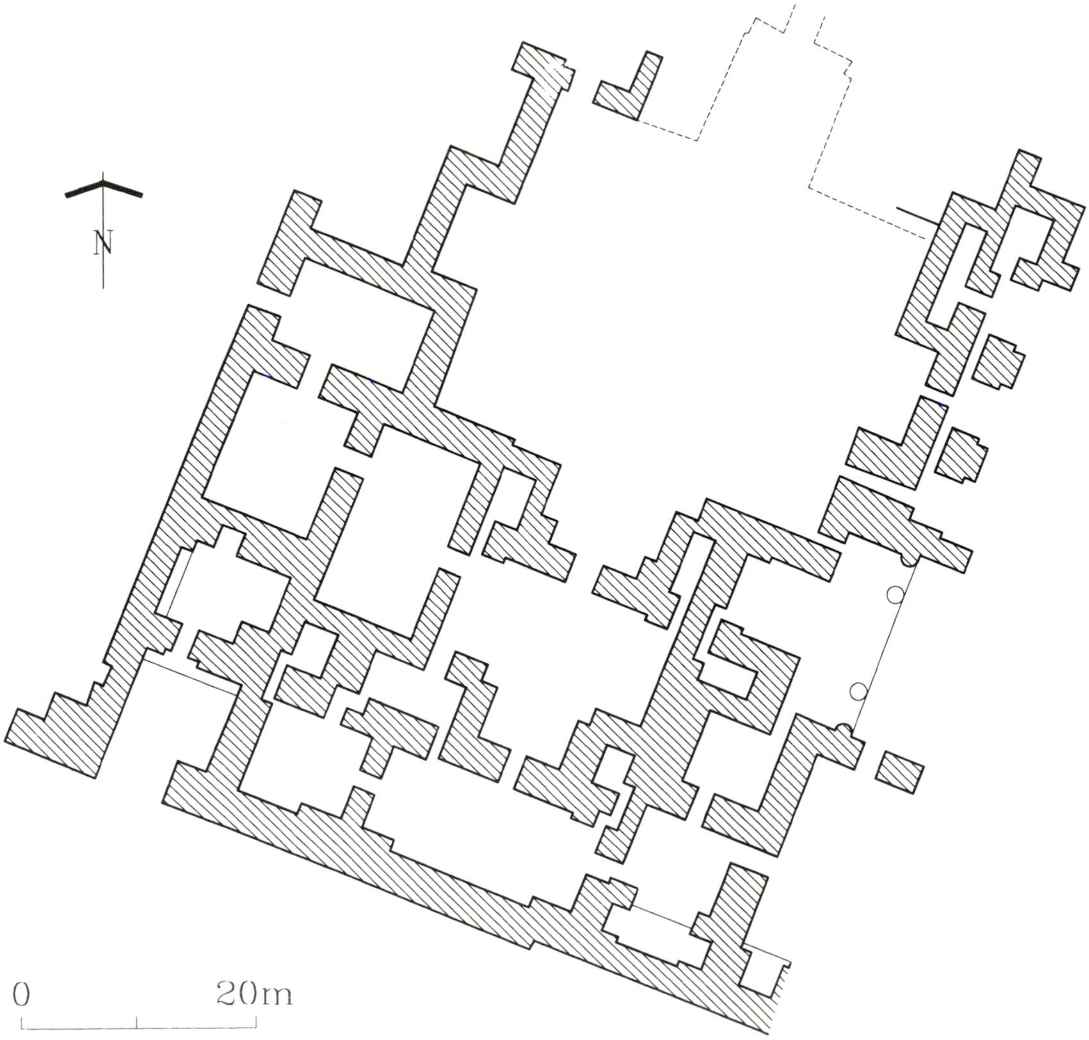

59. House at al-Maʿāriḍ IV, Ctesiphon (1:650).

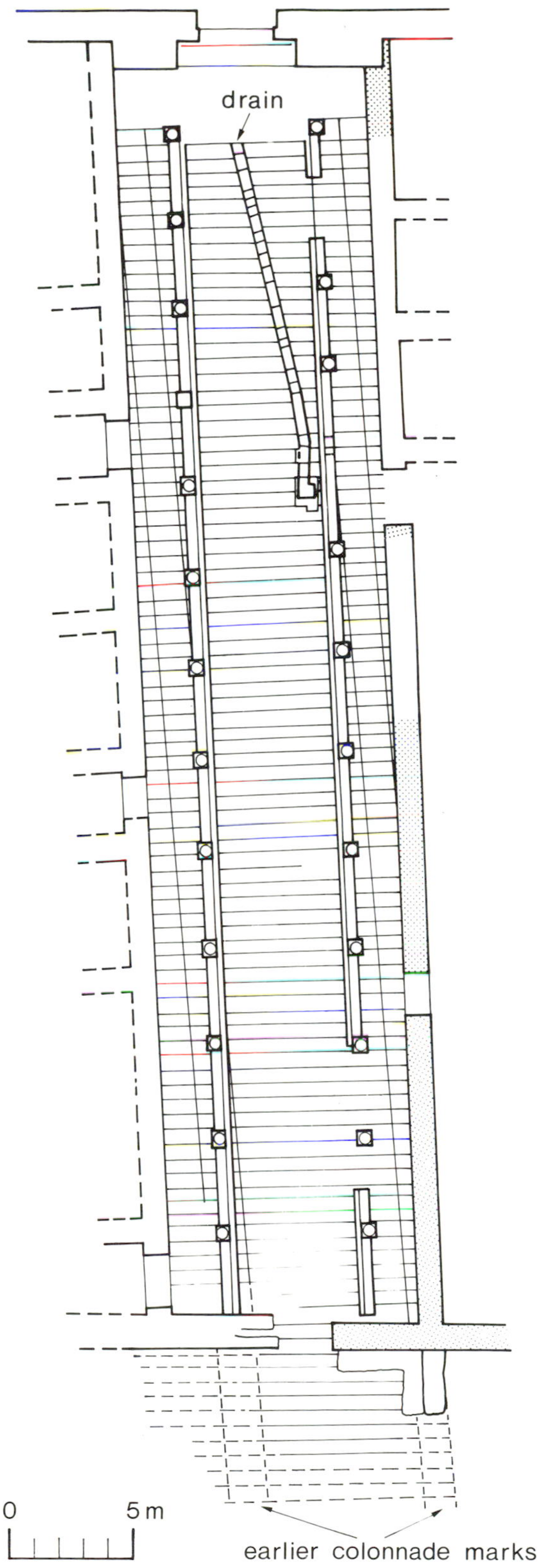

60. Plan of the Columned Street in the Umayyad Palace (1:300).

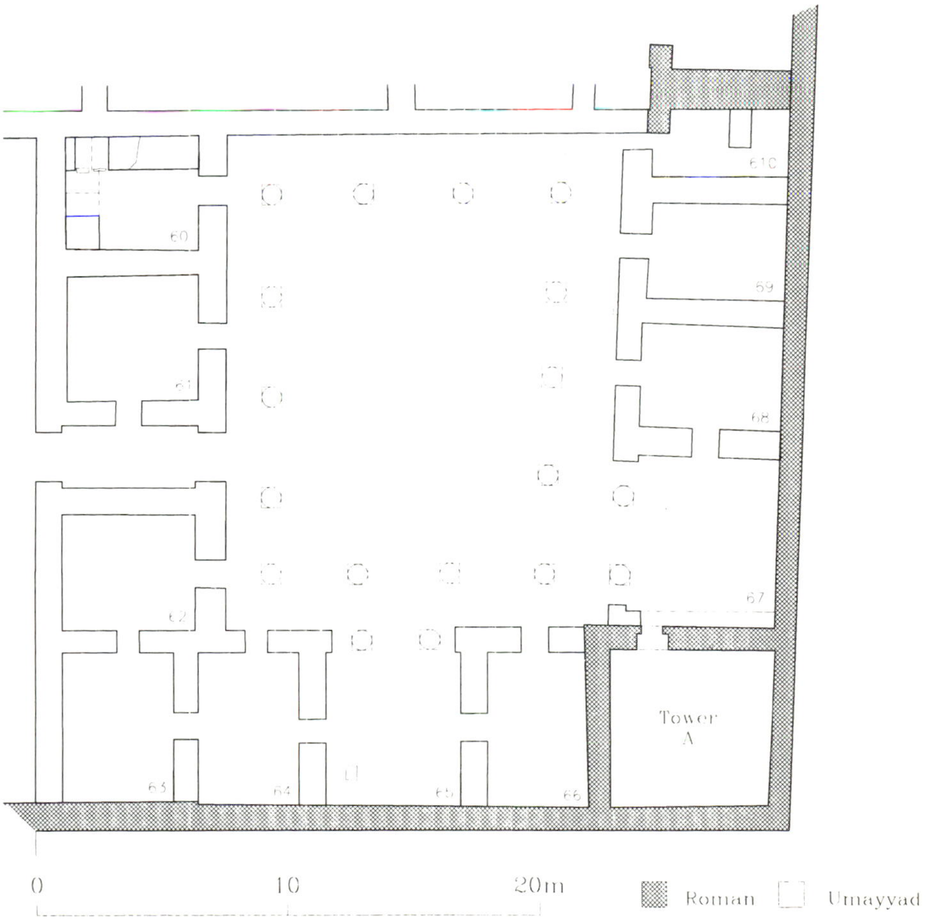

61. Plan of Building 6 (1:300).

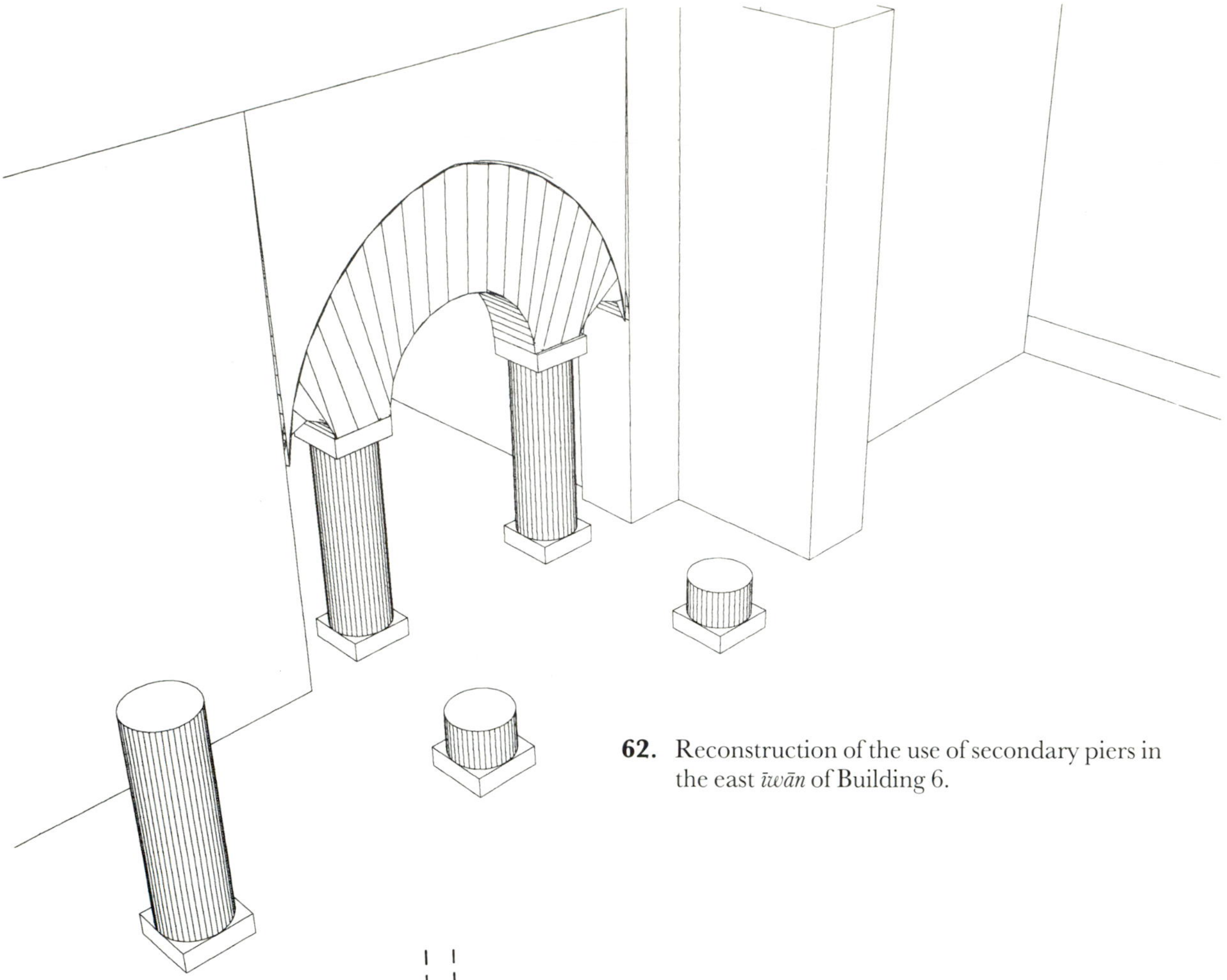

62. Reconstruction of the use of secondary piers in the east *īwān* of Building 6.

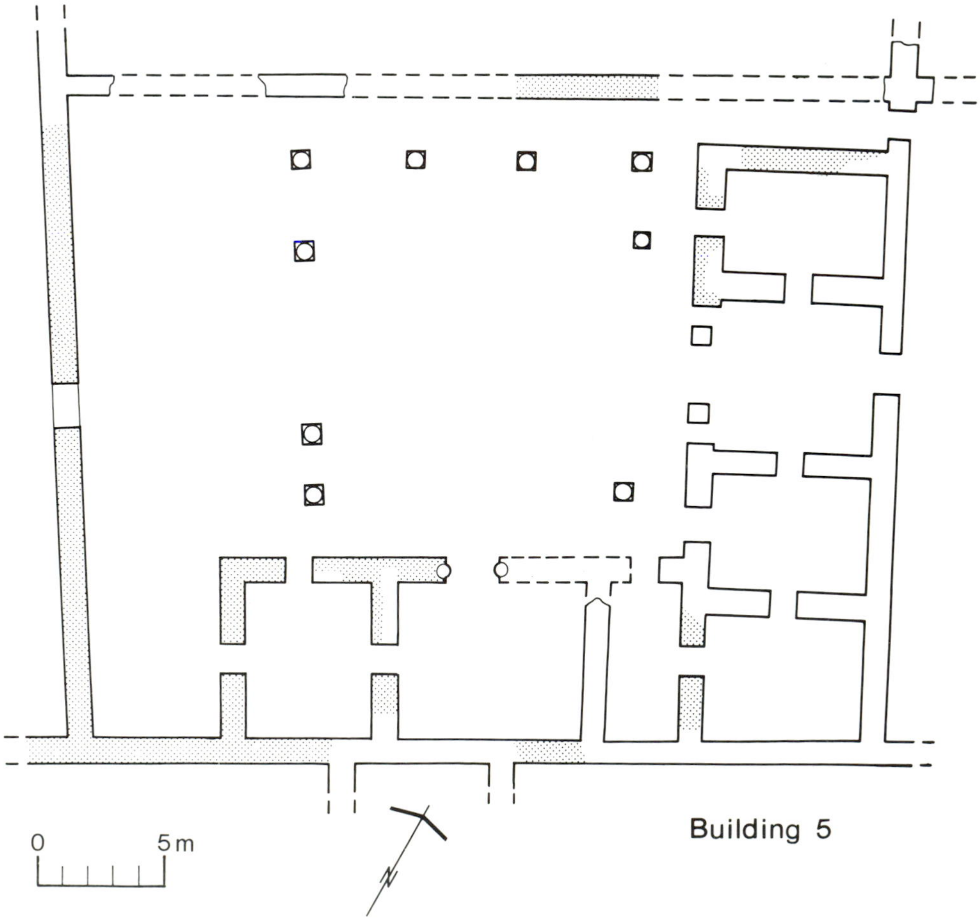

63. Plan of Building 5 (1:300).

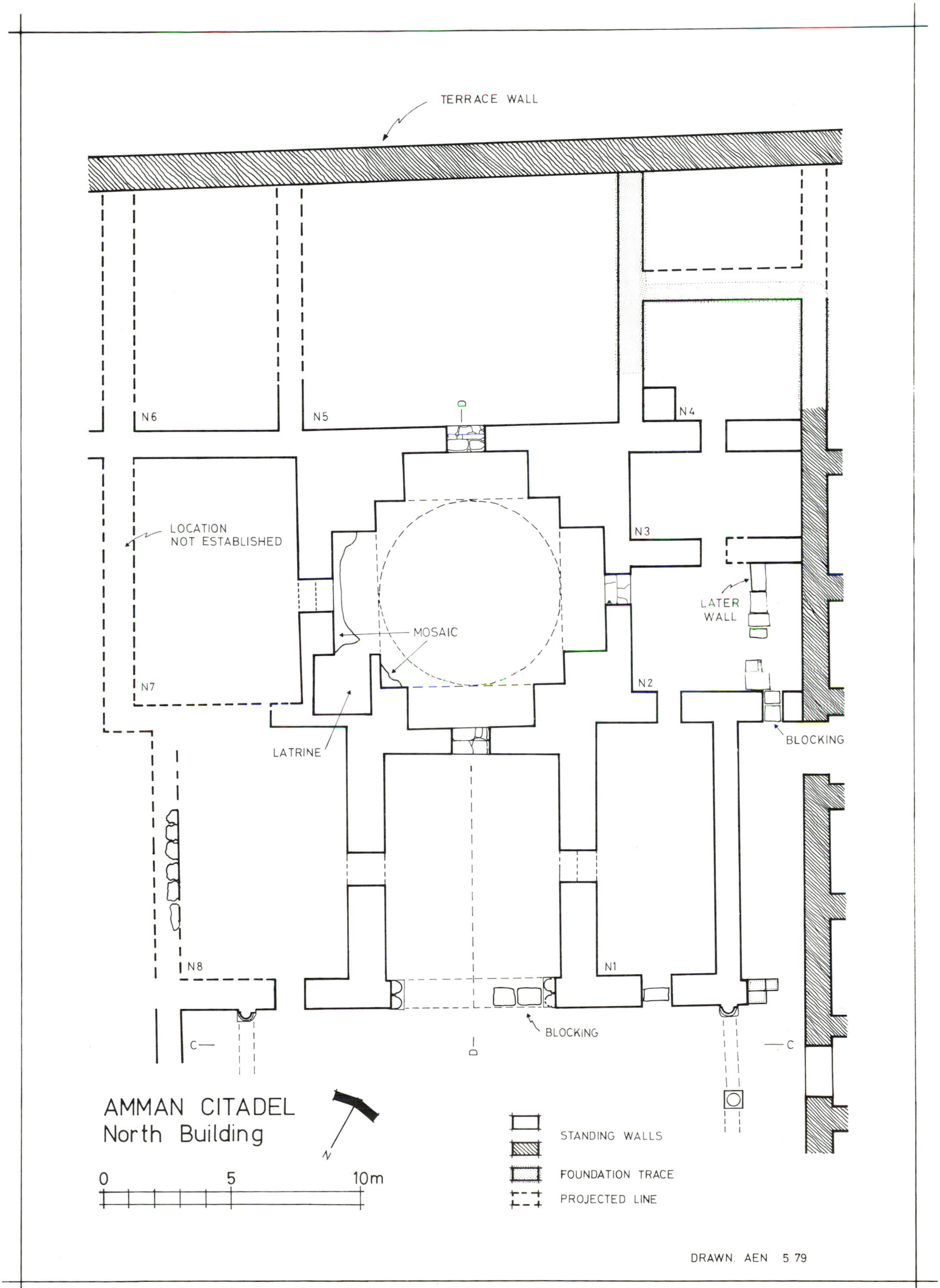

64. North Building: plan (1:200).

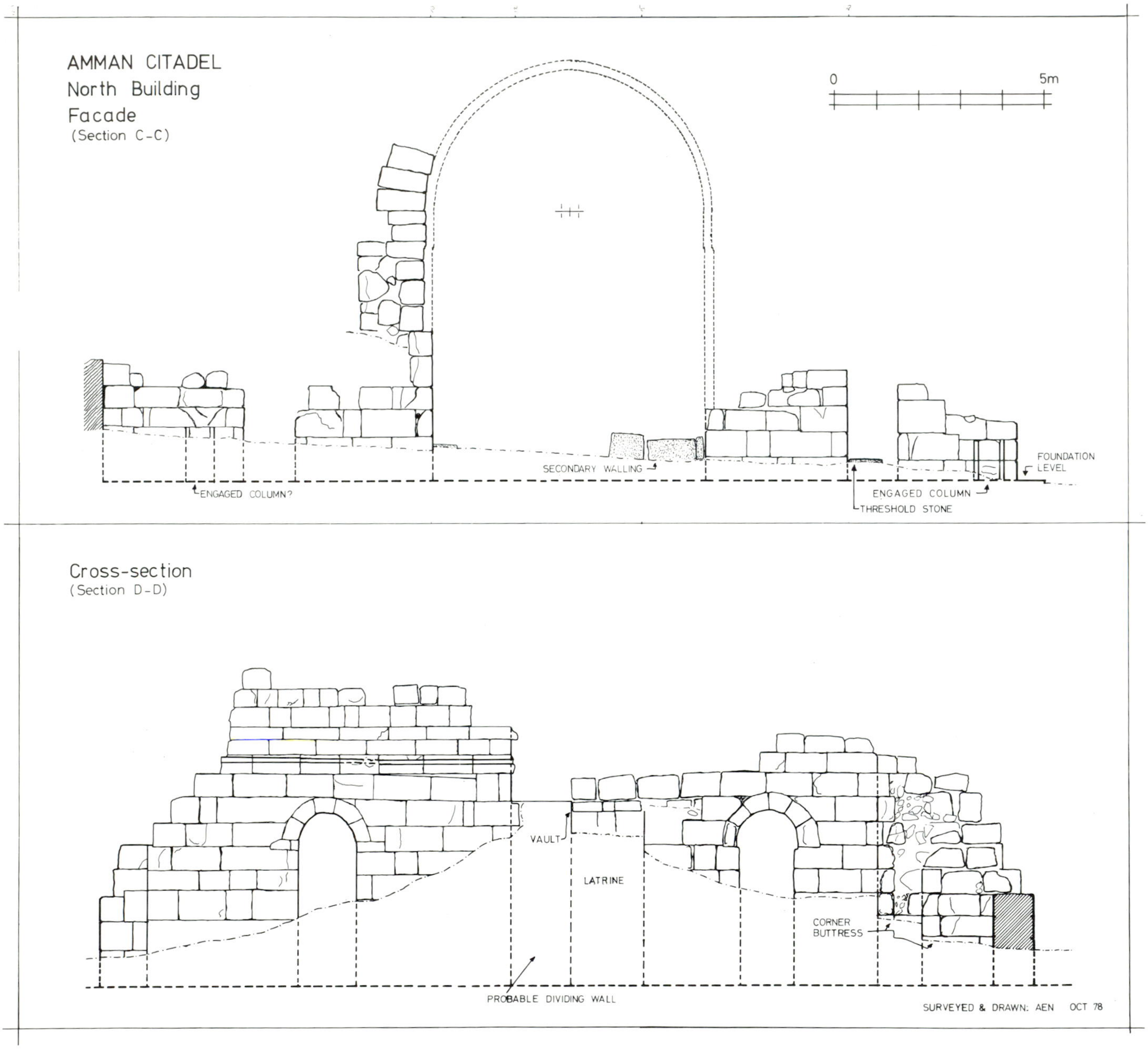

65. North Building: elevation and cross-section (1:150).

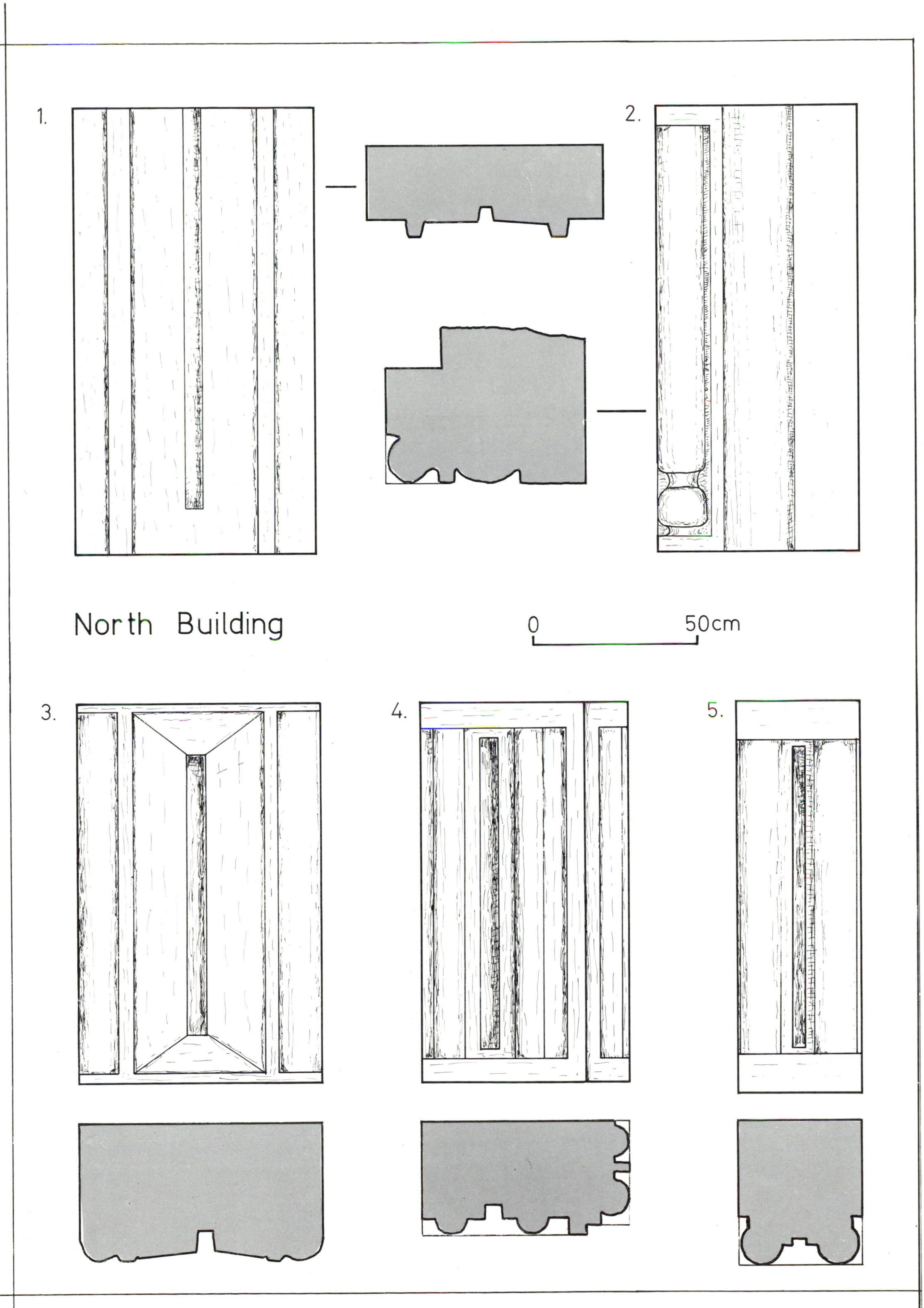

66. North Building: architectural fragments (1:15).

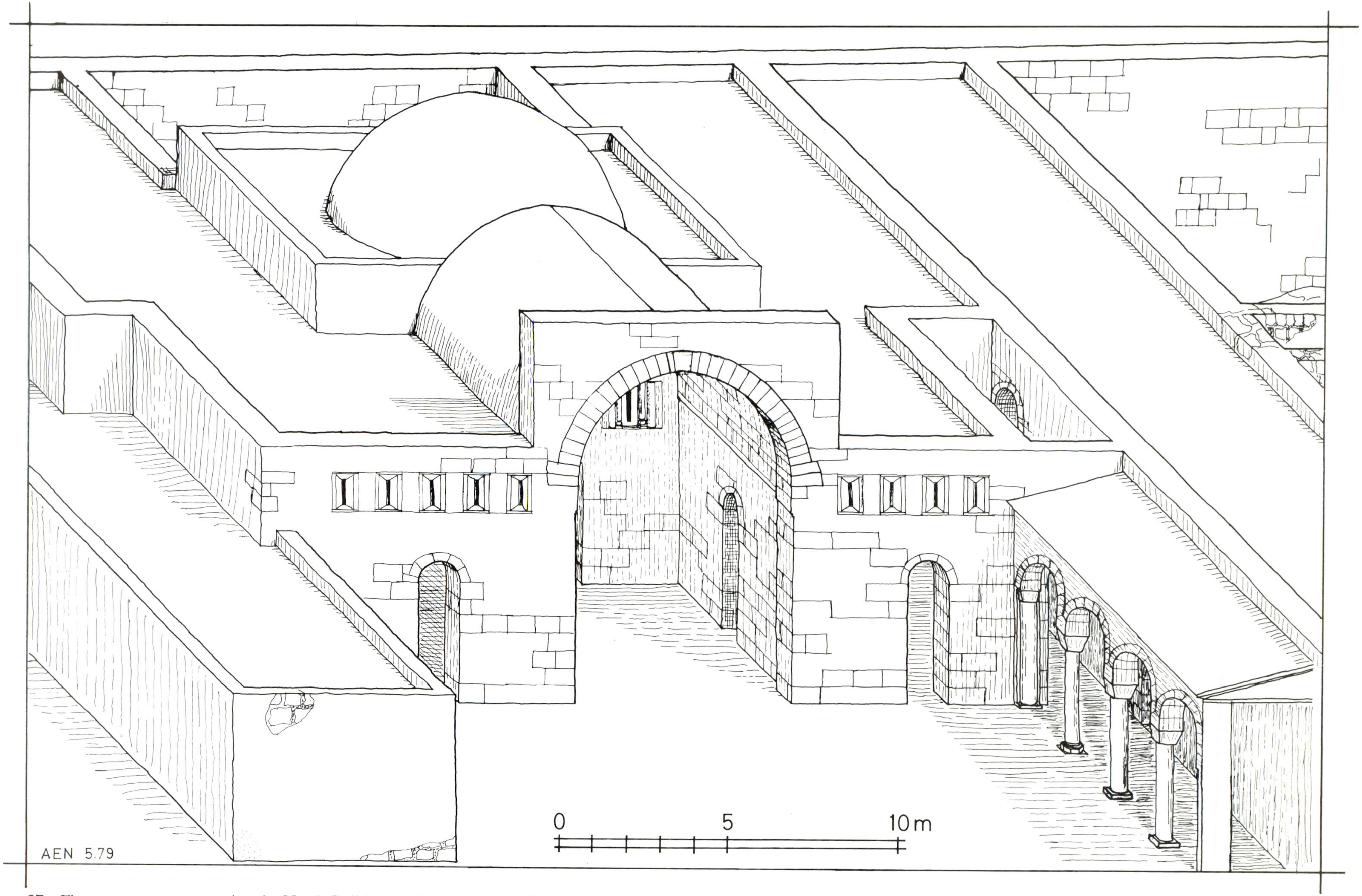

67. First essay at reconstructing the North Building (oblique projection) (1:150).

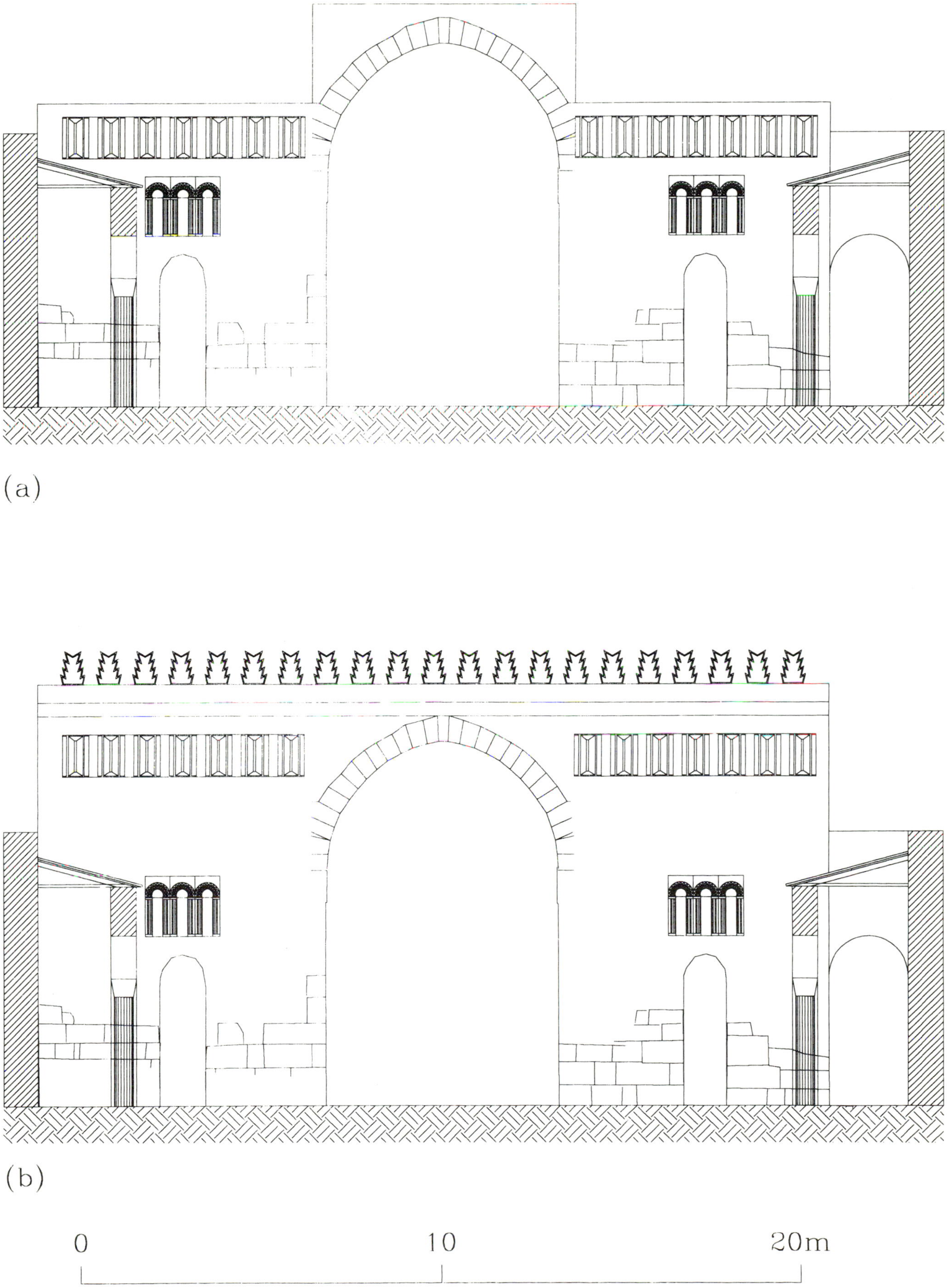

68. Alternative reconstructions of the facade of the North Building (1:150).

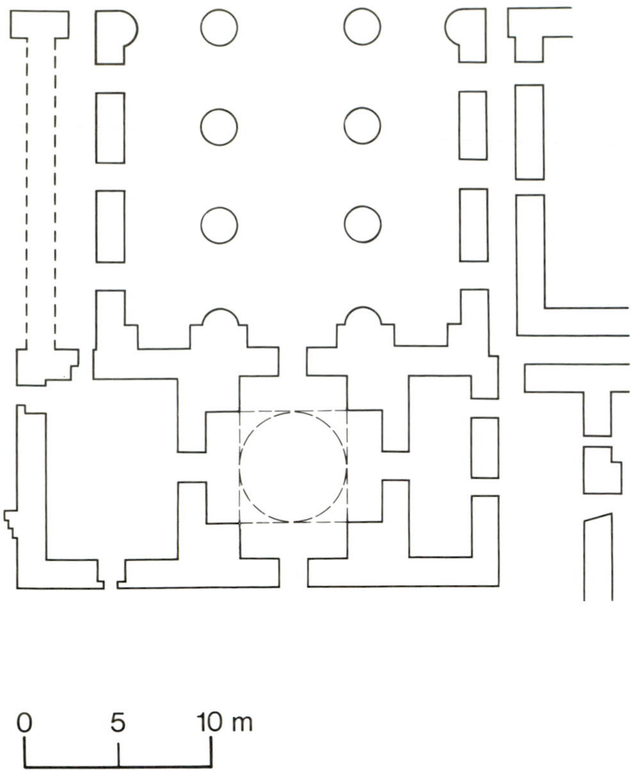

69. *Īwān* and dome chamber plan at Kūfa (1:400).

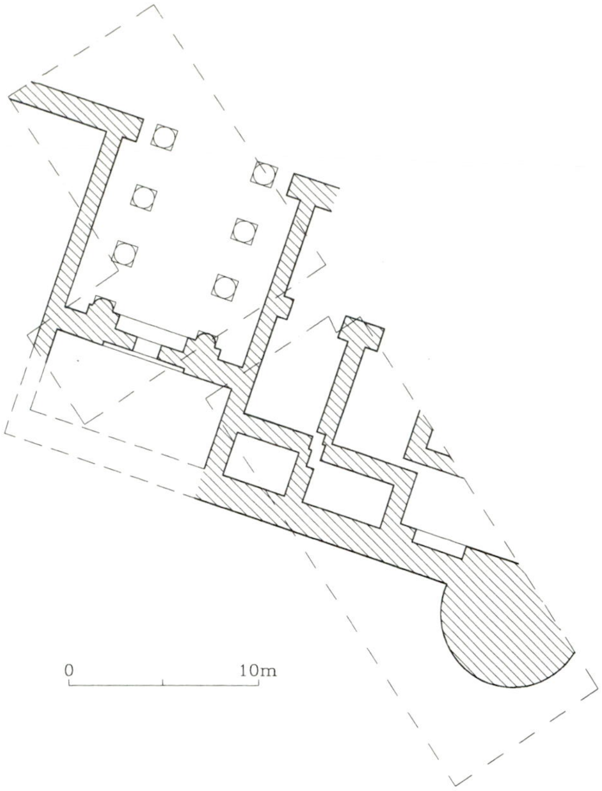

70. *Īwān* at Tulūl al-Ukhayḍir (after Finster and Schmidt 1976) (1:400).

71. Early Abbasid graffito of an *īwān* facade from Ctesiphon (after Abd al-Fattah 1985–6).

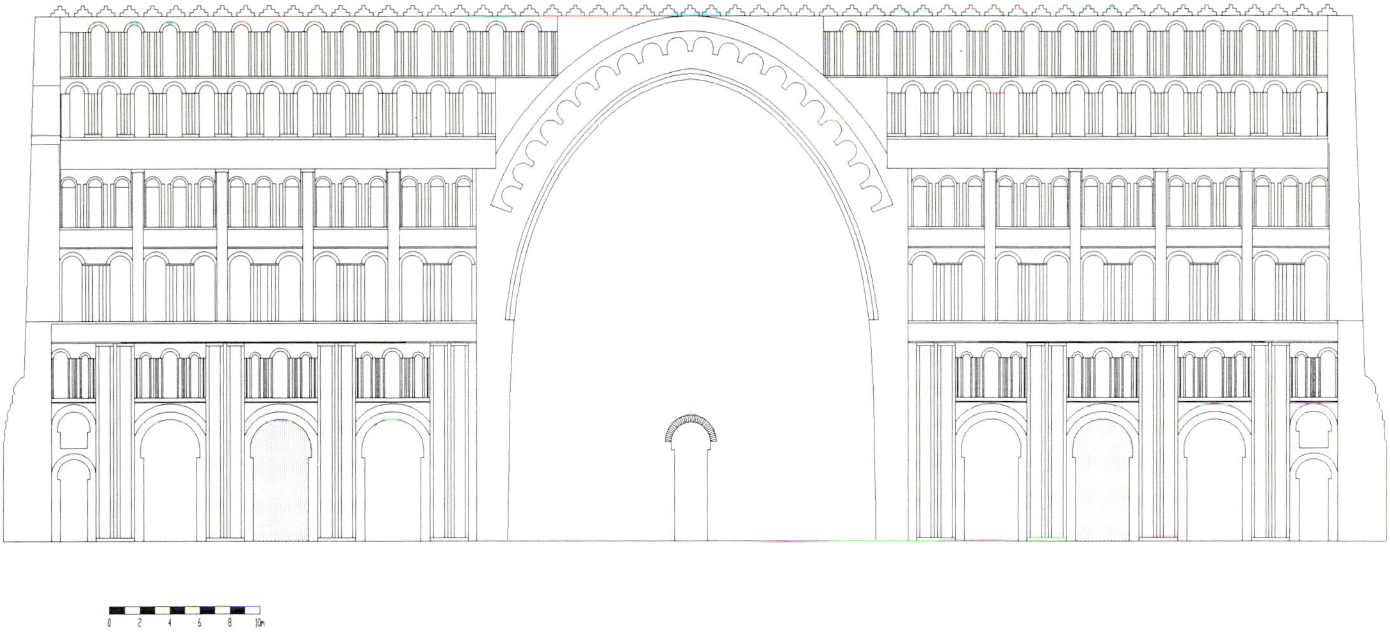

72. Tāq-i Kisrā, Ctesiphon (1:500).

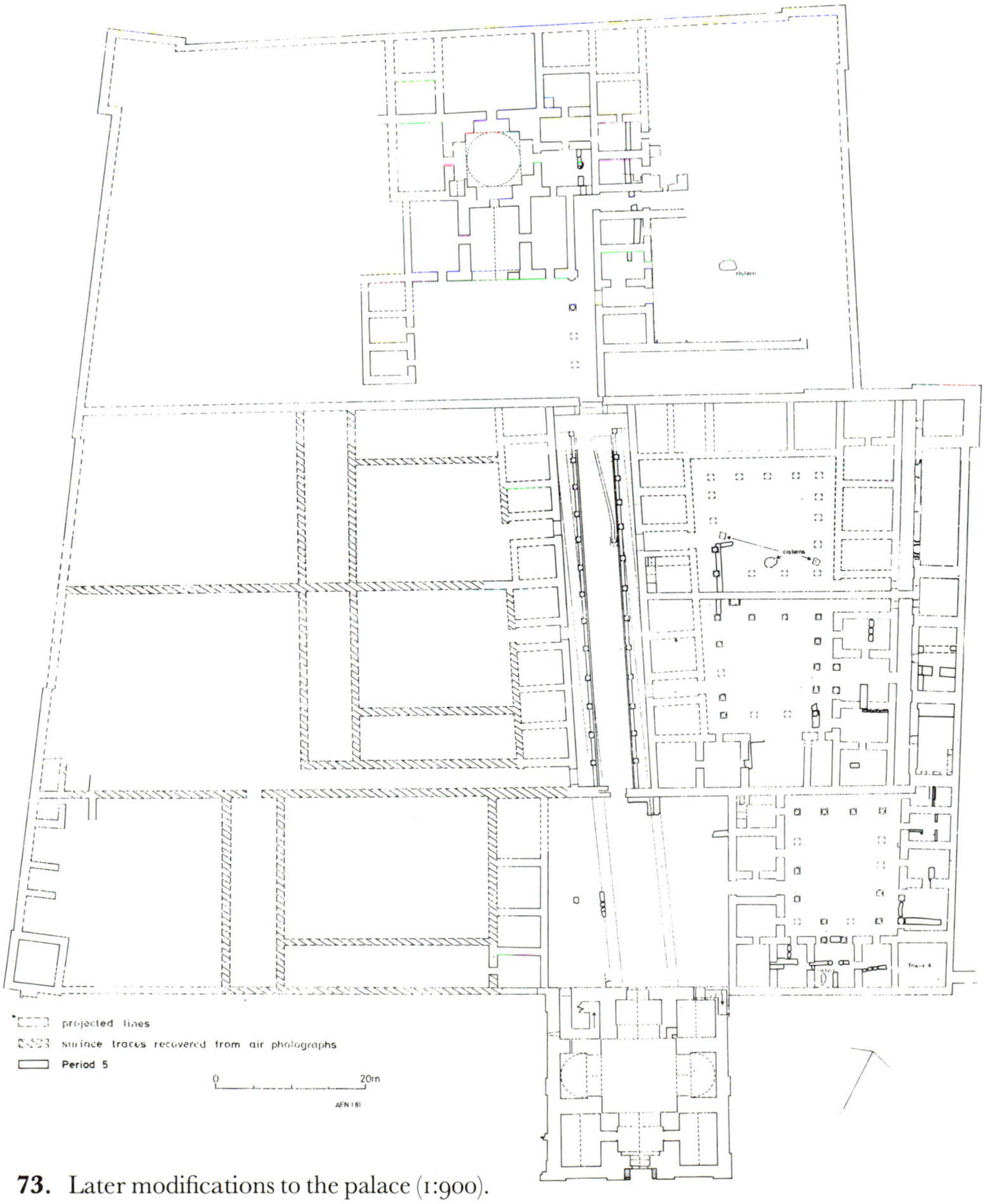

73. Later modifications to the palace (1:900).

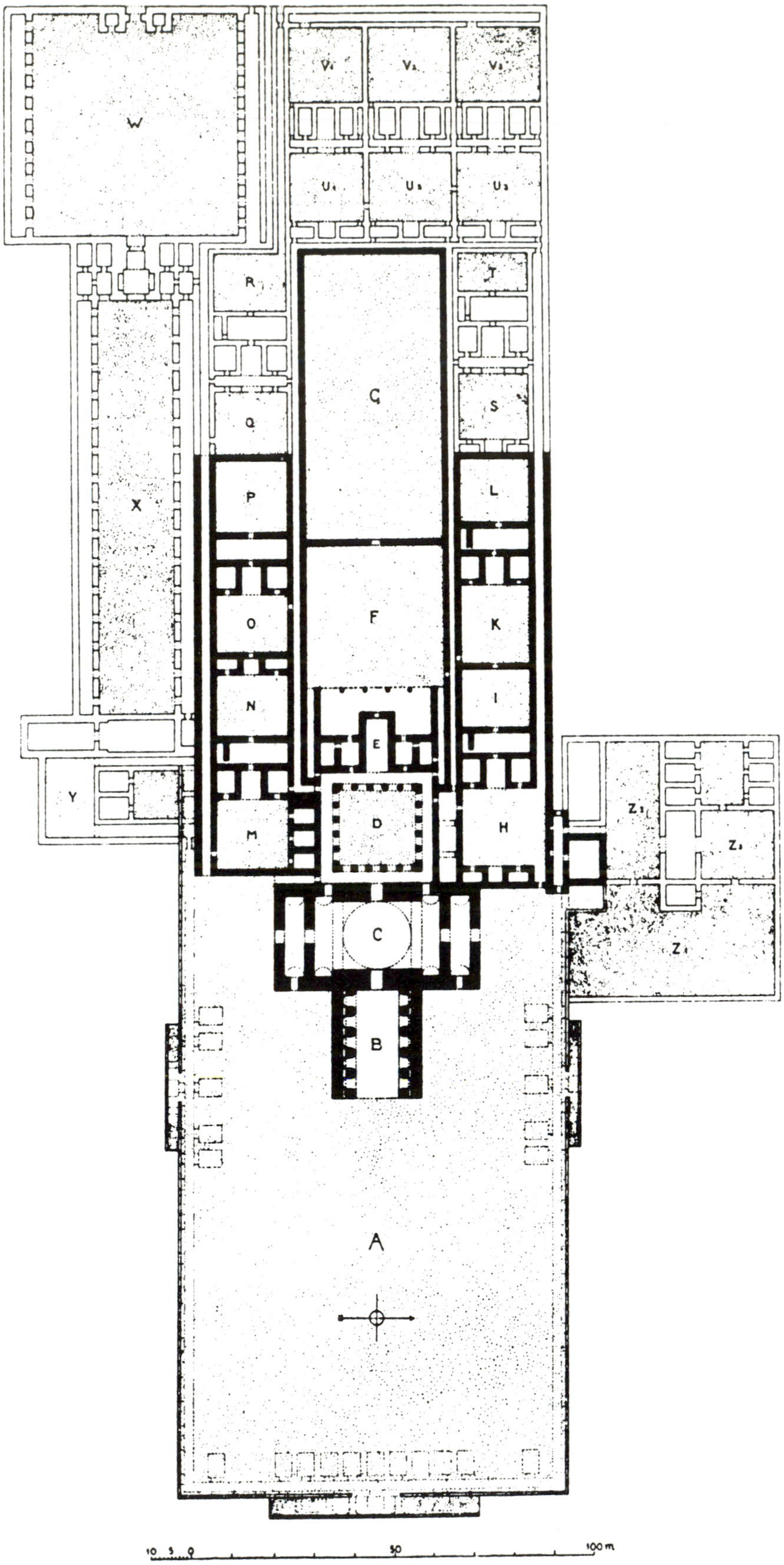

74. Plan of 'Imārat-i Khusrau, Qaṣr-i Shīrīn (after Pope 1938) (1:1500).

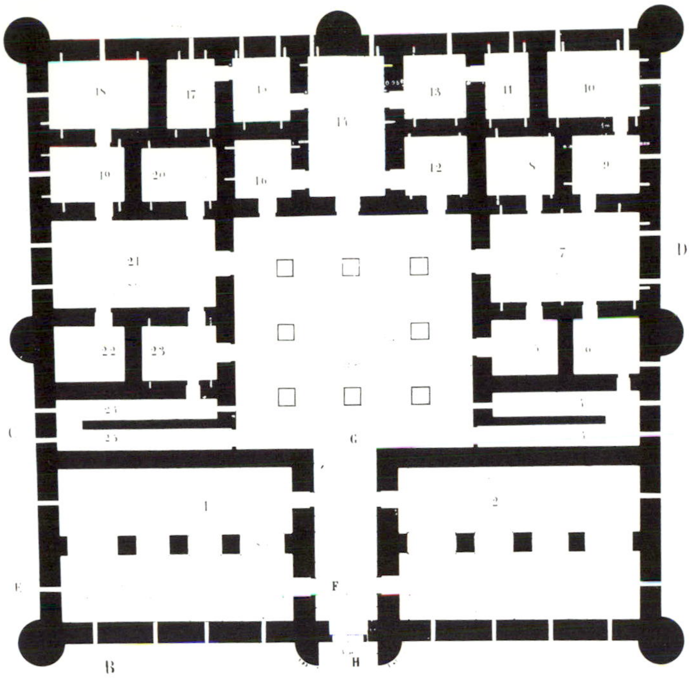

75. Plan of Qaṣr Kharāna (after Jaussen & Savignac) (1:1750).

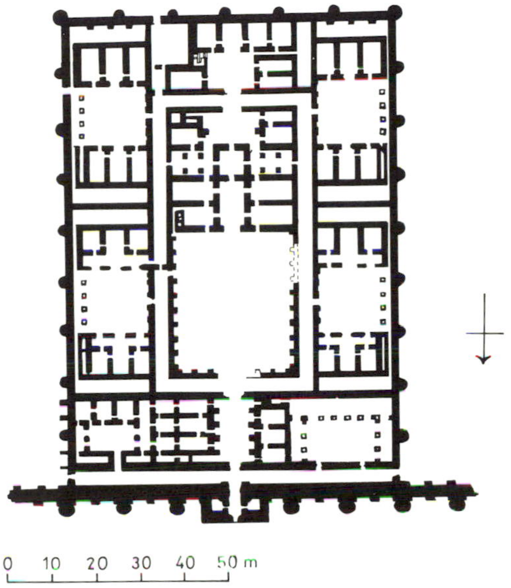

77. The Central Block at al-Ukhayḍir (after Creswell) (1:1750).

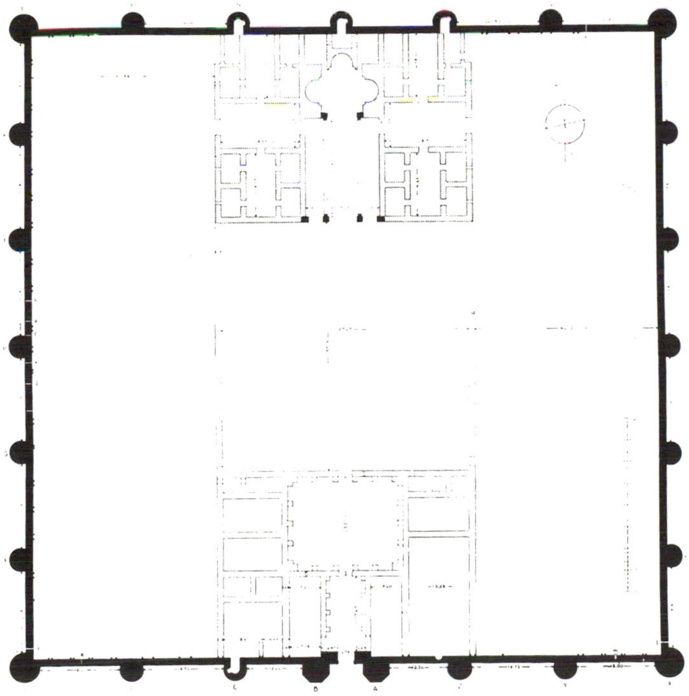

76. Plan of Qaṣr Mshattā (after Creswell 1969) (1:1750).

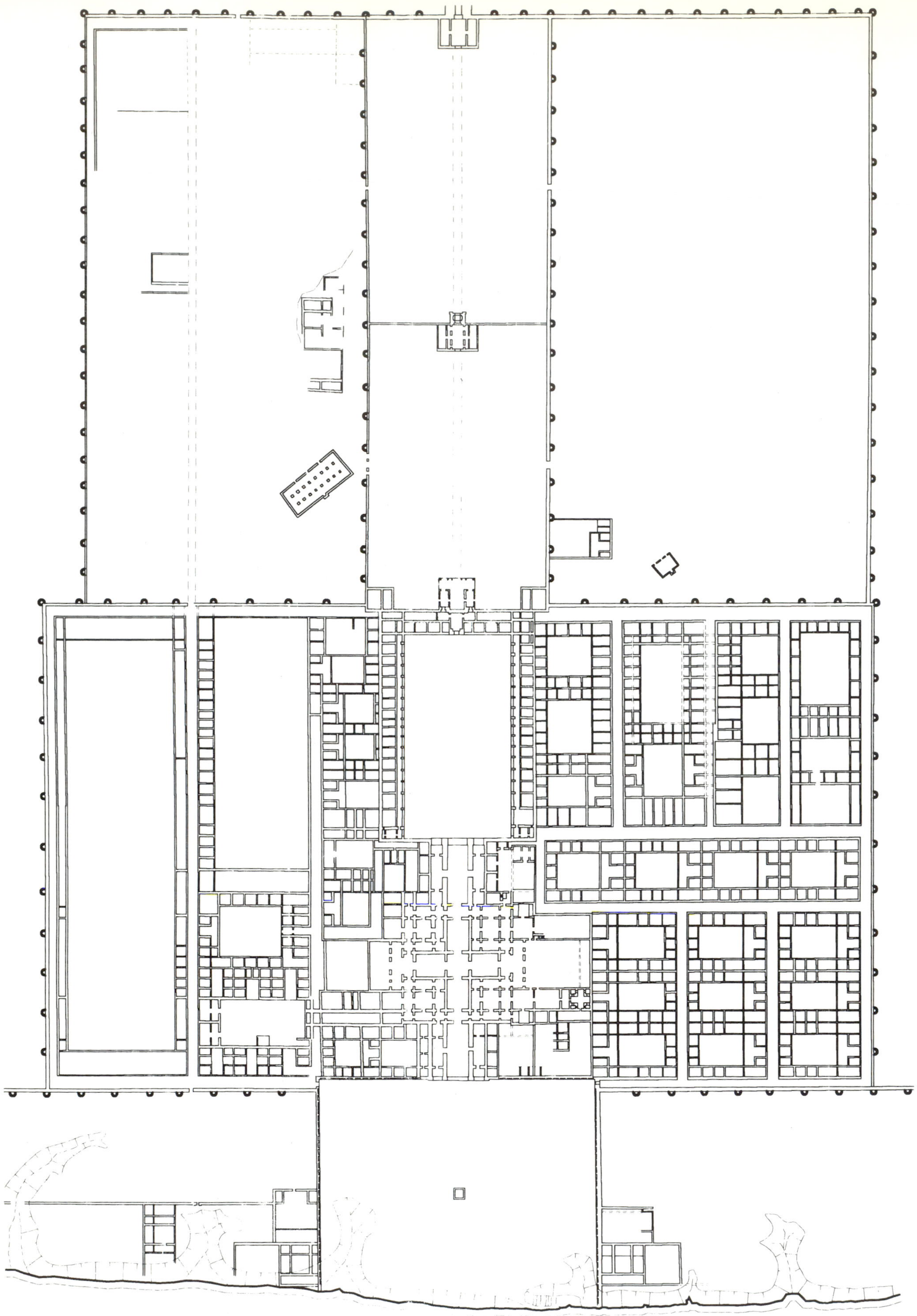

78. Plan of the palace of Balkuwārā, Sāmarrā' (Herzfeld Archive, Freer Gallery of Art) (1:3000).

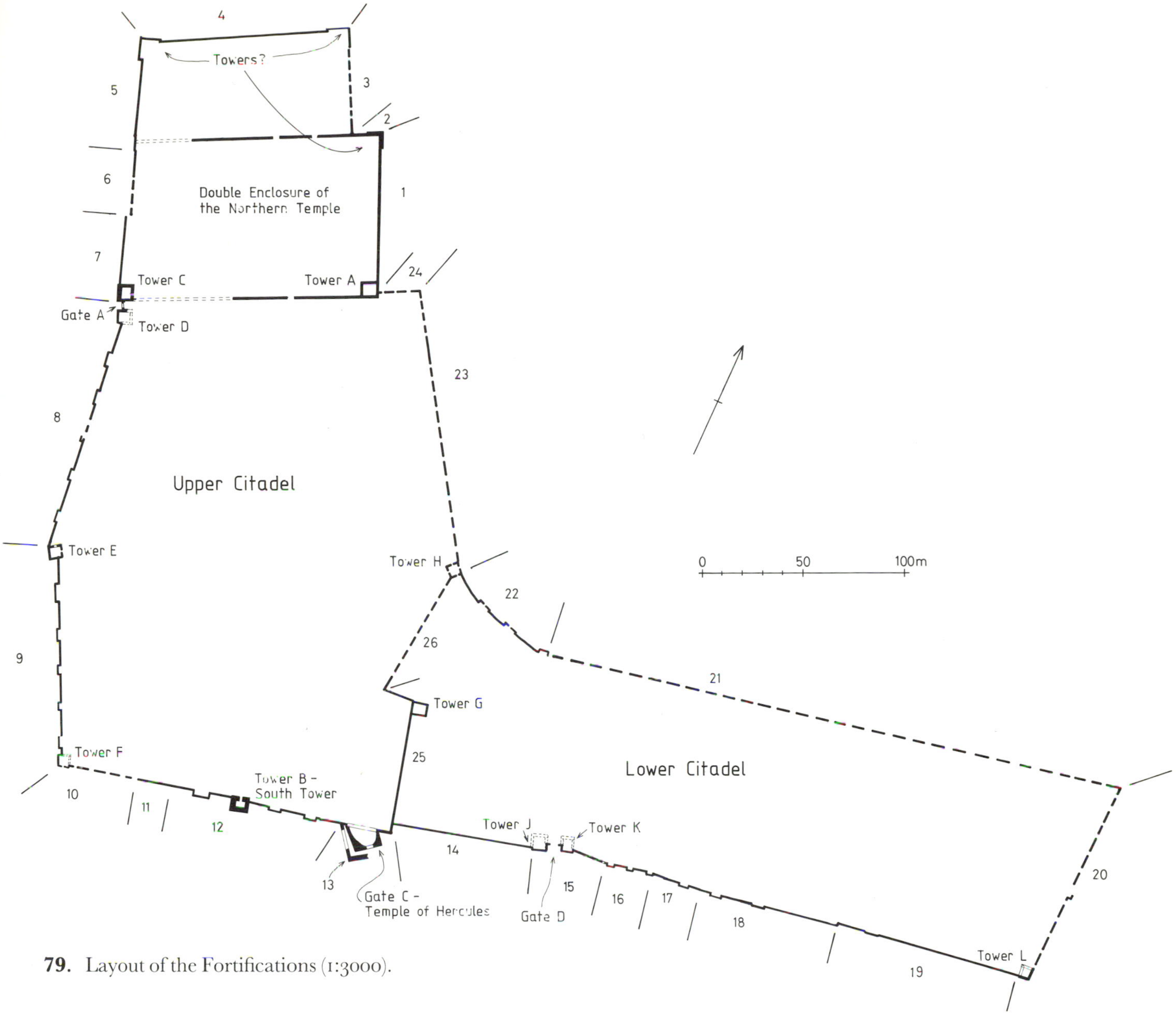

79. Layout of the Fortifications (1:3000).

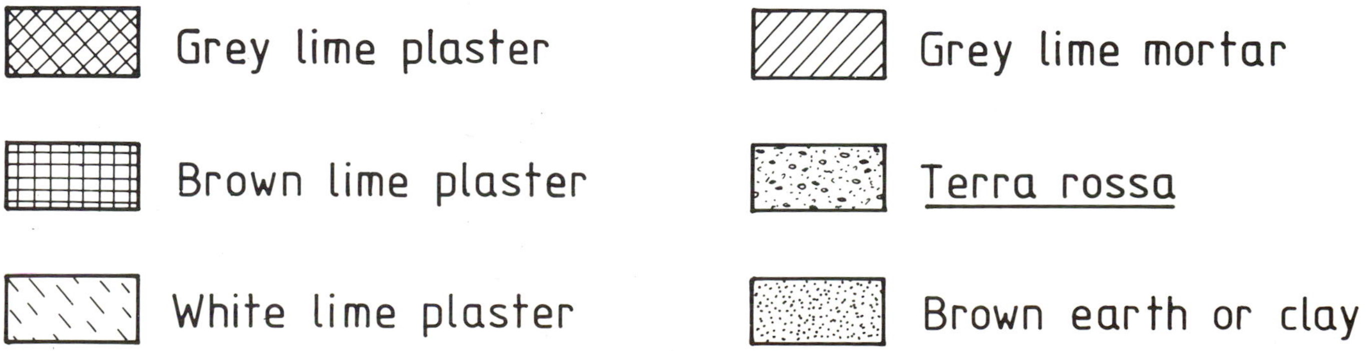

80. Key to symbols used in the fortification drawings.

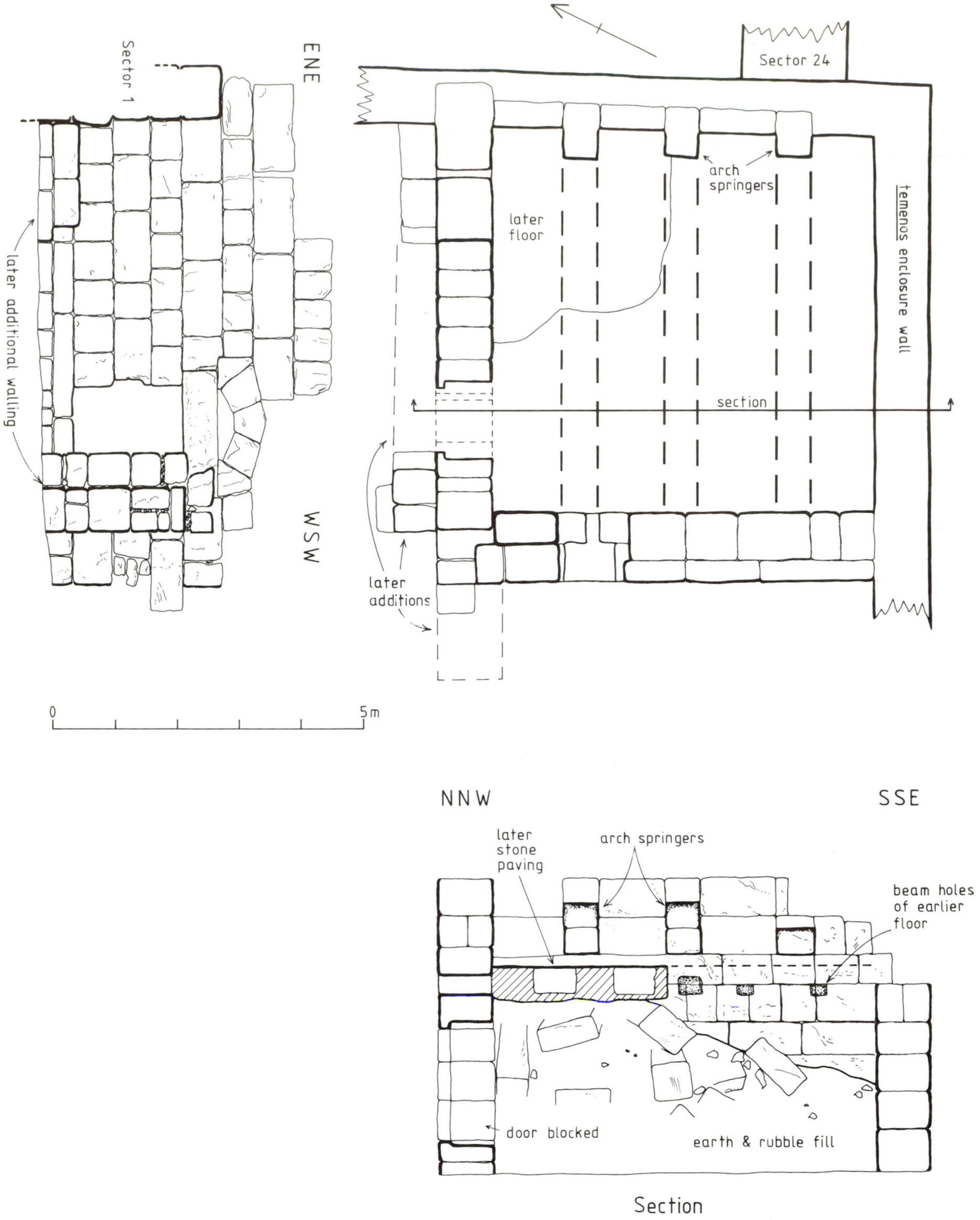

81. Tower A: plan, elevation and section (1:100).

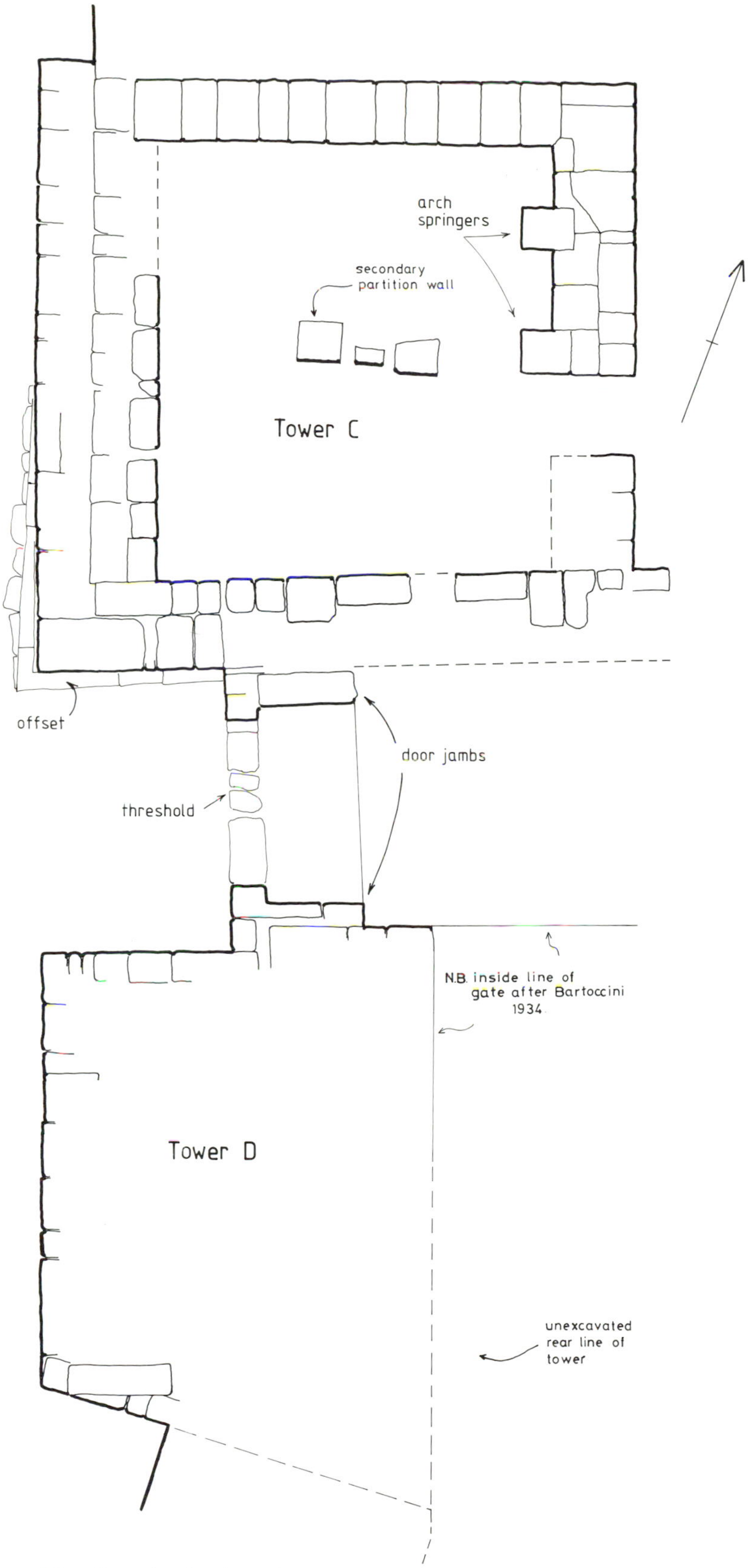

82. Gate A: plan (1:100).

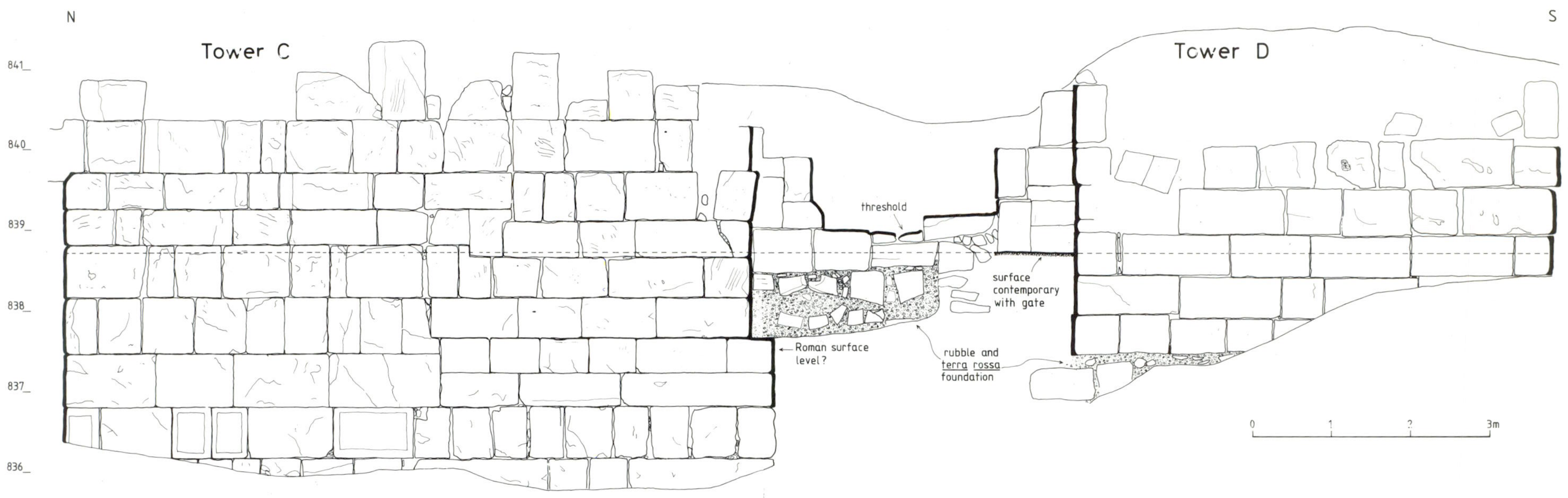

83. Gate A: front elevation of the facade (1:75).

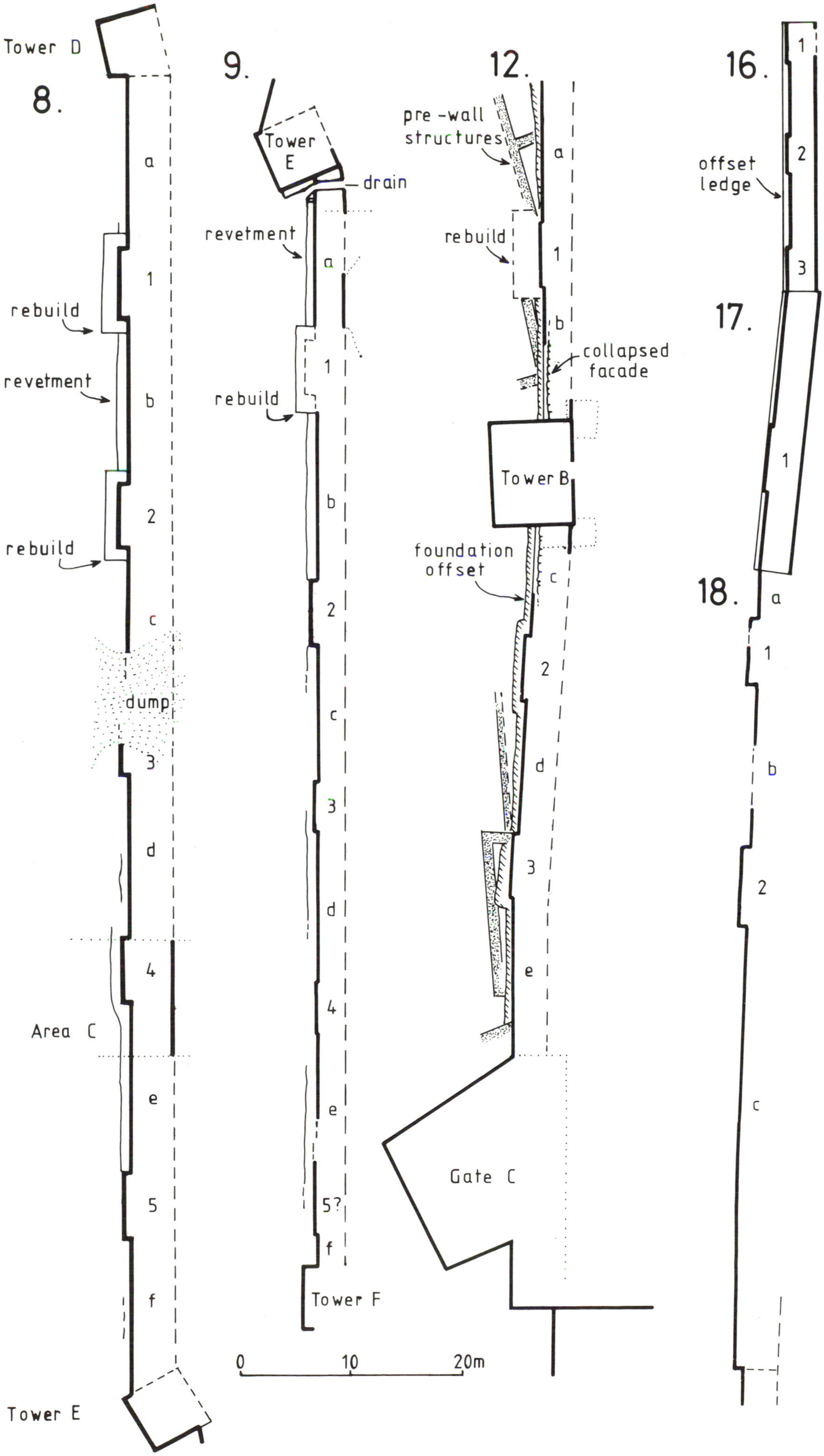

84. Plans of Wall Sectors 8, 9, 12, 16–18 (1:500).

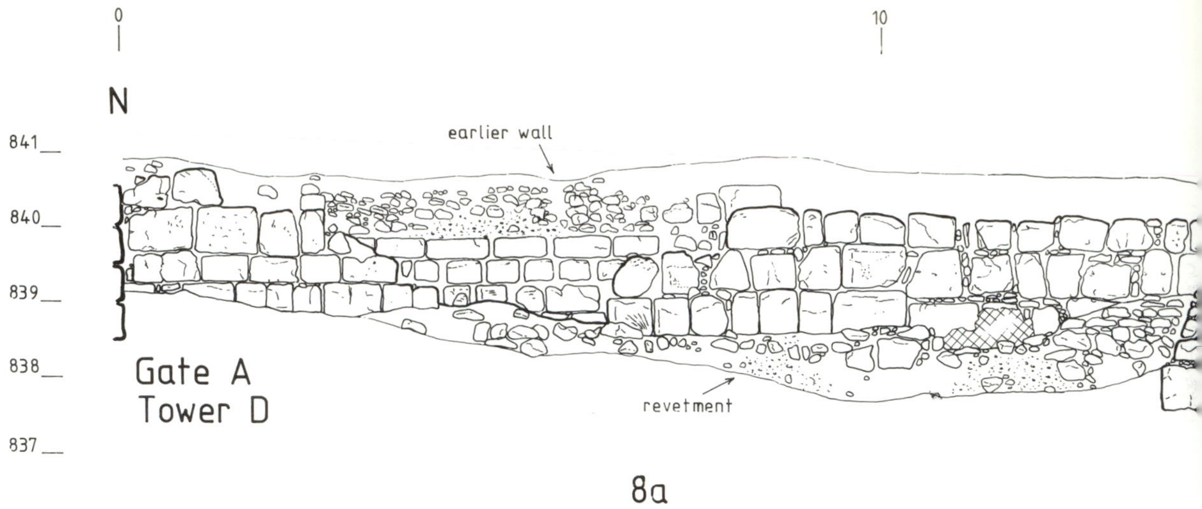

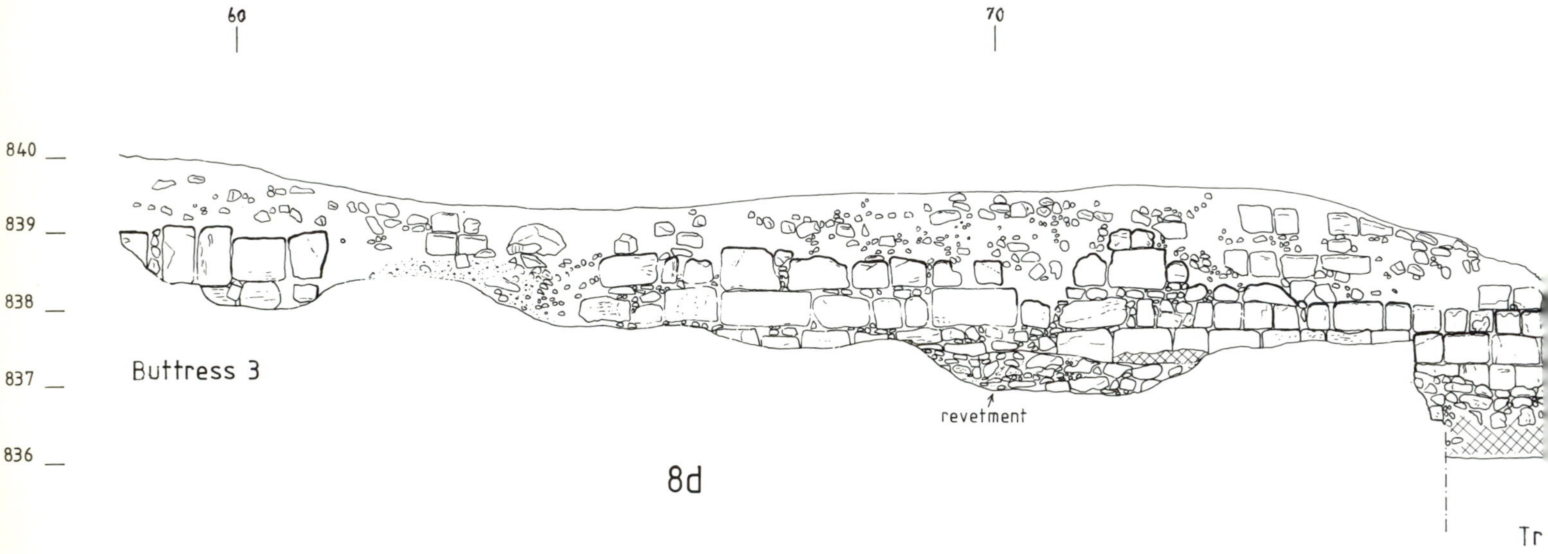

85. Sector 8: elevation (1:100).

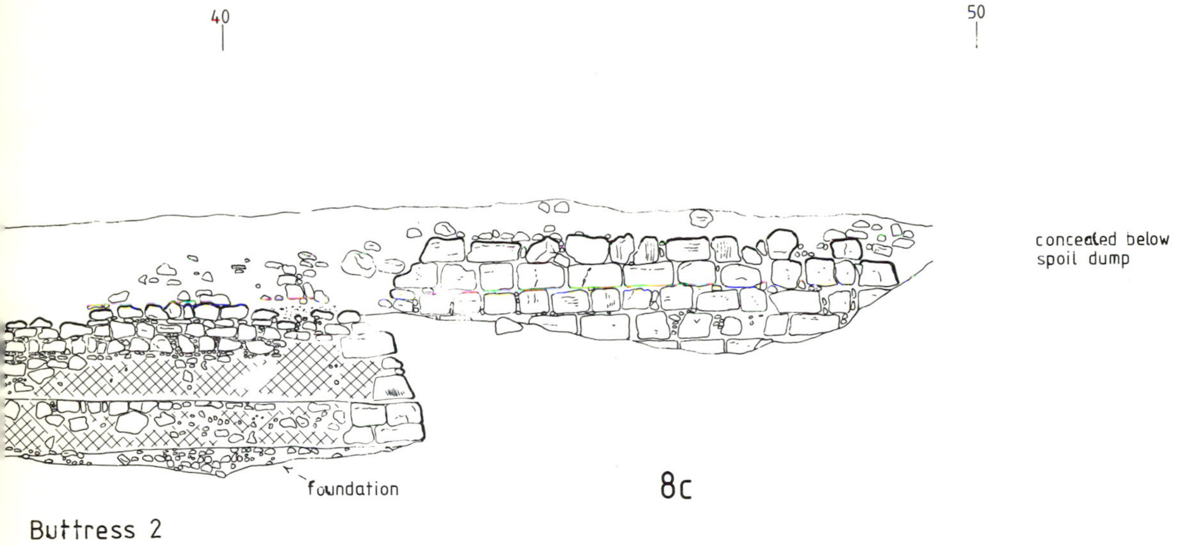
40
50
concealed below
spoil dump
foundation
Buttress 2

8c

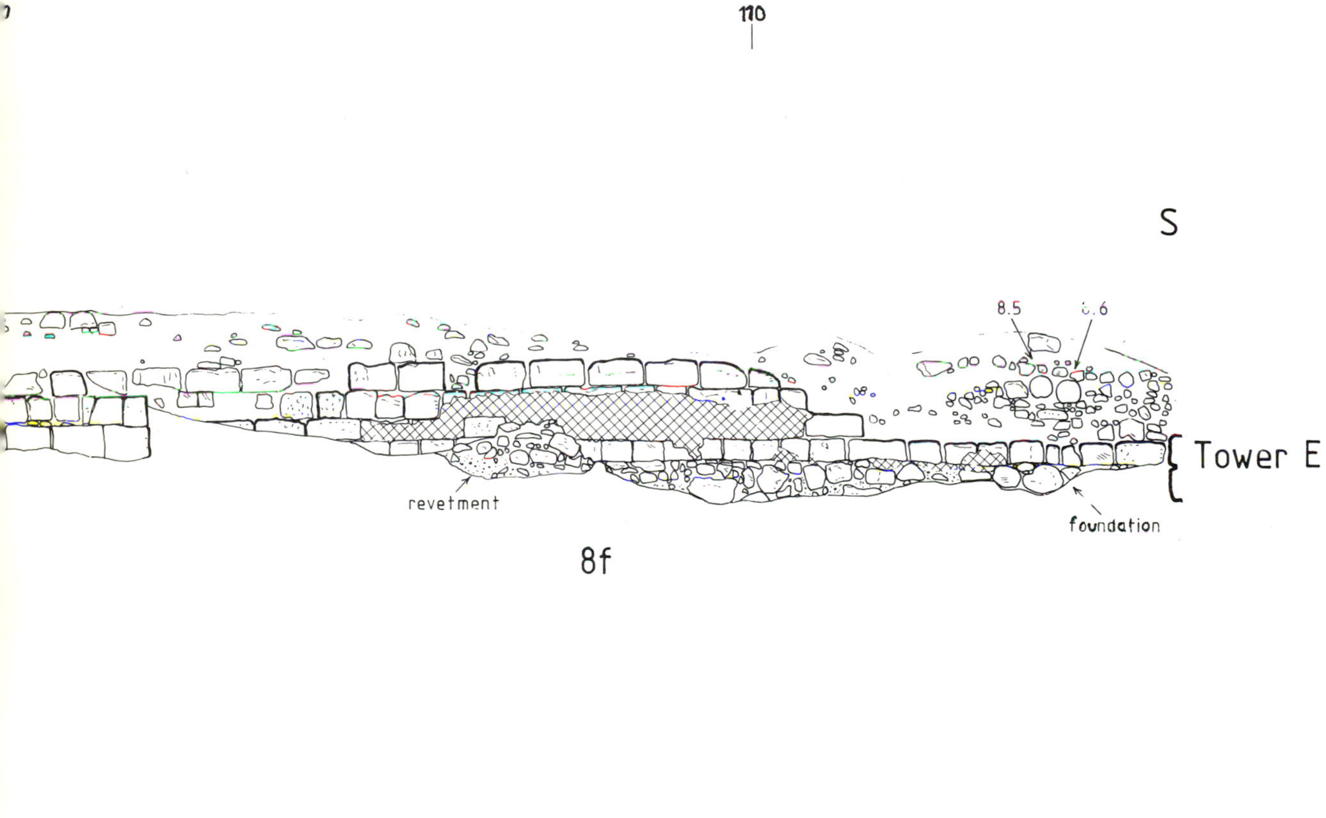
110
S
8.5
Tower E
revetment
foundation

8f

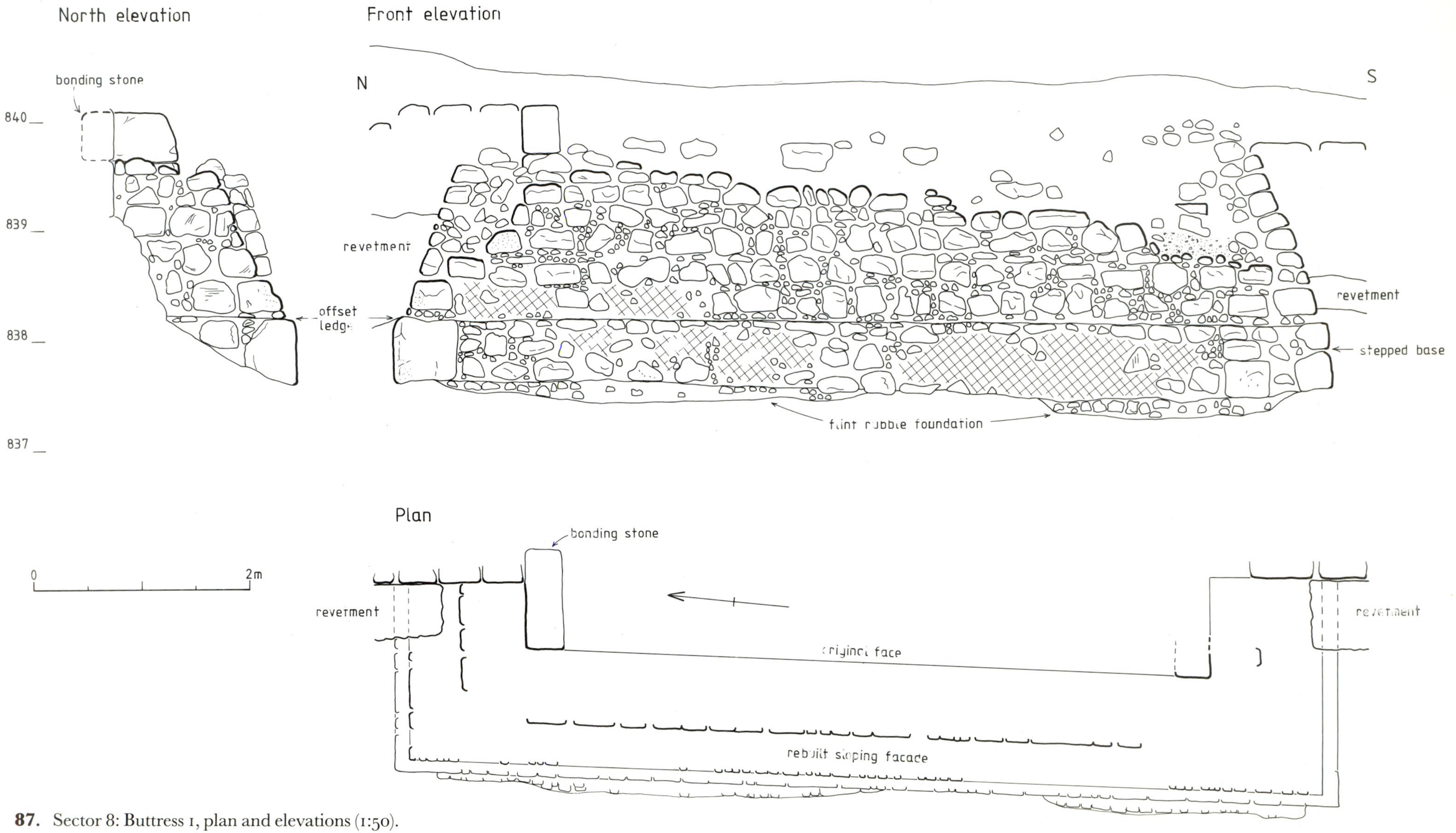

87. Sector 8: Buttress 1, plan and elevations (1:50).

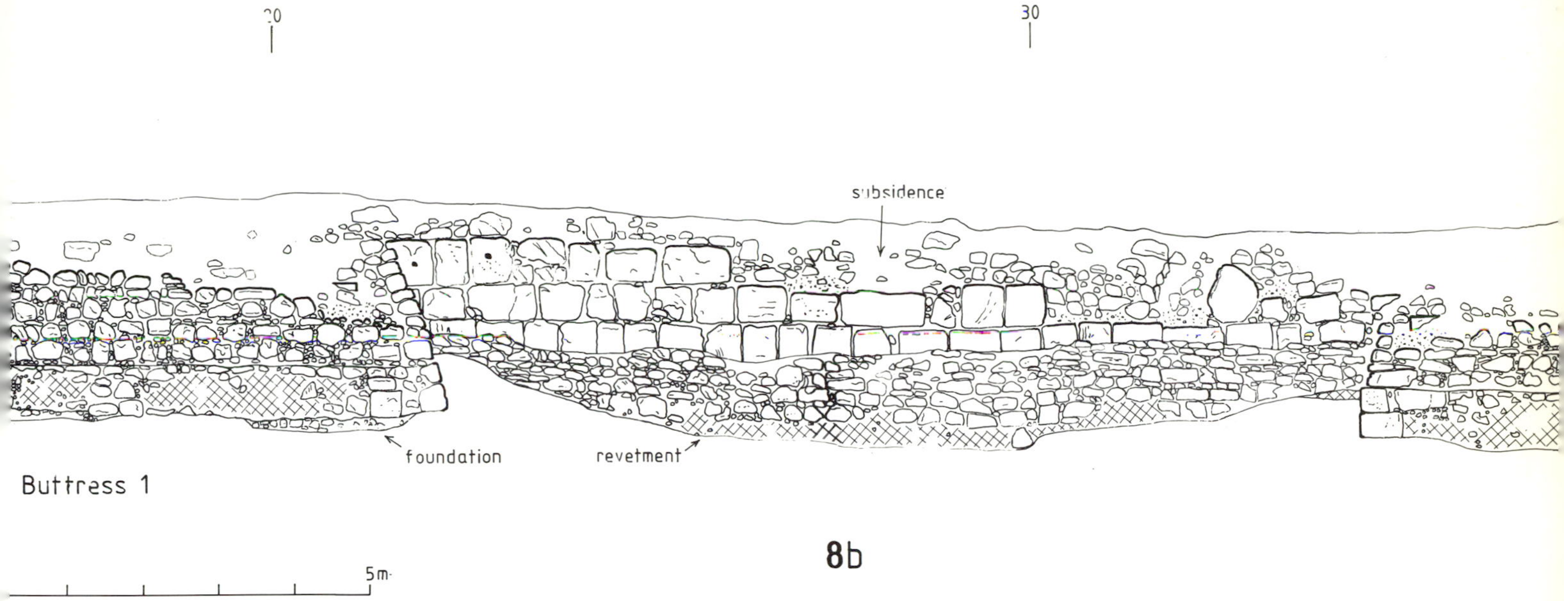

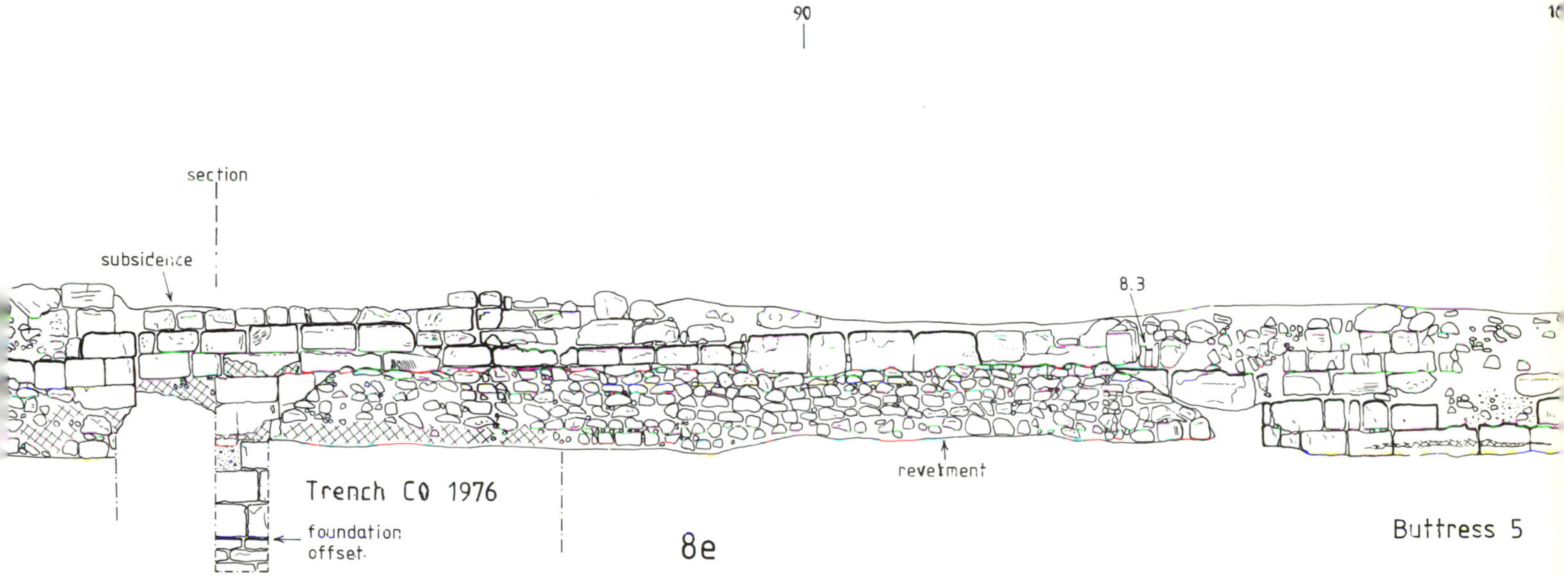

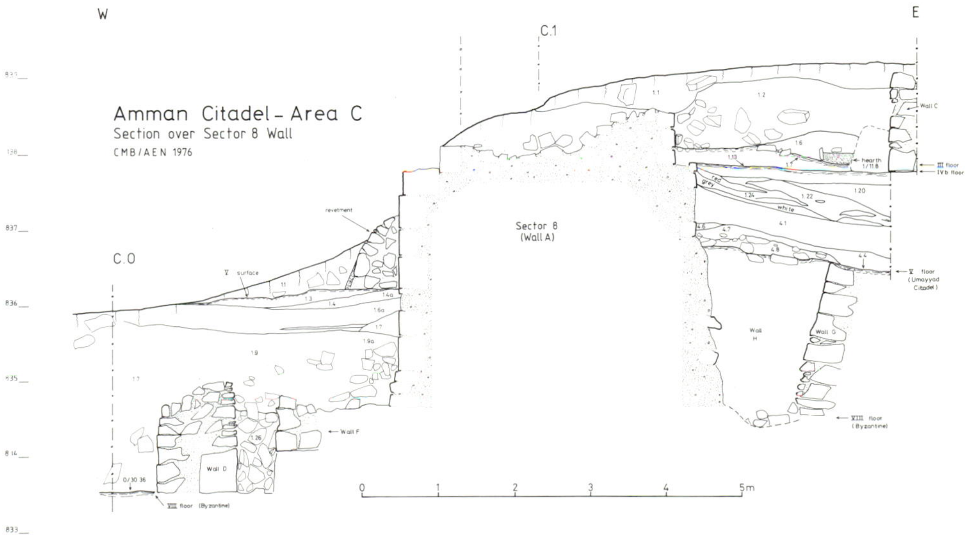

86. Sector 8: section over fortification wall in Area C (1:100).

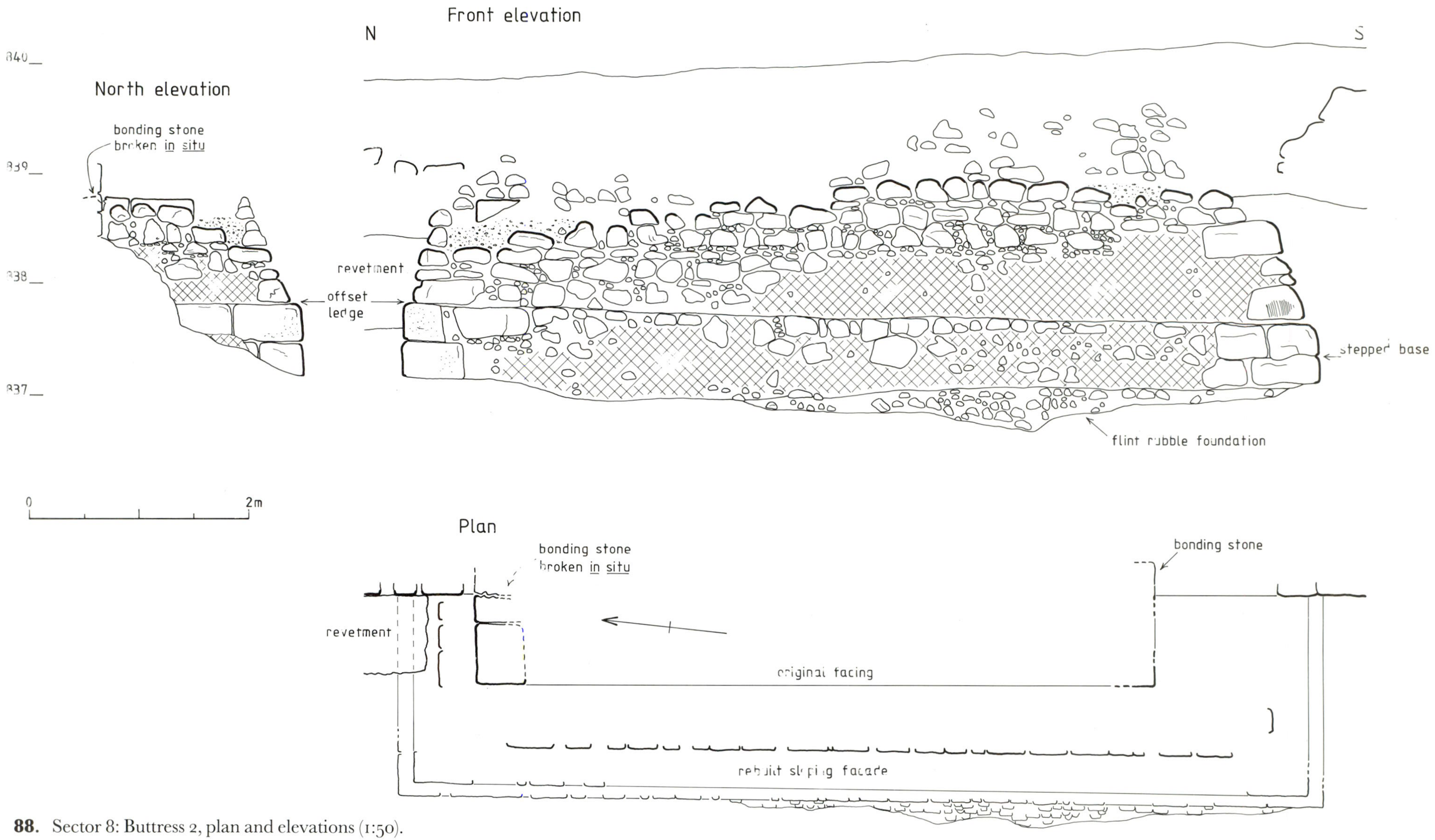

88. Sector 8: Buttress 2, plan and elevations (1:50).

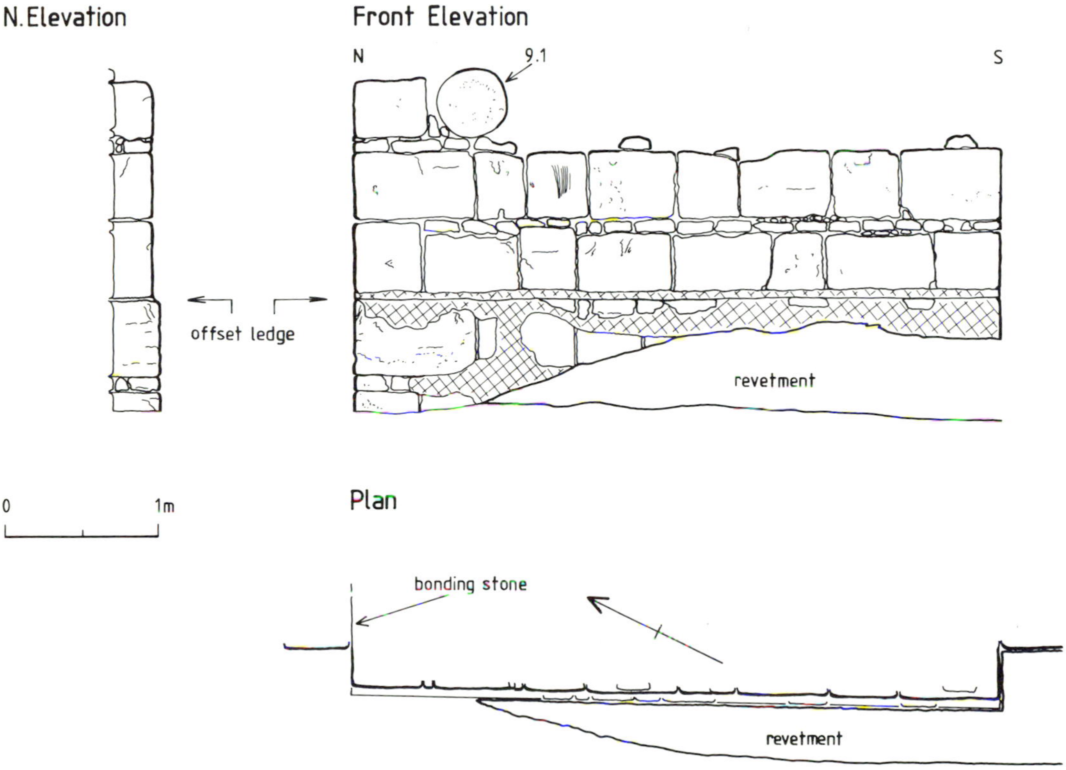

90. Sector 9: Buttress 3, plan and elevations (1:50).

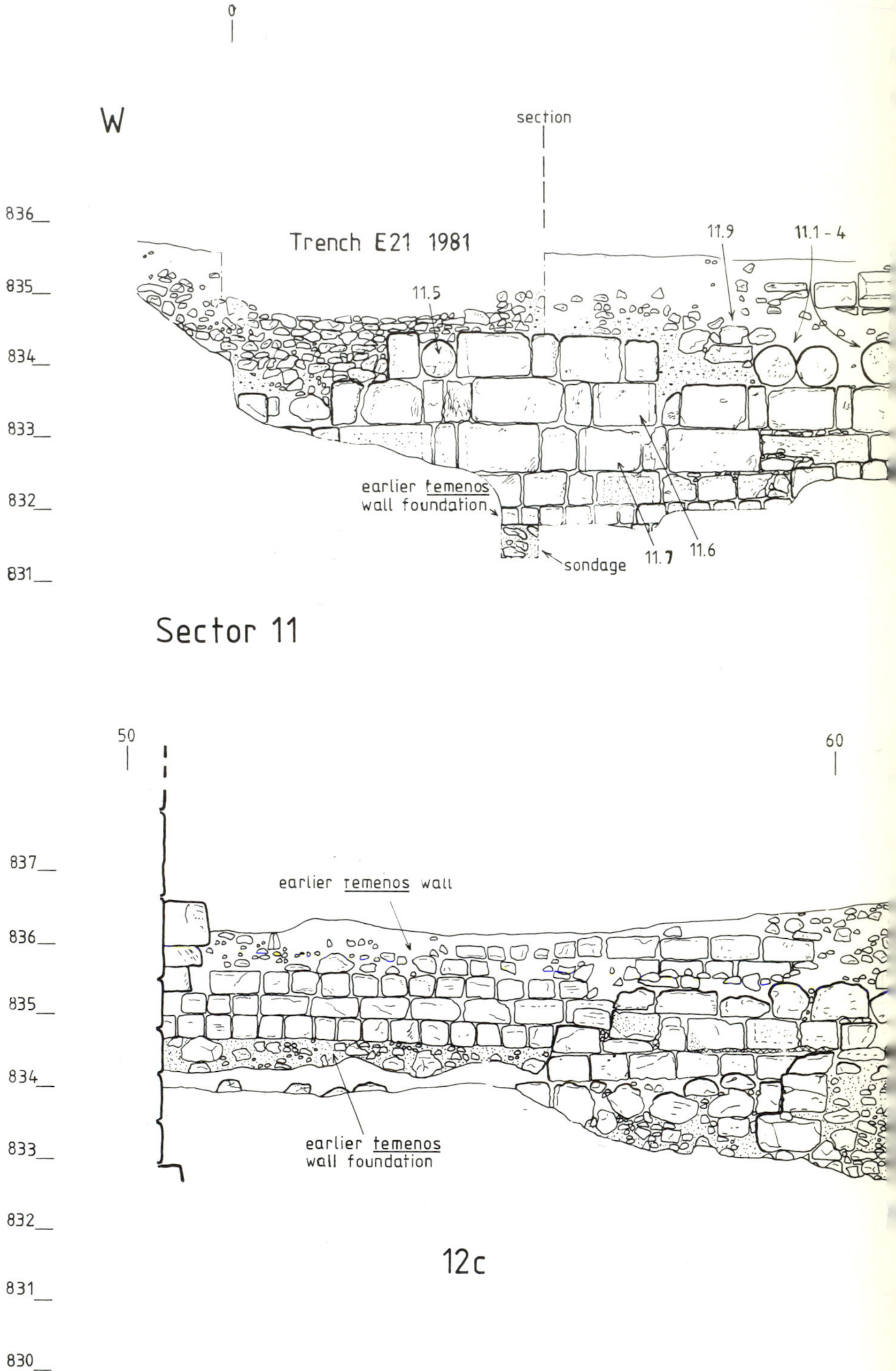

91. Sectors 11 and 12: elevations (1:100).

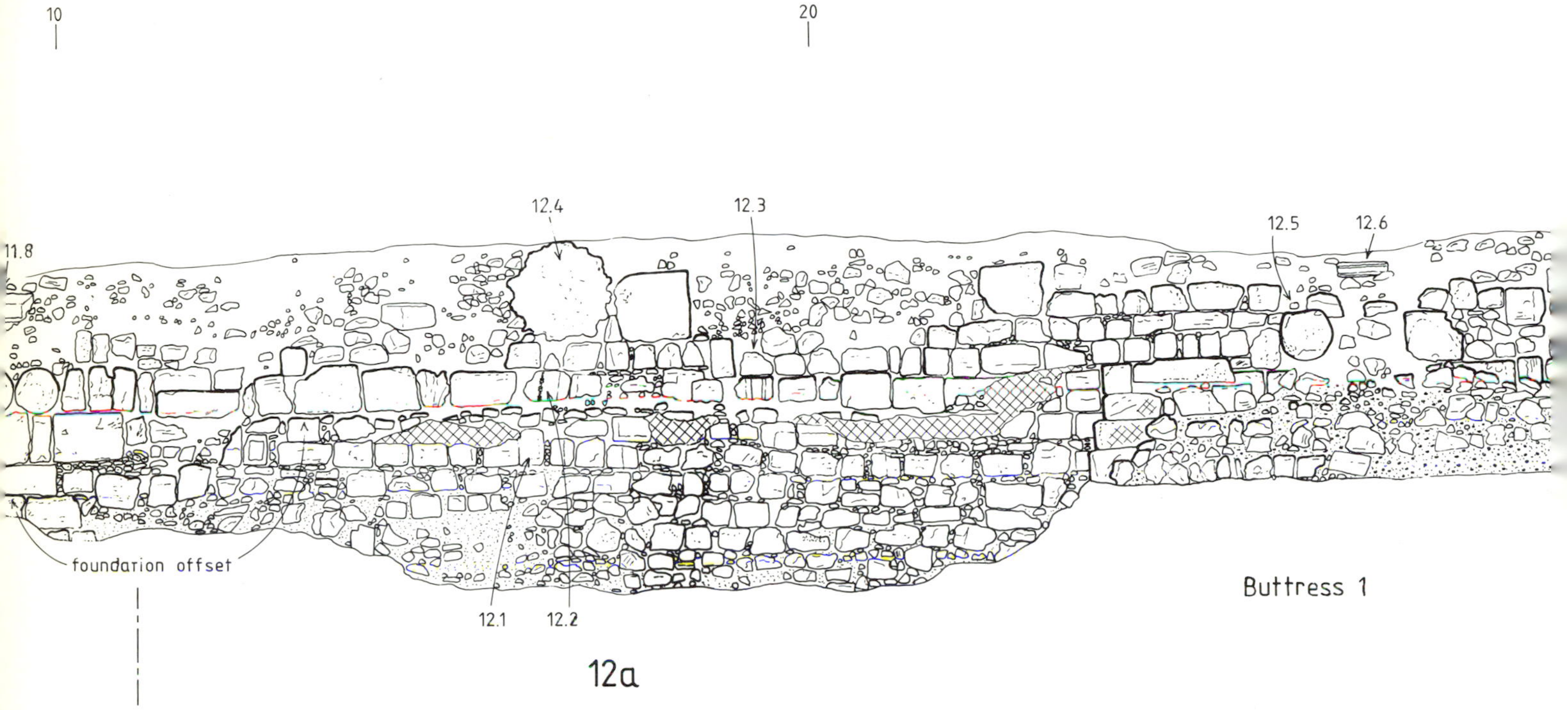
10
20
11.8
12.4
12.3
12.5
12.6
foundation offset
12.1
12.2
Buttress 1

12a

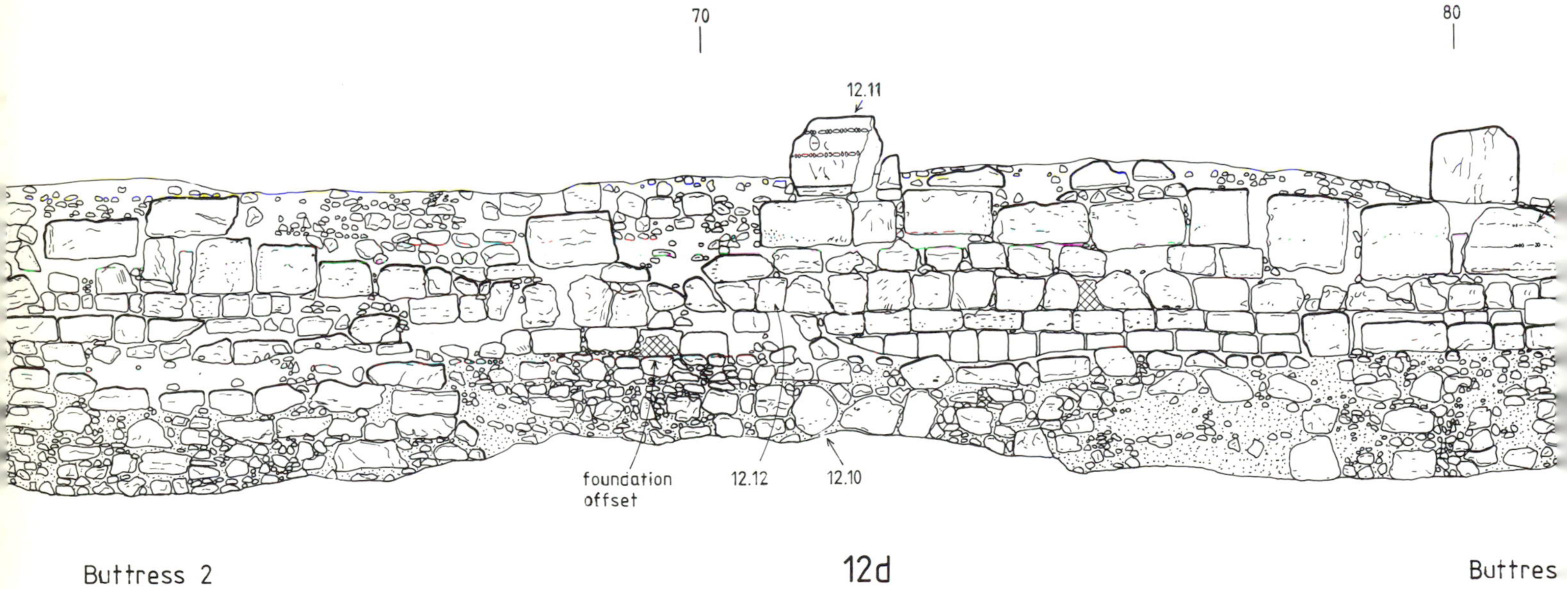
70
80
12.11
foundation offset
12.12
12.10
Buttress 2
Buttres

12d

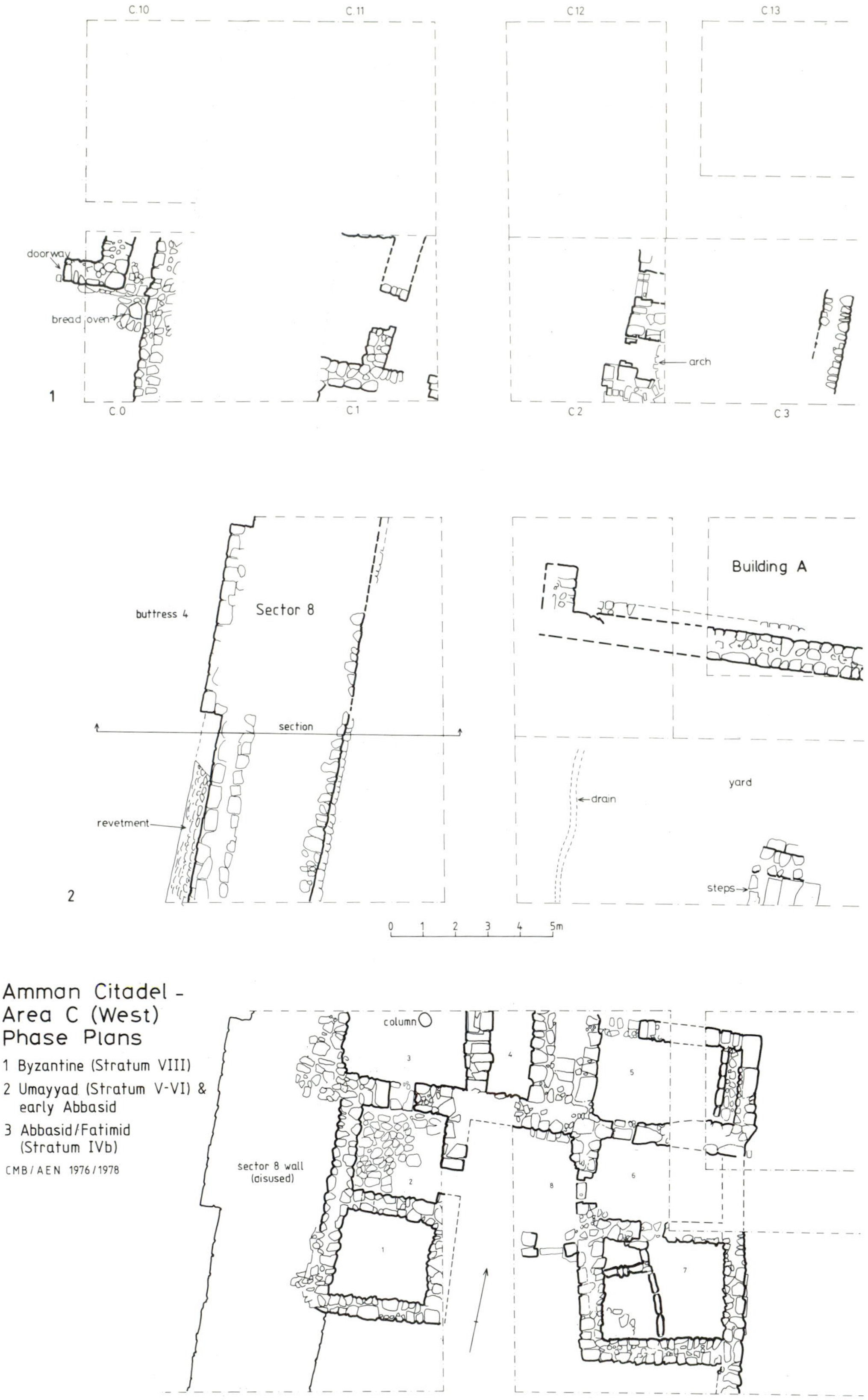

89. Area C (west): phase plans (1:200).

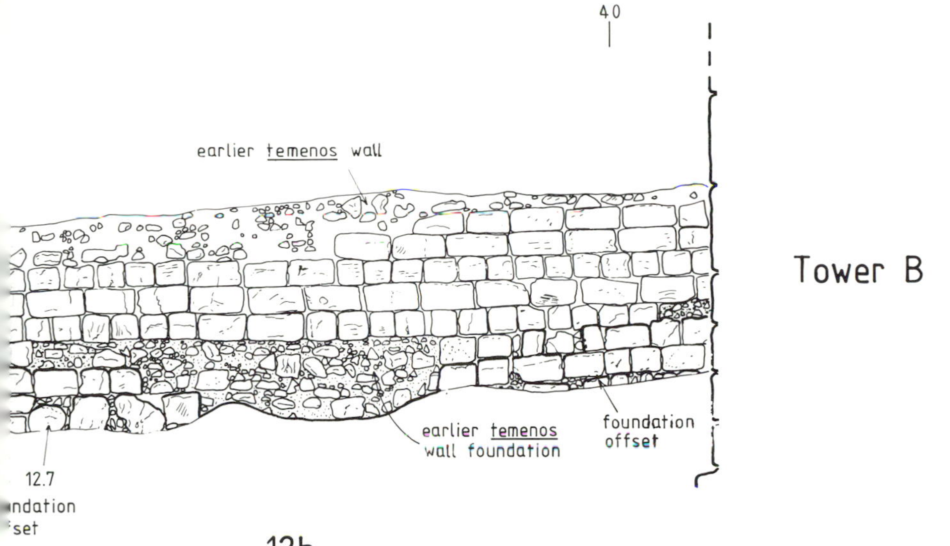
40
earlier temenos wall
Tower B
earlier temenos wall foundation
foundation offset
12.7
ndation
set

12b

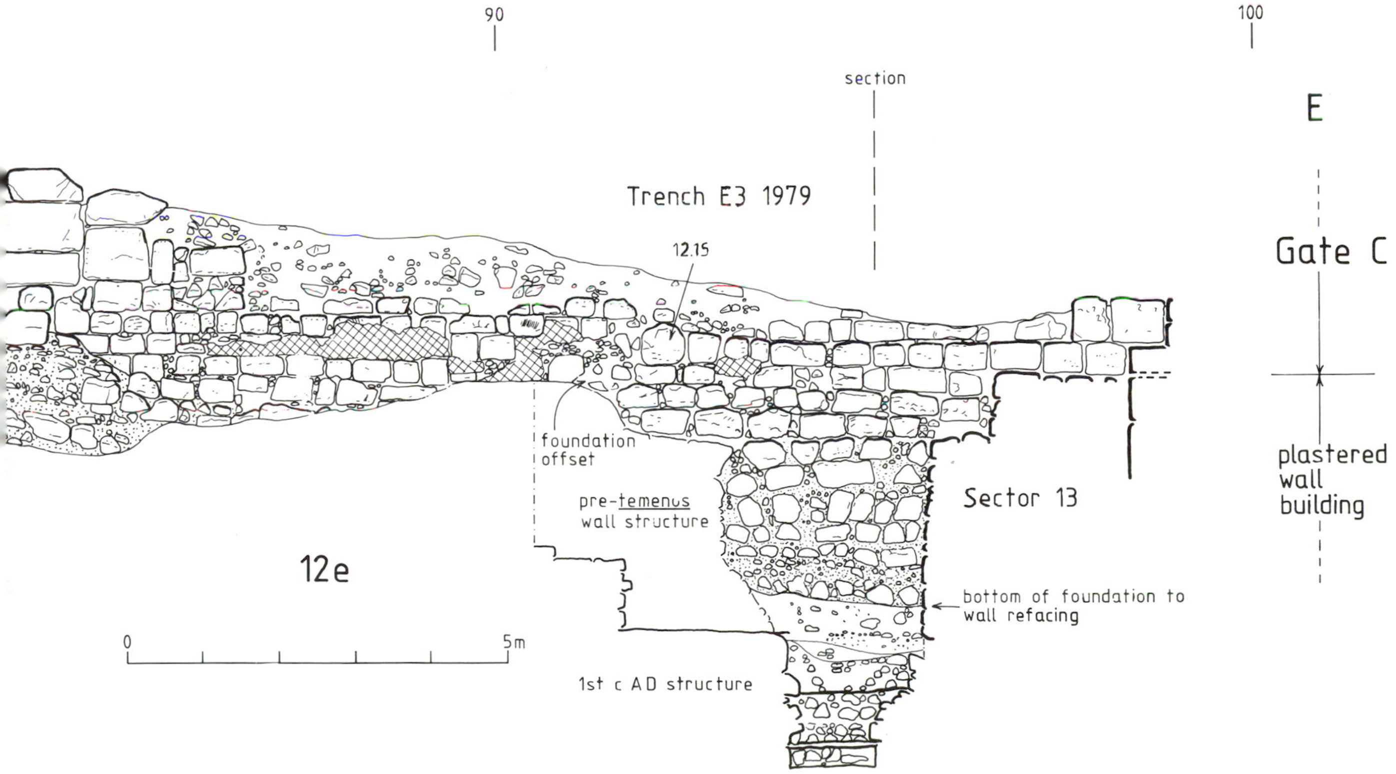
90
100
section
E
Trench E3 1979
12.15
Gate C
foundation offset
plastered wall building
pre-temenos wall structure
Sector 13
bottom of foundation to wall refacing
0
5m
1st c AD structure

12e

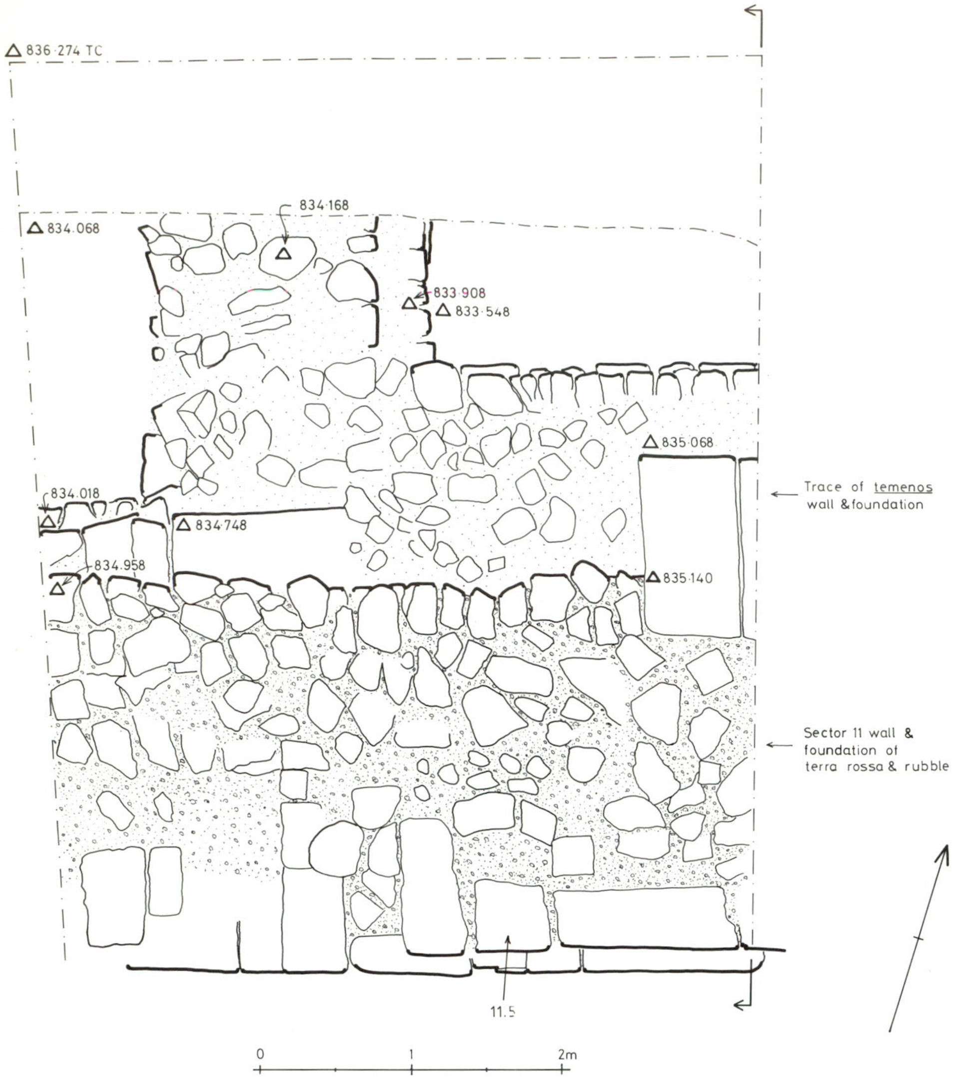

92. Trench E21: plan (1:50).

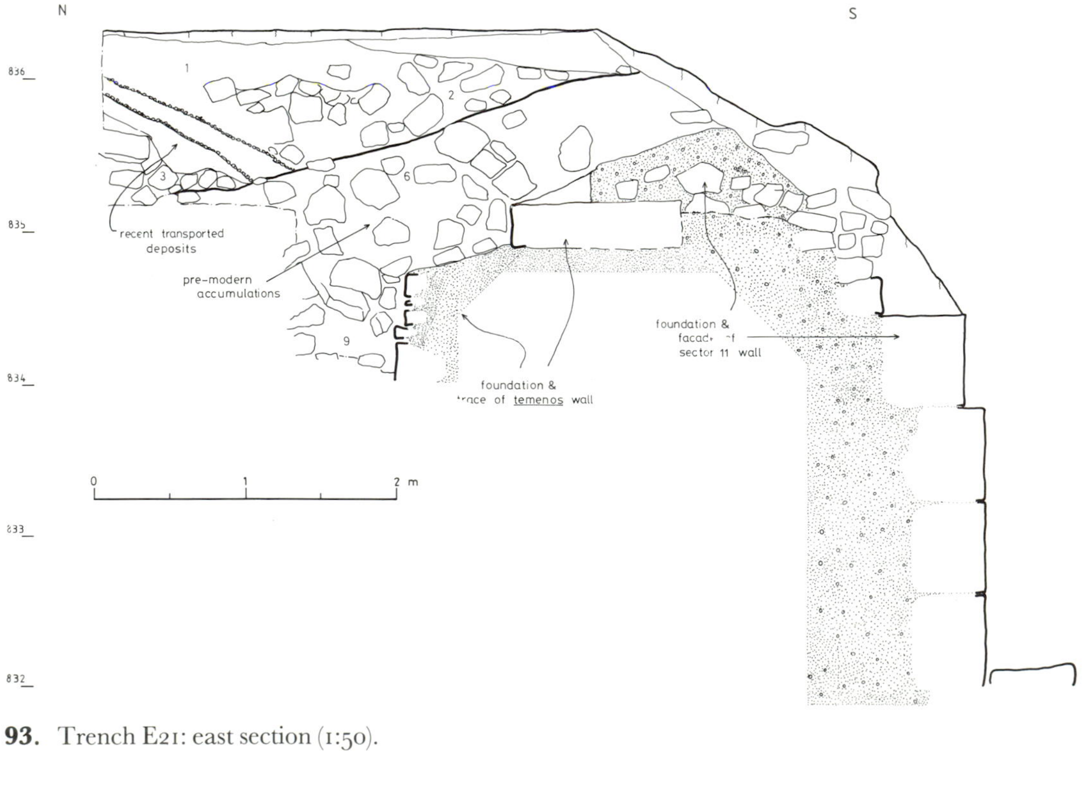

93. Trench E21: east section (1:50).

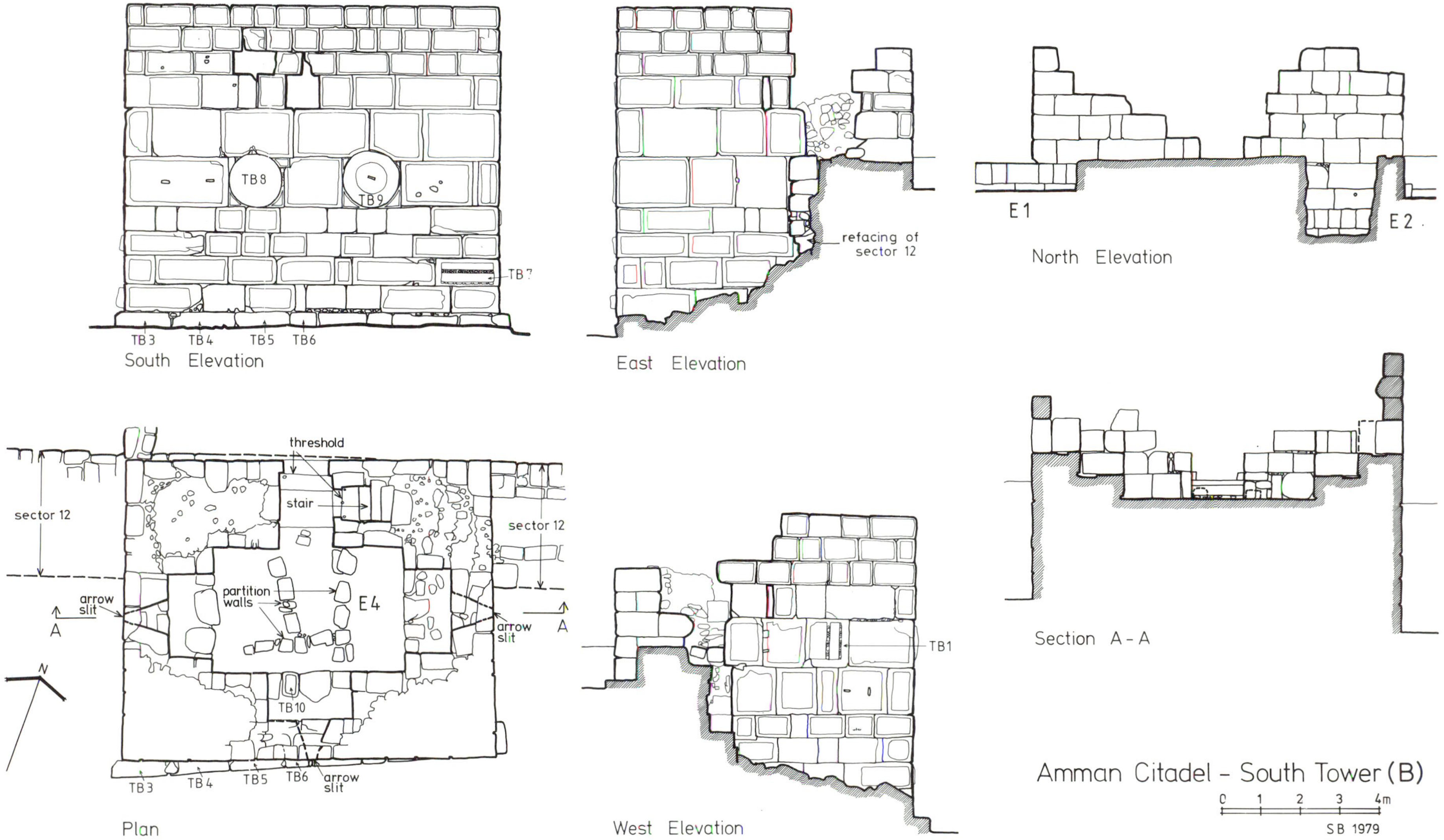

94. Tower B: plan and elevation (1:150).

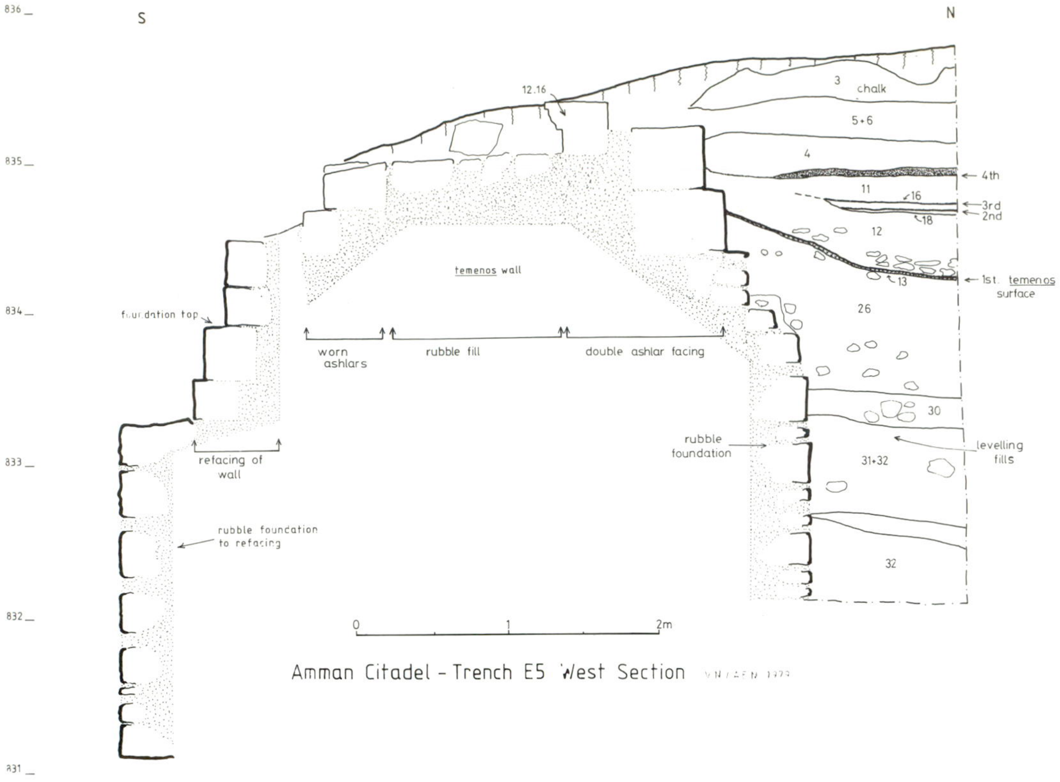

95. West section of trench E5 over *temenos* wall (1:50).

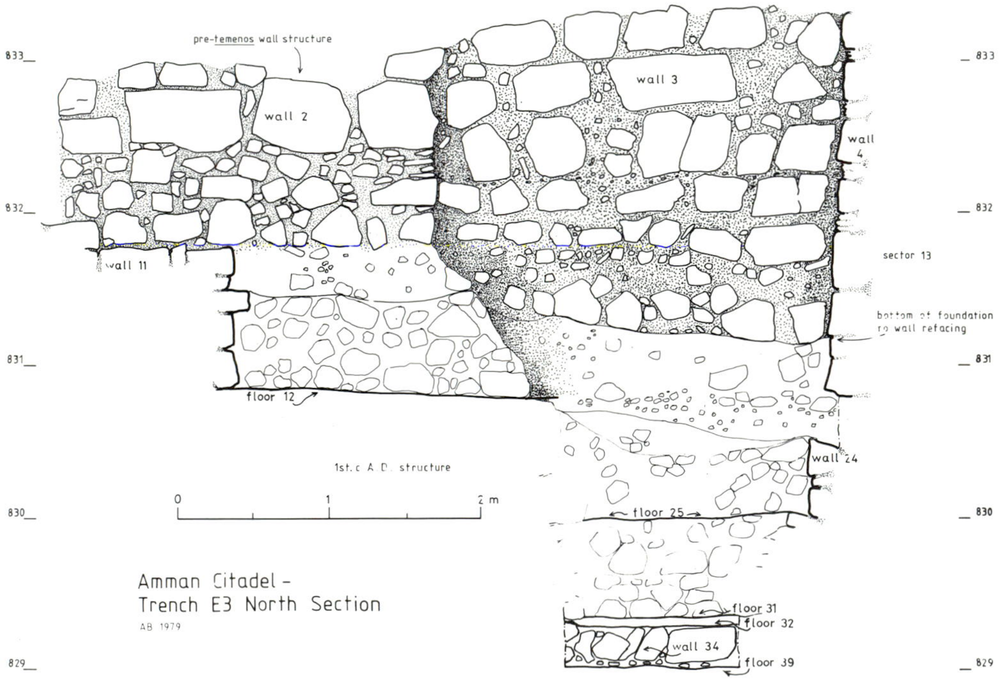

96. Trench E3: north section (1:50).

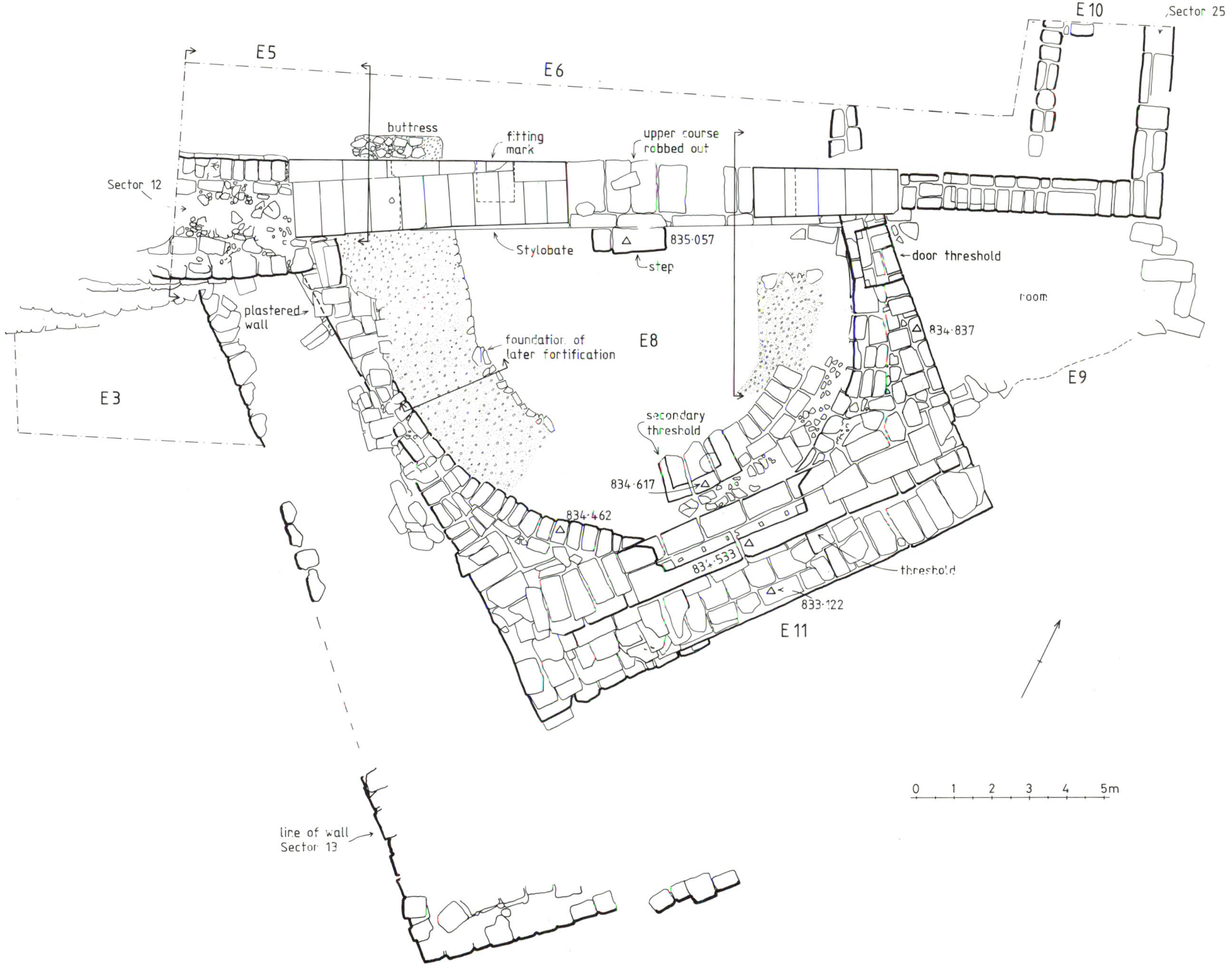

97. Gate C: general plan with position of trenches and sections marked (1:150).

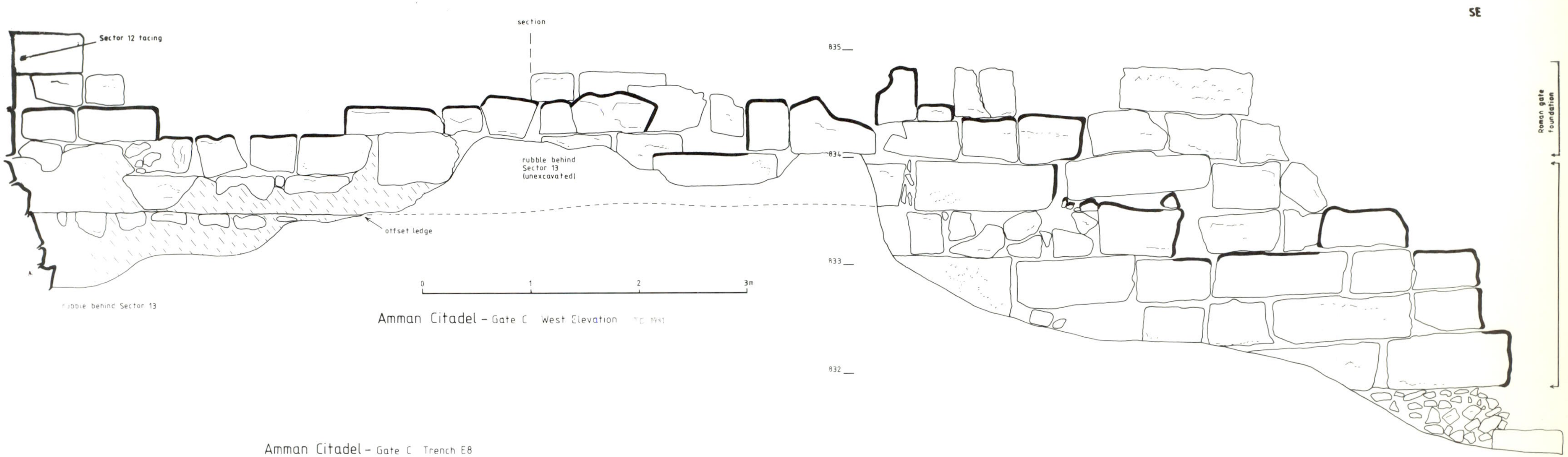

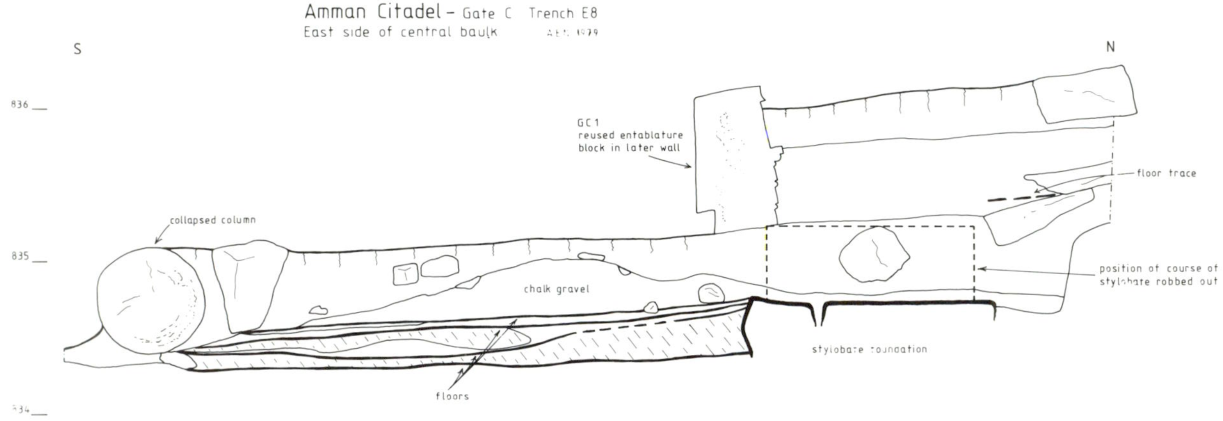

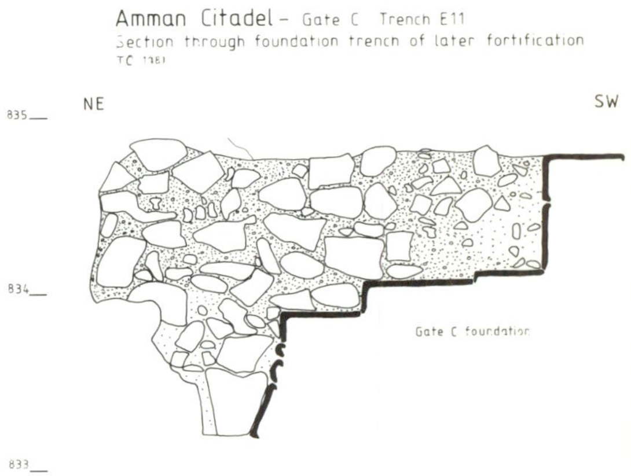

98. Gate C: (a) west elevation; (b) trench E8: central baulk section; (c) trench E11: section through foundation trench.(1:50).

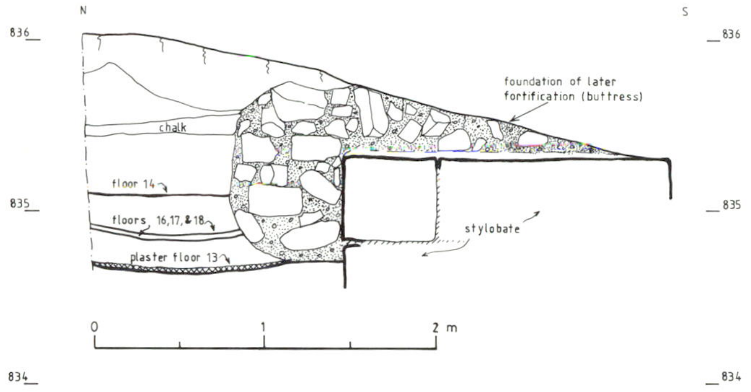

99. Trench E5: east section (1:50).

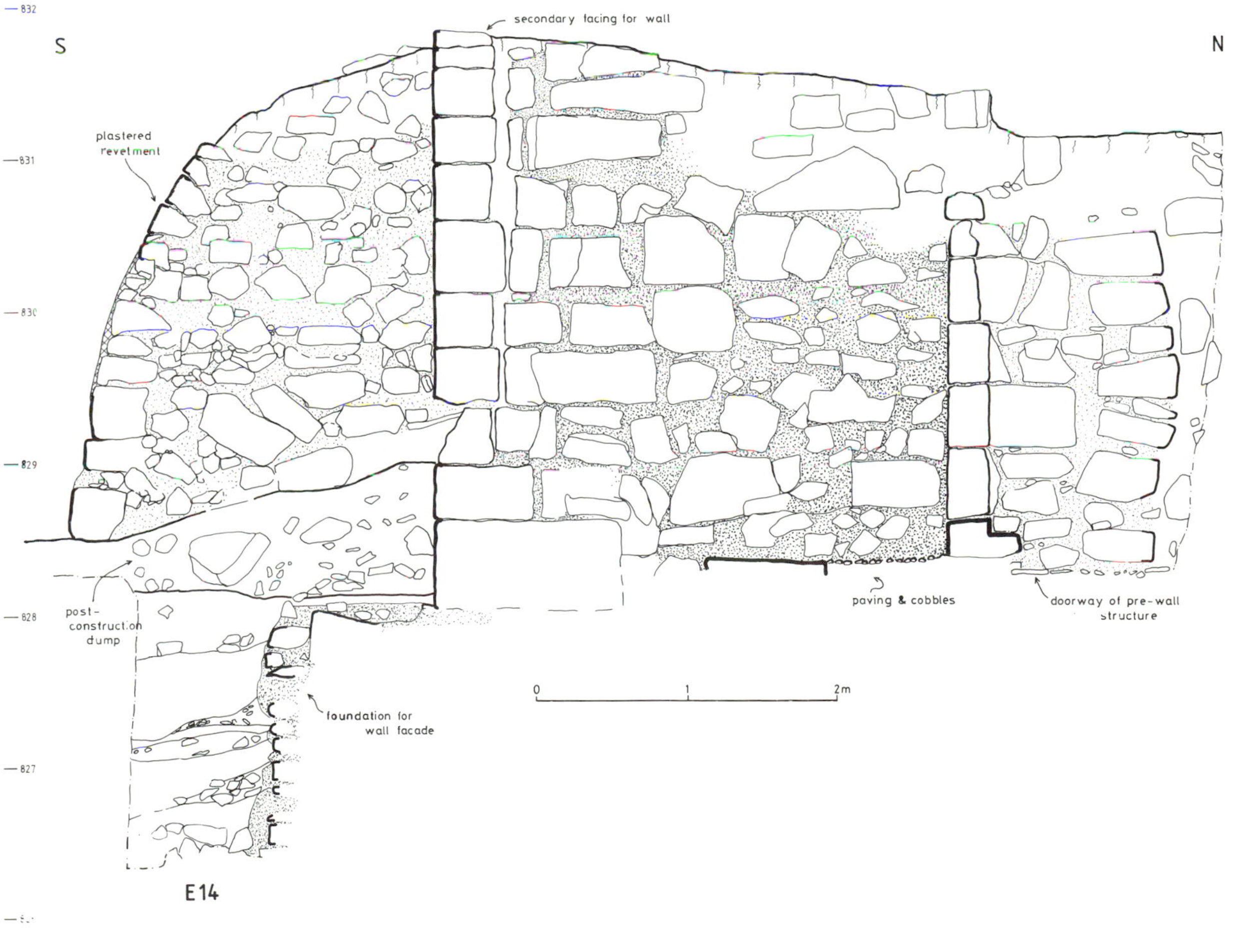

100. Sector 14A: cross-section of wall looking west (1:50).

Figure 101 is placed after figure 107

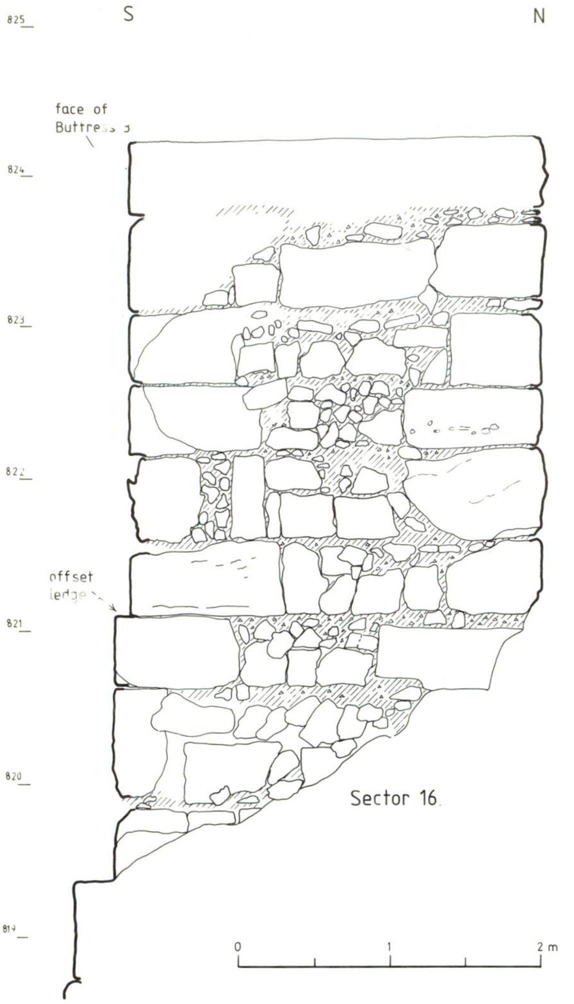

102. Sector 16: cross-section of Wall looking west (1:50).

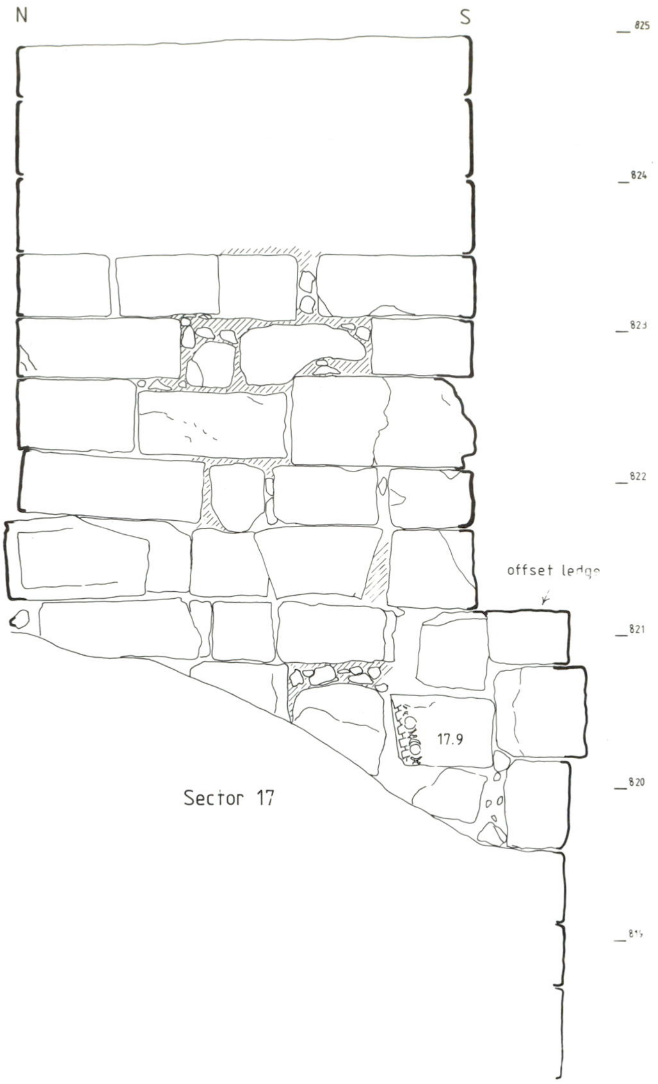

103. Sector 17: cross-section of Wall looking east (1:50).

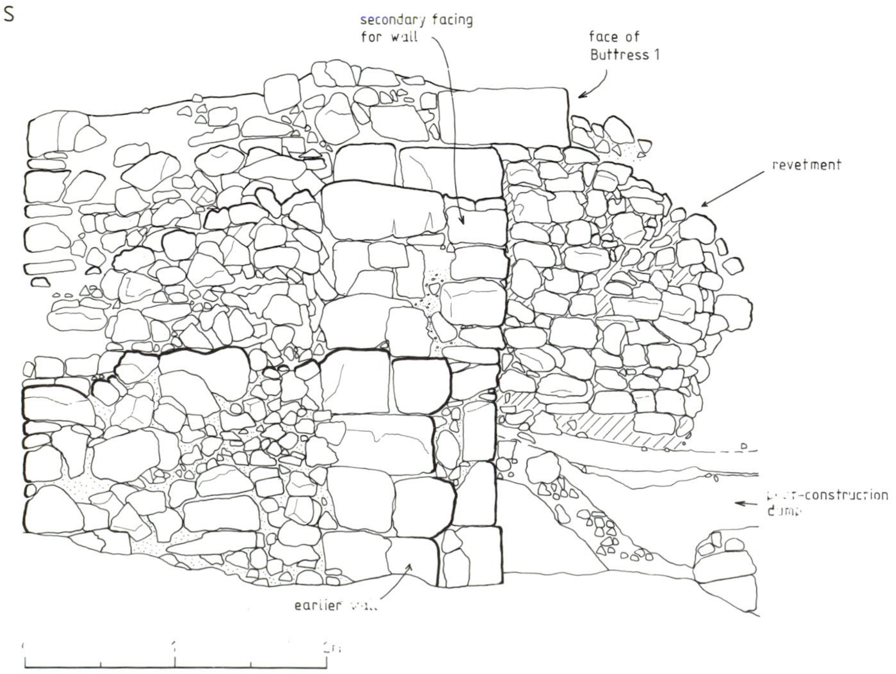

104. Sector 22: cross-section of Wall looking west (1:50).

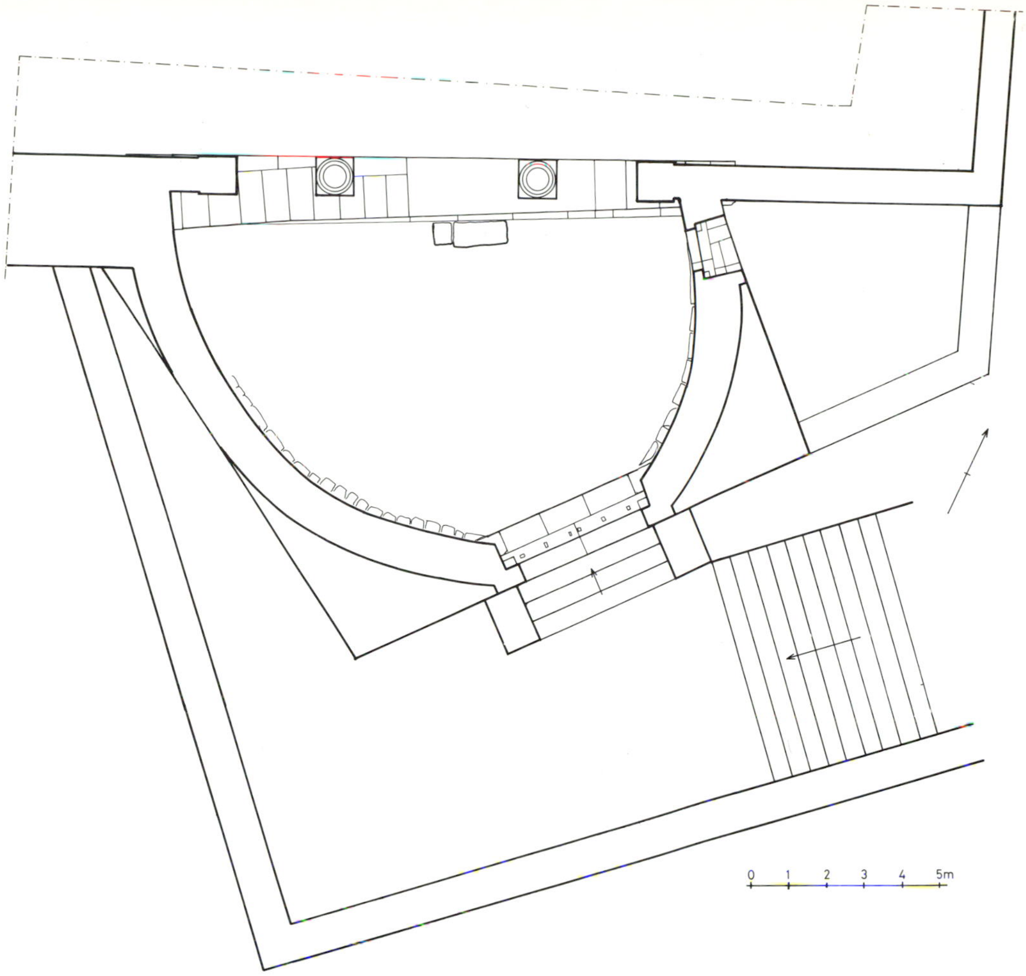

106. Gate C: suggested reconstruction of Roman Period gate plan (1:200).

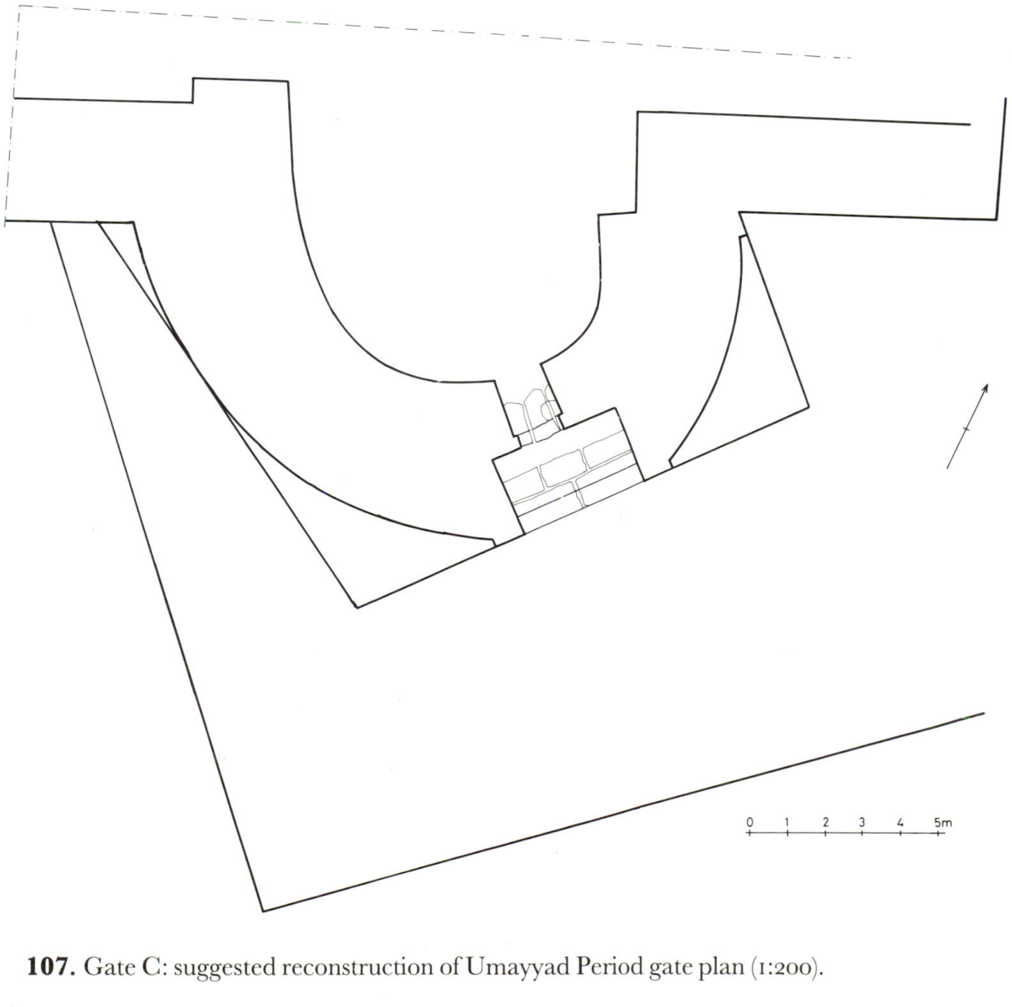

107. Gate C: suggested reconstruction of Umayyad Period gate plan (1:200).

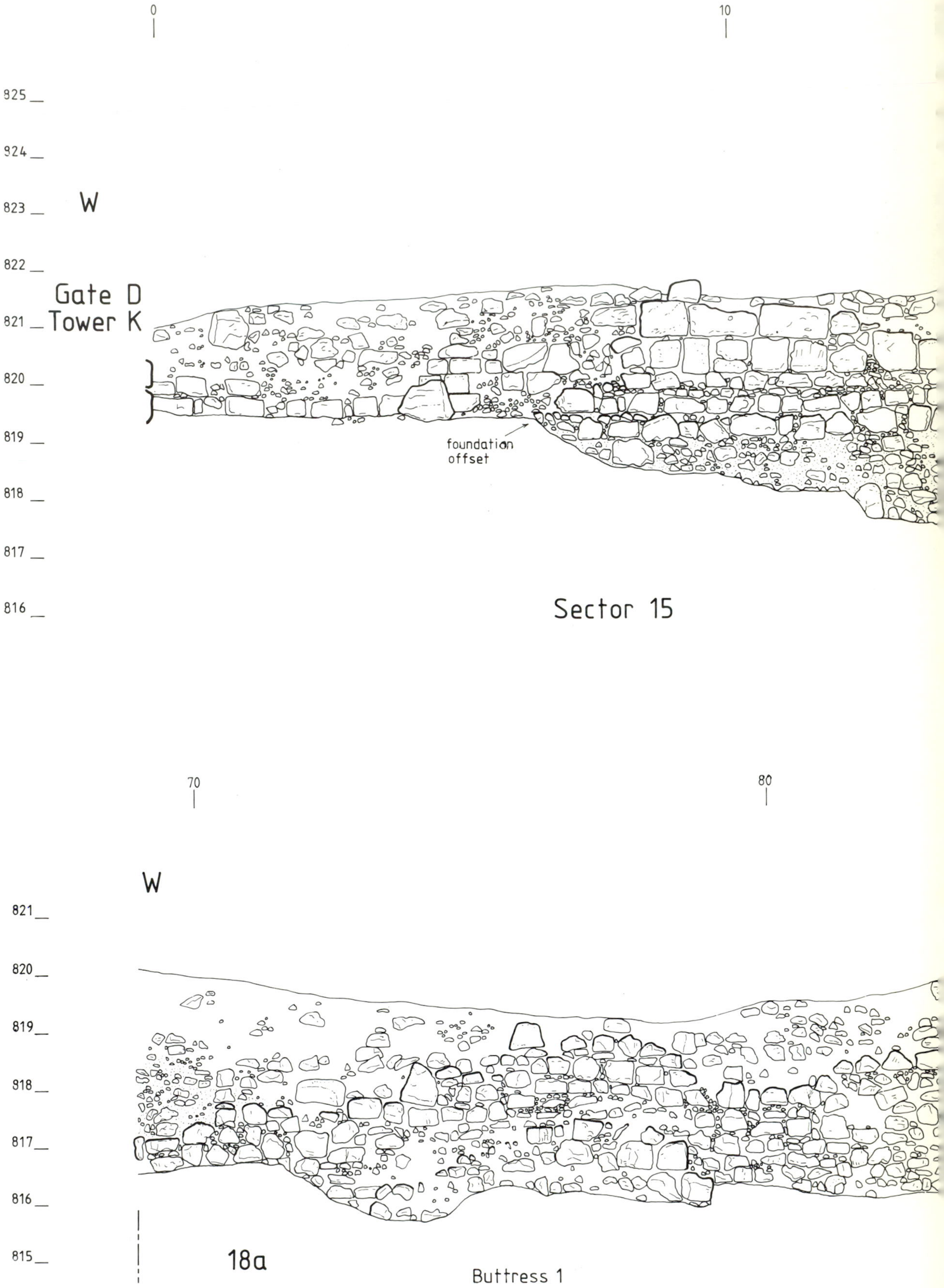

101. Elevations: Sectors 15, 16, 17, 18 (1:100).

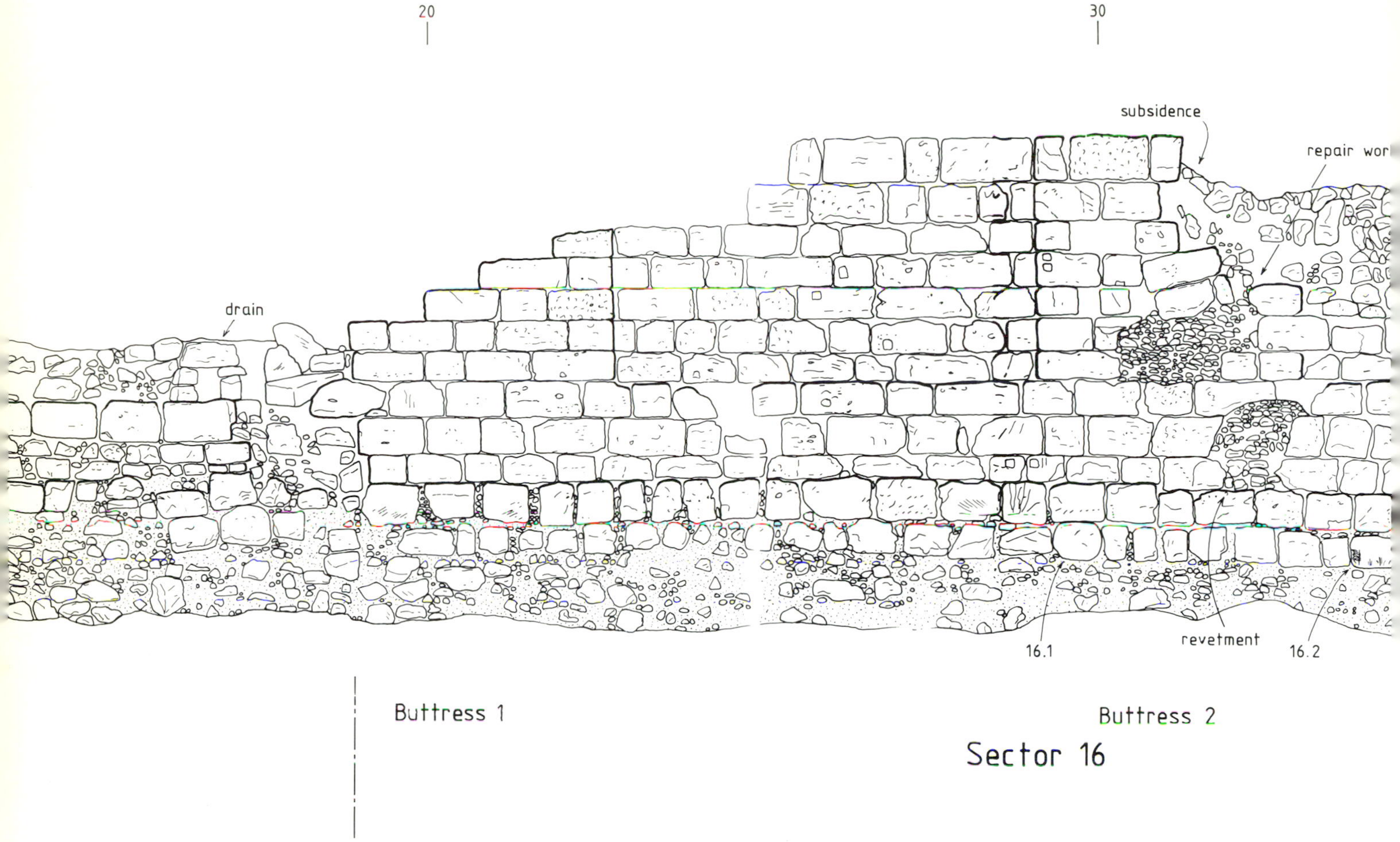

Sector 16

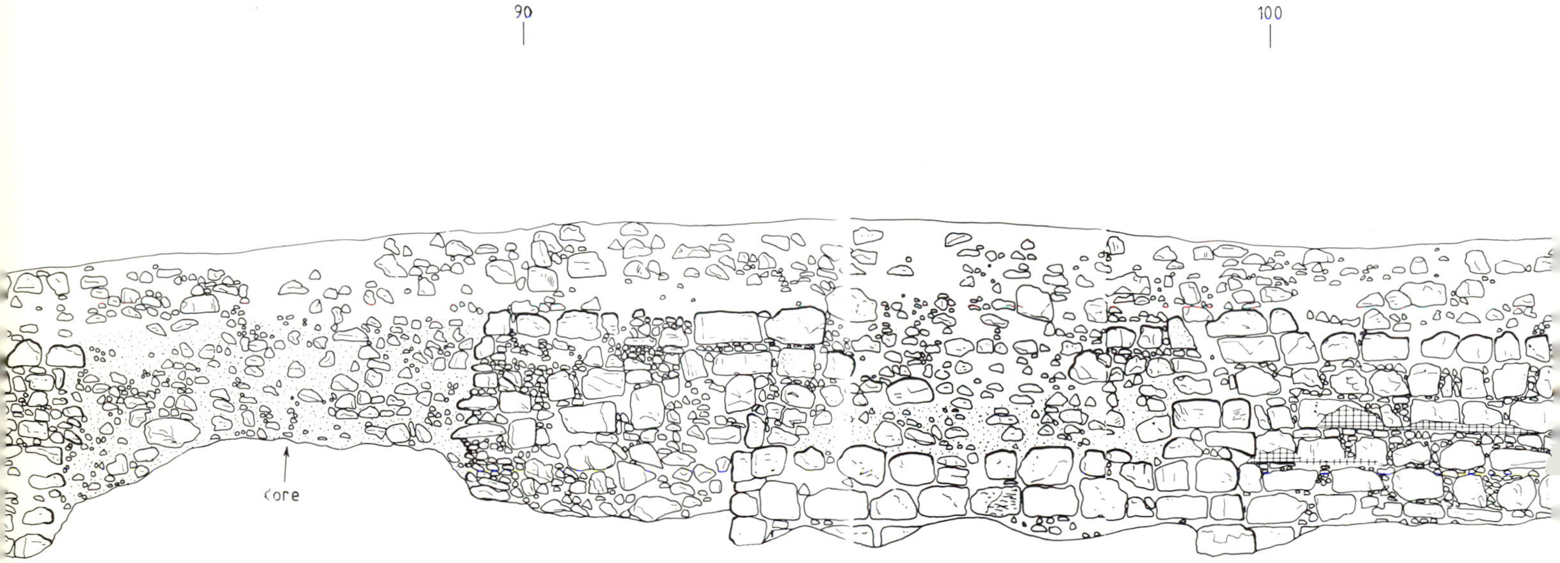

18b

Buttress 2

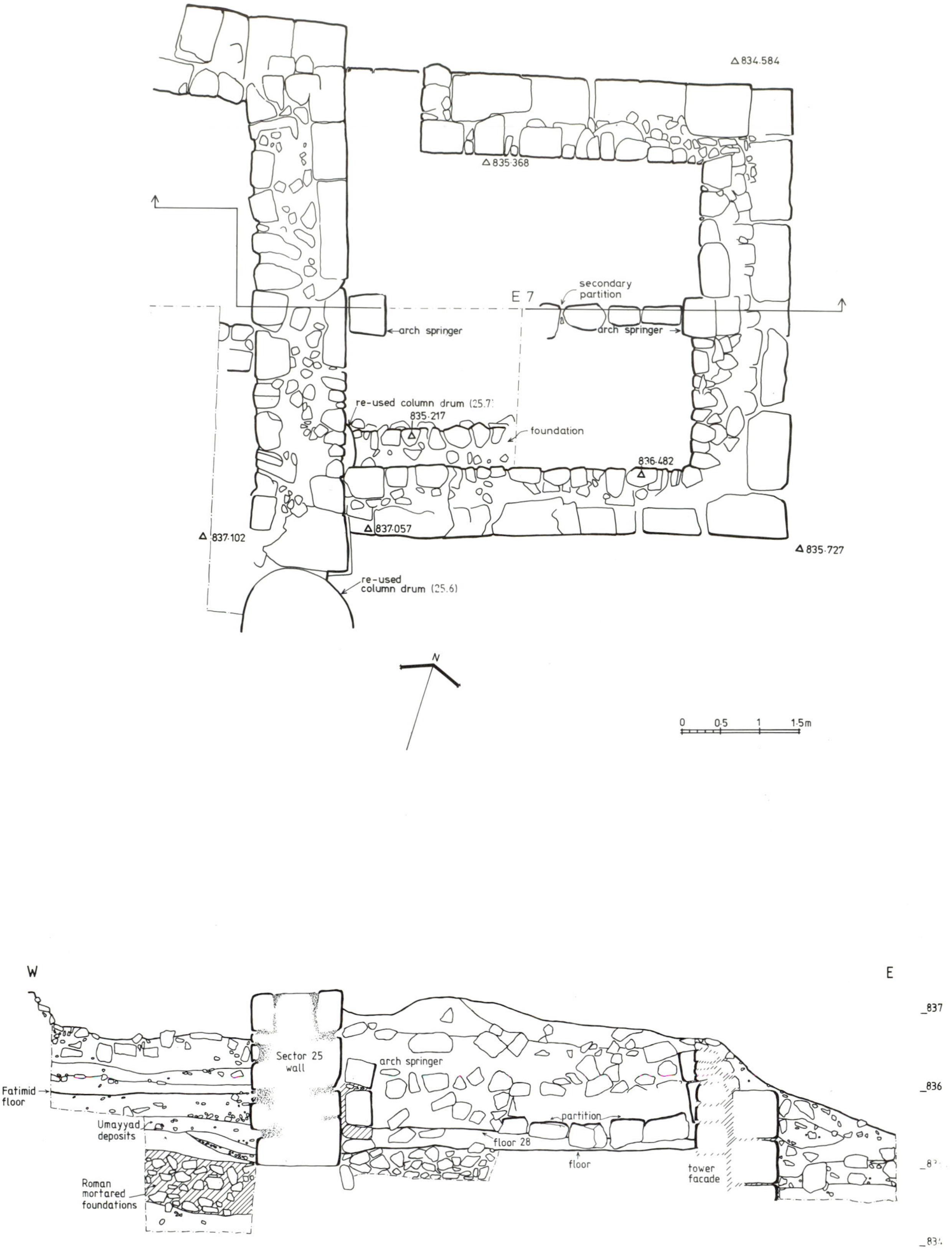

105. Tower G: plan and cross-section (1:75).

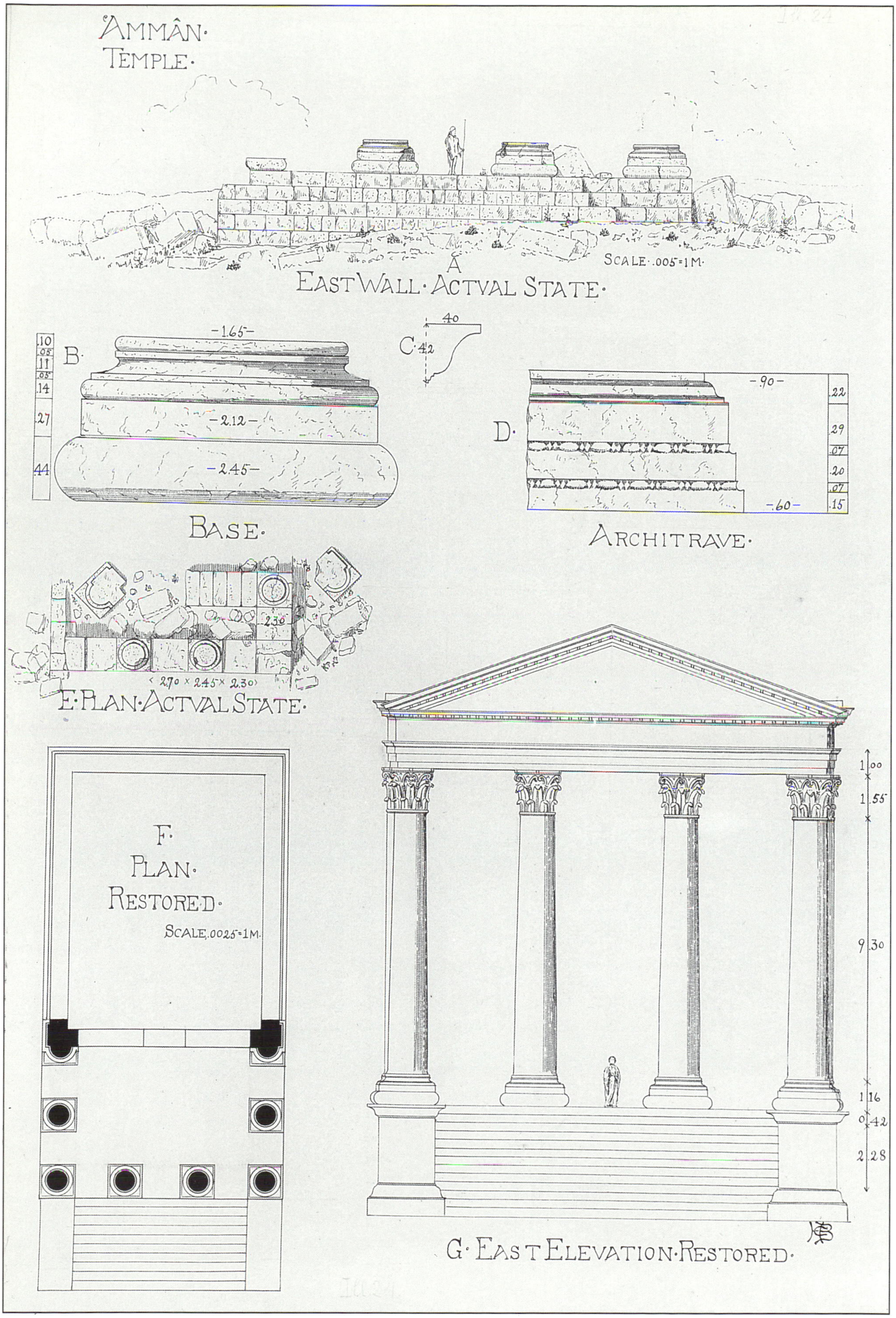

110. Butler's drawings of the Temple of Hercules (after Butler 1913–19, ill.24).

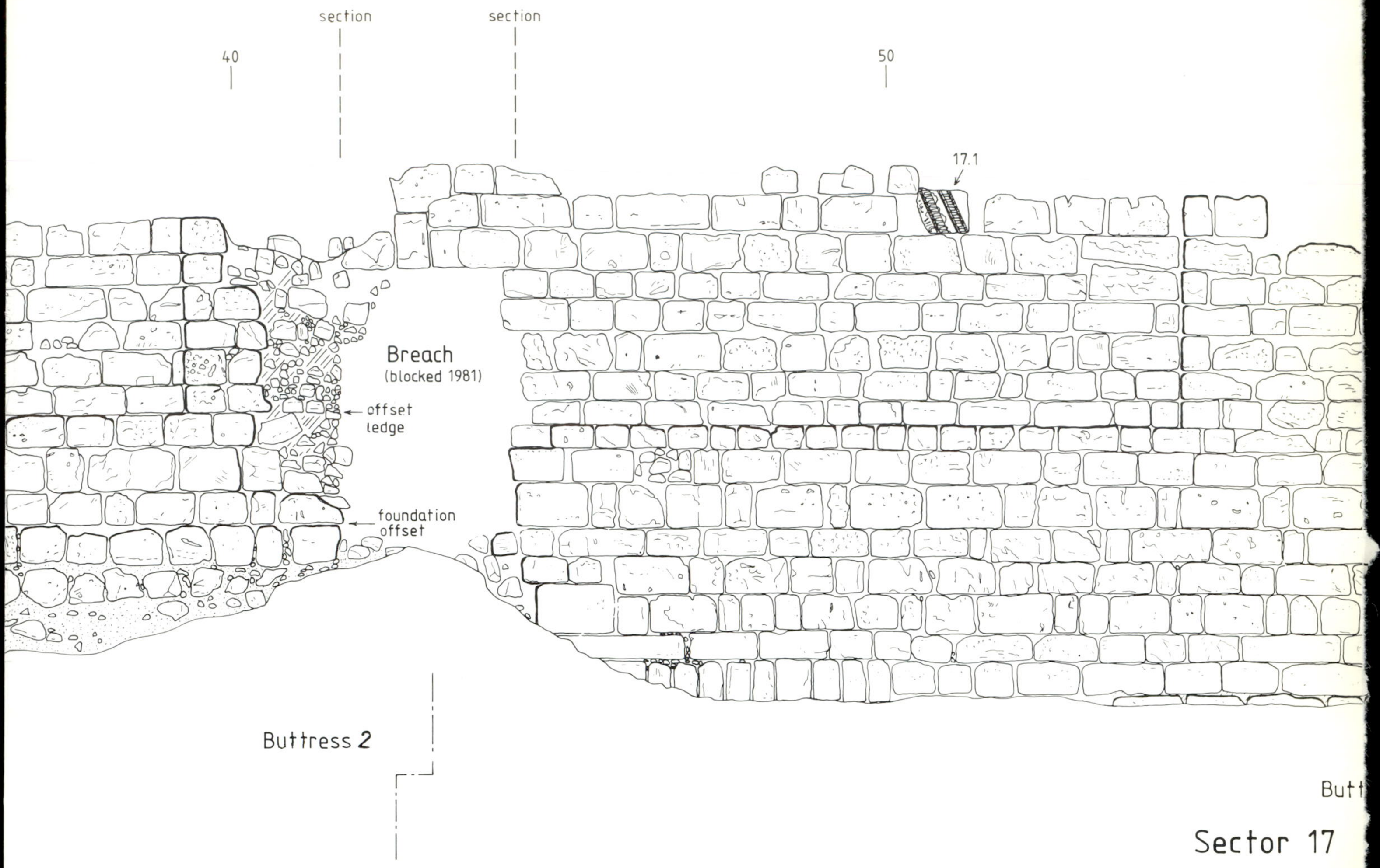

Sector 17

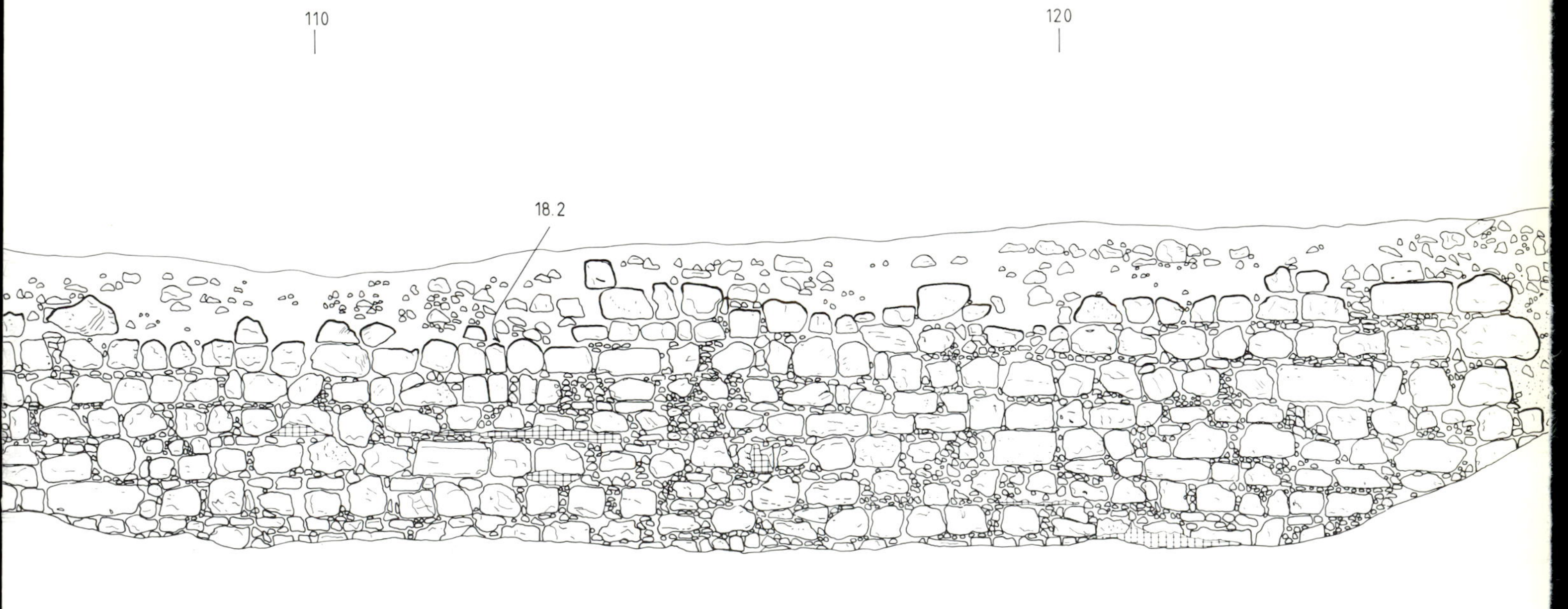

18c

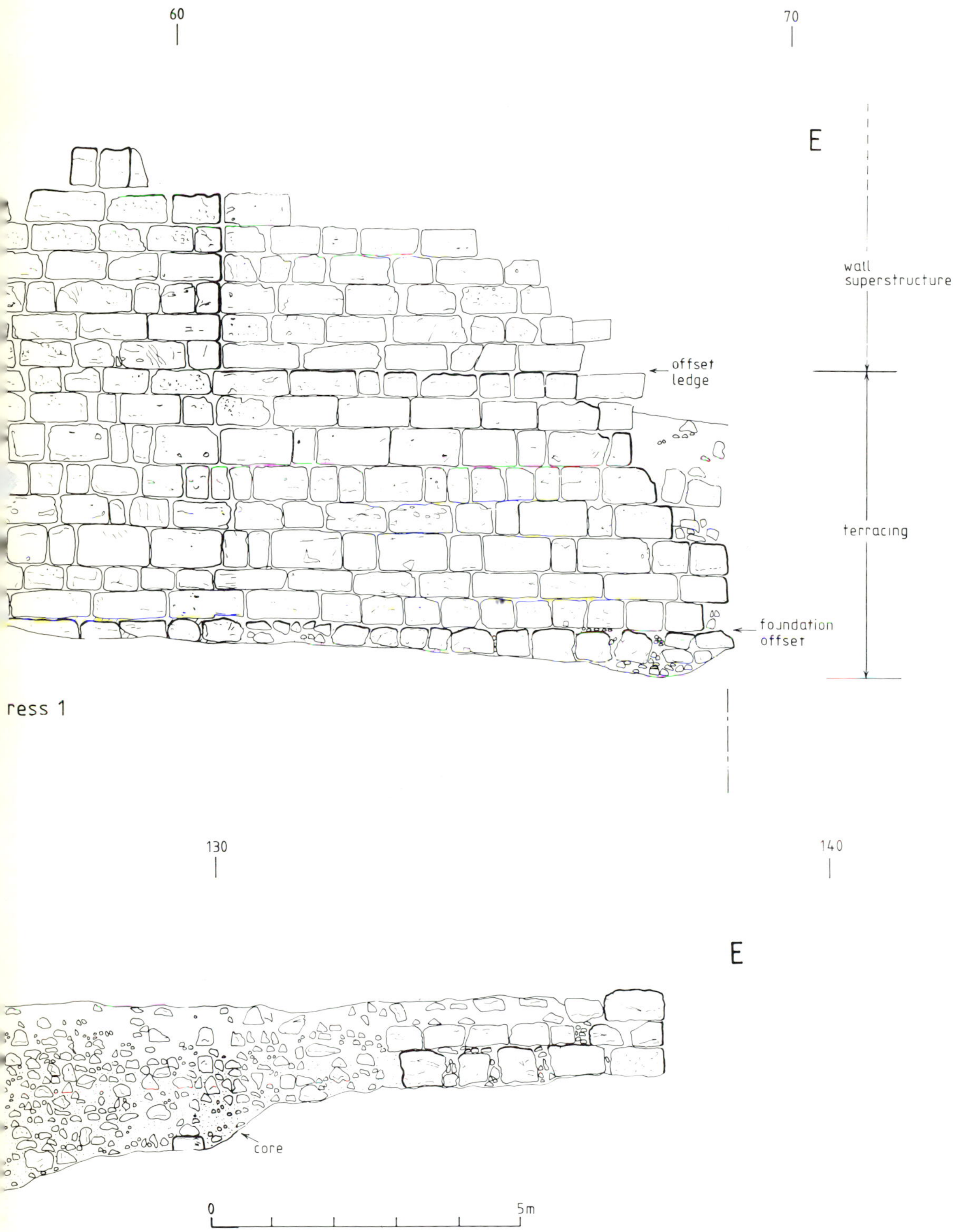
60
70
E
wall
superstructure
offset
ledge
terracing
foundation
offset
ress 1
130
140
E
core
0
5m

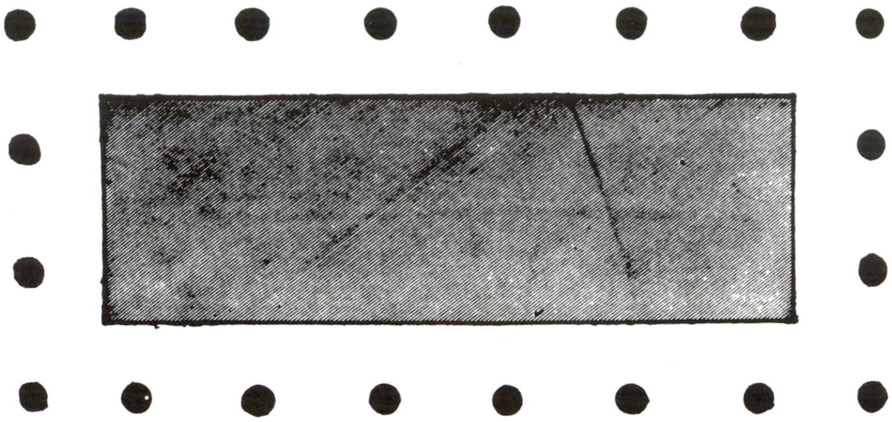

108. Merrill's restored plan of the Temple of Hercules (after Merrill 1882, p.264).

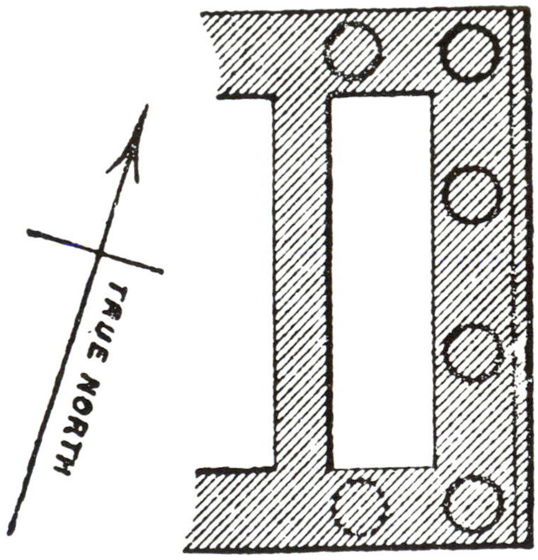

109. Conder's plan of the Temple of Hercules (after Conder 1889, p. 32).

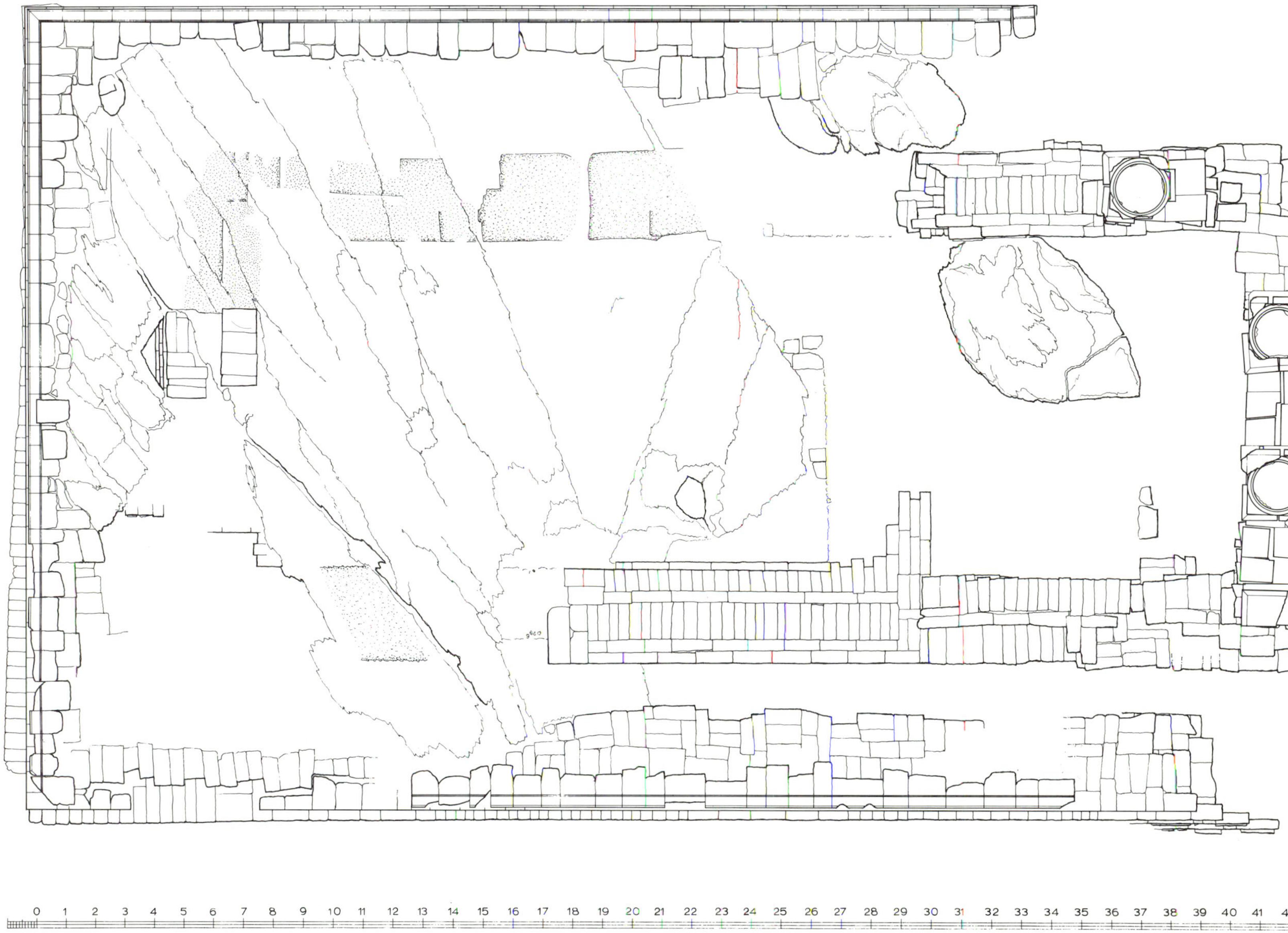
0 1 2 3 4 5 6 7 8 9 10 11 12 13 14 15 16 17 18 19 20 21 22 23 24 25 26 27 28 29 30 31 32 33 34 35 36 37 38 39 40 41 42 43 44
Only exposed in situ masonry and rock are shown. Leveling of the rock for foundations is indicated by stippling.
Richard Brotherton 1981

111. Plan of the Temple of Hercules (Brotherton).

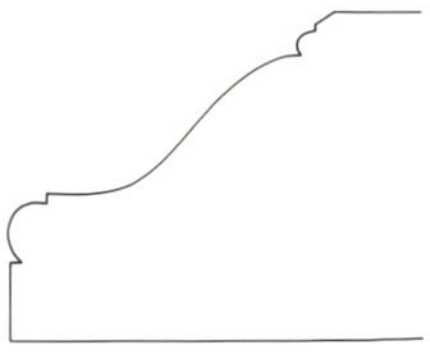

112. Podium base moulding from the Temple of Hercules (Mackenzie) (1:20).

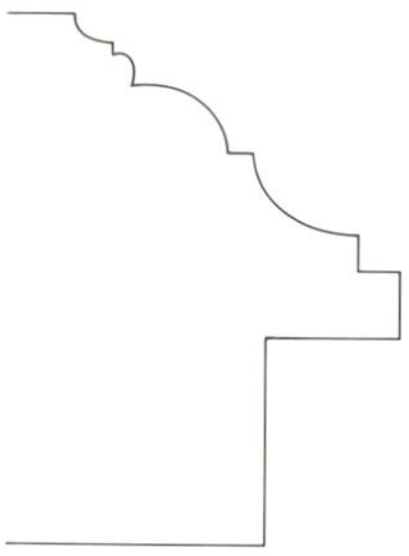

113. Podium cap moulding from the Temple of Hercules (Mackenzie) (1:20).

114. Column base and plinth from the Temple of Hercules (Mackenzie) (1:20).

115. Capital from the Temple of Hercules (Mackenzie) (1:20).

116. Architrave from the Temple of Hercules (Mackenzie) (1:20).

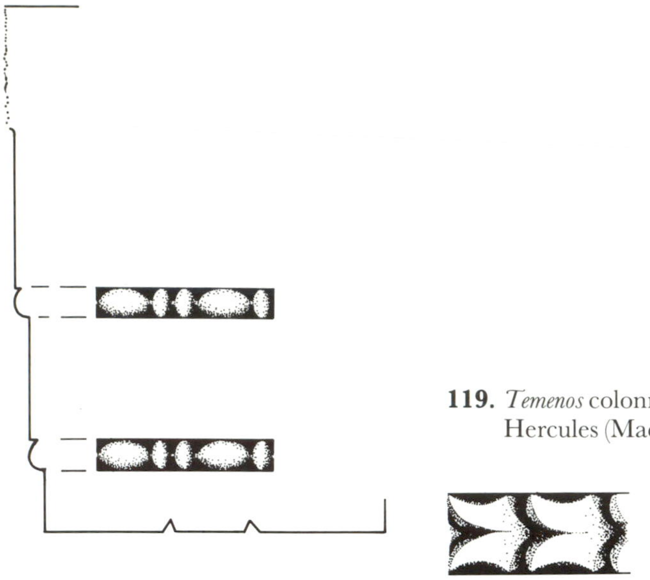

119. *Temenos* colonnade architrave from the Temple of Hercules (Mackenzie) (1:10).

118. *Temenos* colonnade capital from the Temple of Hercules (Mackenzie) (1:10).

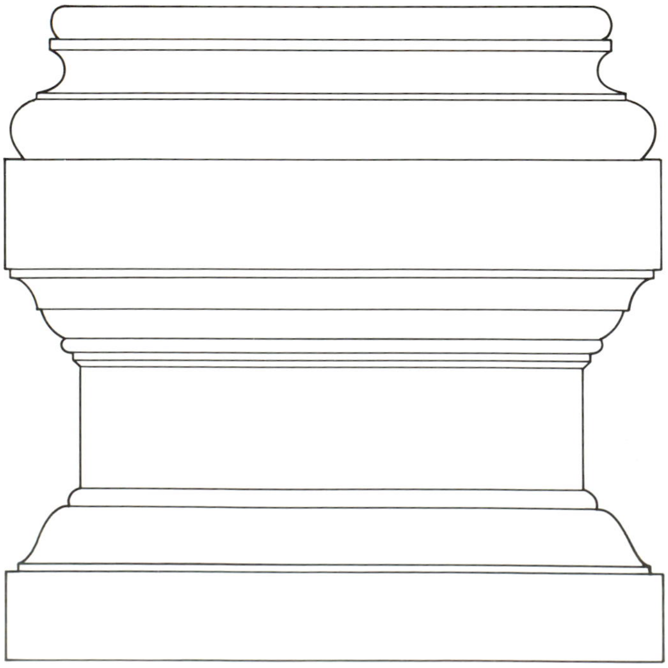

117. *Temenos* colonnade column base and plinth from the Temple of Hercules (Mackenzie) (1:10).

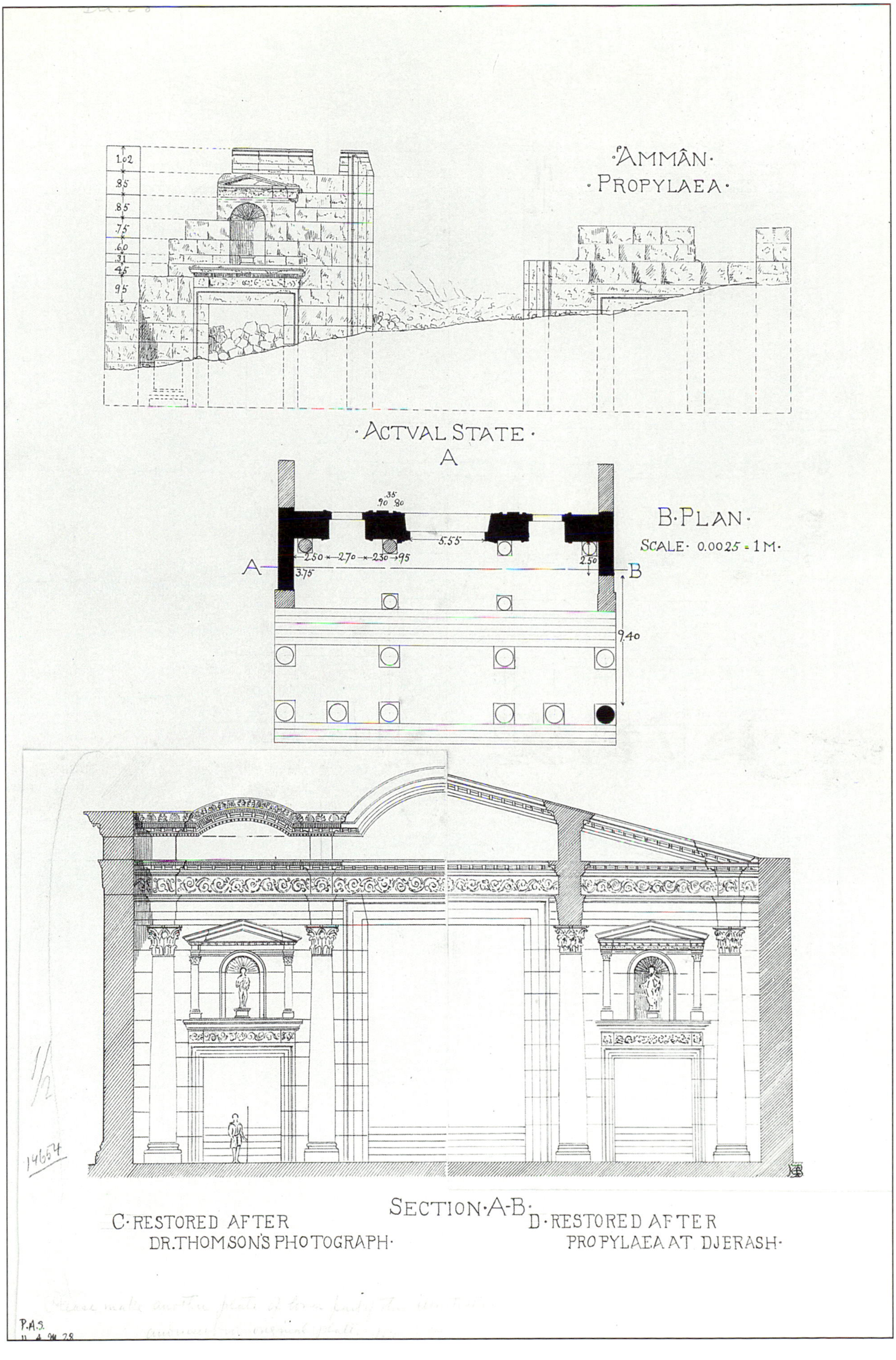

120. The Propylaeon (after Butler 1913–19, ill. 28).

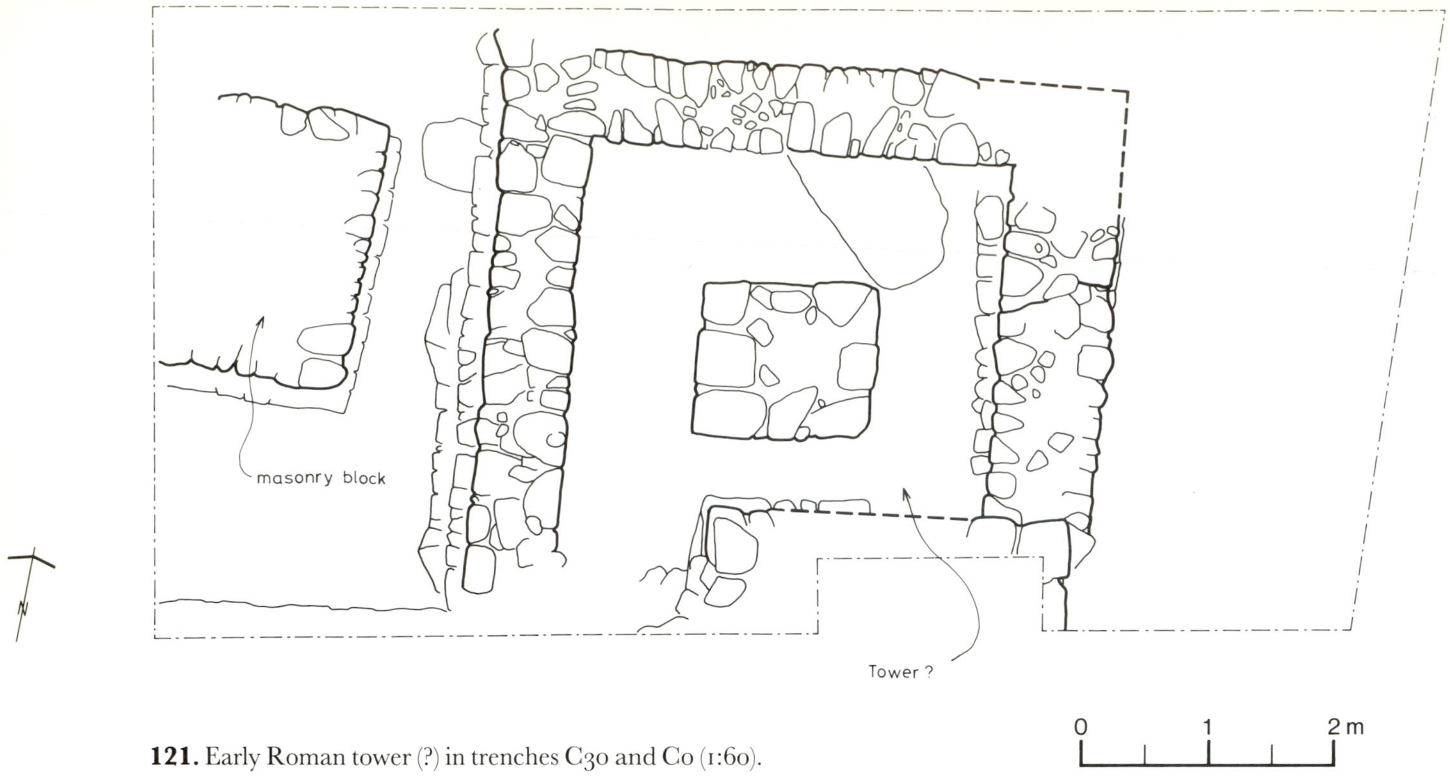

121. Early Roman tower (?) in trenches C30 and C0 (1:60).

122. Plan of Stratum VIII Byzantine building outside the fortification wall in trench C10 (1:60).

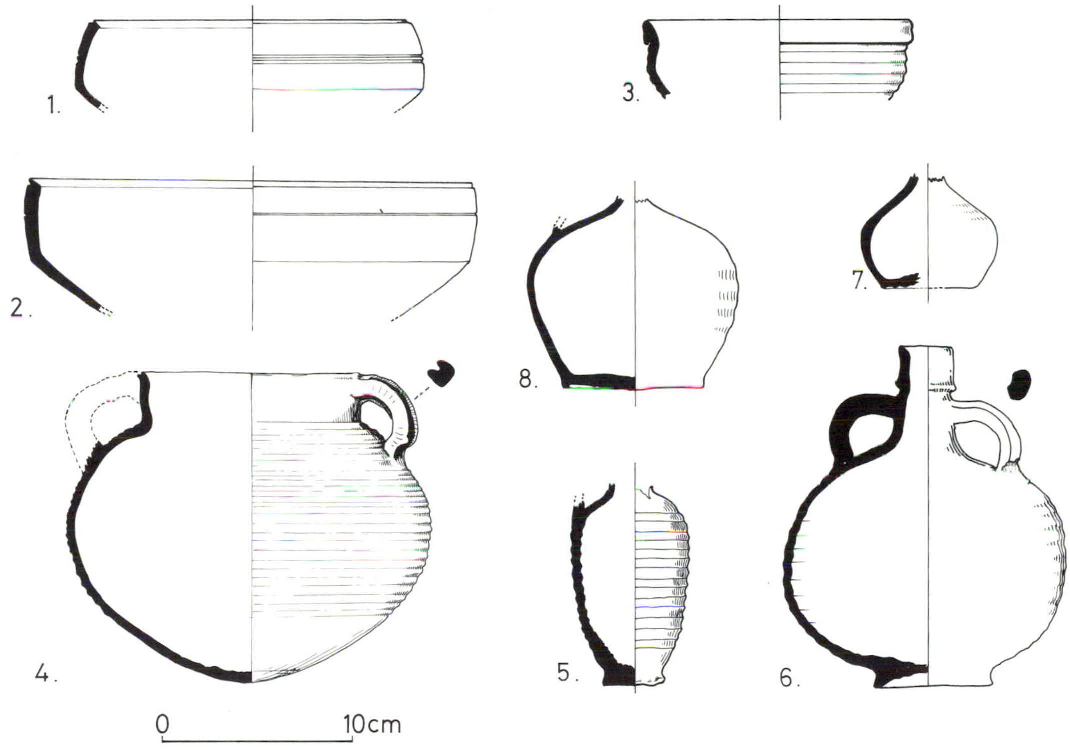

123. Early Byzantine pottery from destruction of building outside the fortification wall (1:4).

No. Reg. Deposit
1. 947 C10.2.8
Bowl, red ware and surface, line incised at rim, and two lines incised at waist.

2. 932 C10.2.8
Bowl with vertical lip, lines incised at rim and waist. Red ware and surface.

3. 946 C10.2.8
Bowl with folded rim and ribbed exterior. 2.5YR 5/6 red – 7.5YR 6/4 light brown.

4. 720 C0.1.17
Two-handled cooking pot with ribbed body; sand temper. 2.5YR 6/6 light red with burning on base.

5. 948 C10.2.8
Small bottle with trace of single handle and ribbed exterior; missing handle neck and rim. 2.5YR 5/6 red – 10YR 6/3 pale brown. Inclusions of lime and sand.

6. 873 C10.2.8
Globular bottle, two handles, ring base. Red ware with greyish patches.

7. 945 C10.2.8
Small bottle with rounded body, flat base. Neck and handle missing. 5YR 6/4 light reddish brown.

8. 944 C10.2.8
Small bottle with rounded body, flat base, and single handle. Neck and handle missing. Exterior 5YR 6/4 light reddish brown, black core. Inclusions: fine lime, sand and basalt.

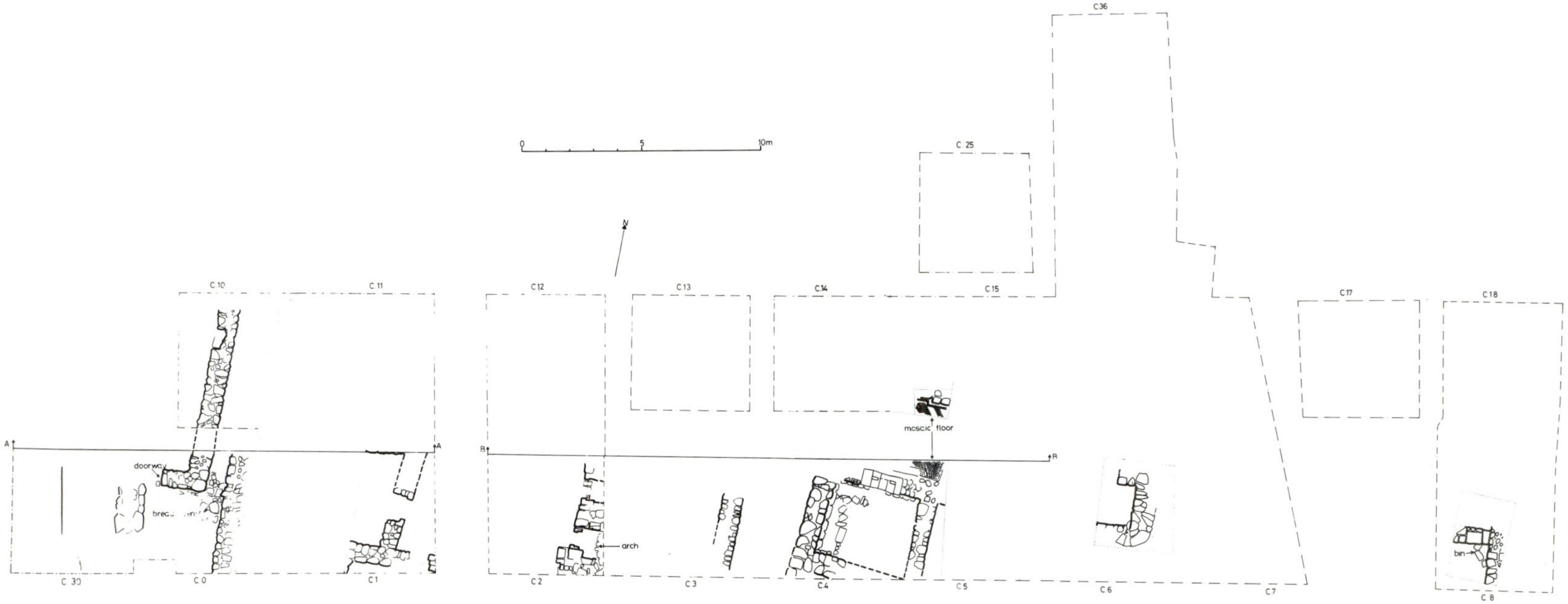

124. Remains of Stratum VII–VIII (Byzantine–Early Umayyad) in Area C (1:250).

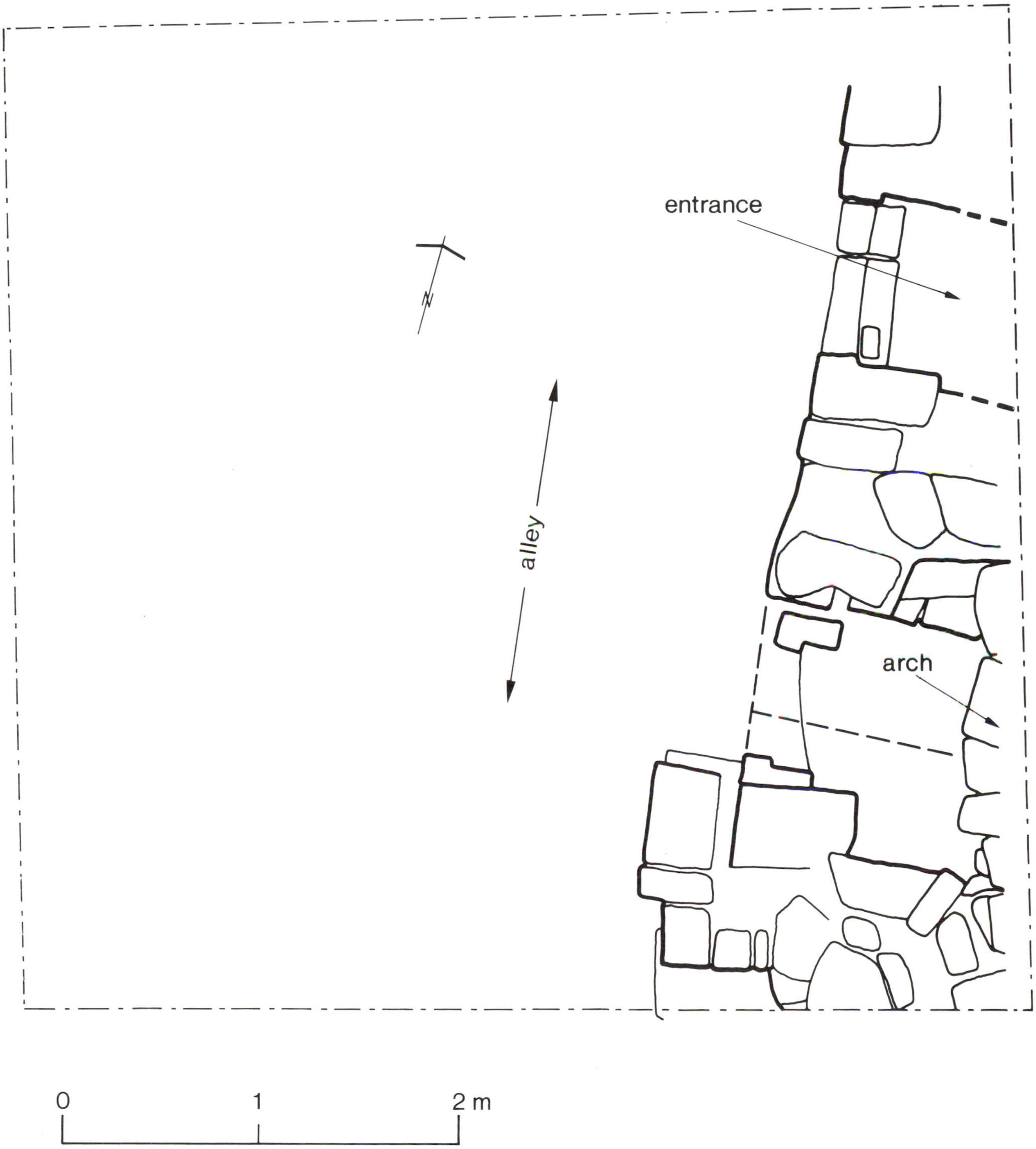

125. Plan of Byzantine Building (b) in trench C2 (1:30).

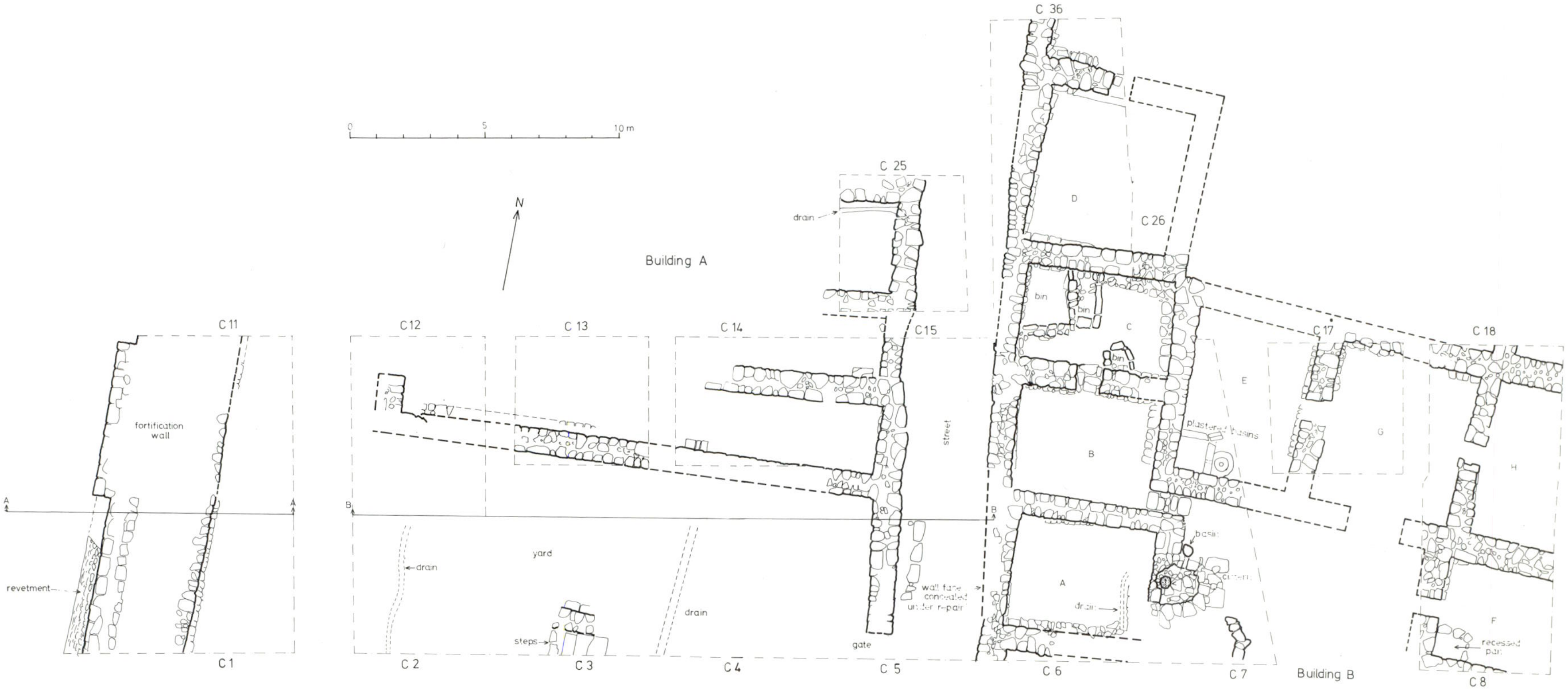

126. Remains of Stratum V (Umayyad Citadel) in Area C (1:250).

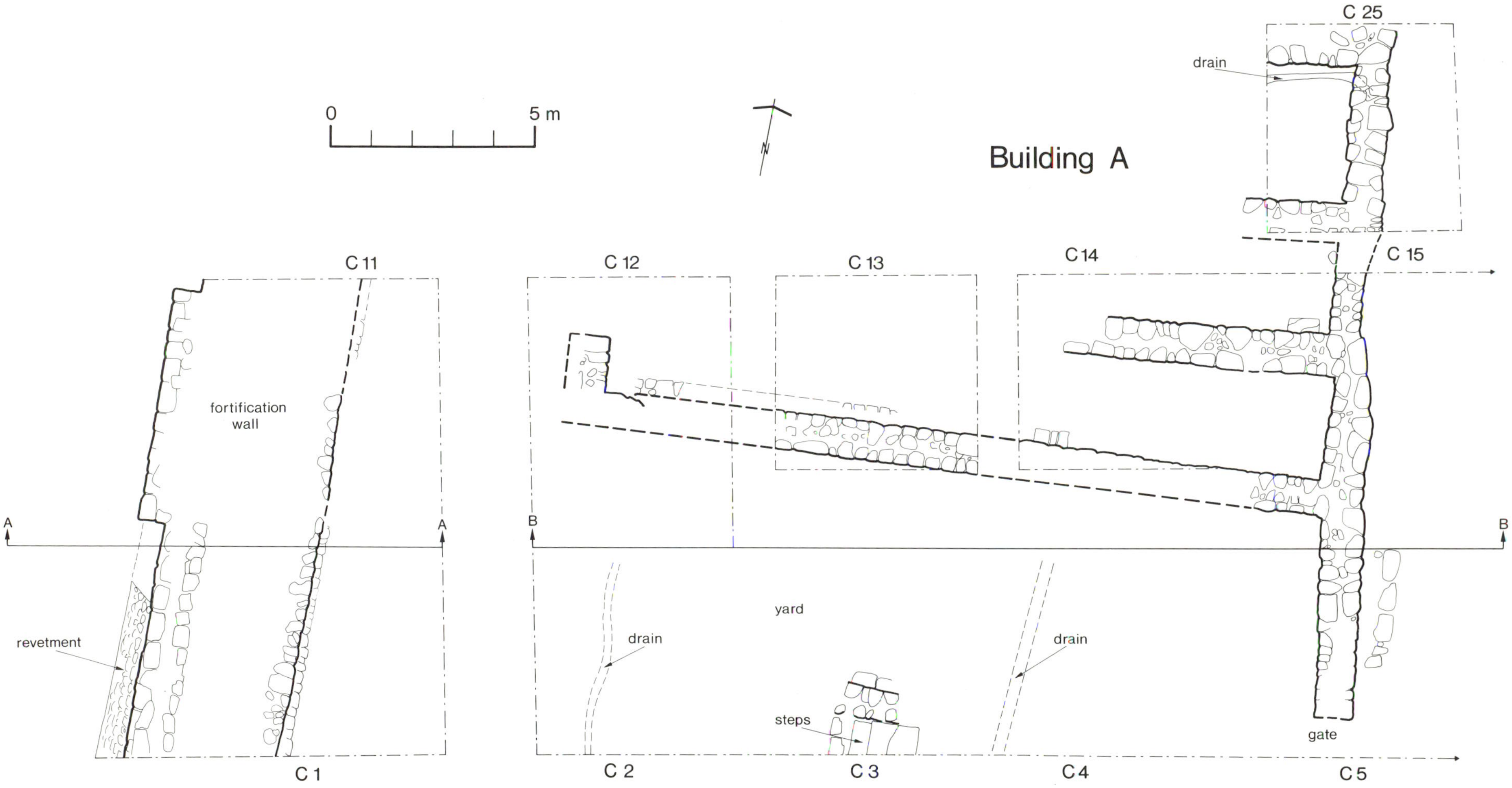

127. Plan of remains of Umayyad Citadel Building A in Area C (1:150).

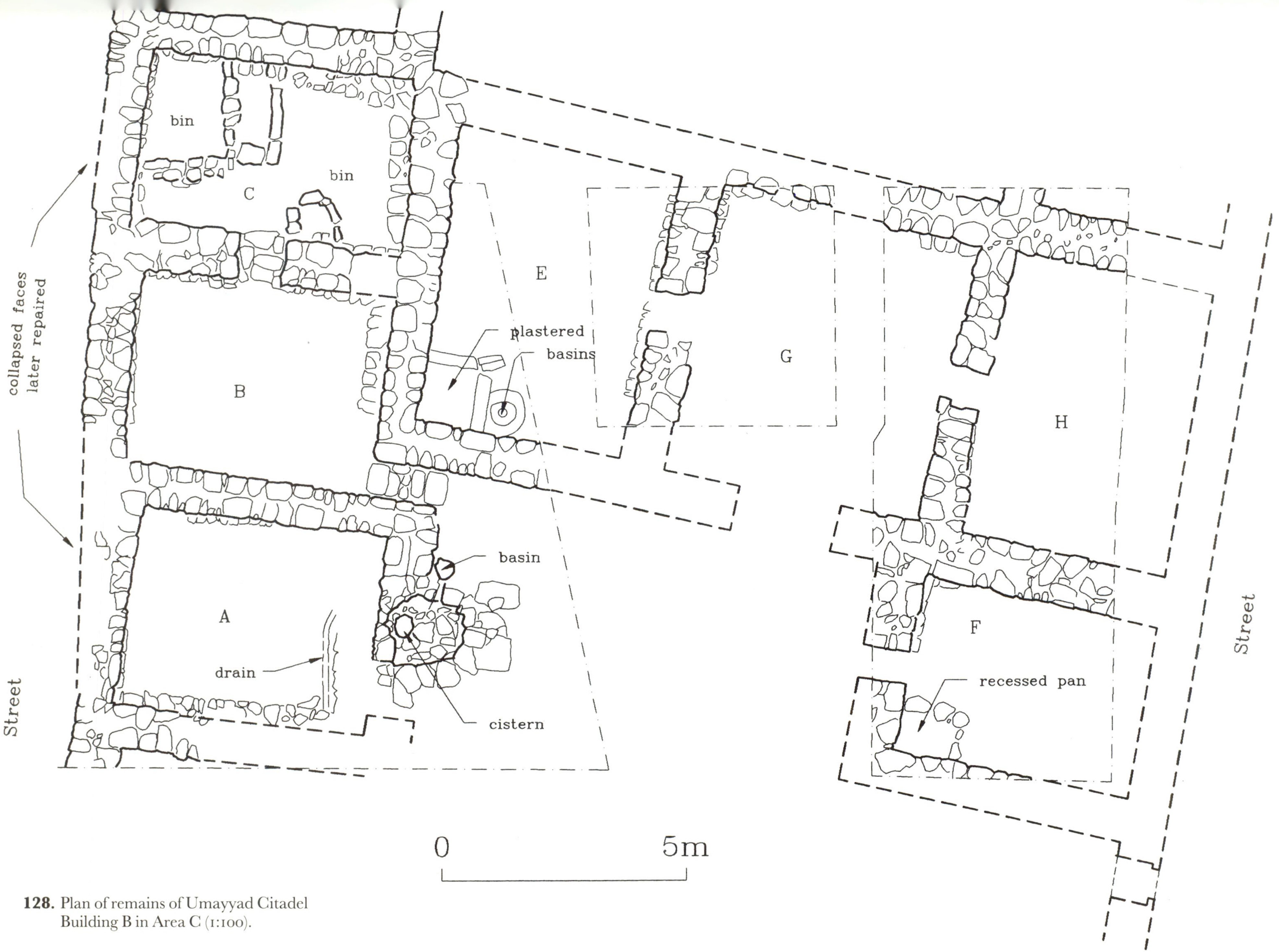

128. Plan of remains of Umayyad Citadel Building B in Area C (1:100).

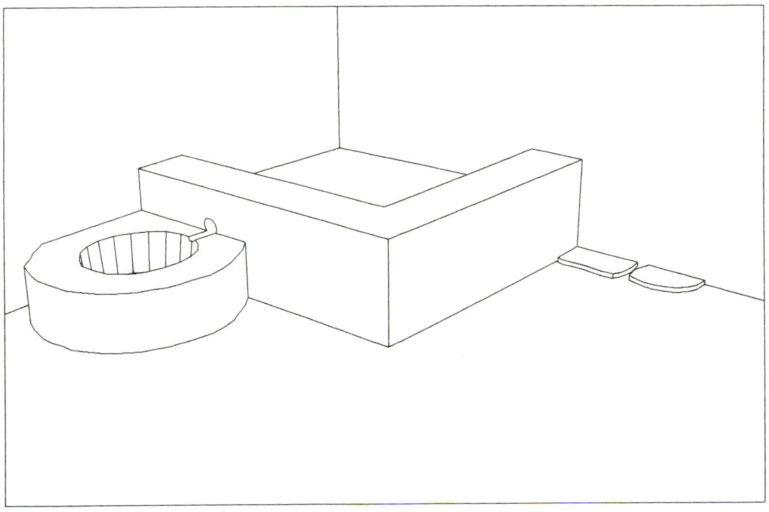

129. Perspective reconstruction of basins in Umayyad Citadel Building B.

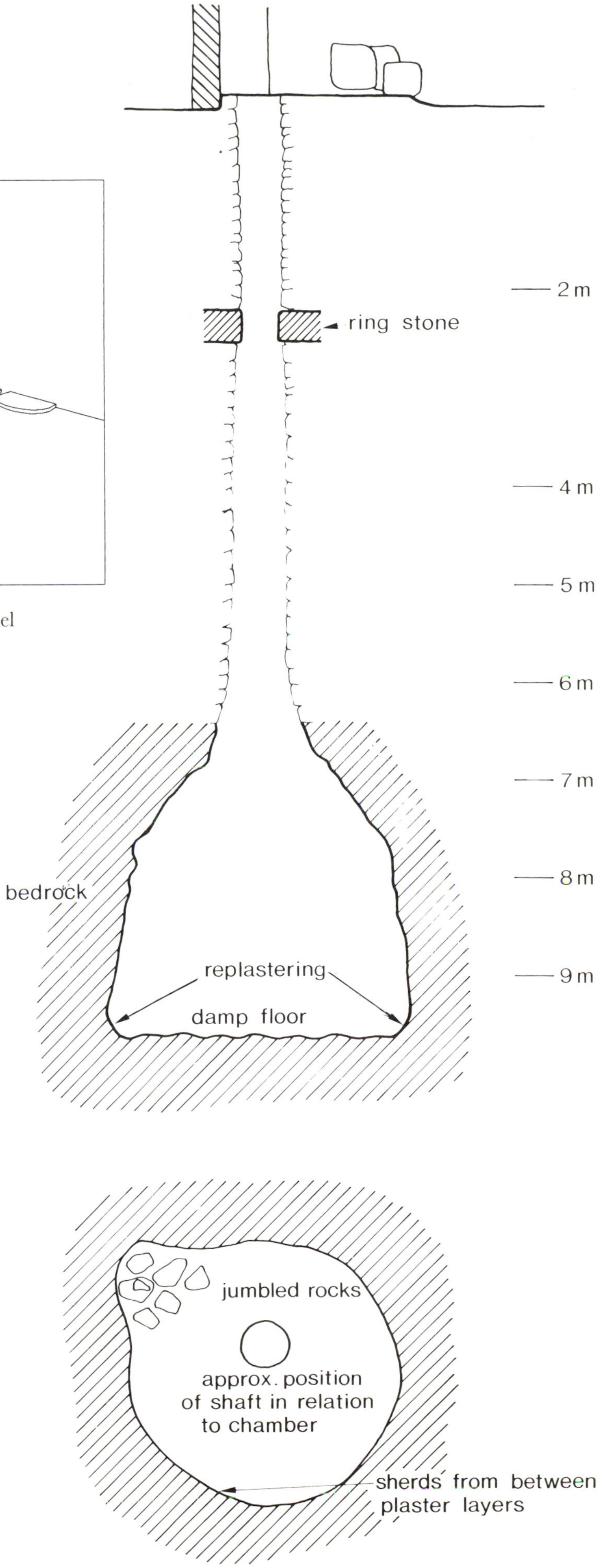

130. Cross-section of cistern in Umayyad Citadel Building B.

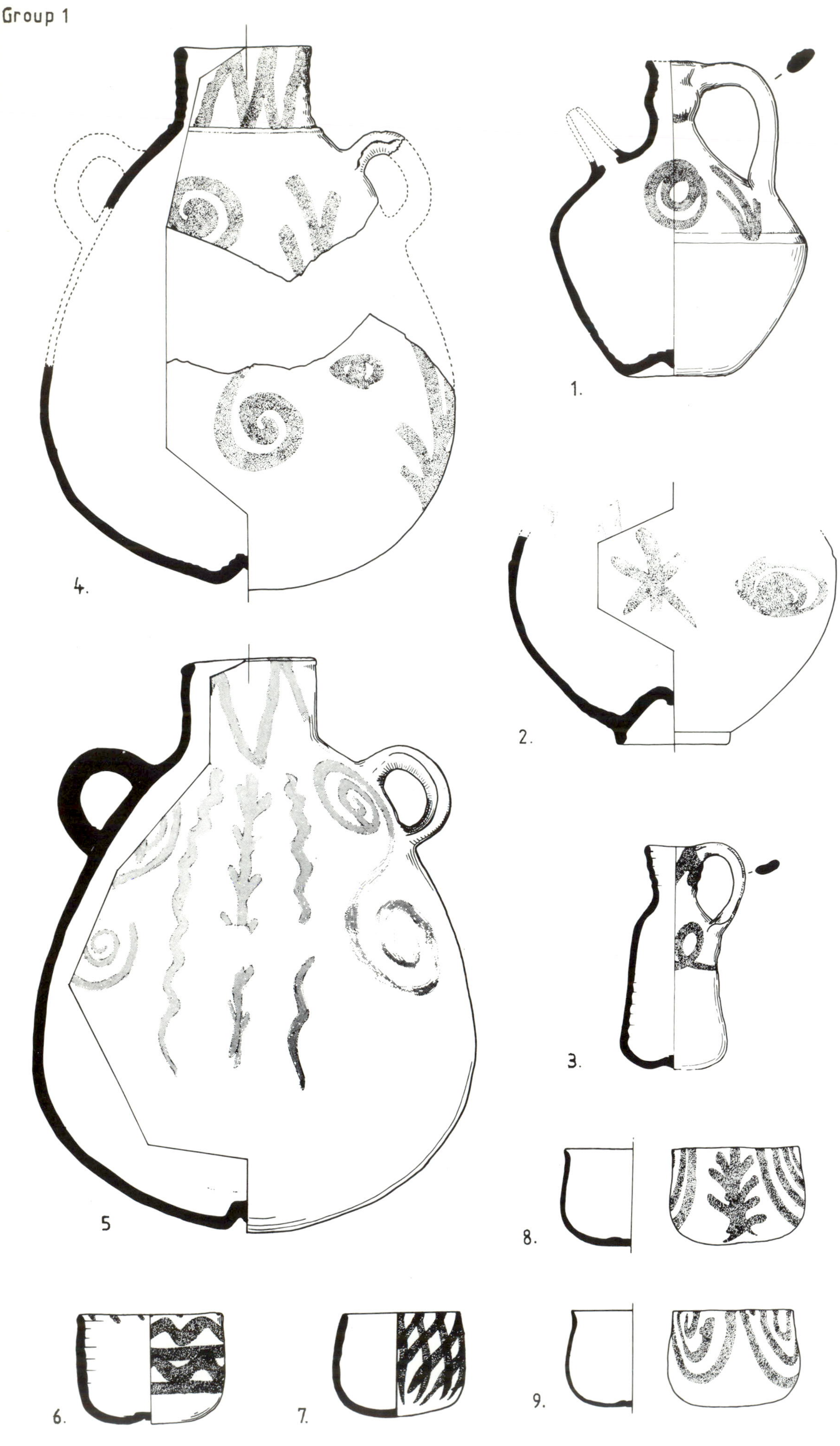

131. Umayyad pottery from the earthquake destruction o Building B (1:4).

No. Reg. Deposit

1. 719 C8.1.5
Spouted jar, intact except for handle rim and spout; 1 hand painted decoration of whorls and sprigs; 5Y 8/3 pale yellov 5YR 7/4 pink. Pnt.: 10R 4/6

2. 77/6 C6.1.9
Part of vessel with ring base recessed in centre. Form probably a 2-handled pot, cf. Harding (1951a), no.39. Painted pattern of stars and whorls. 10YR 7/4 pale browr 2.5YR 5/6 red; Pnt.: 10R 3/4 dark red.

3. 817 C6/16B.4
Jar, intact. 1 handle, painted decoration of zigzags and spi 5Y 8/2 white/2.5YR 6/6 ligh Pnt.: 10R 4/6 red.

4. 835 C6/16B.5
Bag jar, broken, incomplete; Straight vertical rim, pronounced collar on neck; painted decoration of whorls sprigs and zigzags. 10YR 8/3 pale brown/2.5YR 6/6 light red. Pnt.: 10R 3/4 dusky red.

5. 722 C8.1.5
Bag jar, broken, incomplete; painted design of whorls, spri and zigzags; 5Y 8/2 white/ 10YR 7/3 v. pale brown, pnt. 10R 3/4 dark red.

6. 828 C16.4.9
Cup, broken, complete; pain decoration of spots on rim, horizontal straight and wavy 10R 3/6 red over slip or wash 5Y 8/2 pale yellow. Ware: 10

7. 715 C8.1.5
Cup, broken, complete; painted decoration of cross-hatching 10R 3/6 dark red. Ware: 5Y 8/2 white/7.5YR 6/4 light brown.

8. 831 C6/16B.4
Cup, broken, complete; painted decoration of concentric semicircles and sprigs 10R 3/4 dark red; 5Y 8/2 white/2.5YR 6/6 light red.

9. 832 C6/16B.5
Cup, broken, complete; painted decoration of concentric semicircles 10R 3/4 dark red. Ware: 2.5YR 6/6 light red.

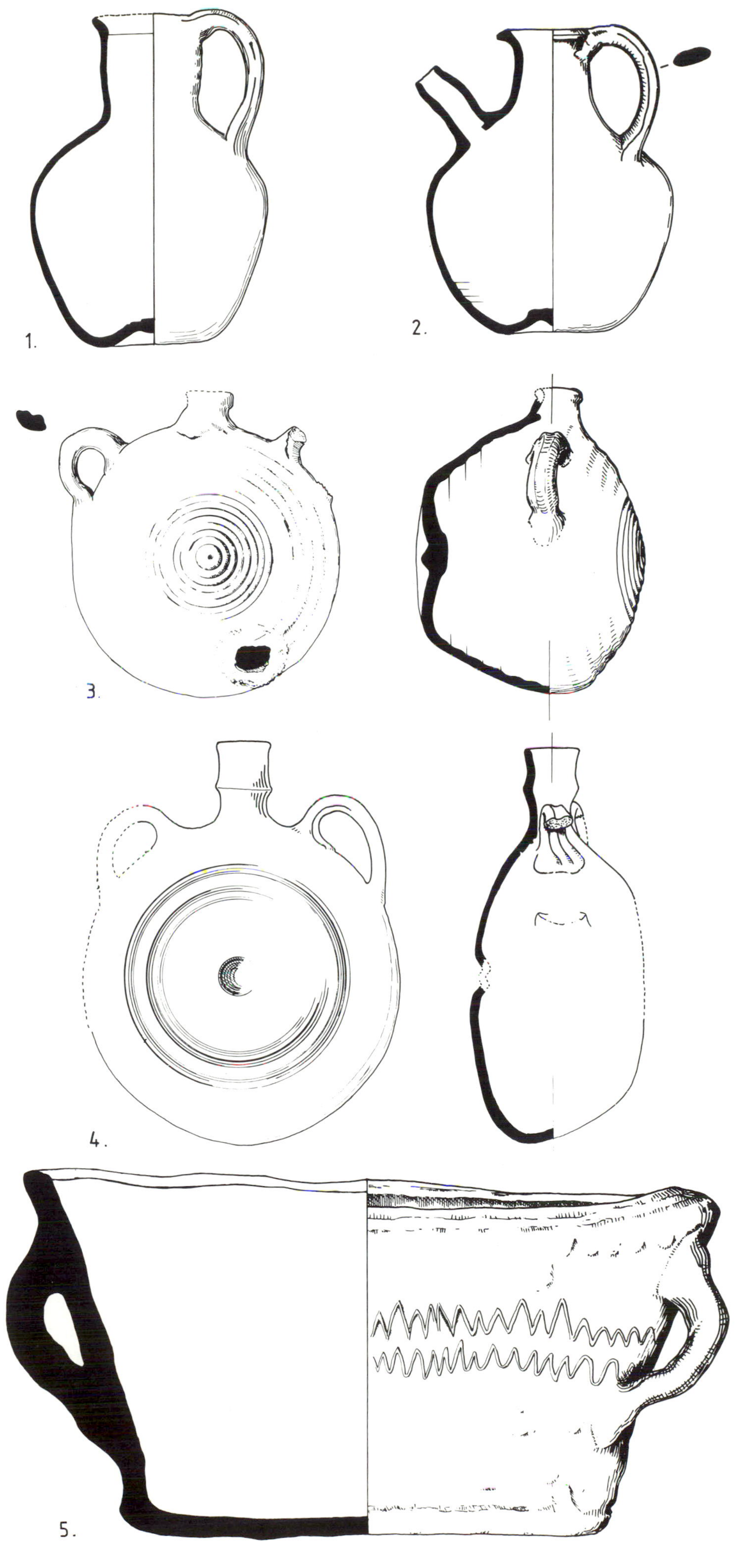

132. Umayyad pottery from the earthquake destruction of Building B (1:4).

No. Reg. Deposit

1. 714 C8.1.5
Jug, intact exc.rim. 2.5Y 8/2 white/7.5YR 6/4 light brown.

2. 829 C6/16B.4
Spouted jar, broken, complete. 5Y 8/2 pale yellow/2.5YR 6/6 light red.

3. 721 C8.1.5
Pilgrim Xask, intact, exc. rim and handle, ancient hole in base. 2 handles, base on side. 5Y 8/3 pale yellow/7.5YR 6/4 pale brown.

4. 870 C16.1.9
Pilgrim Xask, 2 handles, broken, incomplete. 10YR 7/3 v.pale brown /2.5YR 6/4 reddish brown.

5. 830 C16.1.9
Basin, coil-made. 2 handles irregularly placed; decoration of 2 incised wavy lines. Complete, broken. 2.5Y 8/2 white/2.5YR 6/4 light reddish brown.

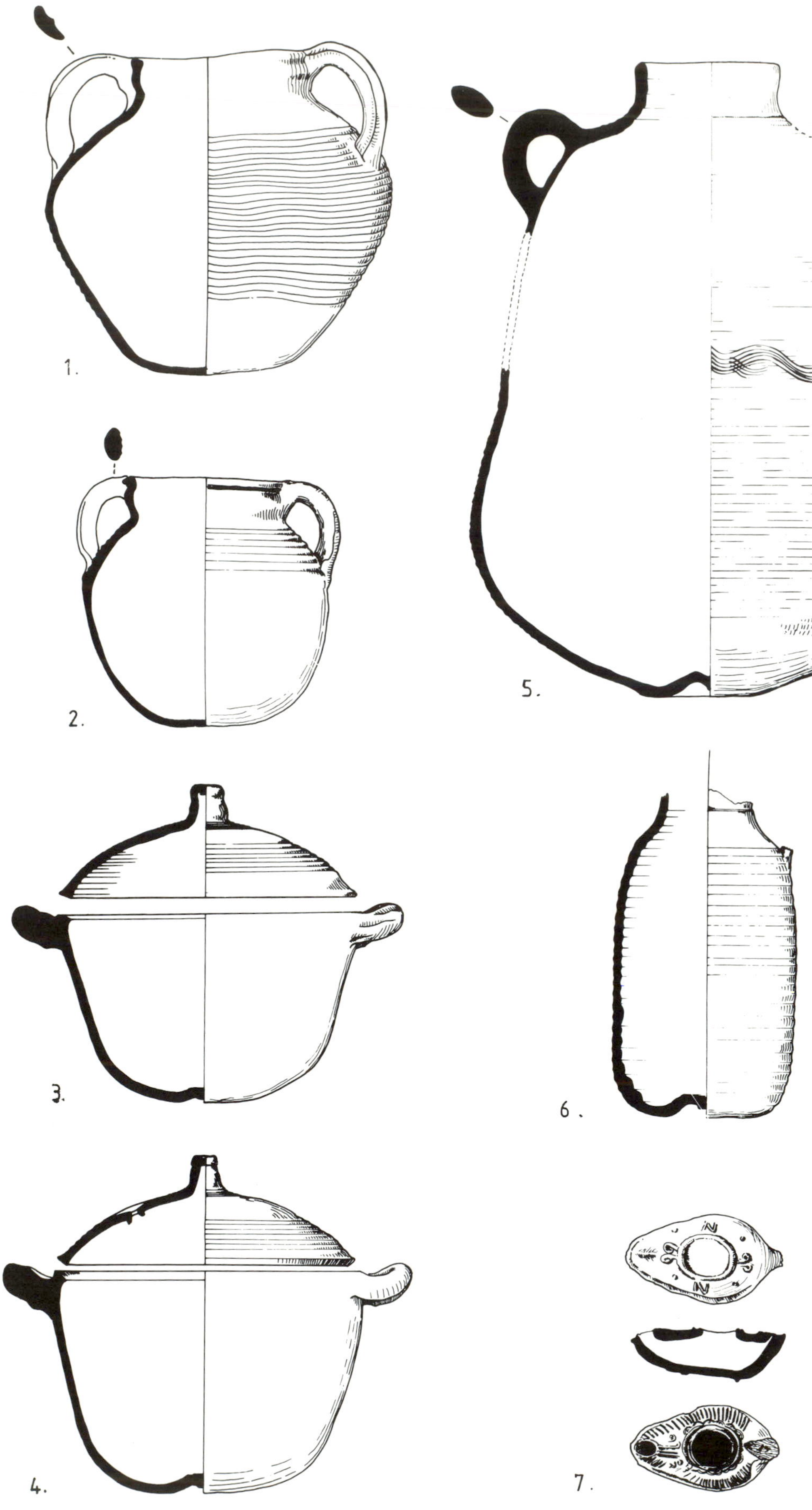

133. Umayyad pottery from the earthquake destruction of Building B (1:4).

No. Reg. Deposit

1. 840 C6/7B.4
2 handled cooking pot, broken, incomplete, ribbed exterior. N4 dark grey.

2. 713 C8.1.5
2 handled cooking pot, broken, nearly complete; light ribbing on shoulders. N4 dark grey/ 5YR 6/6 reddish yellow.

3. 718 C16.1.9
Lidded cooking pot, broken, complete. N4 dark grey.

4. 717 C8.1.5
Lidded cooking pot, broken, nearly complete. N4 dark grey.

5. 741 C6.1.9
Bag jar, broken, incomplete; 2 handles, plain vertical rim: ribbing and a band of wavy combing around waist. 10YR 8/4 v.pale brown/2.5YR 6/8 light red.

6. 716 C8.1.5
Jar, intact exc. handle and rim missing. 5YR 8/3 pale yellow/10R 6/8 light red.

7. 691 C16.1.10
Moulded lamp, handle missing: 2.5YR 5/6 red.

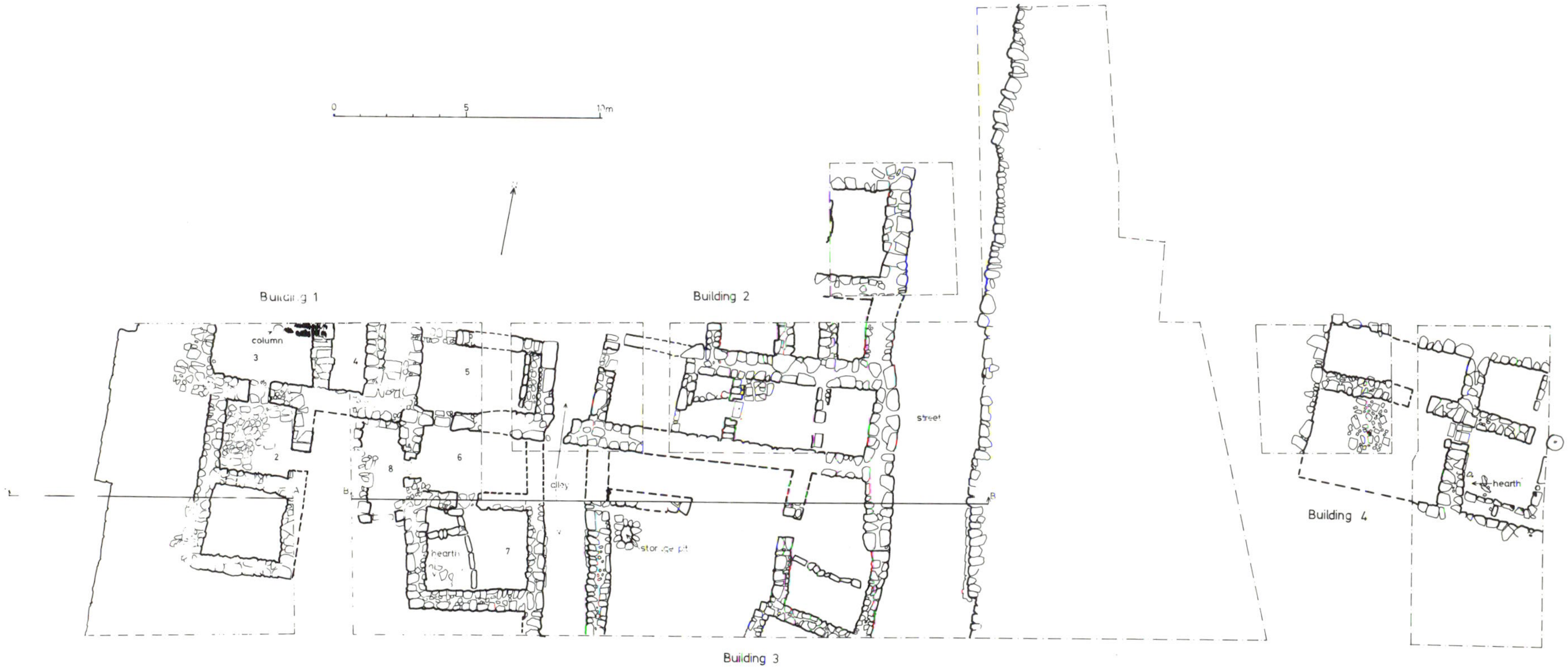

134. Plan of Stratum IVb–III (Abbasid–5th/11th Century) in Area C (1:250).

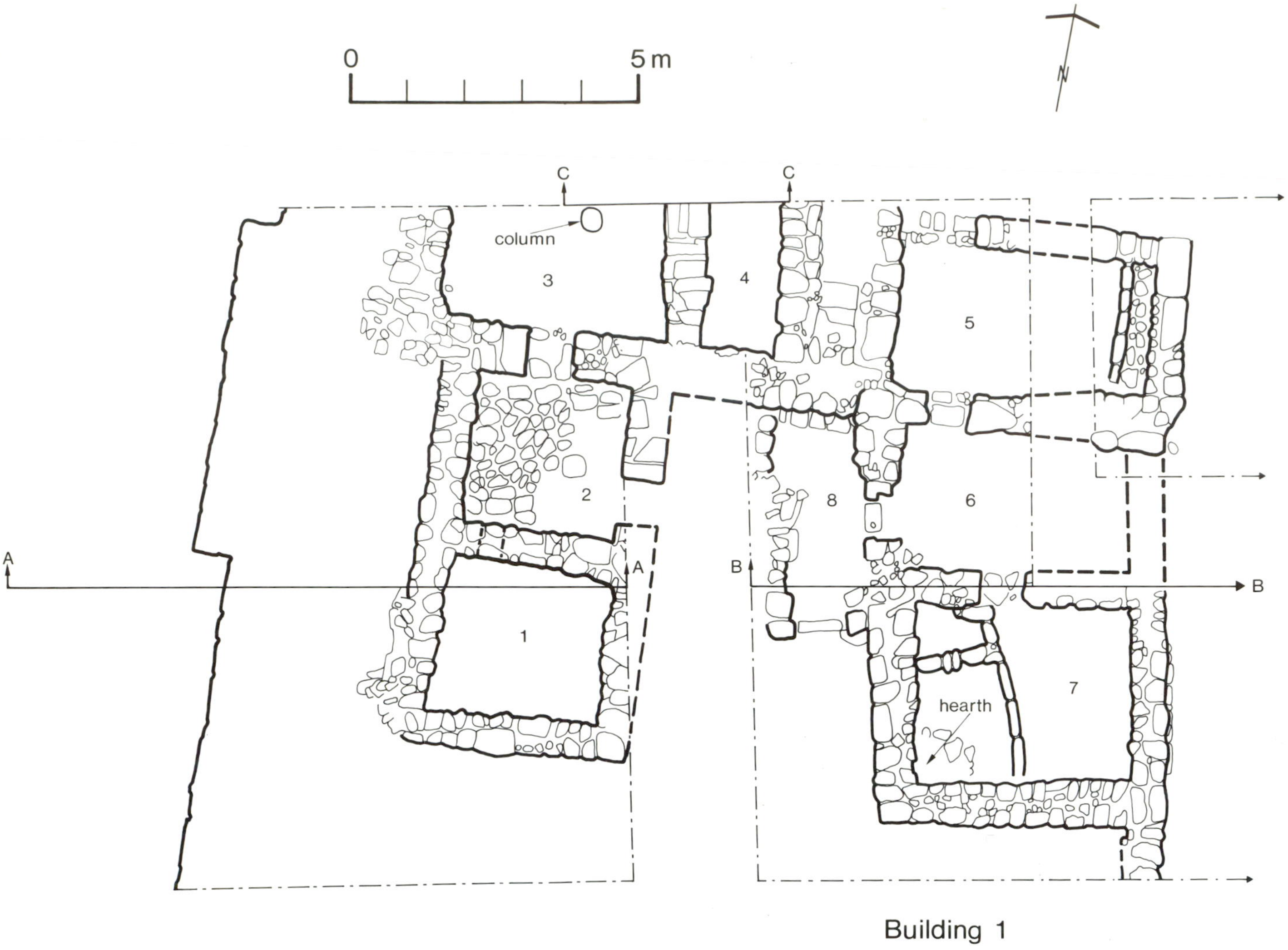

135. Plan of remains of Abbasid-Fatimid Building 1 (Strata IVb–III) in Area C (1:120).

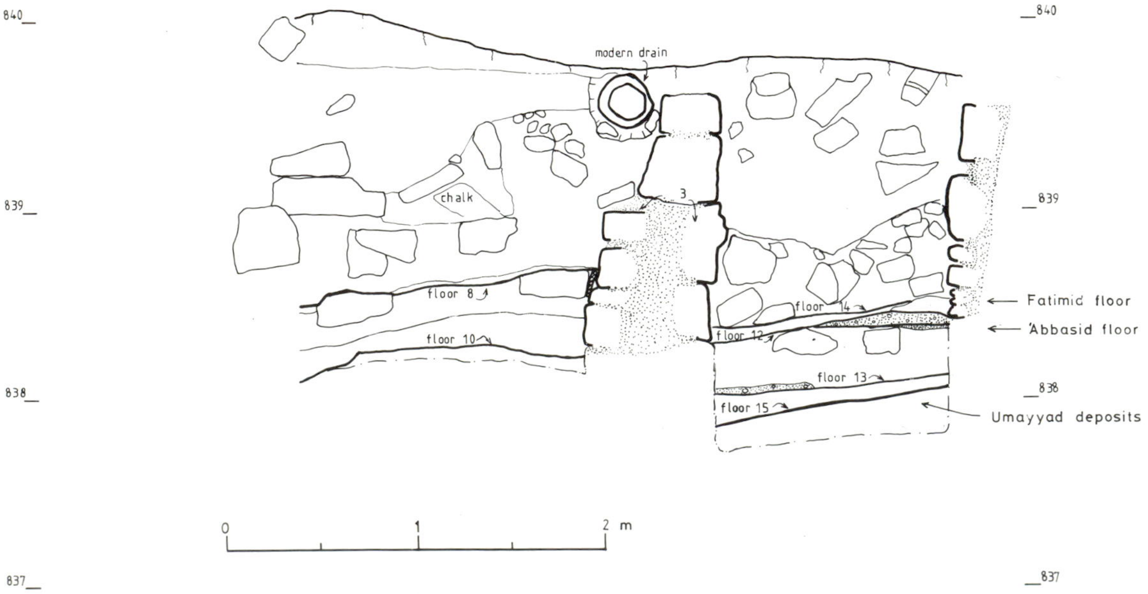

136. The sequence of floors in Abbasid-Fatimid Building 1 (C–C on figs. 124, 126 and 134)(1:40).

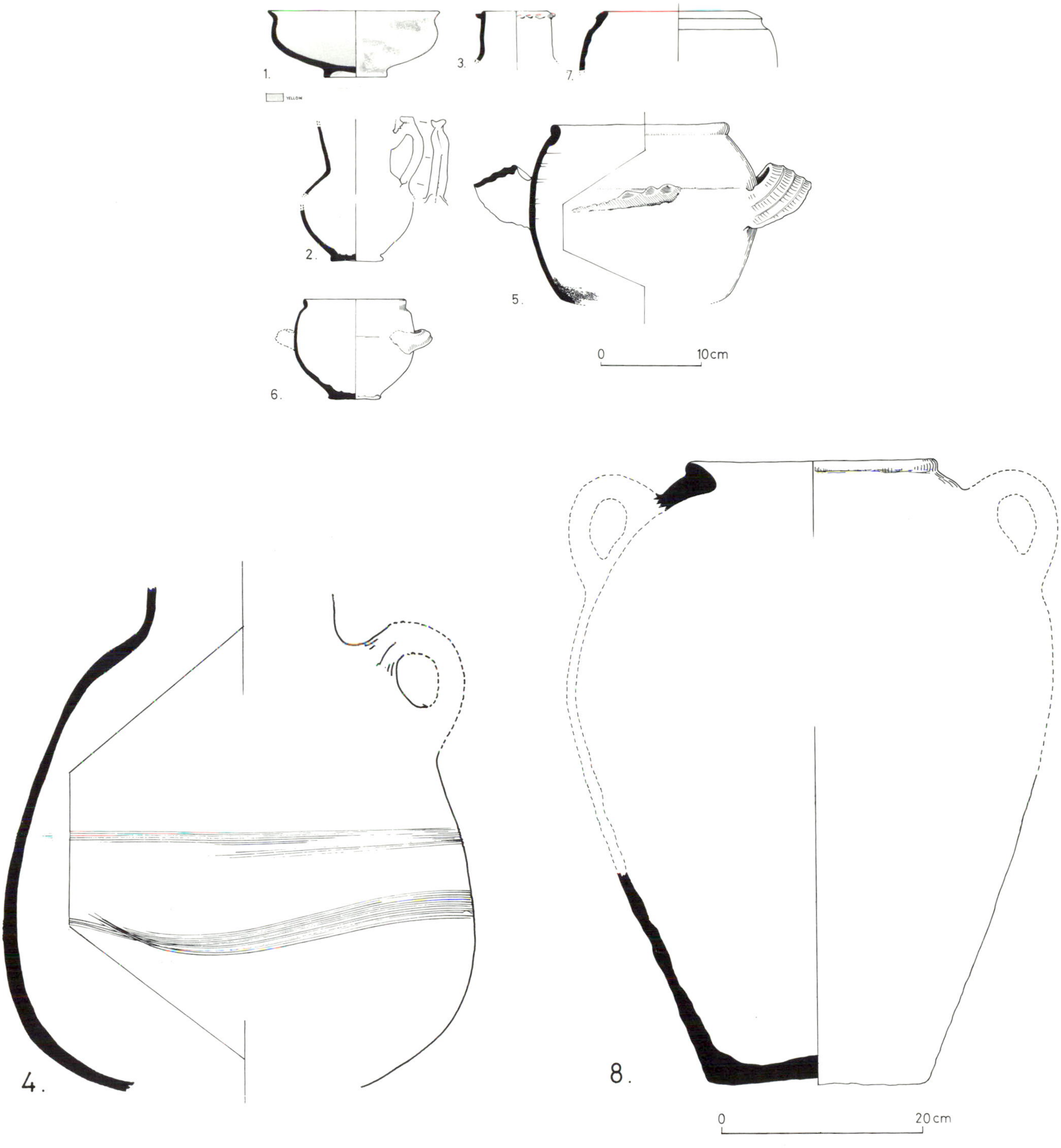

137. Pottery from the destruction of Abbasid-Fatimid Building 1 (1:6).

No. Reg. Deposit

1. 588 C12.1.1
Glazed bowl, complete, broken. Everted rim, ring base. 7.5YR 6/4 pink, white slip, yellow glaze on interior and part of exterior.

2. 76/175 C11.1.7
Jar, incomplete. Flaring rim and turban handle. 5Y 7/6 yellow.

3. 76/169 C11.1.7
Jar rim. Decoration of knife nicking. 7.5YR 7/6 reddish yellow.

4. 833 C11.1.7
Bag jar, incomplete. 1 extant handle, wavy line combing. 7.5YR 6/4 light brown.

5. 841 C11.1.7
Cooking pot, incomplete. 2 strap handles, 2 thumb-impressed lugs. 10R 4/4 red, brown glaze inside base.

6. 628 C11.1.7
Miniature cooking pot, incomplete. 2 horizontal handles. 10R 4/6 red, brown glaze inside base.

7. 77/5 C11.1.7 Cooking pot rim. 10R 4/4 red.

8. 834 C11.1.7 Storage jar, incomplete. 2 handles, 10YR 7/3 v.pale brown.

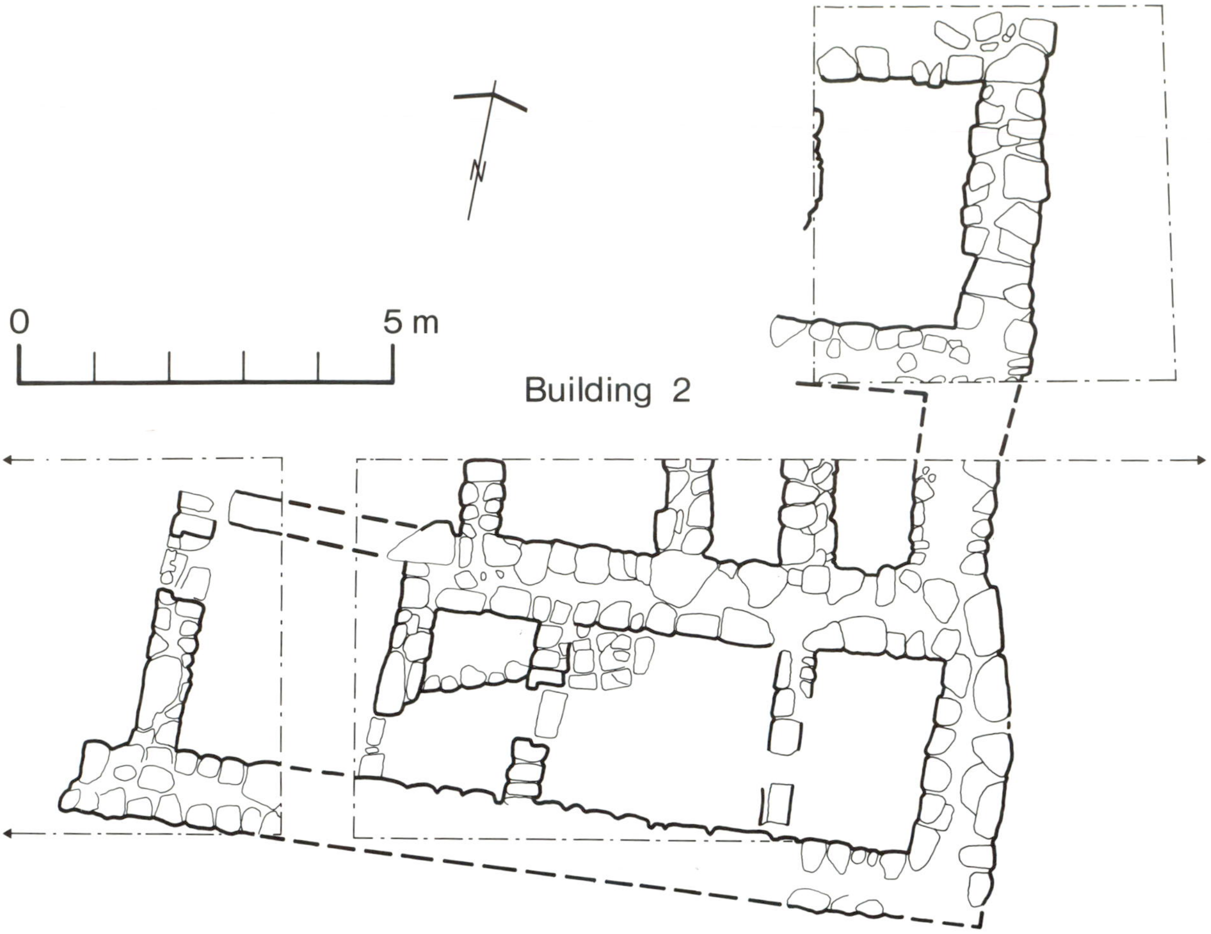

138. Plan of remains of Abbasid-Fatimid Building 2 (Strata IVb–III) in Area C (1:100).

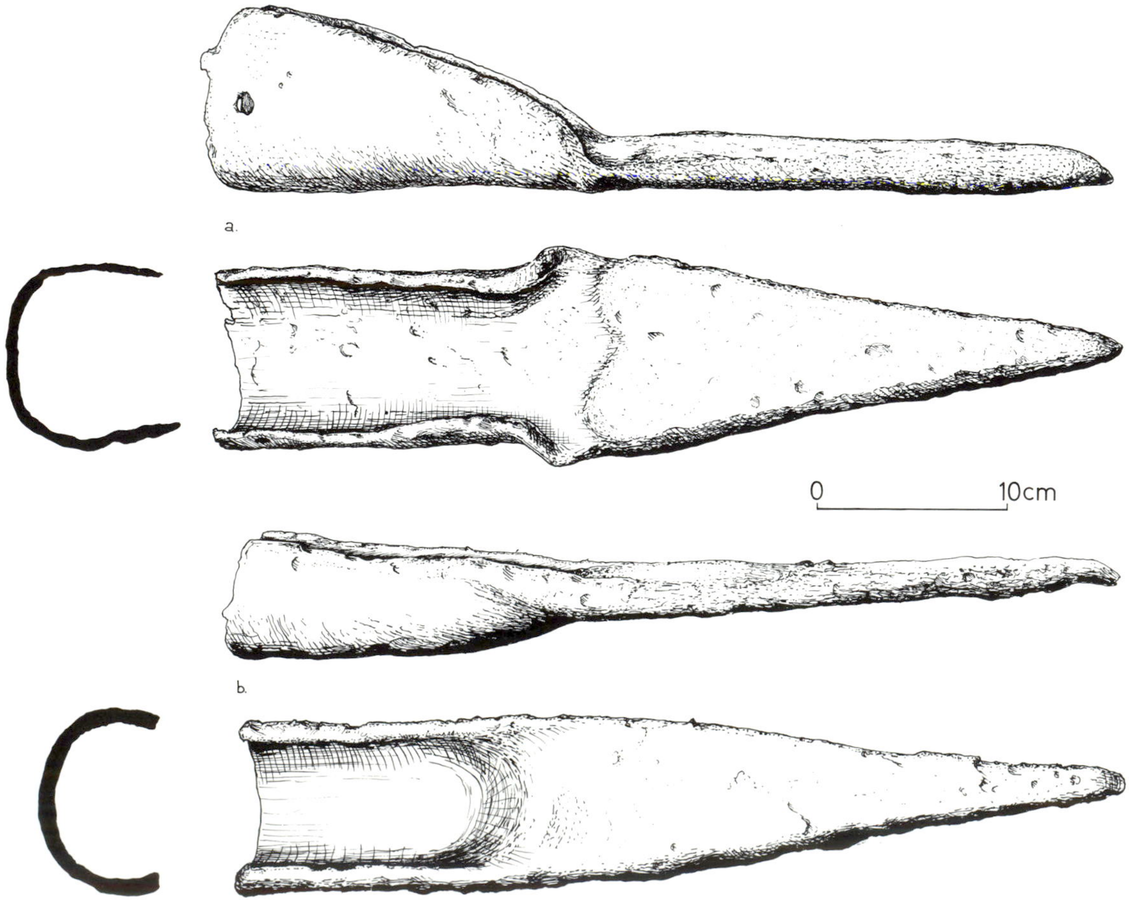

139. 5th/11th century ploughshares from the destruction of Abbasid-Fatimid Building 2 (1:4).

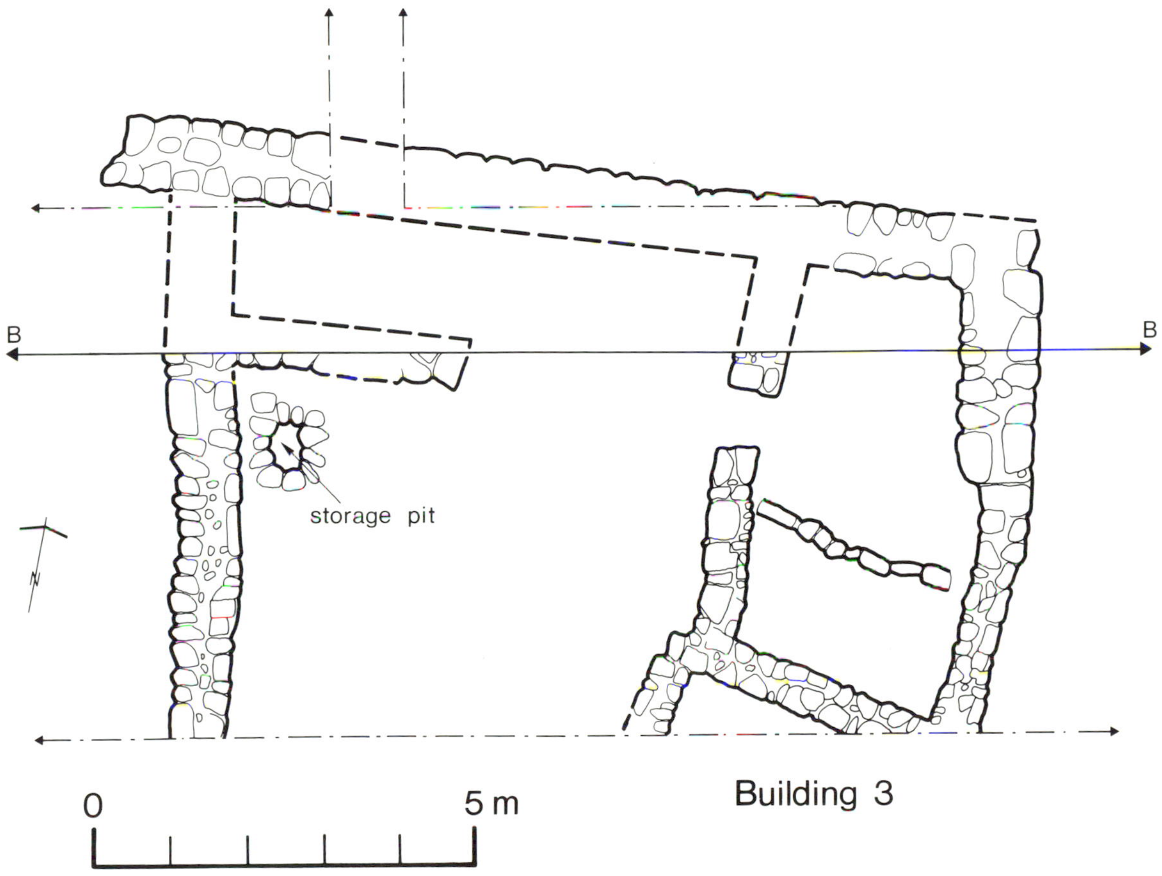

140. Plan of remains of Abbasid-Fatimid Building 3 (Strata IVb–III) in Area C (1:100).

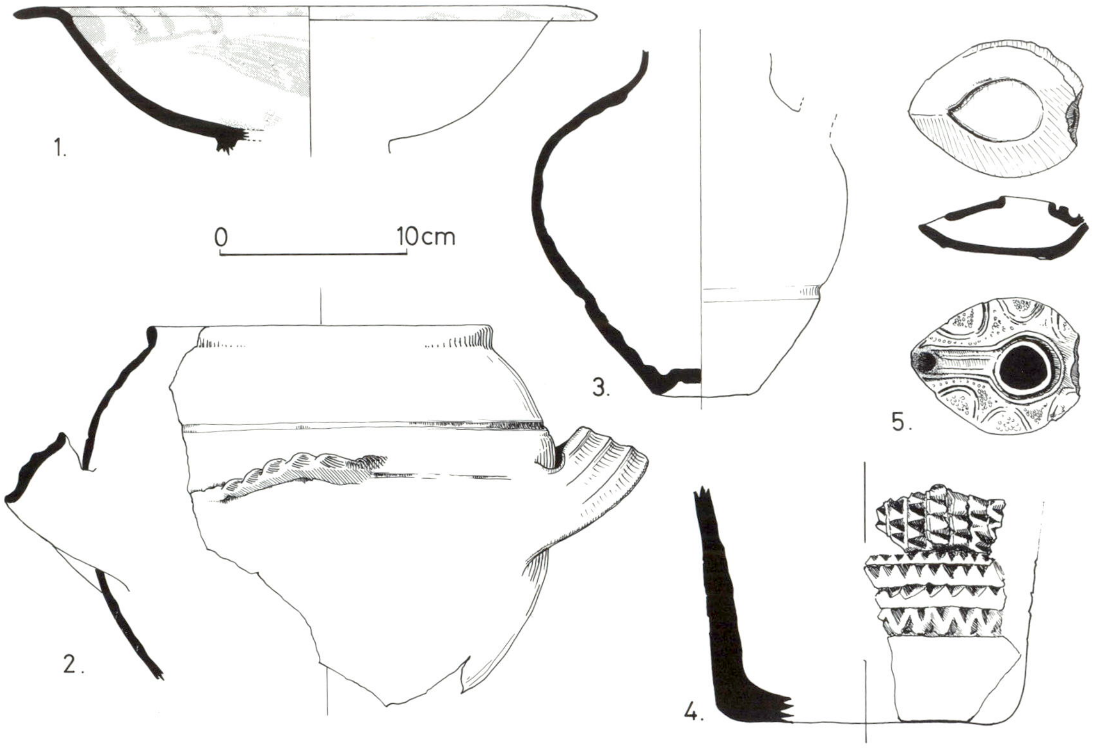

141. 5th/11th century pottery from the destruction of Abbasid-Fatimid Building 3 (1:4).

No. Reg. Deposit
1. 548 C5.3.5
Bowl, incomplete. Everted rim. Body 7.5YR 5/4 brown, white slip, blue-green glaze (deteriorated).

2. 535 C5.1.7
Cooking pot, broken, incomplete. 2 strap handles, 2 thumb-impressed decorative lugs. 10R 4/6 red, brown glaze inside base.

3. 76/98 C5.1.6
Jar, incomplete. 1 handle, recessed base. 5YR 7/6 reddish yellow.

4. 76/135 C5.3.5
Deep bowl, incomplete. Incised dog-tooth pattern. 7.5YR 6/4 light brown.

5. 619 C4/5B.9
Moulded lamp, handle missing. Pattern of bunches of grapes and semi-circles. 7.5YR 6/4 pink.

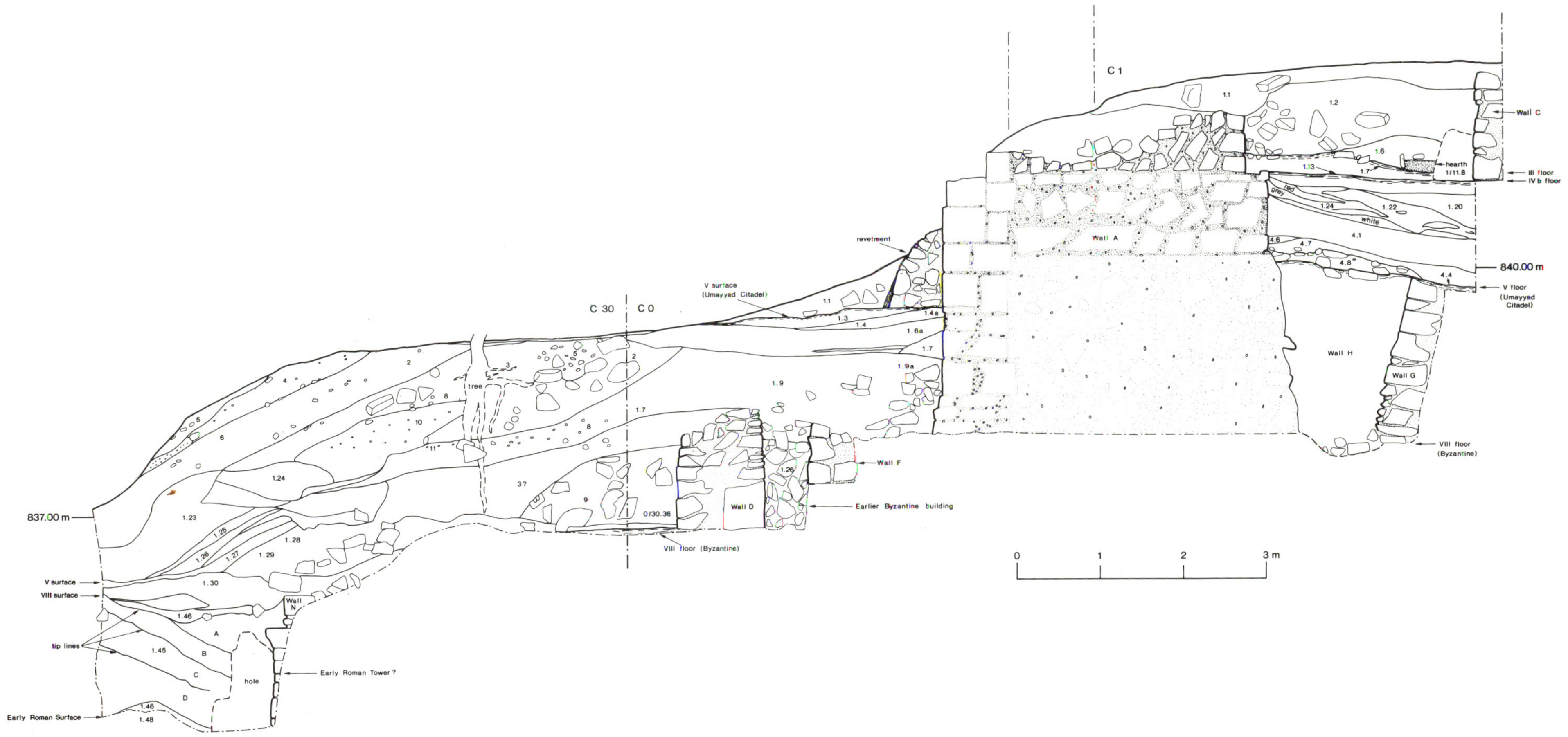

142. Section over Sector 8 fortification wall in Area C, and the area outside the wall, looking north (A–A on figs. 124, 126, and 134) (1:75).

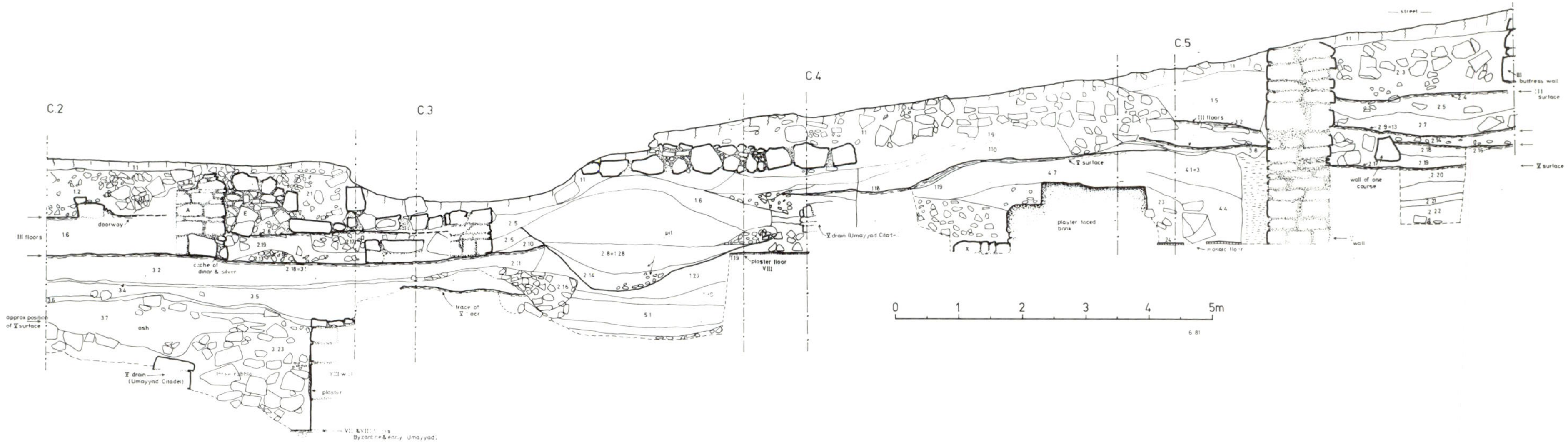

143. North Section of Trenches C2 – C5 (B–B on figs 124, 126, & 134) (1:100).

144. Byzantine remains in Area B (Stratum VIII) (1:200).

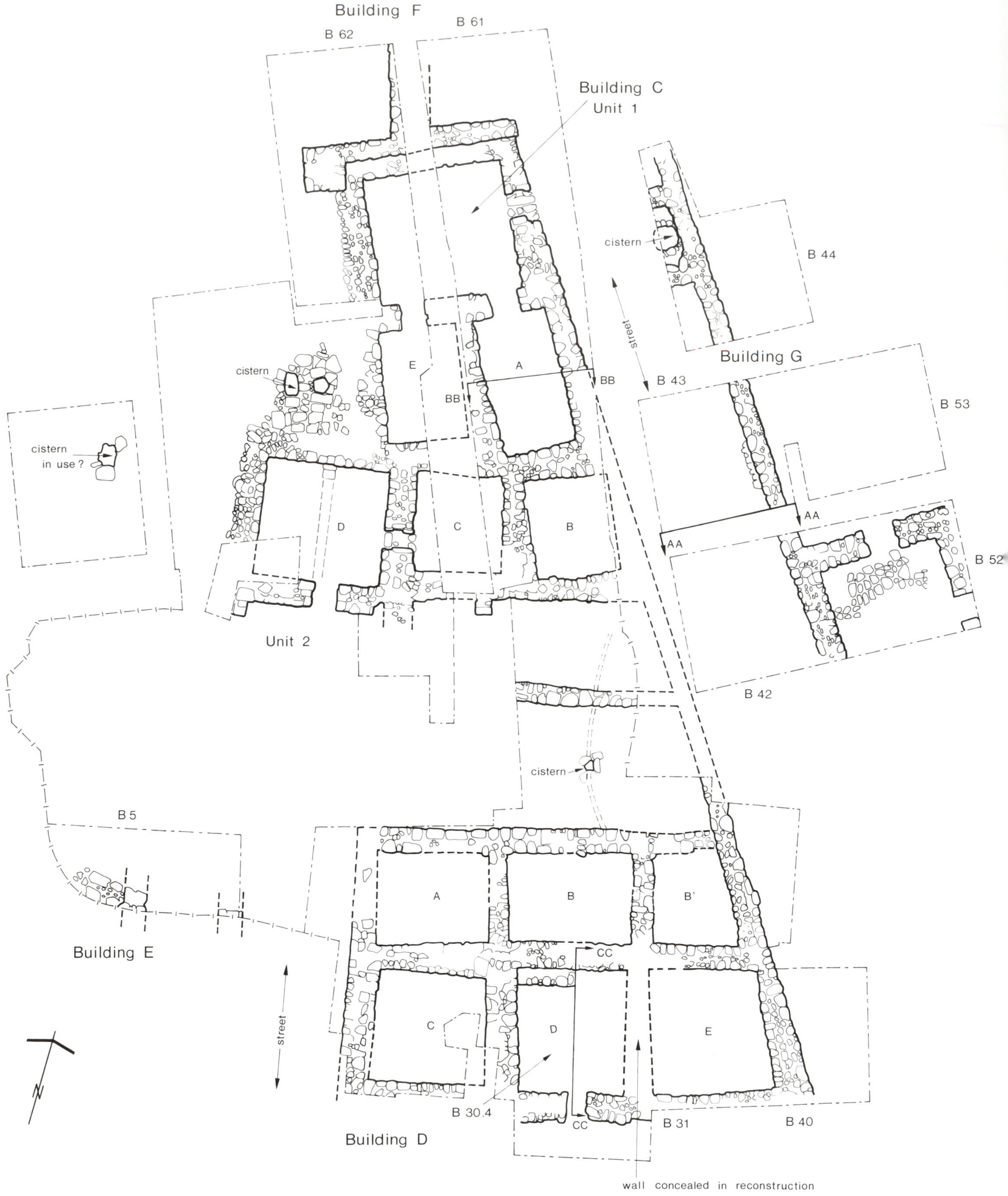

145. Phase plan of Stratum V (Umayyad Citadel) in Area B (1:200).

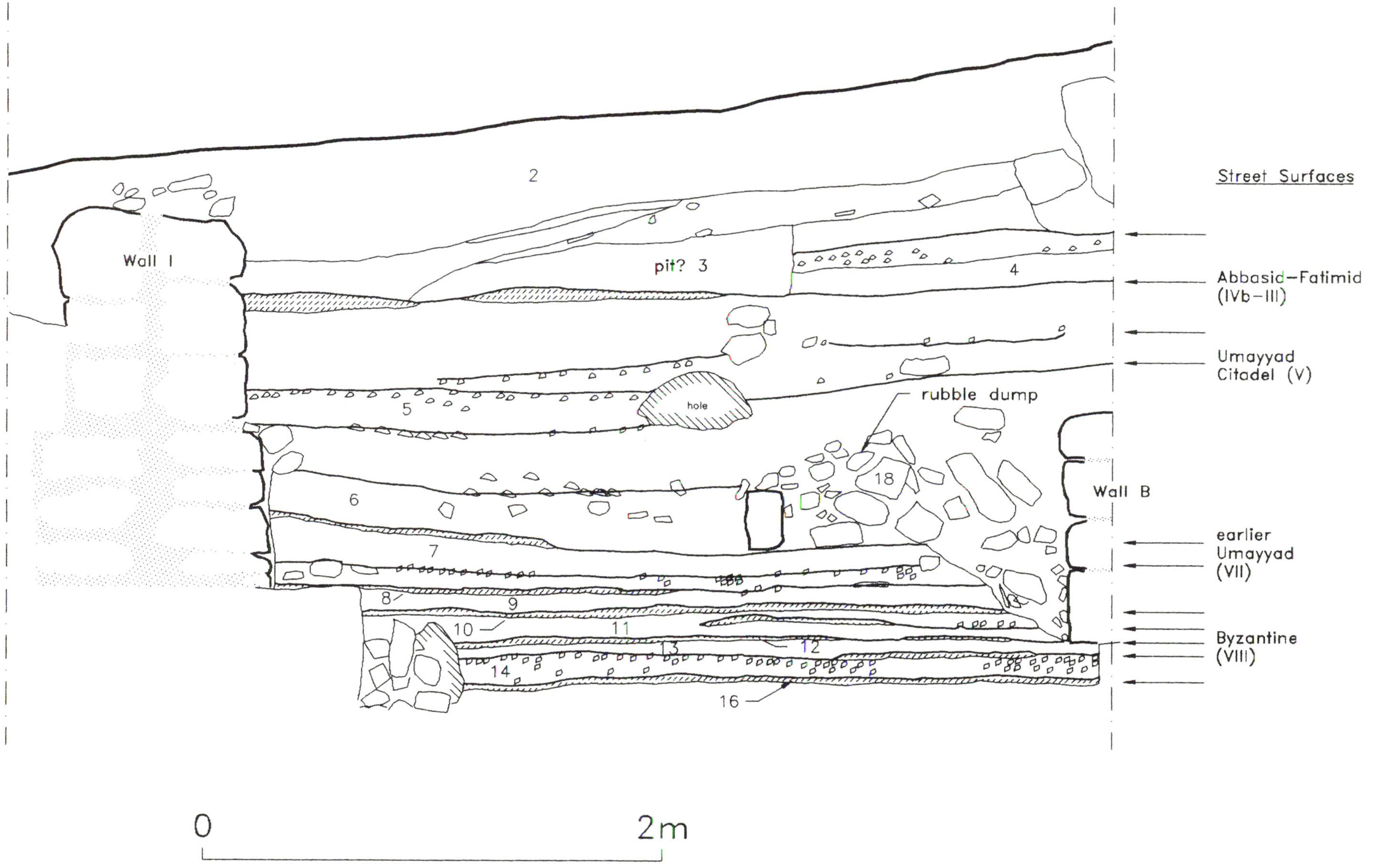

146. Cross-section of the street in Area B, showing development of surfaces from Stratum VIII (Byzantine) to Stratum III (CC–CC on figs 145–6) (1:25).

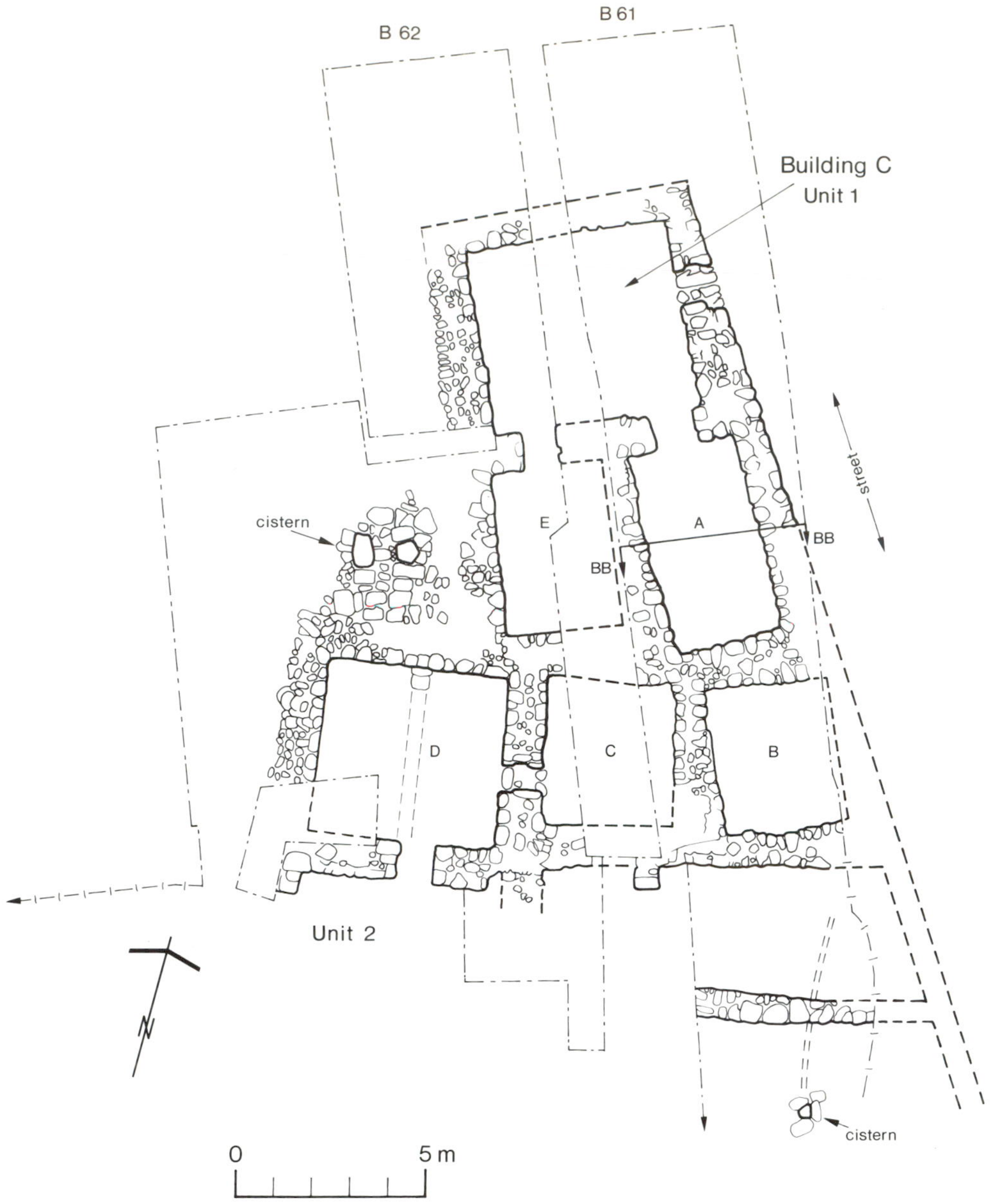

147. Umayyad Building C in Area B (1:200).

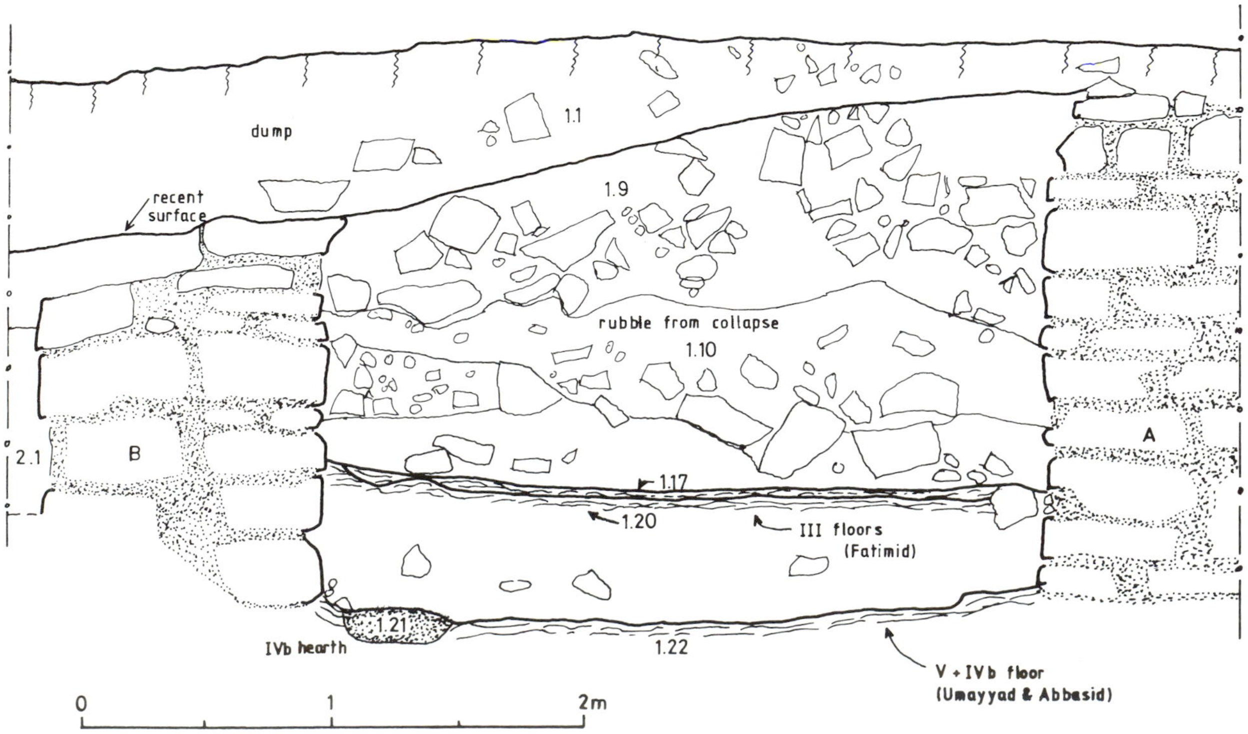

148. Section of Room A, Building C (BB–BB on figs 145–6) (1:30).

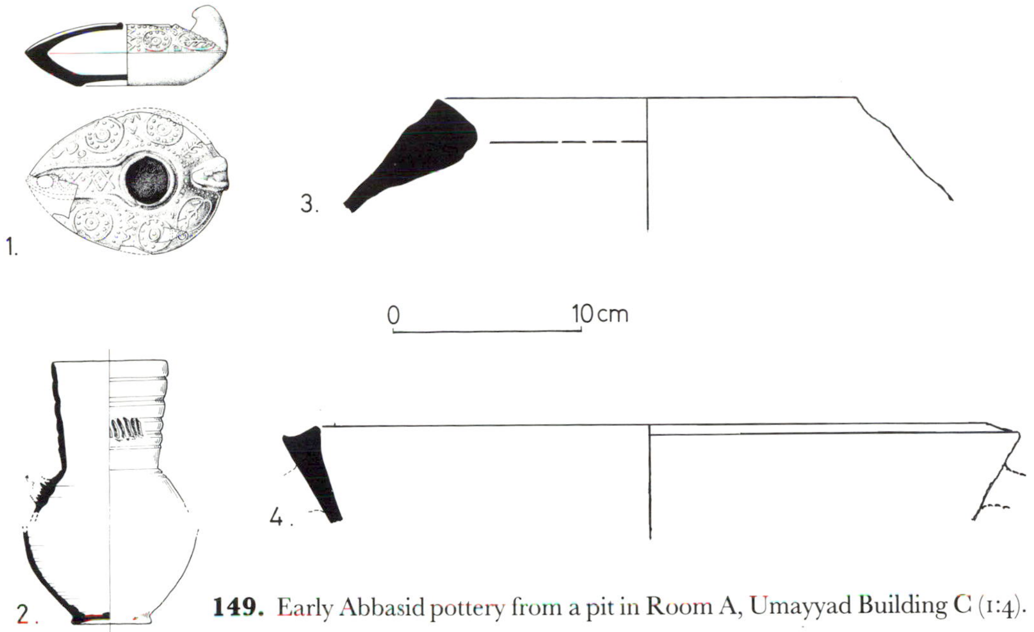

149. Early Abbasid pottery from a pit in Room A, Umayyad Building C (1:4).

No. Reg. Deposit
1. 950 B26.1.24
Moulded lamp, broken, incomplete; pattern of circles and dots. 10YR 8/3 v.pale brown.

2. 988 B26.1.24
Miniature jar with tall Xaring neck, incomplete. 1 round- section handle. Gouged lines on neck. 2.5Y 7/4 pale yellow/ 7.5YR 6/4 light brown.

3. TS492 B26.1.24
Storage jar rim. 7.5YR 8/4 pink.

4. TS494 B26.1.24
Basin rim. At least 1 handle. 5YR 7/6 reddish yellow.

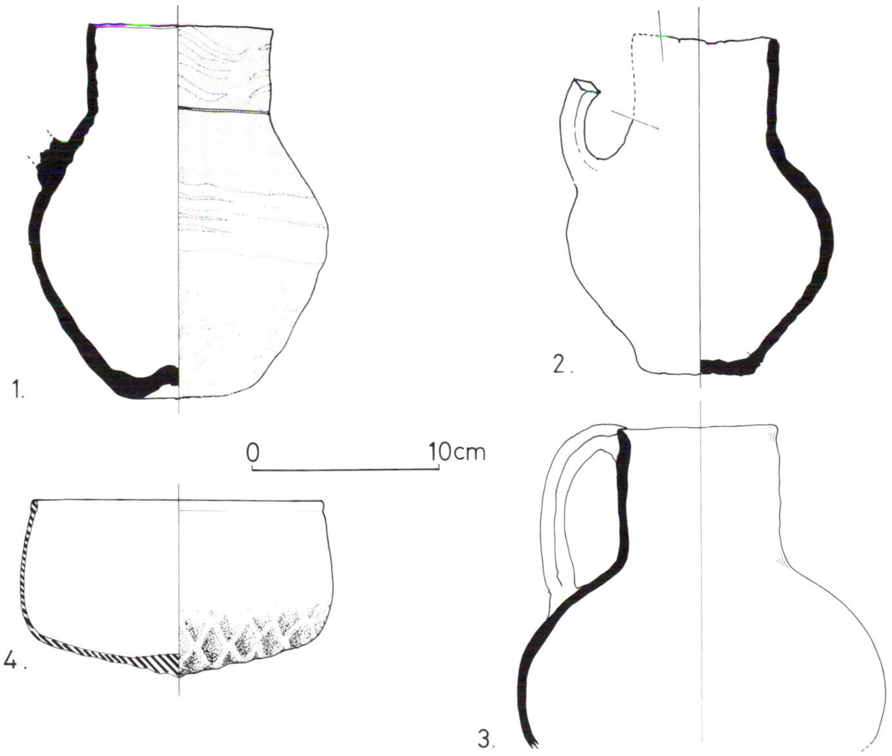

150. Fatimid pottery and glass from a pit in Room A, Umayyad Building C.

No. Reg. Deposit
1. 951 B26.1.18
Jar, broken, incomplete. 1 handle faint white painted lines on neck and shoulder. 2.5YR 5/6 red.

2. 952 B26.1.18
Jar, broken, incomplete. 2.5YR 6/6 light red/N4 dark grey in places.

3. TS224 B26.1.18
Tall-necked jar, incomplete. 5YR 7/8 reddish yellow.

4. 978 B26.1.18
Bowl, glass, mould-blown.

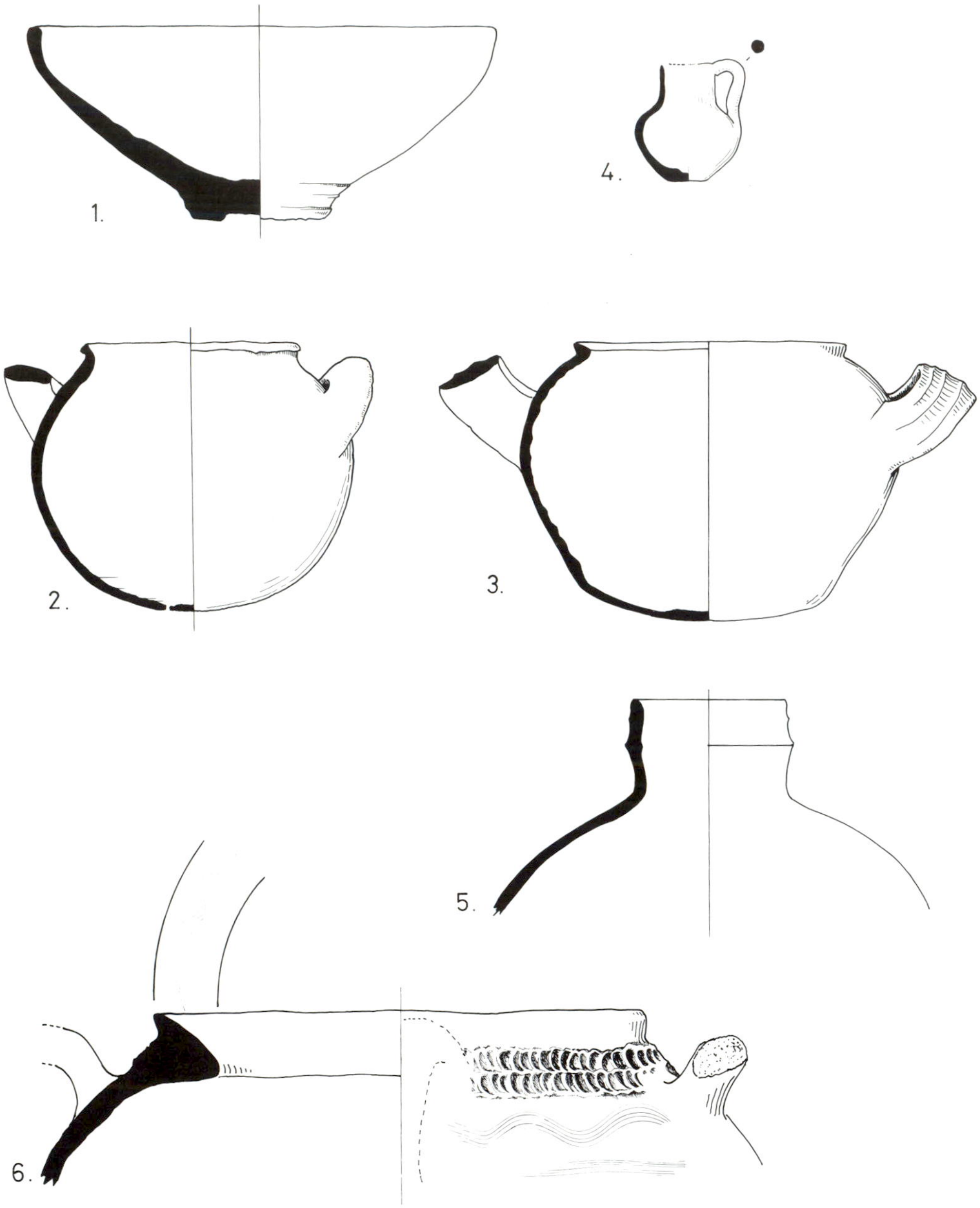

151. 5th/11th century destruction deposit from Umayyad building C (1:4).

No. Reg. Deposit

1. 910 B19/25B.1
Bowl, incomplete. 5YR 6/6 reddish yellow/ N5 dark grey.

2. 939 B25.4.1
Cooking pot, incomplete. 2 horizontal handles, hole drilled in base. 7.5YR 6/4 light brown/N4 dark grey.

3. 880 B25.3.2
Cooking pot, intact. 2 strap handles. 2.5YR 5/6 red.

4. 879 B25.3.2
Juglet, intact. 1 handle. 5YR 6/8 reddish yellow.

5. 77/97 B19/25B.1
Jar, 5YR 3/3 dark reddish brown/5YR 6/4 light reddish brown.

6. TS225 B19/25B.1
Storage jar rim. 2 handles, thumb impressed pattern below rim, combing in wavy and straight lines. 5YR 7/6 reddish yellow.

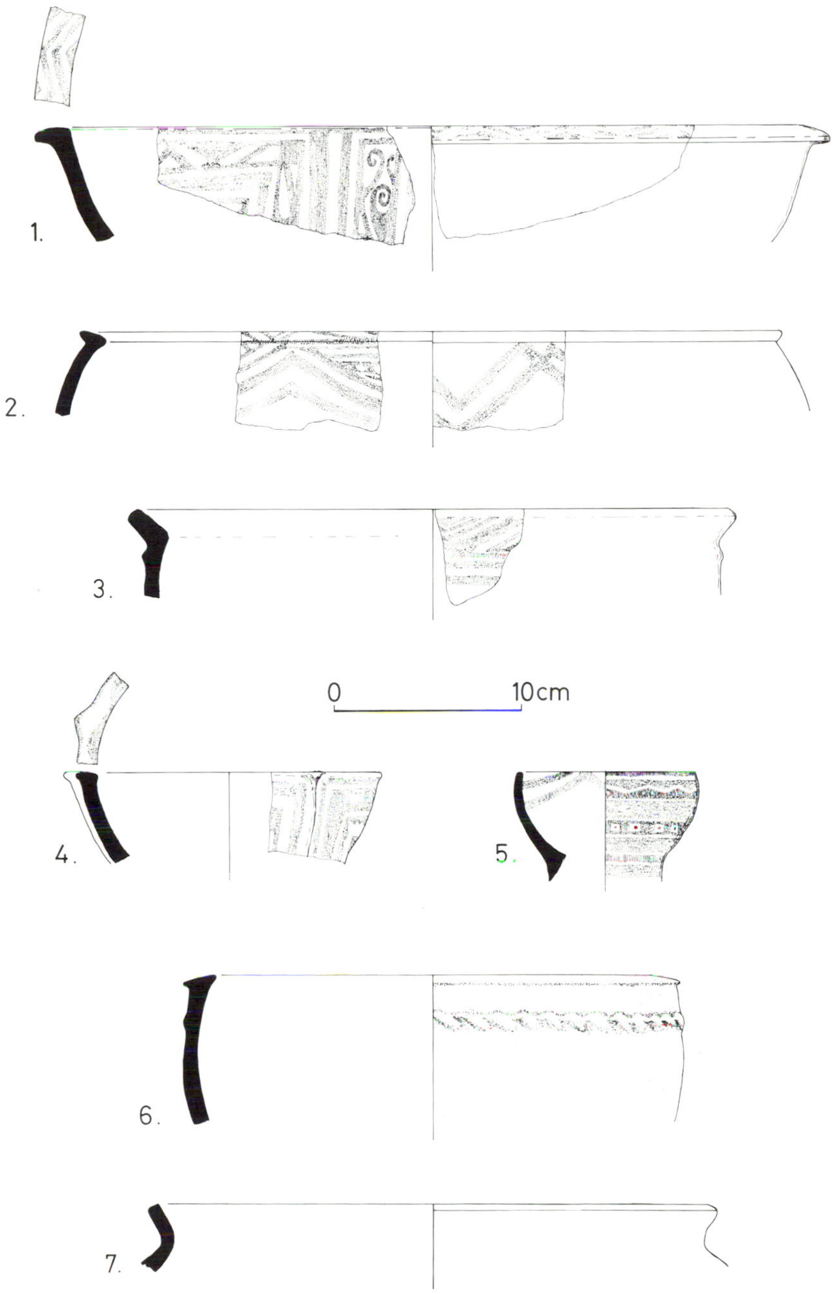

152. Ayyubid or early Mamluk pottery from Umayyad Building C (1:4).

No. Reg. Deposit

1. TS475 B24.6.2
Deep bowl, everted rim. 2.5YR 6/8 light red/5YR 7/8 reddish yellow and N4 dark grey. Inside slip 7.5YR 6/6 reddish yellow and painted design 10R 3/6 dark red.

2. TS480 B24.6.2
Deep bowl, everted rim. 10R 6/8 light red/N4 dark grey. Painted design 10R 3/4 dusky red.

3. TS477 B24.6.2
Deep bowl, slightly everted rim with ridge beneath. 2.5Y 8/2 white. Painted design 10R 3/2 dusky red.

4. TS476 B24.6.2
Thickened rim of jar or bowl. 7.5YR 6/4 light brown. Slip outside 7.5YR 8/4 pink. Painted design 10R 3/1 reddish grey.

5. TS478 B24.6.2
Jar rim 10R 6/8 light red. Painted design 10R 2.5/1 reddish black.

6. TS479 B24.6.2
Deep bowl. Thumb-moulded rope decoration outside. 2.5YR 6/6 light red.

7. TS497 B24.6.2 Cooking pot rim. 5YR 7/6 reddish yellow/N4 dark grey.

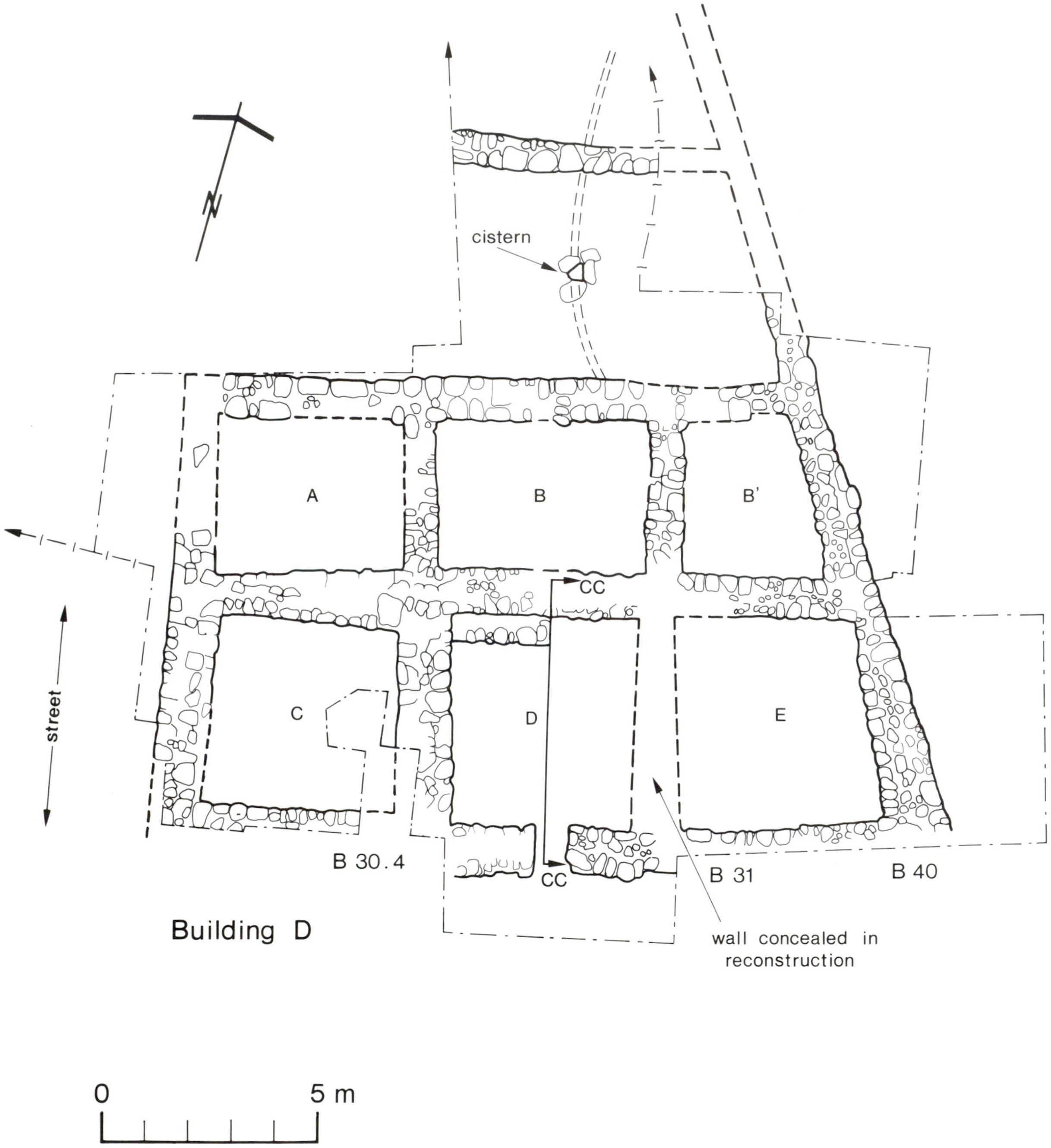

153. Umayyad Building D in Area B (1:150).

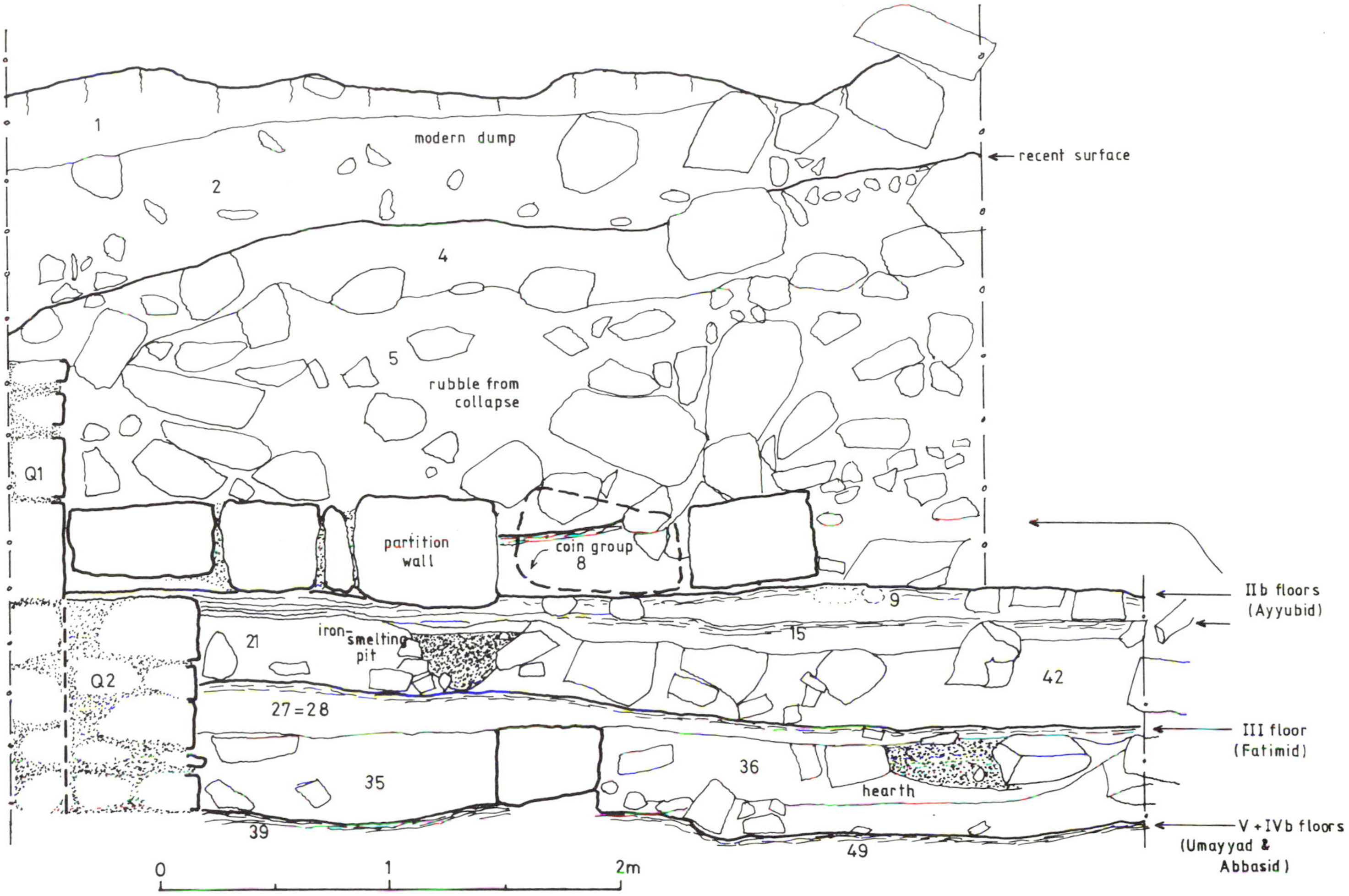

154. Section of Room D, Building D (AA–AA on figs 145–6) (1:30).

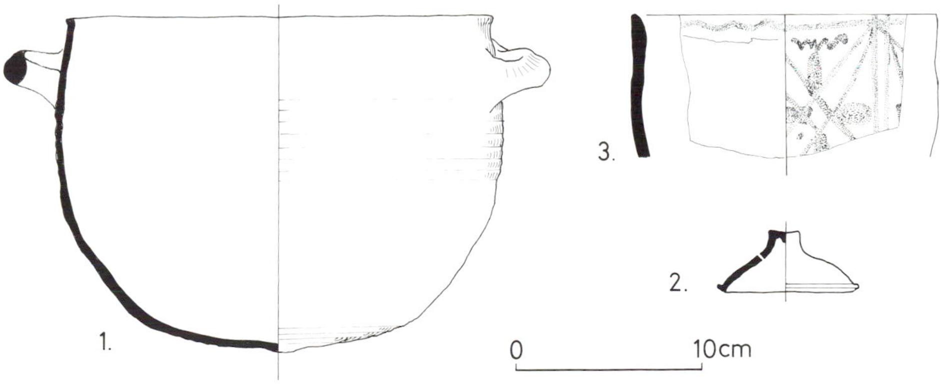

155. Early Abbasid pottery from a secondary Xoor in Room D, Umayyad Building D (1:4).

No. Reg. Deposit

1. 975 B30.4.38
Lidded cooking pot, incomplete (lid missing). 2 horizontal handles, faint traces of ribbing. 10R 2.5/2 v. dusky red.

2. 941 B30.4.39
Lid for miniature cooking pot (cf.74.12) broken, complete. 7.5YR 6/4 light brown.

3. TS496 B30.4.46
Bowl, 5YR-7.5YR 7/6 reddish yellow. White wash 5Y 8/2 on exterior. Painted decoration of lines and squiggles 10R 3/4 dusky red.

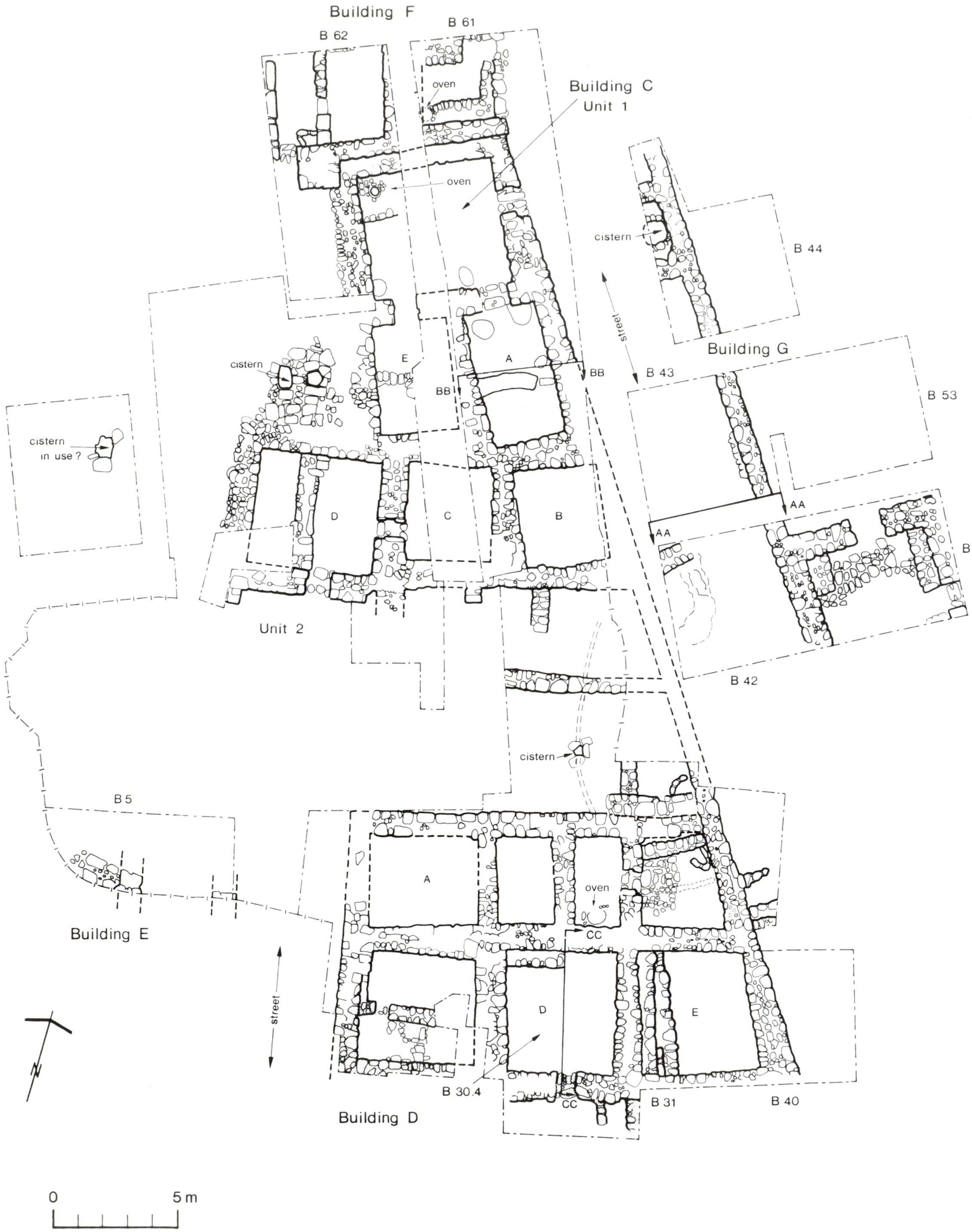

156. Strata IV–IIb in Area B: areas occupied later than the Umayyad period (1:200).

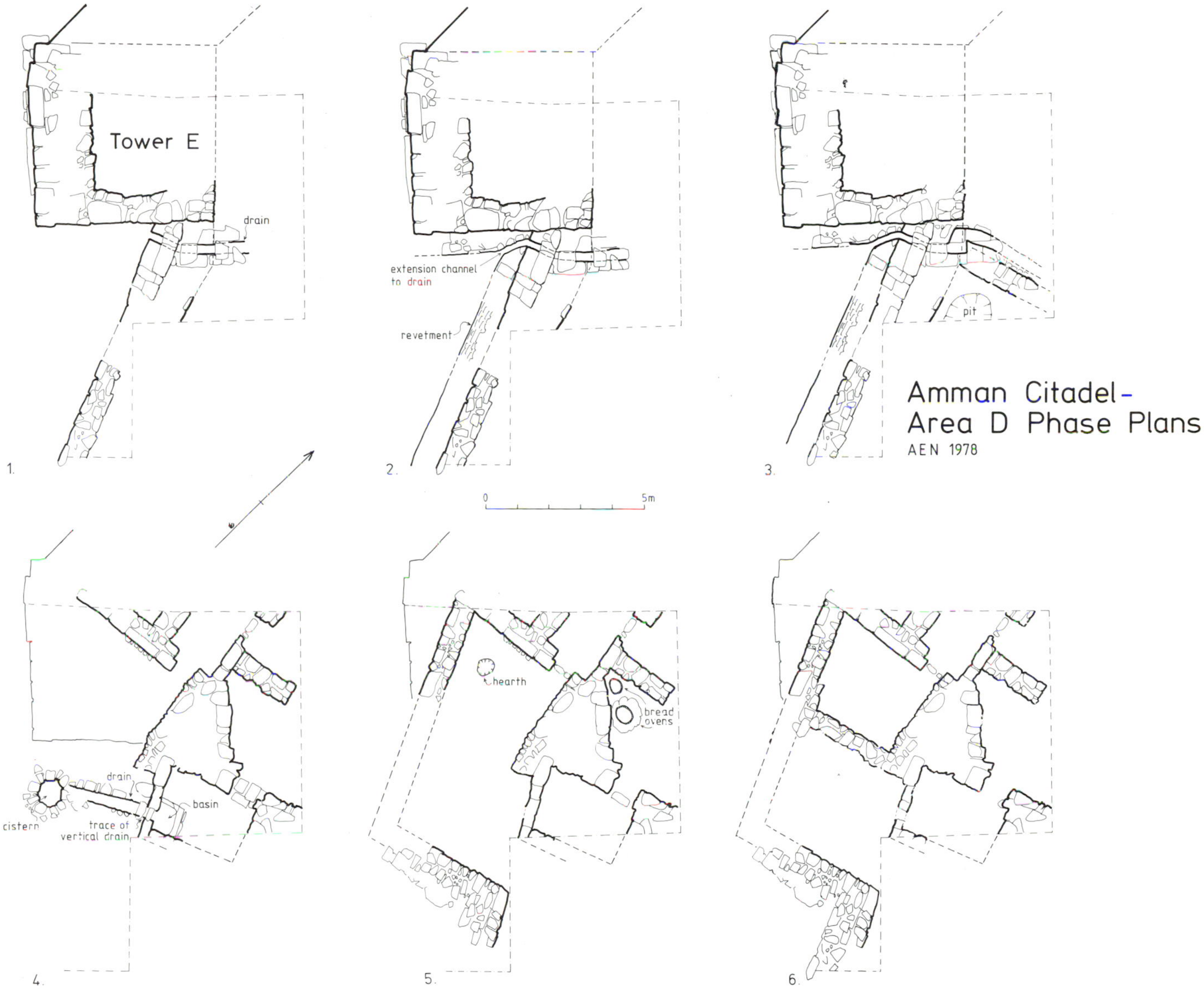

157. Area D: phase plans (1:200).

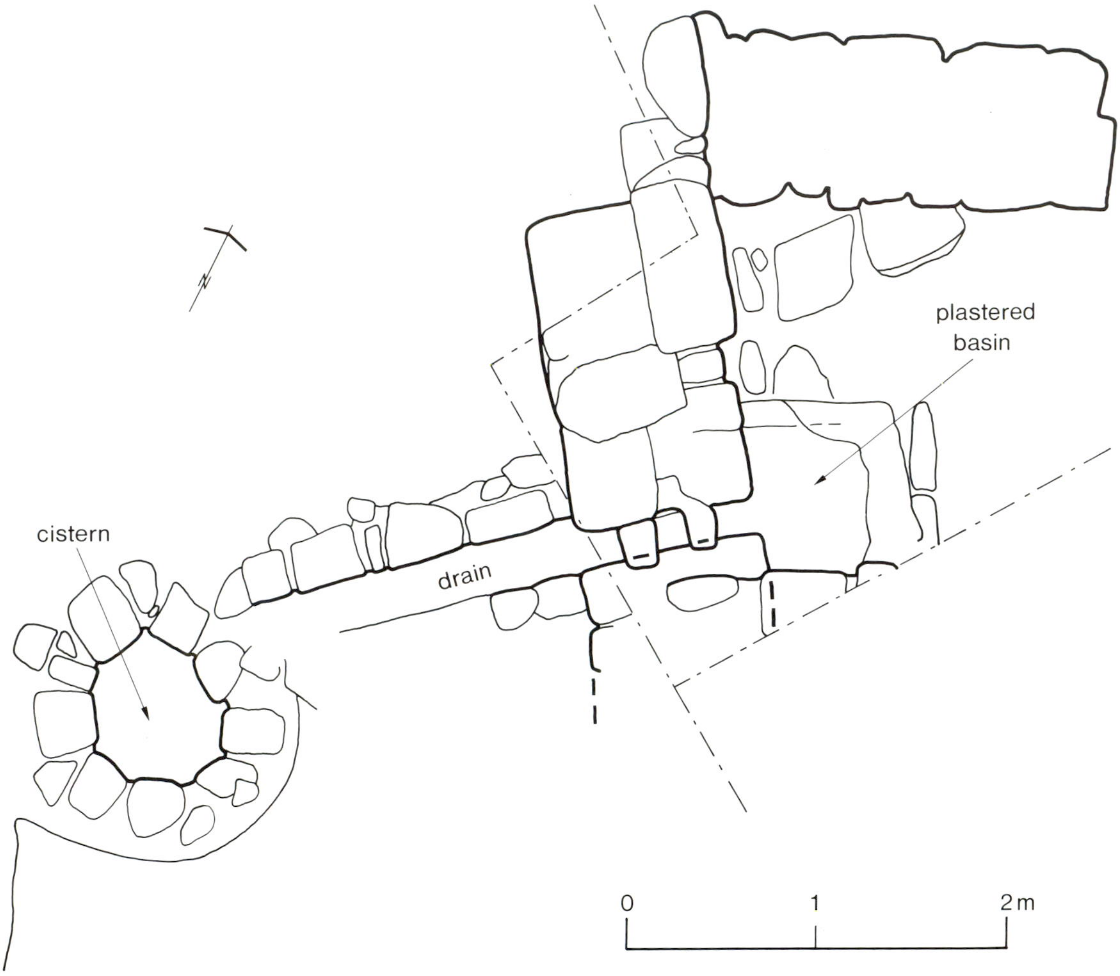

158. Drain details of Phase 4 (Abbasid-Fatimid) in Area D (1:40).

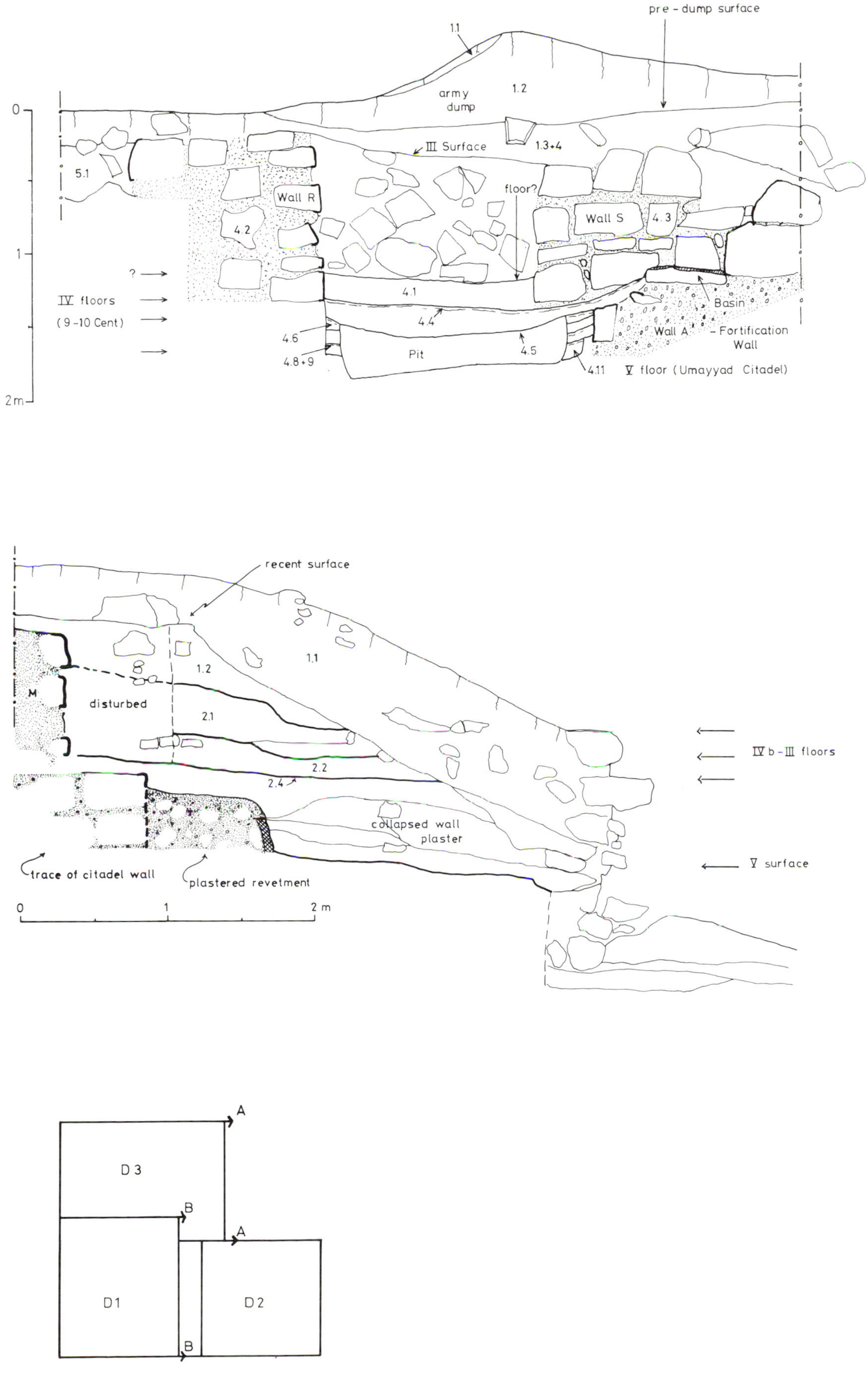

159. D area sections (1:40).

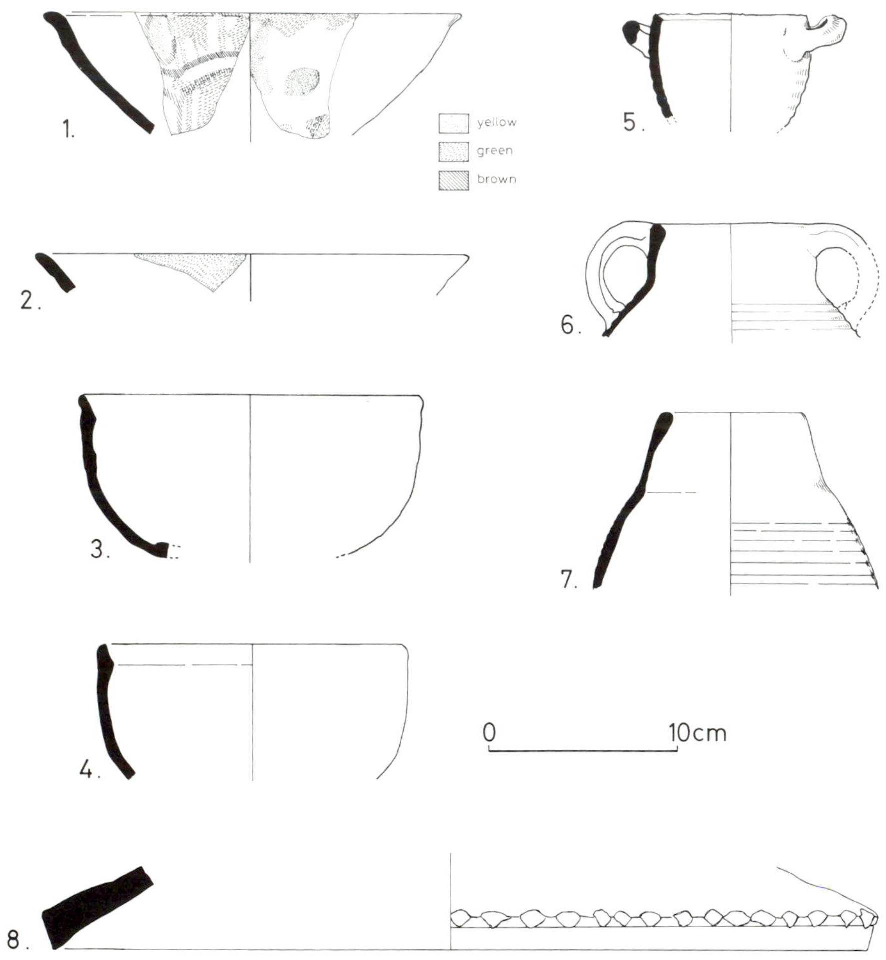

160. Abbasid pottery from an occupation deposit in house Phase 2 in Area D (1:4).

No. Reg. Deposit
1. TS485 D3.4.4
Bowl thickened rim, body 5Y 8/4 yellow. Glazed inside and out with transparent glaze and colourants: yellow and green outside; design of loops and circles in brown, and drips of yellow and green inside.

2. TS498 D3.1.14
Flaring rim of bowl. 10YR 8/3 v. pale brown; white slip, green and yellow mottled splash glaze inside. Clear glaze outside.

3. TS217 D3.1.14
Cup. 2.5Y 8/3 pale yellow.

4. TS482 D3.1.14
Cup. 5Y 8/2 white.

5. 934 D3.1.16
Miniature lidded cooking pot, incomplete (cf.74.6). 2 horizontal handles, very faint ribbing. 2.5Y 7/2 light grey.

6. TS222 D3.1.16
Small 2-handled cooking pot. Light ribbing. 10R 5/6 red.

7. TS472 D3.1.16
Small holemouth bag jar, lightly ribbed. 7.5YR 7/4 pink.

8. TS493 D3.1.14
Basin lid. Thumb impressing on rim. 5YR 7/4 pink.

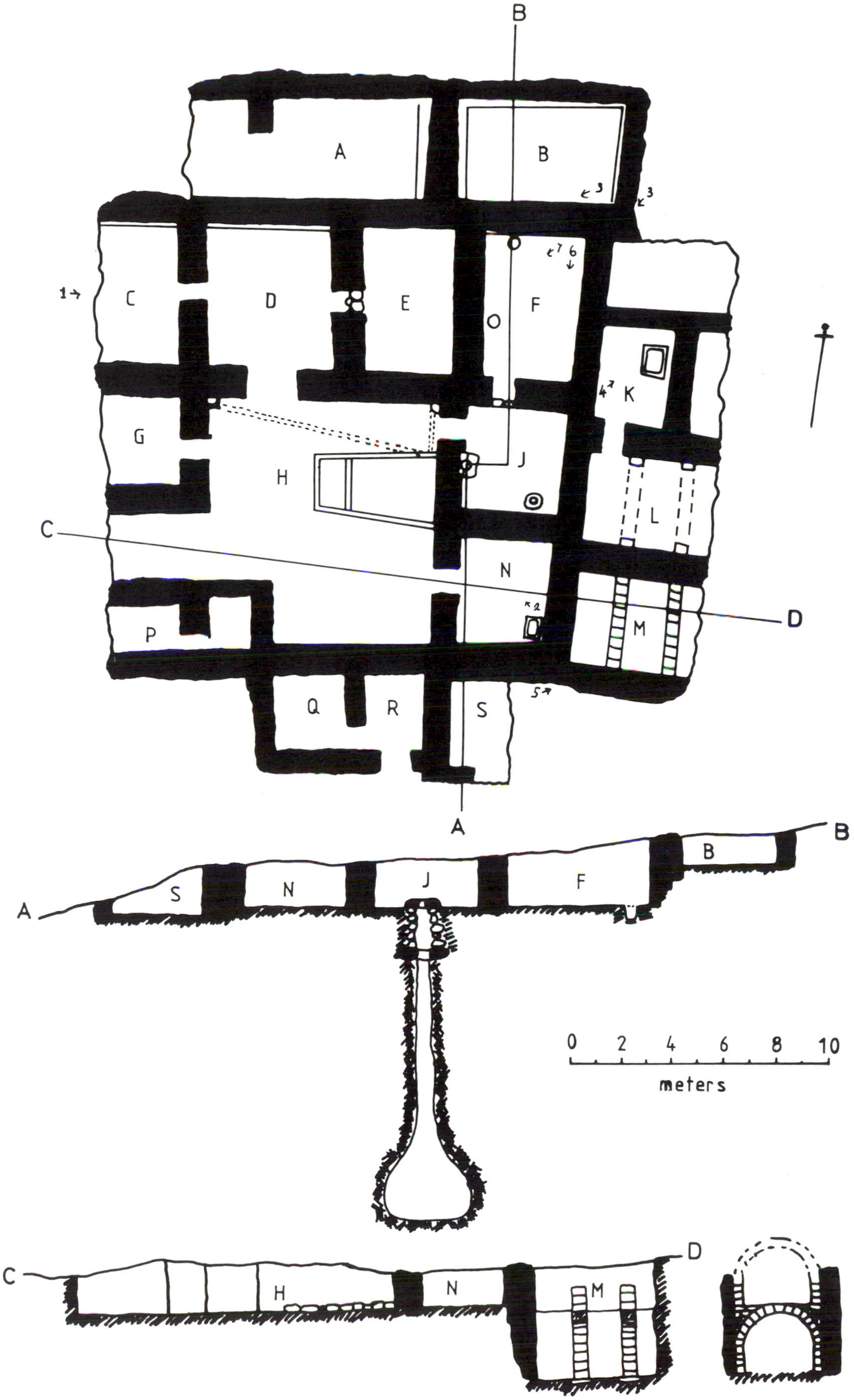

161. Museum Site (after Harding 1951a) (1:200).

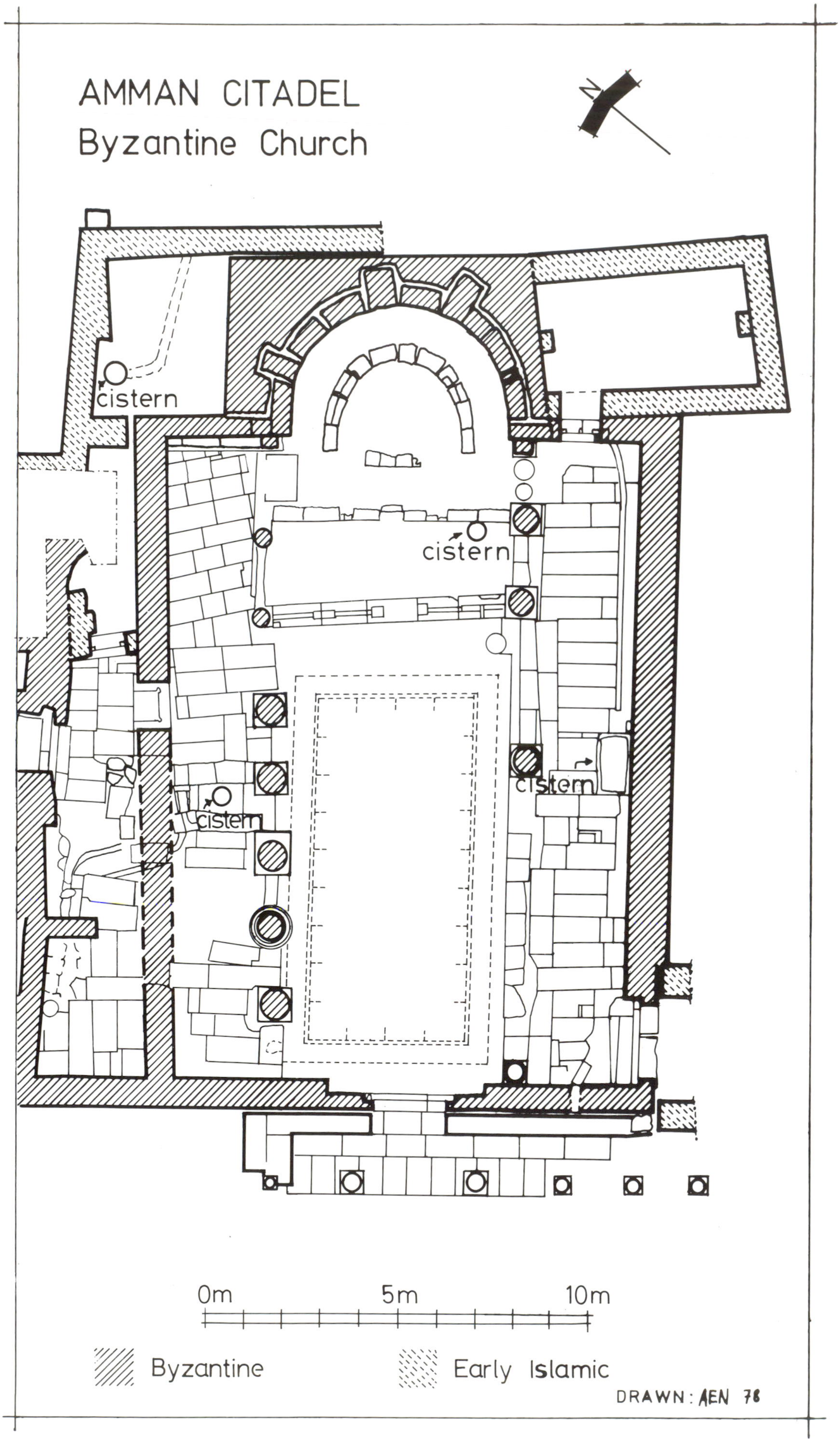

162. Church (after Zayadine 1977–8) (1:150).

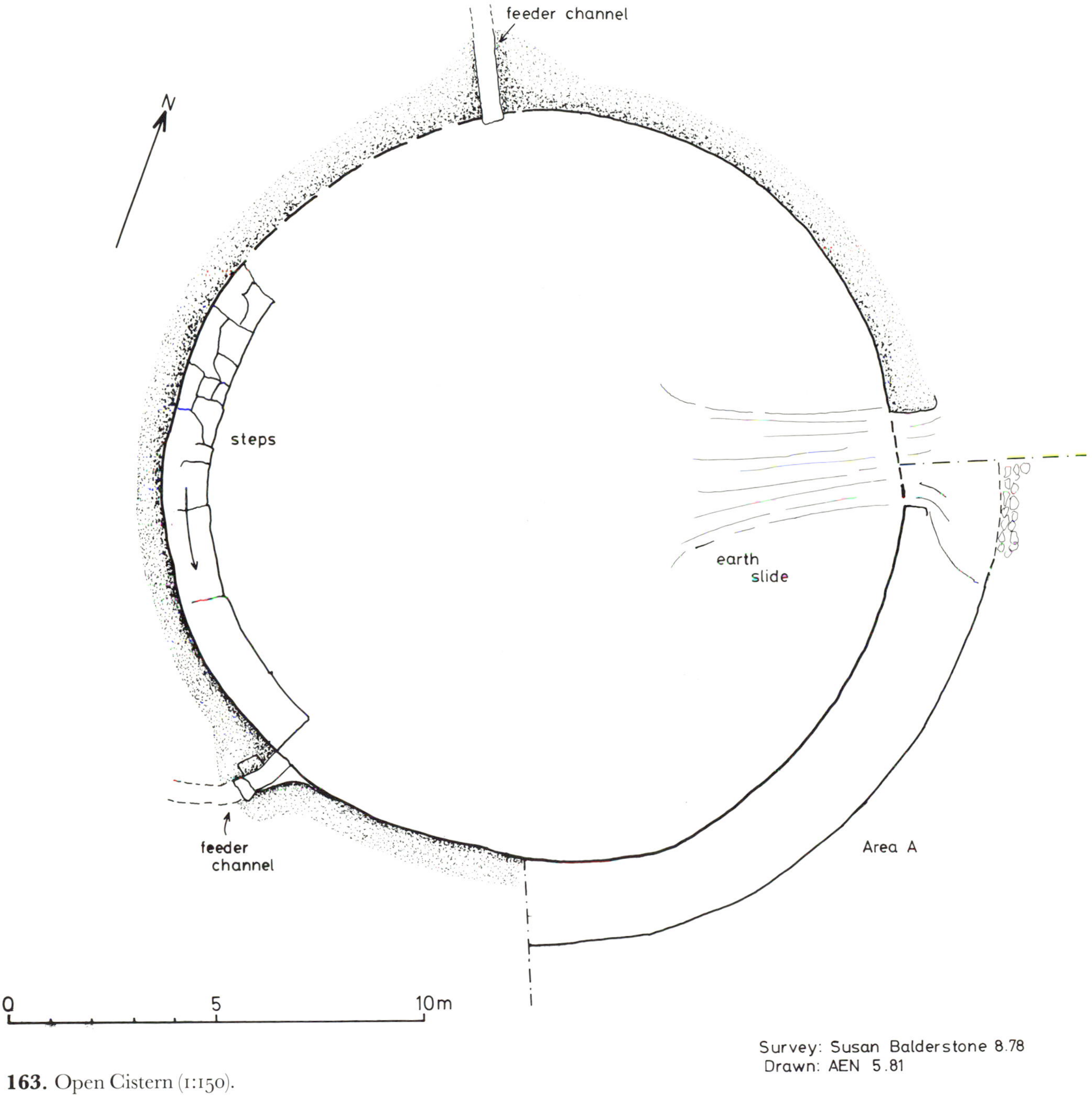

163. Open Cistern (1:150).

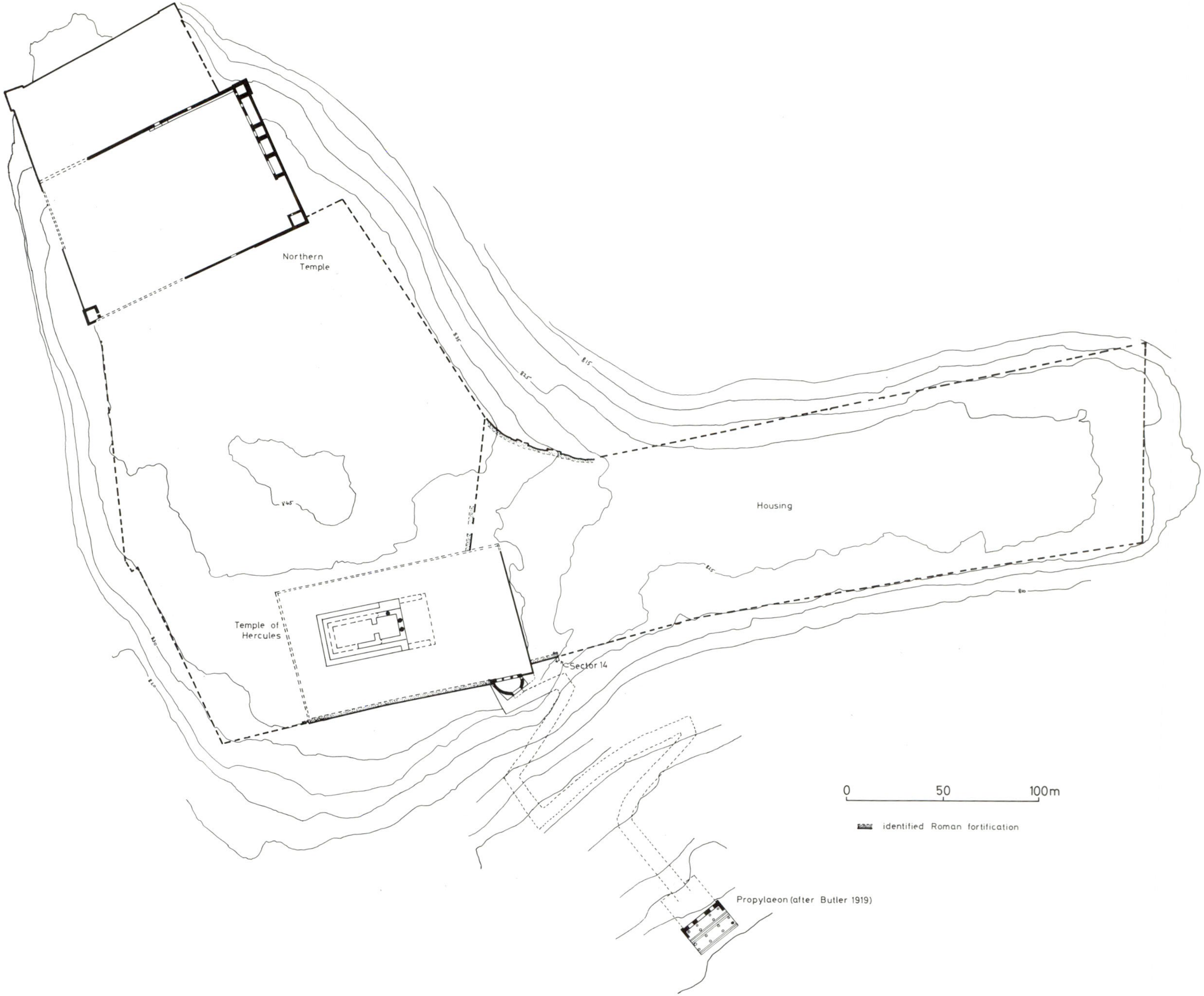

164. Qal'at 'Ammān: 2nd-century AD layout (1:3000).

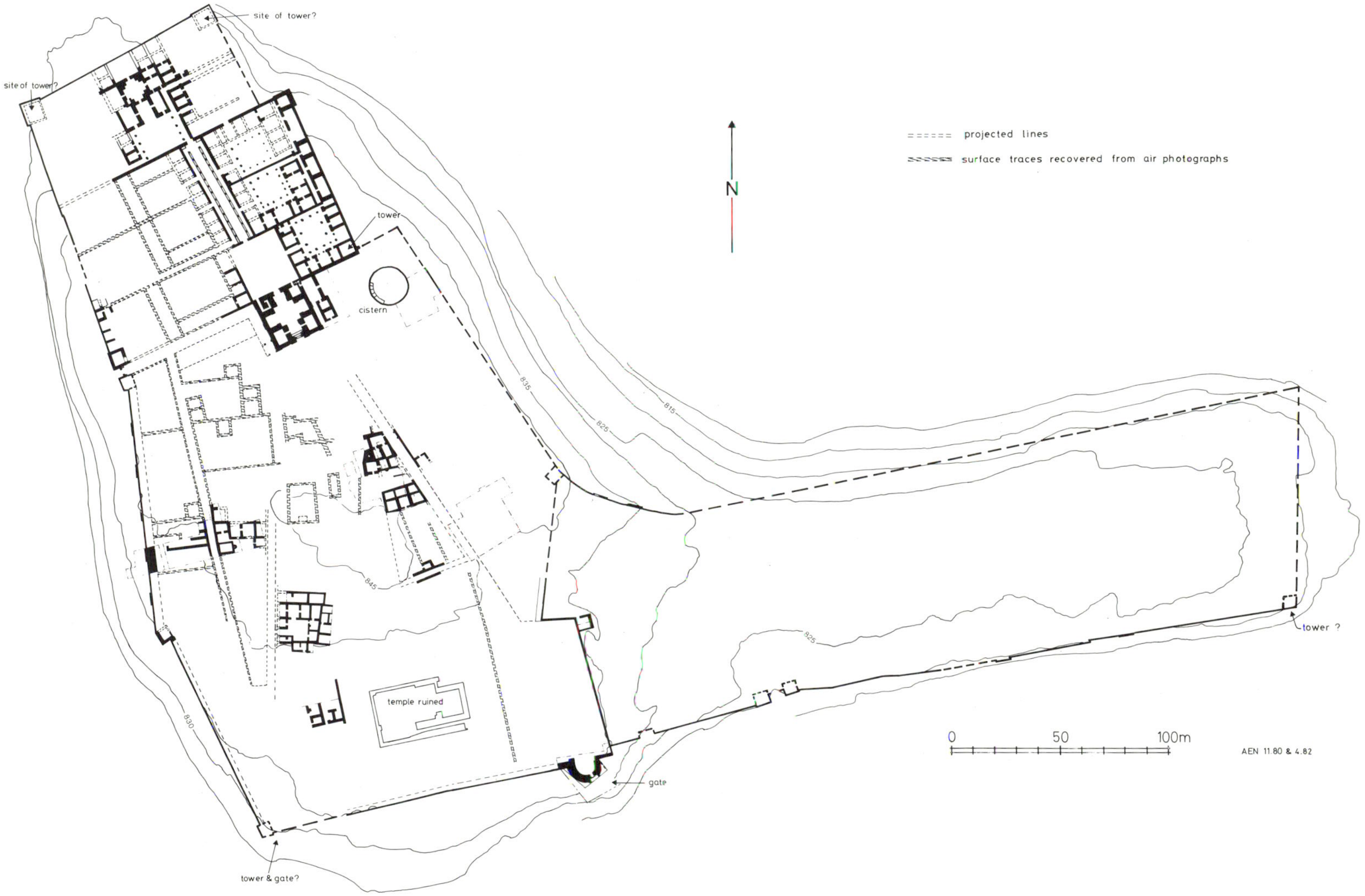

165. The Umayyad Citadel (1:3000).

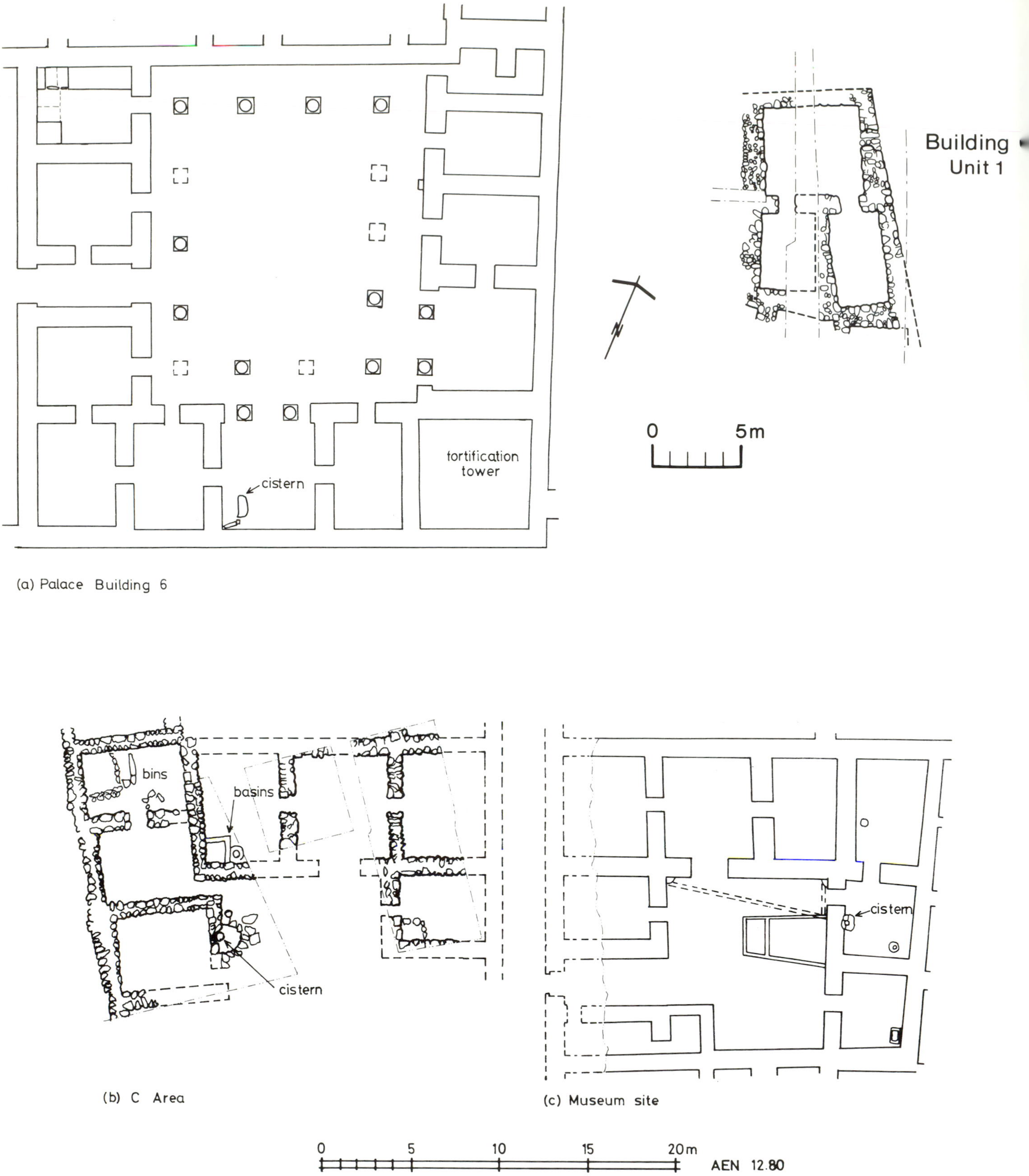

166. Umayyad Citadel comparative house plans (1:300).

167. Distribution of earthquake destruction evidence from the earthquake of 129–30/747–8 (1:2500).

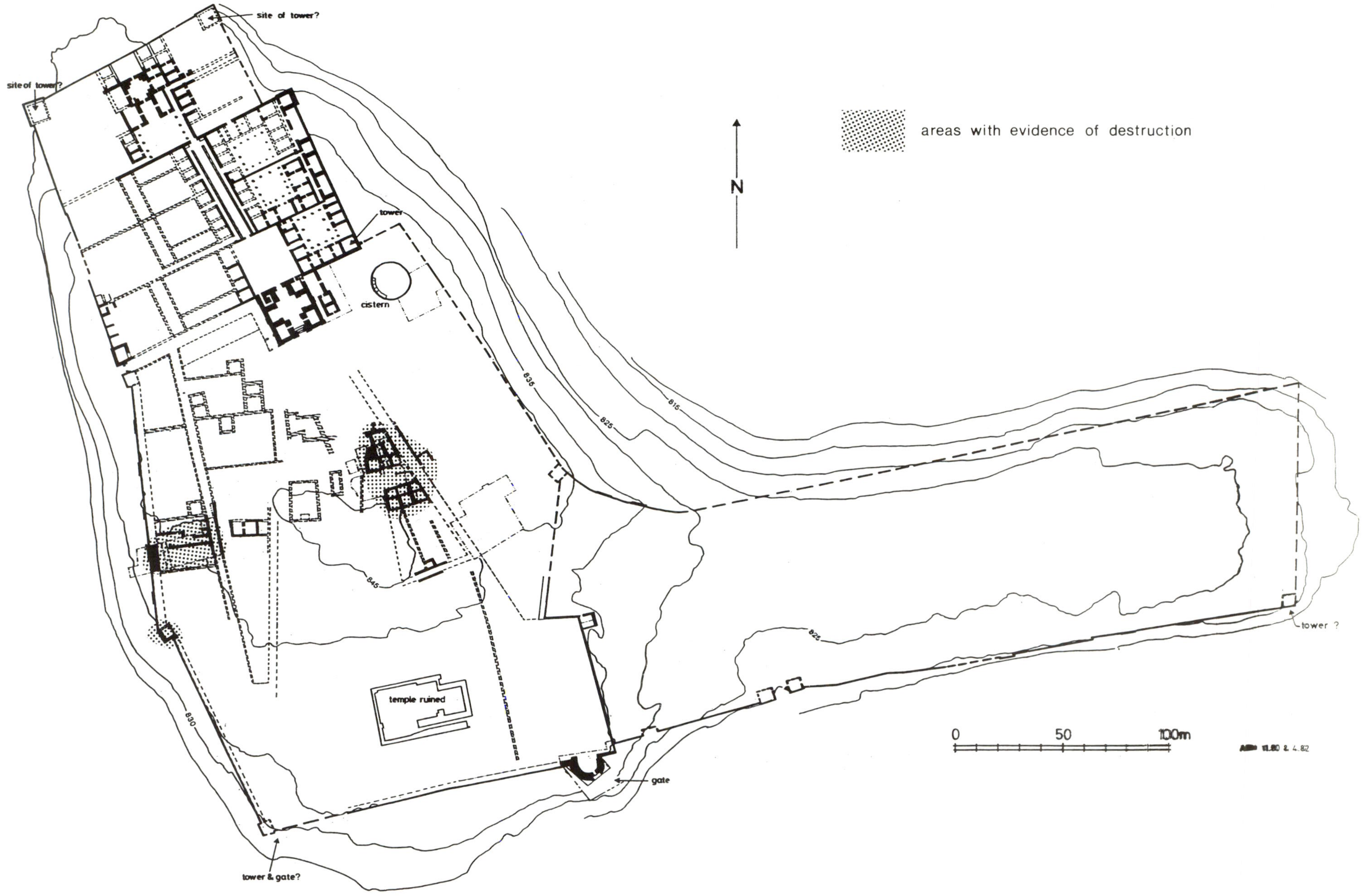

168. Distribution of earthquake destruction evidence from the earthquake of 460/1068 (1:2500).

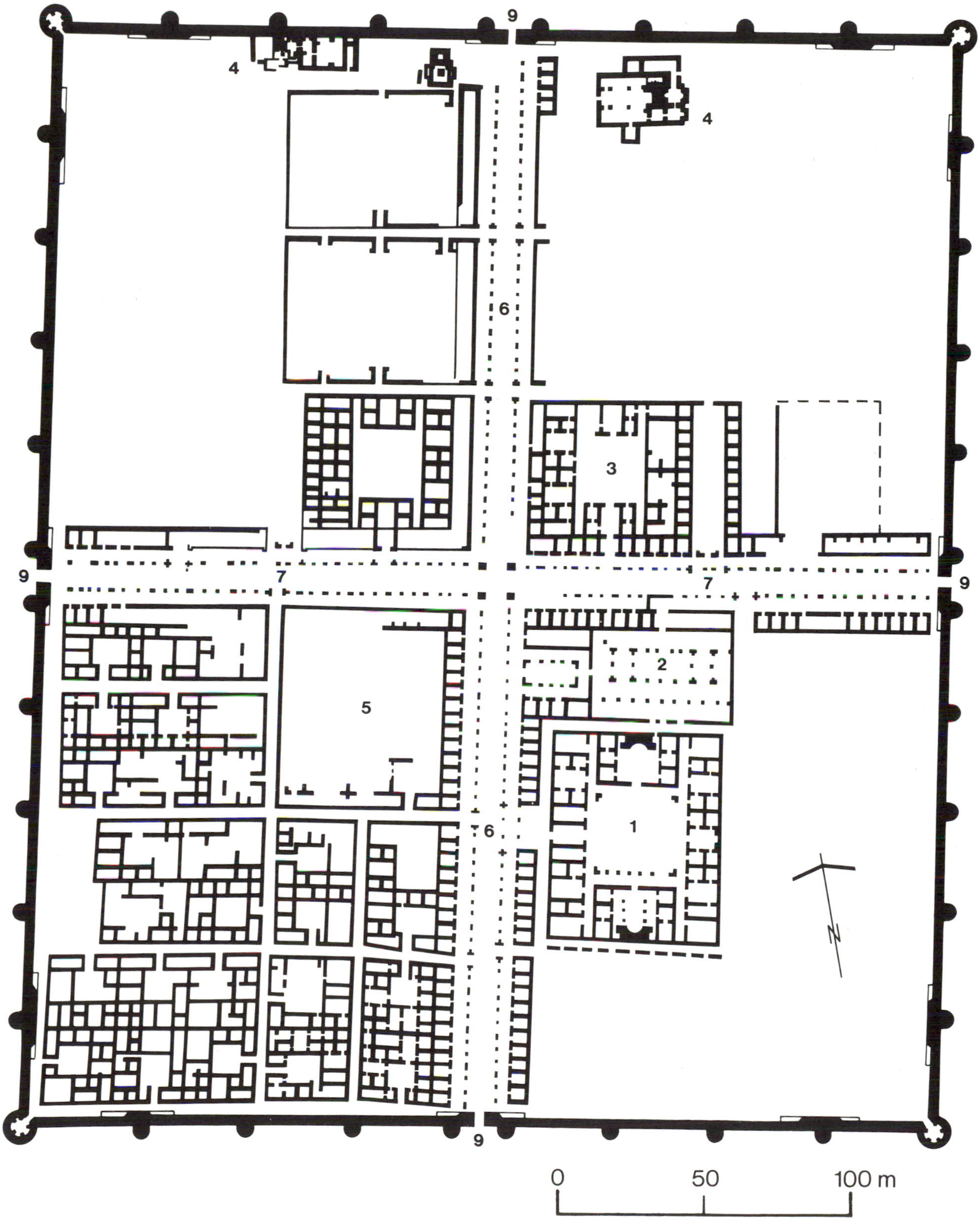

169. 'Anjar (after Chehab 1975) (1:2000).

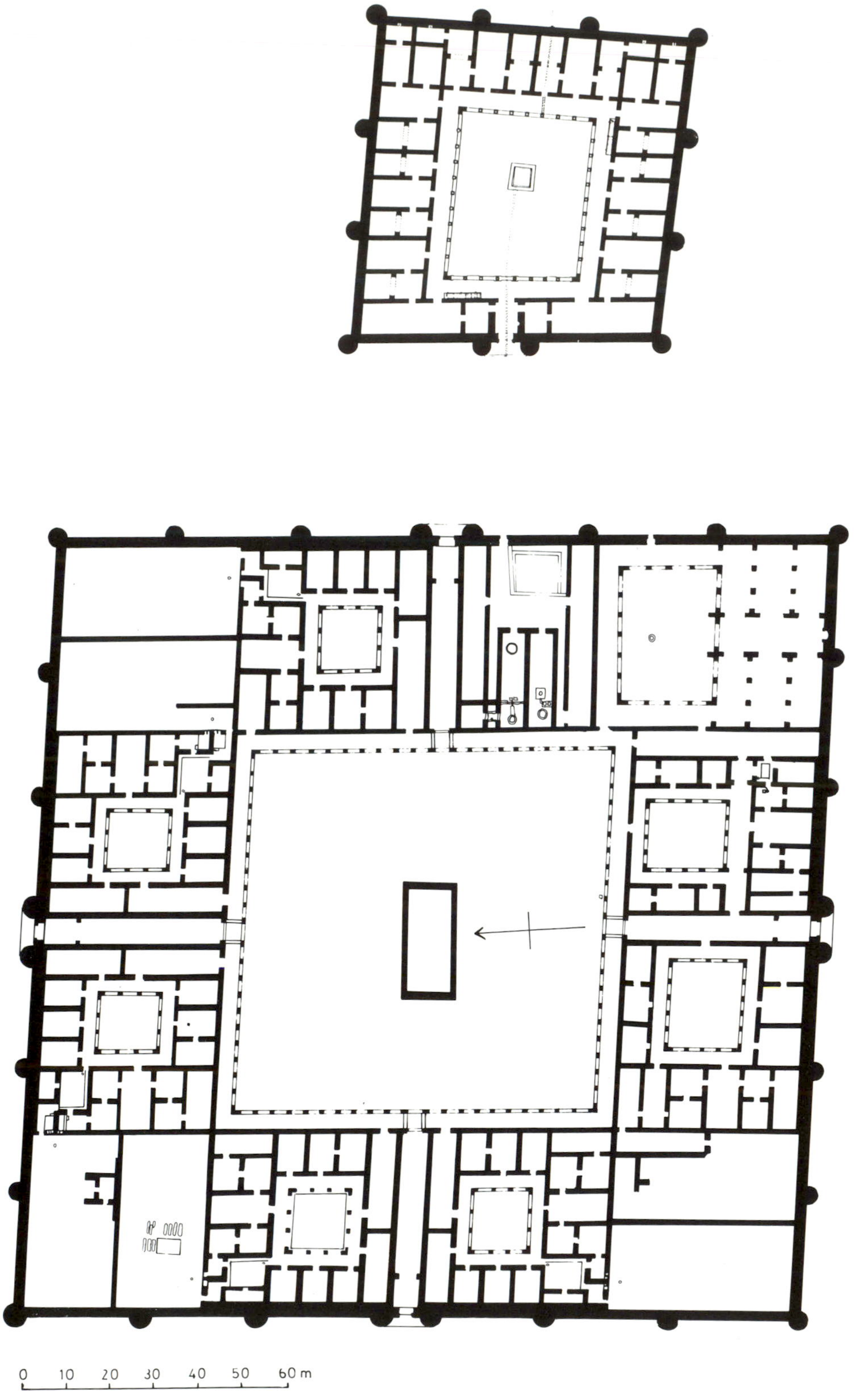

170. Qaṣr al-Ḥayr al-Sharqī (after Grabar et al. 1978) (1:1500).

PLATES

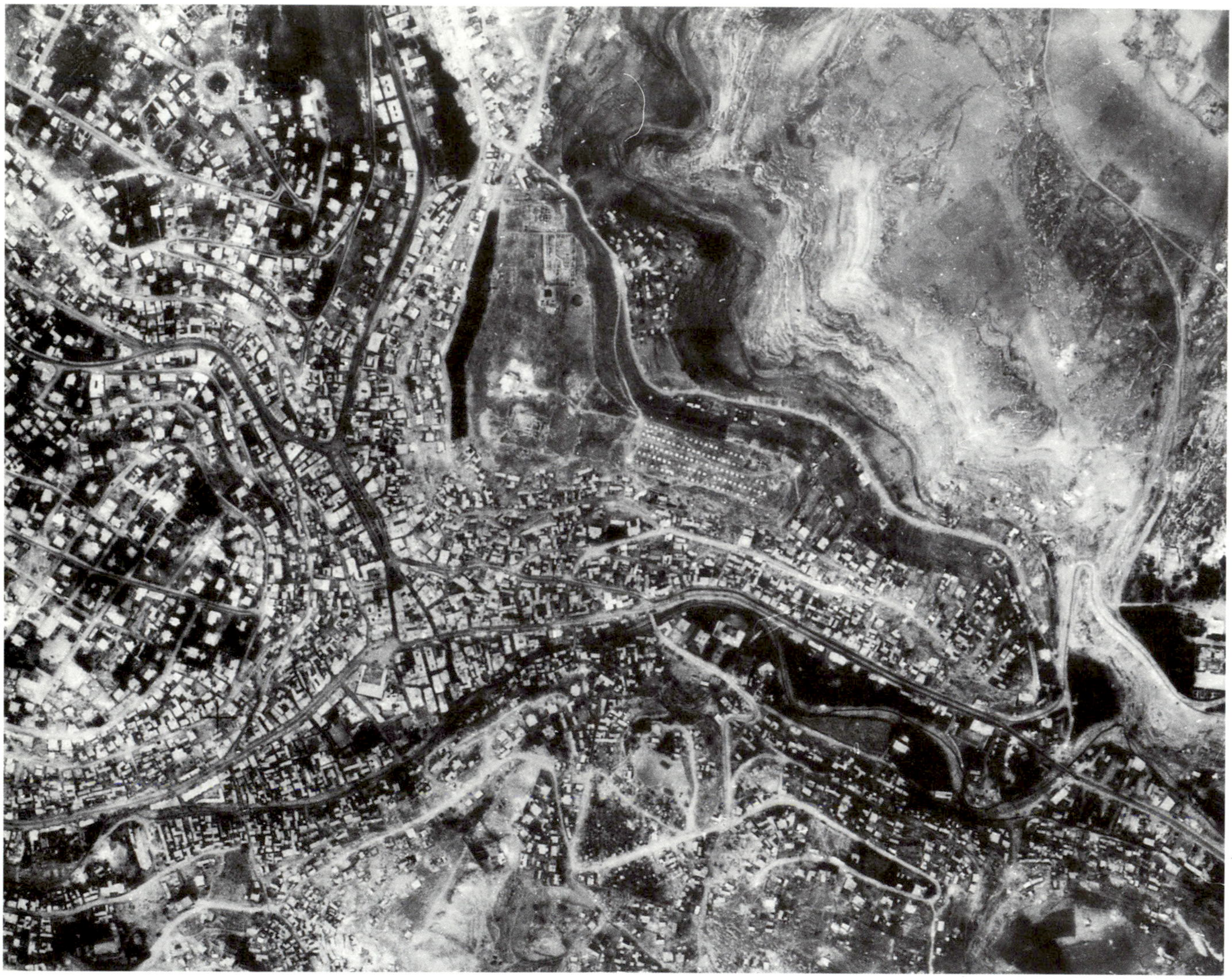

Vertical air photograph of ʿAmmān in 1953 (Aerofilms ltd.).

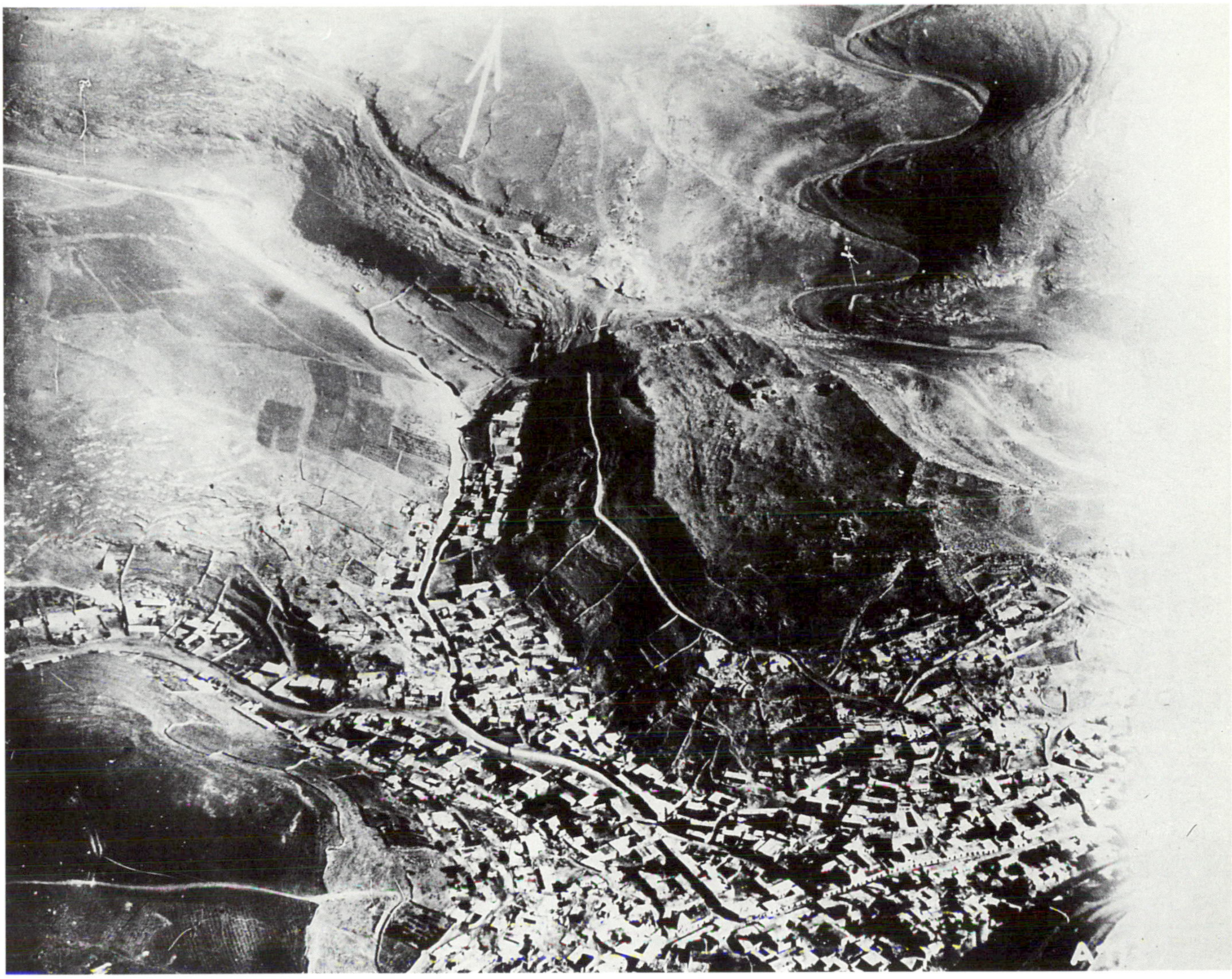

A. Air photograph of ʿAmmān and the Qalʿa taken during the First World War by a German aviator, looking north (Royal Geographical Society, ʿAmmān).

B. The Lower City in October 1881 before the appearance of the Circassian settlement, looking east (Palestine Exploration Fund, no. 546).

Plate 3

Panorama of the Lower City taken from the Lower Terrace of the Qal'a in 1875, eastern part

Plate 4

Panorama of the Lower City taken from the Lower Terrace of the Qal'a in 1875, western part

(American Palestine Exploration Society, nos 89–90).

(American Palestine Exploration Society, nos 91–2).

Plate 5

A. The Nymphaeum in 1867 (Palestine Exploration Fund, no. 550).

B. The Odeum, in July-August 1867 (Palestine Exploration Fund, no. OC308).

A. The vaulted conduit of the *sayl ʿAmmān*, looking west (Palestine Exploration Fund, no. 547).

B. The Qabr al-Sulṭān (Palestine Exploration Fund, no. 564).

A. The Western Tomb (Palestine Exploration Fund, no. 579).

B. The Byzantine Cathedral in 1867, looking south-southwest (Warren photograph, Palestine Exploration Fund, no. 560).

A. The Umayyad Congregational Mosque in 1867, looking south (Warren photograph, Palestine Exploration Fund, OC317).

B. Enlargement of view of the mosque from plate 2b, looking northeast.

A. The north wall and minaret of the mosque, from the inside in 1921 (Creswell Archive).

B. The north wall of the mosque from the outside in 1921 (Creswell Archive).

Plate 10

A. Kufic inscription from the mosque (Palestine Exploration Fund, Garstang photograph no. G184, taken in 1923?).

B. The modern mosque, as first constructed in 1923 (Philby collection no. PJ2898/3131, St Anthony's College, Oxford).

'Ammān and the Qal'a in 1953, air view looking northwest (Aerofilms Ltd.).

Panorama of the south side of the Qal'a.

Plate 13

Qalʻat ʻAmmān in 1979, looking southeast from Jabal Luwaybda.

The Reception Hall of the Palace, before excavation in 1881 (Palestine Exploration Fund, no. 556).

The Reception Hall of the Palace, looking northwest.

A. The Reception Hall of the Palace, looking northeast.

B. The Reception Hall of the Palace, looking south.

The south *īwān* in 1898 (Dept. of Art and Archaeology Princeton).

A. The interior of the Reception Hall, looking northeast.

B. The north *īwān* in 1867 (Palestine Exploration Fund, no. OC393).

A. The east *īwān*.

B. The west *īwān*.

A. The north *īwān*.

B. The south *īwān*.

A. The southeast corner of the central court in 1867 (Palestine Exploration Fund, no. OC320).

B. 'Squinch' in the east *īwān*.

C. Seat outside the south door.

A. 1

B. 6

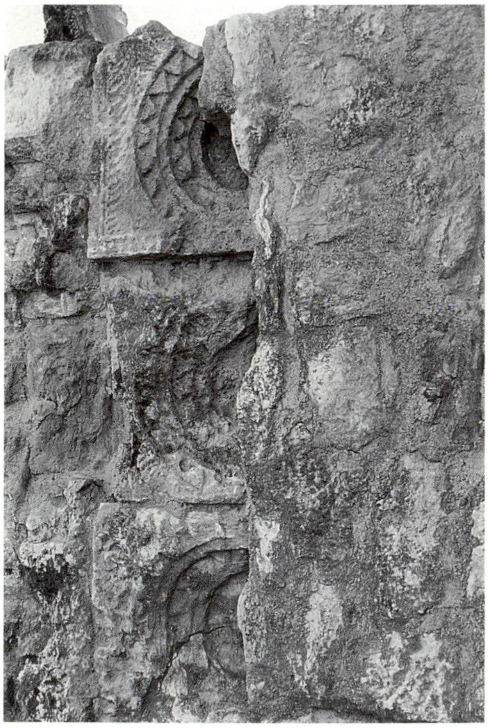
C. 7–9

D. 12

E. 13

F. 20

G. 21

H. 22

A. 23–4

B. 25–6

C. 26–7

D. 28–9

E. 30

F. 31–2

G. 33–4

H. 35–6

A. 40

B. 41

C. 47–8

D. 49–50

E. 52–3

F. 54–5

G. 56

H. 57–8

A. 59–60

B. 61–2

C. 64

D. 65–6

E. 68–9

F. 70

G. 72–3

H. 74–5

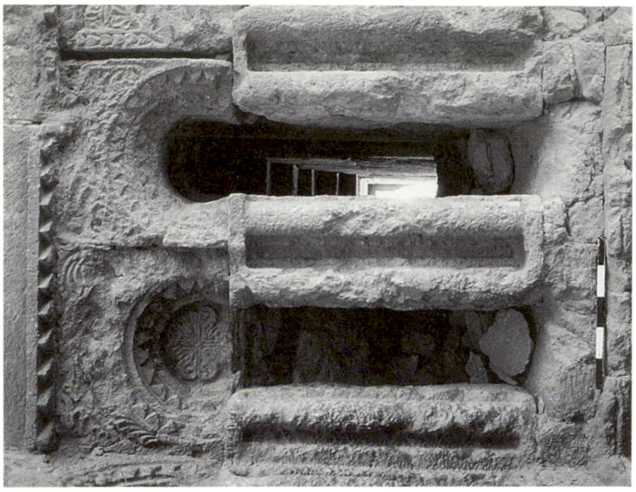
A. 76–7

B. 78

C. 79–80

D. 81–2

E. 83–4

F. 85–6

G. 87

H. 90–1

A. 92

B. 93–4

C. 95

D. 96–7

E. 98

F. 99–100

G. 101–2

H. 106

A. SE

B. SW

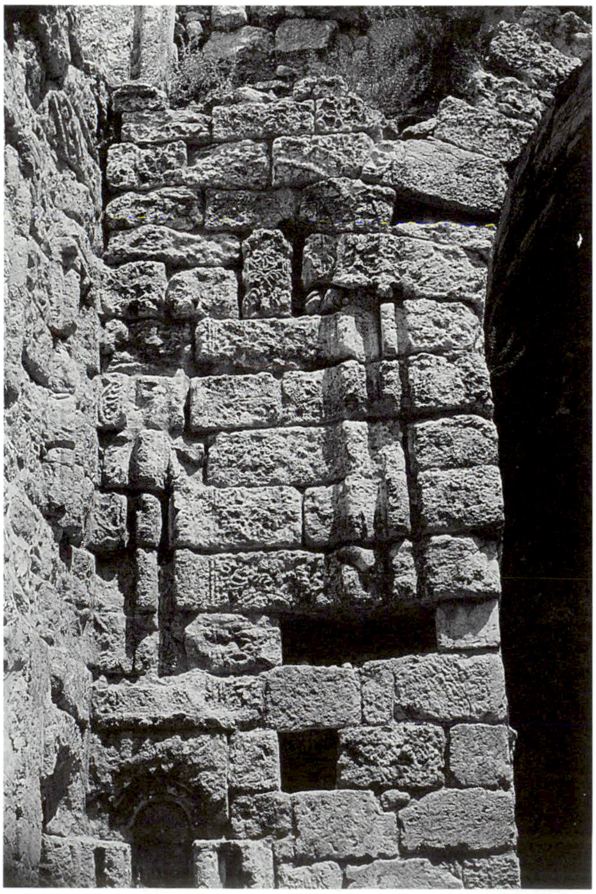

C. EN

D. ES

E. NW

F. NE

G. WS

H. WN

A. SN/4

B. SN/6

C. SN/20

D. SN/7

E. SN/24

F. SB/1

A. C/1

B. C/2

C. C/4

D. C/5

E. F/1

F. B/7

A. Columned Street, looking north, in 1943 (HKJ Dept. of Antiquities).

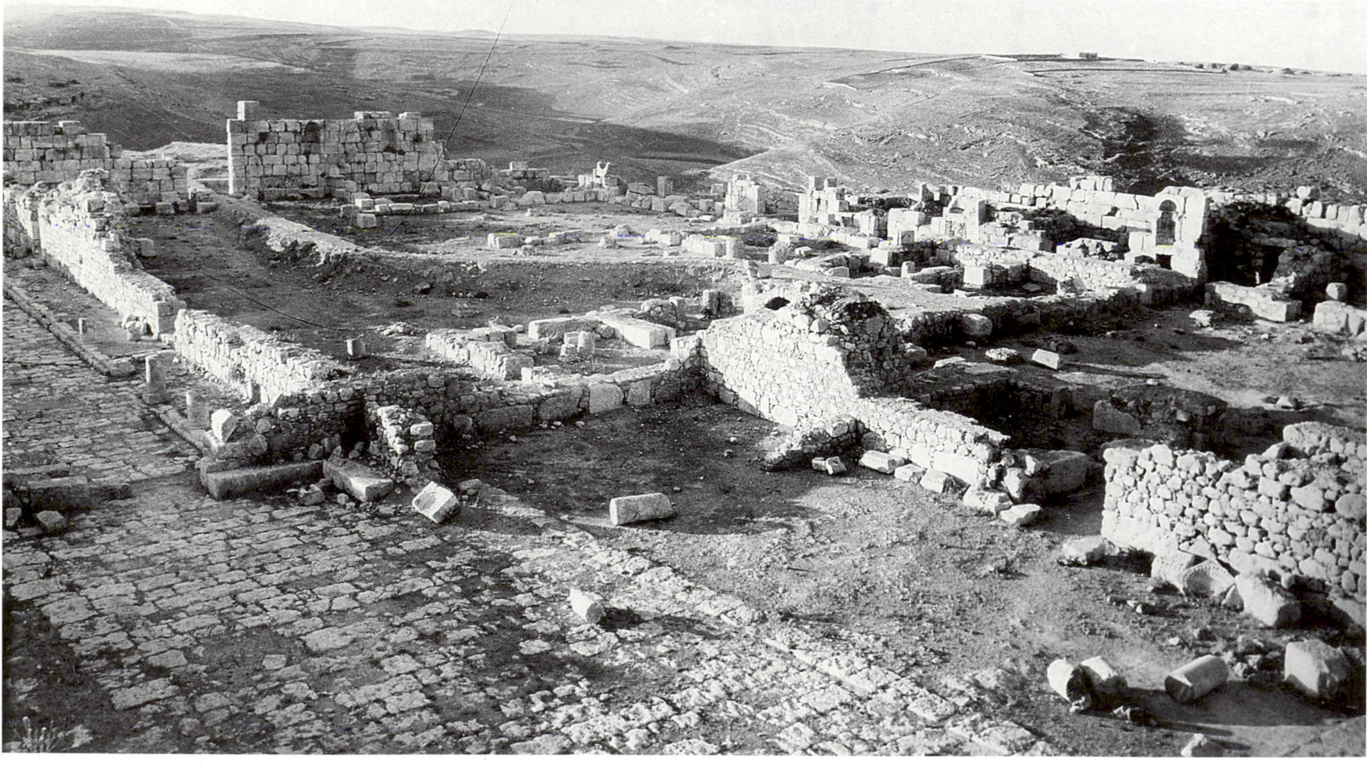

B. East Side of the First Enclosure, looking northeast, in 1943 (HKJ Dept. of Antiquities).

A. East side of the First Enclosure, looking south, in 1943 (HKJ Dept. of Antiquities).

B. Staircase in Room 40.

A. Column from the Columned Street.

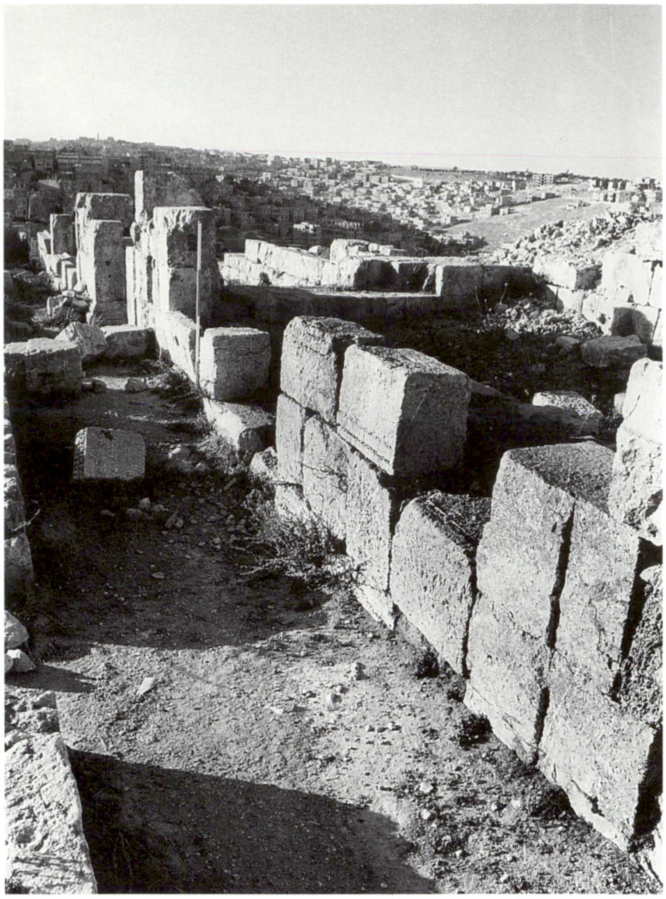

C. The rooms of the east side.

B. Period 4 rubble and mortar pier from Building 5.

Facade of the North Building.

A. The *īwān* vault in the North Building.

B. The dome chamber in the North Building.

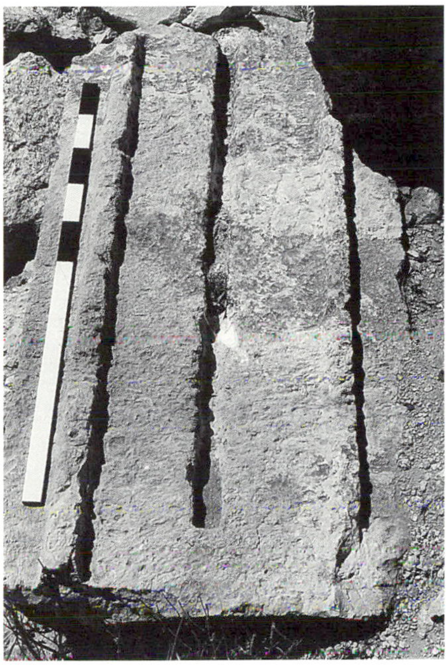

A. NB/1

B. NB/3

C. NB/4

D. NB/5

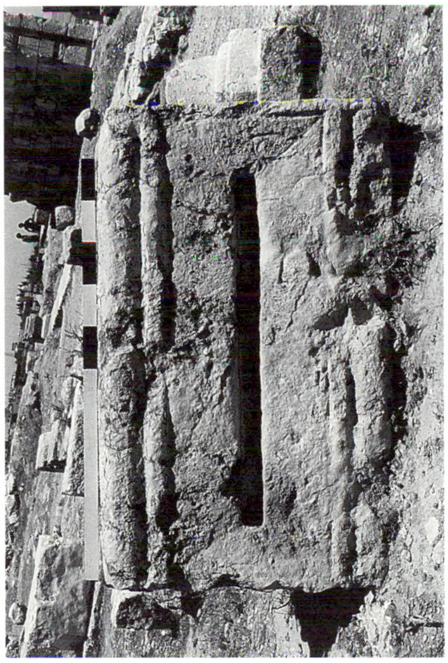

E. NB/6

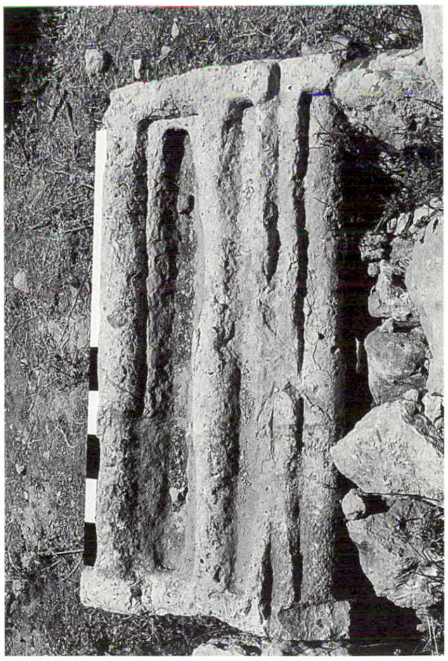

F. NB/13

A. NB/19

B. NB/20

C. NB/21

D. Period 4 double engaged colonette of rubble and gypsum mortar at the mouth of the *īwān*.

E. Doorway to roon N2, rebuilt and subsequently blocked.

F. Fallen arch of rubble and mortar in room N2.

A. Tower A, looking southeast.

B. Tower A, interior, looking northeast.

A. Wall Sector 1, *Temenos* Enclosure wall, exterior looking northwest.

B. Wall Sector 2 in the 1920s, before dumping from the Italian excavations, showing a doorway in the face of the wall (Palestine Exploration Fund, Garstang photograph no. G148).

A. East end of wall Sector 4, showing the buttress at the east end.

B. Wall Sector 4, detail of masonry and later plastering.

C. West End of Wall Sector 4, looking southwest.

A. Wall Sector 5, general view, showing traces of later revetment.

B. Wall Sector 7, looking southeast.

A. Gate A, looking northeast.

B. Passageway of Gate A, showing different foundation levels of Towers C and D.

A. Wall Sector 8, rebuilt Buttress 1.

B. Wall Sector 8, rebuilt Buttress 2.

A. Wall Sector 8, detail of Umayyad facing masonry.

B. Wall Sector 8, original Buttress 4 and later revetment in Area C

A. Wall Sector 8, inside face in Area C.

B. Wall Sector 9, Buttress 4.

A. Wall Sector 11.

B. Wall Sector 11, foundations excavated in trench E21, looking southeast.

A. Tower B, looking northeast.

B. Tower B, north facade.

A. Interior of Tower B, looking southwest.

B. Entrance and staircase to roof in Tower B.

A. Wall Sector 12, Umayyad refacing east of Tower B.

B. The Roman inside face of Wall Sector 12 and its junction with Gate C, looking southeast.

A. Gate C, looking southwest.

B. Gate C, looking southeast.

A. Masonry of Gate C overlying the so-called 'plastered wall building'.

B. The main outer threshold of Gate C.

C. The secondary inner threshold of Gate C.

D. The threshold of the side-room of Gate C.

A. Foundation trench of the Umayyad curved foundation in Gate C, with section of foundation in situ.

B. Wall Sector 13 below Gate C.

A. Cross-section of Wall Sector 14.

B. Gate D.

A. Wall Sector 15.

B. Facade of Wall Sectors 16 and 17.

A. Inside face of join of wall, Sectors 16 and 17.

B. Facade of Wall Sector 17.

A. Reused masonry in Wall Sector 17.

B. Wall Sector 18.

A. Wall Sector 19: inside face in Area A.

B. Superimposed walls at the southeast corner of the Citadel.

A. Cross-section of Wall Sector 22.

B. Rebuilt facade of Sector 22.

A. Tower G, looking southwest.

B. Interior of Tower G, looking northeast.

A. Fragment 11.10

B. Fragment 12.4

C. Fragment TB.7

D. Fragment TB.12

E. Fragment 12.6

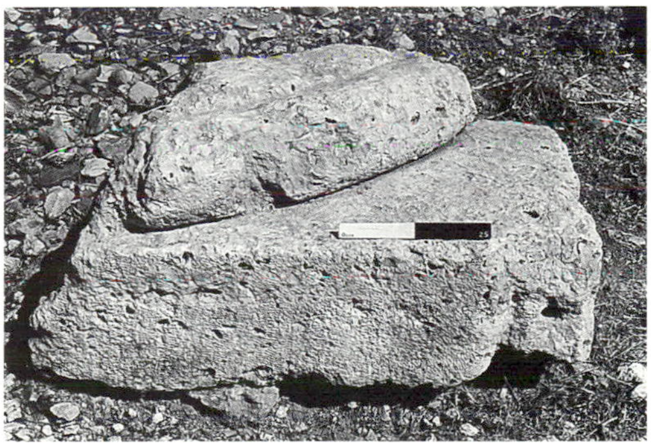

F. Fragment 12.8

G. Fragment 12.11

H. Fragment 12.17

Plate 60 Architectural fragments reused in the fortification walls.

A. Fragment 15.1

B. Fragment 16.4

C. Fragment 17.4

D. Fragment 17.11

E. Fragment 17.15

F. Fragment 17.16

G. Fragment 19.1

H. Fragment 25.12

A. The Temple of Hercules before excavation in 1881, looking northeast (Palestine Exploration Fund, neg. no. 555)

B. The Temple of Hercules, looking east, in 1981.

A. The Temple of Hercules, east-end masonry

B. The Temple of Hercules, elevation of podium.

A. podium cap

B. plinth and base

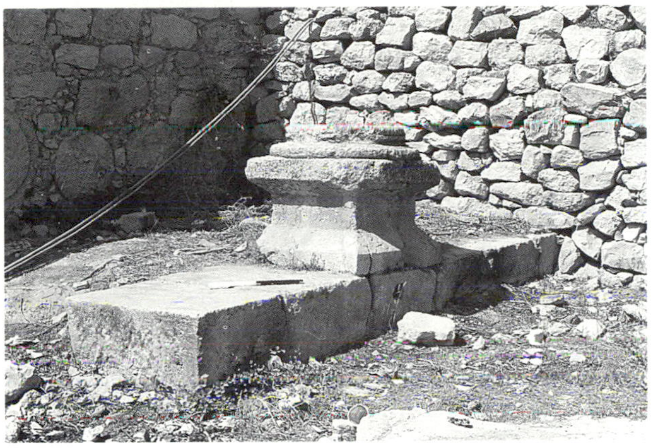

C. *temenos* stylobate

D. *temenos* capital

E. column base

F. fallen column

G. architrave.

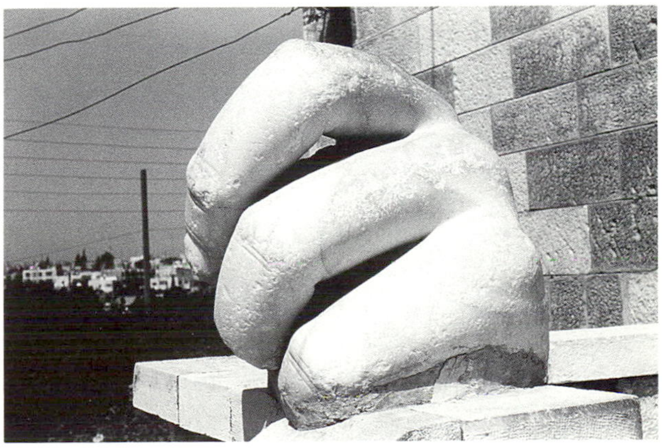

H. hand from a cultic statue, possibly one of Hercules

A. The Propylaeon, looking northeast in 1875 (American Palestine Exploration Society, no. 96).

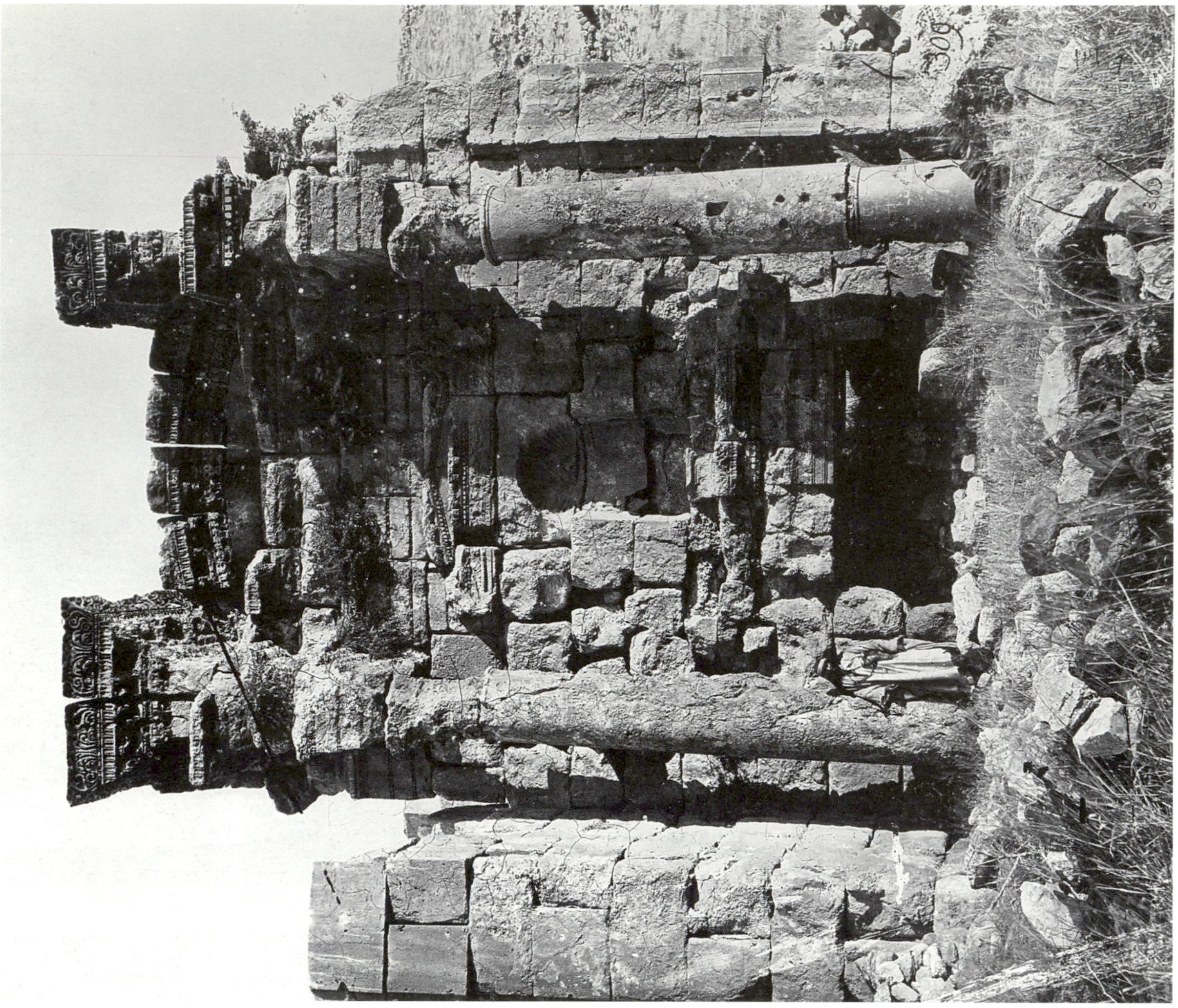

B. The south facade of the Propylaeon in July-August 1867 (Palestine Exploration Fund, no. OC309/561).

C. The north facade of the Propylaeon in 1911 (Bell Archive).

A. Possible Late Hellenistic/Early Roman tower in trenches C30 and C0, looking north.

B. Later walls terracing the slope outside the fortification wall in trenches C30 and C0, looking east.

C. Early Byzantine building outside the fortification wall in trenches C0 and C10, looking south.

Panorama of Area C within the fortification wall, looking south.

A. Doorway of Byzantine Building (a) in trench C1, looking east.

B. Byzantine Building (b) in trench C2, looking east.

A. Area C street, showing later Stratum III surface and buttressing of Umayyad Building B.

B. Room B, Stratum V Umayyad Building B in Area C, looking NW.

A. Storeroom C, Stratum V Umayyad Building B in Area C, looking west.

B. Cistern with surround in courtyard of Stratum V, Umayyad Building B in Area C, looking west.

A. Basins in Room E, Stratum V Umayyad Building B in Area C, looking south.

B. Skeleton of adult killed in the collapse of Umayyad Building B on the threshold of Room B, during the earthquake of 129–30/747–8.

A. Building 1, in trenches C1–C12 (Strata IVb–III: 4th/10th–5th/11th centuries), looking northwest.

B. Room of Umayyad Building B, reoccupied during the Fatimid period (Stratum III Building 4).

A. General view of Area B, looking south.

B. The bulldozed basin in Area B.

A. Byzantine remains in trenches B20 and B23, looking east.

B. Plastered basin in trench B20.

C. Byzantine-Umayyad cistern arch in trench B23, looking east.

A. The east side of unit 1 in Umayyad Building C, looking south.

B. Fatimid bread oven in the northwest corner of the courtyard in unit 1 in Umayyad Building C.

C. Plastered drain and cistern in Umayyad Building D (trench B19).

A. Fatimid Stratum III reconstruction of Umayyad Building D, looking south. Note bread oven in upper-right corner.

B. Byzantine (Stratum VIII) steps underlying Umayyad Building D, looking west.

A. Umayyad remains east of the B area street in trench B52, looking east.

B. Ayyubid surface levels in Room D, Umayyad Building D, looking east.

A. Tower E in Area D, looking north.

B. Abbasid-Fatimid (Stratum IVb–III) house overlying Tower E in Area D.

A. Detail of drains adjacent to Tower E.

B. Abbasid basin, drain and cistern in Area D.

A. Qal'a, Church, looking southeast.

B. Apse of the Citadel church, looking northeast.

A. Open Cistern belonging to the Umayyad construction.

B. Open Cistern, detail of steps.